MUIR'S
HISTORICAL ATLAS
ANCIENT AND CLASSICAL

Sixth Edition

EDITED BY

the late **R. F. TREHARNE**, M.A., Ph.D.
PROFESSOR OF HISTORY, UNIVERSITY COLLEGE OF WALES, ABERYSTWYTH

AND

HAROLD FULLARD, M.Sc.
CARTOGRAPHIC EDITOR

BOOK CLUB ASSOCIATES LONDON

CONTENTS OF
ANCIENT AND CLASSICAL ATLAS

* *Maps marked with an asterisk are coloured physically*

*1 THE WORLD AS KNOWN TO THE ANCIENTS 1:70M.
World according to Herodotus c. 450 B.C.
World according to Eratosthenes c. 200 B.C.
World according to Strabo c. 18 A.D.
World according to Ptolemy c. 150 A.D.

2A THE CRADLES OF CIVILISATION IN THE XV CENTURY B.C. 1:25M.
B *Achaean Greece according to Homer c. 1200 B.C. 1:8M.*
C *Troy 1:500,000*
D *The Assyrian Empire in the First Half of the VII Century B.C. 1:15M.*

3A THE NILE AND EUPHRATES VALLEYS c. 1200 B.C. 1:10M.
B *Ancient Egypt 1:5M.*

4A ISRAELITE CONQUEST OF CANAAN 1:2M.
B *Jerusalem before the Exile 1:50,000*
C *Syria and the Hebrew Kingdoms 1:5M.*
D *Palestine in the time of Christ 1:2M.*
E *Jerusalem before 70 A.D. 1:50,000*
F *Paul's Missionary Journeys 1:30M.*

5A PHOENICIAN AND GREEK COLONIES 1:20M.
B *Persian Empire c. 500 B.C. 1:20M.*

*6-7 ANCIENT GREECE 1:2M.
A *Acropolis 1:15,000*
B *Ancient Athens 1:50,000*
C *The Shores of Propontis 1:3M.*
D *Crete 1:3M.*

8 GREECE AND THE AEGEAN IN THE V CENTURY B.C. 1:3M.

9A PELOPONNESIAN WAR 1:8M.
B *Empire of Alexander the Great 1:20M.*
C *Empires of Alexander's Successors c. 300 B.C. 1:40M.*

*10-11 ROMAN EMPIRE 1:15M.
A *Imperial and Senatorial Provinces c. 14 A.D. 1:40M.*
B *Roman Conquest of the Mediterranean 1:30M.*
C *Republican Rome 1:60,000*
D *Imperial Rome 1:60,000*

*12 ANCIENT ITALY: NORTHERN SECTION 1:3M.

*13 ANCIENT ITALY: SOUTHERN SECTION 1:3M.
A *Republican Forum 1:15,000*
B *Imperial Fora 1:15,000*

14A ITALY UNDER THE ROMAN REPUBLIC 1:5M.
B *Latium 1:2½M.*
C *Racial Distribution c. 400 B.C. 1:15M.*

15 WEST ROMAN EMPIRE IN THE TIME OF AUGUSTUS 1:10M.

16 EAST ROMAN EMPIRE IN THE TIME OF AUGUSTUS 1:10M.

*17 ROMAN BRITAIN: PHYSICAL 1:3M.
A *Britain according to Ptolemy*
B *Hadrians Wall 1:1,500,000*

18-19 THE REALMS OF CIVILISATION, c. 200 A.D. AND THE NATURAL CONDITIONS AFFECTING THEIR RELATIONS 1:30M.
A *The Empire of Asoka, c. 250 B.C. 1:50M.*
B *Gupta Empire, c. 400 A.D., and Iran 1:50M.*

20 EUROPE ON THE EVE OF THE BARBARIAN INVASIONS, c. 395 A.D. 1:25M.

George Philip and Son Limited
12-14 Long Acre London WC2E 9LP

First published 1938
Sixth Edition 1963
Reprinted 1966 1969 1971 1973 1974 1976
© *George Philip and Son Limited 1963*

This edition published 1976 by
Book Club Associates
By arrangement with George Philip
and Son Limited

PRINTED IN GREAT BRITAIN BY GEORGE PHILIP PRINTERS LIMITED, LONDON

INTRODUCTION

THE ANCIENT WORLD

Plate 1 shows the area within which the whole drama of ancient history was played—the development not only of the civilisation of the West, upon which our attention is mainly concentrated, but of the remote and independent civilisations of China and India. But by far the greater part of the area shown on this map—the whole of northern Europe and Asia and the whole of Africa south of the Atlas mountains, except the narrow valley of the Nile—was practically untouched by the influence of the various civilisations, and was known to them, vaguely, as the region from which incursions of barbarians broke into the more civilised regions.

The small maps at the foot of the page give a diagrammatic illustration of the expansion of human knowledge about the earth's surface among the Greeks and Romans between the time of Herodotus (c. 450 B.C.) and the time of Ptolemy (c. 150 A.D.). Herodotus knew of the existence of India, but knew nothing of its shape, and the great civilisation of China lay altogether beyond his horizon. Ptolemy knew that China existed, but no more than that. The expansion of knowledge about the world and its peoples among the Greeks and Romans was thus very slight during the six centuries covered by these diagrams.

The beginnings of civilisation in the western part of the region covered by the main map took place in the two riverine districts of Egypt and Mesopotamia. The relations between these two regions are more clearly illustrated in **Plate 3**. They were brought into contact with one another at an early date; the wanderings of Abraham ranged from Ur of the Chaldees, which was probably the chief centre of the Sumerian or Euphratic civilisation, through Syria to Egypt. Which of these two centres of development was the older, scholars are not yet ready to affirm with confidence. They probably had independent beginnings, but contributed something to each other's development. Excavators are beginning to reveal to us a third riverine civilisation, on the lower Indus, which was probably an offshoot from Sumer, but it seems to have had almost no influence upon the development of Indian civilisation, which seems to have been of much later origin. In distant China another riverine civilisation grew up, in the basins of the Hwang-ho and (later) of the Yang-tse-kiang. No direct contact seems to be traceable between the civilisation of China and those of Egypt and Babylonia. Isolated by the huge mountain-mass which is shown on the map, and by the great deserts of the north-east, the marvellous civilisation of China seems to have had from the first an isolated existence, though its influence spread over the Indo-China peninsula to the south-west of China, and over Japan, Korea and Manchuria in the north.

In the west, the riverine stage of civilisation was followed by a marine stage, when first the Minoans (whose brilliant civilisation has only recently been discovered,) and later the Phœnicians, the Greeks and (to some extent) the Etruscans made the Mediterranean the centre of the rising European civilisation, which was to be unified by the conquests of Rome. Throughout the " classical " era, and down to the great discoveries of the fifteenth and sixteenth centuries, the Mediterranean and the countries bordering upon it remained the arena of western civilisation; these lands are, indeed, the only part of the wide area shown in the main map of which the classical geographers had any real knowledge.

Meanwhile, from Egypt, and still more from Babylonia, the impetus to progress in civilisation had passed to the uplands of the Near East: to the Hittites and the Lydians in Asia Minor, to the Assyrians in upper Mesopotamia, to the Persians and the Medians on the high ground that looks down upon Mesopotamia in the East. Here arose huge but short-lived empires which strove for the control of the Fertile Crescent that curves round the Syrian deserts from Palestine to Mesopotamia. With these wide empires first the Greeks and then the Romans were brought into contact and conflict; and it was in struggles against them that the nascent European system of freedom-under-law underwent its first ordeals. For a time, under Alexander and his successors, this wide region of the Near East was brought under the influence of the European civilisation. But this influence was short-lived. The Romans only succeeded in preserving control over the western fringes of this area. But this was enough to ensure that Christianity, born in Palestine, should be one of the most powerful moulding influences in the development of the European civilisation.

As for India, the real beginning of her distinctive civilisation may be traced to the coming of the Aryans, about 2,000 years before Christ. But this civilisation, though it was temporarily influenced by the coming of Alexander, and by a series of barbarian irruptions from Central Asia, had its own independent existence, almost as isolated as that of China. There was, indeed, always a thin stream of trade between India and Europe, and an intermittent trickle even from China to Europe; but the European civilisation in effect knew nothing of the great civilisations of the East, at any rate until the later middle ages.

If by the " Ancients " we mean the Greeks and the Romans, the world really known to them was but a small fragment of the wide area represented in this map.

Plate 2 illustrates the ancient civilisations of the Near East which preceded the rise of Greek and Roman civilisation. The date 1400 B.C. is chosen for the first map, 2*a*, because by that date the main powers of the Near East had got themselves into position. (1) *Egypt*, whose records date back to at least 4,000 B.C., had reached a great height of development in the Early and Middle Kingdoms before 2000 B.C. Its development had then been interrupted by the conquest of the Hyksos (c. 1800–1600), who were probably Hittites (*see* below) with a following of Semitic tribes. The expulsion of the Hyksos (1580 B.C.) was followed by a great imperialist period, when Egypt conquered Nubia and Syria, especially under Thutmose III., c. 1500 B.C. The Egyptian empire was at the height of its power under Amenhotep III. at the date of the map; all the Semitic tribes of Syria were obedient to it; and the other empires were all in relation with it. (2) In *Babylonia* the beginnings of civilisation were as ancient as in Egypt. The Sumerians, a non-Semitic people who lived near the mouth of the Euphrates, had invented cuneiform writing, which was adopted by all the peoples of the Near

East. Their power was subsequently merged in that of the Semitic Akkadians of Babylonia, whose empire reached its height under the great codifier Hammurabi, c. 2200 B.C.—the Amraphel of Genesis and the contemporary of Abraham. But the development of Babylon, like that of Egypt, had been checked by a barbarian irruption—that of the Aryan Kassites (c. 1800–1200 B.C.) : on all sides the barbarian irruptions of c. 1800 B.C. mark an epoch like the later barbarian irruptions into the Roman Empire. (3) The *Semitic* peoples, who probably sprang from Arabia, occupied the whole area (coloured green on the map) from the mountains of Persia and Armenia to the Mediterranean : a wide crescent of settled ground, from Palestine through Mesopotamia to the Persian gulf, curving round the great desert whence Bedouin movements continually sprang. Apart from Babylonia, the greatest of the Semitic peoples were the *Assyrians*, who were beginning to be active at the date of the map, and were later (*see* 2d) to unite nearly the whole Semitic area under their rule ; the *Amorites*, who stretched from Syria into Northern Mesopotamia ; the *Canaanites*, who occupied the coastlands of Syria, and were beginning to be active in trade in the Phoenician cities ; and a multitude of smaller tribes, among whom the Habiru (? Hebrews) are mentioned as giving trouble in the Amarna letters. The Semitic peoples drew their civilisation partly from Babylon, partly from Egypt, and linked the two. (4) The *Hittite* empire, whose greatness has only recently been disclosed by archaeological research, had its centre in south-east Asia Minor (Cappadocia) and the Taurus mountains, whence they waged frequent war against the

FIG. 1.—THE MINOAN CENTRES IN CRETE

Egyptians and other Powers. Their greatness was at its height at the date of the map, 1400 B.C. They had only recently emerged, and had probably been the chief disturbing factor in the irruptions of c. 1800 B.C. There were also scattered Hittite tribes in Syria and Palestine : Abraham bought his grave from a Hittite clan. It is not known to what stock the Hittites belonged, but they were not Semites. Their neighbours and rivals were the people of *Mitanni*, in North Mesopotamia—an Indo-European tribe, probably related to the Medes. (5) In Crete and the Aegean Sea a brilliant civilisation, known as *Minoan*, was at its height at the date of the map. Its existence has only been disclosed in the twentieth century by archaeological research. The Minoans were not Greeks ; their downfall was probably due to the invasions of the Greeks from the north ; but Greek civilisation owed much to them. *Cnossus*, in Crete, was the centre of a sea-empire of which Greek legends and Egyptian monuments preserve traces. *Mycenae* in European Greece was a secondary centre of Minoan civilisation, and *Troy* (2c), at the mouth of the Dardanelles, was another. The influence of the

Minoans spread as far west as Sicily and South Italy, where their relics have been discovered.

The second map, 2b, illustrates the geography of Greece as it is described by Homer, for the period of the Trojan War (c. 1200 B.C.). The first wave of Greek conquest, that of the " Achaeans," had displaced the Minoan kingdom, while still keeping its Greek centre, Mycenae, as its capital ; and the Trojan War was an expedition of all the Achaean chiefs. The second wave of Greek conquest, that of the Dorians (c. 1000 B.C.) brought about a complete reconstruction of the political geography of Greece, which governed the great age of Greek history. The Homeric poems (? c. 850 B.C.) preserve the memory of the older geography, here represented.

The third map, 2d, shows, at its height, the empire of the Assyrians, who were the dominating factor in the Near East from c. 1000 B.C. to c. 600 B.C., the older Powers of Egypt, Babylonia, and the Hittites having fallen into decrepitude. Between the date of the first map on this plate, and the date of this, the Israelites had settled in Palestine, and had reached the culminating point of their power in the empire of David (c. 1000 B.C. : *see* **Plate 4**). The history of the divided kingdoms of Israel and Judah was dominated by the struggle against Assyria, which forms the background of the greater part of the Old Testament. The great age of Assyrian history began with Tiglath-Pileser III. (745), and reached its height under Sennacherib (705) and Esarhaddon (681). These monarchs ruled over the whole of Mesopotamia and Syria, thus uniting the whole Semitic stock outside Arabia ; they also occupied Egypt for a time. Their most dangerous enemies were, in the north, the *Medes* (Indo-European peoples in the uplands of Iran), the kingdom of *Urartu* (in Armenia : another ancient Power recently rescued from oblivion by archaeology) ; and in the south the ancient realm of *Elam*, and the *Chaldaeans* who were reviving the civilisation of ancient Babylonia. At the end of the seventh century B.C. the Medes and the Chaldeans united and rapidly overwhelmed Assyria (fall of Nineveh, 612 B.C.), which was more completely ruined than any other empire in history. For a short time a Chaldaean Empire took the place of the Assyrians, reaching its height under Nebuchadnezzar (605 B.C.) ; while the Medes extended their conquests in the north, and overthrew the empire of *Phrygia*, which had been built up in central Asia Minor by invaders from Europe. But both the Median and the Chaldaean empires were short-lived ; in the middle of the sixth century both were overthrown and incorporated by Cyrus in the vast Persian empire (*see* **Plate 5b**).

Plate 3. This map gives a fuller treatment of the region in which the first civilisations arose, and the lands between them. It shows, in brown, the wide desert regions which separated Babylonia from Egypt—the most difficult of geographical obstacles to intercourse. The deserts were, of course, crossed by caravan routes, using the oases, some of which are marked on the map. Round them curves the Fertile Crescent, with its agricultural (green) and pastoral (yellow) regions, which was the home of the chief Semitic peoples. A glance at this map is enough to show why Palestine was the inevitable clash-point in the constantly renewed conflict between the Egyptian Empire and the successive empires of the Euphrates and Tigris valleys—Babylonia, Assyria, Persia ; and why Megiddo was the natural scene of their Armageddon.

The second map (3b) illustrates in greater detail the area of the Egyptian Empire ; though it is necessary to check this map by the main map, which shows how narrow was

the peopled region of Egypt south of the delta, and how inaccessible except from the north. Egypt, indeed, may be compared to a lily, with the well watered region of the delta as the flower, the Nile valley as the stem, and the region of the Fayoum, round lake Moeris, as a bud. The true Egypt—occupied by a white-skinned people who gave birth to the Egyptian civilisation—extended only as far south as the First Cataract, where " Nubia," the land of black-skinned peoples, began. During the period of the Egyptian Empire's greatest power, its sway was extended as far southwards as the Sixth Cataract, but this region (part of the modern Sudan) was never fully incorporated in Egypt. The flat and well-watered lands of the delta never played so great a part in history as the narrow valley of the river; and there was always a clear distinction between Upper Egypt, with its capital at Thebes (temples of Karnak) and Lower and Middle Egypt, with its capital at Memphis (modern Cairo, where the pyramids declare the greatness of its rulers). But these two regions were, according to legend, united as early as the First Dynasty, perhaps 5,000 years B.C. Lower Egypt controlled the western part of the Sinai Peninsula, with its copper and turquoise mines; upper Egypt had ports on the Red Sea, whence trade was carried on in gold, gems, spices and hides. From the ports of the delta trade was carried on with the peoples of Syria and the western Mediterranean, including the Greeks. Protected by the desert and the sea, Egypt could live an isolated life in security. The ambitions of her rulers tempted them to conquer an external empire, and for about 500 years, from the 17th to the 12th century B.C., they controlled most of Syria, and gave civilisation to its peoples. But this empire was broken by the attacks of the Hittites from the north, and of the " peoples of the sea " (probably Minoans) a section of whom, known as the Philistines, were allowed to settle on the coast of Palestine, under the nominal suzerainty of the Pharaohs. After this period of imperialism, Egypt was the victim of successive conquests, first by the Assyrians, then by the Persians, then by Alexander the Great and his Macedonians, and ultimately by the Romans. Egypt was drawn into the common life of the Mediterranean world, and her great Greek port in the Mediterranean, Alexandria, became one of the principal centres of Greek thought and later of Christianity. Her own civilisation became stagnant, though she contributed to the ferment of mystical religious thought which marked the first century of the Christian era. But through all these conquests the life of her people went on unchangingly.

Plate 4 illustrates the history of the Israelites down to the time of Christ.

The first map illustrates the slow conquest of parts of Palestine by the tribes of Israel, and their long struggles with the Semitic Canaanites, whom they gradually absorbed, and with the non-Semitic Philistines. Their piecemeal conquests divided them into four separate blocks. Two tribes, Judah and Simeon, seem to have come in from the southern desert: Simeon melted away among the Bedouin tribes; Judah had a hard struggle to establish a foothold on the high ground above the Dead Sea, and could not even conquer Jerusalem from the Canaanites until the time of David. The other tribes entered the country from the east of the Jordan; the tribes of Reuben and Gad, and half of the tribe of Manasseh settled on the further side of Jordan and formed a second block. The most powerful tribes—Ephraim, Benjamin and half of Manasseh—occupied the highlands round

Mounts Ebal and Gerizim, with Shechem as their holy place, but only slowly conquered the fertile plain of Jezreel and the sea coast. In the north—in Galilee and northwards—the four tribes of Dan, Naphtali, Issachar and Zebulun established themselves with difficulty. First Ephraim, under Gideon and Abimelech, then Benjamin, under Saul, strove to bring these divided clans under a single control, and to keep the surrounding tribes at bay. Finally, about 980, Judah under David established for the first time the unity of the Children of Israel.

The second map illustrates (a) the consolidated kingdom of David, with its capital in the recently conquered city of Jerusalem, and its control over neighbouring tribes; (b) the wide extension of the Davidic empire under Solomon which almost amounted to a hegemony of Syria; and (c) its rapid collapse after his death, and the formation of the tiny kingdoms of Israel and Judah.

The third map shows the political condition of Palestine at the time of Christ: it is now a Roman province, including several vassal States held by the family of Herod, one of which contained Galilee. Two small plans show respectively Jerusalem as it was under David and Solomon and down to the exile, and as it was in the time of Christ; and a final small map shows the chief journeys of St. Paul.

Plate 5. The first map on this Plate (5a) illustrates the work of three sea-going peoples who brought the Western Mediterranean into contact with the civilisation of the Eastern Mediterranean. First among these, in order of time, were the *Phoenicians*—Canaanites from the cities of the Syrian coast, especially Tyre. Their greatest period was between the fall of the Egyptian Empire in Syria, and the conquest of Syria by the Assyrians—c. 1200–750 B.C.; Solomon's ally, Hiram of Tyre, ruled at the period of their greatest splendour, c. 950 B.C. They are said to have established themselves in Southern Spain (Tarshish or Tartessus) as early as 1100 B.C. They planted colonies in Cyprus, Western Sicily, Malta, Sardinia, Corsica, and along the north coast of Africa. The greatest of these, Carthage, traditionally dates from 813 B.C. It became the centre of the Punic Empire when Tyre fell under the dominion of Assyria and Persia. There was constant conflict between the Phoenicians and the Greeks when the latter began (in the eighth century B.C.) to invade their monopoly of sea-going trade.—The *Etruscans* appear to have migrated from Asia Minor to Western Italy at an unknown date. The Greeks, in the eighth century, found them planted, with twelve thriving cities, in Etruria; they also occupied the Po valley; they later (seventh century) conquered Latium and Campania; and their pirate-ships dominated the Tyrrhenian or Etruscan sea, where they frequently fought the Greeks.—The *Greeks* spread outwards from continental Greece in two great stages: (1) At a very early date, say from 1200 B.C. onwards, Achaeans and Aeolians, and later Ionians, settled in the Aegean islands and the coast of Asia Minor; the Achaeans or Aeolians in the north; the Ionians farther south (Phocaea, Chios, Samos, Ephesus, Miletus); after the Dorian migration into Greece, Dorian colonists spread to the southern islands, to Crete, and to the southern part of the west coast of Asia Minor. (2) Between 750 and 550 B.C. there was a remarkable outburst of colonising activities. Some hundreds of Greek colonies were planted (a) on the north shore of the Aegean (mainly by Chalcis and Eretria, cities of Euboea); (b) in the sea of Marmora, the Bosporus, and all round the Black Sea (mainly by Miletus and Megara); (c) in the Ionian Islands and the coast of Epirus (mainly by Corinth); (d) in Southern Italy, which came to be

known as Magna Graecia (mainly by the Achaeans of the Gulf of Corinth, but also by Chalcis, which founded Cumae, whence the alphabet spread to the Latins); (e) in Sicily (mainly by Chalcis in the north-east, and by Corinth, Megara, and other Dorian cities in the south-east and south); (f) in the Western Mediterranean, from the Alps to the Pyrenees, in Corsica and on the west coast of Spain, notably Massilia (Marseilles) (mainly Phocaean); (g) on the north coast of Africa, in Cyrenaica (the island of Thera).

The rapid expansion of these three naval Powers represents the first extension of civilisation into the west.

The second map (5b) illustrates the gigantic Persian Empire, which with incredible swiftness incorporated all the civilisations of the East in a single vast dominion, in the second half of the sixth century B.C. The Persians

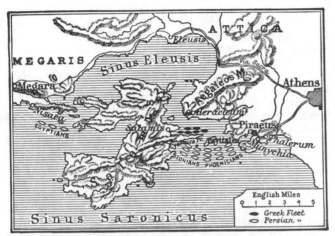

FIG. 2.—BATTLE OF SALAMIS

were an Indo-European people, akin to the Medes: their home, Persia proper, corresponds to the modern district of Fars. The Persian Cyrus, ruling over a little kingdom called Anshan, rebelled in 549 against the Medes, and made himself master of their whole vast empire; overthrew and annexed the Lydian Empire of Croesus (546), with its capital at Sardes, and then came in contact with the Greeks of Ionia, whom he forced to submit; captured Babylon (539) and made himself master of the whole Babylonian Empire, including Phoenicia and Syria where he restored the Jews to Jerusalem; and also extended his sway widely over the countries to the east, possibly as far as Bactria and Afghanistan. Cyrus' son Cambyses conquered Egypt (525), and the whole eastern world was brought under a single rule. The next king, Darius (521–486), had at first to deal with revolts; but he suppressed them and gave to his empire an efficient organisation under twenty satrapies or viceroyalties; he extended his power eastwards as far as the Indus and sea of Aral; he invaded Europe by the Bosporus, and crossed the Danube; and it was this gigantic Power which, from 490 B.C. onwards, menaced the very existence of the little Greek states.

The double-page **Plate 6-7** is intended to illustrate the whole history of Greece proper. The boundaries shown are those of the fifth century B.C. The map is coloured physically, to bring out the mountain features which naturally split up continental Greece into a large number of separate city-states, each with its dependent country-side. The map shows the relationship of Greece Proper to the northern realm of Macedonia, which was to be the

means, under Alexander, of disseminating Greek culture over a great part of Asia. The map shows only European Greece: the islands of the Aegean and the Greek-settled coastland of Asia Minor, are shown in the next map, **Plate 8.**

The smaller maps on this plate show (a) the principal buildings of ancient Athens, clustered round the great fortified rock of the Acropolis; on which stood the Parthenon and the Erechtheum; (b) the extent of Athens in the time of Pericles, with the Long Walls, planned by Themistocles, which linked it to the port of the Piræus, thus making the centre of a maritime empire independent of attacks on the mainland; (c) the Propontis, through which the main trade of Greece with the Black Sea passed, and the numerous Greek settlements on its shores. One interpretation of the Trojan war is that it was a struggle for the control of this important trade-route, which could be interrupted by Troy (Ilium); (d) the island of Crete, which was the centre of the prehistoric Minoan Empire, but played an unimportant part in Greek history.

Plate 8 is a supplement to **Plate 6-7**, showing not only continental Greece, but the islands of the Aegean and the wealthy Greek cities on the coast of Asia Minor, through which the Greeks were brought into conflict with the Persians. The map is coloured to show the four racial or linguistic groups which the Greeks recognised among themselves. Green is the colour of the Ionians, whose only representative on the mainland was Athens, the natural capital of the Ionian peoples, though in the earliest period this pre-eminence might have been claimed by the great colonising city of Miletus in Asia Minor. A mere glance at the distribution of the green colour in this map is enough to show why Athens became the capital of a maritime empire. Of these four races: (1) the *Achaeans* represent the ruling race of the heroic age, displaced by later migrations; (2) the *Dorians* were the latest Greek immigrants in the tenth century B.C.; Sparta, the greatest Dorian centre, retained leadership throughout the classic period; (3) the *Ionians* were in the classic age the chief rivals of the Dorians and the chief source of Greek art and thought, first in Asia Minor and later in Athens; they were probably, in the main, not only pre-Dorian but pre-Achaean; (4) the *Aeolians* broadly represent all the other pre-Dorian Hellenic peoples. These divisions have not much historical value, except that they counted for a good deal among the Greeks themselves—especially the distinction between Dorian and Ionian, which was brought into sharp antithesis by the conflict of the Spartans and the Athenians.

Plate 9a shows the division of Greece between the two sides in the Peloponnesian War. The Athenian Empire, beginning as a confederacy of maritime states for common action against the Persians after the Persian invasion, developed into an empire when the treasury of the league was transferred from the sacred island of Delos to Athens (450 B.C.). Its members were later grouped into five districts, (1) Ionia, (2) Hellespont, (3) Thrace, (4) Caria, (5) the islands. Direct Athenian settlements or *cleruchies* were made in Euboea, Andros, Naxos, Aegina, Melos, Scyros, Imbros, Lemnos, Sinope, several cities in Chalcidice, and the island of Lesbos. The critical struggle for Syracuse is illustrated by **Fig. 3.**

The principal map on **Plate 9b** shows the huge empire of Alexander, who brought all Greece under his sway and then conquered the Persian Empire (334–323 B.C.). This conquest was the means of extending the influence of Greek civilisation over the East, as far as the Indus valley;

and this period of expansion is known as the " Hellenistic " period. Alexander's conquering march is shown on the map. An empire which was so swiftly created could not be expected to last long. It broke up into sections under

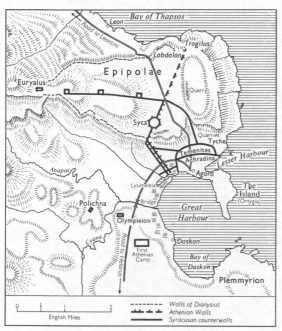

FIG. 3.—SYRACUSE

Alexander's generals, who are known as the Diadochi or successors. This division is shown in the smaller map, 9c. The chief of these kingdoms were : (1) Asia Minor and Syria under Seleucus and his successors the Seleucids; (2) Egypt under the Ptolemies ; (3) Macedonia under the successors of Antigonus Gonatas ; (4) Pergamum under the Attalids. It was with these Powers that the expanding empire of Rome was brought into conflict ; their weakness made its conquests easier, and they were gradually merged in the Roman Empire.

Plate 10–11. This double-page plate is intended to illustrate the whole history of Rome and her Empire. On the main map, which is meant for general reference, note the way in which the empire was linked together by great roads, only the principal of which can be shown. It is probable that transport on these great roads was as swift and efficient as at any period in European history down to the coming of the railway ; while the sea formed an equally valuable means of holding this Mediterranean empire together. Note, secondly, the distinction between the limits of the empire as they were when the empire was first systematically organised under Augustus, and the extensions subsequently made down to the time of Trajan : these extensions, shown by a scarlet line, include, in the west, Britain and Mauretania ; in the centre, Dacia ; in the east Cappadocia, Armenia, Mesopotamia and inland Syria. If Augustus' attempt to subjugate northern Germany had not been disastrously defeated, the Roman Empire might have had a shorter and more defensible frontier, along the line of the Elbe, the Bohemian mountains and the Carpathians.

The first of the smaller maps (11b) shows (a) the area of the Carthaginian Empire, which was the first external foe of Rome, then (240 B.C.) a purely Italian power ; and (b) the stages in the growth of the Roman Empire. The

first advances were due to the Punic wars, of which the first gave to Rome the islands of Corsica and Sardinia, and the second Sicily and the Carthaginian coast of Spain. Then came a period of strenuous warfare, extending over eighty years (201–120 B.C.), which gave to Rome Cisalpine Gaul, bringing Italy up to the Alps, the greater part of Spain, south-eastern Gaul (Narbonensis), the home-territory of Carthage (which became the province of Africa), Macedonia, Greece, and the province of Asia (western Asia Minor) : by this time (120 B.C.) Rome had become the dominant power in the Mediterranean. The third stage—the last century of the Republic, down to the death of Julius Cæsar, 44 B.C.—saw Cæsar's conquest of Gaul, the conquest of the African coast (Numidia and Cyrenaica), Syria, and the north and south coasts of Asia Minor. Before his death (14 A.D.) the emperor Augustus had completed the conquest of Spain, subjugated the Alpine regions of Rhaetia, Noricum and Pannonia, and the Balkan regions of Illyricum and Moesia, thus securing the whole line of the Danube as a frontier ; he had annexed Egypt, and had brought the central part of Asia Minor under his control ; the boundaries of the empire had been rounded off. His successors added Britain, Mauretania Thrace, Cappadocia and inland Syria ; the final conquests, which were to be impermanent, included Dacia, in Europe, and Armenia and Mesopotamia in Asia.

The second of the smaller maps (10a) shows how Augustus divided the empire between himself and the Senate for administrative purposes, keeping for himself the warlike frontier provinces where armies had to be maintained, and leaving to the control of the Senate the more peaceful provinces.

Finally, this Plate contains two plans of the city of Rome, one for the Republican, the other for the Imperial period.

Plate 12-13. This large double plate, like the corresponding plate of Greece, is intended for general reference in studying the whole history of Italy. It shows (by underlining) the numerous Greek colonies of " Magna Graecia." It also shows, in different symbols, the Roman and the Latin colonies by means of which the country was held down as it was conquered ; and the great network of roads by which it was held together, and all its parts were made swiftly accessible. Note how the organising genius of Augustus extended the northern boundary of Italy, the heart of the empire, from the indefensible foothills of the mountains to the watershed.—The two plans, which show the forum of republican Rome, and the grandiose fora of imperial Rome, may be regarded as supplements to the plans of the city on the preceding plate.

Plate 14 is a politically coloured supplement to **Plate 12-13**, meant to illustrate, in particular, the methods whereby Rome conquered Italy. The process begins with the unification, after much fighting, of Latium, of which a more detailed map is given in the inset, **Plate 14b**. The second inset, **14c**, is meant to illustrate roughly the distribution of the racial stocks in Italy at an early date : the flood of conquered slaves which later poured into the peninsula turned it into a *colluvies gentium*. In the main map the Roman and Latin colonies are indicated, in most cases with the dates of their foundation. Note that Italy Proper excluded the whole valley of the Po and its tributaries. This, the most fertile part of Italy, had once been largely occupied by the Etruscans, while in the east and west the Venetian and Ligurian races remained distinct. Conquered by the invading Gauls, this district became known as Gallia Cisalpina, and even after it was

conquered, it was administered as a provincia until Augustus revised the imperial system. Its boundary was the little river Rubicon, which Cæsar crossed when he declared war upon the republic.

Plates 15 and **16**, coloured politically, show more clearly than is possible in **Plate 10–11** (with which they should be compared) Augustus' division of the Empire into provinces. The post-Augustan provinces are coloured buff. The whole coast of the Black Sea was under imperial control, but only the Crimean peninsula was organised as a province.

Plate 17, while primarily designed to illustrate the Roman occupation of Britain, also gives the names and distribution of the British tribes whom the Romans found in the island; and, being coloured physically, it shows how hills, forests, and marshes broke up the country—obstacles which the Roman roads largely overcame. Though the Romans held Britain for nearly four centuries, little is known about their organisation : it is not even possible to give the boundaries of the provinces into which the island was divided. But note (1) the system of fortification against the northern savages—more fully shown in the inset, **17b**; (2) the road-system, with London as its centre, because London was the lowest crossing-place on the Thames for the roads coming from the south-east coast; (3) the location of the three main armies of occupation (legions), at York, Chester, and Caerleon; (4) the few organised towns—Colchester, Gloucester, Lincoln, York, and St. Albans; (5) the Saxon shore (from the Wash to the Severn), fortified during the fourth century as a protection against the German pirates.

Plate 18–19. This plate is intended to illustrate the geographical relations between western civilisation with the Roman Empire as its guardian, and the other civilisations which existed in the world before the breakdown of the Roman Empire began. The map is coloured to show broadly the character of the soil, and of its natural products. Note that there are three fertile and productive regions, each of which gave birth to a civilisation of its own—Europe in the west, India and China in the east. But note also that they are separated from one another by huge barriers of mountains, deserts, or semi-desert countries, which occupy the central area in the map. Out of this region nomadic tribes burst in at intervals upon each of the great civilisations, which strove in vain to keep them at arm's length. For this purpose, the frontier-fortresses of the Roman Empire may be compared with the Great Wall of China. About 200 A.D., the date of this map, the Chinese Empire, which was probably the most advanced of these civilisations, had extended its nominal sway over a vast region of Central Asia, in the hope of keeping the barbarians in check. India (then passing through one of her periodic phases of disorder), saw a large part of her richest territories under the control of a Central Asiatic dynasty; Rome had pushed out her frontiers to the north and east in the hope of reducing the danger, but was soon to lose these gains. But between these rival civilisations—all threatened, from the same source, by a common danger—there was practically no contact.

The two insets show two stages in ancient history of India. In 250 B.C., when Rome had not yet begun the conflict with Carthage that was to make her the predominant power in the Mediterranean, almost the whole of India was under the enlightened and tolerant rule of the great Asoka, one of the noblest of monarchs. In 400 A.D., when the Roman Empire was already in ruins, a new Indian Empire had arisen under the Guptas and for a moment it promised to reduce the whole sub-continent to subjection; but before the English conquest India was never to know unity. At the same period of collapse in the west, the Sassanid kingdom, heir of the Parthians and of the Persians, was reviving past glories.

Plate 20 shows the "Lower" Empire, as it was reconstructed by Diocletian (286–305 A.D.) and Constantine (306–337 A.D.) after the first irruptions of the German barbarians in 250 A.D. and the following years. The frontiers have greatly shrunk, both in Europe (Dacia) and in Asia (Mesopotamia and Armenia). There is a sharp division between the western (Latin) and the eastern (Greek) halves of the empire. Constantinople has replaced Rome as the centre of supreme authority; and the methods of government have become those of oriental despotism, save that the Roman system of law still prevails. The empire is now divided into four great Prefectures or satrapies, and the prefectures are in their turn divided into Dioceses. In the west, the Prefecture of Gaul includes the Dioceses of Britain, Gaul and Spain; the Prefecture of Italy includes the Dioceses of Italy, Illyricum and Africa. In the east, the Prefecture of Illyria includes the Dioceses of Macedonia (including Greece) and Dacia; the Prefecture of the east includes the Dioceses of Pontus, Asia, the Orient (Syria) and

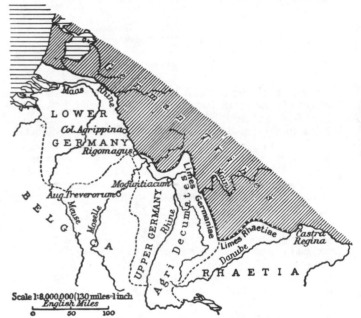

FIG. 4.—THE ROMAN LIMES IN GERMANY

Egypt. Along the weak northern frontier the German tribes are always dangerous and the fortifications of the Limes between the Rhine and the Danube have not availed to prevent the occupation of the angle between the two rivers by the Allemanni and Suevi. These barbarians were being enlisted in large numbers to fill the depleted ranks of the legions. Some of them had been converted to Christianity, which had become, under Constantine, almost the official religion of the empire. Their real veneration for the great structure of civilised society did not prevent them from desiring to enrich themselves by overrunning it; and the downfall of the Empire under whose shelter the civilisation of Europe had absorbed the learning of Greece, the law of Rome, and the religion of Christianity was at hand. "Ancient" history had reached its term.

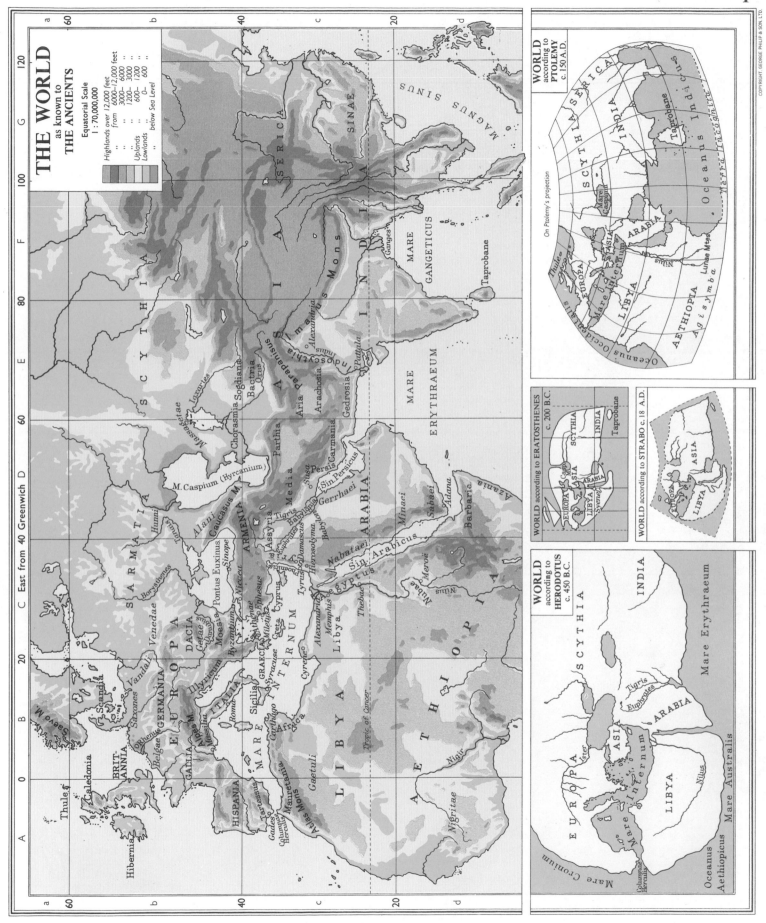

THE WORLD
as known to
THE ANCIENTS

Equatorial Scale
1 : 70,000,000

Highlands over 12,000 feet		
from	6000–	12,000 feet
"	3000–	6000 "
"	1200–	3000 "
Uplands "	600–	1200 "
Lowlands "	0–	600 "
	below Sea Level	

WORLD
according to
PTOLEMY
c. 150 A.D.

On Ptolemy's projection

WORLD according to **ERATOSTHENES** c. 200 B.C.

WORLD according to **STRABO** c.18 A.D.

WORLD
according to
HERODOTUS
c. 450 B.C.

1

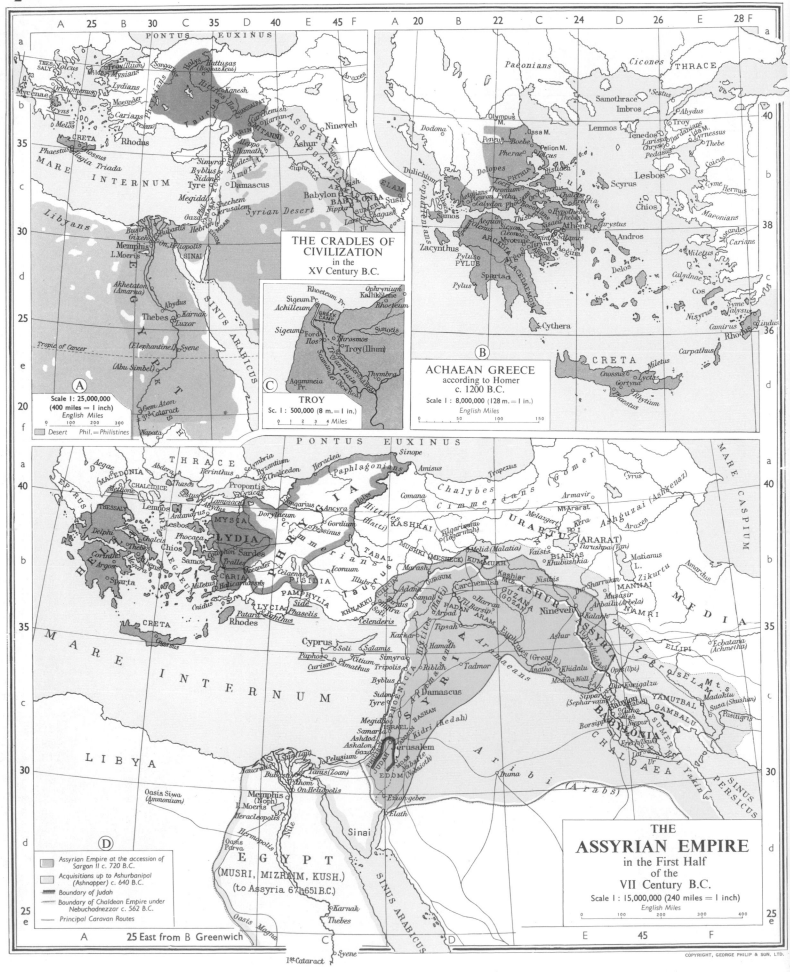

2

THE CRADLES OF CIVILIZATION in the XV Century B.C. — Scale 1 : 25,000,000 (400 miles = 1 inch)

TROY — Sc. 1 : 500,000 (8 m. = 1 in.)

ACHAEAN GREECE according to Homer c. 1200 B.C. — Scale 1 : 8,000,000 (128 m. = 1 in.)

THE ASSYRIAN EMPIRE in the First Half of the VII Century B.C. — Scale 1 : 15,000,000 (240 miles = 1 inch)

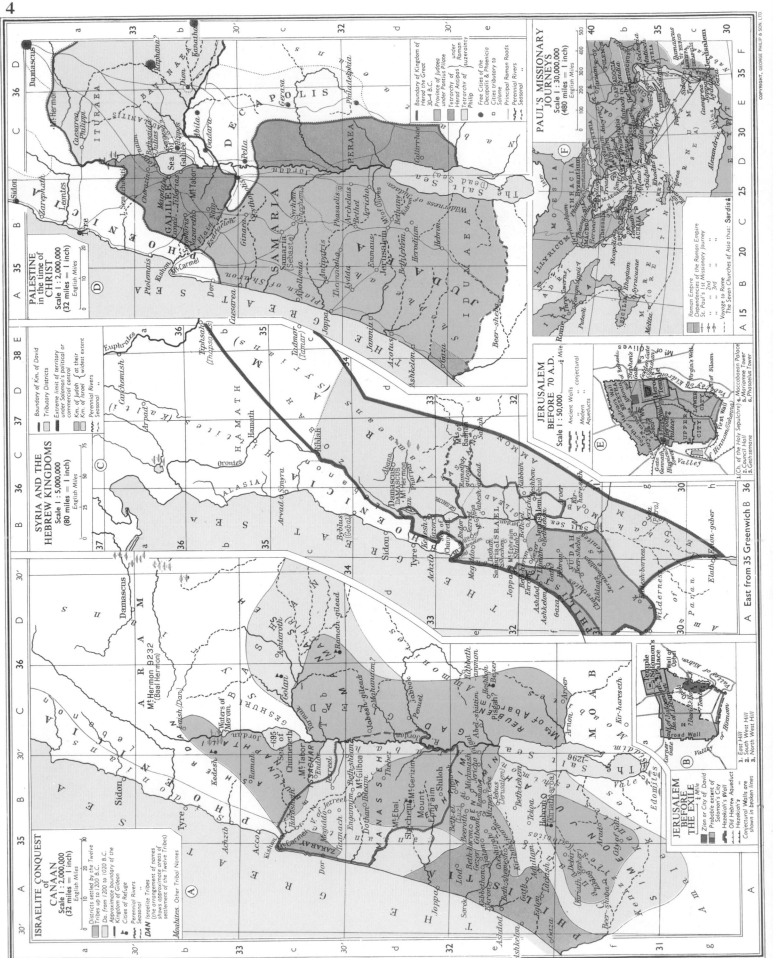

4

ISRAELITE CONQUEST of CANAAN
Scale 1 : 2,000,000
(32 miles = 1 inch)

Districts settled by the Twelve Tribes up to 1200 B.C.
Do. from 1200 to 1020 B.C.
Approximate boundary of the Kingdom of Gideon
Cities of Refuge
Perennial Rivers
Seasonal
DAN Israelite Tribes
(the arrangement of names shows approximate areas of settlement of the Twelve Tribes)
Moabites, Other Tribal Names

SYRIA AND THE HEBREW KINGDOMS
Scale 1 : 5,000,000
(80 miles = 1 inch)

Boundary of Km. of David
Tributary Districts
Extreme limit of territory under Solomon's political or commercial control
Km. of Judah { at their
Km. of Israel { widest extent
Perennial Rivers
Seasonal

PALESTINE in the time of CHRIST
Scale 1 : 2,000,000
(32 miles = 1 inch)

Boundary of Kingdom of Herod the Great 30–4 B.C.
Province of Judea under Pontius Pilate
Tetrarchy of } under
Herod Antipas } Roman
Tetrarchy of } suzerainty
Philip
Free Cities of the Decapolis & Phoenicia
Cities tributary to Salome
Principal Roman Roads
Perennial Rivers
Seasonal

PAUL'S MISSIONARY JOURNEYS
Scale 1 : 30,000,000
(480 miles = 1 inch)

Roman Empire
Dependencies of the Roman Empire
St. Paul's 1st Missionary Journey
2nd
3rd
Voyage to Rome
The Seven Churches of Asia thus: Sardis

JERUSALEM BEFORE 70 A.D.
Scale 1 : 50,000
Ancient Walls
Modern } conjectural
Aqueducts
1.Ch. of the Holy Sepulchre
2.Council Hall
3.Gethsemane
4.Maccabaean Palace
5.Mariamne Tower
6.Phasaelus Tower

JERUSALEM BEFORE THE EXILE
Zion or City of David
Probable extent of Solomon's City
Hezekiah's Wall
Old Hebrew Aqueduct
Hezekiah's
Conjectural Walls are shown in broken lines

COPYRIGHT, GEORGE PHILIP & SON, LTD.

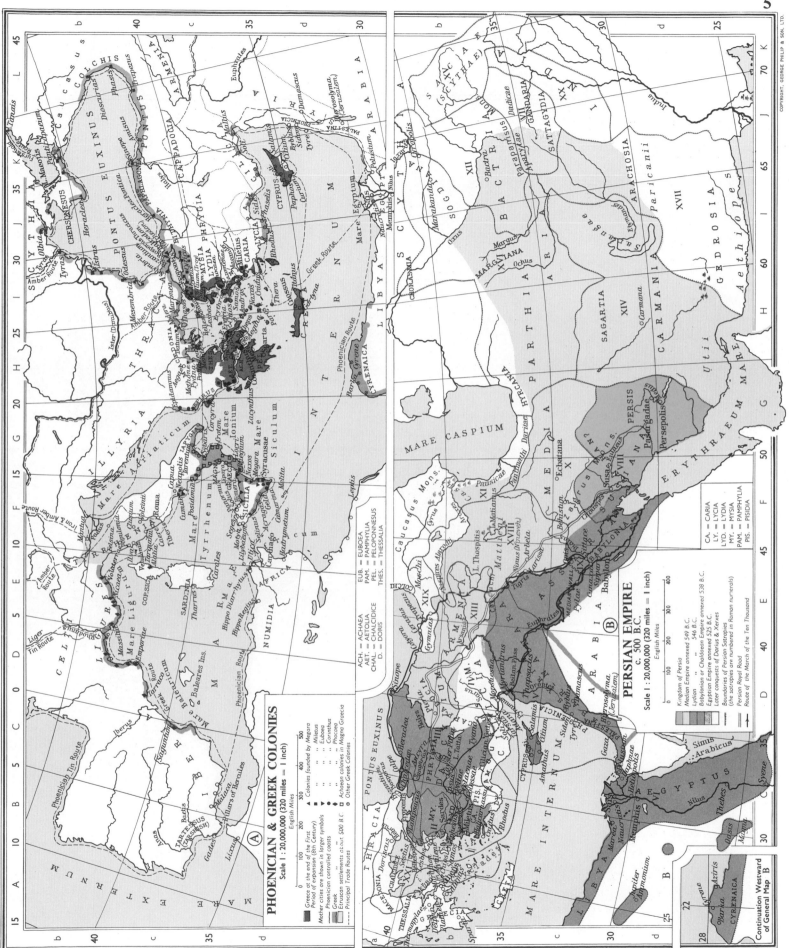

PHOENICIAN & GREEK COLONIES

Scale 1 : 20,000,000 (320 miles = 1 inch)

English Miles

100   200   300   400   500

Greece at the end of the First
Period of expansion (8th Century)
Mother cities are shown in larger symbols
Phoenician controlled coasts
Greek   "
Etruscan settlements about 500 B.C.
Principal Trade Routes

Colonies founded by Megara
        "   "   Miletus
        "   "   Corinth
        "   "   Phocaea
Achaean colonies in Magna Graecia
Other Greek Colonies

ACH. = ACHAEA
AET. = AETOLIA
CHAL. = CHALCIDICE
D. = DORIS

EUB. = EUBOEA
PAM. = PAMPHYLIA
PEL. = PELOPONNESUS
THES. = THESSALIA

PERSIAN EMPIRE
c. 500 B.C.

Scale 1 : 20,000,000 (320 miles = 1 inch)

English Miles

100   200   300   400

Kingdom of Persia
Median Empire annexed 549 B.C.
Lydian   "   "   546 B.C.
Babylonian or Chaldaean Empire annexed 538 B.C.
Egyptian Empire annexed 525 B.C.
Later conquests of Darius & Xerxes
Boundaries of Persian Satrapies
(the satrapies are numbered in Roman numerals)
Persian Royal Road
Route of the March of the Ten Thousand

CA. = CARIA
LY. = LYCIA
LYD. = LYDIA
MY. = MYSIA
PAM. = PAMPHYLIA
PIS. = PISIDIA

Continuation Westward
of General Map B

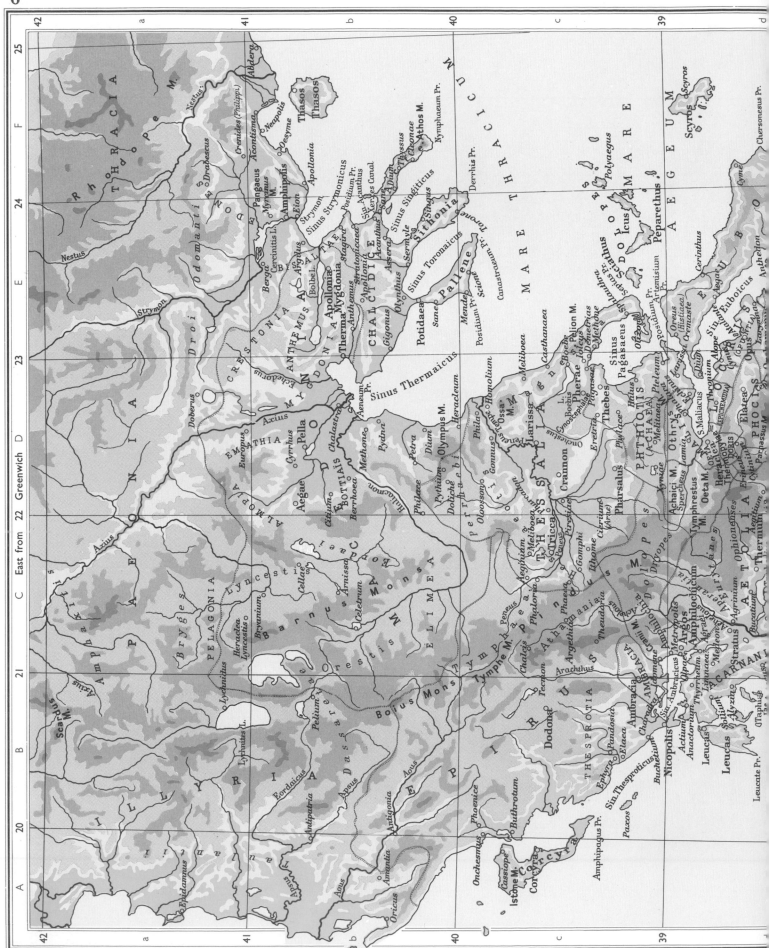

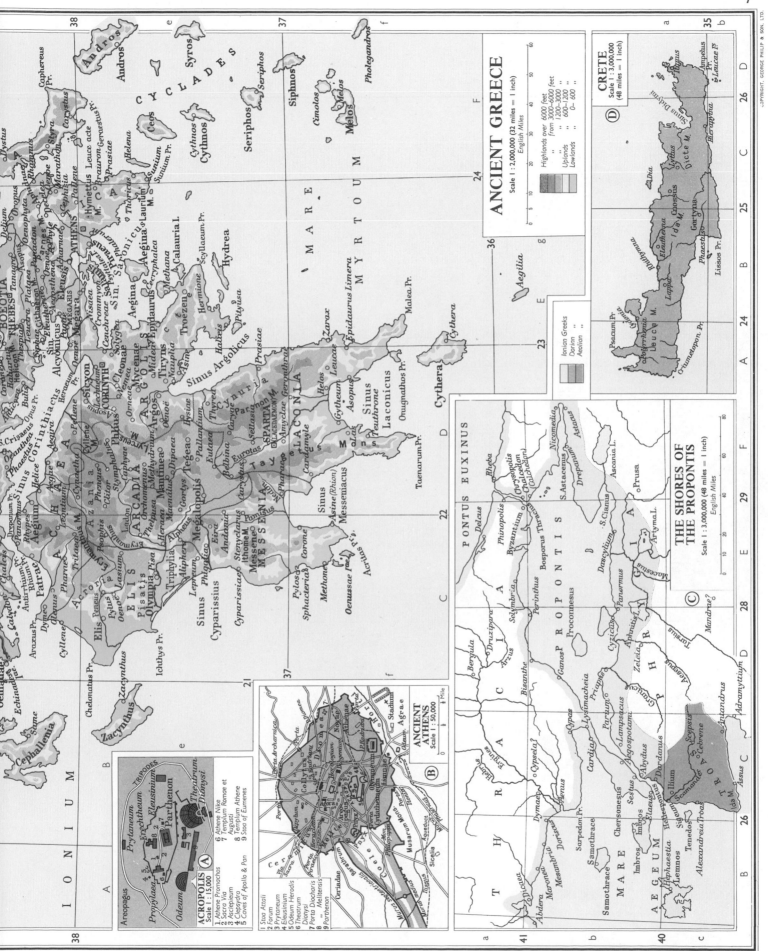

ANCIENT GREECE

Scale 1 : 2,000,000 (32 miles = 1 inch)

English Miles

Highlands over 6000 feet
from 3000–6000 feet
,,   1200–3000   ,,
Uplands   ,,   600–1200   ,,
Lowlands   ,,   0– 600   ,,

Ionian Greeks
Dorian   ,,
Aeolian   ,,

CRETE
Scale 1 : 3,000,000
(48 miles = 1 inch)

THE SHORES OF THE PROPONTIS
Scale 1 : 3,000,000 (48 miles = 1 inch)
English Miles

ACROPOLIS Scale 1 : 15,000

Areopagus   Prytaneum   TRIPODES
Propylaea   Erechtheum   Eleusinium   Theatrum Dionysi
Parthenon   Odeum

1 Athene Promachos
2 Sacra Via
3 Asclepieum
4 Clepsydra
5 Caves of Apollo & Pan
6 Athene Nike
7 Templum Romae et Augusti
8 Templum Athene
9 Stoa of Eumenes

ANCIENT ATHENS
Scale 1 : 50,000

1 Stoa Attali
2 Forum
3 Prytaneum
4 Eleusinium
5 Odeum Herodis
6 Theatrum Dionysi
7 Porta Diocharis
8   ,,   Melitensis
9 Parthenon

COPYRIGHT, GEORGE PHILIP & SON, LTD.

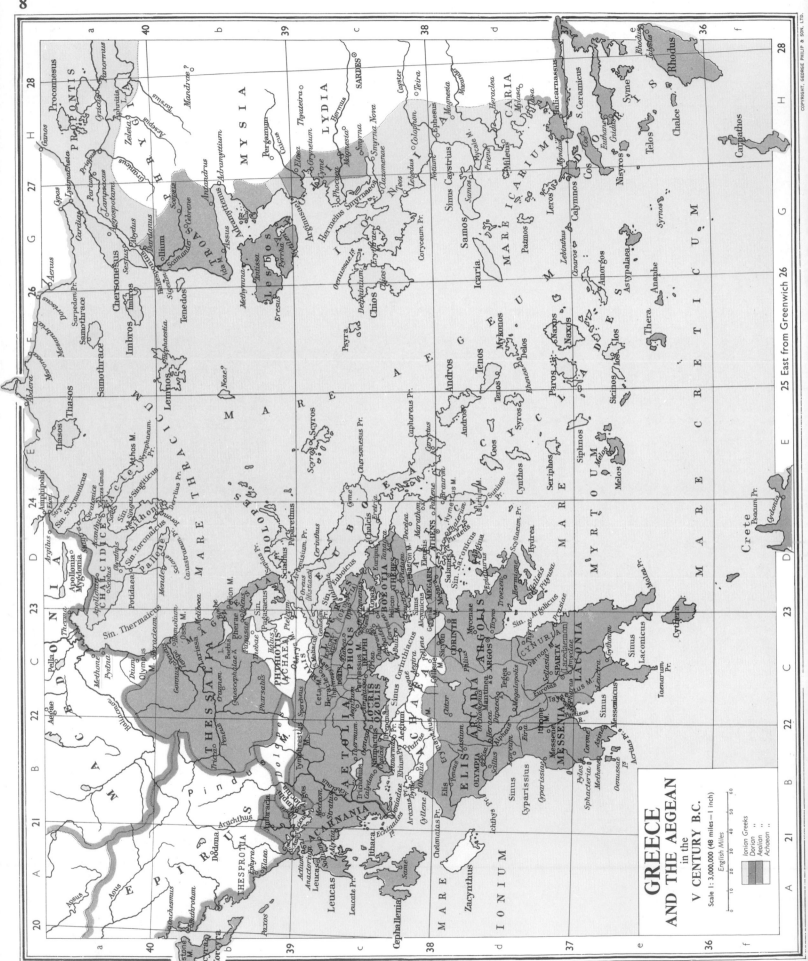

GREECE AND THE AEGEAN in the V CENTURY B.C.

Scale 1: 3,000,000 (48 miles = 1 inch)

English Miles

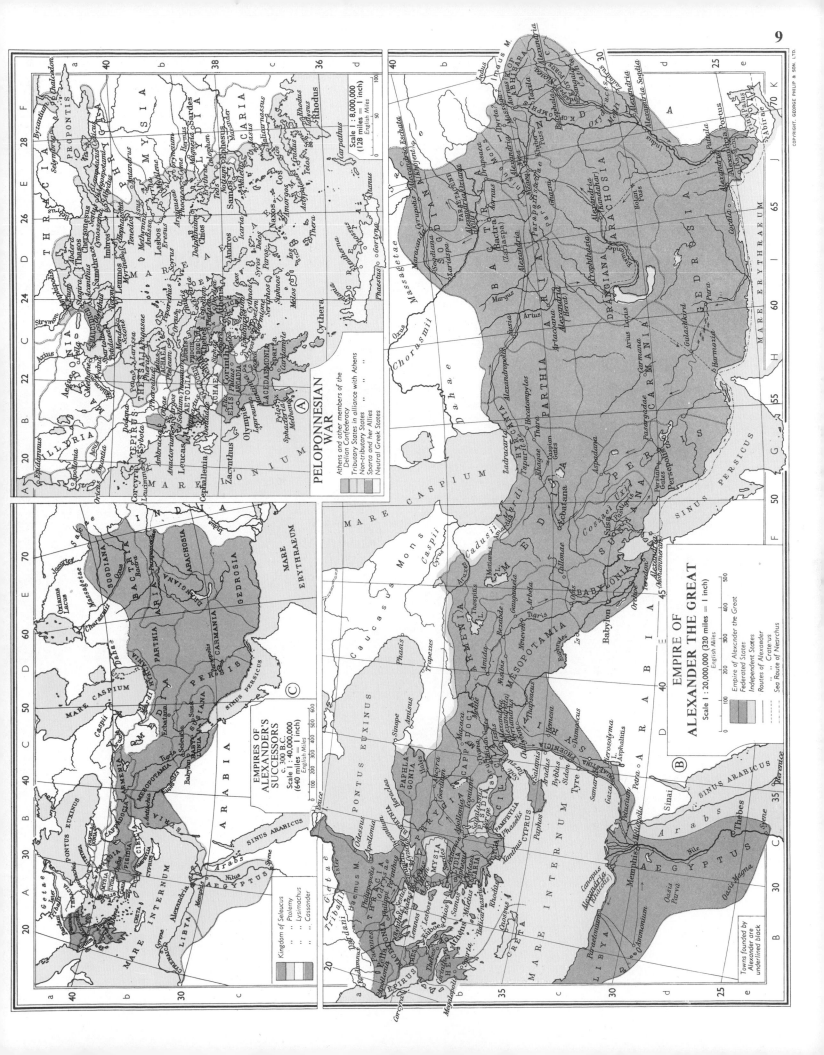

PELOPONNESIAN WAR

Scale 1 : 8,000,000
(128 miles = 1 inch)
English Miles

Athens and other members of the Delian Confederacy
Tributary States in alliance with Athens
Non-tributary States   "   "
Sparta and her Allies   "   "
Neutral Greek States

A

EMPIRE OF ALEXANDER THE GREAT

Scale 1 : 20,000,000 (320 miles = 1 inch)
English Miles
0   100   200   300   400   500

Empire of Alexander the Great
Federated States
Independent States
Routes of Alexander
Crater·us
Sea Route of Nearchus

Towns founded by Alexander are underlined black

B

EMPIRES OF ALEXANDER'S SUCCESSORS

c. 300 B.C.
Scale 1 : 40,000,000
(640 miles = 1 inch)
English Miles
0   100   200   300   400   500   600

Kingdom of Seleucus
"   "   Ptolemy
"   "   Lysimachus
"   "   Cassander

C

15 10 A B C 5 D 10 E 15 F 20 G 25

b
50
c
45
d
40
e
35
f

CALEDONIA

OCEANUS

GERMANICUS

MARE SUEVICUM

HIBERNIA

Osii

Veltae

Vallum Hadriani

Eburacum

Scandiae

Cimbri

Chersonesus

Saxones

Rugii

Guttones

Deva

Lugdunum

Burgundiones

OCEANUS HIBERNICUS

OCEANUS BRITANNICUS

SARM

GERMANIA

Cherusci

Suevi-Semnones

Marcomanni

Colonia Agrippina

Sugambri

Chatti

Quadi

Carpates Montes

LUGDUNENSIS

Lutetia

Argentoratum

RHAETIA

NORICUM

PANNONIA (SUPERIOR) (INF.)

DACIA

ATLANTICUS

MARE CANTABRICUM

AQUITANIA

GERMANIA SUPERIOR

Helvetii

Vindelicia

Carnuntum

Aquincum

Brigantium

Mediolanum

Burdigala

Lugdunum

ILLYRICUM

MOESIA (SUPERIOR)

HISPANIA

TARRACONENSIS

Tolosa

Narbo

Massilia Martius

Arelate

Genua

Ravenna

Ariminum

Ancona

DALMATIA

Salonae

Naissus

MACEDONIA

LUSITANIA

Emerita Augusta

Caesaraugusta

Tarraco

Dertosa

Saguntum

Valentia

CORSICA

SARDINIA

Roma

Ostia

Tarracina

MARE TYRRHENUM

Thessalonica

BAETICA

Corduba

Hispalis

Gades

Carthago Nova

Baleares Iae Maior Minor

Pityusae Iae

Capua

Beneventum

Brundisium

Tarentum

MACEDONIA

IONIUM MARE

ACHAEA Sparta

Tingis

MAURETANIA TINGITANA

MAURETANIA CAESARIENSIS

Caesarea

Hippo Regius

Carthago

Utica

SICILIA

Syracusae

MARE INTERNUM

NUMIDIA

AFRICA

Hadrumetum

Thapsus

MARE

a 50
b 40
c 30

HIBERNIA

OCEANUS GERMANICUS

MARE SUEVICUM

BRITANNIA

ATLANTICUS OCEANUS

GERMANIA

SARMATIA

LUGDUNENSIS

BELGICA

GALLIA

AQUITANIA

NARBONENSIS

RHAETIA

NORICUM

PANNONIA

DACIA

TARRACONENSIS (HISPANIA CITERIOR)

ITALIA

DALMATIA

MOESIA

PONTUS EUXINUS

LUSITANIA

HISPANIA

BAETICA

CORSICA

SARDINIA

Roma

MACEDONIA

THRACIA

BITHYNIA

PONTUS

GALATIA

CAPPADOCIA

PARTHIA

SICILIA

ACHAEA

ASIA

CILICIA

SYRIA

MARE

INTERNUM

CRETA

CYPRUS

AFRICA

CYRENAICA

AEGYPTUS

ARABIA

Ⓐ MAURETANIA
**IMPERIAL &
SENATORIAL
PROVINCES**
c. 14 A.D.
Scale 1 : 40,000,000
(640 miles = 1 inch)
English Miles
0   200   400   600

▓ Imperial Provinces
░ Senatorial „

Tripolitana

Leptis Magna

Oea

Syrtis Maior

Ptolemaïs

Arsinoë

Cyrene

Apollonia

Pentapolis

Barka

Nasamones

CYRENAICA

CRETA

Gortyna

A.C. Alpes Cottiae
A.M. Alpes Maritimae
A.P. Alpes Penninae

	Highlands over 12,000 feet
	„ „ 6000-12,000
	„ „ 3000- 6000
	Uplands „ 1200- 3000
	„ „ 600- 1200
	Lowlands „ 0- 600
	„ below Sea Level

E 15 F 20 G East from

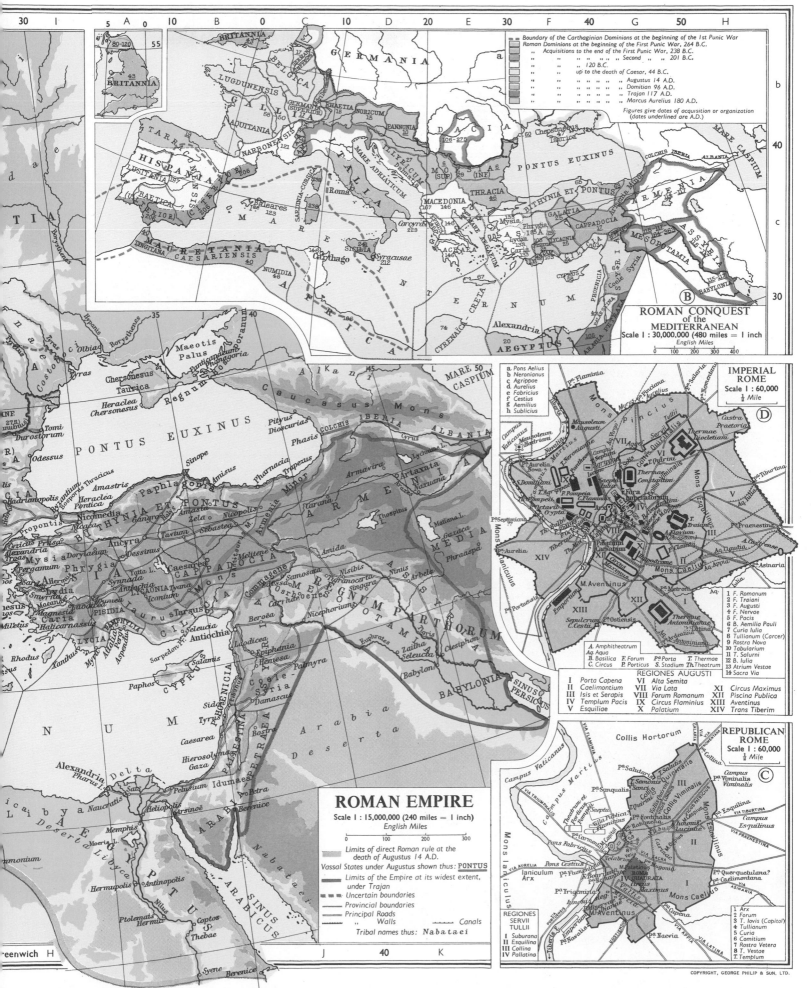

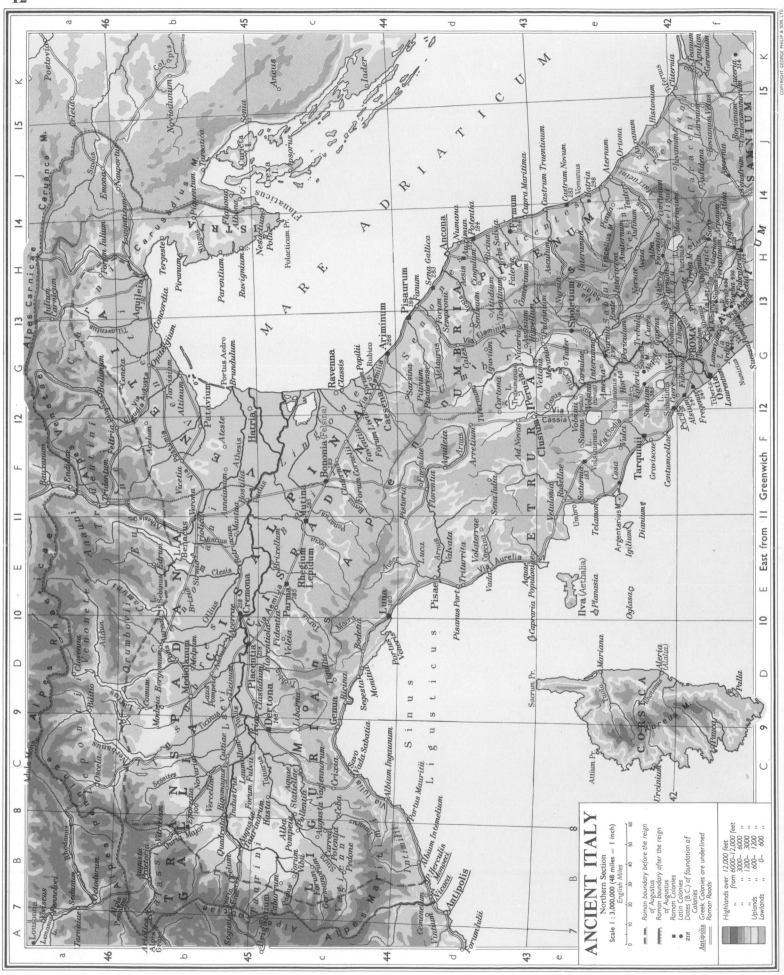

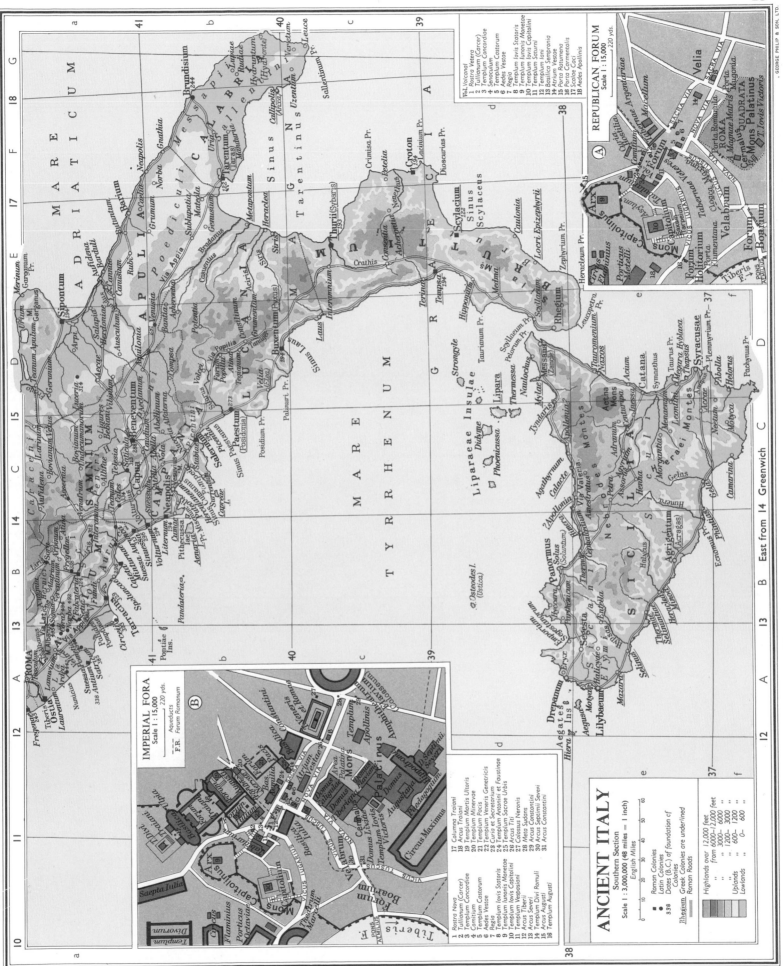

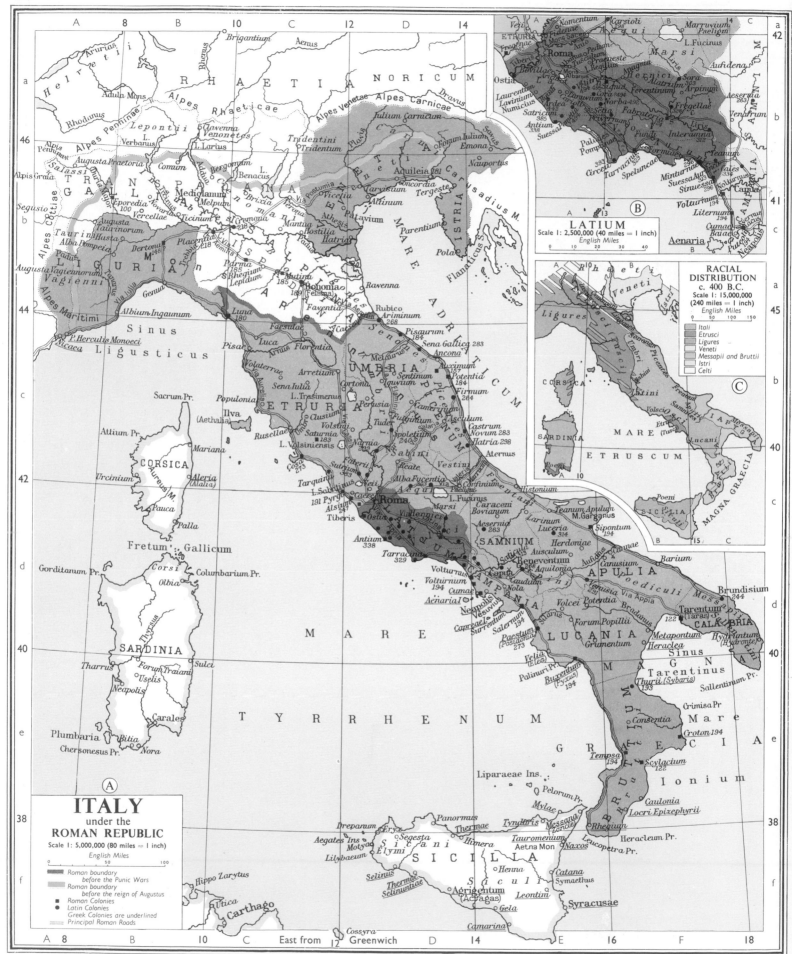

ROMAN EMPIRE
in the time of
AUGUSTUS
I. ITALIA &
WESTERN PROVINCES
Scale 1 : 10,000,000 (160 miles = 1 inch)
English Miles

Limits of direct Roman rule at the death of Augustus 14 A.D.
Territories subsequently acquired
Provincial boundaries
Chief Roads
"   Walls
Tribal names thus: HELVETII
A.C.   Alpes Cottiae
A.M.   Alpes Maritimae
A.P.   Alpes Penninae

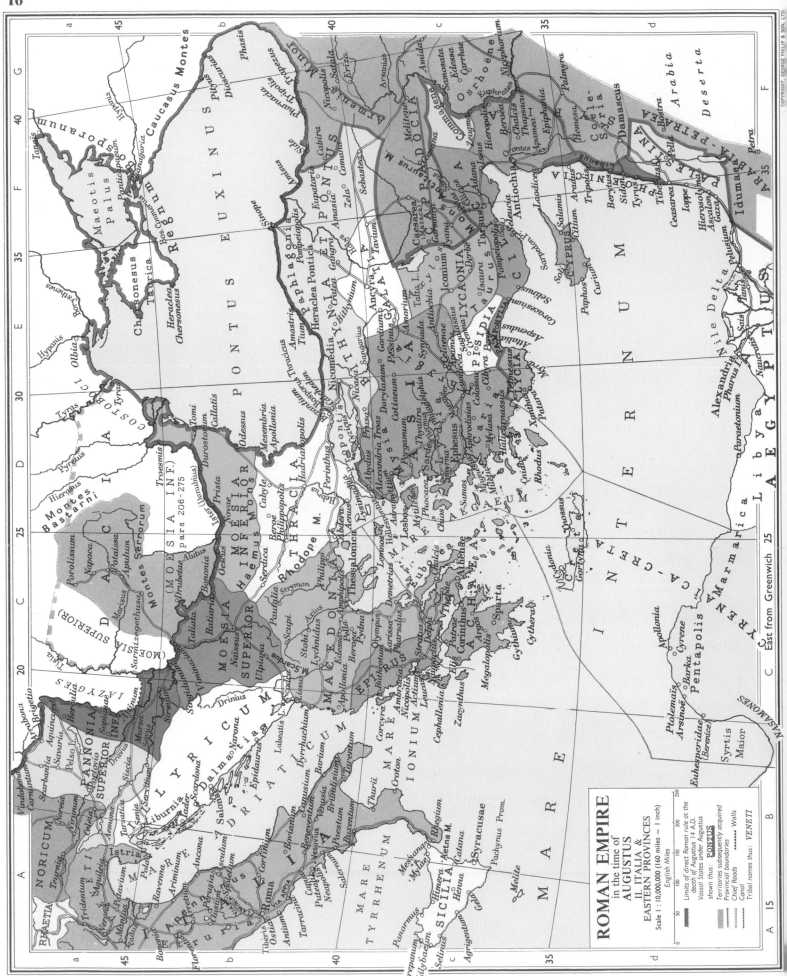

ROMAN EMPIRE
in the time of
AUGUSTUS

II. ITALIA &
EASTERN PROVINCES

Scale 1 : 10,000,000 (160 miles = 1 inch)

English Miles

Limits of direct Roman rule at the
death of Augustus 14 A.D.
Vassal States under Augustus
shown thus: **PONTUS**
Territories subsequently acquired
Provincial boundaries
Chief Roads
Walls
Canal
Tribal names thus: VENETI

INDEX

Note—Each Map in the Atlas is divided into Squares by the lines of latitude and longitude, and these Squares are indicated by Reference Letters in the map borders. These Reference Letters, following each name in the Index, indicate the Square, and the succeeding Numeral indicates the Number of the Map in which each place will be found. Thus:—"Babylonia, Fc, 9b" shows that Babylonia will be found on Map 9b, and in the Square indicated by the Reference Letters "Fc".

The following abbreviations are used:—A., *Amphitheatrum* (Amphitheatre); Aest., *Aestuarium* (Estuary); Aq., *Aquaeductus* (Aqueduct); C., *Castellum* (Castle); E., East(ern); F., Fl., *Flumen* (River); Ins., *Insula(ae)* (Island(s)); I(s). *Island(s)*; K., *Kingdom;* L., *Lacus* (Lake, Loch); M., *Mons* (Mountain); Mtes., *Montes* (Mountains); Mt(s). *Mountain(s)*; N., North(ern); Pa., *Porta* (Gate); Pr., *Promontorium* (Promontory); R., River; S., South(ern); Th., *Theatrum* (Theatre); Val., *Valley;* W., West(ern).

Abana, R., Cd, 4c
Abarim, Mts. of, Ce, 4a
Abar-Nahara, Db, 5b
Abdera (Hispania), Be, 15
Abdera (Thracia), Hb, 5a; Da, 9a
Abella, Cb, 13
Abellinum, Cb, 13
Abel-shittim Ce, 4a
Abergavenny (Gobannium), Ce, 17
Abhira, Ec, 18b
Abhisara, Kingdom of, Kc, 9b
Abila, Cb, 4d
Abirae, Je, 9b
Abodu (Abydus), Bc, 3b
Abolla, Df, 13
Abone, De, 17
Abu Simbel Bd, 3a
Abus, Cb., 15
Abus Fl., Fc, 17
Abydus (Abodu), Bc, 3b
Abydus (Mysia), Db, 16
Acanthus, Eb, 6
Acarnania, Cd, 6
Acco, Bc, 4a
Acelum, Fb, 12
Acerrae, Db, 12
Achaea, Cd, 7
Achaea, Phthiotis, Dc, 6
Achaia, Ed, 18
Achaici, M., Dd, 6
Acharnae, Ed, 7
Achelous, F., Cd, 6
Acherontia (Bruttium), Ec, 13
Acherontia (Lucania), Db, 13
Achilleum, Inset, 2c
Achmetha (Ecbatana), Fc, 2d
Achzib, Bb, 4a
Aciris, F., Eb, 13
Acium, De, 13
Acontisma, Fb, 6
Acrae, Ce, 13
Acragas, Fc, 5a
Acritas Pr., Cf, 7
Acropolis, Inset, 7a
Acroria, Ce, 7
Acte, Argolis, Ee, 7
Acte, Chalcidice, Fc, 15
Actium, Bd, 6
Ad Novas, Fd, 12
Adana, Arabia, Gf, 18
Adana, Syria, Dc, 2d
Addua, F., Db, 12
Adramyttenus, Gb, 8
Adramyttium, Cc, 7c
Adranum, Ce, 13
Adria, Ba, 4f
Aduatuca, Db, 15
Adula Mons, Ca, 12
Adullam, Ae, 4a
Aebudae, Inset, 17a
Aecae Da, 13
Aeclanum, Da, 13
Aedes Apollinis, Inset, 13a
Aedes Magnae Matris, Inset, 13a
Aedes Vestae, Inset, 13a
Aedui, Cc, 15
Aegae (Achaea), Dd, 7
Aegae (Euboea), Ed, 6
Aegae (Macedonia), Ca, 9a
Aegates, Ins., Ad, 13
Aegilia, Eg, 7
Aegina, Ee, 7
Aeginium, Cc, 6
Aegira, Dd, 7
Aegitium, Dd, 6
Aegium, Dd, 7
Aegospotami, Ea, 9a
Aegosthena, Ed, 7
Aegusa, Ae, 13
Ægyptus, Fe, 18
Aeminium, Ad, 15
Aemona, Aa, 16
Aenaria Ins., Bb, 13

Aeneum Pr., Db, 6
Aenus, Cb, 7c
Aenus, F., Ec, 15
Aeolis, Bb, 5b; Bb, 9b; Gc, 8
Aequi, He, 12
Aesepus, F., Dc, 7c
Aesernia, Ca, 13
Aesica (Great Chesters), Inset, 17
Aesis, Hd, 12
Aesis, F., Hd, 12
Aestii, Ha, 10
Aethalia, Ee, 12
Aethiopes, Id, 5b
Aethiopia, Bd, 1
Aetna M., Ce, 13
Aetolia, Bb, 9a
Aetolians, Bb, 2b
Africa, Dd, 18
Africa, Diocese of, Eg, 20
Africa (*vetus provincia*), De, 15
Agammeia Pr., Inset, 2c
Agathyrnum, Cd, 13
Agedincum, Cc, 15
Agger Servii Tullii, Inset, 11d
Aginnum, Cd, 15
Agisymba, Inset, 1
Agora, Inset, 7b
Agrae, Inset, 7b
Agraei, Cd, 6
Agri Decumates, Dc, 15
Agrigentum (Acragas), Be, 13
Agrinium, Cd, 6
Agrippae, Inset, 11d
Agyrium, Ce, 13
Ai, Be, 4a
Ajodhya, Fc, 18b
Akeman Street, Ee, 17
Akhetaton (Tell-el-Amarna), Bc, 3b
Akhlamu, Db, 3a
Akkad, Db, 3a
Alalia (Aleria), De, 12
Alani, Gc, 18
Alasa (Cyprus), Ba, 3a
Alasia, Cb, 4c
Alatrium, Ba, 13
Alauna (Maryport), Cb, 17
Alba, Cd, 15
Alba Fucentia, He, 12
Alba Pompeia, Cc, 12
Albania, Gb, 11b
Albanus, L., Aa, 13
Albanus, M., As, 13
Albis, R., Fc, 20
Albium Ingaunum, Cc, 12
Albium Intemelium, Bd, 12
Albona, Jb, 12
Alchester, Ee, 17
Aleppo (Halap), Ca, 3a
Aleria (Alalia), De, 12; Dd, 10
Alesia, Cc, 15
Alexandreia Troas, Cc, 7c
Alexandretta (Alexandria), Db, 9b
Alexandria Aegyptus, Ed, 18
Alexandria, Asia, Ec, 1
Alexandria (Alexandretta), Db, 9b
Alexandria (Bactria), Ib, 9b
Alexandria (Gedrosia), Jd, 9b
Alexandria (Herat), Ic, 9b
Alexandria (India), Jb, Kd, 9b
Alexandria (Kandahar), Jc, 9b
Alexandria (Mohammerah), Fc, 9b
Alexandria (Porus), Kc, 9b
Alexandria (Rhacotis), Bc, 9b
Alexandria Eschata (Khojent), Ja, 9b
Alexandria Oxiana (Kilif), Jb, 9b
Alexandria Portus (Karachi), Jc, 9b
Alexandria Sogdia, Kd, 9b

Alexandria Troas, He, 11
Alexandropolis, Hb, 9b
Aliphera, Ce, 7
Allemanni, Ed, 20
Allifae, Ca, 13
Allobroges, Dc, 15
Almopia, Db, 6
Alope, Dd, 6
Alpes, Ed, 20
Alpes Carnicae, Ga, 12
Alpes Cottiae, Ab, 12
Alpes Maritimi, Bc, 12
Alpes Montes, Dc, 15
Alpes Penninae, Ba, 12
Alpes Rhaeticae, Ea, 12
Alpes Venetae, Ga, 12
Alpheus, F., C, 7
Alpis Graia, Ab, 12
Alpis Pennina, Bb, 12
Alsium, Gf, 12
Alta Semita, Inset, 11d
Altinum Venetia, Gb, 12
Altinum Pannonia, Ba, 16
Alutus, F., Gd, 10
Alyzia, Bd, 6
Alzi, Ca, 3a
Amalekites, Bf, 4a
Amantia, Aa, 9a
Amardus, F., Fb, 9b
Amasia, Fb, 16
Amastris, Cd, 11
Amathus, Cc, 5b
Ambracia, Bb, 9a
Ameria, Ge, 12
Amestratus, Ce, 13
Amida, Gc, 16
Amisia, F., Db, 15
Amisus, Fb, 16
Amiternum, He, 12
Ammon, Ce, 4c
Ammonites, Cd, 4a
Ammonium, Bd, 9b
Amor, Cb, 3a
Amorgos, Fe, 8
Amorites, Cb, 3a
Amorium, Ec, 16
Ampelus Pr., Da, 7d
Amphaxitis, Ca, 6
Amphilochia, Cc, 6
Amphipagus Pr., Bc, 6
Amphipolis, Ca, 9a
Amphissa, Dd, 6
Amphitheatrum Flavium, Inset, 13b
Amphylia, Eb, 4f
Amyclae, De, 7
Anactorium, Bb, 9a
Anagnia, Ba, 13
Anaphe, I., Fe, 8
Anapus, F., De, 13
Anas, R., Bf, 20
Anatho, Ec, 2d
Anauni, Ea, 12
Ancaster (Causennae), Fd, 17
Ancona, Hd, 12
Ancus, Kc, 12
Ancyra (Phrygia), Cb, 2d
Andania, De, 7
Andematunnum, Dc, 15
Anderida (Pevensey), Gf, 17
Anderida Silva, Fe, 17
Andhra, Jf, 19
Andhra, Kingdom of, Cc, 18a
Andros, Fe, 7
Angli, Ec, 20
Anglii, Db, 15
Anio, F., Gf, 12
Anneianum, Fb, 12
Anping, Nd, 19
Anshan, Fc, 5b
Antaeopolis (Du-kau), Bc, 3b
Antandrus, Eb, 9a
Anthedon, Ed, 6
Anthemus, Eb, 6

Antiachia, Ie, 11
Anticyra, Dd, 7
Antigonia, Bb, 6
Anting, Md, 19
Antinopolis, Ig, 11
Antioch (Pisidia), Eb, 4f
Antiochia, Fd, 18
Antiochia (Syria), Fc, 16
Antiochus, Kingdom of, Fb, 4f
Antipatria, Ab, 6
Antipatris, Ac, 4d
Antipolis, Bd, 12
Antirrhium Pr., Cd, 7
Antissa, Eb, 9a
Antitaurus M., Fc, 16
Antium, Aa, 13
Antonia, Inset, 4e
Antoniniana Aq., Inset, 11d
Anxa, Fb, 13
Anxanum, Je, 12
Aornus (Abhisara), Kc, 9b
Aornus (Bactria), Jb, 9b
Aous, F., Ab, 6
Apamea (Phrygia), Ec, 16
Apamea (Syria), Fc, 16
Aparytae, Jb, 5b
Aperantia, Cd, 6
Aphidnae, Ed, 7
Aphnitis, L., Db, 7c
Aphrodis ias, Dc, 16
Aphroditopolis (Middle Egypt), Bb, 3b
Aphroditopolis (Upper Egypt), Bc, 3b
Apodotia, Cd, 6
Apollinopolis magna Bd, 3a
Apollinopolis-parva (Nebut), Cd, 3b
Apollo and Pan, Caves of, Inset, 7a
Apollonia (Edones), Fb, 6
Apollonia (Illyria), Aa, 9a
Apollonia (Judea), Ac, 4d
Apollonia (Macedonia), Bb, 16
Apollonia ((Pentapolis), Cd, 16
Apollonia Phrygia, Cb, 9b
Apollonia (Sicilia), Cd, 13
Apollonia (Thracia), Db, 16
Apollonia Mygdonia, Eb, 6
Appia, Aq., Inset, 11d
Apsorus, Jc, 12
Apsus, F., Ab, 6
Apuli, Cb, 14c
Apulia, Ea, 13
Apulum, Ca, 16
Aquae, Inset, 17a
Aquae (Buxton), Ec, i7
Aquae Flaviae, Ad, 15
Aquae Populoniae, Ed, 12
Aquae Sextiea, Dd, 15
Aquae Statiellae, Cc, 12
Aquae Sulis (Bath), De, 17
Aquae Tarbellicae, Bd, 15
Aquileia (Etruria), Fd, 12
Aquileia (Rhaetia), Ec, 15
Aquileia (Venetia), Hb, 12
Aquilonia, Da, 13
Aquincum, Ba, 16
Aquitania, Dd, 20
Arabah, Bg, 4c; Cd, 4a
Arabia, Ge, 18
Arabia Deserta, Lh, 20
Arabia, Felix, Fe, 18
Arabian Desert, Bc, 3a; Cc, 3a
Arabia, Petraea, Fe, 18
Arabs (Aribi), Ec, 2d
Arachosia, Id, 18
Arachthus, F., Cc, 6
Aram, Db, 4a
Aramaeans (Syrians), Cd, 4c
Arar, F., Cc, 15
Ararat, Mt., Eb, 2d

Ararat (Urartu), Eb, 2d
Arausio, Cd, 15
Araxes, F., Fb, 9b
Araxus, Pr., Cd, 7
Arbailu (Arbela), Eb, 2d
Arbela, Gd, 18
Arbela (Arbailu), Eb, 2d
Arcadia, Cc, 9a
Archelais, Bd, 4d
Arcus Augusti, Inset, 13b
Arcus Constantini, Inset, 13b
Arcus Septimii Severi, Inset, 13b
Arcus Severi, Inset, 13b
Arcus Tiberii, Inset, 13b
Arcus Titi, Inset, 13b
Arcus Traiani, Inset, 13b
Ardea, Aa, 13
Ardeatina, Pa., Inset, 11d
Arden, Forest of, Ed, 17
Arduenna Silva, Db, 15
Area Palatina, Inset, 13b
Arelate, Cd, 15
Areopagus, Inset, 7a
Argentarius, M., Fe, 12
Argentoratum, Dc, 15
Argethia, Cc, 6
Argilus, Eb, 6
Arginusae, Eb, 9a
Argolis, De, 7
Argos, De, 7
Argos (Amphilocia), Bb, 9a
Aria, Id, 18
Aribi (Arabs), Ec, 2d
Aricia, Ab, 14b
Ariminum, Gc, 12
Arinna, Ca, 3a
Ariolica (Transpadana), Ab Eb, 12
Arius, F., Ib, 9b
Arius Lacus, Hc, 9b
Arjunayana, Ec, 18b
Armavir, Ea, 2d
Armavira, Kd, 11
Armenia, Ke, 11
Armenia Minor, Fb, 16
Armorica, Bc, 15
Arne, Dc, 6
Arnissa, Cb, 6
Arnon, R., Cf, 4a
Arnus, F., Ed. 12
Aroer, Bf, 4c
Arpad, Da, 4c
Arpi, Da, 13
Arpinum, Ba, 13
Arrabona, Ba, 16
Arretium, Fd, 12
Arsanias, F., Db, 5b
Arsinoé (Aegyptus), If, 11
Arsinoé (Egypt), Bc, 3a
Arsinoé (Pentapolis), Cd, 16
Artacoana, Ic, 9b
Artaxata, Gc, 18
Artemisium, Ec, 6
Artyma, L., Eb, 7c
Arurias, F., Aa, 14a
Arvad, Bc, 4c
Arverni, Cc, 15
Arzanibiu, Ca, 3a
Arzawa, Ba, 3a
Arzus, F., Da, 7c
Ascania, L., Fb, 7c
Asclepieum, Inset, 7a
Asculum, He, 12
Ashdod, Ae, 4a
Asher, Bb, 4a
Ashguzai (Ashkenaz), Fb, 2d
Ashkelon, Ae, 4a
Ashkenaz (Ashguzai), Fb, 2d
Ashtaroth, Dc, 4a
Ashur, Da. 3a
Ashur (Assyria), Eb. 2d
Asia, If, 20
Asia, Diocese of, If, 20

Asinaria, Pa., Inset, 11d
Asine (Argolis), De, 7
Asine (Rhion), Cf, 7
Askalon, Bb, 3a
Asopus, Df, 7
Asopus, F., De, Ed, 7
Aspadana, Hd, 18
Aspendus, Ec, 16
Asphaltitis, L., Dc, 9b
Asphynis, Cd, 3b
Assera, Eb, 6
Assisium, Gd, 12
Assorus, Ce, 13
Assus, Eb, 9a
Assyria, Da, 3a
Astacus (Acarnania), Cd, 6
Astacus (Phrygia), Fb, 7c
Atella, Cb, 13
Astigi, Ae, 15
Astures, Ad, 15
Asturica Augusta, Ad, 15
Astypalaea, I., Ge, 8
Asylum, Inset, 13a
Atalante, Ed, 6
Atavi, Cb, 18
Aternum, Je, 12
Aternus, F., He, 12
Ateste, Fb, 12
Athamania, Cc, 6
Athenae, Hf, 20
Athene Nike, Inset, 7a
Athene Promachos, Inset, 7a
Athens, Ancient, Inset, 7b
Athesis, F., Fb, 12
Athos, M, Fb, 6
Athribis (Hat-bri-ebe), Ba, 3b
Atina (Latium), Ba, 13
Atina (Lucania), Db, 13
Atlas, M., Cg, 20
Atrebates, Ee, 17
Atrium Vestae, Inset, 13a, b
Atropatene, Mf, 20
Attalia, Db, 4f
Attica, Cb, 9a
Attidium, Gd, 12
Attium Pr., Ce, 12
Aufidena (Apulia), Ea, 13
Aufidena (Samnium), Ca, 13
Aufidus, F., Ea, 13
Aufinum, He, 12
Augusta Praetoria, Bb, 12
Augusta Rauricorum, Dc, 15
Augusta Taurinorum (Turin),
  Bb, 12
Augusta Treverorum, Dc, 15
Augusta Vagiennorum, Bc, 12
Augusta Vindelicorum, Ec, 15
Augustobona, Cc, 15
Augustobriga, Bd, 15
Augustodunum, Cc, 10
Augustodurum, Bc, 15
Augustonemetum, Cc, 15
Augustoritum, Cc, 15
Aulis, Ed, 7
Aunedonnacum, Cc, 15·
Aurasius, M., De, 15
Aurelia, Pa., Inset, 11d
Aurelia Nova, Pa., Inset, 11d
Aureliani, Dd, 20
Aurelius, Inset, 11d
Aureus M., De, 12
Aurunci, Ba, 13
Ausculum, Da, 13
Auser, F., Ec, 12
Australe Pr., Inset, 17a
Autricum, Cc, 15
Auximum, Hd, 12
Avaricum, Cc, 15
Aveia, He, 12
Avenio, Cd, 15
Aventicum, Dc, 15
Aventinus, Inset, 11d
Aventinus M., Inset, 11c; 11d
Avernuslacus, Cc, 14b
Aviones, Db, 15
Axius, F., Ca, 9a
Axylos, Ec, 16
Azania, Gg, 18
Azania, De, 7
Aziris, Inset, 5b
Azotus, Ad, 4d

BAAL HERMON (Mt. Hermon),
  Cb, 4a
Babel (Babylon), Ec, 2d
Babylon, Db, 3a
Babylon (Babel), Ec, 2d
Babylon (Cairo), Bb, 3b
Babylonia, Fc, 9b
Bactra, Jb, 5b; Jb, 9b

Bactria, Id, 18
Bactria (Zariaspa), Jb, 9b
Baetica, Ae, 15
Baetis, F., Ae, 15
Bagacum, Cb, 15
Bagistana, Gd, 18
Baiae, Cc, 14b
Bairat, Bb, 18a
Baithan, Jf, 19
Bakarei, Jg, 19
Baleares, Df, 20
Bannaventa, Ed, 17
Bantia, Db, 13
Bar Hill, Ba, 17
Barathrum, Inset, 7b
Barbaria, Gg, 18
Barbarike, Ie, 18
Barcino, Cd, 10
Barduli, Ea, 13
Barga, Ca, 3a
Barium, Ea, 13
Barka, Cd, 16
Barnus, M., Cb, 6
Bashan, Dc, 4a
Bashan, Mts. of, Ce, 4c
Basilica Aemilia, Inset, 13b
Basilica Constantini, Inset, 13b
Basilica Iulia, Inset, 13b
Basilica Sempronia, Inset, 13a
Basilica Ulpia, Inset, 13b
Bastarnae, Id, 20
Bastarni M., Da, 16
Bastetani, Be, 15
Basti, Be, 15
Bastuli, Be, 15
Batanaea, Db, 4d
Batava, Ec, 15
Batavi, Cb, 15
Bath (Aqua Sulis), De, 17
Bauxanum, Fa, 12
Beeroth, Be, 4a
Beer-sheba, Af, 4a
Behistun, Fc, 5b
Beilan Pass, Db, 5b
Beirut, Cb, 3a
Belbina, De, 7
Belgae, De, 17
Belgae, Bb, 1
Belgica, Cc, 15
Bellunum, Ga, 12
Benacus, L., Eb, 12
Benares (Kasi), Cb, 18a
Beneventum, Ca, 13
Benjamin, Be, 4a
Benwell (Condercum), Inset, 17
Berenice (Aegyptus), Cd, 3a
Berenice (Arabia-Petraea), Jg, 11
Berenice (Euhesperiade), Cd, 16
Berga, Eb, 6
Bergomum, Db, 12
Bergula, Da, 7c
Beroe, Db, 16
Beroea (Macedonia), Cb, 16
Beroea (Syria), Fc, 16
Berrhoea, Db, 6
Berytus, Fd, 16
Bethany, Bd, 4d
Beth-el (Luz), Be, 4a
Bethesda, Pool of, Inset, 4e
Beth-horon, Be, 4a
Bethlehem, Be, 4a
Bethsaida Julias, Cb, 4d
Beth-shean, Bd, 4a
Beth-shemish, Ae, 4a
Betriacum, Eb, 12
Bezabde, Eb, 9b
Bezer, Ce, 4a
Bezetha, Inset, 4e
Bhojas, Bb, 18a
Biainas, Eb, 2d
Bibracte, Cc, 15
Bibrax, Cc, 15
Bilbilis, Bd, 15
Bilitio, Da, 12
Birdoswald (Camboglanna),
  Inset, 17
Birrens (Blatobulgium), Ca, 17
Bisalate, Eb, 6
Bisanthe, Db, 7c
Bishri, Mt., Ca, 3a
Bit Yakin, Fc, 2d
Bithynia, Fc, 18; Je, 20
Bithynia-et-Pontus, Eb, 16
Bithynium, Eb, 16
Bitia, Be, 14a
Bituriges-Cubi, Cc, 15
Bituriges-Vivisci,·Bc, 15
Blatobulgium (Birrens), Ca, 17
Boderia Aest., Inset, 17a
Bodetia, Dc, 12

Bodh Gaya, Cb, 18a
Bodotria Aest., Da, 17
Boebe, Dc, 6
Boebis, L., Dc, 6
Boeotia, Cb, 9a
Boeotians, Cb, 2b
Boghaz Keui (Hattusas), Cb, 2a
Boii, Fc, 12
Boius, M., Bb, 6
Bokhara, Id, 18
Bolan Pass, Jd, 9b
Bolbe, L., Eb, 6
Bolbitinic Mouth, Ba, 3b
Bolerium Pr., Af, 17
Bononia (Felsina), Fc, 12
Bononia (Gesoriacum), Cb, 15
Bononia (Moesia), Cb, 16
Borcovicium (Housesteads)
  Inset, 17
Boreale Pr., Inset, 17a
Borsippa, Db, 3a
Borysthenes, R., Jd, 20
Bosporus Cimmerius, Fa, 16
Bosporus Thracius, Fa, 7c
Bostra, Jf, 11
Bottais, Db, 6
Bovianum Undecumanorum,
  Ca, 13
Bovianum Vetus, Ca, 13
Bovillae, Ab, 14b
Bowness, Cb, 17
Bracara Augusta, Ad, 15
Bradanus, F., Eb, 13
Brancester (Branodunum) Gd, 17
Branodunum (Brancester),
  Gd, 17
Brauron, Ee, 7
Bravoniacum (Kirkby Thore),
  Db, 17
Bravonium, Dd, 17
Bremenium, Da, 17
Bremetennacum (Ribchester),
  Dc, 17
Brigantes, Db, 17; Inset, 17a
Brigantium, Ac, 12
Brigantium (Hispania), Ad, 15
Brigantium (Rhaetia), Dc, 15
Brigetio, Ba, 16
Britannia (Roman Diocese),
  Cc, 20
Brixellum, Ec, 12
Brixia, Eb, 12
Broad Wall, Inset, 4b
Brocavum (Brougham), Db, 17
Brough (Petuaria), Fc, 17
Brough (Verterae), Db. 17
Brougham (Brocavum), Db, 17
Bructeri, Db, 15
Brundisium, Ge, 20
Brundulum, Gb, 12
Bruttii, Ed, 13
Bruttium, Ed, 13
Bryanium, Cb, 6
Bryges, Ca, 6
Bubastis (Pebeseth), Ba, 3b
Bucatium, Cd, 6
Bucephala, Kc, 9b
Buchetium, Bc, 6
Bulis, Dd, 7
Burdigala, Ce, 20
Burgh by Sands, Cb, 17
Burgundiones, Fd, 20
Burrium, De, 17
Busiris, Cc, 2a
Buthrotum, Bc, 6
Buto, Ba, 3b
Bututuntum, Ea, 13
Buxentum, Db, 13
Buxton (Aquae), Ec, 17
Byblus, Dc, 9b
Byblus (Gebal), Bd, 4c
Byzantium, Ib, 5a; Fa, 9a
Byzantium (Constantinopolis),
  Ie, 20

CABILLONUM, Cc, 15
Cabira, Fb, 16
Caburrum, Bc, 12
Cabyle, Db, 16
Cadusii, Fb, 9b
Caecina, Ed, 12
Caelia, Ea, 13
Caelimontana, Pa., Inset, 11c
Caelimontium, Inset, 11d
Caer Gai, Cd, 17
Caer Sws, Cd, 17
Caere, Ge, 12
Caerleon (Isca), De, 17
Caernarvon (Segontium), Bc, 17
Caesar Augusta, Ce, 20

Caesarea (Cappadocia), Kf, 20
Caesarea I. (Gallia), Bc, 15
Caesarea (Judaea), Ab, 4d;
  Ed, 16
Caesarea (Mauretania), Df, 20
Caesarea (Mazaca), Fc, 16
Caesarea Philippi, Ca, 4d
Caesariensis, Ce, 15
Caesarodunum, Cc, 15
Caesena, Gc, 12
Caetobriga, Ae, 15
Caicus, F., Eb, 2b
Caieta, Ba, 13
Caistor, Fc, 17
Calabria, Fb, 13
Calacte, Cd, 13
Calagurris, Bd, 15
Calauria, I., Ee, 7
Calcaria (Tadcaster), Ec, 17
Calchedon (Chalcedon), Ib, 5a
Calebites (Kenizzites), Af, 4a
Caledonia, Ab, 20
Caledonii, Inset, 17a
Cales (Campania), Ca, 13
Cales (Umbria), Gd, 12
Calleva Atrebatum (Silchester),
  Fe, 17
Callinicum, Kf, 20
Callipolis, Fb, 13
Callirrhoe, Cd, 4d
Callonae, Fc, 9b
Calpe, Ca, 5b
Calpe, M., Ae, 15
Calvary, Inset, 4e
Calydnae, Ec, 2b
Calydon, Cd, 7
Calymnos, Ge, 8
Camarina, Fc, 5a
Cambodunum, Ec, 15
Camboglanna (Birdoswald),
  Da, 17
Cambridge (Durolipons),
  Gd, 17
Camelon, Ca, 17
Camerinum, Hd, 12
Camirus, Ec, 2b
Campania, Cb, 13
Campus Agrippae, Inset, 11d
Campus Esquilinus, Inset, 11c
Campus Martius, Inset, 11c
Campus Vaticanus, Inset, 11c
Campus Viminalis, Inset, 11c
Camulodunum (Colchester),
  Ge, 17
Camuni, Eb, 12
Cana, **Bb, 4d**
Canaan, Dc, 2a
Canaanites, Af, Bd, 4a
Canastraeum Pr., Ec, 6
Cane, Gf, 18
Cannae, Ea, 13
Canopic Mouth, Ba, 3b
Canopus, Bc, 9b
Canovium, Cc, 17
Cantabri, Bd, 15
Canterbury (Durovernum),
  Ge, 17
Cantii, Ge, 17
Canusium, Ea, 13
Capena, Ge, 12
Capernaum, Cb, 4d
Capetani, Be, 10
Caphereus Pr., Fd, 7
Caphyae, Bc, 7
Capitol, Inset, 11d
Capitolinus, M., Insets, 13a, b
Capitolium, Insets, 13a, b
Cappadocia, Kf, 20
Capraria, Dd, 12
Capreae Ins., Cb, 13
Capsa, Df, 15
Capua, Ca, 13
Caraceni, Jf, 12
Carales, De, 15
Carana, Ke, 11
Carcer, Insets, 13a, b
Carchemish, Da, 4c
Cardamyle, Cc, 9a
Cardia, Cb, 7c
Cardiff, Ce, 17
Carduchi, Eb, 5b
Caria, Fc, 9a
Carians, Bb, 2a
Carinae, Inset, 11c
Carlisle (Luguvalium), Db, 17
Carmana, Hc, 5b
Carmania, Hc, 9b; He, 18
Carmel, Mt., Ac, 4a

Carmentalis, Pa, Inset, 11'
Carni, Ga, 12; Dc, 18
Carnuntum, Ba, 16
Carolis, Ef, 20
Carpathos I., Hf, 8
Carpatus Mons, Hd, 20
Carpetani, Bd, 15
Carpis, Ee, 15
Carrawburgh (Procolitia),
  Inset, 17
Carrea Potentia, Bc, 12
Carrhae, Fc, 16; Ab, 18b
Carriden, Ca, 17
Carsioli, He, 12
Carsulae, Ge, 12
Cartenna, Ce, 15
Carteia, Ae, 15
Carthago, Ff, 20
Carthago Nova, Cf, 20
Caruanca, M., Ja, 12
Carusadius, M., Hb, 12
Caryae, De, 7
Carystus (Euboea), Fd, 7
Carystus (Laconia), De, 7
Caspian Gates, Gb, 9b
Caspii, Fa, 9b
Cassanitae, Ge, 18
Cassiope, Ac, 6
Castell Collen, Cd, 17
Casthanaea, Dc, 6
Castle Flemish, Be, 17
Castlecary, Ca, 17
Castledykes, Ca, 17
Castlehill, Ba, 17
Castlesteads, Inset, 17
Castra Exploratorum, Ca, 17
Castra Praetoria, Inset, 11d
Castrense, A., Inset, 11d
Castrum Novum, He, 12
Castrum Truentinum, He, 12
Castulo, Be, 15
Casuentus, F., Eb, 13
Catana (Catane), De, 13
Cataractonium (Catterick
  Bridge), Eb, 17
Cathaei, Kc, 9b
Catterick Bridge (Catarac-
  tonium), Eb, 17
Catuvellauni, Fe, 17
Cauca, Bd, 15
Caucasus Mts., Fb, 16
Caudium, Ca, 13
Caulonia, Ed, 13
Causennae (Ancaster), Fd, 17
Cauvery, R., Jf, 19
Cayster, R., Hc, 8
Cayster Plain, Cb, 5b
Ceba, Cc, 12
Cebenna, M., Cd, 15
Cebrene, Cc, 7c
Cecryphalea, Ee, 7
Celaenae, Bb, 9b
Celeia, Ba, 16
Celenderis, Cb, 2d
Celetrum, Cb, 6
Cellae, Cb, 6
Celti, Da, 5a
Celtiberi, Bd, 15
Celtica, Cc, 15
Celtici, Ae, 15
Cemenelum, Bd, 12
Cenabum, Cc, 15
Cenaeum Pr., Cc, 8
Cenchreae, Be, 7
Cenomani, Eb, 12
Centumcellae, Fe, 12
Centuripa, Ce, 13
Ceos, Fe, 7
Cephallenia Bd, 7; Cc, 16
Cephallenians, Bb, 2b
Cephalœdium, Be, 13
Cephisia, Ed, 7
Cephisus, Dd, 6
Ceramicus, Inset, 7b
Cerasus, Da, 5b
Cercinitis L., Eb, 6
Ceriadae, Inset, 7b
Cerinthus, Ed, 6
Cermalus, Insets, 13a, b
Cespius, M., Inset, 11c
Ceylon (Simkala), Fe, 18b
Ceylon (Tamraparni), Cd, 18a
Chaeronea, Dd, 7
Chalastra, Db, 6
Chalce, He, 8
Chalcedon, Ie, 20
Chalcedon (Calchedon), Ib, 5a
  Fa, 9a
Chalcidice, Ca, 9a

Chalcis (Aetolia), Cd, 7
Chalcis (Epirus), Cc, 6
Chalcis (Euboea), Ed, 6
Chalcis, Syria, Fc, 16
Chaldaea, Ec, 2d
Chalybes, Da, 2d
Chalybon, Db, 9b
Chambal, R., Je, 19
Chang-an, Md, 19
Chang-Jeh, Md, 19
Charadra, Bc, 6
Charidemi Pr., Be, 15
Chatti, Cb, 18
Chauci, Db, 15
Chelonatus Pr., Ce, 7
Chephirah, Be, 4a
Chera, Jf, 19
Chera, Kingdom of, Ee, 18b
Cherethites, Af, 4c
Chersonesus (Thrace), Da, 9a
Chersonesus Cimbrica, Da, 10
Chersonesus Pr., Be, 14a
Chersonesus, Pr., Fd, 6
Chersonesus Taurica, Ea, 16
Cherusci, Db, 15
Chester (Deva), Dc, 17
Chesterford, Gd, 17
Chesterholm (Vindolanda),
   Inset, 17
Chester-le-Street, Eb, 17
Chesters (Cilurnum), Inset, 17
Chiang-Hsia, Nd, 19
Chiao Chow, Ne, 19
Chichester (Novio magus),
   Ff, 17
Ching-chao, Md, 19
Ching-chow, Nd, 19
Ching Chow, Nd, 19
Chinnereth, Sea of, Cc, 4a
Chios, Fc, 8
Choaspes, R., Fc, 5b
Chola, Jf, 19
Chola, K. of, Bc, 18a; Ed, 18b
Chorasmia, Hc, 18
Chorasmii, Ha, 9b
Chorazin, Cb, 4d
Chryse, Eb, 2b
Chrysopolis, Ie, 20
Cibalae, Gd, 20
Cibyra, Dc, 1b
Cicones, Da, 2b
Cierium, Dc, 6
Cilicia, Jf, 20
Cilicia (Khilakku), Cb, 2d
Cilician Gates, Cb, 5b
Cilurnum (Chesters), Inset, 17
Cimbrica Chersonesus, Da, 15
Ciminius, L., Ge, 12
Cimmerians, Cb, 2d
Cimmerians (Gomer), Ea, 2d
Cimolos, Ff, 7
Cinaros, Ge, 8
Cingulum, Hd, 12
Circeii, Ba, 13
Circesium, Lf, 20
Circus Flaminius, Inset, 13a
Circus Maximus, Inset, 13b
Cirrha, Dd, 7
Cirta, Ef, 20
Cispadana, Ec, 12
Citerior, Hispania, Be, 15
Cithaeron M., Ed, 7
Citium (Cyprus), Ed, 16
Citium (Macedonia), Db, 6
City of Salt, Bf, 4a
Clanis, F., Ge, 12
Clanoventa (Ravenglass), Cb, 17
Classis, Gc, 12
Clastidium, Db, 12
Claterna, Fc, 12
Claudia, Aq., Inset, 11d
Clausentum, Ef, 17
Clavenna, Da, 12
Clazomenae, Ic; 5a, Gc, 8
Cleonae (Argolis), De, 7
Cleonae (Chalcidice), Fb, 6
Clepsydra, Inset, 7a
Clesis, Eb, 12
Cliternia, Kf, 12
Clitor, De, 7
Cloaca Maxima, Inset, 13a
Clota Aest, Ba, 17
Clunia, Bd, 15
Clupea, Ee, 15
Clusium, Fd, 12
Cnidus, Ic, 5a
Cnossus, Dc, 16
Cocala, Jd, 9b
Coele, Inset, 7b
Coelesyria, Fd, 18

Colapis, F., Kb, 12
Colchester (Camulodunum),
   Ge, 17
Colchis, Kd, 11
Collina, Inset, 11c
Collina, Pa., Inset, 11c
Collis Hortorum, Inset, 11c
Collis Quirinalis, Inset, 11c
Collis Viminalis, Inset, 11c
Collytus, Inset, 7b
Colonia Agrippina, Ec, 20
Colophon, Eb, 9a
Colossae, Bb, 5b
Colosseum, Inset, 13b
Colossus Neronis, Inset, 13b
Columbarium Pr., Bd, 14
Columna Traiani, Inset, 13b
Columnae Herculis, Ae, 15
Comana (Bithynia), Fb, 16
Comana (Cappadocia), Fc, 16
Comitium, Insets, 13a, b
Commagene, Fc, 16
Compsa, Db, 13
Comum, Db, 12
Concordia (Venetia), Gb, 12
Condate, Bc, 15
Condercum (Benwell), Inset, 17
Coneta, Gb, 12
Confluentes, Db, 15
Conimbriga, Ad, 15
Consentia, Ec, 13
Consilinum, Db, 13
Constantinopolis (Byzantium),
   Ie, 20
Contestani, Be, 15
Contrebia, Bd, 15
Copae, Ed, 7
Copais, L., Ed, 7
Coptos (Kebtu), Cd, 3b
Cora, Aa, 13
Coracesium, Ec, 16
Corbridge (Corstopitum), Db, 17
Corcyra, Ac, 6
Corduba, Be, 15; Cf, 20
Corfinium, He, 12
Corinium, Inset, 17a
Corinium (Cirencester), Ee, 17
Corinth, De, 7
Corinthus, Bd, 18
Corioli, Ab, 14b
Coritani, Fc, 17
Corner Gate (Old Gate),
   Inset, 4b
Cornovii, Dd, 17
Cornus, Dd, 15
Corodamum Pr., Ie, 18
Corone, Cf, 7
Coronea, Dd, 7
Corsi, Bd, 14a
Corsica, Ce, 12
Corstopitum (Corbridge), Db, 17
Cortona, Gd, 12
Coryceum Pr., Gc, 8
Cos, He, 8
Cossaei, Fc, 9b
Cossura, I., Ee, 15
Costoboci, Da, 16
Cotiaeum, Dc, 16
Cotini, Dc, 18
Cotyora, Da, 5b
Cramond, Ca, 17
Cranii M., Cc, 6
Crannon, Dc, 6
Cratea, Eb, 16
Crathis, F., Ec, 13
Cremna, Ec, 16
Cremona, Eb, 12
Crenides, Fa, 6
Crestonia, Eb, 6
Creta, Hf, 20
Crete, Inset, 7d
Crexa I., Jc, 12
Crimisa Pr., Fc, 13
Crisa, Dd, 7
Criumetopon Pr., Aa, 7d
Crixia, Cc, 12
Crococalana, Fc, 17
Crocodilopolis-Arsinoe (Shedet),
   Bb, 3b
Crommyon, Ee, 7
Croton, Gc, 5a
Crypta, Inset, 11d
Ctesiphon, Kf, 11
Cularo, Dc, 15
Cullu, De, 15
Cumae, Fb, 5a
Cunaxa, Lb, 5b
Cunetio, Ee, 17
Cupra Maritima, Hd, 12
Cures, Ge, 12

Curia, Inset, 13b
Curia (Rhaetia), Dc, 15
Curia Hostilia, Inset, 13a
Curia Iulia, Inset, 11d
Curicta I., Jb, 12
Curium, Jd, 5a
Curium (Cyprus), Ed, 16
Cusae (Gosu), Bc, 3b
Cutch, Ie, 19
Cutha, Ec, 2d
Cuttiae, Cb, 12
Cyclades, Ed, 8
Cydathenaeum, Inset, 7b
Cydonia, Cc, 16
Cyllene, Cd, 7
Cyllene M., De, 7
Cyme, Aeolis, Gc, 8
Cyme, Euboea, Fd, 6
Cynaetes, Ae, 15
Cynaetha, Dd, 7
Cynopolis, Bb, 3b
Cynoscephalae, Dc, 6
Cynossema, Ea, 9a
Cynuria, De, 7
Cynus, Ed, 6
Cyparissiae, Ce, 7
Cypas, Cb, 7c
Cypsela, Cb, 7c
Cyprus, Ec, 16
Cyrenaica, Ed, 18
Cyrenaica-Creta, Cd, 16
Cyrene, Hg, 20
Cyropolis, Jb, 5b
Cyrrhus, Db, 6
Cyrus, R., Fa, 2d; Ld, 11
Cythera, I., Df, 7
Cythnos, Fe, 7
Cytinium, Dd, 6
Cyzicus, Ha, 8

DACIA, Ca, 16
Dacia, Diocese of, He, 20
Dadicae, Kb, 5b
Dahae, Hb, 9b
Daix, R., Hb, 18
Dalmatia, Ge, 20
Damascus, Da; 4d
Damnonii, Ba, 17
Dan, Bd, 4c
Dan (Tribe), Ae, Cb, 4a
Danubius (Ister), F., Db, 16
Danum (Doncaster), Ec, 17
Daphnae, Cc, 5b
Dardani, Aa, 9b
Dardanians, Eb, 2b
Dardanus, Cb, 7c
Daritae, Gb, 5b
Dascylium, Cb, 5b
Dascylium, Eb, 7c
Dassaretae, Bb, 6
Datum, Hb, 5a
Davaka, Kingdom of, Fc, 18b
David's House, Inset, 4b
Debir (Kiriath-sepher), Af, 4a
Decapolis, Cb, 4d
Deceangli, Cc, 17
Decelea, Cb, 9a
Delcus, Ea, 7c
Delium, Cb, 9a
Delos, Dc, 9a
Delphi, Hc, 5a
Delphi (Indraprastha), Ec, 18b
Delphinium, Gc, 8
Demetae, Be, 17
Demetrias, Dc, 6
Derbe, Eb, 4f
Der ez Zor, Da, 3a
Derrhis Pr., Fc, 6
Dertona, Cc, 12
Dertosa, Cd, 15
Deserta Libyca, Hg, 11
Dessinus, Ie, 11
Deva (Chester), Dc, 17
Devagiri, Ed, 18b
Devarashtra, Ed, 18b
Dhauli, Cc, 18a
Dia, Ca, 7d
Dialas, R., Fc, 5b
Dianium, Hispania, Ce, 15
Dianium, Italy, Fe, 12
Dicaea, Bb, 7c
Dicte M., Ca, 7d
Didyme, Cd, 13
Diogenium, Inset, 7b
Diomea, Inset, 7b
Dion, Db, 4d
Dioscoridis I., Hf, 18
Dioscurias, Lb, 5b
Dioscurias Pr., Fd, 13
Diospolis Parva, Cc, 3b
Dipaea, De, 7

Dipylum, Inset, 7b
Dium (Chalcidice), Fb, 6
Dium (Euboea), Dd, 6
Dium (Macedonia), Db, 6
Divodurum, Dc, 15
Divona, Cd, 15
Doberus, Da, 6
Dobuni, De, 17
Dodona, Bc, 6
Doliche, Db, 6
Dolopes, Cc, 6
Dolopes, Is., Ec, 6
Domus Augustana, Inset, 13b
Domus Caligulae, Inset, 13b
Domus Flaviana, Inset, 13b
Domus Livia, Inset, 13b
Domus Septimii Severi,
   Inset, 13b
Domus Tiberiana, Inset, 13b
Doncaster (Danum), Ec, 17
Dor, Ac, 4a
Dorchester. Ee, 17
Dorchester (Durnovaria), Df, 17
Doris, Dd, 6
Doris, He, 8
Doriscus, Ba, 5b
Dorylaeum, Ec, 16
Dothan, Be, 4c
Drabescus, Fa, 6
Drangiana, Id, 18
Drapsaca, Jb, 9b
Dravus, F., Ba, 16
Drepanum (Phrygia), Fb, 7c
Drepanum (Sicilia), Ad, 13
Drepanum Pr., Cd, 7
Drinius, F., Bb, 16
Droi, Ea, 6
Droitwich (Salinae), Dd, 17
Drubetae, Cb, 16
Drumburgh, Inset, 17
Druzipara, Da, 7c
Dryopes, Cc, 6
Dubris, He, 17
Du-kau (Antaeopolis), Bc, 3b
Dulichium, Bb, 2b
Duma, Dc, 2d
Dumnonii, Bf, 17
Dur Kurigalzu, Ec, 2d
Dur Shaarukin, Eb, 2d
Duranius, F., Cd, 15
Durius, F., Ad, 15
Durnovaria(Dorchester), Df, 17
Durobrivae, Fd, 17
Durobrivae (Rochester), Ge, 17
Durocobrivae, Fe, 17
Durocortorum, Cc, 15
Durolipons, Gd, 17
Durostorum, Db, 16
Durotriges, Df, 17
Durovernum (Canterbury),
   Ge, 17
Durovigutum (Godmanchester),
   Gd, 17
Dymae, Cb, 7c
Dyme, Cd, 7
Dyrrhachium, He, 20
Dyrta Kb, 9b
Dystus, Fd, 7

EAST, DIOCESE OF THE (Orientis),
   Kg, 20
East, Prefecture of the, Jg, 20
East Roman Empire, If, 20
Ebal, Mt., Bd, 4a
Ebchester (Vindomora), Inset, 17
Eburacum (York), Eb, 17
Ebusus, Ce, 15
Ecbatana, Fc, 5b; Gd, 18
Ecbatana (Achmetha), Fc, 2d
Ecdippa, Ba, 4d
Echedorus, F., Db, 6
Echinades Ins., Cd, 7
Echinus, Dd, 6
Ecnomus Pr., Be, 13
Edessa (Macedonia), Cb, 16
Edessa (Syria), Fc, 16
Edetani, Bd, 15
Edom, Bg, 4c
Edomites, Bf, 4a
Edones, Ea, 6
Edrum, Eb, 12
Eglon, Ae, 4a
Egypt, Bc, 3
Egypt, Diocese of (Ægyptus),
   Ih, 20
Egypt (Musri, Mizraim, Kush),
   Cd, 2d
Eileithyiapolis, Bc, 3a
Eion, Eb, 6
Eira, Ce, 7

Eium, Ca, 9a
Ekron, Ae, 4a
Elaea, Aeolis, Hc, 8
Elaea, Thesprotia, Bc, 6
Elaeus, Ba, 9b
Elam, Eb, 3a
Elatea, Dd, 6
Elath, Ah, 4c
Elburz, Cb, 18b
Elea, Db, 13
Elephantine I., Bd, 3a
Eleusinium, Inset, 7a
Eleusis, Ed, 7
Eleutherae, Ed, 7
Eleutherna, Ba, 7d
Eleutherus, F., Cb, 3a
Elimberrum, Cd, 15
Elimea, Cb, 6
Elis, Ce, 7
Ellipi, Fc, 2d
Elymi, Ae, 13
Emathia, Da, 6
Emerita Augusta, Bd, 18
Emmaus, Ad, 4d
Emona, Ja, 12
Emporiae, Db, 5a
Emporium, Inset, 11c
Emporium Segestanorum, Ad, 13
En Mont (Hermonthis), Cd, 3b
Endidae, Fa, 12
Endor, Bc, 4a
Enet (Tentyra), Cc, 3b
Engannim, Bd, 4a
Entella, Be, 13
Eordaei, Cb, 6
Eordaicus, F., Bb, 6
Epeans, Bb, 2b
Ephesus, Hd, 8
Ephraim, Bd, 4a
Ephraim, Mt., Bd, 4a
Ephyra, Bc, 6
Epidamnus, Gb, 5a
Epidaurus (Argolis), Ee, 7
Epidaurus (Illyricum), Bb, 16
Epidaurus Limera, Df, 7
Epidium Pr., Aa, 17
Epiphania, Fc, 16
Epirus, Bc, 6
Eporedia, Bb, 12
Erandapalla, Ec, 18b
Erech, Eb, 3a
Erechtheum, Inset, 7a
Eresus, Fb, 8
Eretria (Euboea), Ed, 7
Eretria (Phthiotis), Dc, 6
Ergines, Ca, 7c
Eridu, Eb, 3a
Erineus, Dd, 6
Eriza, Fc, 16
Ermine Street, Fd, 17
Erymanthus, M., Ce, 7
Erythrae, Eb, 9a
Erythraeum Mare, Gd, 5b
Eryx, Ad, 13
Esdraelon, Plain of, Bb, 4d
Esquiliae, Inset, 11d
Esquilina, Inset, 11c
Esquilina, Pa., Inset, 11c
Etruria, Fd, 12
Etrusci (Tusci), Bb, 14c
Etymander, R., Ic, 5b
Euboea, Db, 9a
Euganei, Eb, 12
Euhesperidae (Berenice), Cd, 16
Eulaeus, F., Gc, 5b
Eupatoria, Fb, 16
Euphrates, R., Db, 3; Gd, 18
Euripus, Dc, 8
Europa, Bb, 1
Europa, Eb, 12
Europus, Da, 6
Eurotas, F., De, 7
Eurytanes, Cd, 6
Eutaea, De, 7
Euthane, He, 8
Exeter (Isca Dumnoniorum),
   Cf, 17
Ezion Geber, Bh, 4c

FABRATERIA, Ba, 13
Faesulae, Fd, 12
Fair Havens, Cc, 4f
Faleria, Hd, 12
Falerii, Ge, 12
Fanum, Hd, 12
Faventia, Fc, 12
Felsina, Fc, 12
Feltria, Fa, 12
Ferentinum, Ba, 13
Fidenae, Gf, 12
Fidentia, Ec, 12

Filey, Fb, 17
Firmum, Hd, 12
Fiscellus, M., He, 12
Flaminia, Pa., Inset, 11d
Flanona, Jb, 12
Flaviobriga, Bd, 15
Flavium A. (Colosseum),
  Inset, 11d
Flevo L., Db, 15
Florentia, Fd, 12
Florentiola, Dc, 12
Flumen Senus, Inset, 17a
Flumen Vidua, Inset, 17a
Flumentana, Pa., Inset, 11
Folkestone, He, 17
Fontinalis, Pa., Inset, 11c
Forden, Cd, 17
Forest of Arden, Ed, 17
Forest of Dean, Dc, 17
Formiae, Bb, 14b
Forum Appii, Aa, 4f
Forum Augusti, Inset, 13b
Forum Boarium, Inset, 13b
Forum Cornelii, Fc, 12
Forum Fulvii, Cb, 12
Forum Germanorum, Bc, 12
Forum Holitorium, Inset, 13a
Forum Iulii, Dd, 15
Forum Iulium (Roma), Inset, 13b
Forum Iulium (Venetia), Ha, 12
Forum Livii, Gc, 12
Forum Nervae, Inset, 13b
Forum Pacis, Inset, 13b
Forum Popilii (Cispadana),
  Gc, 12
Forum Popilii (Lucania), Db, 13
Forum Romanum, Inset, 13b
Forum Sempronii, Gd., 12
Forum Traiani, Inset, 13b
Forum Traiani, Sardinia, Be, 14a
Forum Vibii, Bc, 12
Fosse Way, Ed, 17
Franci, Ec, 20
Fregellae, Ba, 13
Fregenae, Gf, 12
Frentini, Je, 12
Frento, F., Kf, 12
Fretum Gaditanum, Ae, 15
Fretum Gallicum, Cb, 15
Fretum Gallicum (Corsica),
  Dd, 15
Frisii, Ec, 20
Fucinus, L., Hf, 12
Fulaeus, F., Eb, 3a
Fulginium, Ge, 12
Fundi, Ba, 13

GABAEUM Pr., Bc, 15
Gad (Tribe), Cd, Ce, 4a
Gadara, Cb, 4d
Gades, Bf, 20
Gaetuli, Bc, 1
Galatia, Jf, 20
Galilee, Bb, 4d
Galilee, Sea of, Cb, 4a
Gallaecia, Ad, 15
Gallia, Dd, 20
Gallia Cisalpina, Eb, 12
Gambalu, Fc, 2d
Gandaria, Kc, 5b
Gandhara, Jd, 19
Gandhara, Kingdom of, Eb, 18b
Ganganorum Pr., 17, Bd
Ganges, R., Je, 19
Gangra, Eb, 16
Ganos, Db, 7c
Garganum Pr., Ea, 13
Garganus, M., Da, 13
Gariannonum, Hd, 17
Garsaura, Ec, 16
Garumna, F., Bd, 15
Gath, Ae, 4a
Gaugamela, Eb, 9b
Gaul (Gallia), Diocese of, Dd, 20
Gaul (Gallia), Prefecture of,
  Dd, 20
Gaulanitis, Cb, 4d
Gaya, Fc, 18b
Gaza, Ae, 4a
Gazaca, Gd, 18
Geba, Be, 4a
Gebal (Byblus), Bd, 4c
Gedrosia, Ie, 18
Gela, Ce, 13
Gelas, F., Ce, 13
Gelligaer, Ce, 17
Gem Aton, Bd, 3a
Genath (Gate Genath), Inset, 4e
Geneva, Dc, 15
Genua, Cc, 12

Genusium, Eb, 13
Gepidae, Hd, 20
Geraestus Pr., Fe, 7
Gerania, M., Cc, 8
Gerasa, Cc, 4d
Gergesa, Cb, 4d
Gergovia, Cc, 15
Gerizim, Mt., Bd, 4a
Germania, Eb, 15
Germania Inferior, Db, 15
Germania Superior, Dc, 15
Geronthrae, Df, 7
Gerrha, He, 18
Gerrhaei, Ge, 18
Gerunda, Cd, 15
Gerunium, Da, 13
Geshuri, Cc, 4a
Gesoriacum (Bononia), Cb, 15
Getae, Ba, 9b
Gezer, Ae, 4a
Ghazni, Jc, 9b
Gibbethon, Ae, 4a
Gibeon, Be, 4a
Gigonus, Eb, 6
Gihon Sinnor, Inset, 4b
Gilboa, Mt., Bd, 4a
Gilead, Cd, 4a
Gilgal, Ce, 4a
Ginaea, Bc, 4d
Gizeh, Cc, 2a
Glenlochar, Bb, 17
Glevum (Gloucester), De, 17
Gloucester (Glevum), De, 17
Gnathia, Fb, 13
Gobannium (Abergavenny),
  Ce, 17
Godavari, R., Jf, 19
Godmanchester (Durovigutum),
  Gd, 17
Golan Cc, 4a ,
Golden Gate(Jerusalem),Inset,4e
Goldsborough, Fb, 17
Gomer (Cimmerians), Ea, 2d
Gomphi, Cc, 6
Gonnus, Dc, 6
Gorditanum Pr., Bd, 14
Gordium, Ec, 16
Gortyna, Id, 5a
Gortys, De, 7
Goshen (Egypt), Ba, 3b
Gosu (Cusae), Bc, 3b
Gozan (Guzana), Eb, 2d
Graecia, Ab, 5b
Granicus, Ba, 9b
Granicus, F., Db, 7c
Graviscae, Fe, 12
Great Chesters (Aesica), Inset, 17
Great Sea, The, Ac, 4a
Greece, 7
Greece (Achaea), Cb, 4
Grumentum Db, 13
Grumum, Eb, 13
Gryneium, Eb, 9a
Gujarat, Ec, 18b
Gulashkird, Hd, 9b
Gurgum, Db, 2d
Guttones, Db, 18
Guzana (Gozan), Eb, 2d
Gwalior, Ec, 18
Gymnias, Da, 5b
Gytheum, Df, 7

HABIRU (Shasu), Cb, 3a
Habitancum, Da, 17
Hadrianopolis, Db, 16; Ie, 20
Hadrumetum, Ee, 15
Haemus, M., Ba, 9b
Hagia Triada, Bc, 2a
Halap (Aleppo), Ca, 3a
Haliacmon, F., Db, 6
Haliartus, Ed, 7
Halicarnassus, Bb, 5b; Ec, 9a
Halicyae, Ae, 13
Halieis, Ee, 7
Halton (Onnum), Ea, 17
Halus, Dc, 6
Halycus, F., Be, 13
Halys, R., Eb, 16
Hamath, Cb, 4c
Han Dominions, Nd, 19
Han-chung, Md, 19
Hanigalbat, Ca, 3a
Hardknot, Cb, 17
Harmozia, He, 18
Harosheth, Bc, 4a
Harran, Ca, 3a
Hasta, Baetica, Ae, 15
Hasta, Liguria, Cc, 12
Hatra, Gd, 18

Hatria (Picenum), Je, 12
Hatria (Venetia), Gb, 12
Hatti (Hittites), Cb, Db, 2d
Hattusas (Boghaz Keui), Cb, 2a
Hazor, Bd, 4c
Hebron (Kiriath-arba), Be, 4a
Hebrus, F., Db, 16
Hecatompylos, Gg, 9b
Helena (Graecia), Fe, 7
Helice, Dd, 7
Helicon M., Dd, 7
Heliopolis (On), Ba, 3b
Hellas, Ab, 9b
Hellespontus, If, 20
Helorus, Df, 13
Helos, Df, 7
Helvetii, Dc, 15
Hemesa, Fd, 16
Henen-seten (Heracleopolis
  magna), Bb, 3b
Henna, Ce, 13
Hephaestia, Bc, 7c
Heraclea, Caria, Hd, 8
Heraclea Chefsonesus, Eb, 16
Heraclea (Lucania), Eb, 13
Heraclea Lyncestis, Ca, 6
Heraclea (Malis), Dd, 6
Heraclea Minoa, Be, 13
Heraclea Pontica, Eb, 16
Heracleopolis magna (Henen-
  seten), Bb, 3b
Heracleum, Db, 6
Heracleum (Theseum), Inset, 7b
Heracleum Pr., Ee, 13
Heraea, Ce, 7
Heraei M., Ce, 13
Heraeum, Pr., Dd, 7
Herat, see Alexandria
Herculaneum, Cb, 13
Herculia, Ba, 16
Herculis Pr., Be, 17
Herdoniae, Da, 13
Hermeius Smyrnaeos, Gc, 8
Hermione, Ee, 7
Hermon, Mt., Cb, 4a
Hermonthis (En Mont), Cd, 3b
Hermopolis Magna (Hmunu),
  Bc, 3b
Hermopolis, Ig, 11
Hermus, F., Dc, 16
Hernici, Ba, 13
Herod Agrippa, Kingdom of,
  Fc, 4f
Herod's Palace, Inset, 4e
Herod's Temple, Inset, 4e
Herodium, Bd, 4d
Heruli, Jd, 20
Heshbon, Ce, 4a
Heshmon, Ce, 4a
Hestiaeotis, Cc, 6
Hibernia, Bc, 20
Hiddekel (Tigris), F., Ec, 2d
Hiera, Ad, 13
Hierapolis, Kf, 20
Hierapytna, Ca, 7d
Hierasus, F., Da, 16
Hieropolis, Fc, 16
Hierosolyma, Fd, 18
Hierosolyma (Jerusalem), Dc, 5b
High Street, Db, 17
Himalaya Mts., Ba, 18a
Himera, Fc, 5a
Himera, F., Ce, 13
Hindu, Kush, Ba, 18a
Hinnom (Gehenna), Valley of,
  Insets, 4e, 4b
Hippicus Tower, Inset, 4e
Hippo Diarrhytus, Ec, 5a
Hippo Regius, Ec, 5a
Hippo Zarytus, De, 15
Hipponium, Ed, 13
Hipponon, Bb, 3b
Hippós, Cb, 4d
Hirpini, Ca, 13
Hirpalis, Ae, 15
Hispania, Ce, 20
Hispellum, Gd, 12
Histiaea, Ed, 6
Histonium, Je, 12
Hit, Bb, 18b
Hittites (Hatti), Cb, Db, 2d
Hittites (Hatti), Ca, 3a
Hittites (Kalti), Cb, 4c
Hmunu (Hermopolis Magna)
  Bc, 3b
Holyhead, Bc, 17
Homolium, Dc, 6
Honan, Nd, 19
Horncastle, Fc, 17

Horologium, Inset, 7b
Horta, Ge, 12
Horti, Inset, 7b
Hostilia, Fb, 12
Housesteads (Vercovicium),
  Inset, 17
Hsu Chow, Nd, 19
Huai, R., Od, 19
Hui-hi, Od, 19
Hunni, Db, 1
Huntcliff, Fb, 17
Hurmunduri, Db, 18
Hyccara, Bd, 13
Huntcliff, Fb, 17
Hydrea, Ee, 7
Hydronte, Gb, 13
Hydruntum, Gb, 13
Hymettus, M., Ee, 7
Hypanis, F., Ea, 9b
Hypanis, F., Fa, 16
Hypothebae (Thebes), Cb, 2b
Hypsas, F., Ae, 13
Hypsele, Bc, 3b
Hyrcania, Hd, 18
Hyrcanium (M. Caspium), Db, 1
Hysiae, De, 7

IADER (Illyricum), Bb, 16
Ialysus, Fc, 9a
Iambia, Fe, 18
Ianiculum Arx, Inset, 11
Iapygia, Cb, 14c
Iasa, Hd, 8
Iasus, Ec, 9a
Iaxartes, F., Eb, 1
Iazyges, Ec, 18
Iberia, Cc, 5a
Iberia (Caucasus), Kd, 11
Iberus, R., Ce, 20
Ibleam, Bd, 4a
Icaria, Gd, 8
Iceni, Gd, 17
Ichthys Pr., Ce, 7
Icknield Wat, Gd, 17
Iconium, Ec, 16
Icosium, Ce. 15
Ictis, Ab, 15
Icus, Ec, 6
Ida, M., Ba, 7d
Ida, Mt. (Troy), Eb, 2b
Idomene, Cc, 6
Idumaea, Ae, 4d
Igilgili, De, 15
Igilium, Ee, 12
Iguvium, Gd, 12
Ilchester, De, 17
Ilerda, Cd, 15
Ilici, Be, 15
Ilillubri, Cb, 2d
Illyria, Ba, 6
Illyria, Diocese of, Ge, 20
Illyria, Prefecture of, Hf, 20
Illyricum, Bb, 16; Gd, 20
Ilos, Inset, 2c
Ilva, Fb, 5a
Imaus Mons, Ec, 1; Kc, 9b
Imbros, Fa, 8
India, Fc, 1
Indoscythia, Ec, 1
Indraprastha (Delhi), Ec, 18b
Indus, R., Ie, 19
Indus, R., Ie, 19
Inessa, Ce, 13
Ingira, Cb, 2d
Insubres, Db, 12
Interacrea, He, 12
Interamna (Etruria), Ge, 12
Interamna (Latium), Ba, 13
Interamna (Picenum), He, 12
Interamnium, Ec, 13
Intimilii, Bd, 12
Inveravon, Ca, 17
Inveresk, Da, 17
Iol Caesarea, Ce, 15
Iolcus, Dc, 6
Iomnium, Ce, 15
Ionia, Gc, 8
Ioppe, Ed, 16
Ios I., Fe, 8
Ipsus, Bb, 9c
Irchester, Fd, 17
Iria, Dc, 12
Iria Flavia, Ad, 15
Irina Palus, Ke, 9b
Is, Ec, 9b

Isaura, Ec, 16
Isauria, Jf, 20
Isca (Caerleon), De, 17
Isca Dumnoniorum (Exeter),
  Cf, 17
Isca Silurum, Bb, 15
Iseum, Inset, 11d
Isin, Eb, 3a
Isis et Serapis, Inset, 11d
Israel, Dc, 2d
Israel, Kingdom of, Be, 4c
Issachar, Bc, 4a
Issus, Db, 9b
Istakr (Persepolis), Cb, 18b
Ister (Danubius), F., Hb, 5a

Istone, M., Ac, 6
Istri, Ba, 14c
Istria, Hb, 12
Istrus, Ib, 5a
Isurium, Eb, 17
Italia, Ed, 10
Italia, Diocese of, Fe, 20
Italy, Ancient, 12-13
Italica, Ae, 15
Italy, Prefecture of, Fe, 20
Itanus, Da, 7d
Ithaca, Bd, 7
Ithaca, Cc, 6
Ithome, M., Ce, 7
Ituna Aest., Cb, 17
Ituraea, Ca, 4d
Iulia, Aq., Inset, 11
Iuliobona, Cc, 15
Iuliobriga, Bd, 15
Iuliomagus, Bc, 15
Iulium Carnicum, Ha, 12
Iunonis Reginae, Templum,
  Inset, 11
Iuvanum (Samnium), Jf, 12
Iuvavum, Ec, 15
Iverni, Inset, 17a

JABBOK, R., Cd, 4a
Jabesh Gilead, Be, 4c
Jalandhar, Eb, 18b
Jamnia, Ad, 4d
Jaugada, Cc, 18a
Jaxartes, R., Ic, 18
Jebus (Jerusalem), Be, 4a
Jerameelites, Af, 4c
Jericho, Be, 4a
Jerusalem, Jg, 4b, 4e, 20
Jerusalem (Hierosolyma), Dc 5
Jerusalem (Jebus), Bf, 4c
Jeshimon, Be, 4a
Jezreel, Bc, 4a
Jezreel, Valley of, Bc, 4a
Joppa, Ad, 4a
Jordan, R., Cb, 3a; Cd, 4a
Judæa, Bd, 4a
Judæa, Wilderness of, Bd, 4d
Judah, Be, 4d
Judah, Kingdom of, Bf, 4c
Judgement, House of, Inset, 4b
Jumna, R., Je, 18
Junagarh, Ec, 18b
Jupiter Ammonium, Bd, 5b
Juti, Eb, 20

KABUL, Id, 19
Kadesh, Cb, 3a
Kadesh Barnea, Ag, 4c
Kalakh, Da, 3a
Kalinga, K. of, Cc, 18a
Kallikolone, Inset, 2c
Kalsi, Ba, 18a
Kalti (Hittites), Da, 4c
Kamarapura, Kingdom of,
  Gc, 18b
Kambojas, Ca, 18a
Kanatha, Db, 4d
Kanchi, Ed, 18b
Kanesh, Db, 2a
Kaplavasti, Cb, 18a
Karachi (Alexandria Portus),
  Je, 9b
Kara-shahr, Kc, 19
Karkar, Db, 2d
Karnak Temples, Cd, 3b
Kartripura, K. of, Eb, 18b
Kashgar, Jd, 19
Kashiari, Mt., Da, 3a
Kashkai, Db, 2d
Kashmir, Ba, 18a
Kasi (Benares), Cb, 18a
Katna, Da, 3a
Kaviripaddanam, Kf, 19
Ke Chow, Nd, 19
Kebtu (Coptos), Cd, 3b

Kedah (Kidri), Dc, 2d
Kedesh, Bd, 4c
Kedesh, Bb, 4a
Kenites, Bf, 4a
Kenizzites (Calebites), Af, 4a
Kera, Eb, 2d
Keralaputra, K. of, Bc, 18a
Khabur, F., Da, 3a
Khesout (Xois), Ba, 3b
Khidalu, Ec, 2d
Khilakku (Cilicia), Cb, 2d
Khojent (Alexandria Eschata), Ja, 9b
Khotan, Kd, 19
Khubushkia, Eb, 2d
Khyber P., Kc, 9b
Kidri (Kedah), Dc, 2d
Kidron, R., Bd, 4d
Kidron, Val. of, Insets, 4e, 4b
Kilif (Alexandria Oxiana), Jb, 9b
Kir-haresheth, Cf, 4a
Kiriath-arba (Hebron), Be, 4a
Kiriath-jearim, Be, 4a
Kiriath-sepher (Debir), Af, 4a
Kirkby Thore (Bravoniacum), Db, 17
Kish, Db, 3a
Kishon, R., Bc, 4a
Kistna, R., Jf, 19
Kizzuwatna, Ca, 3a
Kode, Cb, 3a
Konkan, S., Jf, 19
Korkai, Jg, 19
Kosala, K. of, Bb, 18a
Kottura, Fd, 18b
Kuang Han, Md, 19
Kuang-ling, Nd, 19
Kuang-Yang, Nd, 19
Kucha, Kc, 19
Kudal, Jg, 19
Kumani, Ca, 3a
Kummeh, Bd, 3a
Kummukh, Ca, 3a
Kurti, Da, 3a
Kush, Bd, 3a
Kushan Dominions, Id, 18
Kusinagara, K. of, Cb, 18a
Kuti, Da, 3a

Labeatis, L., Bb, 16
Lacedaemon (Sparta), De, 7
Lacedaemonia, Cc, 9a
Lachish, Ae, 4a
Lacinium Pr., Fc, 13
Laconia, Df, 7
Lactodorum, Ed, 17
Ladon, F., Ce, 7
Laevi, Cb, 12
Lagash, Eb, 3a
Lagentium, Ec, 17
Laish (Dan), Cb, 4a
Lalita Patan, Cb, 18a
Lambaesis, De, 10
Lamia, Dd, 6
Laminium, Be, 15
Lampsacus, Ba, 2d; Cb, 7c
Lancaster, Db, 17
Langobardi, Fc, 20
Lanuvium, Aa, 13
Laodicea, Dc, 16
Laodicea (Syria), Fc, 16
Lappa, Ba, 7d
Larinum, Ca, 13
Larissa, Assyria, Eb, 5b
Larissa, Dardanians, Eb, 2b
Larissa, Thessalia, Dc, 6
Larissa Cremaste, Dd, 6
Larius, L., Da, 12
Larsa, Eb, 3a
Larymna, Ed, 6
Las, Df, 7
Lasea, Db, 4f
Lasium, Ce, 7
Latina, Pa., Inset, 11d
Latini, Aa, 13
Latium, Aa, 13
Latopolis, Cd, 3b
Laumellum, Cb, 12
Laurentum, Gf, 12
Lauriacum, Ec, 15
Laurium M., Ee, 7
Lauriya Araraj, Cb, 18a
Laus, Dc, 13
Laus Pompeia, Db, 12
Lavatrae, Eb, 17
Lebadea, De, 7
Lebanon, Ho. of, Inset, 4b
Lebanon, Mts., Cb, 3a
Lebedus, Gc, 8

Lebinthus, I., Gd, 8
Lechaeum, De, 7
Leicester (Ratae), Ed, 17
Lemanus, L., Dc, 15
Lemnos, Bc, 7c
Leontes, R., Ba, 4d
Leontini, Ce, 13
Leontium, Cd, 7
Lepontii, Ca, 12
Lepreum, Ce, 7
Leptis Magna, Ef, 10
Leptis Minor, Ee, 10; Ee, 15
Leros I., Gd, 8
Lesbos, Gb, 8
Letocetum, Ed, 17
Letopolis, Ba, 3b
Leuca, M., Aa, 7d
Leucae, Df, 7
Leucae Is., Db, 7d
Leucas, Bd, 6
Leuce, Gc, 13
Leucimma Pr., Ab, 9a
Leucopetra Pr., De, 13
Leucos Limen, Bc, 3a
Leuctra, Boeotia, Ed, 7
Leuctra, Laconia, Ce, 8
Liang Chow, Md, 19
Liao-tung, Oc, 19
Libanus, M., Fd, 16
Libarna, Cc, 12
Libnah, Af, 4c
Liburnia, Bb, 16
Libya, Dd, 16
Libyans, Bc, 2a
Liger, R., Cd, 20
Ligures, Eb, 5a
Ligures Bebiani, Ca, 13
Liguria, Bc, 12
Lilybaeum, Ae, 13
Limes, Dc, 15
Limnae, Inset, 7b
Limnaea, Cd, 6
Limonum, Cc, 15
Lincoln (Lindum), Fc, 17
Lindinis, De, 17
Lindum (Lincoln), Fc, 17
Lindus, Fc, 2b
Lingones, Fc, 12
Lipara, Gc, 5a
Liparaeae Ins., Cd, 13
Liris, F., Ba, 13
Lissos Pr., Bb, 16
Lissus, Bb, 16
Liternum, Cb, 13
Littlechester, Ed, 17
Littus Saxonicum, Hd, 17
Lixus, Bc, 5a
Llandovery, Cd, 17
Llanio, Bd, 17
Locri (Magna Graecia), Gc, 5a
Locri, R., Cb, 2b
Locri Epizephyrii, Ed, 13
Locris (Epicnemidia), Dd, 6
Locris (Opuntia), Ed, 6
Locris Ozolis, Dd, 7
Lod, Ae, 4a
Logia Sinus, Ab, 17
Londinium, Ge, 17
Longaticum, Jb, 12
Loudoun Hill, Ba, 17
Lousonna, Aa, 12
Lower City, Inset, 4e
Lower Egypt, Ba, 3b
Loyang, Nd, 19
Luca, Ed, 12
Lucani, Cb, 14c
Lucania, Db, 13
Luceria, Da, 13
Lu-chiang, Nd, 19
Lucus Augusti, Ad, 15
Lugdunensis, Bc, 15
Lugdunum, Cc, 15
Lugdunum Batavorum, Cb, 15
Lugii, Fb, 15
Luguvalium (Carlisle), Db, 17
Luae, Mtes., Inset, 1
Luna, Ec, 12
Lung-Hsi, Md, 19
Lupiae, Gb, 13
Lusitani, Ae, 15
Lusitania, Ae, 15
Lutetia, Dd, 20
Luxor, Cd, 2a
Luz (Beth-el), Be, 4a
Lycaonia, Fd, 18
Lychnidus, Ba, 6
Lychnites, L., Ba, 6
Lychnitus, L., Ld, 11
Lycia, Ed, 18

Lycians, Bb, 2a
Lycopolis (Syout), Bc, 3b
Lyctus, Dd, 2b
Lydda, Ad, 4d
Lydia, If, 20
Lydians, Bb, 2a
Lympne (Portus Lemanis), He, 17
Lyncestis, Cb, 6
Lyrceus M., De, 7
Lyrnessus, Eb, 2b
Lysimacheia, Cb, 7c
Lysimachia, Acarnania, Cd, 6
Lysimachia, Thracia, Aa, 9
Lyttus, Ca, 7d

Macae, He, 18
Macedonia, Cb, 6; Hf, 20
Macedonia, Diocese of, He, 20
Macestus, F., Eb, 7c
Machir (Manasseh), Dc, 4a
Macra, Dc, 12
Madaktu, Fc, 2d
Madraka, Eb, 18b
Madura, Ed, 18b
Maeander, F., Dc, 16
Maegaeum, Cb, 4f
Maenalus, De, 7
Maeonians, Eb, 2b
Maeotis, L., Ka, 5a
Maeotis Palus, Kd, 20
Magadha, Kingdom of, Fc, 18b
Magna Graecia, Gc, 5a
Magnae (Carvoran), Inset, 17
Magnesia (Caria), Hd, 8
Magnesia (Graecia), Dc, 6
Magnesia (Lydia), Dc, 16
Magnis, Dd, 17
Magnus Portus (Portsmouth Harb.), Ef, 17
Maha Kosala, Fc, 18b
Mahanadi, R., Ke, 19
Mahanaim, Cd, 4a
Mahendragiri, Mt., Fd, 18b
Maior, I., Ce, 15
Malaca, Cc, 5a
Malatia (Melid), Db, 2d
Malaya, Ec, 18b
Malea Pr., Ef, 7
Malis, Dd, 6
Mallus, Kc, 5a
Malwa, Je, 19
Mamucium (Manchester), Dc, 17
Manasseh (Machir), Dc, Bd, 4a
Manchester (Mamucium), Dc, 17
Mandrae, Ec, 7c
Manduria, Fb, 13
Manju Patan, Ke, 19
Mannai, Fb, 2d
Mansera, Ba, 18a
Mantinea, Cc, 9a
Mantua, Eb, 12
Maracanda, Jb 9b
Marakanda, Jb, 5b
Marash, Ca, 3a
Marathon, Ed, 7
Marcelli, Th., Inset, 11d
Marcellum, Inset, 13a
Marcomanni, Fd, 20
Mardi, Fb, 9b
Mardin, Da, 3a
Mare Adriaticum, Ge, 20
Mare Ægæum, If, 20
Mare Africum, Fc, 5a
Mare Australis, Inset, 1
Mare Balearicum, Dc. 5a
Mare Cantabricum, Bc, 18
Mare Caspium, Ne, 20
Mare Creticum, Ee, 8
Mare Cronium, Inset, 1
Mare Egyptum, Jd, 5a
Mare Erythraeum, Ec, 9c
Mare Etruscum, Bc, 14c
Mare Externum, Ac, 5a
Mare Gangeticus, Fd, 1
Mare Icarium, Gd, 8
Mare Internum, Dd, 18
Mare Ionium, Gf, 20
Mare Ligurum, Eb, 5a
Mare Myrtoum, Ef, 7
Mare Siculum, Gc, 5a
Mare Suevicum, Gb, 20
Mare Thracicum, Ec, 6
Mare Tyrrhenum, Ff, 20
Marea, Bc, 5b
Margiana, Id, 18
Margus, F., Margiana, Ib, 5b
Margus, F., Moesia, Gd, 10
Mari, Db, 2a
Mariana, De, 12

Maridunum (Carmarthen), Be, 17
Marisus, F., Ca, 16
Marmarica, Cd, 16
Maronea, Ib, 5a
Marrucini, Je, 12
Marruvium, Hf, 12
Marsi, Hf, 12
Maryport (Alauna), Cb, 17
Massaga, Kc, 9b
Massagetae, Hc, 18
Massilia, Ee, 20
Mateola, Eb, 13
Mathura (Meerut), Ec, 18b
Matiana, L., Le, 11
Matianus, L., Fb, 2d
Mattieni, Eb, 5b
Mauretania, Df, 20
Mausoleum Augusti, Inset, 11d
Mausoleum Hadriani, Inset, 11d
Mazaca (Cæsarea), Fc, 16
Mazara, Ae, 13
Medeon, Cd, 6
Media, Gd, 18
Median Wall, Ec, 2d
Mediolanum, Db, 12
Mediolanum Santonum, Bc, 15
Medma, Dd, 13
Medus, F., Gc, 5b
Meerut (Mathura), Ec, 18b
Meerut (Mirath), Bb, 18a
Megalopolis, De, 7
Megara, Hc, 5a
Megara (Sicilia), Gc, 5a
Megara Hyblaea, De, 13
Megaris, Ed, 7
Megiddo, Bc, 4a
Melandra Castle, Ec, 17
Melazgert, Eb, 2d
Meliboea (Hestiaeotis), Cc, 6
Meliboea (Magnesia), Dc, 6
Melid (Malatia), Db, 2d
Melita, Inset, Ab, 4f
Melite, Ff, 20
Melite, Db, 9b
Melitene, Fc, 16
Melli, Kc, 9b
Mellte, Inset, 7b
Melos, Ff, 7
Melpum, Db, 12
Memphis, Jh, 20
Memphis (Men-nofer), Bb, 3b
Memphis (Noph), Cd, 2d
Menaenum, Ce, 13
Menapii, Cb, 15
Mende, Hc, 5a; Ec, 6
Mendes, Ba, 3b
Menet Hufu (Speos Artemidos) Bc, 3b
Men-nofer (Memphis), Bb, 3b
Merinum, Ea, 13
Meroë, Cd, 1; Be, 3a
Merom, Waters of, Cb, 4a
Merv, Db, 18b
Mesambria, Bb, 7c
Mesembria, Ib, 5a; Db, 16
Mesheck (Mushki), Db, 2d
Mesopotamia, Eb, 9b
Messana, Gf, 20
Messana (Zancle), Dd, 13
Messapii, Fb, 13
Messene, Ce, 7
Messenia, Ce, 7
Meta Sudans, Inset, 13b
Metapontum, Eb, 13
Metaris, Aest, (The Wash), Gc, 17
Metaurus, F., Gd, 12
Metellinum, Ae, 15
Methana, Ee, 7
Methone (Macedonia), Db. 6
Methone (Messenia), Cf, 7
Methone (Thessalia), Ec, 6
Methydrium, De, 7
Metropolis, Cd, 6
Mevania, Ge, 12
Michmash, Be, 4a
Midea, De, 7
Miletus, Hd, 8
Miletus (Creta), Dd, 2b
Milid, Ca, 3a
Min Yueh, Ne, 19
Minaei, Gf, 18
Mincius, F., Eb, 12
Minius, F., Ad, 15
Minnagara, Ie, 19

Minor I., Cd, 15
Minturnae, Ba, 13; Bb, 14b
Mirath (Meerut), Bb, 18a
Misenum Pr., Cb, 13
Mitanni, Ca, 3a
Mitylene, Gb, 8
Mizpeh, Be, 4a
Moab, Cf, 4a
Moabites, Cf, 4a
Modicia, Db, 12
Moeris, L., Bb, 3b
Moesia Inferior, Db, 16
Moesia Superior, Cb, 16
Moguntiacum, Ec, 20
Mohammerah (Alexandria), Fc, 9b
Mona, Bc, 17
Monavia, Bb, 17
Monitia, Dc, 12
Mons Albanus, Ab, 14b
Mons Apenninus, Ed, 10; Fd, 12
Mons Caelius, Inset, 11c
Mons Esquilinus, Inset, 11d
Mons Ianiculus, Inset, 11d
Mons Pincius, Inset, 11d
Mons Sacer, Ab, 14b
Montes Bastarnici, Hc, 10
Montes Serrorum, Ca, 16
Monumentum Philopappi, Inset, 7b
Mopsuestia, Db, 5b
Morgantia, Ce, 13
Mosa, F., Dc, 15
Moschi, Ea, 5b
Mosella, F., Db, 15
Motya, Ae, 13
Motyca, Cf, 13
Mugonia, Pa., Inset, 11c
Munda, Be, 15
Murattash, Da, 3a
Mursa, Gd, 20
Murus Aurelius, Inset, 11d
Murus Hadriani, Cb, 20
Murus Medius, Inset, 7b
Murus Phalericus, Inset, 7b
Murus Septentrionalis, Inset, 7b
Musarum Mons, Inset, 7b
Musasir, Eb, 2d
Mushki (Mesheck), Db. 2d
Musri, Ca, 3a
Mutina, Ec, 12
Muziris, Jf, 19
Mycale, M., Hd, 8
Mycalessus, Ed, 7
Mycenae, De, 7
Mygdonia, Db, 6
Mykonos, Fd, 8
Mylae, Dd, 13
Mylasa, Bb, 9b
Myndus, Hd, 8
Myos Hormos, Bc, 3a
Myra, Ec, 16
Myrcinus, Eb, 6
Myriandrus, Db, 5b
Myrina, Db, 9a
Mysia, Ic, 5a
Mysians, Bb, 2a
Mytilene, Eb, 9a

Nabaite (Nebaioth), Dc, 2d
Nabataeans, Cd, 4d
Nabataei, Fe, 18
Naevia, Pa., Inset, 15c
Naharin, Ca, 3a
Nain, Bb, 4d
Nairi, Da, 3a
Naissus, He, 20
Namri, Fb, 2d
Nandangarh, Cb, 18a
Napata, Be, 3a
Napoca, Ca, 16
Nar, F., Ga, 12
Narbada, R., Je, 19
Narbada (Normada), R., Bb, 18a
Narbo, De, 20
Narbo Martius, Cd, 15
Narbonensis, Cd, 15
Narmada (Narbada), R., Bb, 18a
Narnia, Ge, 12
Narona, Bb, 16
Nasamones, Cd, 16
Natron Lakes, Ba, 3b
Naucratis, Cc, 5b
Naulochus, Dd, 13
Nauplia, De, 7
Nauportus, Jb, 12
Navalia, Inset, 11d
Navalis, Pa., Inset, 11c

Navio, Ec, 17
Naxos, Euboea, Fd, 8
Naxos, Sicilia, Gc, 5a; Dc, 13
Naxuana, Le, 11
Nazareth, Bb, 4d
Neae, Fb, 8
Neaethus, F., Ec, 13
Neapolis, Be, 14a
Neapolis (Africa), Ee, 15
Neapolis (Apulia), Fb, 13
Neapolis, Campania, Cb, 13
Neapolis (Macedonia), Fb, 6
Neath (Nidum), Ce, 17
Nebaioth (Nabaite), Dc, 2d
Nebrodes Montes, Ce, 13
Nebut (Apollinopolis parva),
    Cd, 3b
Nedon, F., De, 7
Neetum, Cf, 13
Nemausus, Cd, 15
Nemea, De, 7
Nemetacum, Cb, 15
Nepal, Kingdom of, Fc, 18b
Nepete, Ge, 12
Nerium Pr., Ad, 15
Neronianus, Inset, 11d
Nersae, He, 12
Nervii, Cb, 15
Nesactium, Jc, 12
Nestus, F., Fa, 6
Newcastle (Pons Aelius),
    Inset, 17
Nicaea, Db, 16
Nicaea (Bactria), Jc, 9b
Nicaea (India), Kc, 9b
Nicaea (Liguria), Eb, 5a; Dd, 15
Nicephorium, Fc, 16
Nicomedia, Db, 16
Nicopolis (Armenia Minor),
    Fb, 16
Nicopolis (Epirus), Bd, 6
Nidum (Neath), Ce, 17
Nigir, R., Bd, 1
Nigliva, Cb, 18a
Nigritae, Ad, 1
Nile, R., Bc, 3a
Nilus, Ec, 4f
Nineveh, Da, 3a; Eb, 2d
Ningus, F., Hb, 12
Ninus, Lf, 20
Nippur, Eb, 3a
Nisaea, Ee, 7
Nishapur, Cb, 18b
Nisibis, Eb, 2d
Nisyros, I., He, 8
Nisyrus, Ec, 2b
Niy, Ca, 3a
No (Ammon, Thebes), Cd, 3b
Nola, Cb, 13
Nomentum, Ge, 12
Nomentana Pa., Inset, 11d
Noph (Memphis), Cd, 2d
Nora, Be, 14a
Norba (Apulia), Fb, 13
Norba (Hispania), Ae, 15
Norba (Latium), Aa, 13
Noreia, Ec, 10
Noricum, Fd, 20
Northern Hiung-nu, Kc, 19
Notium, Ec, 9a
Nova Via, Insets, 13a, b
Novae, Ie, 20
Novae Athenae, Inset, 7b
Novantae, Bb, 17
Novantarum Pr., Inset, 17a
Novaria, Cb, 12
Noviodunum, Kb, 12
Noviomagus (Chichester), Ff, 17
Noviomagus (Germania),
    Db, Dc, 15
Noviomagus (Lugdunensis),
    Cc, 15
Nubae, Cd, 1
Nubian Desert, Bd, 3a
Nuceria, Gd, 12
Nuceria Alfaterna, Cb, 13
Numana, Hd, 12
Numantia, Bd, 15
Numicius, F., Aa, 13
Numidia, De, 15
Nursia, He, 12
Nymphaeum Pr., Fb, 6
Nysa, Jc, 9b

OASIS MAGNA, Bd, 2d
Oasis Parva, Bd, 2d
Oasis Siwa (Ammonium), Bb, 2d
Oceanus Aethiopicus, Inset, 1
Oceanus Atlanticus, Ad, 20
Oceanus Britannicus, Bc, 18

Oceanus Germanicus, Db, 20
Oceanus Hibernicus, Bc, 17
Oceanus Indicus, Inset, 1
Oceanus Occidentalis, Inset, 1
Ocelum, Bb, 12
Ochus, F., Ib., 5b
Ocriculum, Ge, 12
Ocrinum Pr., Af, 17
Octapitarum Pr., Ae, 17
Octaviae, P., Inset, 11d
Octavii, P., Inset, 11d
Octodurum, Ba, 12
Octodurus, Dc, 15
Odessus, Db, 16
Odeum, Inset, 7a
Odomanti, Ea, 6
Odrysae, Ba, 9b
Oea, Ef, 10
Oeneon, Cd, 7
Oeniadae, Bb, 9a
Oenoe (Argolis), De, Ed, 7
Oenoe (Attica), Ed, 7
Oenoe (Elis), Ce, 7
Oenophyta, Ed, 7
Oenthea, Dd, 7
Oenussae, Is. Ionia, Gc, 8
Oenussae Ins., Messenia, Ct. 7
Oescus, Cb, 16
Oesyme, Fb, 6
Oeta, Dd, 6
Oglasa, Ee, 12
Olbia (Sardinia), Dd, 15
Olbia (Scythia), Ea, 16
Old Kilpatrick, Ba, 17
Olenus, Cd, 7
Olicana (Ilkley), Ec, 17
Olisippo, Ae, 15
Olives, Mt. of, Bd, 4d
Olizon, Ec, 6
Ollius, Eb, 12
Oloosson, Dc, 6
Olpae, Cd, 6
Olympieum, Inset, 7b
Olympia, Ce, 7
Olympus, Db, 6
Olynthus, Eb, 6
Omanitae, Hf, 18
Ombos, Bd, 3a
Omphis, Kingdom of, Kc, 9b
On (Heliopolis), Ba, 3b
Onchesmus, Bc, 6
Onchestus, F., Dc, 6
Onnum (Halton), Ea, 17
Onugnathos Pr., Df, 7
Ophel, Inset, 4b
Ophel, Wall of, Inset, 4b
Ophionenses, Cd, 6
Ophrah, Be, 4a
Ophrynium, Inset, 2c
Opis, Ec, 5b
Opis (Upi), Ec, 2d
Opitergium, Gb, 12
Oppius, M., Inset, 11c
Opus, Ed, 6
Opus, Pr., Dd, 7
Orcades, Inset, 17a
Orchoe, Fc, 9b
Orchomenus (Arcadia), De, 7
Orchomenus (Boeotia), Dd, 6
Ordovices, Cd, 17
Orestis, Cb, 6
Oreus, Cb, 9a
Oricus, Aa, 9a
Orneae, De, 7
Orontes, R., Cb, 4c
Oropus, Ed, 7
Ortona, Je, 12
Orumbovii. Db, 12
Osca, Bd, 15
Oscela, Ca, 12
Osci, Bb, 14c
Osii, Eb, 18
Osrhoene, Fc, 16
Ossa, M., Dc, 6
Osteodes, Ins., Bd, 13
Ostia, Gf, 12
Ostiensis, Pa., Inset, 11d
Ostrogothi, Id, 20
Otadini, Da, 17
Othona (Bradwell), Ge, 17
Othrys, M., Dd, 6
Ovilava, Ec, 15
Oxianus Lacus, Ea, 9c
Oxus, R., Ia, 9b
Oxydraces, Kc, 9b
Oxyrhynchus, Bb, 3b

PACHYNUS PR., Df, 13
Padan Aram, Db, 2d
Padmavati, Ec, 18b

Padus, F., Fb, 12
Paedagogium, Inset, 13b
Paeligni, He, 12
Paeones, Aa, 9b
Paeonia, Da, 6
Paeonians, Ca, 2b
Paestum, Cb, 13
Pagae, Ed, 7
Pagasae, Dc, 6
Paithan, Ed, 18b
Palaestina, Fd, 18
Palatinus, M., Inset, 13b
Palatium, Inset, 11d
Palatium Caesarum, Inset, 11d
Palestina, Cc, 5b
Palinuri Pr., Db, 13
Palla, Df, 12
Pallantia, Bd, 15
Pallantium, De, 7
Pallatina, Inset, 11c
Pallavas, Jf, 19
Pallene (Argolis), Ed, 7
Pallene (Chalcidice), Eb, 6
Palma, Ce, 15
Palmyra, Kg, 20
Paludes Pomptinae, Ba, 13
Pamisus, F., Ce, 7
Pamphylia, If, 20
Panacton, Ed, 7
Panarus, F., Ec, 12
Pangaeus, M., Fb, 6
Panjadada, Jd, 19
Pannonia (Interior), Ba, 16
Pannonia (Superior), Ba, 16
Panopolis (Shem), Bc, 3b
Panormus (Achaea), Cd, 7
Panormus (Phrygia), Db, 7c
Panormus (Sicilia), Bd, 13
Pantheon, Inset, 11d
Panticapaeum, Ka, 5a
Pantimathi, Fb, 5b
Paphlagonia, Je, 20
Paphlagonians, Ca, 2d
Paphos, Jd, 5a
Paraetacene, Jb, 9b
Paraetonium, Bc, 9b
Paran, Wilderness of, Ag, 4c
Parapanisadae, Jc, 9b
Parapanisus Mons, Jb, 5b
Parentium, Hb, 12
Paricanii, Jd, 5b
Parisi (Yorkshire), Fc, 17
Parium, Db, 7c
Parma, Ec, 12
Parnassus M., Dd, 6
Parnes M., Ed, 7
Parnon M., De, 7
Paropanisadai, Aa, 18a
Paros, Fd, 8
Parthenicum, Bd, 13
Parthenon, Inset, 7a
Parthia, Cb, 18b
Parthian Empire, Hd, 18
Parushapura, Jd, 19
Pasargadae, Gc, 5b
Pasitigris, F., Fc, 2d
Pataliputra, Cb, 18a
Patara, Dc, 16
Patavium, Fb, 12
Patmos I., Gd, 8
Patrae, Cd, 7
Pattala, Jd, 9b
Pauca, Cf, 12
Pausicae, Fb, 5b
Pautalia, Cb, 16
Pax Iulia, Ae, 15
Paxos, Bc, 6
Pebeseth (Bubastis), Ba, 3b
Pedasus, Eb, 2b
Pedone, Bc, 12
Pedum, Ab, 14b
Pelagonia, Ca, 6
Pelion M., Ec, 6
Pelium, Bb, 6
Pella (Macedonia), Db, 6
Pella (Palestina), Fd, 16; Cc, 4d
Pellene, Dd, 7
Pellene, Dd, 7
Peloponnesus, Hc, 5a
Pelorum Pr., Dd, 13
Pelso, L., Ba, 16
Peltae, Bb, 5b
Pelusic Mouth, Ca, 3b
Pelusium, Cc, 9b
Peneus, F., Cc, 6
Peneus, F., Ce, 7
Pennal, Cd, 17
Penneloci, Aa, 12

Pentapolis, Gf, 10
Pentri, Ca, 13
Penuel, Cd, 4a
Peparethus, Ec, 6
Peraea, Cd, 4d
Perga, Eb, 4f
Pergamum, Dc, 16
Perge, Cb, 9b
Perinthus, Ba, 9b
Per-Ramses, Ca, 3b
Perrhaebi, Dc, 6
Persarum Regnum, Mg, 20
Persepolis, Gd, 5b
Persian Empire, 5b
Persian Gates, Gc, 9b
Persis, Gc, 5b; Cb, 18b
Perusia, Gd, 12
Pessinus, Jf, 20
Petelia, Fc, 13
Petra (Arabia), Fd, 16
Petra (Graecia), Db, 6
Petra (Sela), Bg, 4c
Petra (Sicilia), Ce, 13
Petrianae, Cb, 17
Petuaria (Brough), Fc, 17
Peuce I., Ba, 9b
Pevensey (Anderida), Gf, 17
Phaeca, Cc, 6
Phaestus, Crete, Ba, 7d
Phaestus, Locris Ozolis, Dd, 7
Phalara, Dd, 6
Phalerum, Ee, 7
Phaloria, Cc, 6
Phanagoria, Fa, 16
Pharae (Achaea), Cd, 7
Pharae (Messenia), De, 7
Pharcadon, Dc, 6
Pharnacia, Fb, 16
Pharpar, R., Cd, 4c
Pharsalus, Dc, 6
Pharus I., Dd, 16
Phasaelis, Bc, 4d
Phaselis, Jc, 5a
Phasis, Gb, 16
Phatnitic Mouth, Ba, 3b
Pheneus, De, 7
Pherae, Dc, 6
Phigalia, Ce, 7
Phila, Dc, 6
Philadelphia (Asia), Db, 4f
Philadelphia (Palestine), Cd, 4d
Philippi, Aa, 9b
Philippi, P., Inset, 11d
Philippopolis, Cb, 16
Philistia, Ae, 4a
Philistines, Cc, 2a
Phinopolis, Ea, 7c
Phintias, Be, 13
Phlius, De, 7
Phocaea, Ic, 5a
Phocians, Cb, 2b
Phocis, Dd, 6
Phoenice, Bc, 6
Phoenicia, Fd, 18
Phoenicussa, Cd, 13
Pholegandros, Ff, 7
Phraaspa, Gd, 18
Phrygia, If, 20
Phrygians, Cb, 2a
Phthia, Cb, 2b
Phthiotis, Dc, 6
Phylace, Dc, 6
Phyle, Ed, 7
Picentes, Hd, 12
Picentia, Cb, 13
Picentini, Cb, 13
Picenum, Hd, 12
Picti, Cb, 20
Pictones, Bc, 15
Pillars of Hercules, Bc, 5a
Pinciana, Pa., Inset, 11d
Pindus, Mts., Cc, 6
Ping Chow, Md, 19
Pinna, He, 12
Piquentum, Jb, 12
Pir, Cc, 9a
Piraeus, Ee, 7
Piranum, Hb, 12
Piresiae, Dc, 6
Pisa (Graecia), Ce, 7
Pisae, Ed, 12
Pisanus Port, Ed, 12
Pisatis, Ce, 7
Pisaurum, Gd, 12
Piscina Publica, Inset, 11d
Pisgah, Mt., Ce, 4a
Pishtapura, Fd, 18b
Pisidia, Jf, 20
Pistoria, Ed, 12

Pithecussa Ins., Bb, 13
Pithom, Ba, 3b
Pityus, Ke, 20
Pityusa, I., Ee, 7
Pityusae Ins., Ce, 15
Placentia, Db, 12
Planasia, Ee, 12
Plataea, Cb, 9a
Plavis, F., Ga, 12
Plemmyrium Pr., De, 13
Pleuron, Cd, 7
Plumbaria, Be, 14a
Pnyx, Inset, 7b
Poediculi, Eb, 13
Poeni, Bc, Ac, 14c
Poetovio, Gd, 20
Pola, Hc, 12
Polacticum Pr., Hc, 12
Polemon, K. of, Fb, 4f
Pollentia, Bc, 12
Polyaegus, Fc, 6
Polyrrhenia, Aa, 7d
Pompaelo, Bd, 15
Pompeia, P., Inset, 11d
Pompeii, Cb, 13
Pompeii, Th., Inset, 11d
Pompeiopolis (Paphlagonia),
    Eb, 16
Pompeiopolis (Soli), Ec, 16
Pons Aelius (Newcastle), Eb, 17
Pons Aemilius, Inset, 13a
Pons Aeni, Ec, 15
Pons Aureoli, Db, 12
Pons Cestius, Inset, 11c
Pons Fabricius, Inset, 11c
Pontes, Fe, 17
Pontiae Ins., Ab, 13
Pontus, Jf, 20
Pontus, Diocese of, If, 20
Pontus Euxinus, Je, 20
Populonia, Fb, 5a
Porolissum, Ca, 16
Porta Archarnica, Inset, 7b
Porta Capena, Inset, 11d
Porta Carmentalis, Inset, 13a
Porta Diomea, Inset, 7b
Porta Flumentana, Inset, 13a
Porta Hadriani, Inset, 7b
Porta Itonia, Inset, 7b
Porta Mugonia, Inset, 13a
Porta Piraeica, Inset, 7b
Porta Ratumena, Inset, 13a
Porta Romanula, Inset, 13a
Porticus Metelli, Inset, 13a
Porticus Octaviae, Inset, 13b
Portsmouth Harb. (Magnus
    Portus), Ef, 17
Portuensis, Pa., Inset, 11d
Portus Adurni, Ef, 17
Portus Aedro, Gb, 12
Portus Cale, Ad, 15
Portus Herculis Monoeci, Bd, 12
Portus Itius, Cb, 15
Portus Lemanis (Lympne),
    He, 17
Portus Magnus, Be, 15
Portus Mauritii, Cd, 12
Portus Namnetum, Bc, 15
Portus Veneris (Gallia), Cd, 15
Portus Veneris (Italia), Dc, 12
Porus, Kingdom of, Kc, 9b
Posidium, Pr., Chalcidice, Eb,
Posodium Pr. (Italia), Cb, 13
Posidium Pr. (Pallene), Ec, 6
Posidium Pr. (Phthiotis), Ec, 6
Posidonia (Paestum), Cb, 13
Potaissa, Ca, 16
Potentia (Lucania), Db, 13
Potentia (Picenum), Hd, 12
Potidaea Ca, 9a
Praeneste Gf, 12
Praenestina, Pa., Inset, 11d
Prarjuna, Ec, 18b
Prasiae (Attica), Fe, 7
Prasiae (Laconia), De, 7
Prayaga, Cb, 18a
Priapus, Db, 7c
Priene, Hd, 8
Prista, Db, 16
Privernum, Bb, 14b
Procolitia (Carrawburgh),
    Inset, 17
Proconnesus, Db, 7c
Prophthasia, Ic, 9b
Propontis, Ib, 5a
Propylaea, Inset, 7a
Provincia, Cd, 15
Prusa, Fb, 7c
Prytaneum, Inset, 7a

Psacum, Pr., Aa, 7d
Pselchis, Bd, 3a
Psophis, Ce, 7
Psyra, I., Fc, 8
Psyttalea, I., Ee, 7
Pteleum, Dc, 6
Pteria, Cb, 5b
Ptolemais (Pentapolis), Cd, 16
Ptolemais (Phoenicia), Bb, 4d
Ptolemais Hermiu, Ig, 11
Pura, Ie, 18
Puteoli, Cb, 13
Pydna, Ca, 9a
Pylae, Ec, 5b
Pylae Ciliciae, Ec, 16
Pylos, Bc, 9a
Pylus, Elis, Ce, 7
Pylus, see Pylos
Pyramids, Bb, 3b
Pyramus, F., Db, 5b
Pyrenaei Mtes., De, 20
Pyretus, R., Id, 20
Pyrgi, Ge, 12
Pyrrha, Gb, 8
Pythium, Db, 6
Pytho, Cb, 2b
Pyxus, Db, 13

QUADI, Gd, 20
Quadrata, Cb, 12
Querquetulana, Pa., Inset, 11c

RABBAH, Ce, 4a
Raeburnfoot, Ca, 17
Rakoti (Alexandria), Aa, 3b
Ramah, Asher, Bc, 4a
Ramah, Benjamin, Be, 4a
Ramoth Gilead, Dc, 4a
Rampurwa, Bc, 18a
Raphana, Db, 4d
Ratae (Leicester), Ed, 17
Ratiaria, Cb, 16
Ratumena, Pa., Inset, 11c
Ravenglass (Clanoventa), Cb, 17
Ravenna, Gc, 12
Ravenscar, Fb, 17
Reate, Ge, 12
Reculver (Regulbium), He, 17
Regia, Insets, 13a, b
Regillus, L., Ab, 14b
Regina, Ec, 15
Regma, He, 18
Regni, Ff, 17
Regnum Bosporanum, Fa, 16
Regnum Parthorum, Ke, 11
Regulbium (Reculver), He, 17
Remi, Cc, 15
Renus, F., Fc, 12
Republican Forum, 13a
Rerigonius Sinus, Ba, 17
Resaena, Bb, 18b
Restan, Cb, 3a
Reuben, Ce, 4a
Rha, R., Md, 20
Rhacotis (Alexandria), Bc, 9b
Rhaeti, Ba, 14c
Rhaetia, Ed, 20
Rhagae, Hd, 18
Rhamnus, Fd, 7
Rheba, Fa, 7c
Rhegium (Bruttium), Dd, 13
Rhegium Lepidum, Ec, 12
Rhenea, Fd, 8
Rhenus, F , Ed, 20
Rhion (Asine), Cf, 7
Rhithymna, Ba, 7d
Rhium Pr., Cd, 7
Rhodanus, F., Cd, 15; Ee, 20
Rhodope, M, Fa, 6; Gd, 10
Rhodus, If, 20
Rhoeteum, Inset, 2c
Rhoeteum Pr., Inset, 2c
Rhotanus, F., De, 12
Rhypes, Dd, 7
Rhytium, Dd, 2b
Ribchester (Bremetennacum), Dc, 17
Riblah, Cc, 4c
Richborough (Rutupiae), He, 17
Ricina (Liguria), Dc, 12
Ricina (Picenum), Hd, 12
Rigomagus, Cb, 12
Ripuarii, Ec, 20
Robogdii, Inset, 17a
Robogdium Prom., Aa, 17
Rochester (Durobrivae), Ge, 17
Rockingham Forest, Fd, 17
Roma, Gf, 12
Roma Quadrata, Inset, 13a
Roman Britain, 17

Roman Empire, 10-11; 15; 16
Romanula, Pa., Inset, 11c
Rostra Nova, Inset, 13b
Rostra Vetera, Inset, 13a
Rotomagus, Cc, 15
Rough Castle, Ca, 17
Roxolæni, Fc, 18
Rubi, Ea, 13
Rubico, F., Gc, 12
Rudiae, Gb, 13
Rugii, Fc, Hd, 20
Rummindei, Cb, 18a
Rupnath, Bb, 18a
Rusaddir, Be, 15
Rusellae, Fe, 12
Rusgonia, Ce, 15
Rutuli, Ab, 14b
Rutupiae (Richborough), He, 17
Ruvignium, Hb, 12
Ryknield Way, Ed, 17

SABAEI, Dd, 1
Sabatinus, L., Ge, 12
Sabini, Ge, 12
Sabrina Aest. (Severn), Ce, 17
Sabrina, F., Bb, 15
Sacae (Scythae), Kb, 5b
Sacra Via (Athens), Inset, 7a
Sacra Via (Roma), Inset, 13b
Sacrum Pr., Dd, 12
Saepta, Inset, 11c
Saepta Iulia, Inset, 13b
Saetabis, Be, 15
Saevo M., Ba, 1
Sagalassus, Cb, 9b
Sagartia, Hc, 5b
Sagrus, Je, 12
Saguntum, Cc, 5a
Sai (Sais), Ba, 3b
St. Albans (Verulamium), Fe, 17
Sais (Sai), Ba, 3b
Sais (Zau), Cc, 2d
Sakas, Je, 19
Salamis (Cyprus), Jc, 5a
Salamis (Graecia), Ee, 7
Salapia, Da, 13
Salaria, Pa.,·Inset, 11d
Salassi, Bb, 12
Salcah, Ce, 4c
Saldae, De, 15
Salernum, Cb, 13
Salii, Ec, 20
Salinae (Droitwich), Dd, 17
Salisbury (Sorviodunum), Ee, 17
Sallentini, Fb, 13
Sallentinum Pr., Gc, 13
Salmantica, Ad, 15
Salonae, Bb, 16
Salt Sea, The, Bf, 4a
Salutaris, Pa., Inset, 11
Samal, Ca, 3a
Samaria, Bc, 4d
Samaria (Sebaste), Bc, 4d
Samarobriva, Cc, 15
Samatata, Kingdom of, Fc, 18b
Same, Bd, 7
Samnites, Bb, 14c
Samnium, Ca, 13
Samos, Gd, 8
Samos (Cephallenia), Bb, 2b
Samosata, Je, 11
Samothrace, Fa, 8 ·
Sane, Eb, 6
Sangala, Kc, 9b
Sangarius, Eb, 16
Sanqualis, Pa., Inset, 11c
Santones, Bc, 15
Saradaush, Da, 3a
Sarangae, Ic, 5b
Sardes, Dc, 16
Sardinia-Corsica, Dd, 10
Sardis, Inset, Db, 4f
Sarmatia, Jc, 20
Sarmizegethusa, Ec, 18
Sarnia, Bc, 15
Sarpedon Pr., Cb, 7c
Sarsina, Gd, 12
Sarus, F., Db, 5b
Saspires Alardoii, Ea, 5b
Sassanid Kingdom, Cb, 18b
Satala, Fb, 16
Saticula, Ca, 13
Satiyaputra, K. of, Bc, 18a
Satricum, Aa, 13
Saturnia, Fe, 12
Saurashtra, Je, 19
Savaria, Ba, 16
Savo, Cc, 12
Savus, F., Ba, 16

Saxones, Ec, 20
Saxum Tarpeium, Inset, 13a
Scalae Caci, Inset, 13a
Scallabis, Ae, 15
Scamander, F., Cc, 7c
Scandia, Fa, 20
Scandiae Ins., Ea, 15
Scarbantia, Ba, 16
Scarborough, Fb, 17
Scardona, Bb, 16
Scardus, M., Ba, 6
Scepsis, Cc, 7c
Sciathus, Ec, 6
Scillus, Bd, 8
Scione, Ec, 6
Scodra, Bb, 16
Scoti, Bc, 20
Scotus, De, 8
Scupi, Cb, 16
Scylacium, Ed, 13
Scyllaeum, Dd, 13
Scyllaeum Pr. (Argolis), Ee, 7
Scyllaeum Pr. (Bruttium), Dd, 13
Scyros, Ec, 6
Scyrus, Db, 9a
Scythae (Sacae), Kb, 5b
Scythia, Jb, 19
Scythopolis, Bc, 4d
Sebaste (Samaria), Bc, 4d
Sebastea, Fc, 16
Sebinus, L., Eb, 12
Secia, F., Ec, 12
Second Cataract of Nile, Bd, 3
Secretarium, Inset, 13b
Sedunum, Ba, 12
Segedunum (Wallsend), Ea, 17
Segelocum, Fc, 17
Segesta (Liguria), Dc, 12
Segesta (Sicilia), Ae, 13
Segestanorum, Ad, 13
Segobriga, Bè, 15
Segodunum, Cd, 15
Segontium (Carnarvon), Bc, 17
Segovia, Bd, 15
Segusio, Ab, 12
Seir, Cb, 3a
Sela (Petra), Bg, 4c
Seleucia, Ec, 16
Seleucia (Mesopotamia), Kf, 11
Seleucia (Syria), Fb, 4f
Selgovae, Ca, 17
Selinus (Cilicia), Ec, 16
Selinus (Sicilia), Ae, 13
Sellasia, De, 7
Selymbria, Ea, 7c
Semachonitis, L., Ca, 4d
Semneh, Bd, 3a
Sena Gallica, Hd, 12
Sena Iulia, Fd, 12
Senaculum, Inset, 13a
Sengara, Da, 3a
Senia, Aa, 16
Senones (Gallia), Cc, 15
Senones (Italia), Gd, 12
Sentinum, Gd, 12
Senzar, Ca, 3a
Sepharvaim (Sippar), Ec, 2d
Sepias Pr., Ec, 6
Sepphoris, Bb, 4d
Septimania, Pa., Inset, 11d
Sepulcrum C. Cestii, Inset, 11d
Sequana, R., Dd, 20
Sequani, Dc, 15
Serdica, Cb, 16
Serica, Gc, 1
Seriphos, Fe, 7
Sermyle, Eb, 6
Servitium, Ba, 16
Sessites, F., Cb, 12
Sestus, Ba, 5b
Seteia Aest., Cc, 17
Setia, Ba, 13
Severn (Sabrina Aest.), R., Ce, 17
Shahbazgarhu, Ba, 18a
Sharon, Plain of, Ac, 4d
Shasu (Habiru), Cb, 3a
Shechem, Bd, 4a
Shechem (Sychem), Bc, 4d
Shedet (Crocodilopolis-Arsinoé), Bb, 3b
Shel Gharraf, Eb, 3a
Shem (Panopolis), Bc, 3b
Shephelah, Ad, 4d
Sherwood Forest, Ec, 17
Shiloh, Bd, 4a
Shubari, Da, 3a
Shushan (Susa), Fc, 2d
Shuster, Bb, 18b
Sicani, Ae, 13
Sicca, De, 15

Sicelia, Inset, 7b
Sicilia, Be, 13; Ff, 20
Sicinos, I., Fe, 8
Siculi, Ce, 13
Sicyon, De, 7
Siddapura, Bc, 18a
Siddim, Vale of, Bf, 4a
Side, Bithynia et Pontus, Fb, 16
Side, Pamphylia, Jc., 5a
Sidon, Dc, 5b; Dc, 9b
Sidonians, Bb, 4a
Siga, Be, 15
Sigeum, Ic, 5a
Sigeum Pr., Inset, 2c
Signia, Ba, 13
Sila M., Dd, 13
Silarius, F., Db, 13
Silchester (Calleva Atrebatum), Fe, 17
Siloam, Pool of, Inset, 4e
Silures, Ce, 17
Simeon, Af, 4a
Simkala (Ceylon), Fe, 18b
Simoeis, F., Inset, 2c
Simyra, Bc, 4c
Sinae, Gc, 1
Sinai, Mt., Bc, 3a
Sinai Pen., Bc, 3a
Sind, Ie, 19
Singara, Lf, 20
Singidunum, Cb, 16
Singus, Eb, 6
Sinope, Fb, 16
Sinuessa, Ba, 13
Sinus Acanthus, Eb, 6
Sinus Aelanites, Bc, 3a
Sinus Alcyonicus, Ed, 7
Sinus Ambracius, Bd, 6
Sinus Arabicus, Cd, 3a
Sinus Argolicus, De, 7
Sinus Astacenus, Fb, 7c
Sinus Aualites, Gb, 18
Sinus Caystrius, Hd, 8
Sinus, Ceramicus, He, 8
Sinus Cianus, Fb, 7c
Sinus Corinthiacus, Dd, 7
Sinus Crisaeus, Dd, 7
Sinus Cumanus, Cb, 13
Sinus Cyparissius, Ce, 7
Sinus Didymi, Ca, 7d
Sinus Euboicus, Ed, 6
Sinus Flanaticus, Jb, 12
Sinus Heroopolites, Bc, 3a
Sinus Laconicus, Df, 7
Sinus Laus, Db, 13
Sinus Ligusticus, Dd, 15
Sinus Maliacus, Dd, 6
Sinus Messeniacus, Df, 7
Sinus Oxianus, Hc, 18
Sinus Paestanus, Cb, 13
Sinus Pagasaeus, Dc, 6
Sinus Persicus, Eb, 3a
Sinus Saronicus, Ee, 7
Sinus Scylaceus, Ed, 13
Sinus Singiticus, Eb, 6
Sinus Strymonicus, Eb, 6
Sinus Tarentinus, Fb, 13
Sinus Thermaicus, Db, 6
Sinus Thesproticus, Bc, 6
Sinus Toronaicus, Eb, 6
Siphae, Ed, 7
Siphnos, Ff, 7
Sippar, Ec, 5b
Sippar (Sepharviam), Ec, 2d
Siris, Eb, 13
Siris, F., Eb, 13
Sirmio, Eb, 12
Sirmium, Ge, 20
Siscia, Gd, 20
Sithonia, Eb, 6
Sitifis, De, 15
Sittace, Ec, 5b
Smyrna, Hc, 8
Smyrna Nova, Hc, 8
So-fang, Mc, 19
Sogdiana, Jb, 5b; Jb, 9b
Sogdiana, Ib, 9b
Soleb, Bd, 3a
Soli (Cilicia), Jc, 5a
Soli (Cyprus), Jc, 5a
Soli (Pompeiopolis), Ec, 16
Sollium, Bd, 6
Solomon's Palace, Inset, 4b
Soluntum, Bd, 13
Solus, Fc, 5a
Solygea, De, 7
Sopara, Bc, 18a
Sopianae, Ba, 16
Sora, Ba, 13

Soracte M., Ge, 12
Sorek, R., Ae, 4a
Sorviodunum (Salisbury), Ee, 17
South Shields, Inset, 17b
Southern Hiung-nu, Mc, 19
Spain (Diocese of Hispania), Ce, 20
Spalauthra, Ec, 6
Sparta, De, 7
Spartolus, Ca, 9a
Speluncae, Ba, 13
Speos Artemidos (Menet Hufu), Bc, 3b
Spercheus, F., Dd, 6
Sphacteria, Bc, 9a
Spinis, Ee, 17
Spoletium, Ge, 12
Sravasti, Ke, 19
Srinagar, Ba, 18a
Stabiae, Cb, 13
Stadium (Athens), Inset, 7b
Stadium Domitiani, Inset, 11d
Stagira, Eb, 6
Stanwix, Inset, 17
Stenyclarus, De, 7
Stephen's Gate, Inset, 4e
Stoa Hadriani, Inset, 7b
Stoa of Eumenes, Inset, 7a
Stobi, Cb, 16
Stratonicaea, Eb, 6
Stratonice, Da, 8
Stratus, Cd, 6
Strongyle, Dd, 13
Strymon, F., Cb, 16
Stura, F., Bc, 12
Stymphalus, De, 7
Styra, Fd, 7
Suana, Fe, 12
Sublicius, Inset, 11d
Sublupatia, Eb, 13
Subura, Inset, 11c
Suburana, Inset, 11c
Sucro, F., Be, 15
Sudeti Mts., Eb, 15
Suessa Aurunca, Ba, 13
Suessa Pometia, Aa, 13
Suessula, Ca, 13
Suevi, Ed, 20
Suevi, Semnones, Db, 18
Sugambri, Db, 15
Suindinum, Cc, 15
Sulci, De, 15
Sumer, Eb, 3a
Sunium, Fe, 7
Sunium Pr., Fe, 7
Surashtra, Ec, 18b
Surrentum, Cb, 13
Susa, Fc, 5b
Susa (Shushan), Fc, 2d
Susia, Hb, 9b
Susiana, Fc, 5b; Gd, 18
Sutrium, Ge, 12
Sutu, Db, 3a
Syagros Pr., Hf, 18
Sybaris, Gc, 5a
Sybota, Bb, 9a
Sychem (Shechem), Bc, 4d
Syene, Ce, 5b
Symaethus, F., De, 13
Syme, Ec, 9a
Synnada, Ec, 16
Syout (Lycopolis), Bc, 3b
Syracusae, Gc, 5a; De, 13; Gf, 20
Syria, Dc, 9b
Syria Deserta, Gd, 18
Syrian Desert, Cb, 3a
Syrians (Aramaeans), Dc, 4c
Syrnos I., Ge, 8
Syros, Fe, 7
Syrtis Major, Gg, 20
Syrtis Minor, Fg, 20
Sze Chow, Nd, 19

TAANACH, Bc, 4a
Tabal, Cb, 2d
Tabernae Argentariae, Inset, 13a
Tabernae Veteres, Inset, 13a
Tabor, Mt., Bc, 4a
Tabularium, Inset, 13b
Tadcaster (Calcaria), Ec, 17
Tadmor (Palmyra), Cb, 3a
Tadmor (Tamar), Ec, 4c
Taenarum Pr., Df, 7
Tagus, F., Ae, 15
Tai Yuan, Nd, 19
Taliata (Tamar), Ec, 4c
Taliata, Cb, 16
Talmis, Bd, 3a
Tamar (Tadmor), Ec, 4c
Tamesa Aest., Inset, 17a
Tamesis, F., Bb, 15

Tamralipti, Cb, 18a
Tamraparni (Ceylon), Cd, 18a
Tanager, F., Db, 13
Tanagra, Ed, 7
Tanarus, F., Cc, 12
Tanis (Zoan), Ba, 3b
Tanitic Mouth, Ca, 3b
Taphiae Ins., Bd, 6
Taprobane, Fd, 1
Tapti, R., Je, 19
Tapuritae, Gb, 9b
Taras, Fb, 13
Tarentum, Fb, 13
Tarnaiae, Aa, 12
Tarracina, Ba, 13
Tarraco, De, 20
Tarraconensis, Bd, 15
Tarsatica, Aa, 16
Tarshish (Tartessus), Bc, 5a
Tarsius, F., Dc, 7c
Tarsus, Cb, 5b
Tartessus (Tarshish), Bc, 5a
Tarus, F., Dc, 12
Tarvenna, Cb, 15
Tarvisium, Gb, 12
Tatta, L., Cb, 5b
Taulantii, Aa, 6
Taurianum Pr., Dd, 13
Taurica, Jd, 20
Tauromenium De, 13
Taurini, Bc, 12
Taurus, Jf, 20
Taurus, M., Ec, 16
Taurus Pr., De, 13
Tavium, Ec, 16
Taxila, Eb, 18b
Taygetus, M., De, 7
Teanum, Ca, 13
Teanum Apulum, Da, 13
Teate, Je, 12
Tecmon, Bc, 6
Tegea, De, 7
Tegianum, Db, 13
Tehenu, Ba, 3b
Teira, Hc, 8
Tekoa, Be, 4a
Telamon, Fe, 12
Telesia, Ca, 13
Tell-el-Amarna (Akhetaton),
  Bc, 3b
Telmessus, Dc, 16
Telos, Ec, 9a
Tempe, F., Dc, 6
Temple (Jerusalem), Inset, 4b
Templeborough, Ec, 17
Templum Antonini et Faustinae,
  Inset, 13b
Templum Apollinis, Inset, 13b
Templum Athene, Inset, 7a
Templum Augusti, Inset, 13b
Templum Castorum, Insets, 13a, b
Templum Concordiae,
  Insets, 13a, b
Templum Dianae, Inset, 11c
Templum Divi Romuli, Inset, 13b
Templum Divi Traiani, Inset, 13b
Templum Divorum, Inset, 13b
Templum Iani, Inset, 13a
Templum Iovis Capitolini,
  Insets, 13a, b
Templum Iovis Statoris,
  Insets, 13a, b
Templum Iovis Victoris,
  Insets, 13a, b
Templum Iunonis Lucinae,
  Inset, 11c
Templum Iunonis Monetae,
  Insets, 13a, b
Templum Martis Ultoris,
  Inset, 13b
Templum Minervae, Inset, 13b
Templum Pacis, Insets, 13b
Templum Quirini, Inset, 11c
Templum Romae et Augusti,
  Inset, 7a
Templum Sacrae Urbis, Inset. 13b
Templum Salutis, Inset, 11c
Templum Saturni, Inset, 13a
Templum Semonis Sanci,
  Inset, 11c
Templum Veneris et Romae,
  Inset, 13b
Templum Veneris Genetricis,
  Inset, 13b
Templum Vespasiani, Inset, 13b
Tempsa, Ed, 13
Tena Aest., Inset, 17a

Tenebrium Pr., Ce, 15
Tenedos, Gb, 8
Tenos, Fd, 8
Tentyra (Enet), Cc, 3b
Teos, Eb, 9a
Teredon, Fc, 9b
Tergeste, Hb. 12
Terina, Ec, 13
Teurnia, Ec, 15
Teuthrone, Df, 7
Teutones, Db, 15
Thaenae, Ef, 15
Thalaba, Ge, 18
Thapsacus, Db, 5b
Thapsacus (Tiphsah), Eb, 4c
Thapsus (Africa), Ee, 15; Ff, 20
Thapsus (Silicia), De, 13
Thara, Gb, 9b
Tharrus, Ec, 5a
Tharu, Ca, 3b
Thasos, Fb, 6
Theatrum Dionysi, Inset, 7a
Theatrum et Porticus Pompeii,
  Inset, 11
Theatrum Marcelli, Inset, 13b
Thebae, Achaea, Cc, 16
Thebae, Libya, Cc, 1; Ig, 11
Thebe, Eb, 2b
Thebes (Boeotia), Ed, 7
Thebes (Hypothebae), Cb, 2b
Thebes (No, Ammon), Cd, 3b
Thebes (Phthiotis), Dc, 6
Thebez, Bd, 4a
Thelpusa, Ce, 7
Thera, Dc, 9a
Therma, Eb, 6
Thermae, Be, 13
Thermae Agrippae, Inset, 11d
Thermae Antoninianae, Inset,11d
Thermae Constantini, Inset, 11d
Thermae Diocletiani, Inset, 11d
Thermae Neptuni, Inset, 11d
Thermae Neronianae, Inset, 11d
Thermae Quirini, Inset, 11d
Thermae Salurni, Inset, 11d
Thermae Selinuntiae, Be, 13
Thermae Solis, Inset, 11d
Thermae Traiani, Inset, 11d
Thermae Vestae, Inset, 11c
Thermessa, Cd, 13
Thermopylae, Dd, 6
Thermum, Cd, 6
Thespiae, Ed, 7
Thesprotia, Bc, 6
Thessalia, Dc, 6
Thessaly, see Thessalia
Thessalonica, He, 20
Theudoria, Cc, 6
Theveste, De, 15
Third Cataract of Nile, Be, 3a
Thisbe, Cb, 2b
Thoricus, Fe, 7
Thospitis, L., Eb, 5b
Thrace, see Thracia
Thracia, Fa, 6; Ie, 20
Thracia, Diocese of, Ie, 20
Three Taverns, Aa, 4f
Thronium, Cb, 9a
Throsmos, Inset, 2c
Thule, Inset, 17a
Thurii, Ec, 13
Thusdrus, Ee, 15
Thyateira, Hc, 8
Thyatira, Db, 4f
Thymbra, Inset, 2c
Thyrea, De, 7
Thyrrheum, Bd, 6
Thyrsus, F., Bd, 14a
Thyssus, Fb, 6
Tiberias, Bb, 4d
Tiberina, I., Inset, 11d
Tiberis, F., Gf, 12
Tibur, Gf, 12
Tiburtina, Pa., Inset, 11d
Ticinum, Db, 12
Ticinus, F., Cb, 12
Tifernum, Gd, 12
Tifernus, F., Kf, 12
Tigranocerta, Ke, 11
Tigris (Hiddekel), F., Ec, 2d
Tigris, R., Db, 3
Tigullia, Dc, 12
Til Barsip, Db, 2d
Tilaventus, F., Ga, 12
Tilgarimmu (Togarhah), Db, 2d
Tingis, Bd, 18
Tingitana, Bf, 15
Tingitania, Cg, 20
Tipasa, Ce, 15
Tiphsah (Thapsacus), Eb, 4c

Tipsah, Db, 2d
Tiryns, De, 7
Tisia, F., Ca, 16
Titulcia, Bd, 15
Tium, Eb, 16
Tob, Cc, 4a
Togarmah (Tilgarimmu), Db, 2d
Tolentinum, Hd, 12
Toletum, Bd, 15
Tolosa, De, 20
Tomen-y-mur, Cd, 17
Tomi, Hd, 11
Topra, Bb, 18a
Torone, Ec, 6
Towcester, Ed, 17
Tralles, Bb, 2d
Transpadana, Cb, 12
Trapezus, Ke, 20
Trans Tiberim, Inset, 11d
Trasimenus, L., Gd, 12
Treba, Hf, 12
Trebbia, F., Dc, 12
Trebula, Ge, 12
Treveri, Dc, 10
Triballi, Aa, 9c
Tricca, Cc, 6
Trichonius, L., Cd, 6
Tridentini, Fa, 12
Tridentum, Fa, 12
Trigemina, Pa., Inset, 11c
Trimontium, Da, 17
Trinovantes, Ge, 17
Triphylia, Ce, 7
Tripodes, Inset, 7a
Tripolis, Fg, 20
Tripolis (Phoenicia), Fd, 16
Tripolis (Pontus), Fb, 16
Tripolitana, Ef, 10
Tritaea, Cd, 7
Tritonis, L., Df, 10
Triturrita, Ed, 12
Troas, Db, 4f
Troesmis, Da, 16
Troezen, Ee, 7
Troy (Ilium), Bb, 2a
Tsang-Wu, Ne, 19
Tsang-Wu, Ne, 19
Tuder, Ge, 12
Tullianum, Insets, 13a, b
Tullum, Dc, 15
Tunes, Ee, 15
Tung-hai, Nd, 19
Tun-Huang, Ld, 19
Tuola, F., De, 12
Turdetani, Ae, 15
Turduli, Be, 15
Turushpa (Van), Eb, 2d
Tusci (Etrusci), Bb, 14c
Tusculum, Aa, 13
Tyana, Ba, 3a
Tymphaea, Cc, 6
Tymphe M., Cc, 6
Tymphrestus M., Cd, 6
Tyndaris, Cd, 13
Tyras, Ja, 5a
Tyras, R., Id, 20
Tyre, Bb, 4a; Kg, 20
Tyrrhenia, Fb, 5a
Tyrus, Fd, 18

Ubi, Cb, 3a
Ugarit, Dc, 2a
Ujjain, Je, 19
Ulpiana, Cb, 16
Ulterior Hispania, Ad, 15
Umbria, Gd, 12
Umbri, Gd, 12
Umbro, F., Fe, 12
Upi (Opis), Ec, 2d
Upper City (Jerusalem), Inset. 4e
Upper Egypt, Bc, 3b
Ur, Eb, 3a
Uraipur, Bc, 18a
Uraiyu, Jf, 19
Urartu (Ararat), Eb, 2d
Urbs Salvia, Hd, 12
Urcinium, Ce, 12
Uria, Fb, 13
Urium, Da, 13
Uselis, Be, 14a
Ustica, Bd, 13
Utii, Hd, 5b
Uxantis, Ac, 15
Uxii, Gc, 9b
Uzentum, Gc, 13

Vaccaei, Ad, 15
Vada, Ed, 12
Vada Sabatia, Cc, 12

Vadimonis, L., Ge, 12
Vagienni, Bc, 12
Vaisis, Eb, 2d
Valabhi, Ec, 18b
Valentia (Gallia), Cd, 15
Valentia (Hispania), Be, 15
Vallis Murcia, Inset, 11c
Vallis Quirini, Inset, 11c
Vallum Antonini, Ba, 17
Vallum Hadriani, Da, 17
Valvata, Ed, 12
Van (Turushpa), Eb, 2d
Vandali, Gc, 20
Vanga, Cb, 18a
Vapincum, Dd, 15
Vascones, Bd, 15
Vectis, Ef, 17
Veii, Ge, 12
Velabrum, Insets, 13a, b
Veldidena, Ec, 15
Veleia, Dc, 12
Velia, Inset, 13a
Velia (Elea), Db, 13
Velitrae, Aa, 13
Veltae, Eb, 18
Venafrum, Ca, 13
Venedae, Ib, 20
Veneris et Romae, Inset, 11d
Veneti (Gallia), Bc, 15
Veneti (Italia), Gb, 12; Ec, 15
Venetia, Fb, 12
Vengi, K. of, Fd, 18b
Vengipura, Fd, 18b
Venonae, Ed, 17
Venonetes, Da, 12
Venta, Inset, 17a
Venta Belgarum (Winchester),
  Ee, 17
Venta Icenorum, Hd, 17
Venta Silurum, De, 17
Venusia, Db, 13
Verbanus, L., Ca, 12
Vercellae, Cb, 12
Vercovicium (Housesteads),
  Inset, 17
Veretum, Gc, 13
Verlucio, De ,17
Vernemetum, Ed, 17
Verona, Fb, 12
Verterae (Brough), Db, 17
Vertones Oretani, Ad, 15
Verulamium (St. Albans), Fe, 17
Vesontio, Dc, 15
Vestini, He, 12
Vesunna, Cc, 15
Vesuvius, M., Cb, 13
Vetera, Db, 15
Vettona, Ge, 12
Vetulonia, Ee, 12
Via Aemilia, Ec, Gc, 12
Via Appia, Aa, Eb, 13
Via Asinaria, Inset, 11c
Via Aurelia, Ed, 12
Via Cassia, Fe, 12
Via Claudia Augusta, Gb, 12
Via Clodia, Fe, 12
Via Dolorosa, Inset, 4e
Via Domitia, Cd, 15
Via Flaminia, Gd, 12
Via Galaria, Inset, 11c
Via Iulia, Cc, 12
Via Lata, Inset, 11d
Via Latina, Ba, 13
Via Nomentana, Inset, 11c
Via Ostiensis, Inset, 11c
Via Popilia, Db, 13
Via Portuensis, Inset, 11c
Via Postumia, Fb, 12
Via Praenestina, Inset, 11c
Via Sacra (Athens), Inset, 7b
Via Sacra (Rome), Inset, 11c
Via Salaria, He, 12
Via Tiburtina, Inset, 11c
Via Triumphalis, Inset, 11c
Via Valeria (Italia), He, 12
Via Valeria (Sicilia), Ce, 13
Viadua, F., Fb, 10
Viadua, R., Gc, 20
Vibinum, Da, 13
Vicetia, Fb, 12
Vicus Iugarius, Insets, 13a, b
Vicus Longus, Inset, 11c
Vicus Patricius, Inset, 11c
Vicus Tuscus, Insets, 13a, b
Vienna (Gallia), Cc, 15
Vienna (Vienne), Dd, 20
Villa Publica, Inset, 11c
Viminacium, He, 20
Viminalis, Pa., Inset, 11c
Vindelicia, Ec, 15

Vindobona, Ba, 16
Vindolanda (Chesterholm),
  Inset, 17
Vindomora (Ebchester), Inset, 17
Vindovala, Inset, 17
Vinovia, Eb, 17
Vinocladia, Ef, 17
Vintium, Bd, 12
Virgin's Well, Inset, 4e
Virgo, Aq., Inset, 11d
Viroconium (Wroxeter), Dd, 17
Virodunum, Dc, 15
Virunum, Ec, 10
Visigothi, Hd, 20
Vistula, F,. Gb, 10; Hc, 20
Visurgis, F., Db, 15
Vitricium, Bb, 12
Viviscus, Aa, 12
Volaterrae, Ed, 12
Volcanal, Inset, 13a
Volcei, Db, 13
Volsci, Bb, 14c; Ba, 13
Volsiniensis, L., Fe, 12
Volsinii (novus), Ge, 12
Volsinii (vetus), Ge, 12
Volturnum, Ba, 13
Volturnus, F., Ca, 13
Volubilis, Af, 10
Vomanus, F., Je, 12
Vosegus, M., Dc, 15
Vulci, Fe, 12

Wadi Tumilat, Ba, 3b
Walls (Jerusalem), Inset, 4e
Wallsend (Segedunum), Ea, 17
Walton Castle, He, 17
Warrington, Dc, 17
Wash, The (Metaris Aest.),
  Gc, 17
Watling Street, Dd, 17
Western Satraps, Ec, 18b
Wigan, Dc, 17
Winchester (Venta Belgarum),
  Ee, 17
World (Eratosthenes), 1b
World (Ptolemy), 1a
World (Herodotus), 1a
World (Strabo), 1c
Wroxeter (Viroconium), Dd, 17
Wuchun, Nd, 19
Wu-Wei, Md, 19

Xanthus, Bb, 9b
Xerxes Canal, Eb, 6
Xois (Khesout), Ba, 3b
Xyniae, Dc, 6

Y Gaer, Cd, 17
Yamutbul, Fc, 2d
Yandheya, Ec, 18b
Yang Chow, Ne, 19
Yangtze R., Od, 19
Yarkand, Jd, 19
Yarmuk, R., Cc, 4a
Yavanas, Id, 18
Yenoam, Cb, 3a
Yih Chow, Md, 19
Ying-chuan, Nd, 19
York (Eburacum), Eb, 17
Yu Chow, Nd, 19
Yu-chang, Ne, 19
Yueh-Sui, Me, 19
Yun Chow, Nd, 19
Yun-chung, Nc, 19

Zacynthus, Hc, 5a
Zadadrus, F., Kc, 9b
Zadracarta, Gb, 9b
Zagros Mts., see Zagrus Mons.
Zagrus Mons, Fc, 5b
Zahi, Cb, 3a
Zaitha, Bb, 18b
Zakaray, Ac, 4a
Zama Regia, De, 15
Zamua, Fb, 2d
Zancle (Messana), Dd, 13
Zarax, Ef, 7
Zarephath, Ba, 4d
Zariaspa, Ib, 9b
Zariaspa (Bactria), Jb, 9b
Zau (Sais), Cc, 2d
Zebulun, Bc, 4a
Zela, Fb, 16
Zeleia, Db, 7c
Zephyrium Pr., Ed, 13
Zeugma, Fc, 16
Ziklag, Af, 4a
Zikurtu, Fb, 2d
Zilis, Ae, 15
Zoan (Tanis), Ba, 3b
Zobah, Cc, 4c

PRINTED IN GREAT BRITAIN BY GEORGE PHILIP AND SON, LIMITED, LONDON

BHA

MUIR'S
HISTORICAL ATLAS
MEDIEVAL AND MODERN
Eleventh Edition

EDITED BY

the late R. F. TREHARNE, M.A., Ph.D.
PROFESSOR OF HISTORY, UNIVERSITY COLLEGE OF WALES, ABERYSTWYTH

AND

HAROLD FULLARD, M.Sc.
CARTOGRAPHIC EDITOR

First Edition 1911
Second Edition 1914
Third Edition 1917
Fourth Edition, Enlarged 1920
Fifth Edition 1923
Sixth Edition, Revised and Greatly Enlarged . . . 1927
Seventh Edition 1947
Eighth Edition 1952
Reprinted 1956
Ninth Edition, Revised and Completely Redesigned . 1962
Tenth Edition 1964
Eleventh Edition . . . . ©1969
George Philip & Son Ltd.

PRINTED IN GREAT BRITAIN BY GEORGE PHILIP PRINTERS LIMITED, LONDON

PREFACE

FIFTY YEARS afford a searching test of the qualities of any work designed to satisfy the needs of many thousands of teachers and students in universities and in the higher classes of schools and colleges, especially when the book is planned on a scale which, despite the utmost economy in production, necessarily implies a fairly substantial price. The present editors of Ramsay Muir's *Historical Atlas: Mediaeval and Modern*, may fairly claim that the work which they are now partly refashioning has triumphantly stood that test, amply justifying the pride which Ramsay Muir and George Philip felt in their original edition of it. The *Atlas* has now run through eight editions and many reprints, and has so fully satisfied the need which brought it into being that it still has no serious rival in the British market over its own range and at a comparable price. It is no exaggeration to say that the Ramsay Muir historical atlases, pioneer works at their first appearances, demonstrating for the first time how a modern study of historical geography might illuminate so much of the study of history, played a decisive part in establishing historical geography as an integral part of the study and teaching of history in Britain. In so doing they did much to shape the new canon of our present method of teaching historical geography, especially by their demonstration of the physical basis of the subject, and also by their systematic conventions for representing historical data on coloured maps in such a way as to facilitate comparison between successive maps over long periods of time. To attempt now to recast a work which has not only thoroughly established itself in our educational provision, but has actually helped to shape our thinking and teaching of history, is no light responsibility.

Yet, after fifty years, reshaping there must be: in 1927, after only sixteen years, Ramsay Muir and George Philip themselves drastically refashioned this *Atlas* for its sixth edition. Muir never claimed that the *Atlas* was in any sense a work of original research, save where, as on British India, his own special knowledge enabled him at one or two points to make it so; the present editors can claim no more for this ninth edition. To make an atlas of this kind a work of original research would entail employing a specialist to design each separate map: this work aspires only to render in map form the conclusions of the best modern authorities readily available to the editors at the time when their work of revision was in process. But even this entails change. There are always errors and omissions to be rectified: the inevitable slow accretion of too many names on the successive editions of

certain maps requires periodic pruning: the appearance of new and authoritative books, whether monographs, standard histories or works of reference, and even of new maps and atlases, inevitably necessitates change if the work is to be kept up to date. Most of all, we must keep pace with History itself. The last thirty years have not only seen rapid and tremendous changes in the political maps of the more familiar parts of the world, but have also forced on our attention regions virtually ignored in common history teaching until today. So we have been compelled to make great changes in this standard instrument of teaching history, some of them changes which we adopted grudgingly, others which we know the original editors would themselves have wished to see.

Inflation and rising costs have imposed sharp limits on us. Seeking to keep the price of the *Atlas* within the reach of those for whom it was first designed, we can in fact claim that, allowing for the changes in money value, the *Atlas*, at its present price, is no dearer than it was in 1911. But this has been achieved only by sharp cuts. The stimulating letterpress introduction of the first edition disappeared in 1952. Now one or two familiar maps have been dropped, and a few others reduced from double to single-page size, though we venture to think that the practical value of the *Atlas* to students has not materially suffered thereby. All this, with other rearrangements designed to save space without sacrificing content, has been done to make room for ten totally new plates illustrating world history since 1926, and especially recording the course of the shattering upheavals wrought in the world in that quarter-century of wars and revolutions. The result has been drastically to change the geographical and the chronological balance of the *Atlas*, shifting it much nearer our own contemporary age, and also away from our former European preoccupations.

Even so, the present edition tells as much as did any earlier edition of the *Atlas* of the history of the world before 1926—in fact, considerably more. New maps show the Norman conquest of S. Italy and Sicily, the rise of the house of Luxemburg, the rise of the house of Burgundy, the decline of the Ottoman Empire, Russian expansion in Turkestan, and the south-eastern United States during the Civil War. Many more maps have been redesigned to make them more informative, not merely by adding new names, but also by employing new technical processes of colour-printing to make them tell a more detailed story of the stages of development in many lands and at many periods. In particular several maps of

the more familiar parts of the world—Western and Central Europe, France, Germany, Italy, England and Wales, Scotland, Ireland, North America, South America, South Africa—have been coloured politically in the present edition, whereas in earlier editions they had a basis of physical colouring. Lest this be thought a retreat from one of Ramsay Muir's basic principles in designing the original *Atlas*, the editors assert that in this respect Muir's teaching has by now succeeded so completely that, at a time when modern schools everywhere are teaching physical geography and providing their pupils handsomely with atlases of physical geography, it is no longer necessary to provide physically-coloured maps in a historical atlas except where the subject-matter of the map especially requires a physical basis for its understanding. This change, we think, fully justified by present circumstances, has enabled us to add greatly to the historical content of the present edition. In re-designing these maps and in reviewing the content of many others, thousands of entries have been made: in many maps new place-names have been added, new boundaries shown, in some overcrowded maps the amount of lettering has been reduced. The aim has been throughout to make the *Atlas* an efficient work of reference for the teachers and students, furnishing without overcrowding all the information which they could reasonably expect to find for any but the most specialised and detailed work. Revision of this kind is a never-ending process, and will continue to be recorded in future reprints and editions. The editors owe much to the helpful criticism of users who have reported omissions and errors or who have made other suggestions for improvement; these, whenever advisable, have been incorporated. Further suggestions and criticisms will be welcomed as hitherto, for no work of this kind can hope to attain perfection.

It remains to acknowledge our greatest debts. First of all to Ramsay Muir and George Philip, whose original design we inherited and have tried to preserve as far as we could in greatly changed conditions. The memory of their friendly guidance is a valued inspiration to one of the present editors, who was a pupil of the one and a junior colleague of the other of the makers of this *Atlas*. Then to the late Mr. George Goodall, editor of the seventh edition and joint editor of the eighth, who played a large part in planning some of the changes embodied in the present version—a steady counsellor and shrewd guide whose knowledge and practical experience were always freely given, and who understood the limits of the possible.

R. F. Treharne.
H. Fullard.

CONTENTS

1 THE REALMS OF CIVILISATION C.200 A.D. 1 : 50M.

2 EUROPE ON THE EVE OF THE BARBARIAN INVASIONS
        C.395 A.D. 1 : 25M.
 A *Europe* C.476 A.D. 1 : 40M.

3A ROMAN BRITAIN 1 : 3M.
 B *Britain according to Ptolemy*
 C *Hadrian's Wall* 1 : 1½M.

4A EUROPE C.526 A.D. 1 : 25M.
 B *Europe* C.600 A.D. 1 : 25M.

5 ITALY C.600 A.D. 1 : 5M.
 A *Rome in the Middle Ages* 1 : 100,000
 B *Papal Lands* C.800 A.D. 1 : 8M.

6 THE CONQUESTS OF ISLAM 1 : 30M. 622-945
 A *Iraq, Syria and Mesopotamia* 1 : 15M.
 B *The Disintegration of Islam* 1 : 70M.

7A THE TEUTONIC INVADERS OF BRITAIN 1 : 8M.
 B *England under Offa and Egbert* 1 : 6M.
 C *The Treaty of 886 and the Reconquest of the Danelaw*
         1 : 6M.

8 EUROPE IN THE AGE OF CHARLEMAGNE 1 : 20M.
 A *The Partitions of Verdun 843 and Mersen 870* 1 : 20M.
 B *The Growth of the Frankish Kingdom to 768*
         1 : 20M.
 C *Races of Western and Central Europe* C.800 1 : 40M.

9 EUROPE C.900 A.D. 1 : 20M.

10 GERMANY ABOUT THE YEAR 962 A.D. 1 : 5M.

11 FRANCE AND BURGUNDY ABOUT THE YEAR 1032 A.D.
         1 : 5M.

12 ENGLAND AND HER VIKING INVADERS 1 : 8M.

13 ENGLAND ACCORDING TO THE DOMESDAY SURVEY 1086
         1 : 2½M.

14 SCOTLAND C.500–C.1200 A.D. 1 : 2M.
 A *Ecclesiastical Scotland* C.1500 1 : 8M.

15 IRELAND BEFORE THE ENGLISH INVASION 1 : 2M.
 A *Ecclesiastical Ireland* C.1500 1 : 8M.

16 EUROPE AT THE TIME OF THE FIRST CRUSADE C.1100 A.D.
         1 : 20M.
 A *Advance and Divisions of Christianity to* C.1096
         1 : 60M.

17 THE ANGEVIN EMPIRE AND THE KINGDOM OF FRANCE
      1154-1220 1 : 6M.
 A *Growth of the French Monarchy from Philip Augustus*
    to the Hundred Years' War 1 : 10M.

18A SECOND AND THIRD CRUSADES 1 : 20M.
 B *Fourth and later Crusades* 1 : 20M.
 C *Christian States in Syria* C.1100 1 : 5M.
 D *Jerusalem during the Crusades* 1 : 25,000
 E *Constantinople* 1 : 200,000

19 EASTERN EUROPE C.1250 1 : 15M.

20-21 WESTERN AND CENTRAL EUROPE IN THE EARLY
     THIRTEENTH CENTURY 1 : 6M.
 A *Rise of the Norman Kingdom of Italy and Sicily*
         1 : 6⅓M.
 B *Germany under Frederick Barbarossa* 1 : 12M.

22 WESTERN AND CENTRAL EUROPE C.1500: ECCLESIA-
  STICAL PROVINCES AND MEDIÆVAL UNIVERSITIES
         1 : 10M.
 A *Suburbicarian District of Rome* 1 : 5M.

23A ITALY IN THE XI CENTURY 1 : 10M.
 B *Italy in the XII and XIII Centuries* 1 : 8M.
 C *Iberian Peninsula: the Reconquest* 1037–1270 1 : 10M.
 D *Iberian Peninsula* 1270–1492 1 : 10M.

24 EUROPE C.1360 1 : 20M.

25 ASIA UNDER THE MONGOLS 1 : 45M.

26 THE BALTIC LANDS AND THE HANSEATIC LEAGUE IN
  THE XIV, XV AND XVI CENTURIES 1 : 10M.

27 MEDIÆVAL ENGLAND AND WALES C.1399 1 : 2½M.
 A *London* 1 : 75,000

28A WALES AND THE MARCHES IN THE XIII CENTURY
         1 : 2½M.
 B *The Scottish Borders* 1 : 2½M.
 C *France at the Peace of Bretigny* 1360 1 : 9M.
 D *France in 1429* 1 : 9M.

29A THE ALPINE BARRIER AND THE NEIGHBOURING
        BATTLEFIELDS 1 : 5M.
 B *Growth of the Swiss Confederation* 1 : 2M.

30-31 WESTERN AND CENTRAL EUROPE IN THE LATER
     FIFTEENTH CENTURY 1 : 6M.
 A *Rise of the House of Burgundy* 1 : 6½M.
 B *Rise of the House of Luxemburg* 1 : 10M.

32A ITALY DURING THE RENAISSANCE 1 : 5M.
 B *Italy in the XVII and XVIII Centuries* 1 : 10M.
 C *Italy in the XIX and XX Centuries* 1 : 10M.
 D *Growth of Venice* 1 : 5M.
 E *Growth of Florence* 1 : 5M.

CONTENTS

33A GROWTH OF THE OTTOMAN EMPIRE 1 : 20M.
  B *Algiers* 1 : 30M.
  C *Growth of the Habsburg Dominions to 1914* 1 : 10M.

34 EUROPE IN 1519 1 : 15M.

35 THE WORLD IN 1490 1 : 165M.
  A *The World according to Ptolemy* : 150
  B *The World according to Edrisi* : 1154
  C *The World according to Fra Mauro* : 1459

36 ECCLESIASTICAL ENGLAND TO THE TIME OF HENRY VIII
                                              1 : 3M.
  A *English Dioceses in the Anglo-Saxon Period* C.800
                                              1 : 9M.

37A SCOTLAND IN THE XVI AND XVII CENTURIES 1 : 3M.
  B *Ireland before the Tudor Conquest* 1 : 3M.
  C *The English Plantation of Ireland* 1 : 8M.

38-39 WESTERN AND CENTRAL EUROPE 1555-1648 1 : 6M.
  A *Religions of Central Europe* C.1618 1 : 18M.
  B *Alsace-Lorraine during the Thirty Years' War* 1 : 3M.
  C *Ernestine and Albertine Lands in Saxony* 1 : 3½M.

40A THE WORLD AT THE TREATY OF SARAGOSSA 1529
                                              1 : 165M.
  B *The World according to Behaim* 1492
  C *The World according to Schoner* 1523

41A PORTUGUESE TRADE EMPIRE IN THE FAR EAST C.1580
                                              1 : 50M.
  B *South America* C.1650 1 : 50M.

42 THE WORLD 1588-1650 1 : 165M.
  A *The World according to Mercator* 1587
  B *Australia according to Tasman* 1643

43A WEST INDIES AND CENTRAL AMERICA 1 : 25M.
  B *Political Distribution in 1650* 1 : 50M.
  C *Political Distribution in 1763* 1 : 50M.
  D *Political Distribution in 1855* 1 : 50M.

44 EXPLORATION OF NORTH AMERICA 1 : 35M.

45A EARLY COLONISATION OF NORTH AMERICA 1607-1689
                                              1 : 10M.
  B *New England and the Middle Colonies* 1620-1650
                                              1 : 5M.

46A THE NETHERLANDS IN THE XVII CENTURY 1 : 2½M.
  B *Campaign of Waterloo* 1 : 1M.
  C *The Netherlands: Political Distribution in the later
                                    Middle Ages* 1 : 5M.

47 EUROPE AFTER THE PEACE OF WESTPHALIA 1648 1 : 15M.

48A ENGLAND DURING THE CIVIL WAR 1642-43 1 : 4M.
  B *England during the Civil War 1644-45* 1 : 4M.

49A SCOTLAND SINCE THE RESTORATION 1 : 3M.
  B *Ireland since the XVII Century* 1 : 3M.
  C *The Cromwellian Settlement in Ireland* 1 : 8M

50 CENTRAL AND EASTERN EUROPE IN 1667 1 : 12M.

51 CENTRAL AND EASTERN EUROPE IN 1795 1 : 12M.

52 THE WORLD AT THE TREATIES OF UTRECHT 1713-15
                                              1 : 165M.
  A *India at the beginning of the XVII Century* 1 : 30M.
  B *Gilolo and Ternate* 1 : 2½M.
  C *The Moluccas or Spice Islands* 1 : 20M.

53 FRANCE AND WESTERN GERMANY 1660-1789 1 : 6M.
  A *Paris at the time of the French Revolution* 1 : 50,000

54 EUROPE IN 1740 1 : 15M.

55A THE NARROW SEAS 1 : 6M.
  B *The North Atlantic* 1 : 60M.

56 NORTH AMERICA 1689-1783 1 : 10M.
  A *Quebec* 1 : 250,000
  B *Boston* 1 : 1M.

57 NORTH AMERICA IN THE ERA OF CONFLICT 1750-1783
                                              1 : 5M.
  A *West and South* 1778-1781 1 : 20M.
  B *New York*

58 THE WORLD AT THE TREATY OF PARIS 1763 1 : 165M.
  A *The World according to Homan* 1716
  B *The World according to D'Anville* 1772

59A INDIA IN THE TIME OF CLIVE AND WARREN HASTINGS
                                              1 : 20M.
  B *Calcutta* 1 : 10M.
  C *India in 1805* 1 : 20M.
  D *Madras* 1 : 10M.

60A THE GROWTH OF BRANDENBURG-PRUSSIA 1 : 6M.
  B *The Growth of Prussia* 1 : 6M.

61 GROWTH OF THE RUSSIAN EMPIRE IN EUROPE UP TO
                                       1914 1 : 20M.
  A *Partitions of Poland* 1 : 15M.
  B *Russian Expansion in Turkestan* 1855-1895 1 : 21¼M.

62 EUROPE UNDER NAPOLEON 1810 1 : 15M.

63 THE IBERIAN PENINSULA AT THE TIME OF THE
                                  PENINSULAR WAR 1 : 5M.
  A *Strait of Gibraltar* 1 : 2½M.
  B *The Lines of Torres Vedras* 1 : 1M.

CONTENTS

64 EUROPE AFTER THE CONGRESS OF VIENNA 1815
1 : 20M.

65A and B RECONSTRUCTION OF GERMANY BY NAPOLEON
1 : 10M.
C *The German Confederation* 1 : 12M.
D *Growth of the German Zollverein* 1 : 12M.
E *German Empire* 1871 1 : 20M.
F *Schleswig Holstein* 1864 1 : 5M.

66A ENGLAND BEFORE THE INDUSTRIAL REVOLUTION
C.1701 1 : 4½M.
B *England after the Industrial Revolution* 1911 1 : 4½M.

67A PRINCIPAL ENGLISH CROWN GRANTS 1 : 25M.
B *United States* 1783–1803 1 : 25M.
C *United States* 1803–1830 1 : 30M.
D *United States: Slavery and Emancipation* 1787–1865
1 : 30M.

68 SOUTH AMERICA IN THE XIX AND XX CENTURIES 1 : 30M.
A *North West South America* 1 : 40M.

69A THE WORLD IN 1830 1 : 165M.
B *Arctic Exploration* 1 : 100M.
C *Antarctic Exploration* 1 : 100M.

70-71 THE GROWTH OF THE UNITED STATES AND BRITISH
NORTH AMERICA 1 : 20M.
A *Alaska* 1 : 30M.
B *Alaska Boundary Dispute* 1 : 10M.
C *The Campaigns of* 1812–14 1 : 10M.
D *Niagara Frontier* 1 : 1M.
E *North East Boundary Dispute* 1 : 8M.
F *Jackson's Campaign* 1813–18 1 : 10M.

72 SOUTH EASTERN UNITED STATES DURING THE CIVIL
WAR 1 : 10M.
A *Atlanta and Chattanooga Campaigns* 1 : 5M.
B *Eastern Campaigns* 1 : 5M.
C *Vicksburg Campaigns* 1 : 2½M.

73 INDIA IN 1858 1 : 15M.
A *Partition of Bengal* 1 : 25M.

74 EUROPEAN INFLUENCE AND RUSSIAN EXPANSION IN
ASIA UP TO 1914 1 : 50M.

75 PARTITION OF THE PACIFIC IN THE XIX AND EARLY XX
CENTURIES 1 : 100M.
A *Singapore* 1 : 15M.
B *Samoa* 1 : 15M.
C *Fiji Is.* 1 : 15M.
D *Hawaii* 1 : 15M.
E *Philippines* 1 : 20M.

76 THE WORLD AFTER THE CONGRESS OF BERLIN 1878
1 : 165M.
A *Franco-German War* 1870–71 1 : 5M.
B *Russo-Japanese War* 1904–5 1 : 5M.

77 EXPLORATION AND SETTLEMENT OF AUSTRALASIA
1 : 30M.
A *New Zealand* 1 : 20M.

78 BALKAN PENINSULA 1800–1914 1 : 6M.
A *The Slavonic and Bulgarian Powers in the Balkan
Peninsula* 1 : 20M.

79 THE DECLINE OF THE OTTOMAN EMPIRE 1683–1924
1 : 15M.

80A EXPLORATION AND PARTITION OF AFRICA TO 1914
1 : 40M.
B *Egypt and the Nile Valley* 1 : 16M.

81A SOUTH AFRICA SHOWING THE GROWTH OF BRITISH
POWER DURING THE XIX CENTURY 1 : 20M.
B *South Africa before and after the Great Trek* 1 : 10M.
C *West Africa to 1914* 1 : 20M.
D *Natal and Zululand during the Boer and Zulu Wars*
1 : 4M.

82 EUROPE ON THE EVE OF THE GREAT WAR 1914 1 : 20M.

83 THE WORLD AT THE OUTBREAK OF THE GREAT WAR
1914 1 : 165M.
A and B *The Western Front* 1 : 3M.

84 EUROPE IN 1923 1 : 20M.

85 EUROPE IN 1923: LINGUISTIC DIVISIONS 1 : 20M.

86 THE WORLD ACCORDING TO THE PEACE TREATIES OF
1919–1927 1 : 165M.
A *The Salonica Front* 1 : 4½M.
B *The Italian Front* 1915–1918 1 : 3M.
C *Asiatic Fronts* 1 : 16M.
D *The Dardanelles* 1 : 2M.

87 CENTRAL EUROPE IN 1939 1 : 10M.

88 EUROPE AT THE HEIGHT OF AXIS POWER OCTOBER 1942
1 : 22½M.

89 EUROPE AFTER THE SECOND WORLD WAR 1 : 22½M.

90 JAPANESE EXPANSION 1928–42 1 : 60M.

91 EASTERN ASIA 1945–1969 1 : 30M.

92 INDIA, PAKISTAN, BURMA AND CEYLON 1969 1 : 17½M

93 THE NEAR AND MIDDLE EAST 1939–1969 1 : 17M.

94-95 THE WORLD IN 1969 1 : 100M.
Political Groupings 1 : 300M.

96A ITALIAN EAST AFRICA 1936–41 1 : 40M.
B *West Africa* 1969 1 : 25M.
C *Africa* 1923 1 : 64M.
D *Africa* 1969 1 : 64M.

CLASSIFIED LIST OF MAPS AND SUBJECTS

A

ABBASID Caliphate, 8, 9
Abbasids, Disintegration of Islam under the, 6B
Aden Protectorate, 93
Afghan Supremacy, 59A
Afghanistan, 61B, 74, 92
Africa, 1923, 96C
Africa, 1969, 94, 96D
Africa, Partition and Exploration of, 80A
Ahmadnagar, 52A
Alaska, 71A, 75
Alaska Boundary Dispute, 71B
Alban, Kingdom of, 14
Albania, 78, 82, 84, 85, 88, 89
Albertine Lands in Saxony, 39C
Albigensian Crusade, 20
Albuquerque, Track of, 40
Algeria, 24, 80A, 96C, 96D
Almohad Empire, 18
Alpine Barrier and the Neighbouring Battlefields, 29A
Alsace-Lorraine during the Thirty Years' War, 39B
Anatolia, 33A
Angevin Empire, 17
Anglo-Egyptian Sudan, 80A, 96C
Angola, 80A, 96C, 96D
Annam, 74
Antarctic Exploration, 69C
Antarctica, 95
Antioch, Principality of, 18C
Apulia and Calabria, Duchy of, 21A
Aquitaine, Duchy of, 17
Arab League States, 93, 94-95
Arabia, 1, 6, 25, 41A, 96C
Aragon, 24
Aragon, Kingdom of, 23C, 23D
Archbishoprics in the Baltic Lands, 26
Archbishoprics in England at the Domesday Survey, 13
Archbishoprics in France and Burgundy, 1032 A.D., 11
Archbishoprics in Western and Central Europe in the later 15th century, 30-31
Archiepiscopal Provinces in Western and Central Europe, c.1500, 22
Archiepiscopal Sees in England to the time of Henry VIII, 36
Archiepiscopal Sees in Ireland c.1500, 15A
Archiepiscopal Sees in Scotland c.1500, 14A
Archiepiscopal Sees in Western and Central Europe c.1500, 22
Arctic Exploration, 69B

Argentina, 68
Arles, Kingdom of, 20
Armenia, Kingdom of, 19
Ascanians, Lands held by the, 21B
Asia, 94
Asia, Eastern, 1945-69, 91
Asia, European Influence and Russian Expansion in, 74
Asia under the Mongols, 25
Asia Minor, 86C
Asiatic Fronts in the Great War, 86C
Asoka Empire, 1
Assam, 74
Atlanta and Chattanooga Campaigns, 72A
Australasia, Exploration and Settlement of, 77
Australia, 75, 95
Australia, Commonwealth of, 77
Australia according to Tasman, 42B
Austria, 50, 65A, 84, 85, 87, 88, 89
Austria-Hungary, 82
Austrian Empire, 64, 65B
Austrian Netherlands, 55A
Aversa, County of, 21A
Ayubites, Empire of the, 18B

B

BACHAN, 52C
Bahama Islands, 43A
Balkan Peninsula 1800–1914, 78
Balkan Peninsula, Slavonic and Bulgarian Powers in, 78A
Baltic Lands and the Hanseatic League, 26
Baluchistan, 74
Barcelona, County of, 11, 23C
Bartholemew Diaz, Track of, 35
Basutoland, 80A, 81B, 96C
Batavian Republic, 51
Bavaria, 10
Bechuanaland, 96C
Bechuanaland Protectorate, 80A
Belgian Congo, 80A, 96C
Belgium, 82, 83A, 84, 85, 87, 88, 89
Benevento, D. of, 23A
Bengal, 59A, 59C, 73, 74
Bengal, Partition of, 73A
Berlin, World after the Congress of, 76
Bhonsla's Lands, 73
Bhutan, 73, 74, 91, 92

Bihar and Orissa, 73
Bijapur, 52A
Bishoprics in the Baltic Lands, 26
Bishoprics in England at the Domesday Survey, 13
Bishoprics in England to the time of Henry VIII, 36
Bishoprics in France and Burgundy 1032 A.D., 11
Bishoprics in Ireland, 1150, 15
Bishoprics in Western and Central Europe in the later
                                    15th century, 30–31
Bohemia, 10
Bohemia, Kingdom of, 31, 39
Bohemia and Luxemburg, Lands of the House of, 24
Bohemia-Moravia, Prot. of, 87
Bolivia, 68, 68A
Botswana, 96D
Bosnia, 78, 79
Boston, 56B
Bourbon Lands, 34, 54
Brandenburg, 34
Brandenburg-Prussia, 47, 50, 54
Brandenburg-Prussia, Growth of, 60A
Brazil, 41B, 68
Britain according to Ptolemy, 3B
Britain, Roman, 3A
Britain, Teutonic Invaders of, 7A
British Columbia, 75
British Guiana Boundary, 68B
British Honduras, 75
British Isles, 88
British North America, Growth of, 70–71
British North Borneo, 74, 75, 90
British Somaliland, 80A
Brittany, County of, 11
Brunei, 74, 75, 90, 91
Bulgaria, 24, 78, 79, 82, 84, 85, 88, 89
Bulgaria, Kingdom of, 9, 19
Bulgarian Kingdom, 18B
Bulgarian Powers in the Balkan Peninsula, 78A
Burgundian Kingdom, 4A
Burgundy, Kingdom of, 11, 16
Burgundy, Lands of the House of, 30–31
Burgundy, Rise of the House of, 31A
Burma, 73, 90, 91, 92
Byzantine Territory in Italy c.1000, 23A

                          C

CABOT, Track of, 40
Cabral, Track of, 40
Calabria and Apulia, Duchy of, 21A

Calcutta, 59B
Caledonia, Pictish Kingdom of, 14
Calmar, Lands of the Union of, 34
Cambodia, 74, 91
Cameroon, 96D
Cameroons, 96C
Canada, 56, 69A, 75
Cape of Good Hope, 80A, 81A
Capua, Duchy of, 23A
Capua, Principality of, 21A
Carinthia, 10
Carolina, 67A
Carolingian Empire, 8
Carnatic, 59A, 59C, 59D
Carpini's Route, 25
Castile, Kingdom of, 23C, 23D, 24
Cathay, 25, 35
Central Africa, 96D
Central America, 43A, 94
Central America in 1650, 43B
Central America in 1763, 43C
Central America in 1855, 43D
Central Europe in 1939, 87
Central Europe, Religions of, 39A
Central Provinces, 74
Central and Eastern Europe in 1667, 50
Central and Eastern Europe in 1795, 51
Cephalonia, County of, 24
Ceylon, 52A, 59A, 59C, 73, 92
Chad, 96D
Charles, Kingdom of, 8A
Chile, 41B, 68
China, 41A, 74, 75, 90
China, Great Wall of, 1
Chinese Republic, 91
Christian States in Syria c.1100, 18C
Christianity, Advance and Divisions of, to c.1096, 16A
Church, States of the, 30–31, 32A
Church Lands, 19, 20, 24, 26, 30–31, 34, 38–39, 47, 50, 51,
                                                    53, 54
Cilicia, 18C
Cinque Ports, 27
Civil War, England during the, 48
Civil War, South Eastern United States during the, 72
Cochin China, 74
Colombia, 68, 68A, 75
Columbus, Track of, 40
Commonwealth Countries, 94–95
Communist Bloc, 94–95
Congo, 96D
Congo (former French), 96D
Constantinople, 18E

Cook's Voyages, 58
Cordova, Emirate of, 6, 8, 9
Cossack Penetration, Lines of, 42
Costa Rica, 75
Crete, 78
Crusades, 16, 18
Cuba, 43A, 43B, 43C, 43D, 75
Cyprus, 93
Cyprus, Kingdom of, 18A
Czechoslovakia, 84, 85, 89

D

DAHOMEY, 96B, 96D
Dalmatia, 34
Dalriada, Scottish Kingdom of, 14
Dampiers' Voyages, Track of, 52
Danelaw, Reconquest of the, 7C
Danish Towns in Ireland, 15
Dardanelles, 86D
Delhi, Sultanate of, 25
Denmark, 9, 12, 24, 26, 34, 47, 50, 51, 62, 64, 82, 84, 85, 87, 88, 89
Denmark and Norway, 54
Djagatai Empire, 25
Domesday Survey, England according to the, 13
Dominican Republic, 75
Drake's Voyage, Track of, 42
Dutch East Indies, 74, 75, 90

E

EAST Anglia, 12
East Pakistan, 91, 92
East Roman Empire, 2, 6, 8, 9
East Roman Empire, Themes of the, 9
Eastern Asia 1945–1964, 91
Eastern Association, 48A
Eastern Campaigns of the American Civil War, 72B
Eastern Empire, 16, 24
Eastern Europe, 19
Ecclesiastical England to the time of Henry VIII, 36
Ecclesiastical Fiefs in France and Burgundy 1032 A.D., 11
Ecclesiastical Provinces in Western and Central Europe c.1500, 22
Ecuador, 68, 68A, 75
Egypt, 79, 80A, 93, 96C, 96D
Egypt and the Nile Valley, 80B
Eire, 49B

El Cid, Dominion of, 23C
England, 24, 34, 47, 54, 55A, 62
England during the Civil War, 48
England according to the Domesday Survey 1086, 13
England, Ecclesiastical to the time of Henry VIII, 36
England under Edward the Confessor, 12
England before the Industrial Revolution c.1701, 66A
England after the Industrial Revolution 1911, 66B
England under Offa and Egbert, 7B
England, Treaty of 886 and Reconquest of the Danelaw, 7C
England and her Viking Invaders, 12
England and Wales, Mediæval c.1399, 27
English Dioceses in the Anglo-Saxon Period, 36A
Episcopal Sees in England to the time of Henry VIII, 36
Episcopal Sees in Ireland c.1500, 15A
Episcopal Sees in Scotland 500–1200 A.D., 14
Episcopal Sees in Scotland c.1500, 14A
Episcopal Sees in Western and Central Europe c.1500, 22
Er Riff, 88
Eritrea, 80A, 80B, 93, 96C, 96D
Estonia, 84, 85, 87, 88, 89
Ethiopia, 80A, 96C, 96D
Europe c.476 A.D., 2
Europe c.526 A.D., 4
Europe c.600 A.D., 4
Europe c.768–814, 8
Europe c.900, 9
Europe c.1100, 16
Europe c.1360, 24
Europe 1519, 34
Europe 1648, 47
Europe 1740, 54
Europe 1810, 62
Europe 1815, 64
Europe 1923, 84
Europe 1942, 88
Europe 1969, 89
Europe, Linguistic Divisions, 85
Europe, Races of Western and Central, c.800, 8C
Exploration of Africa, 80
Exploration of the Antarctic, 69C
Exploration of the Arctic, 69B
Exploration of Australasia, 77
Exploration of North America, 44

F

FEDERATED Malay States, 74
Federation of Arabian Emirates, 93
Ferrara, D. of, 32A

Fiji Is., 75c
Finland, 84, 85, 88, 89
Flanders, County of, 11
Florence, Growth of, 32E
Florence, Republic of, 30–31, 32A
Formosa, 91
France, 34, 47, 54, 64, 82, 84, 85, 88, 89
France c.1032 A.D., 11
France in 1429, 28D
France, Kingdom of, 12, 16, 17, 20–21, 24, 38
France at the Peace of Bretigny, 28C
France and Western Germany 1660–1789, 53
Franco-German War, 76A
Franconia, 10
Frankish Empire, 6, 8
Frankish Kingdom growth to 768, 8b
Frankish Kingdom, 4A, 4B, 7A
French Appanages, 20, 30
French Community, 94–95
French Empire, 62
French Equatorial Africa, 80A, 96C
French Indo-China, 75, 90
French Monarchy, Growth of the, 17A
French Royal Domain, 11, 16, 17, 20, 24, 30, 38
French Somaliland, 80A
French West Africa, 80A, 96C

G

GABON, 96D
Galloway, Pictish Sub-Kingdom of, 14
Gambia, 80A, 96B, 96C, 96D
Gascony, Duchy of, 11, 17
Genoa, Republic of, 30, 32A, 38
Genoese Dominions, 19
German Confederation, 64, 65C
German East Africa, 80A
German Empire, 82
German Empire 1871, 65E
German South-West Africa, 80A, 81A
German Zollverein, Growth of the, 65D
Germany, 84, 85, 87, 88, 89
Germany c.962 A.D., 10
Germany, Kingdom of, 16, 20–21, 21B
Germany under Frederick Barbarossa, 21B
Germany, Reconstruction of, by Napoleon 1803, 65A
Germany, Reconstruction of, by Napoleon 1807, 65B
Ghana, 96B, 96D
Gibraltar, 63
Gilolo and Ternate, 52B
Golconda, 52A

Gold Coast, 80A, 96c
Golden Horde, Khanate of the, 19, 24, 25
Granada, Kingdom of, 23C, 23D
Greater Antilles, 43A, 43C
Greece, 78, 79, 82, 84, 85, 88, 89, 93
Guatemala, 75
Guiana, 41B, 55B, 68, 68B, 75
Guienne, Duchy of, 11
Guinea, 96B, 96D
Guyana, 68D
Gwynedd, Principality of, 28

H

HABSBURG Dominions, Growth of the, 33C
Habsburgs, Lands of the, 24, 30–31, 34, 38–39, 53
Hadhramaut, 74
Hadrian's Wall, 3C
Haiti, 75
Han Dominions, 1
Hanseatic League, 26
Hawaii, 75D
Hindustan, 40A
Hispaniola, 43A, 43B
Hohenzollern, Lands of the House of, 30–31, 38–39, 50, 53
Holland, 82, 84, 85
Holy Roman Empire, 16, 20–21, 24, 30–31, 34, 38–39, 54, 65
Honduras, 75
Hungary, 16, 19, 24, 34, 47, 51, 54, 79, 84, 85, 87, 88, 89
Hungary, Imperial, 39
Huguenot Centres in France, 38
Hyderabad, 74

I

IBERIAN Peninsula 1037–1270, 23C
Iberian Peninsula 1270–1492, 23D
Iberian Peninsula at the time of the Peninsular War, 63
Iceland, 88, 89
Iconium, Kingdom of, 18A
Ifni, 96C
Ilkhan Empire, 25
Imperial Free Cities, 53
Imperial Hungary, 39
India, 35, 74
India in 1805, 59C
India in 1858, 73
India at the beginning of the XVII century, 52A

India in the time of Clive and Warren Hastings, 59A
India, Pakistan, Burma and Ceylon 1969, 92
Indies, 42
Indonesia, 91
Industrial Revolution, England before and after the, 66
Iran, 93
Iraq, 6A, 88, 89, 93
Ireland, 24, 34, 47, 54, 62, 89
Ireland since the XVII century, 49B
Ireland, the Cromwellian Settlement in, 49B
Ireland, Ecclesiastical c.1500, 15A
Ireland before the English Invasion, 15
Ireland before the Tudor Conquest, 37B
Islam, Conquests of, 6
Islam, Disintegration under the Abbasids, 6B
Israel, 89, 93
Italian East Africa 1936–41, 96A
Italian Front in the Great War, 86B
Italian Somaliland, 80A, 96C
Italy, 82, 84, 85, 88, 89
Italy, Kingdom of, 9, 16, 20–21, 62
Italy c.600 A.D., 5
Italy in the XI century, 23A
Italy in the XII and XIII centuries, 23B
Italy in the XVII and XVIII centuries, 32B
Italy in the XIX and XX centuries, 32C
Italy during the Renaissance, 32A
Italy and Sicily, Rise of the Norman Kingdom of, 21A
Ivory Coast, 96B, 96D

J

JACKSON'S Campaign, 71F
Jagellons, Lands of the, 26, 31
Jalayas, Dominions of the, 24
Jammu and Kashmir, 92
Japan, 74, 90, 91
Japanese Empire, 75
Japanese Expansion 1928–42, 90
Jerusalem, Kingdom of, 18C
Jerusalem during the Crusades, 18D
Jordan, 89, 93
Joscelin, Lordship of, 18C

K

KAMERUN, 80A
Kashmir, 73, 74
Kenya, 96C, 96D

Khazar Empire, 9
Khmer Empire, 25
Korea, 74, 75, 90, 91
Kublai Khan, Empire of, 25
Kushan Dominions, 1
Kuwait, 93

L

LAOS, 74, 91
Latin Empire, 19
Latvia, 84, 85, 87, 88, 89
Lebanon, 89, 93
Leon, Kingdom of, 9, 23C
Leon and Castile, Kingdom of, 16, 23C
Lesotho, 96D
Lesser Antilles, 43A, 43C
Liberia, 80A, 96B, 96C, 96D
Libya, 80A, 96C, 96D
Lithuania, 24, 84, 85, 87, 88, 89
Lombard Duchies, 23A
Lombard Kingdom, 5
Lombard Territories, 5
Lombardy, Kingdom of, 23A
London, 27
Lothar, Kingdom of, 8A
Lotharingia, 10
Louis, Kingdom of, 8A
Louisiana, 56
Lucca, Republic of, 30, 32A
Luxembourg, 89
Luxemburg, Rise of the House of, 31A

M

MADAGASCAR, 80A
Madras, 59D
Magellan, Track of, 40
Majapahit, 40A
Majorca, Kingdom of, 23D
Malagasy Republic, 96D
Malawi, 96D
Malay Peninsula, 75
Malaya, 90, 91
Mali, 96D
Mameluke Sultans, 24
Manchukuo, 90
Manchuria, 74, 75, 90
Marco Polo's Routes, 25, 35

Matilda, Lands of Countess, 23B
Mauritania, 96D
Mercia, 12
Mersen, Treaty of, 8A, 9
Mesopotamia, 6A
Mexico, 43A, 43B, 43C, 43D, 75
Mien, 25
Milan, Duchy of, 30, 32A, 38
Modena, Duchy of, 32A, 38
Mogul Empire, 41A, 52A
Mohammed Abtin, Dominions of, 24
Moluccas, 52C
Monasteries in England at the Domesday Survey, 13
Monasteries in England to the time of Henry VIII, 36
Monasteries in Ireland c.1150, 15
Monasteries in Scotland c.500–1200 A.D., 14
Monasteries in Western and Central Europe c.1500, 22
Mongol Il-Khans, Empire of the, 19
Mongolia, 74, 75, 90, 91
Montenegro, 78, 82
Moravian Empire, 9
Morocco, 24, 64, 80A, 96C, 96D
Mozambique, 80A, 96C, 96D
Mysore, 59A, 59C, 73, 74

Niger, 96D
Nigeria, 80A, 96B, 96C, 96D
Nigritia, 58
Nizam's Dominions, 59A, 59C, 73
Norman Kingdom of Italy and Sicily, 18A, 21A
Normandy, 12
Normandy, Duchy of, 11, 17
North America 1689–1783, 56
North America 1750–1783, 57
North America, Growth of British, 70–71
North America, Early Colonisation of, 45A
North America, English Crown Grants, 67A
North America, Exploration of, 44
North Atlantic, 55B
North Atlantic Treaty Organisation, 94–95
North East Boundary Dispute, 71E
North East New Guinea, 75
North West Provinces, 73
Northern Ireland, 49B
Northern Rhodesia, 80A, 96C
Northumbria, 12
Norway, 12, 24, 34, 82, 84, 85, 88, 89
Norway, Kingdom of, 9, 26
Novgorod, Republic of, 19
Nyasaland, 80A, 96C

N

NAPLES, Kingdom of, 24, 32A, 62
Naples and Sicily, Kingdom of, 23B
Narrow Seas, 55A
Natal, 80A
Natal and Zululand, 81D
Navarre, Kingdom of, 11, 23C, 30
Near and Middle East, 1939–1969, 93
Nelson's Track, 55B
Nepal, 73, 74, 91, 92
Netherlands, 53, 64, 87, 88, 89
Netherlands in the XVII century, 46A
Netherlands, Political Distribution in the Later Middle Ages, 46C
New England, 67A
New England and the Middle Colonies 1620–1650, 45B
New Guinea, Territory of, 77
New Holland, 42B
New York, 57B
New Zealand, 75, 77, 77A
Newfoundland, 45A
Niagara Frontier, 71D
Nicaea, Empire of, 18B, 19
Nicaragua, 75

O

ODOACER, Kingdom of, 2
Oman, 74, 93
Orange Free State, 80A, 81B
Orange River Colony, 81A
Orange River Sovereignty, 81B
Organisation of American States, 94–95
Ostrogothic Kingdom, 4
Ottoman Empire, 34, 39, 47, 50, 51, 54, 64, 74, 82
Ottoman Empire, Decline of the, 79
Ottoman Empire, Growth of the, 33A
Oudh, 59A, 59C, 62, 73

P

PACIFIC, Partition of the, 75
Pakistan, 92
Palestine, 6A, 88
Panama, 68, 75
Papal Lands c.800 A.D., 5B
Papal States, 24, 32B, 32C, 34, 39, 47

Papal States in XV century and early XVI century, 32A
Papal Territory in Italy c.1000, 23A
Papal Territory in Italy in the XII and XIII centuries, 23B
Papua, Territory of, 77
Paraguay, 68
Paris at the time of the French Revolution, 53A
Paris, World at the Treaty of, 58
Parma, Duchy of, 38
Parthian Empire, 1
Persia, 6, 41A, 74, 93
Peru, 68, 68A
Peru, Lower, 41B
Peru, Upper, 41B
Peru, Vice-Royalty of, 41B, 42
Philippine Islands, 74, 75, 90
Philippines, 75E, 91
Piedmont, Principality of, 38
Poland, 16, 34, 47, 50, 54, 74, 84, 85, 87, 88, 89
Poland, Kingdom of, 19, 21, 24, 31, 39
Poland, Partitions of, 61A
Polygars, 52A
Portugal, 24, 34, 47, 54, 62, 63, 82, 84, 85, 88, 89
Portugal, County of, 23C
Portugal, Kingdom of, 23D
Portuguese Guinea, 80A, 96B, 96C, 96D
Portuguese Trade Empire in the Far East c.1580, 41A
Prussia, 51, 62, 64, 65A, 65B, 65C, 65E
Prussia, Growth of, 60B
Prussia, Kingdom of, 65D
Punjab, 73, 74

Q

QATAR, 93
Quebec, 56A

R

RAJPUTANA, 59A, 59C, 73, 74
Rhine, Confederation of the, 62, 65
Rhodesia, 96D
Rio de Oro, 80A, 96C
Roman Dioceses, 2
Roman Empire, 1, 2, 4A, 4B
Roman Prefectures, 2
Rome in the Middle Ages, 5A
Rome, Suburbicarian District of, 22A
Rubruquis' Route, 25
Rum, Kingdom of, 18A

Rumania, 78, 79, 82, 84, 85, 87, 88, 89
Rus, Kingdom of, 16
Russia, 34, 47, 54, 64, 74, 82
Russian Empire, 62, 74
Russian Empire in Europe, Growth of the, 61
Russian Expansion in Turkestan, 61B
Russian States, 24
Russo-Japanese War, 76B

S

SABAH, 91
Saladin and the Ayubites, Empire of, 18A
Salerno, Duchy of, 23A
Salerno, Principality of, 21A
Salonica Front in the Great War, 86A
Salvador, 75
Samoa, 75B
Saracen Lands in the Iberian Peninsula, 23C
Saracen Territory in Italy c.1000, 23A
Sarawak, 74, 75, 90, 91
Sardinia, Kingdom of, 32B, 32C, 51, 62
Saudi-Arabia, 93, 96D
Savoy, Duchy of, 30, 32A
Savoy, Lands of the Counts of, 23B
Saxony, 10
Saxony, Ernestine and Albertine Lands in, 39C
Schleswig-Holstein 1864, 65F
Scotland, 12, 24, 34, 47, 54, 62
Scotland c.500–c.1200 A.D., 14
Scotland in the XVI and XVII centuries, 37A
Scotland Ecclesiastical c.1500, 14
Scotland since the Restoration, 49A
Scottish Borders, 28B
Seljuk Empire, 16
Seljuk Empire of Rum or Iconium, 18B
Seljuk Kingdom of Rum or Iconium, 19
Seljuk Turkish Amirates, 19
Senegal, 96D
Sequeira, Track of, 40
Serbia, 78, 79, 82
Siam, 74, 75, 90
Siberia, 74
Sibir, Khanate of, 25
Sicily, County of, 21A
Sicily, Kingdom of, 19, 23B, 24, 62
Sicily and Italy, Rise of the Norman Kingdom of, 21A
Siena, Republic of, 30–31, 32A
Sierra Leone, 80A
Sikkim, 29, 91
Sind, 73, 74

Singapore, 75A
Sinkiang, 74, 75
Slovakia, 87
Somali Republic, 96D
Song Empire, 25
South Africa, Republic of, 96D
South Africa, Union of, 80A, 96C
South Africa before and after the Great Trek, 81B
South Africa showing Growth of British Power, 81A
South African Republic, 81B
South America c.1650, 41B
South America in the XIX and XX centuries, 68
South America, North West, 68A
South East Asia Collective Defence Treaty, 94–95
South Eastern United States during the Civil War, 72
South West Africa, 96C, 96D
South Yemen, 93
Southern Rhodesia, 80A, 96C
Spain, 34, 47, 54, 62, 63, 64, 82, 84, 88, 89
Spanish Guinea, 80A, 96C, 96D
Spanish Morocco, 96C
Spanish Netherlands, 38
Spanish Sahara, 96D
Spice Islands, 52C
Staufen, Demesne Lands held by the House of, 21B
Staufen, Duchies held by the House of, 21B
Stephen Dushan, Dominions of, 24
Stephen Dushan, Empire of, 24
Strathclyde, British Kingdom of, 14
Sudan, 96D
Swabia, 10
Swaziland, 80A, 96C, 96D
Sweden, 9, 24, 26, 34, 47, 50, 51, 54, 62, 82, 84, 85, 88, 89
Sweden and Norway, 64
Swiss Confederation, 30, 34, 38, 50, 51
Swiss Confederation, Growth of the, 29B
Switzerland, 47, 54, 64, 82, 84, 85, 87, 88, 89
Syria, 6A, 88, 89, 93
Syria c.1100, Christian States in, 18C

T

TAMURLANE, Empire of, 25
Tanganyika, 96C
Tanzania, 96D
Tasman's Voyages, Track of, 42
Ternate, 52B, 52C
Thailand, 91
Themes of the East Roman Empire, 9
Tibet, 73, 74, 91, 92
Tidor, 52C

Timur, Empire of, 25
Togo, 80A, 96B, 96D
Togoland, 96C
Tongking, 74, 75
Torres Vedras, Lines of, 63B
Trade Routes in Asia in the Middle Ages, 25
Trade Routes of the Baltic Lands and the Hanseatic
League, 26
Trade Routes of the Portuguese Trade Empire in the Far
East c.1580, 41
Transjordan, 88
Transvaal, 80A, 81A
Trebizond, Empire of, 19
Tripoli, 24
Trucial Oman, 93
Tunis, 24, 80A
Tunisia, 88, 89, 96C, 96D
Turkestan, 74
Turkestan, Russian Expansion in, 61B
Turkey, 82, 84, 85, 86, 88, 89, 93
Tuscany, 23B
Tuscany, Duchy of, 23A
Tuscany, Grand Duchy of, 32B, 32C, 38–39
Two Sicilies, Kingdom of the, 18B, 32B, 32C, 50, 51, 54, 64

U

UGANDA, 96C, 96D
Ukraine, 74
Union of South Africa, 80A, 96C
Union of Soviet Socialist Republics, 75, 84, 85, 87, 88, 89
United Arab Republic, 96D
United Kingdom, 55B, 64, 82, 84, 89
United Provinces, 46, 47, 50, 54, 55A
United Provinces, Republic of, 38
United States, 55B, 75, 76
United States 1783–1803, 67B
United States 1803–1830, 67C
United States, Growth of the, 70–71
United States Slavery and Emancipation, 67D
Universities, Mediæval, in Western and Central Europe
c.1500, 22
Upper Burma, 74
Upper Volta, 96D
Uruguay, 68
Utrecht, World at the Treaties of, 52

V

VANDAL Kingdom, 2A, 4A
Vasco da Gama, Track of, 40
Venetian Territories in the XII century, 23B

Venezuela, 41B, 68, 68A, 74
Venice, 54
Venice, Growth of, 32D
Venice, Republic of, 30–31, 32A, 32B, 38–39, 47, 50, 51
Venice, Territories of the Signoria of, 19
Verdun, Treaty of, 8A
Vicksburg Campaigns in the American Civil War, 72C
Vienna, Europe after the Congress of, 64
Vietnam, 91
Villeneuve's Track, 55B
Virginia, 67A
Visigothic Kingdom, 2A, 4A

W

WALES, 34, 47, 54, 62
Wales, Principality of, 27
Wales and the Marches, 28A
Warsaw, Grand-Duchy of, 62
Waterloo, Campaign of, 46B
Welf, Demesne Lands held by the House of, 21B
Welf, Duchies held by the House of, 21B
Wessex, 12
West Africa to 1914, 81C
West Africa 1969, 96B
West Indies, 55B
West Indies and Central America, 43A
West Indies and Central America 1650, 43B
West Indies and Central America 1763, 43C
West Indies and Central America 1855, 43D
West Pakistan, 92
West Roman Empire, 2
Western Front in the Great War, 83A and B
Western Germany 1660–1789, 53
Western Samoa, 75B
Western and Central Europe in the early XIII century, 20–1

Western and Central Europe c.1500, 22
Western and Central Europe in the later XV century, 30–31
Western and Central Europe 1555–1648, 38–39
Westphalia, Europe after the Peace of, 47
Wettin, Lands of the House of, 30–31, 38–39
Wittelsbach, Lands of the House of, 30–31, 38–39
World 1490, 35
World 1588–1650, 42
World 1713–15, 52
World 1763, 58
World 1830, 69
World 1878, 76
World 1914, 83
World 1919–1927, 86
World 1969, 94–95
World according to Behaim, 40B
World according to D'Anville, 58B
World according to Edrisi, 35B
World according to Fra Mauro, 35C
World according to Homan, 58A
World according to Mercator, 42A
World according to Ptolemy, 35A
World according to Saragossa, 40A
World according to Schöner, 40C

Y

YEMEN, 93
Yugoslavia, 84, 85, 88, 89

Z

ZAMBIA, 96D
Zipangu, 25
Zululand, 81D

THE REALMS OF CIVILISATION

c. 200 A.D.

AND THE NATURAL CONDITIONS AFFECTING THEIR RELATIONS

Scale 1:50,000,000 (800 miles=1 inch)

Statute Miles

0 200 400 600 800 1000

Boundary of the Roman Empire
"   "   "   Parthian Empire
"   "   "   Asoka Empire c.250 B.C.
Boundary of the Kushan Dominions
"   "   "   Han Dominions
The Great Wall of China

GRASSLANDS & STEPPES

- Loess & other easily cultivated porous soils
- Less easily cultivated soils
- Steppes, scrub & semi-desert with Savannah

Mainly agricultural & pastoral with sedentary population

Mainly pastoral or hunting with nomadic population

FOREST REGIONS

- Mainly Coniferous
- " Deciduous with meadows
- " Tropical

Mainly hunting with some primitive cultivation

ARID OR "BARRIER" REGIONS

- Desert & Arctic Tundra
- Alpine or montane
- Swamp

Uninhabited or with scanty nomadic population

ABBREVIATIONS

CAP.	CAPPADOCIA
CIL.	CILICIA
EP.	EPIRUS
GAN.	GANDHARA
LYC.	LYCIA
LYD.	LYDIA
MAC.	MACEDONIA
NUM.	NUMIDIA
PAM.	PAMPHYLIA
PAN.	PANNONIA
PHOEN.	PHOENICIA

COPYRIGHT, GEORGE PHILIP & SON, LTD.

CALEDONIA
HIBERNIA
BRITANNIA
OCEANUS ATLANTICUS
Oceanus Germanicus
GALLIA
HISPANIA
Tagus
Pyrenaei
Mare Cantabricum
CORSICA
SARDINIA
Roma
ROMAN EMPIRE
MARE INTERNUM
MAURETANIA
Atlas Mons
AFRICA
Tropic of Cancer

SCANDIA
Mare Suevicum
German
VENEDA
SARMATIA
Bastarnae
Roxolani
DACIA
MOESIA
THRACIA
Byzantium
PONTUS EUXINUS
MACEDONIA
Athenae
Ionium

Rha
Alani
Caucasus Mons
ARMENIA
MARE CASPIUM
MEDIA
Ctesiphon
Seleucia
MESOPOTAMIA
ASSYRIA
SYRIA
PHOEN.
Damascus
AEGYPTUS
SINUS ARABICUS
ARABIA
ARABIA FELIX
ARABIA DESERTA
Sinus Persicus
Gerrha
PERSIS
Persepolis
Pasargadae
Susa
CARMANIA
PARTHIAN EMPIRE
PARTHIA
HYRCANIA
MARGIANA
ARIA
BACTRIA
SOGDIANA
Bokhara
CHORASMIA
Oxus
Jaxartes
SCYTHIA

KUSHAN DOMINIONS
KUSHAN EMPIRE
Kabul
GANDHARA
Taxila
KASHMIR
Kashgar
Yarkand
Khotan
Kuchao
Kara-shahr
An Hiung-nu
Southern Hiung-nu
Northern Hiung-nu

GEDROSIA
DRANGIANA
SIND
Barbarike
INDUS
ASOKA EMPIRE
RAJPUTANA
MALWA
MAGADHA
Pataliputra
NEPAL
Indraprastha
Ganges
Kosala
AVANTI
KALINGA
KONKAN
ANDHRA
Godavari
Krishna
Pratishan
MUZIRIS
CHERA
CHOLA
PANDYA
Muziris

CHINESE DOMINIONS
CHOW
HIAO
Chang-an
Han-ching
Loyang
Min Yueh
Tsang-wu

Equator

MARE MEDITERRANEUM

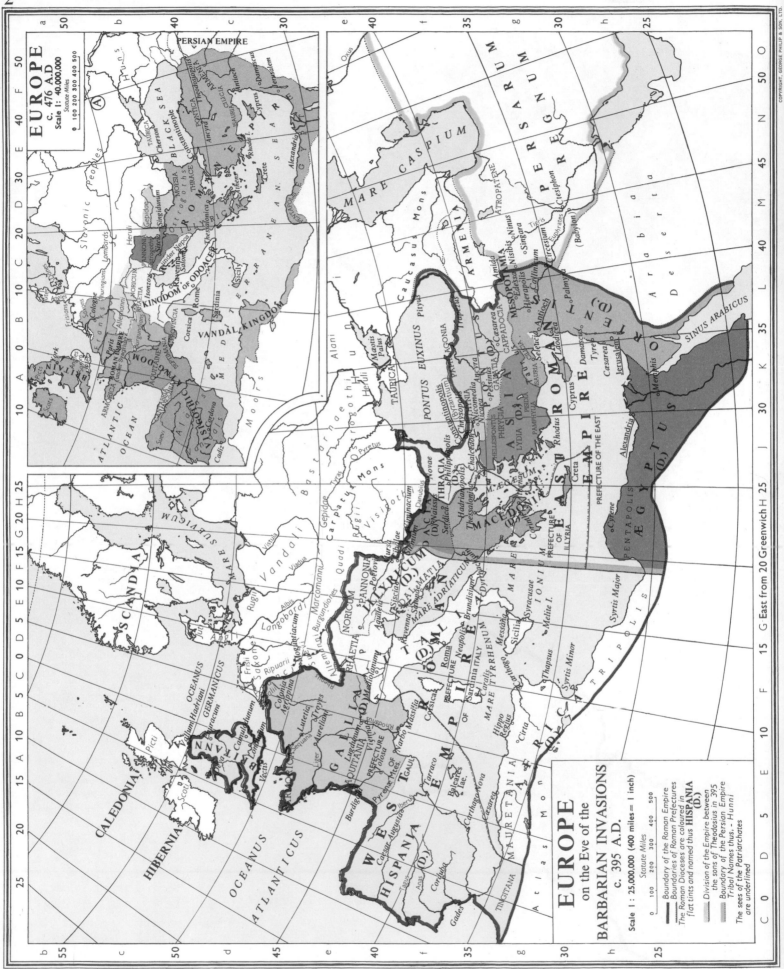

2

EUROPE
c. 476 A.D.
Scale 1: 40,000,000
Statute Miles
0 100 200 300 400 500

PERSIAN EMPIRE

EUROPE
on the Eve of the
BARBARIAN INVASIONS
c. 395 A.D.

Scale 1 : 25,000,000 (400 miles = 1 inch)
Statute Miles
0 100 200 300 400 500

Boundary of the Roman Empire
Boundaries of Roman Prefectures
The Roman Dioceses are coloured in
flat tints and named thus **HISPANIA** (D.)
Division of the Empire between
the sons of Theodosius in 395
Boundary of The Persian Empire
Tribal Names thus.- Hunni
The sees of the Patriarchates
are underlined

G East from 20 Greenwich H 25

Roman Britain

BRITAIN according to PTOLEMY

ROMAN BRITAIN

Scale 1:3,000,000 (48 miles = 1 inch)
Statute Miles

Roman Roads thus
Tribal names   REGNI
Modern names within brackets
Forests
Marshes
Roman permanent forts
  civil sites
Signal Stations

Highlands over 3000 feet
  "   from 1200-3000 feet
Uplands   "   600-1200 "
Lowlands   "   300- 600 "
  "   "   0- 300   "

HADRIAN'S WALL

Scale 1:1,500,000 (24 miles = 1 inch)

West from Greenwich

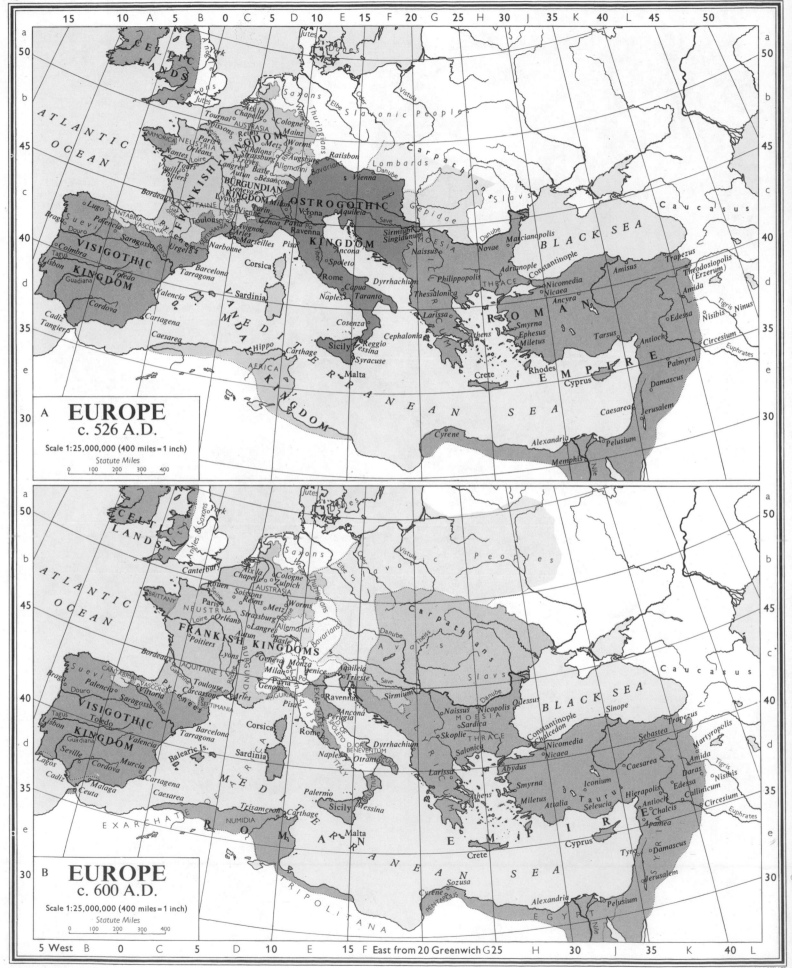

4

A EUROPE c. 526 A.D.

Scale 1:25,000,000 (400 miles = 1 inch)

Statute Miles
0   100   200   300   400

B EUROPE c. 600 A.D.

Scale 1:25,000,000 (400 miles = 1 inch)

Statute Miles
0   100   200   300   400

5 West B 0 C 5 D 10 E 15 F East from 20 Greenwich G 25 H 30 J 35 K 40 L

PANNONIA

FRIULI

Papal Lands
Before A.D. 754
754-774
774-814

PAPAL LANDS
c. A.D. 800
Scale 1:8,000,000
Statute Miles

Ferrara Cabellum
Bononia   Comiaclum
Faventia   Ravenna
                Cesenae
                Ariminum
Castrum Felicitatis   Pisaurum
              Urbinum Fanum
                  Senogalliae
              Aesium Ancona
                      Humana
Populonium   Eugubium
        Rosellae Perusia
    Suana Balneum
    Luscana Regis Spoletium
        Bitervum   Ameria
              Horta Narnia
            Sutrium SABINENSIS
                    Sora
            Roma   Arpinum
        Ceccanum   Arces
                  Aquinum
                  Theanum Capua

ADRIATIC

DALMATIA

Over 3000 feet
1200-3000 ,,
600-1200 ,,
0- 600 ,,

Chur
St. Gotthard P.
Brenner P.
Bernardino P.
Bellinzona Chiavenna Botzen
Sion   Val Tellina Trent Feltre Belluno
L. Como   Drave
L. Maggiore Bergamo Trieste
Aosta Bergomum Treviso save
Little Novara Milan Brescia Verona Vicenza VENETIA Istria
St. Bernard P. Mediolanum Padua Venice
Ivrea   Pavia Cremona Mantua Patavium Pola
Mt Cenis P. Vercelli Piacenza Po
Turin Asti Tortona Placentia Parma Ferrara Comacchio
Alba   Modena Reggio Bologna Ravenna
        (Mutina) (Bononia) EXARCHATE
Genoa   Faenza Rimini
Savona   (Ariminum)
Gulf of Lucca Faesulae Pesaro PENTAPOLIS
Genoa Pisa Florence (Pisaurum) Zara
Ventimiglia   Arno Urbino
Nice   Siena Taginae Ancona
    Piombino Trasimene Perugia Osimo (Auximum)
    Elba Chiusi UMBRIA Assisi Camerino Fermo
        Orvieto Tuder Nursia Ascoli (Firmum)
              Spoleto DUCHY OF
CORSICA   Viterbo Spoletium SPOLETO Chieti
(to Exarchate of Africa) Sutrium Reate
Aleria   Civita Vecchia Tiber
Ajaccio
              Rome DUCHY Mt Gargano
      Ostia (Roma) Lucera Sipontum
            Mt Cassino OF
        Terracina CAMPANIA Capua Tanustum Bari
SARDINIA   Gaeta Benevento APULIA
Torres Garigliano (Beneventum) CALABRIA
(to Exarchate of Africa) Naples BENEVENTUM Brindisi
Galtelli Sorrento (Neapolis) Salerno (Brundisium)
            Capri Amalfi (Salernum) Tarentum
        Paestum BASILICATA Lecce
              Otranto

TYRRHENIAN

SEA

Cosenza Cortona
(Consentia) BRUTIUM
Lipari Is. Squillace

Trapani Palermo Messina Locri
      (Panormus) Reggio (Rhegium)
Lilybaeum Taormina
        (Tauromenium)
        Mt Etna
    Trocala SICILY
        Catana
Girgenti   (Catane)
(Agrigentum) Leontini
      Syracuse
      (Syracusa)

ROME
in the Middle Ages
Scale 1:100,000
Statute Miles

Vatican
St. Peter's
Castle of S. Angelo
Leonine City
S. Potenzo
S. Agostino S. Susanna
Cancelleria S. Silvestro
S. Lorenzo in Damaso Baths of Diocletian
Pantheon S. Maria Maggiore
Palazzo S. Lorenzo
Venezia Fuori le Mura
Capitol S. Agata
S. Maria S. Pietro
in Trastevere S. Prassede
Trans Tiberis House of S. Clemente
  Palatine Colosseum S. Croce
S. Cecilia Aventine S. Sabina Baths of Titus
  S. Prisca S. Sisto S. Stefano
    S. Balbina Baths of Caracalla
      S. Cesareo

ITALY
c. A.D. 600
Scale 1:5,000,000 (80 miles=1 inch)
Statute Miles

East from Greenwich

Lombard Territories
Other lands owed a real or nominal
allegiance to the Eastern Empire

THE CONQUESTS OF ISLAM 622-945

Scale 1:30,000,000 (480 miles = 1 inch)

Statute Miles
0 100 200 300 400 500 600

COPYRIGHT. GEORGE PHILIP & SON LTD.

The DISINTEGRATION of ISLAM under the ABBASIDS

Scale 1:70,000,000

Ommeyad Emirate from 755

K. of Idrisids 788-921

K. of Aghlabids 800-909

Fatimite anti-Caliphate 909

K. of Sejuls

K. of Ulla 874-905

K. of Samanids from 874

K. of Tahirids

K. of Saffarids from 866

K. of Hamdanids 924-1003

K. of Karmati 890-990

K. of Tulunids 868-905

K. of Ikshids 935-969

ZANJ

ETHIOPIA (ABYSSINIA)

IRAQ SYRIA and MESOPOTAMIA

Scale 1:15,000,000 (240 miles = 1 inch)

Statute Miles
0 50 100 150 200 250

Desert

Main map place names

Conquests of Mahommed 622-32
Conquests of the First Four Caliphs 632-661
Conquests 661-750 (Ommeyad Caliphs of Damascus)
Conquests 750-945 (Abbasid Caliphs of Baghdad: Aghlabids and Idrisids of N. Africa: Ommeyad Emirs of Cordova)
Dates: x638 battle or siege: (642-47) Conquest or foundation

FRANKISH EMPIRE

EASTERN ROMAN EMPIRE

MEDITERRANEAN SEA

BLACK SEA

CASPIAN SEA

RED SEA

PERSIAN GULF

ARABIA (630-31)

PERSIA (637-50)

SYRIA (634-40)

EGYPT (MISR) (639-42)

KHORASAN

AFGHANISTAN (661, 711)

MESOPOTAMIA (634-41)

ARMENIA (642-52, 711)

TABARISTAN (765)

AZERBAIJAN

KIRMAN

FARS

KHUZISTAN

HEJER

NEJD

AL NUFUD

HADHRAMAUT

YEMEN

OMAN

BAHREIN

MAHRA

TRIPOLITANIA

CYRENAICA (642-43)

BARKA

LIBYAN DESERT

NUBIA

ETHIOPIA (ABYSSINIA)

AXUM

Idrisids

Aghlabids

Berbers

Garamantes

Tawarik

Ahaggar

Tibbu

Fezzan

East from Greenwich

Mecca (630)
Medina (622) (Yathreb)
Mt. Ohod x625
Jeddah
Yanbu
Yambo

Baghdad (762)
Ctesiphon (638)
Kufah
Basra (638)
Kerbala x680
Kadisia x635
al Anbar
Hit
Samarra
Mosul (641)
Tikrit
Takrit
Amida
Edessa
Melitene

Damascus (635)
Aleppo (Haleb)
Hims
Beyrout (635)
Jerusalem (638)
Baalbek
Tadmor
Siffin
Jabia
Bosra
Muta x630
Petra
Ascalon
Caesarea (640)
Ramleh
Alnadan

Cairo (al Fustat) (641)
Alexandria (642)
Damietta
Rosetta
Memphis
Fayum
Assuan

Antioch (638)
Tarsus
Tripoli
Laodicea

Ecbatana (644) (Hamadan)
Nehavend x642
Susa (Shushan)
Trostar
Ahwaz
Shiraz
Yezd
Ispahan (643)
Nishapur
Merv
Herat (651)
Qayin
Kabul (664)
Kandahar
Ghazni
Balkh (705)
Bukhara (674)
Samarkand
Khwarizm (713-15)
Ferghana

Constantinople
Adrianople
Thessalonica
Nicaea
Ephesus
Rhodes x654, 672
Crete (825)
Sicily
Palermo (831)
Syracuse (878)
Malta (870)
Rome
Ravenna
Venice
Genoa
Pisa
Marseilles
Narbonne (720)
Carcassonne (725)
Toulouse
Bordeaux
Poitiers
Tours x732
Lyons
Avignon
Barcelona (713)
Valencia
Cartagena
Cordova (711-18)
Toledo (712)
Seville (713)
Granada
Malaga (711)
Lisbon
Oviedo
Gibraltar (711)
Tangier (705)
Ceuta (709)
Tlemcen (70)
Tunis (670)
Kairouan (670)
Tripoli
Leptis

Inset A — IRAQ SYRIA and MESOPOTAMIA

ARMENIA (642-52, 717)
MESOPOTAMIA (634-41)
PERSIA (637-50)
SYRIA (634-40)
PALESTINE (634-40)
ARABIA (630-31)
EGYPT

L. Van
L. Urmia
Shiz
Kirmisin
Ecbatana (644) (Hamadan)
Nehavend x642
Susa (Shushan)
Trostar
Ahwaz
Basra (638)
Mansurabad
Baghdad (762)
Ctesiphon (638)
Jilfa
al Anbar
Kufah
Kerbala x680
Kadisia x635
Samarra
Hit
Mosul (641)
Nisibis
Amida
Ras el Ain
al Ruha
Harran
Melitene
Siffin
Aleppo (Haleb)
Hims
Baalbek
Damascus (635)
Tadmor
Jabia
Bosra
Yarmak x635
Jerusalem (638)
Beyrout (635)
Tripoli
Antioch (638)
Laodicea
Tarsus
Cyprus (649)
Caesarea (640)
Ramleh
Ascalon
Alnadan
Muta x630
Petra
Sinai
Alla
Cairo (al Fustat) (641)
Alexandria (642)
Damietta
Rosetta
Memphis
Fayum

Lakhmids
Ghassanids
AL NUFUD
PERSIAN GULF
MEDITERRANEAN SEA
Euphrates
Tigris
Great Zab
Little Zab
Orontes R.

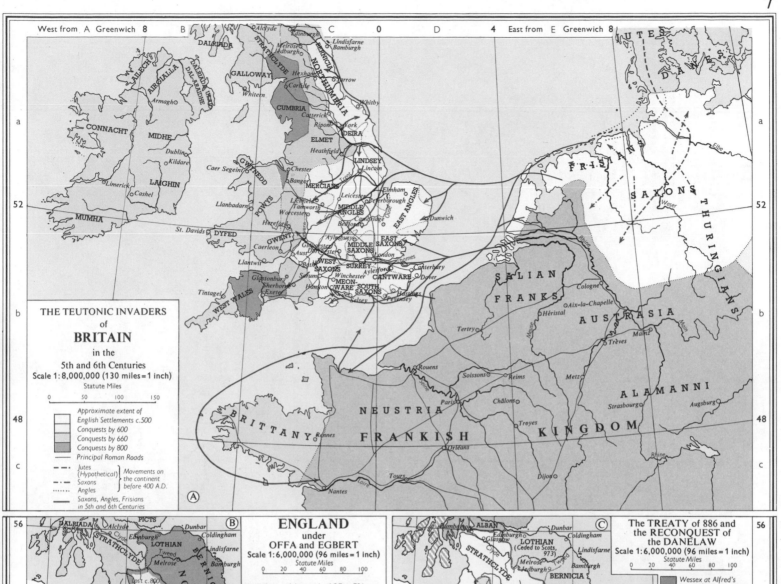

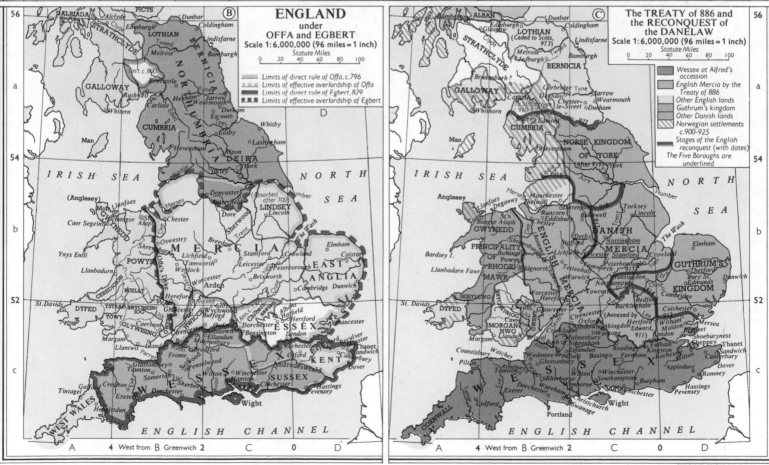

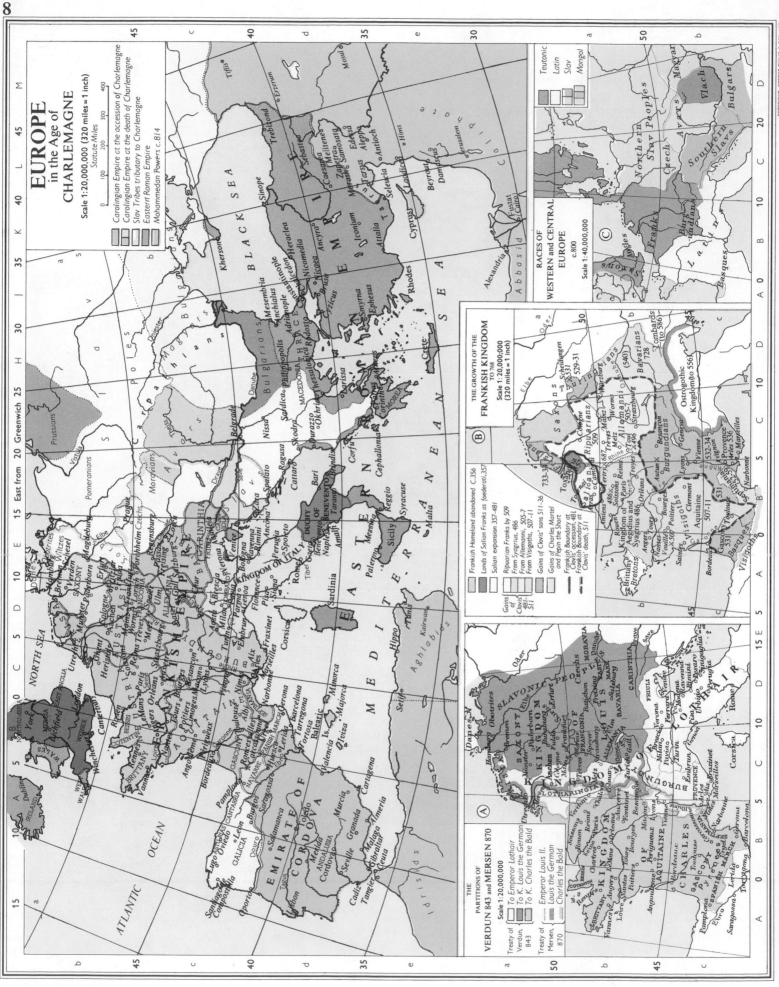

8

EUROPE
in the Age of
CHARLEMAGNE

Scale 1:20,000,000 (320 miles=1 inch)

Statute Miles

0 100 200 300 400

Carolingian Empire at the accession of Charlemagne
Carolingian Empire at the death of Charlemagne
Slav Tribes tributary to Charlemagne
Eastern Roman Empire
Mohammedan Powers c.814

RACES OF
WESTERN and CENTRAL
EUROPE
c.800
Scale 1:40,000,000

Teutonic
Latin
Slav
Mongol

THE GROWTH OF THE
FRANKISH KINGDOM
TO 768

Scale 1:20,000,000
(320 miles=1 inch)

Frankish Homeland abandoned c.356
Lands of Salian Franks as foederati, 357
Salian expansion 357-481

Gains of Clovis:
Ripuarian Franks by 509
From Syagrius, 486
From Allemanni, 505-7
From Visigoths, 507-11

Gains of Clovis' sons 511-36
Gains of Charles Martel and Pepin the Short

Frankish Boundary at Clovis' accession, 481
Frankish Boundary at Clovis' death, 511

THE
PARTITIONS OF
VERDUN 843 and MERSEN 870

Scale 1:20,000,000

Treaty of Verdun, 843:
To Emperor Lothair
To K. Louis the German
To K. Charles the Bald

Treaty of Mersen, 870:
Emperor Louis II.
Louis the German
Charles the Bald

THEMES OF THE EAST ROMAN EMPIRE in the X. Century

ASIA		EUROPE	
1	Opsikion	16	Chaldea
2	Optimaton	17	Mesopotamia
3	Paphlagonia	18	Lykandos
4	Bukellarian	19	Cyprus
5	Anatolic		**EUROPE**
6	Thracesian	20	Thrace
7	Samos	21	Macedonia
8	Aegean	22	Strymon
9	Cibyrrhaeot	23	Thessalonica
10	Seleucia	24	Hellas
11	Cappadocia	25	Peloponnesus
12	Charsianon	26	Nicopolis
13	Armeniac	27	Dyrrhachium
14	Sebastea	28	Cephallenia
15	Colonea	29	Longibardia
		30	Calabria
		31	Cherson

EUROPE c. 900 A.D.

Scale 1:20,000,000 (320 miles = 1 inch)

Statute Miles

0   100   200   300   400

Lands of Arnulf & Louis the Child (Germany)
"   "   Charles the Simple (France)
"   "   Rudolf of Burgundy
"   "   Louis of Provence
Boundaries fixed by the Treaty of Mersen, 870
"   of Themes of East Roman Empire
"   of vassal states of E. Roman Empire
"   of acquisitions of E. Roman Empire

→← Viking raids   →← Saracen raids
↑ Magyar "   --- Route of the Varangians

IDRISID S. DOMINIONS
Tlemçen 788-921

COPYRIGHT, GEORGE PHILIP & SON, LTD.

GERMANY
about the year 962 A.D.
Scale 1:5,000,000 (80 miles = 1 inch)
Statute Miles

Boundary of the Kingdom proper
Boundaries of the Great Duchies and Marches

BALTIC SEA

KINGDOM OF DENMARK
Schleswig
HOLSTEIN
Rügen I.
Colberg
Lübeck
Obotrites
Mecklenburg
Schwerin
Wollin (Jomsburg)
Usedom
Stettin
Garz
Pyritz
POMERANIA
(Conquered by Germany 995)
Hamburg
Lüneburg
Mecklenburg
Redarians
Warthe
Meseritz
Posen
Gnesen
LANDS OF THE BILLUNGS
Bremen
Verden
Salzwedel
Wiltzes
Lusatians
NORDMARK
Havelberg
Hevellians
POLAND
Groningen
Norden
ENGERN
Walsleben
Werben
Spree
Oder
Deventer
Osnabrück
Minden (Duchy)
Brunswick
Magdeburg
Brandenburg
OSTMARK
LAUSITZ, LUSATIA
(Tributary to Germany 963 Kingdom 1025)
Glogau
Utrecht
Münster
Gandersheim
Hildesheim
Halberstadt
Warnsted
Quedlinburg
Wettin
Milzienians
Meissen
Bautzen
Liegnitz
Breslau
Nimwegen
Detmold
Goslar
Harz
Nordheim
Pohlde
Wolfenbüttel
Halle
Leipzig
M. of
THURINGIA
MARCH OF MEISSEN
SILESIA
Breda
Wesel
Dortmund
Paderborn
Nordhausen
Memleben
Merseburg
MERSEB
Molzen
Leitmeritz
Giant Mts.
Birthen
Kaisersworth
Ruhr
Nordheim
Wern
Flarchheim
Höhen
MARCH
OF
ZEITZ
Erz Gebirge
Eger
Sudetes
LOWER
LOTHARINGIA (Duchy 959)
Cologne
HESSE
Fritzlar
Gerstungen
Erfurt
Weimar
Saale
Prague
OLMÜTZ
Brünn
MORAVIA
Bruges
Ghent
Louvain
Maastricht
BRABANT
Aix la Chapelle
Bonn
Wester Wald
Coblenz
Fulda
Hersfeld
Thuringian Forest
THURINGIA
BOHEMIA
(Tributary to Germany from 950 Under Poland 1003-4) (Kingdom 1088)
(From 955 to Bohemia 1003-29) (Under Poland)
FLANDERS
HAINAUT
Namur
Meuse
Liège
Limburg
Anderbach
Lahr
Wetzlar
Frankfurt
Mainz
Tribur
Bleichfeld
Bamberg
Pilsen
Bohemian Forest
Cambrai
LOTHARINGIA (Duchy)
Bouillon
Luxemburg
Moselle
Trèves
Ingelheim
Böckelheim
WEST (Duchy) EAST
Würzburg
FRANCONIA
Nuremberg
MARGRAVIATE OF NORDGAU (From Bavaria 976)
Ratisbon (Regensburg)
Verdun
UPPER
Diedenhofen (Thionville)
Metz
LOTHARINGIA (Duchy 959)
Bar
Toul
Nancy
Saarbrücken
Speyer
Worms
Neckar
Wimpfen
Weinsberg
Eichstadt
Passau
Linz
Krems
Vienna
Pressburg
MARCH OF AUSTRIA
(Kingdom from 1000)
KINGDOM OF FRANCE
Clairvaux
Langres
Strassburg
Lunéville
ALSACE
Waiblingen
Staufen
WÜRTTEMBERG
Tübingen
Danube
Ulm
Augsburg
Freising
Isar
Mühldorf
Altenburg
HUNGARY
Verdun
Zabern
Zähringen
Falkenstein
Zollern
Swabian Jura
Sigmaringen
Lech
feld
Lech
Polling
Salzburg
BAVARIA (Duchy)
Luxeuil
Vosges
Black Forest
Rhine
Constance
L. of Constance
Habsburg
THURGAU
Zürich
St. Gall
AARGAU
(Duchy)
Lucerne
Wilten
Brenner Pass
Inn
Eppenstein
(MARCH)
Raab
Mur
COUNTY OF
Basle
BURGUNDY
Besançon
Citeaux
Neuchâtel
Berne
Freiburg
Lausanne
Engelberg
Chur
SWABIA
ALPS
CARINTHIA (Duchy 976)
Villach
STYRIA (MARCH)
Drave
Cluny
Dijon
UPPER
Rhine
St. Gotthard Pass
Splügen P.
Meran
Brixen
Botzen
FRIULI
Laibach
KINGDOM OF BURGUNDY (ARELATE)
Mâcon
Geneva
L. of Geneva
Simplon P.
Gr. St. Bernard Pass
Como
Brescia
Trent
MARCH OF
Bellunu
VERONA (To Bavaria 952 to Carinthia 976)
Aquileia
CARNIOLA (MARCH)
Trieste
CROATIA
Lyons
Vienne
Aosta
Little St. Bernard Pass
Ivrea
Milan
Bergamo
Lodi
Adige
Verona
Treviso
VENICE
Venice
ISTRIA (MARCH)
LOWER
Mt. Cenis Pass
Turin
Pavia
Cremona
Po
Piacenza
Roncaglia
KINGDOM OF ITALY
ADRIATIC SEA

East from 10 Greenwich

FRANCE & BURGUNDY
showing
the Feudal Lordships
about the year 1032 A.D.

Scale 1:5,000,000 (80 miles = 1 inch)

Statute Miles

0   50   100

Archbishopric
Bishopric
(D) Duchy
(C) County
(V) Viscounty
(S) Seigneurie
(M) Marquisate

Boundary of France
  ,,   of Royal Domain
  ,,   of Burgundy
  ,,   of Ecclesiastical Fiefs

East from 4 Greenwich

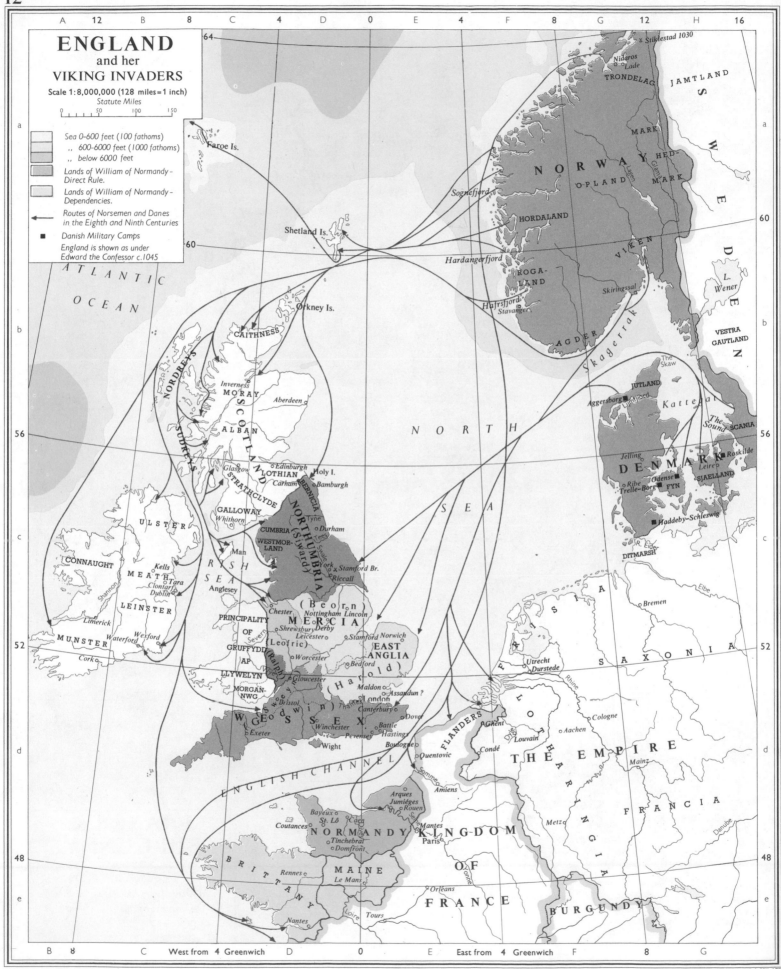

ENGLAND
and her
VIKING INVADERS

Scale 1:8,000,000 (128 miles=1 inch)

Statute Miles

50	100	150

Sea 0–600 feet (100 fathoms)

,, 600–6000 feet (1000 fathoms)

,, below 6000 feet

Lands of William of Normandy – Direct Rule.

Lands of William of Normandy – Dependencies.

Routes of Norsemen and Danes in the Eighth and Ninth Centuries

■ Danish Military Camps

England is shown as under Edward the Confessor c.1045

ATLANTIC OCEAN

Faroe Is.

NORDREYS

Shetland Is.

Orkney Is.

CAITHNESS

Inverness

MORAY

Aberdeen

ALBAN

SCOTLAND

SUDREYS

ULSTER

CONNAUGHT

MEATH

Kells

Tara

Clontarf

Dublin

LEINSTER

Limerick

MUNSTER

Waterford

Wexford

Cork

IRISH SEA

Man

Anglesey

Glasgow

STRATHCLYDE

LOTHIAN

Edinburgh

Carham

GALLOWAY

Whithorn

Holy I.

Bamburgh

BERNICIA

CUMBRIA

WESTMOR-LAND

NORTHUMBRIA
(Siward)

Tyne

Durham

Tees

Swale

York

Stamford Br.

Riccall

Chester

(Beorn)

Nottingham Lincoln

MERCIA

Shrewsbury

Derby

Leicester

Stamford

Norwich

PRINCIPALITY OF GRUFFYDD AP LLYWELYN

Leofric

Worcester

Bedford

EAST ANGLIA
(Harold)

(Ralph)

Gloucester

Severn

MORGAN-NWG

Maldon

Assandun ?

London

Thames

Canterbury

Dover

WESSEX
(Harold)

Godwin

Swein

Bristol

Winchester

Battle

Hastings

Pevensey

Exeter

Wight

FLANDERS

Ghent

Louvain

ENGLISH CHANNEL

Quentovic

Condé

Somme

Amiens

Arques

Jumiéges

Rouen

Bayeux

St. Lô

Caen

Coutances

NORMANDY

Tinchebrai

Domfront

Mantes

Paris

KINGDOM OF FRANCE

BRITTANY

Rennes

MAINE

Le Mans

Nantes

Loire

Tours

Orléans

Yonne

Boulogne

THE EMPIRE

LOTHARINGIA

Utrecht

Dursted

Rhine

Aachen

Cologne

Mainz

Metz

SAXONIA

Bremen

Elbe

FRISIA

R. Eider

DITMARSH

Haddeby-Schleswig

Trelle-Borg

Ribe

JUTLAND

Aggersborg

Limfjord

Jelling

Odense

FYN

DENMARK

SJAELLAND

Leire

Roskilde

SCANIA

The Sound

Kattegat

The Skaw

VESTRA GAUTLAND

L. Wener

SWEDEN

JAMTLAND

NORWAY

TRONDELAG

Nidaros

Lade

Stiklestad 1030

MARK

HED-MARK

OPLAND

Glama

Logen

Sognefjord

HORDALAND

Hardangerfjord

ROGA-LAND

Hafrsfjord

Stavanger

Skiringssal

AGDER

VIKEN

Skagerrak

NORTH SEA

BURGUNDY

Danube

NORTH

SEA

FRANCIA

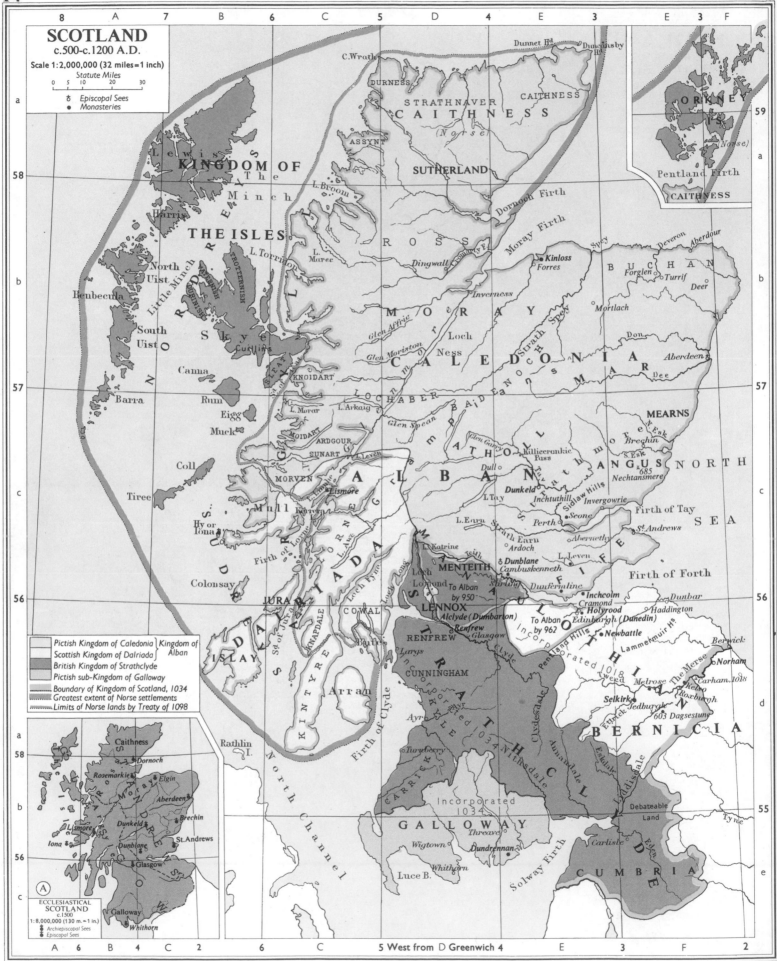

14

SCOTLAND
c.500-c.1200 A.D.
Scale 1:2,000,000 (32 miles = 1 inch)

Statute Miles
0 5 10   20   30

♱ Episcopal Sees
● Monasteries

KINGDOM OF

THE ISLES

Lewis

Harris

North Uist

Benbecula

South Uist

Barra

L. Torridon

L. Maree

L. Broom

The Minch

Little Minch

North Minch

Skye

Cuillins

Canna

Rum

Eigg

Muck

Coll

Tiree

Colonsay

Hy or Iona

Mull

Staffa

MORVEN

MOIDART

SUNART

ARDGOUR

KNOIDART

SLEAT

L. Morar

L. Arkaig

GLEN MORE

LOCHABER

BADENOCH

ATHOLL

L. Tay

L. Earn

Perth

Scone

Abernethy

St. Andrews

Dunkeld

Inchtuthill

Invergowrie

Sidlaw Hills

Strath Earn

Ardoch

Dull

Killiecrankie Pass

Glen Garry

ANGUS

NORTH

MEARNS

N. Esk

Brechin

S. Esk

685 Nechtansmere

Aberdeen

Dee

Don

MAR

BUCHAN

Aberdour

Deveron

Turrif

Deer

Forglen

Mortlach

Spey

Kinloss

Forres

Inverness

Strath Spey

Strath

Dingwall

Cromarty F.

Moray Firth

Dornoch Firth

MORAY

ROSS

Glen Affric

Glen Moriston

Loch Ness

CALEDONIA

SUTHERLAND

ASSYNT

STRATHNAVER

(Norse)

CAITHNESS

DURNESS

C. Wrath

Dunnet Hd.

Duncansby Hd.

CAITHNESS

ORKNEY IS.

(Norse)

Pentland Firth

CAITHNESS

59

DALRIADA

ALBAN

JURA

ISLAY

ARRAN

KINTYRE

KNAPDALE

COWAL

Bute

Larges

Firth of Lorne

Sd. of Jura

Loch Awe

Loch Fyne

Loch Long

Firth of Clyde

Rathlin I.

North Channel

Lismore

Kerrera

L. Leven

L. Etive

L. Awe

LORN

MENTEITH

L. Katrine

L. Lomond

Loch Lomond

Teith

LENNOX

Alclyde (Dumbarton)

Renfrew

Glasgow

RENFREW

CUNNINGHAM

To Alban by 950

To Alban by 962

Incorporated 962

STIRLING

Stirling

Cambuskenneth

Dunblane

Dunfermline

Inchcolm

Holyrood

Edinburgh (Dunedin)

Cramond

Newbattle

Haddington

Dunbar

Pentland Hills

FIFE

Firth of Tay

SEA

Firth of Forth

L. Leven

Incorporated 1018

LOTHIAN

Lammermuir Hs.

Berwick

Norham

Carham, 1018

Kelso

Roxburgh

Melrose

The Merse

Selkirk

Jedburgh

603 Dagsestune

Ettrick

BERNICIA

STRATHCLYDE

Clyde

Clydesdale

Ayr

KYLE

CARRICK

Turnberry

Nithsdale

Annandale

Eskdale

Liddisdale

Incorporated 1034

GALLOWAY

Threave

Wigtown

Dundrennan

Whithorn

Luce B.

Solway Firth

Debateable Land

Carlisle

Eden

CUMBRIA

Tyne

55

56

57

58

LEGEND:
- Pictish Kingdom of Caledonia
- Scottish Kingdom of Dalriada — Kingdom of Alban
- British Kingdom of Strathclyde
- Pictish sub-Kingdom of Galloway
- Boundary of Kingdom of Scotland, 1034
- Greatest extent of Norse settlements
- Limits of Norse lands by Treaty of 1098

ECCLESIASTICAL SCOTLAND
c.1500
1:8,000,000 (130 m. = 1 in.)
♰ Archiepiscopal Sees
♱ Episcopal Sees

Caithness

Dornoch

Rosemarkie

Elgin

Aberdeen

Brechin

Dunkeld

Lismore

Iona

St. Andrews

Dunblane

Glasgow

Galloway

Whithorn

MORAY

ROSS

ST. ANDREWS

GLASGOW

8 A 7 B 6 C 5 D 4 E 3 F

A 6 B 4 C 2 6 C 5 West from D Greenwich 4 E 3 F 2

COPYRIGHT. GEORGE PHILIP & SON. LTD.

15

ECCLESIASTICAL
IRELAND
c. 1500
1:8,000,000 (130m=1 in.)
Archiepiscopal Sees
Episcopal Sees

IRELAND
before the
ENGLISH INVASION
Scale 1:2,000,000 (32 miles=1 inch)
Statute Miles

0   10   20   30   40

Bishoprics existing in 1150
Monasteries
Anglo-Norman Castles erected
during reign of Henry II
Irish Clans thus: O'Dowd
Danish Towns underlined in Red

Over 3000 feet
1200-3000 ,,
600-1200 ,,
0- 600 ,,

COPYRIGHT. GEORGE PHILIP & SON, LTD.

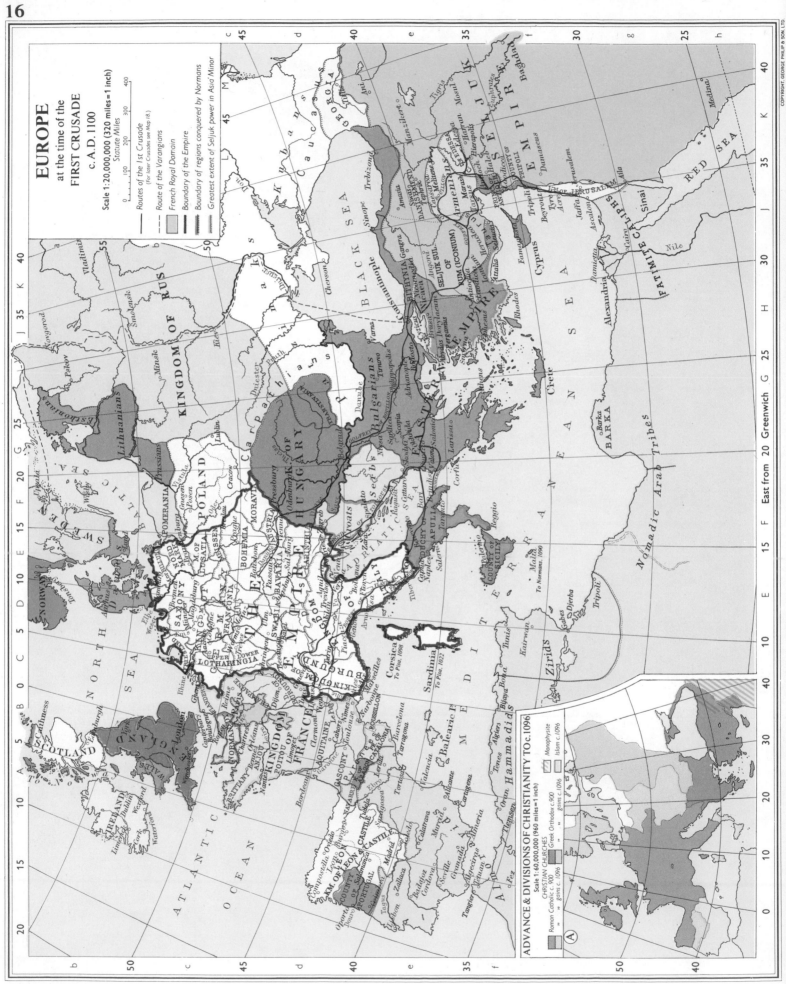

16

EUROPE
at the time of the
FIRST CRUSADE
c. A.D. 1100

Scale 1:20,000,000 (320 miles = 1 inch)
Statute Miles
0   100   200   300   400

Routes of the 1st Crusade
(For later Crusades see Map 18.)
Route of the Varangians
French Royal Domain
Boundary of the Empire
Boundary of regions conquered by Normans
Greatest extent of Seljuk power in Asia Minor

ADVANCE & DIVISIONS OF CHRISTIANITY TO c. 1096

Scale 1:60,000,000 (960 miles = 1 inch)

CHRISTIAN CHURCHES
Roman Catholic c. 900
"   "   gains c. 1096
Greek Orthodox c. 900
"   "   gains c. 1096
Monophysite
Islam c. 1096

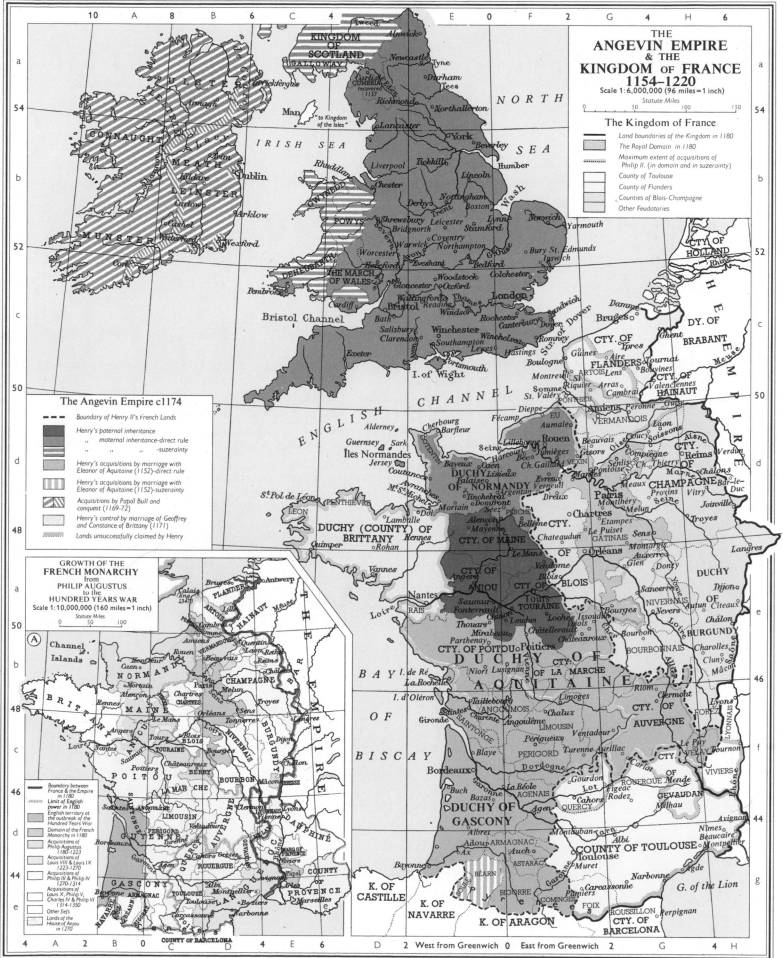

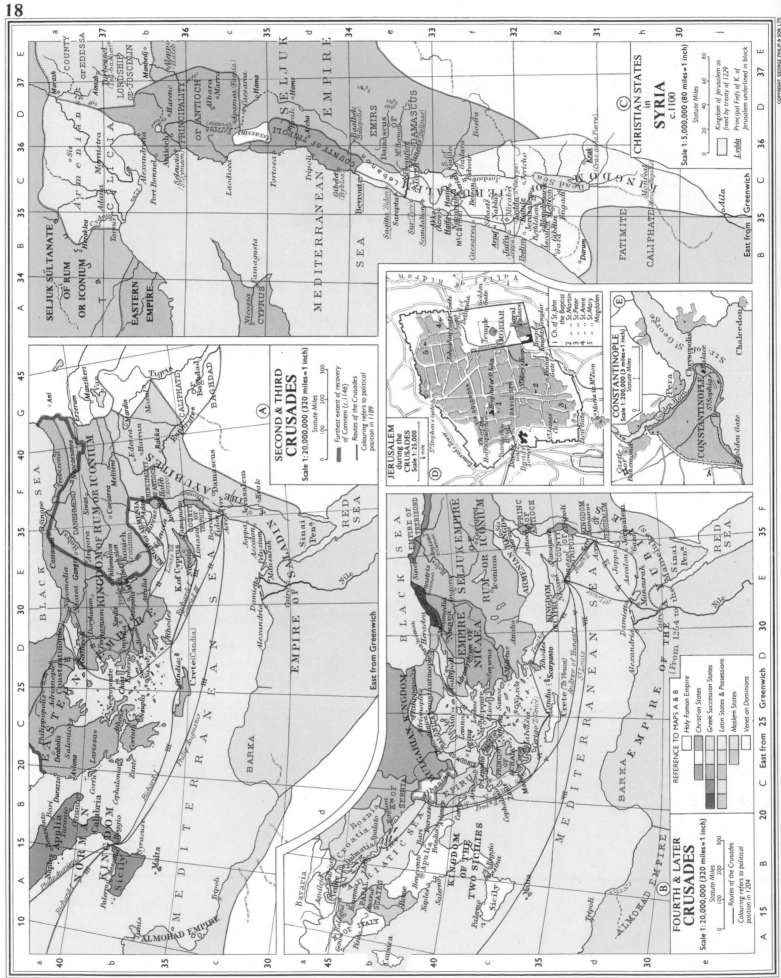

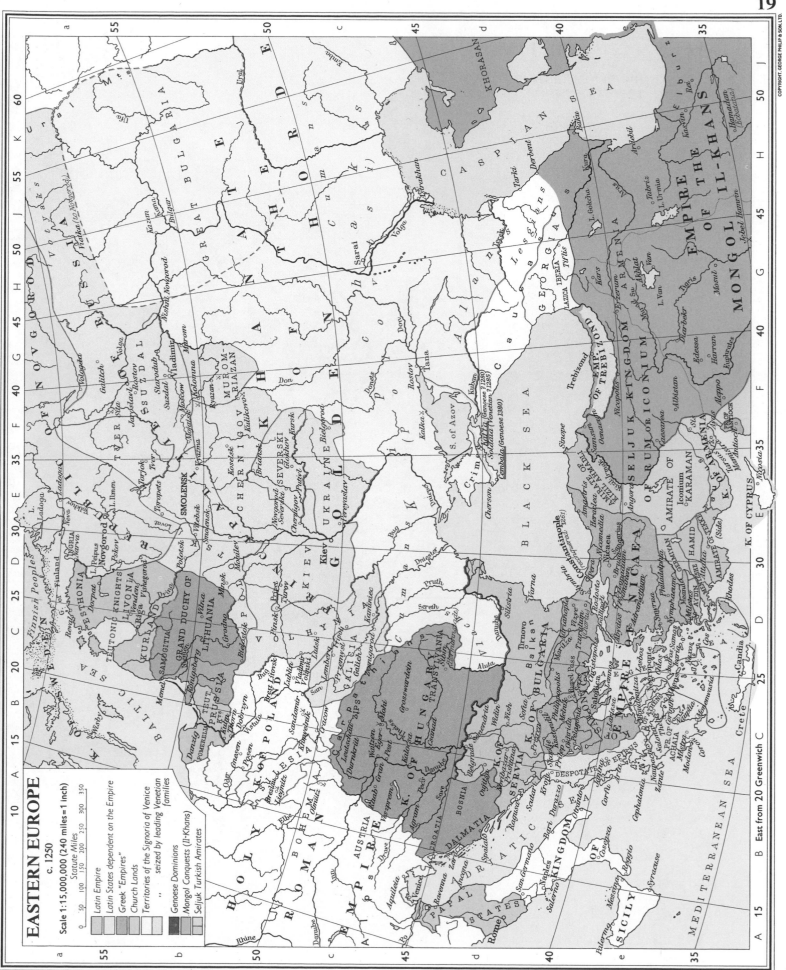

EASTERN EUROPE
c. 1250

Scale 1:15,000,000 (240 miles=1 inch)

Statute Miles
0 50 100 150 200 250 300 350

Latin Empire
Latin States dependent on the Empire
Greek "Empires"
Church Lands
Territories of the Signoria of Venice
"   "   seized by leading Venetian families
Genoese Dominions
Mongol Conquests (Il-Khans)
Seljuk Turkish Amirates

19

EMPIRE OF THE IL-KHANS

MONGOL

KHORASAN

CASPIAN SEA

GREAT BULGARIA

K H A N A T E   O F   T H E

G O L D E N   H O R D E

REP. OF NOVGOROD

GRAND DUCHY OF VLADIMIR-SUZDAL

RUSSIAN REPUBLICS

GRAND DUCHY OF LITHUANIA

POLAND

K. OF HUNGARY

HOLY ROMAN EMPIRE

BLACK SEA

EMPIRE OF TREBIZOND

SELJUK KINGDOM OF RUM OR ICONIUM

ARMENIA

K. OF CYPRUS

EMPIRE OF NICAEA

K. OF BULGARIA

K. OF SERVIA

BOSNIA

DALMATIA

CROATIA

PAPAL STATES

SICILY

MEDITERRANEAN SEA

ADRIATIC

East from 20 Greenwich

GEORGIA

BALTIC SEA

TEUTONIC KNIGHTS

ESTHONIA

LIVONIA

KURLAND

SAMOGITIA

PRUSSIA

POMERELIA

SMOLENSK

TVER

CHERNIGOV

KIEV

UKRAINE

PODOLIA

GALICIA

TRANSYLVANIA

AUSTRIA

BOHEMIA

SILESIA

SWEDEN

FINLAND

Finnish Peoples

Ural

CRETE

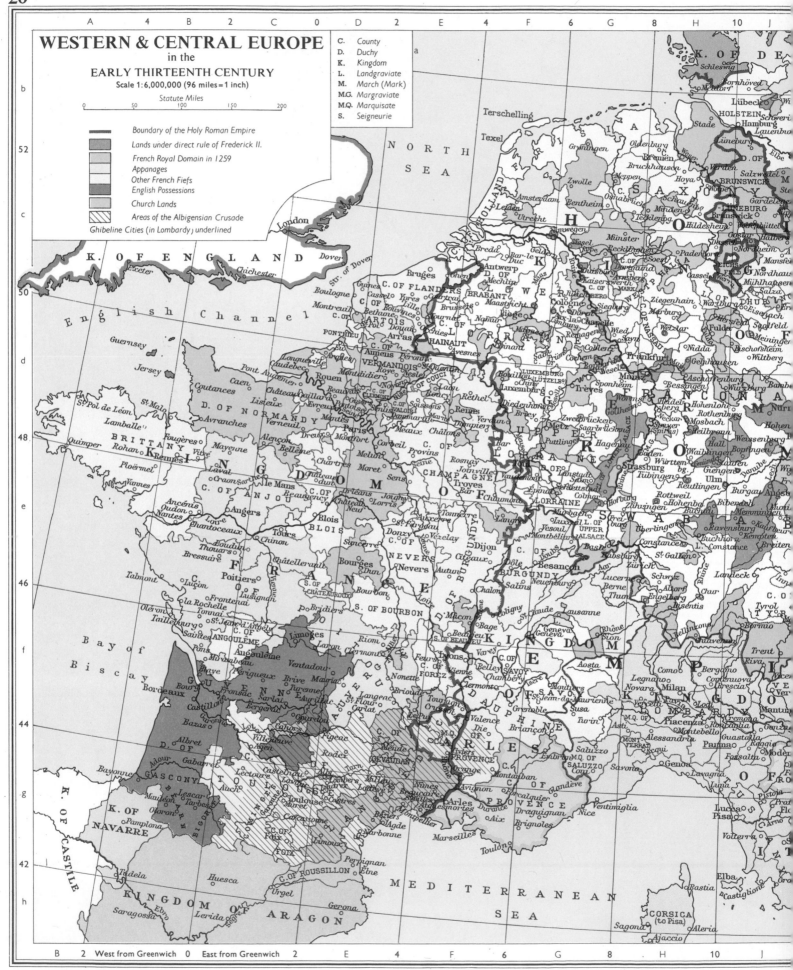

WESTERN & CENTRAL EUROPE
in the
EARLY THIRTEENTH CENTURY
Scale 1:6,000,000 (96 miles = 1 inch)

Statute Miles

0   50   100   150   200

C.	County
D.	Duchy
K.	Kingdom
L.	Landgraviate
M.	March (Mark)
M.G.	Margraviate
M.Q.	Marquisate
S.	Seigneurie

Boundary of the Holy Roman Empire
Lands under direct rule of Frederick II.
French Royal Domain in 1259
Appanages
Other French Fiefs
English Possessions
Church Lands
Areas of the Albigensian Crusade
Ghibeline Cities (in Lombardy) underlined

NORTH SEA

K. OF ENGLAND

English Channel

Bay of Biscay

K. OF CASTILE

K. OF NAVARRE

KINGDOM OF ARAGON

MEDITERRANEAN SEA

Map A — Rise of the Norman Kingdom of Italy & Sicily

Note: Dates indicate Norman Conquest

Rise of the
NORMAN KINGDOM
of
ITALY & SICILY
Scale 1:6,300,000 (100 miles=1 inch)
Statute Miles
0   50   100

Duchy of Apulia and Calabria c. 1085

County of Sicily by 1091

Principality of Salerno by 1077

County of Aversa by 1029

Principality of Capua by 1060 (including County of Aversa)

Papal Territories (including Benevento)

N. Frontier of Kingdom under Roger II.

Map B — Germany under Frederick Barbarossa

GERMANY
under
FREDERICK BARBAROSSA
Scale 1:12,000,000 (192 miles=1 inch)
Statute Miles
0   50   100   150

Limits of the Empire at the accession of Frederick Barbarossa 1152

Duchies held by the House of Staufen before 1176

Demesne lands of the House of Staufen before 1176

Duchies held by the House of Welf before 1176

Demesne lands of the House of Welf before 1176

Lands held by the Ascanians

COPYRIGHT, GEORGE PHILIP & SON, LTD.

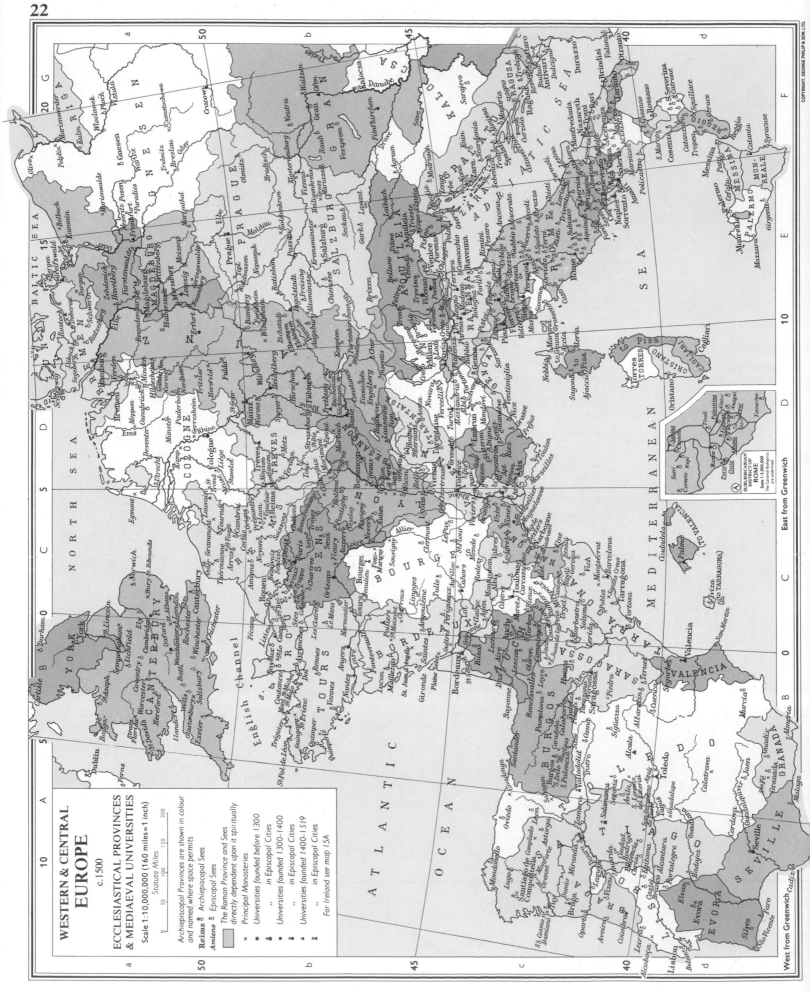

**WESTERN & CENTRAL
EUROPE**
c.1500

**ECCLESIASTICAL PROVINCES
& MEDIAEVAL UNIVERSITIES**

Scale 1:10,000,000 (160 miles=1 inch)

Statute Miles

Archiepiscopal Provinces are shown in colour
and named where space permits

Reims ✠ Archiepiscopal Sees

Amiens ⚑ Episcopal Sees

	The Roman Province and Sees
	directly dependent upon it spiritually
×	Principal Monasteries
×	Universities founded before 1300
	in Episcopal Cities
	Universities founded 1300–1400
	in Episcopal Cities
	Universities founded 1400–1519
	in Episcopal Cities
	For Ireland see map 15A

**SUBURBICARIAN
DISTRICT OF
ROME**
Scale 1:5,000,000
The Cardinal Bishoprics
are underlined

West from Greenwich

East from Greenwich

COPYRIGHT, GEORGE PHILIP & SON, LTD.

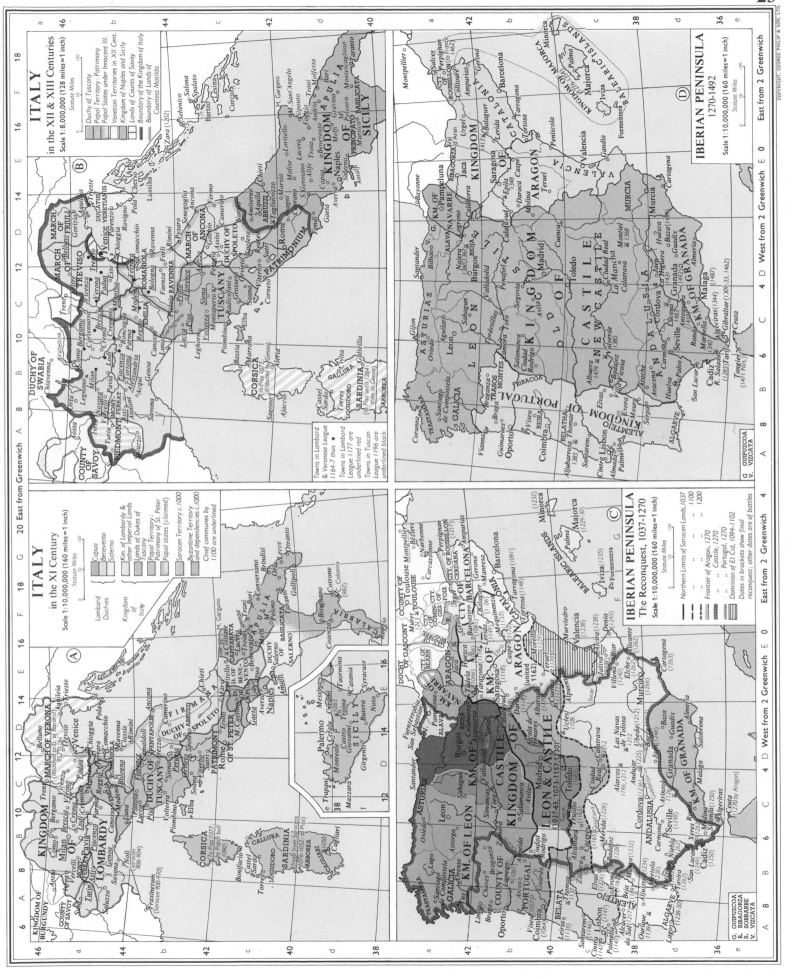

ITALY
in the XII & XIII Centuries
Scale 1:8,000,000 (128 miles=1 inch)

Duchy of Tuscany
Papal Territory: Patrimony
Papal States under Innocent III.
Venetian Territories in XII Cent.
Kingdom of Naples and Sicily
Lands of Counts of Savoy
Boundary of the Kingdom of Italy
Boundary of Lands of Countess Matilda

Towns in Lombard
& Veronese League
1164-7 thus
Towns in Lombard
League 1177 are
underlined red
Towns in Tuscan
League 1196 are
underlined black

ITALY
in the XI Century
Scale 1:10,000,000 (160 miles=1 inch)

Lombard Duchies

Capua
Benevento
Salerno

Km. of Lombardy &
other Imperial Lands
Lands of Dukes of
Tuscany
Papal Territory:
Patrimony of St. Peter
Papal states (claimed)
Byzantine Territory
and dependencies c.1000
Chief communes by
1100 are underlined

Km. of Lombardy &
other Imperial Lands
Papal Territory of St. Peter c.1000
Saracen Territory c.1000

IBERIAN PENINSULA
1270-1492
Scale 1:10,000,000 (160 miles=1 inch)

IBERIAN PENINSULA
The Reconquest, 1037-1270
Scale 1:10,000,000 (160 miles=1 inch)

Northern Limits of Saracen Lands, 1037
" " " 1100
" " " 1200
Frontier of Aragon, 1270
" Castile, 1270
" Portugal, 1270
Dominion of El Cid, 1094-1102
Dates in brackets show final
reconquest; other dates are of battles

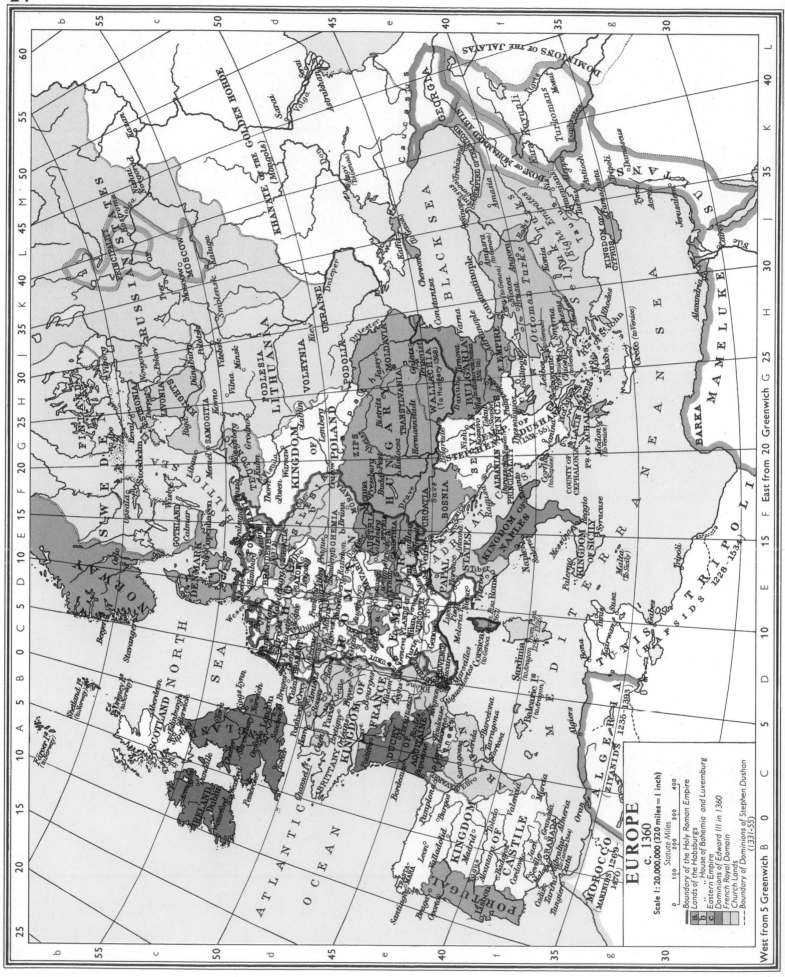

EUROPE
c. 1360

Scale 1 : 20,000,000 (320 miles = 1 inch)

Statute Miles

0   100   200   300   400

Boundary of the Holy Roman Empire
a — Lands of the Habsburgs
b — " House of Bohemia and Luxemburg
c — Eastern Empire
Dominions of Edward III in 1360
French Royal Domain
Church Lands
Boundary of Dominions of Stephen Dushan

West from 5 Greenwich B   0   C   East from 20 Greenwich G   25   H

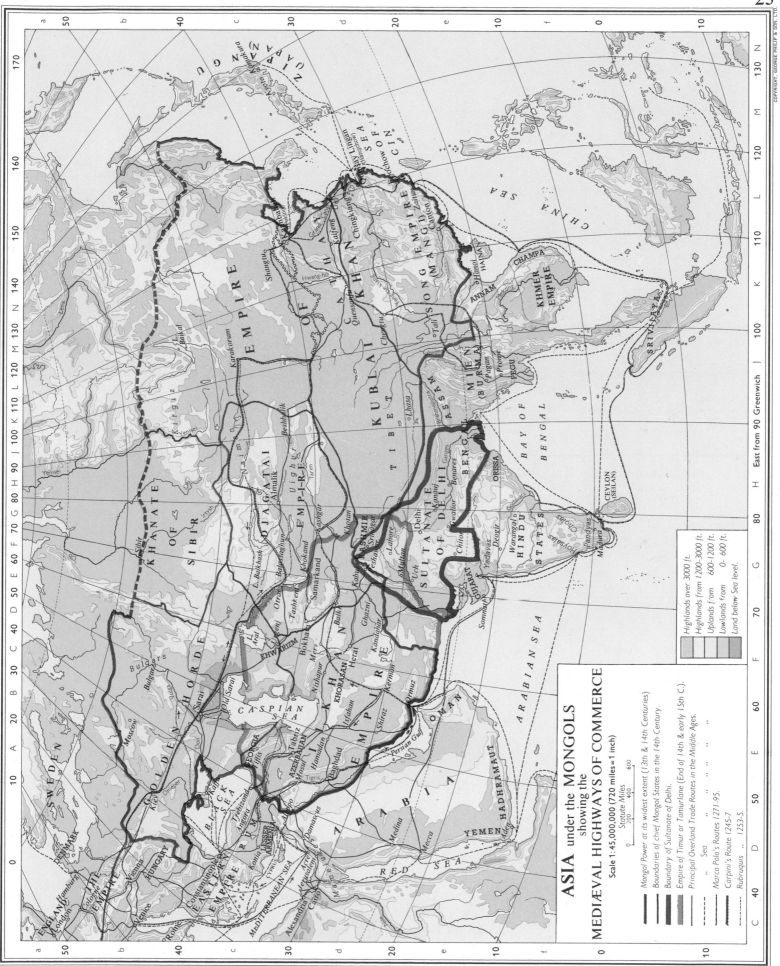

ASIA under the MONGOLS
showing the
MEDIÆVAL HIGHWAYS OF COMMERCE

Scale 1:45,000,000 (720 miles=1 inch)

Statute Miles
200   400   600

Mongol Power at its widest extent (13th & 14th Centuries)
Boundaries of chief Mongol States in the 14th Century.
Boundary of Sultanate of Delhi.
Empire of Timur or Tamurlane (End of 14th & early 15th C.).
Principal Overland Trade Routes in the Middle Ages.
       „   Sea
Marco Polo's Routes 1271-95.
Carpini's Route 1245-7
Rubruquis „ 1253-5.

Highlands over 3000 ft.
Highlands from 1200-3000 ft.
Uplands from 600-1200 ft.
Lowlands from 0- 600 ft.
Land below Sea level.

East from 90 Greenwich

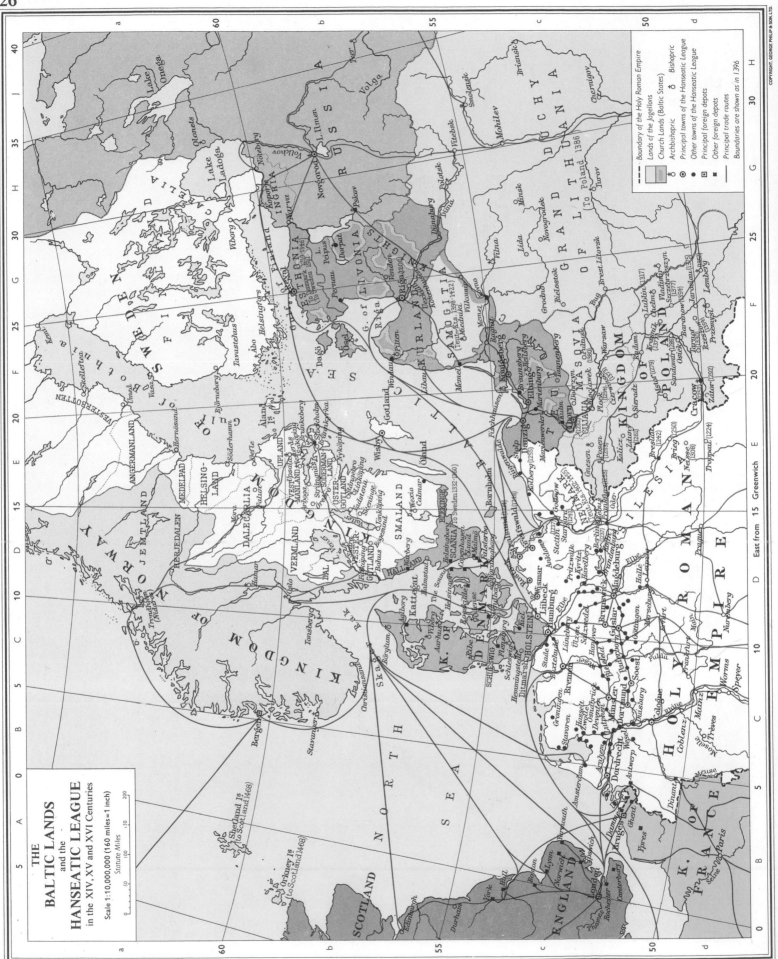

THE
BALTIC LANDS
and the
HANSEATIC LEAGUE
in the XIV, XV and XVI Centuries

Scale 1:10,000,000 (160 miles=1 inch)

Statute Miles

0   50   100   150   200

Legend:
- Boundary of the Holy Roman Empire
- Lands of the Jagellons
- Church Lands (Baltic States)
- ♰ Archbishopric   ♱ Bishopric
- ● Principal towns of the Hanseatic League
- ○ Other towns of the Hanseatic League
- ◻ Principal foreign depots
- ◼ Other foreign depots
- Principal trade routes
- Boundaries are shown as in 1396

COPYRIGHT, GEORGE PHILIP & SON, LTD.

East from 15 Greenwich

SCOTLAND

ENGLAND

K. OF FRANCE

NORTH SEA

KINGDOM OF NORWAY

SWEDEN

DENMARK

BALTIC SEA

HOLY ROMAN EMPIRE

KINGDOM OF POLAND

GRAND DUCHY OF LITHUANIA

RUSSIA

LIVONIA

ESTHONIA

CURLAND

SAMOGITIA

27

MEDIÆVAL ENGLAND & WALES
c. 1399

Scale 1:2,500,000 (40 miles = 1 inch)

Statute Miles
0   10   20   30   40   50

● Boroughs regularly represented from 1366 to 1485.
⊙ Boroughs occasionally represented in Mediæval Parliaments.
  Boroughs represented in the Model Parliament of 1295 are underlined.
⚲ Principal Castles.
✦ Boroughs with Castles.
Dover The Cinque Ports.
░░░ Lands of the Duchy of Lancaster.

A LONDON Scale 1:75,000 ½ Mile

COPYRIGHT, GEORGE PHILIP & SON, LTD.

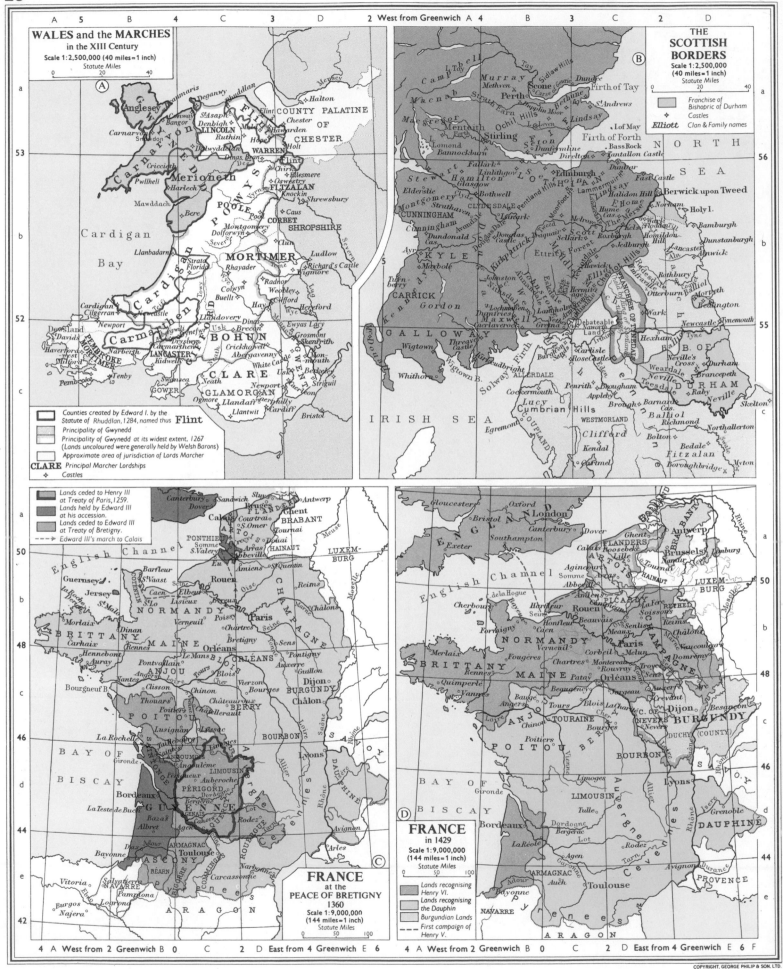

WALES and the MARCHES in the XIII Century
Scale 1:2,500,000 (40 miles=1 inch)
Statute Miles
0   20   40

West from Greenwich

THE SCOTTISH BORDERS
Scale 1:2,500,000 (40 miles=1 inch)
Statute Miles
0   20   40

Franchise of Bishopric of Durham
Castles
Elliott Clan & Family names

Counties created by Edward I. by the Statute of Rhuddlan, 1284, named thus **Flint**
Principality of Gwynedd
Principality of Gwynedd at its widest extent, 1267 (Lands uncoloured were generally held by Welsh Barons)
Approximate area of jurisdiction of Lords Marcher
CLARE Principal Marcher Lordships
Castles

Lands ceded to Henry III at Treaty of Paris, 1259.
Lands held by Edward III at his accession.
Lands ceded to Edward III at Treaty of Bretigny.
Edward III's march to Calais

FRANCE at the PEACE OF BRETIGNY 1360
Scale 1:9,000,000 (144 miles=1 inch)
Statute Miles
0   50   100

FRANCE in 1429
Scale 1:9,000,000 (144 miles=1 inch)
Statute Miles
0   50   100

Lands recognising Henry VI.
Lands recognising the Dauphin
Burgundian Lands
First campaign of Henry V.

4 A West from 2 Greenwich B 0 C 2 D East from 4 Greenwich E 6
4 A West from 2 Greenwich B 0 C 2 D East from 4 Greenwich E 6 F

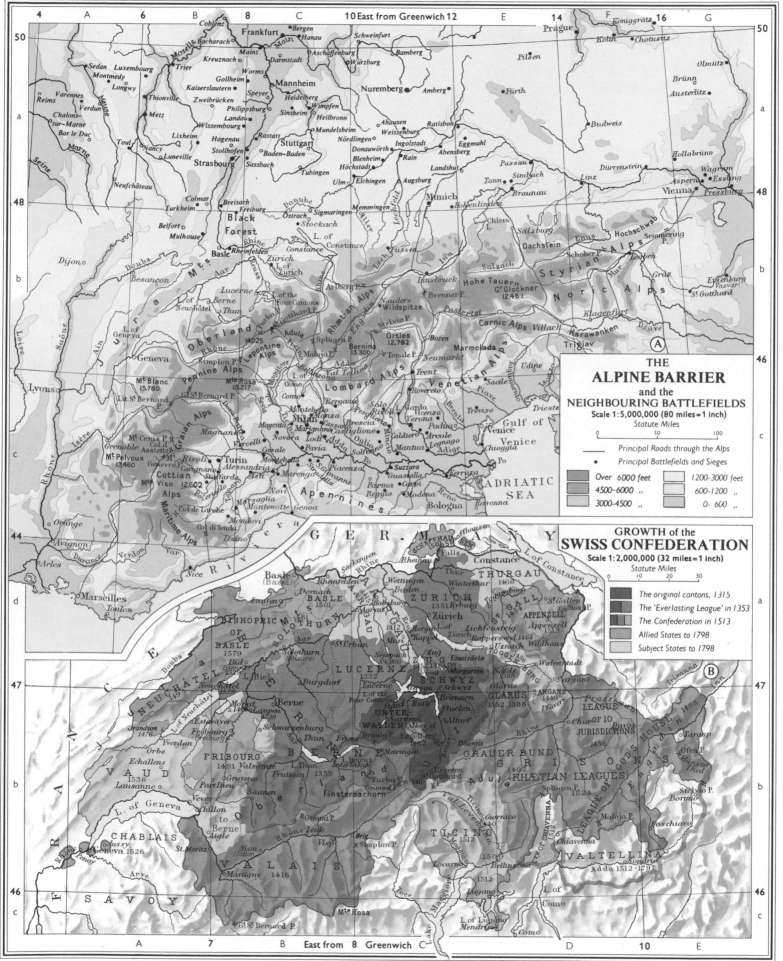

East from Greenwich

THE
ALPINE BARRIER
and the
NEIGHBOURING BATTLEFIELDS
Scale 1:5,000,000 (80 miles=1 inch)
Statute Miles

0	50	100

————— Principal Roads through the Alps

• Principal Battlefields and Sieges

Over 6000 feet	1200-3000 feet
4500-6000 ,,	600-1200 ,,
3000-4500 ,,	0- 600 ,,

GROWTH of the
SWISS CONFEDERATION
Scale 1:2,000,000 (32 miles=1 inch)
Statute Miles

0	10	30

The original cantons, 1315
The 'Everlasting League' in 1353
The Confederation in 1513
Allied States to 1798
Subject States to 1798

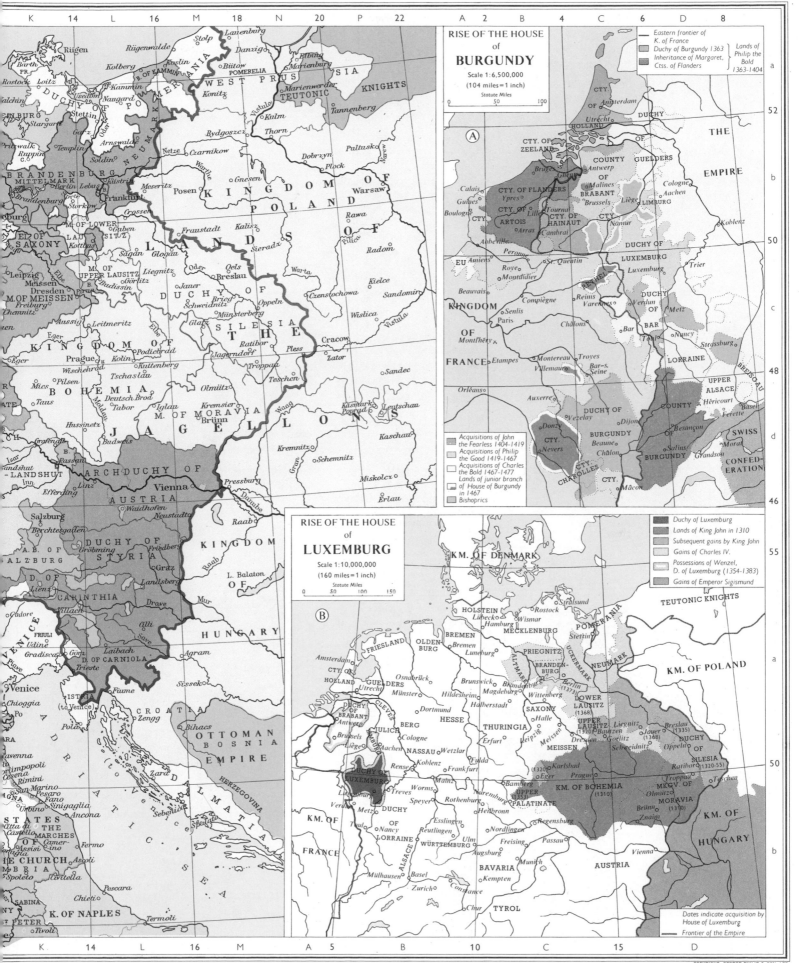

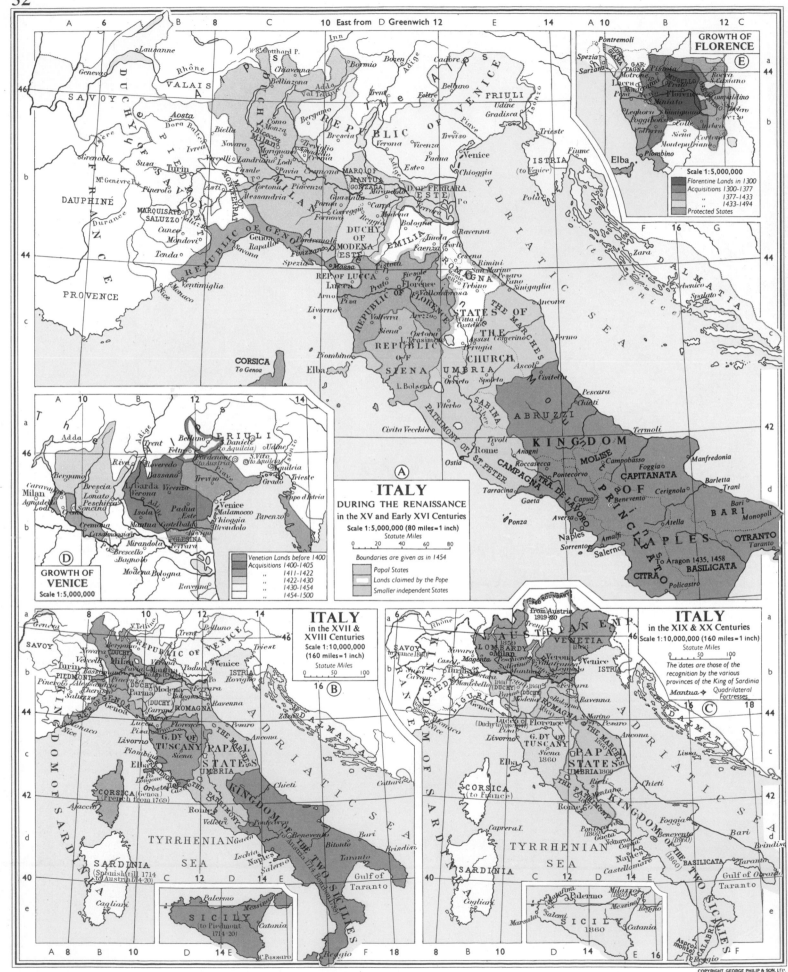

GROWTH OF FLORENCE

Scale 1:5,000,000

- Florentine Lands in 1300
- Acquisitions 1300-1377
- " 1377-1433
- " 1433-1494
- Protected States

ITALY
DURING THE RENAISSANCE
in the XV and Early XVI Centuries
Scale 1:5,000,000 (80 miles=1 inch)
Statute Miles
0   20   40   60   80

Boundaries are given as in 1454

- Papal States
- Lands claimed by the Pope
- Smaller independent States

GROWTH OF VENICE
Scale 1:5,000,000

- Venetian Lands before 1400
- Acquisitions 1400-1405
- " 1411-1422
- " 1422-1430
- " 1430-1454
- " 1454-1500

ITALY
in the XVII &
XVIII Centuries
Scale 1:10,000,000
(160 miles=1 inch)
Statute Miles
0   50   100

ITALY
in the XIX & XX Centuries
Scale 1:10,000,000 (160 miles=1 inch)
Statute Miles
0   50   100
The dates are those of the
recognition by the various
provinces of the King of Sardinia
Mantua ✦ Quadrilateral
Fortresses

COPYRIGHT. GEORGE PHILIP & SON, LTD.

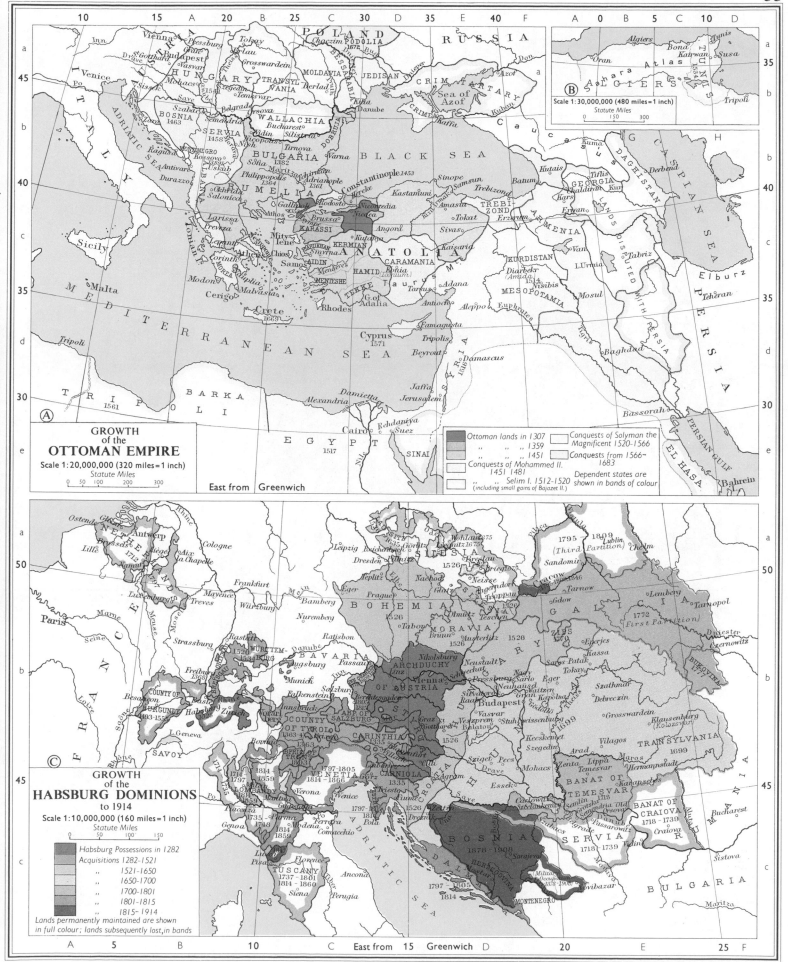

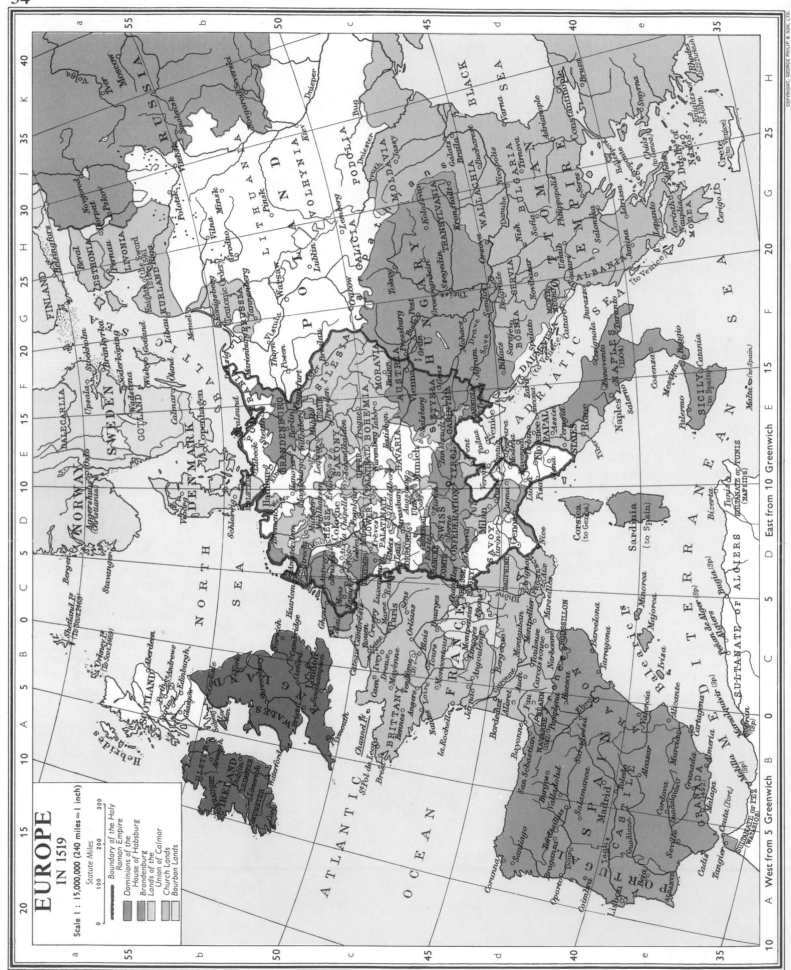

34

EUROPE
IN 1519

Scale 1 : 15,000,000 (240 miles = 1 inch)

Statute Miles
0   100   200   300

⎯⎯⎯ Boundary of the Holy
        Roman Empire
        Dominions of the
        House of Habsburg
        Brandenburg
        Lands of the
        Union of Calmar
        Church Lands
        Bourbon Lands

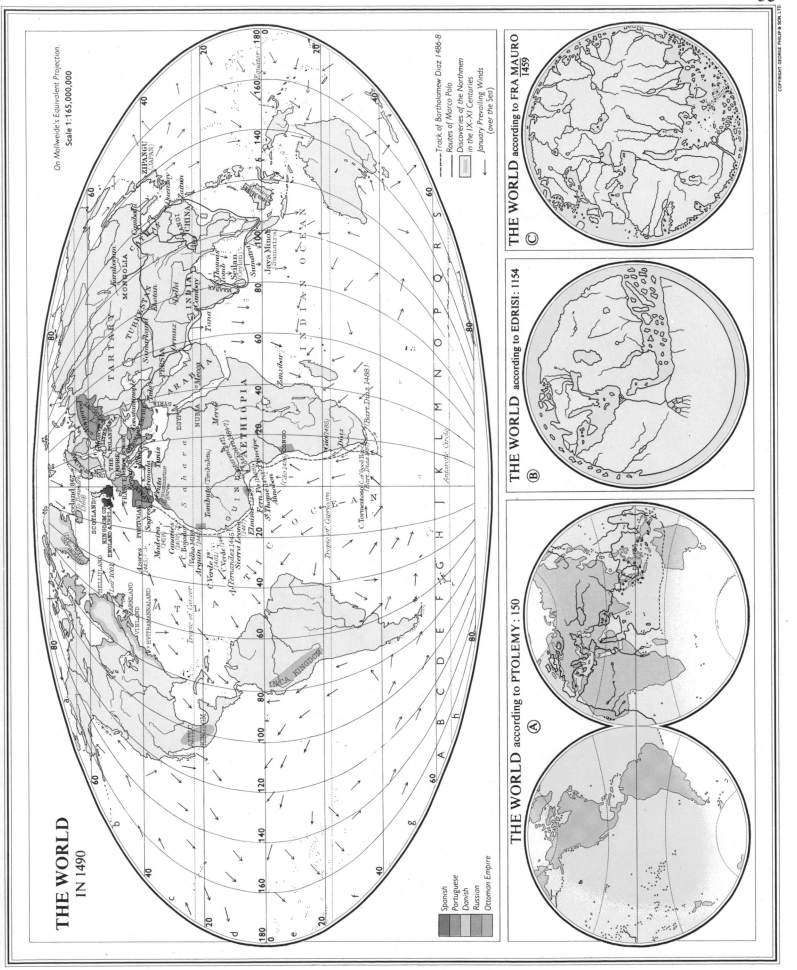

THE WORLD
IN 1490

On Mollweide's Equivalent Projection.
Scale 1:165,000,000

ZIPANGU (JAPAN)

Quelpart
CHINA
CAMBALU
Karakorum
MONGOLIA
TURKESTAN
Khotan
TARTARY
Samarkand
Delhi
INDIA
PERSIA
Ormuz
Cambay
MALABAR
St. Thomas' Tomb
Seilan (Ceylon)
Sumatra
Java Minor (Sumatra)

INDIAN OCEAN

ARABIA
Mecca
Zanzibar
EGYPT
NUBIA
Merve
AETHIOPIA
Tombuto (Timbuktu)
GUINEA
CONGO
Abyssinia

Tropic of Capricorn

Tropic of Cancer

A T L A N T I C   O C E A N

HELLULAND
MARKLAND
VINLAND
HVITRAMANNALAND

Azores
Madeira
Canaries
C. Bojador
C. Verde Is.
Sierra Leone
Elmina
Fern. Po
St. Thomé
C. Torrentoso
C. of Good Hope

INCA KINGDOM

AZTEC KINGDOM

SCOTLAND
KINGDOM OF ENGLAND & IRELAND
FRANCE
PORTUGAL
SPAIN
Tunis
Sahara

----- Track of Bartholomew Diaz 1486-8
—— Routes of Marco Polo
—— Discoveries of the Northmen in the IX–XI Centuries
→ January Prevailing Winds (over the Sea)

Spanish
Portuguese
Danish
Russian
Ottoman Empire

THE WORLD according to PTOLEMY: 150
A

THE WORLD according to EDRISI: 1154
B

THE WORLD according to FRA MAURO 1459
C

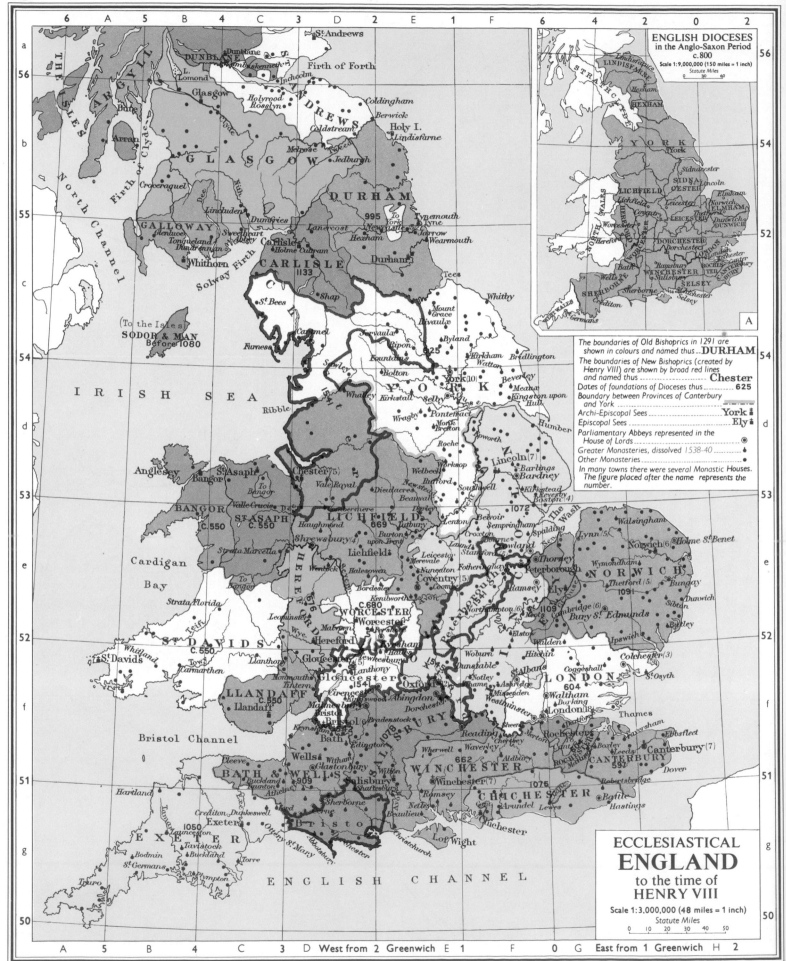

ECCLESIASTICAL
ENGLAND
to the time of
HENRY VIII

Scale 1:3,000,000 (48 miles = 1 inch)
Statute Miles

ENGLISH DIOCESES
in the Anglo-Saxon Period
c. 800
Scale 1:9,000,000 (150 miles = 1 inch)
Statute Miles

The boundaries of Old Bishoprics in 1291 are
shown in colours and named thus .... **DURHAM**
The boundaries of New Bishoprics (created by
Henry VIII) are shown by broad red lines
and named thus .... **Chester**
Dates of foundations of Dioceses thus **625**
Boundary between Provinces of Canterbury
and York ....
Archi-Episcopal Sees .... **York**
Episcopal Sees .... **Ely**
Parliamentary Abbeys represented in the
House of Lords ....
Greater Monasteries, dissolved 1538-40 ....
Other Monasteries ....
In many towns there were several Monastic Houses.
The figure placed after the name represents the
number.

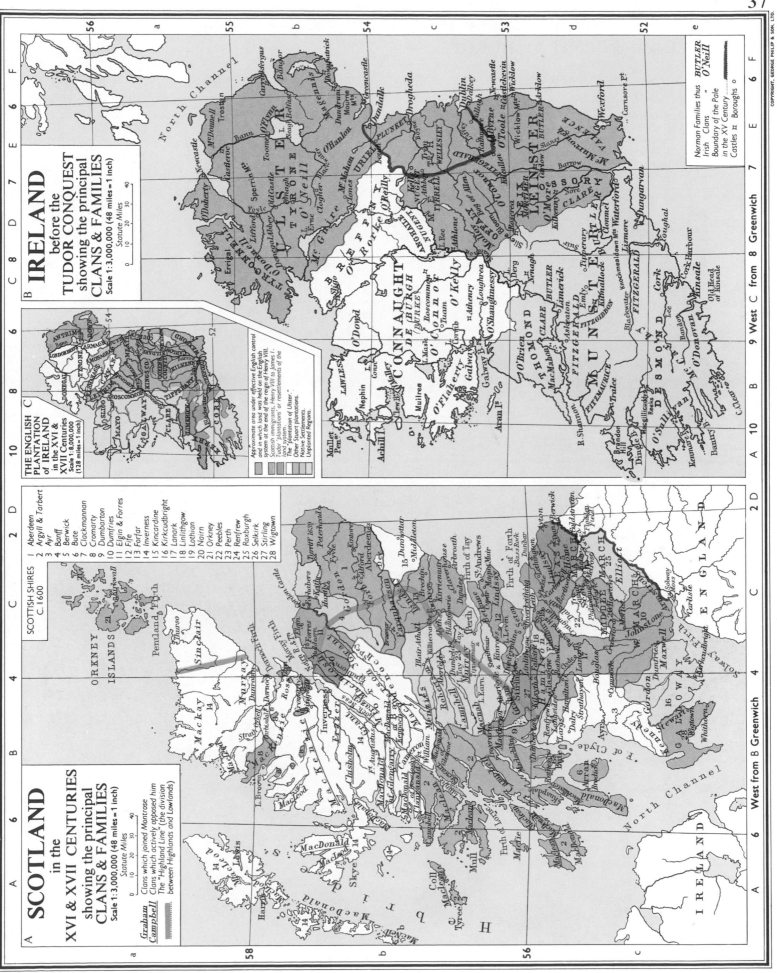

SCOTLAND in the XVI & XVII CENTURIES showing the principal CLANS & FAMILIES
Scale 1:3,000,000 (48 miles = 1 inch)

B IRELAND before the TUDOR CONQUEST showing the principal CLANS & FAMILIES
Scale 1:3,000,000 (48 miles = 1 inch)

C THE ENGLISH PLANTATION of IRELAND in the XVI & XVII Centuries
Scale 1:8,000,000 (128 miles = 1 inch)

SCOTTISH SHIRES C. 1600

1 Aberdeen
2 Argyll & Tarbert
3 Ayr
4 Banff
5 Berwick
6 Bute
7 Clackmannan
8 Cromarty
9 Dumbarton
10 Dumfries
11 Elgin & Forres
12 Fife
13 Forfar
14 Inverness
15 Kincardine
16 Kirkcudbright
17 Lanark
18 Linlithgow
19 Lothian
20 Nairn
21 Orkney
22 Peebles
23 Perth
24 Renfrew
25 Roxburgh
26 Selkirk
27 Stirling
28 Wigtown

Graham Campbell — Clans which joined Montrose
Campbell — Clans which actively opposed him
The "Highland Line" (the division between Highlands and Lowlands)

Norman Families thus **BUTLER**
" Irish Clans " **O'Neill**
Boundary of the Pale in the XV Century
Castles ¤   Boroughs o

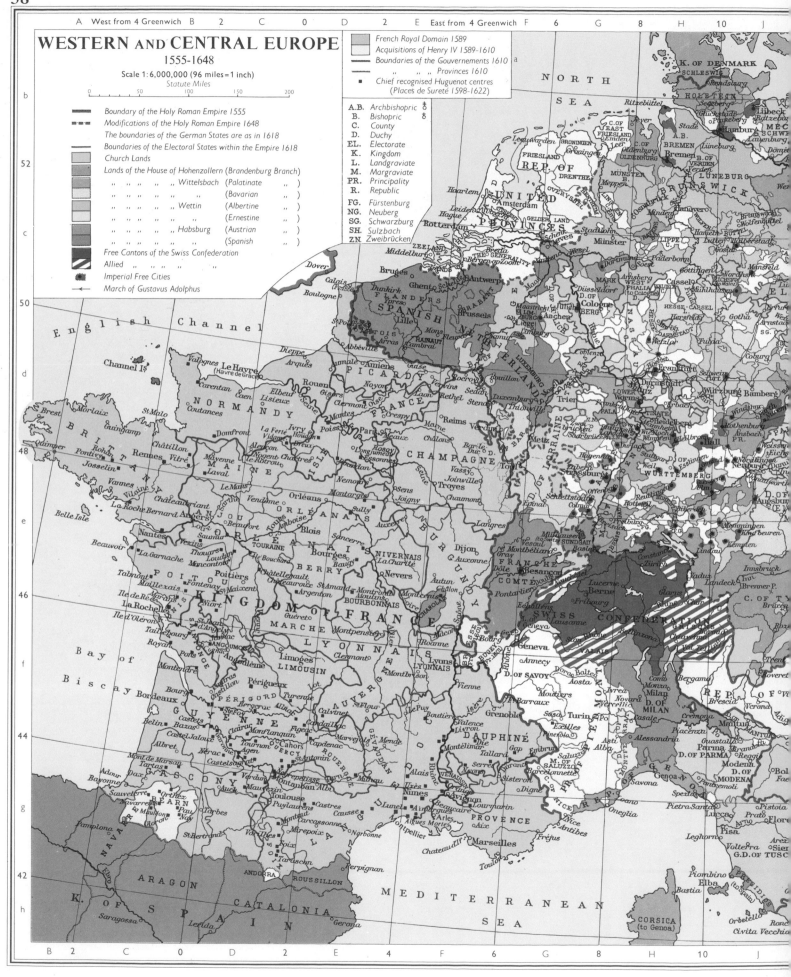

38

WESTERN AND CENTRAL EUROPE
1555-1648

Scale 1:6,000,000 (96 miles = 1 inch)

Statute Miles

French Royal Domain 1589
Acquisitions of Henry IV 1589-1610
Boundaries of the Gouvernements 1610
    ,,   ,,   ,,   Provinces 1610
Chief recognised Huguenot centres
(Places de Sureté 1598-1622)

Boundary of the Holy Roman Empire 1555
Modifications of the Holy Roman Empire 1648
The boundaries of the German States are as in 1618
Boundaries of the Electoral States within the Empire 1618
Church Lands
Lands of the House of Hohenzollern (Brandenburg Branch)
  ,, ,, ,, ,, Wittelsbach (Palatinate ,,)
  ,, ,, ,, ,, (Bavarian ,,)
  ,, ,, ,, Wettin (Albertine ,,)
  ,, ,, ,, (Ernestine ,,)
  ,, ,, ,, Habsburg (Austrian ,,)
  ,, ,, ,, (Spanish ,,)
Free Cantons of the Swiss Confederation
Allied ,, ,, ,,
Imperial Free Cities
March of Gustavus Adolphus

A.B. Archbishopric
B. Bishopric
C. County
D. Duchy
EL. Electorate
K. Kingdom
L. Landgraviate
M. Margraviate
PR. Principality
R. Republic
FG. Fürstenburg
NG. Neuberg
SG. Schwarzburg
SH. Sulzbach
ZN. Zweibrücken

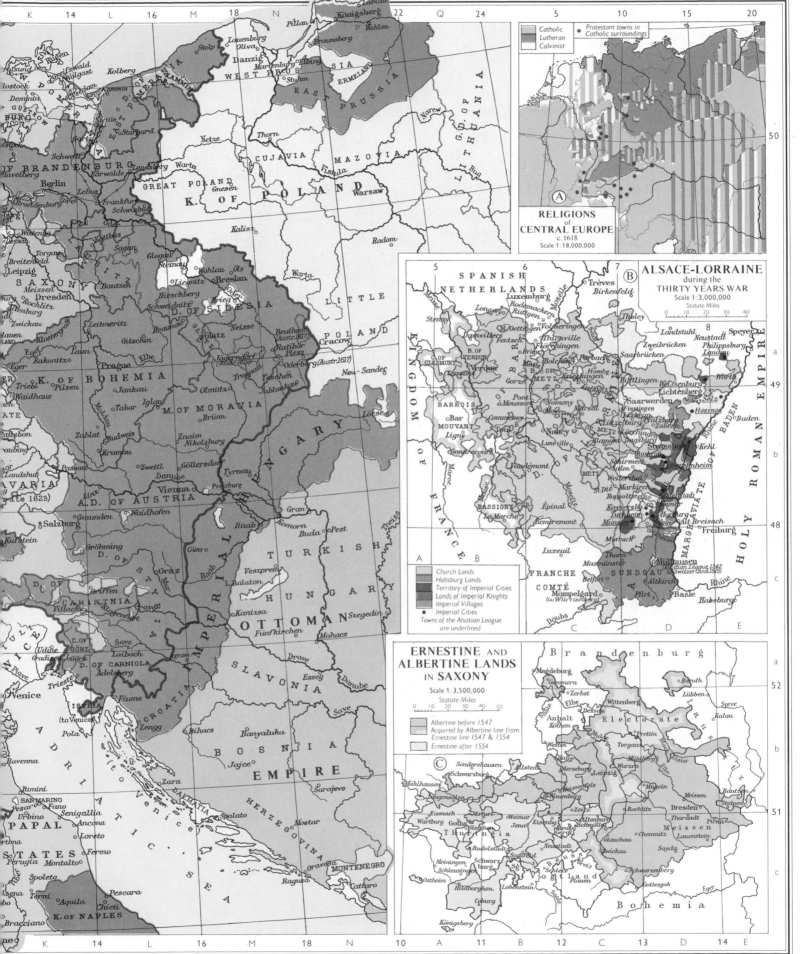

RELIGIONS
of
CENTRAL EUROPE
c. 1618
Scale 1:18,000,000

Catholic
Lutheran
Calvinist
● Protestant towns in Catholic surroundings

B ALSACE-LORRAINE
during the
THIRTY YEARS WAR
Scale 1:3,000,000
Statute Miles
0 10 20 30 40

Church Lands
Habsburg Lands
Territory of Imperial Cities
Lands of Imperial Knights
Imperial Villages
● Imperial Cities
Towns of the Alsatian League are underlined

ERNESTINE AND
ALBERTINE LANDS
IN SAXONY
Scale 1:3,500,000
Statute Miles
0 10 20 30 40 50

Albertine before 1547
Acquired by Albertine line from Ernestine line 1547 & 1554
Ernestine after 1554

COPYRIGHT, GEORGE PHILIP & SON, LTD.

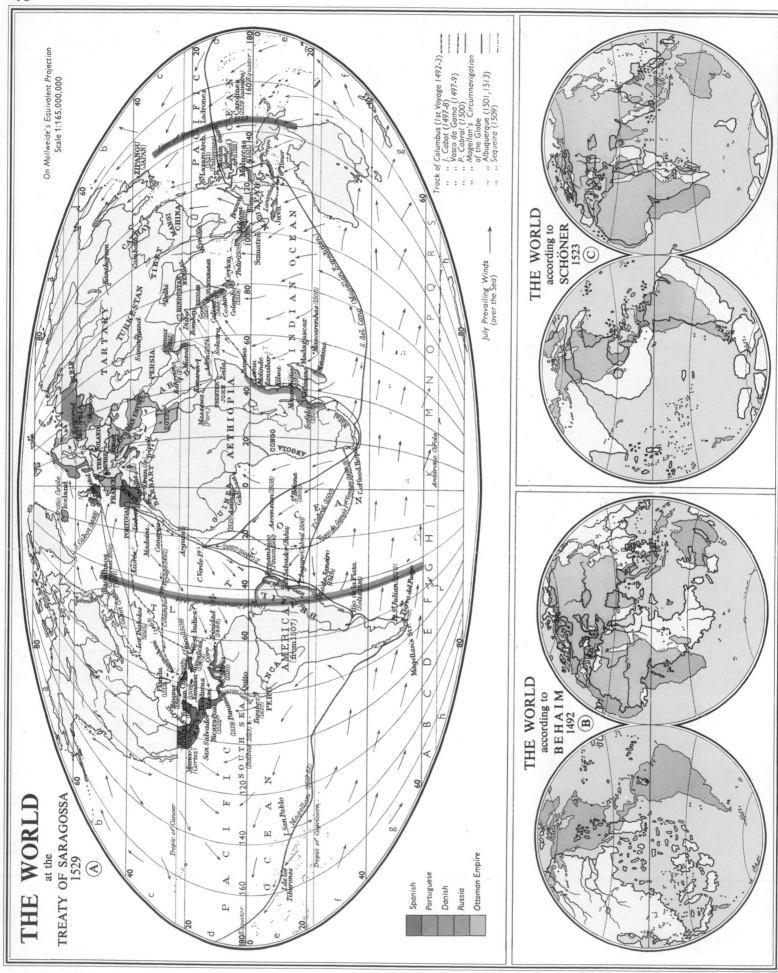

THE WORLD
at the
TREATY OF SARAGOSSA 1529 Ⓐ

On Mollweide's Equivalent Projection
Scale 1:165,000,000

Track of Columbus (1st Voyage 1492-3)
     :: J. Cabot (1497-8)
     :: Vasco da Gama (1497-9)
     :: P. Cabral (1500)
     :: Magellan's Circumnavigation
         of the Globe
     :: Albuquerque (1501, 1513)
     :: Sequeira (1509)

July Prevailing Winds ⟶
(over the Sea)

Spanish
Portuguese
Danish
Russia
Ottoman Empire

THE WORLD
according to
SCHÖNER 1523 Ⓒ

THE WORLD
according to
BEHAIM 1492 Ⓑ

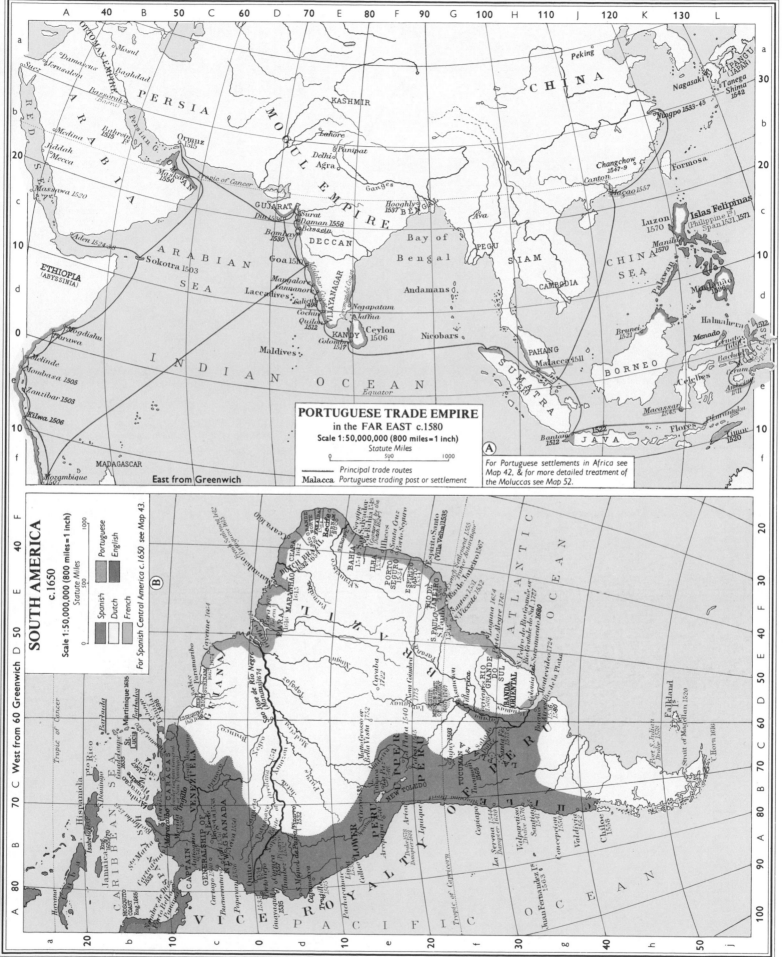

PORTUGUESE TRADE EMPIRE
in the FAR EAST c.1580
Scale 1:50,000,000 (800 miles=1 inch)
Statute Miles
0 _____ 500 _____ 1000

——— Principal trade routes
Malacca Portuguese trading post or settlement

For Portuguese settlements in Africa see Map 42, & for more detailed treatment of the Moluccas see Map 52.

SOUTH AMERICA
c.1650
Scale 1:50,000,000 (800 miles=1 inch)
Statute Miles
0 ____ 500 ____ 1000

Portuguese
English
Spanish
Dutch
French

For Spanish Central America c.1650 see Map 43.

COPYRIGHT. GEORGE PHILIP & SON. LTD.

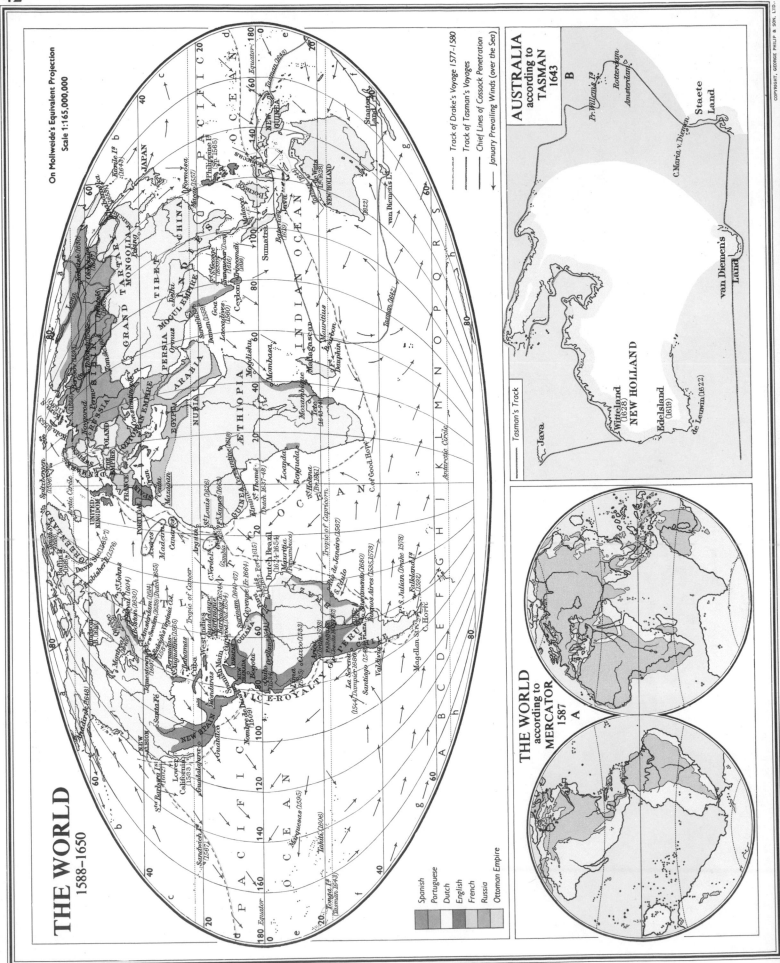

THE WORLD
1588–1650

On Mollweide's Equivalent Projection
Scale 1:165,000,000

Track of Drake's Voyage 1577–1580
Track of Tasman's Voyages
Chief Lines of Cossack Penetration
January Prevailing Winds (over the Sea)

Spanish
Portuguese
Dutch
English
French
Russia
Ottoman Empire

AUSTRALIA
according to
TASMAN
1643

B

Pr. Willems I.s
Rotterdam
Amsterdam
C. Maria v. Diemen

Staete
Land

van Diemens
Land

NEW HOLLAND

Witteland
(1628)

Edelsland
(1619)

de Leeuwin (1622)

Java

Tasman's Track

THE WORLD
according to
MERCATOR
1587

A

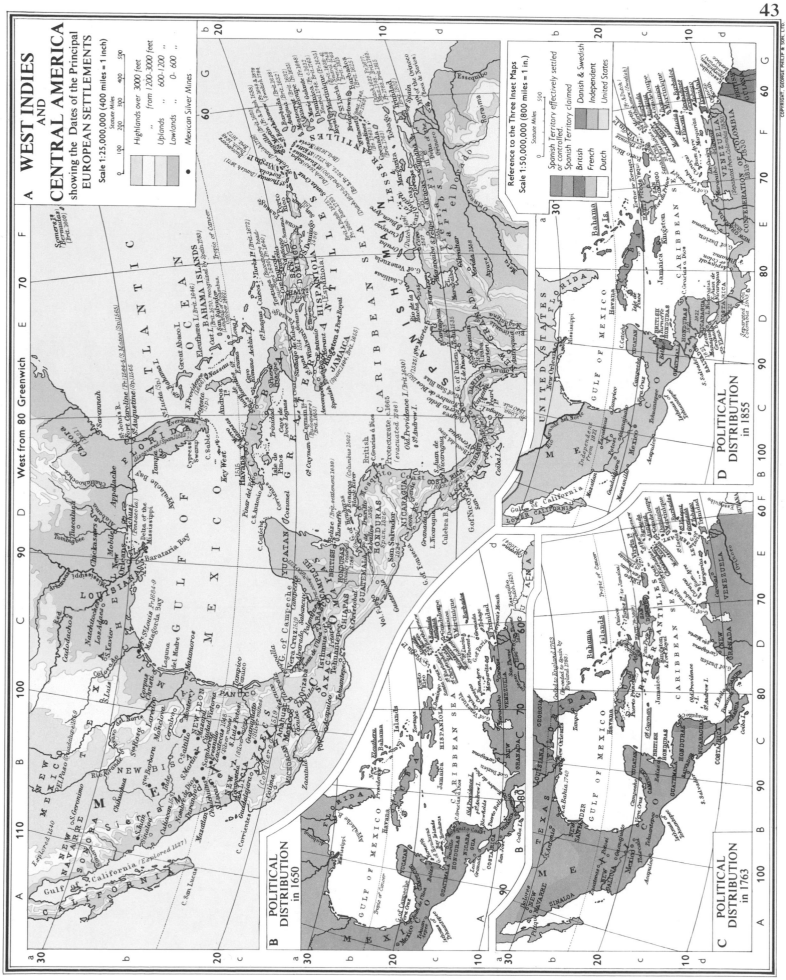

A WEST INDIES AND CENTRAL AMERICA
showing the Dates of the Principal EUROPEAN SETTLEMENTS

B POLITICAL DISTRIBUTION in 1650

C POLITICAL DISTRIBUTION in 1763

D POLITICAL DISTRIBUTION in 1855

COPYRIGHT. GEORGE PHILIP & SON, LTD.

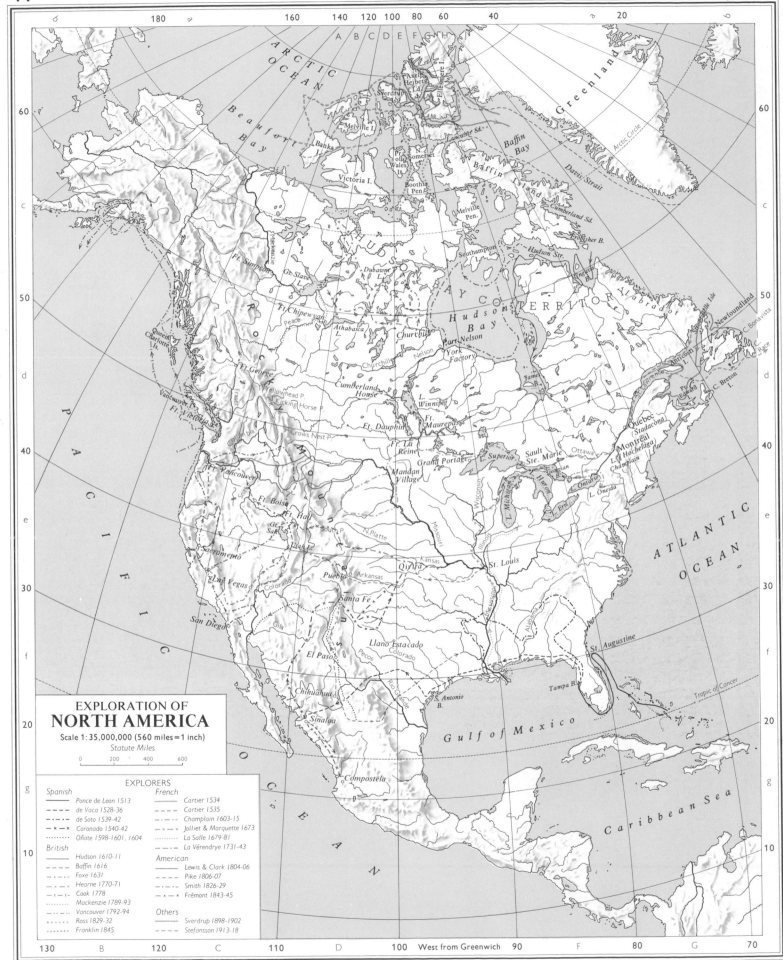

EXPLORATION OF
NORTH AMERICA

Scale 1 : 35,000,000 (560 miles = 1 inch)

Statute Miles

0   200   400   600

EXPLORERS

Spanish
Ponce de Leon 1513
de Vaca 1528-36
de Soto 1539-42
Coronado 1540-42
Oñate 1598-1601, 1604

British
Hudson 1610-11
Baffin 1616
Foxe 1631
Hearne 1770-71
Cook 1778
Mackenzie 1789-93
Vancouver 1792-94
Ross 1829-32
Franklin 1845

French
Cartier 1534
Cartier 1535
Champlain 1603-15
Jolliet & Marquette 1673
La Salle 1679-81
La Vérendrye 1731-43

American
Lewis & Clark 1804-06
Pike 1806-07
Smith 1826-29
Frémont 1843-45

Others
Sverdrup 1898-1902
Stefansson 1913-18

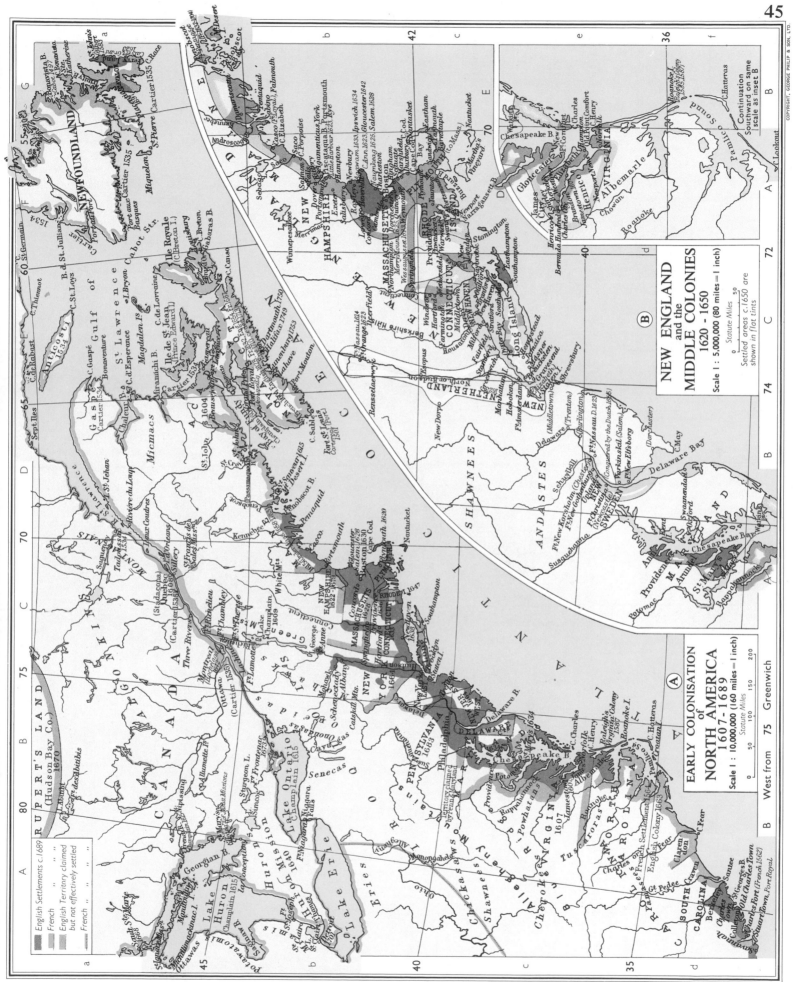

45

EARLY COLONISATION of NORTH AMERICA 1607-1689

Scale 1 : 10,000,000 (160 miles = 1 inch)

Statute Miles
0   50   100   150   200

NEW ENGLAND and the MIDDLE COLONIES 1620 - 1650

Scale 1 : 5,000,000 (80 miles = 1 inch)

Statute Miles
0   50

Settled areas c.1650 are shown in flat tints

English Settlements c.1689
French   "   "   "
English Territory claimed but not effectively settled
French   "   "   "

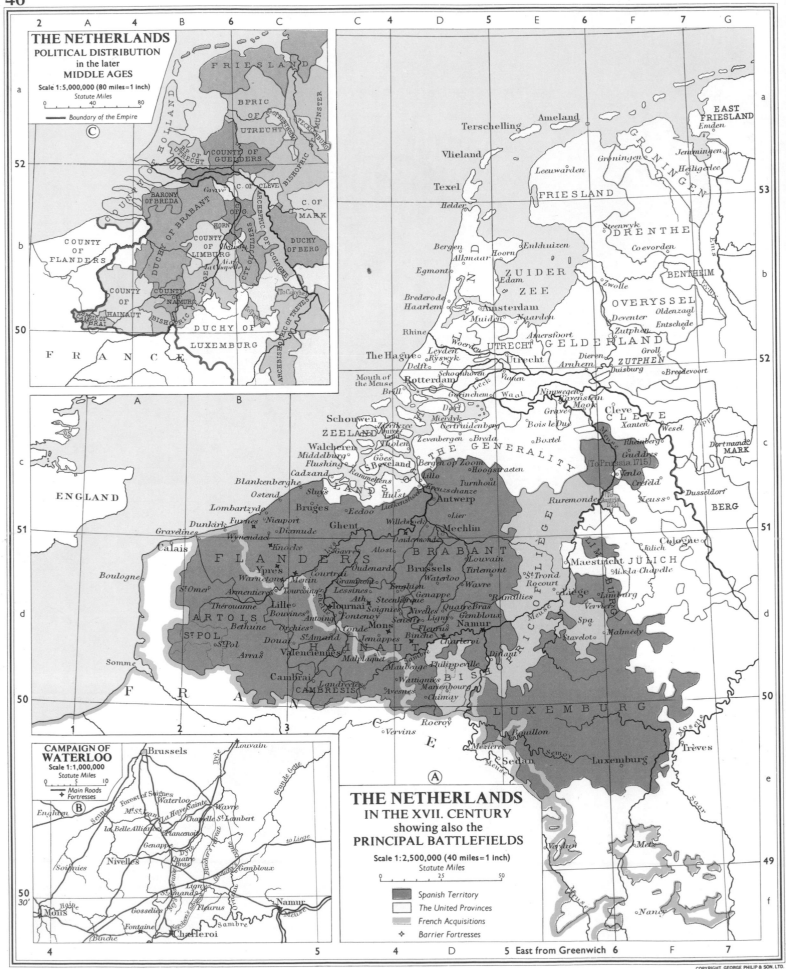

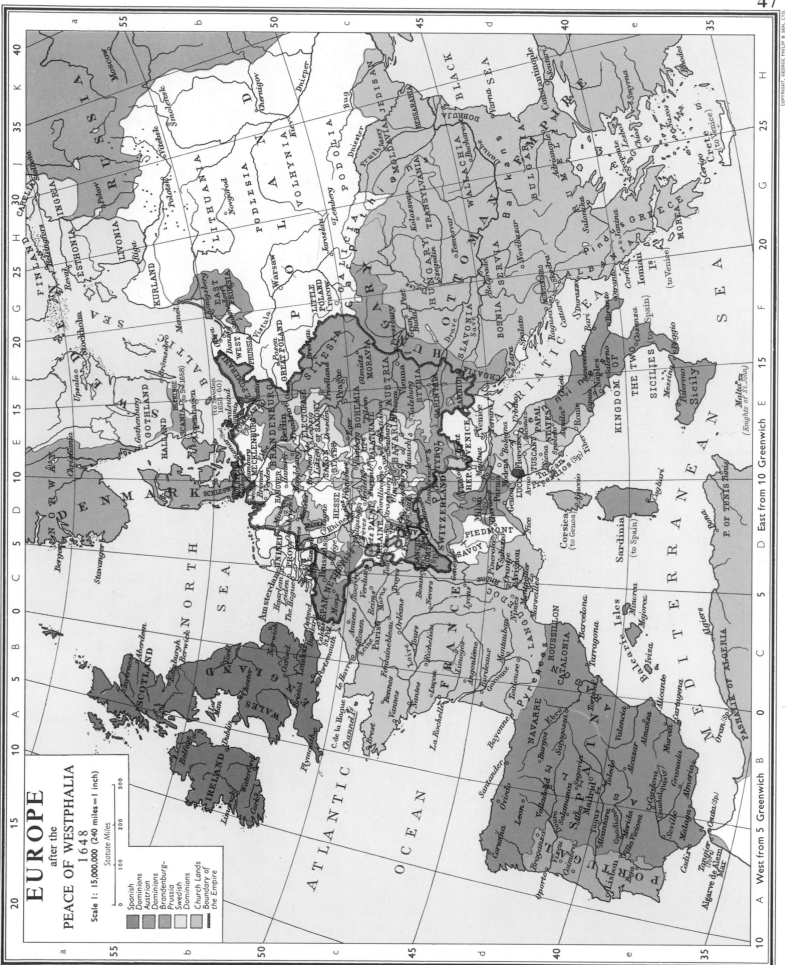

EUROPE
after the
PEACE OF WESTPHALIA
1648
Scale 1: 15,000,000 (240 miles = 1 inch)

Statute Miles
0   100   200   300

Spanish Dominions
Austrian Dominions
Brandenburg-Prussia
Swedish Dominions
Church Lands
Boundary of the Empire

47

COPYRIGHT, GEORGE PHILIP & SON, LTD.

48

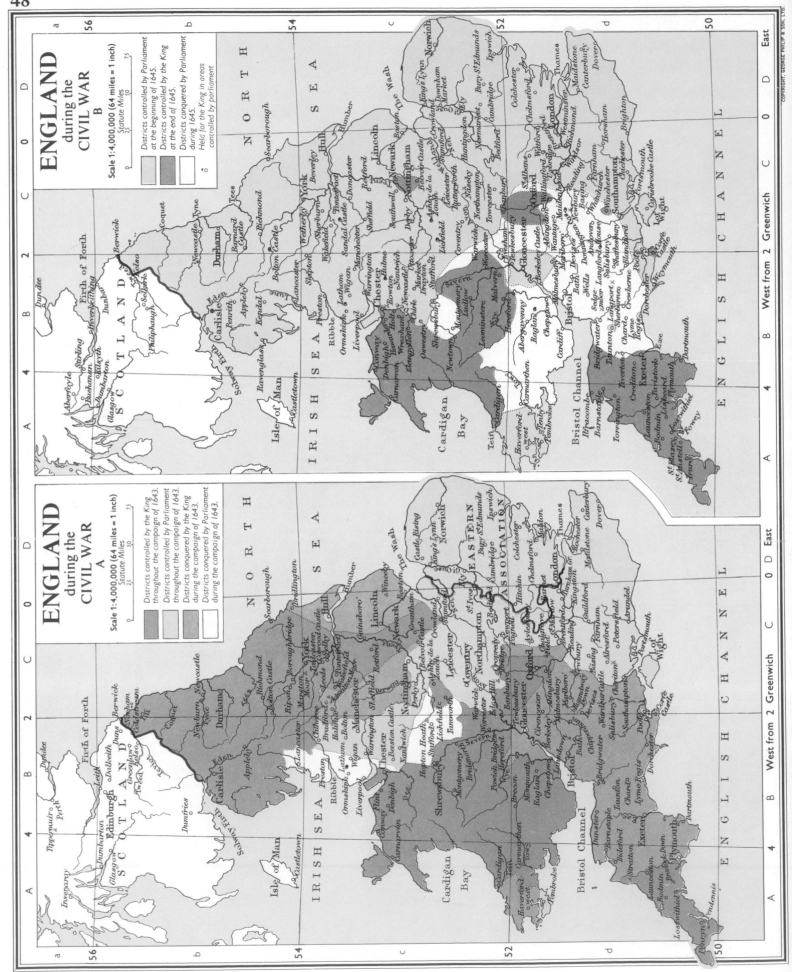

ENGLAND
during the
CIVIL WAR
B

Scale 1:4,000,000 (64 miles = 1 inch)
Statute Miles

Districts controlled by Parliament at the beginning of 1645.
Districts controlled by the King at the end of 1645.
Districts conquered by Parliament during 1645.
Held for the King in areas controlled by parliament

COPYRIGHT, GEORGE PHILIP & SON, LTD.

ENGLAND
during the
CIVIL WAR
A

Scale 1:4,000,000 (64 miles = 1 inch)
Statute Miles

Districts controlled by the King throughout the campaign of 1643.
Districts controlled by Parliament throughout the campaign of 1643.
Districts conquered by the King during the campaign of 1643.
Districts conquered by Parliament during the campaign of 1643.

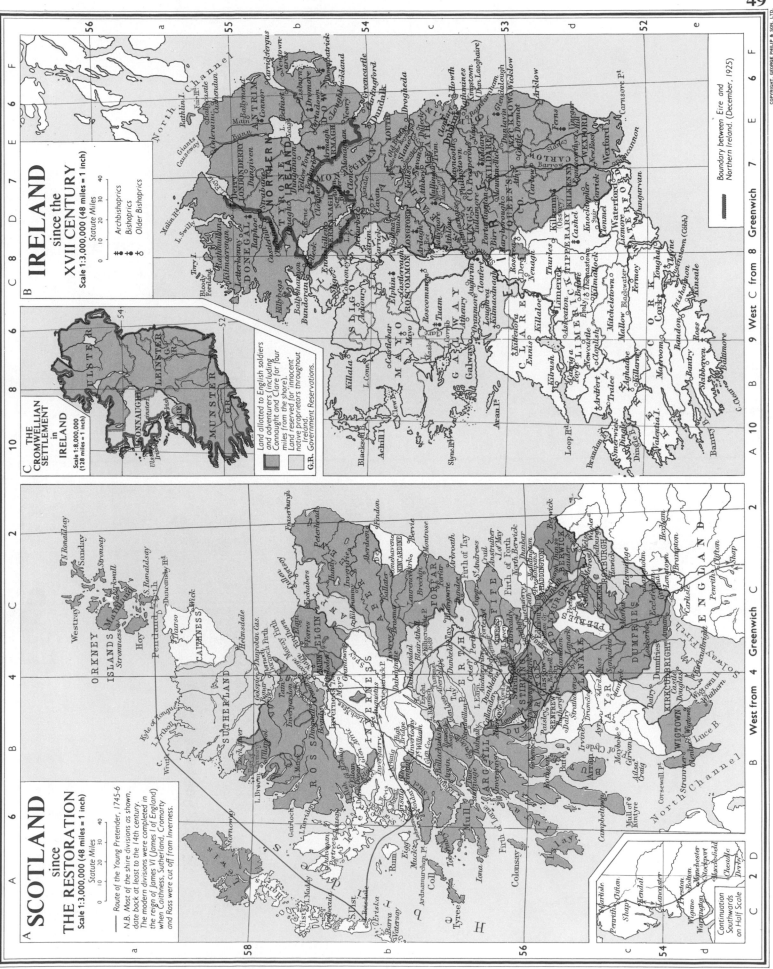

A SCOTLAND since THE RESTORATION

Scale 1:3,000,000 (48 miles = 1 inch)

Statute Miles
0 10 20 30 40

— — — Route of the Young Pretender, 1745-6
N.B. Most of the shire divisions as shown,
date back at least to the 14th century.
The modern divisions were completed in
the reign of James VI (James I of England)
when Caithness, Sutherland, Cromarty
and Ross were cut off from Inverness.

B IRELAND since the XVII CENTURY

Scale 1:3,000,000 (48 miles = 1 inch)

Statute Miles
0 10 20 30 40

✠ Archbishoprics
☩ Bishoprics
† Older Bishoprics

C THE CROMWELLIAN SETTLEMENT in IRELAND

Scale 1:8,000,000 (128 miles = 1 inch)

Land allotted to English soldiers
and adventurers (including
Connaught and Clare for four
miles from the shore).
Land reserved for 'innocent'
native proprietors throughout
Ireland.
G.B. Government Reservations.

Boundary between Eire and
Northern Ireland. (December, 1925)

Continuation
Southwards
on Half Scale

	Austrian Dominions
	Spanish Dominions
	Hohenzollern Dominions (Brandenburg-Prussia)
	Swedish Dominions
	Church Lands
	Boundary of the Empire

20East from Greenwich25

CENTRAL & EASTERN EUROPE in 1667

Scale 1:12,000,000 (192 miles = 1 inch)

Statute Miles

0   50   100   200   300

CRETE
(To Venice 1212
Turk. 1669)
On same scale

To Venice 1699-1718
Turk. 1669

Austrian Dominions
Kingdom of Prussia
Swedish Dominions
Church Lands
Boundary of the Empire

0   A   5   D   20 East from Greenwich 25   F   30   G   35

a

N O R W A Y

Trondhjem

FINLAND

Gulf of Bothnia

S W E D E N

C A R E L I A

60

Bergen

Christiania

DALECARLIA

Gävle

Willmanstrand

Wäräla

L. Ladoga

60

Upsala

Nystad Åland

Anigla

Åbo

Helsingfors

Svedborg

Viborg 1721

Kronstadt

Fredrikshald

Stockholm

Gulf of Finland

St. Petersburg

b

L. Wener

Nerköping

Dagö

ESTHONIA 1721

Reval

Narva 1721

INGRIA

Novgorod

L. Ilmen

Volga

b

L. Wetter

Linköping

Osel

G. of Riga

Dorpat 1721

LIVONIA 1721

L. Peipus

Pskov

N O R T H

Gotland

Riga

Tver

Gothenburg

Öland

B A L T I C   S E A

Mitau

KURLAND

Polotsk

Vitebsk

Smolensk

Moscow

Kaluga

55

Karlskrona

Memel

Libau

Dvina

WHITE RUSSIA

1772

Mscislaw

55

S E A

Christianstad

Bornholm

Memel

Kovno

Vilna

Beresina

Mohilev

Minsk

Heligoland (To Denmark)

SCHLESWIG

Fünen

Zeeland Copenhagen

Stralsund 1793

Danzig

EAST Königsberg

Gross Jägersdorf

Grodno 1795

Niemen

BLACK RUSSIA 1795

Chernigov

Amsterdam

BATAVIAN REPUBLIC

Altona Hamburg

Lübeck

Wismar

SWEDISH POMERANIA

Elbing

Marienburg

WEST PRUSSIA Kulm 1772

NETZE

Mazovia

Bug

Brest Litovsk

PODLESIA

Pripet 1793

Czartorysk

c

Ghent Malines

Crefeld

Oldenburg

Bremen

Verden

HANOVER

Magdeburg

BRANDENBURG

Berlin

Stettin

POMERANIA

Thorn

Posen

Dobrzyn

SOUTH PRUSSIA

Warsaw

Praga

Radzyn

Dubienka

LITTLE RUSSIA

Kiev

c

Brussels Liège

Düsseldorf

Cassel

Leipzig

Frankfurt

Cottbus

Oder

SAXONY

Kalisz 1793

Breslau

Radom

Sandomir

Lublin

VOLHYNIA

Aix-la-Chapelle

Cologne

Elberfeld

SAXE-WEIMAR

Dresden

SILESIA

Szczekorny 1795

Raslawice

Baslawice

Lemberg

50

Coblenz

FRENCH REPUBLIC

Mainz

Ehrenbreitstein

Frankfurt

Neustadt

Neisse

Grocow Crocow

GALICIA 1772

UKRAINE

Poltawa

50

Treves

Darmstadt

Prague

BOHEMIA

Olmütz Teschen

Simdec

PODOLIA

Nemirov

Targowica

Strassburg

Mannheim

Nuremberg

Ratisbon

MORAVIA

Brünn

Carpathian

Bar

Dniester

d

Vosges

ALSACE

Stuttgart

Ingolstadt

Danube

BAVARIA

Augsburg

Munich

ZIPS

Hungarian Ore Mts

Munkacz

Theiss

BUKOWINA 1775

BESSARABIA

Balta

Bug

Yekaterinoslav

d

Basle

Berne

SWISS CONFEDERATION

St. Gothard

Klagenfurt

Salzburg

TYROL

CARINTHIA

Vienna

Pressburg

STYRIA

Graz

Grat Buda

Tokaj

Pest

HUNGARY

JEDISAN 1792

Ochakov

Kherson

Geneva

SAVOY

Turin

Milan

KINGDOM OF PIEDMONT

REP. OF VENICE

CARNIOLA

Laibach

Drave

Mohacs

Zenta

TRANSYLVANIA

Jassy MOLDAVIA

Seredu

Focsani

Bender

Akerman

Odessa

Kinburn

Perekop

e

Lyon

Nice

Toulon

Bassano

Padua

Mantua

Venice

CROATIA

Save

SLAVONIA

Peterwardein

BANAT OF 1718

Temesvar

TEMESVAR

Transylvanian Alps

WALLACHIA

Bucharest

Galatz

Braila

Ismail

Ilia

DOBRUJA

Kozlov (Eupatoria) 1783

Bakhchisarai

Sevastopol

Kaffa

CRIMEA

e

Marseilles

GENOA

REP. of Loano

Parma

Modena

Giustalla

ADRIATIC SEA

DALMATIA

BOSNIA

Belgrade

Passarowitz

Smederevo

Semendria (To Austria 1718-1739)

SERVIA

Nish

Danube

Giurgevo

Silistria

Ruschuk

Sistova

Kutchuk Kainarji

Varna

B L A C K   S E A

CORSICA

REP. OF GENOA

Lucca

Florence

TUSCANY

PAPAL STATES

HERZEGOVINA

MONTE-NEGRO

Scutari

Novibazar

Sofia

B a l k a n s

B U L G A R I A

Philippopolis

Adrianople

Constantinople

Bosporus

Rome

Pontecorvo

KINGDOM OF THE TWO SICILIES

Monastir

Rhope

S. of Marmara

Angora

40

SARDINIA

Naples

Beneveto

Salonica

Dardanelles

O T T O M A N   E M P I R E

Smyrna

Konia

40

TYRRHENIAN SEA

Corfu

Pindus

ALBANIA

GREECE

AEGEAN SEA

Taurus

Palermo

SICILY

Messina

Morea

Athens

Cerigo

Cesme

Rhodes

CRETE (Turkish 1669) On same scale

Canea

Candia

35   25

CENTRAL & EASTERN **EUROPE** in 1795

Scale 1:12,000,000 (192 miles = 1 inch)

Statute Miles

0   50   100   200   300

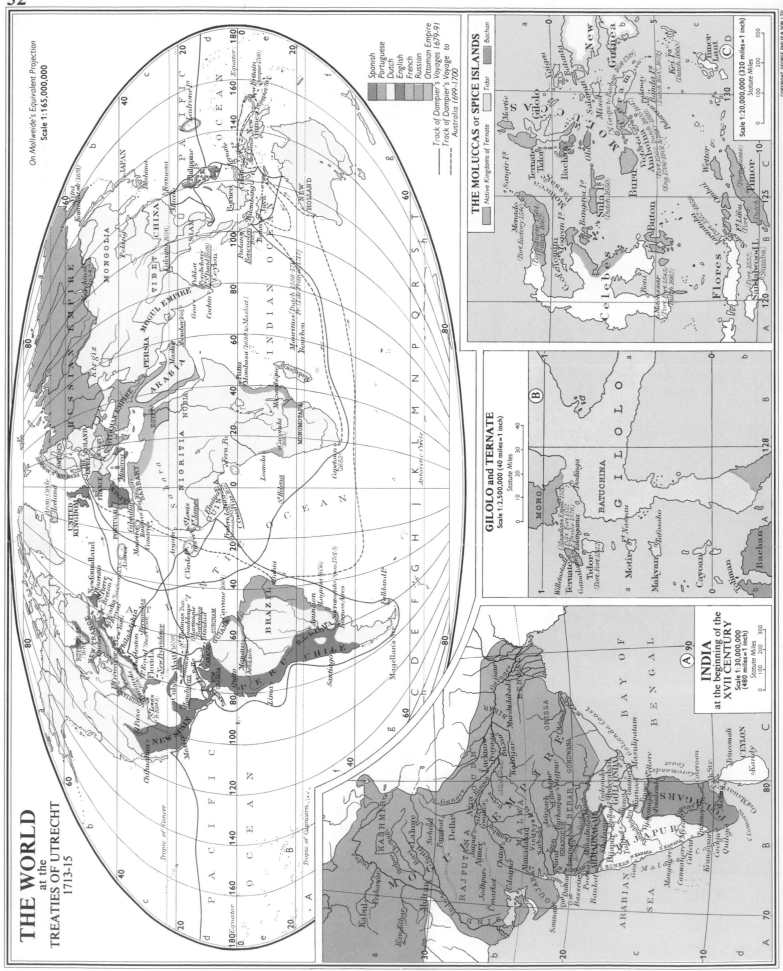

52

THE WORLD
at the
TREATIES OF UTRECHT
1713-15

On Mollweide's Equivalent Projection
Scale 1:165,000,000

Spanish
Portuguese
Dutch
English
French
Russian
Ottoman Empire 1679-91

Track of Dampier's Voyages
Track of Dampier's Voyage to
Australia 1699-1700

THE MOLUCCAS or SPICE ISLANDS
Native Kingdoms of Ternate
Tidor
Bachan

Scale 1:20,000,000 (320 miles = 1 inch)
Statute Miles

GILOLO and TERNATE
Scale 1:2,500,000 (40 miles = 1 inch)
Statute Miles

INDIA
at the beginning of the
XVII CENTURY
Scale 1:30,000,000 (480 miles = 1 inch)
Statute Miles

COPYRIGHT, GEORGE PHILIP & SON, LTD.

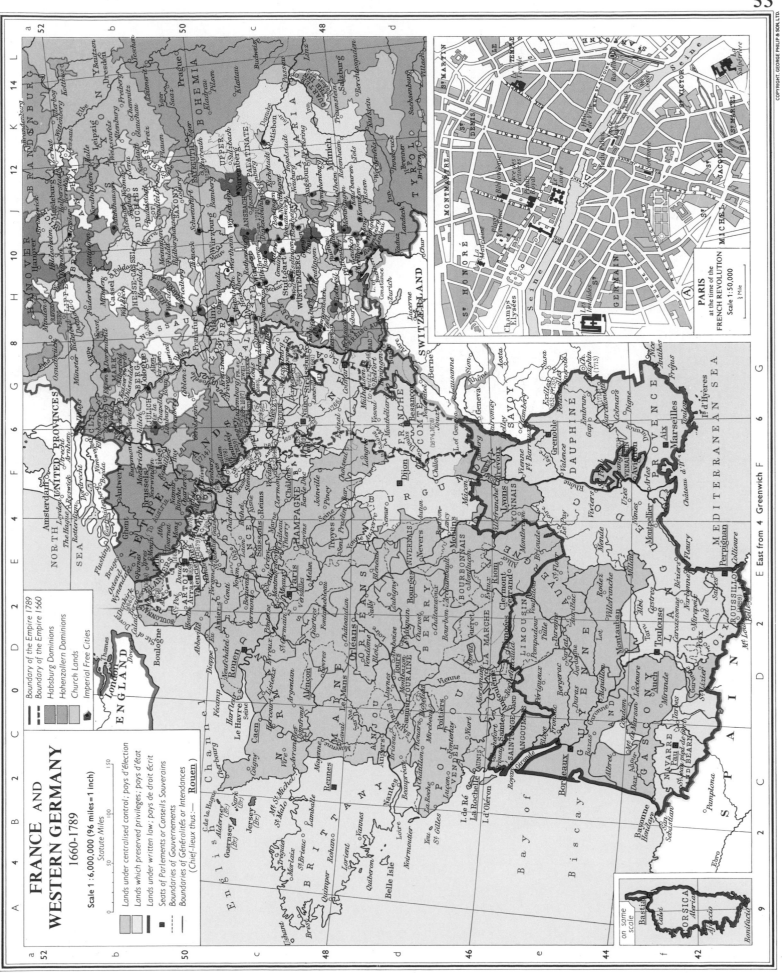

FRANCE AND WESTERN GERMANY
1660-1789

Scale 1 : 6,000,000 (96 miles=1 inch)

Statute Miles

Boundary of the Empire 1789
Boundary of the Empire 1560
Habsburg Dominions
Hohenzollern Dominions
Church Lands
Imperial Free Cities

Lands under centralised control: pays d'Élection
Lands which preserved privileges: pays d'état
Lands under written law: pays de droit écrit
Seats of Parlements or Conseils Souverains
Boundaries of Gouvernements
Boundaries of Généralités or Intendances
(Chief-lieux thus:— Rouen)

PARIS
at the time of the
FRENCH REVOLUTION
Scale 1:50,000

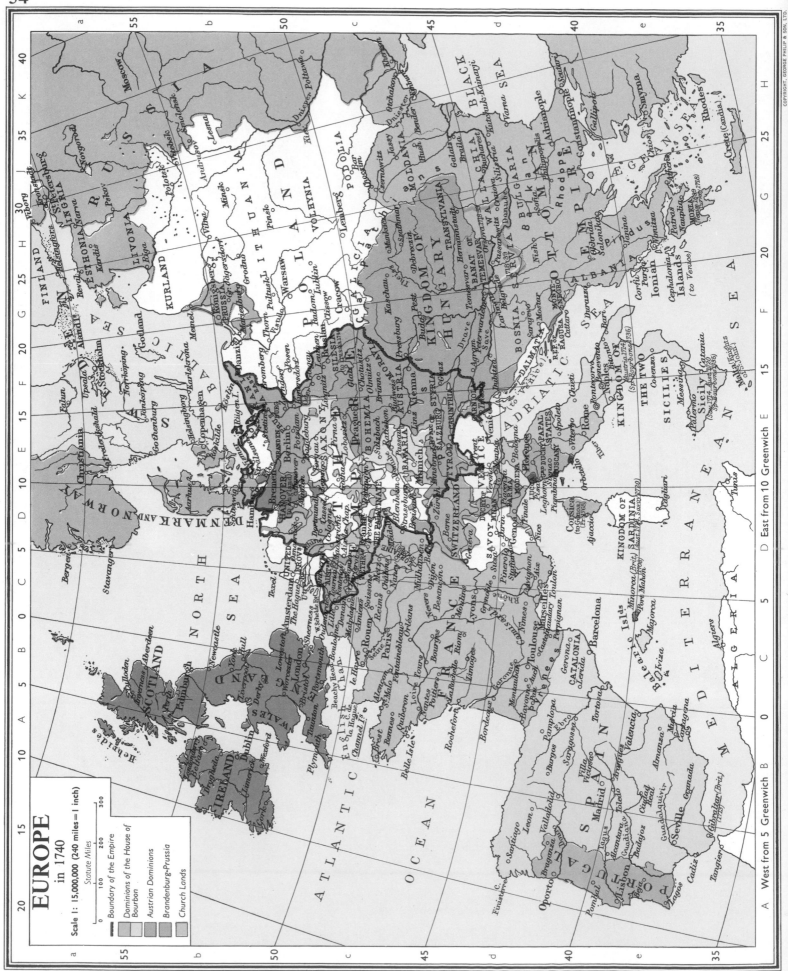

EUROPE
in 1740

Scale 1 : 15,000,000 (240 miles = 1 inch)

Statute Miles

0   100   200   300

Boundary of the Empire
Dominions of the House of Bourbon
Austrian Dominions
Brandenburg-Prussia
Church Lands

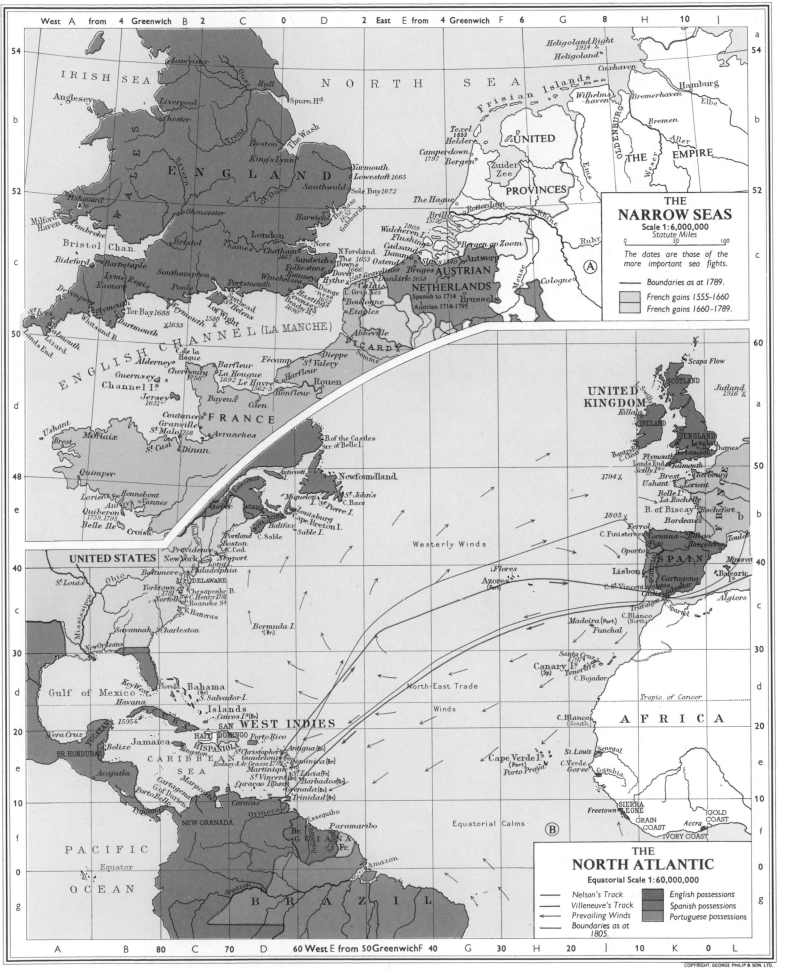

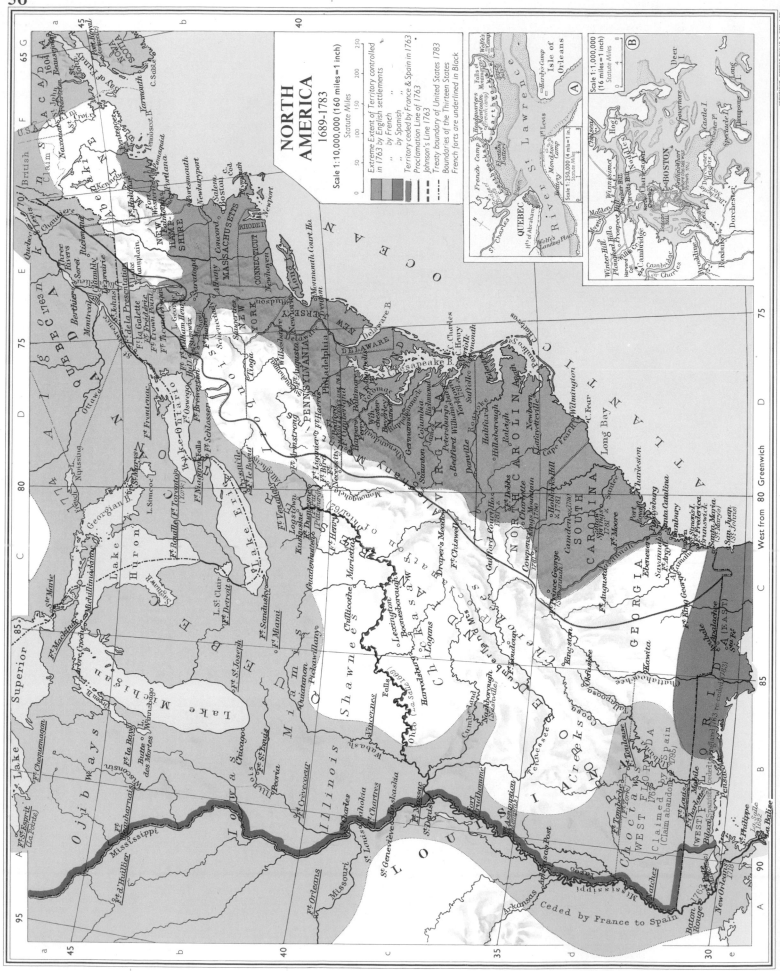

NORTH AMERICA
1689-1783

Scale 1:10,000,000 (160 miles=1 inch)

Statute Miles

0   50   100   150   200   250

Extreme Extent of Territory controlled
in 1763 by English settlements
"   "   "   by French
"   "   "   by Spanish
Territory ceded by France & Spain in 1763
Proclamation Line of 1763
Johnson's Line 1763
Treaty boundary of United States 1783
Boundaries of the Thirteen States
French forts are underlined in Black

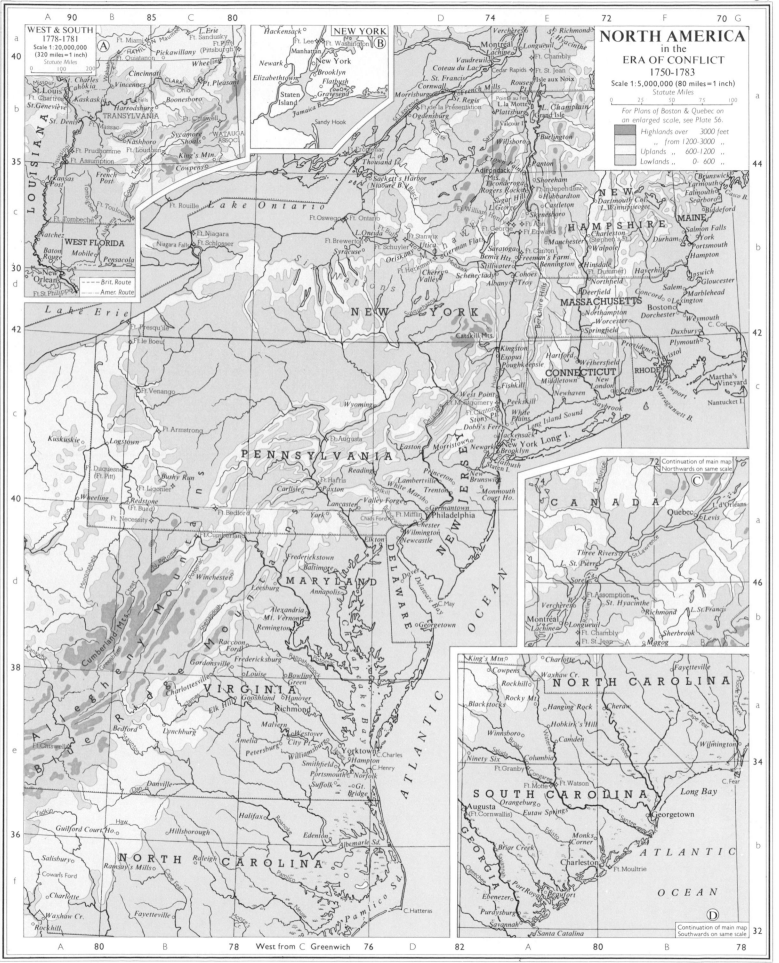

WEST & SOUTH
1778-1781
Scale 1:20,000,000
(320 miles=1 inch)
0 100 200 Statute Miles

NEW YORK

NORTH AMERICA
in the
ERA OF CONFLICT
1750-1783
Scale 1:5,000,000 (80 miles=1 inch)
Statute Miles
0 25 50 75 100

For Plans of Boston & Quebec on
an enlarged scale, see Plate 56.

Highlands over 3000 feet
,, from 1200-3000 ,,
Uplands ,, 600-1200 ,,
Lowlands ,, 0- 600 ,,

— — — Brit. Route
— · — · — Amer. Route

72 Continuation of main map
Northwards on same scale

Continuation of main map
Southwards on same scale

West from Greenwich

COPYRIGHT, GEORGE PHILIP & SON, LTD.

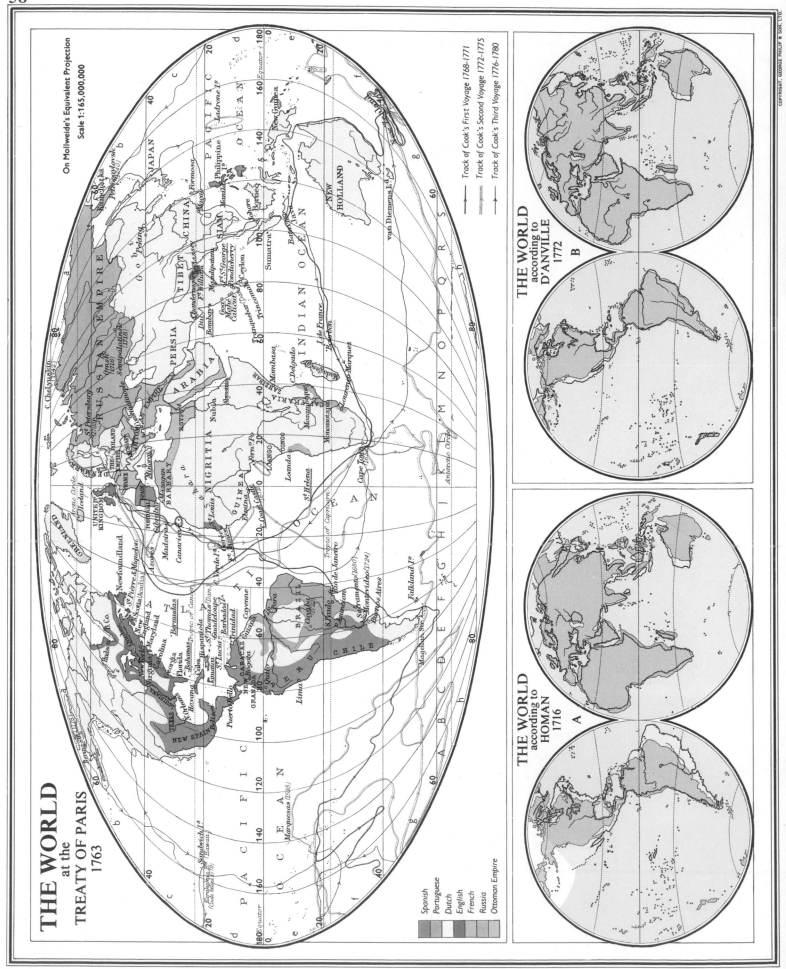

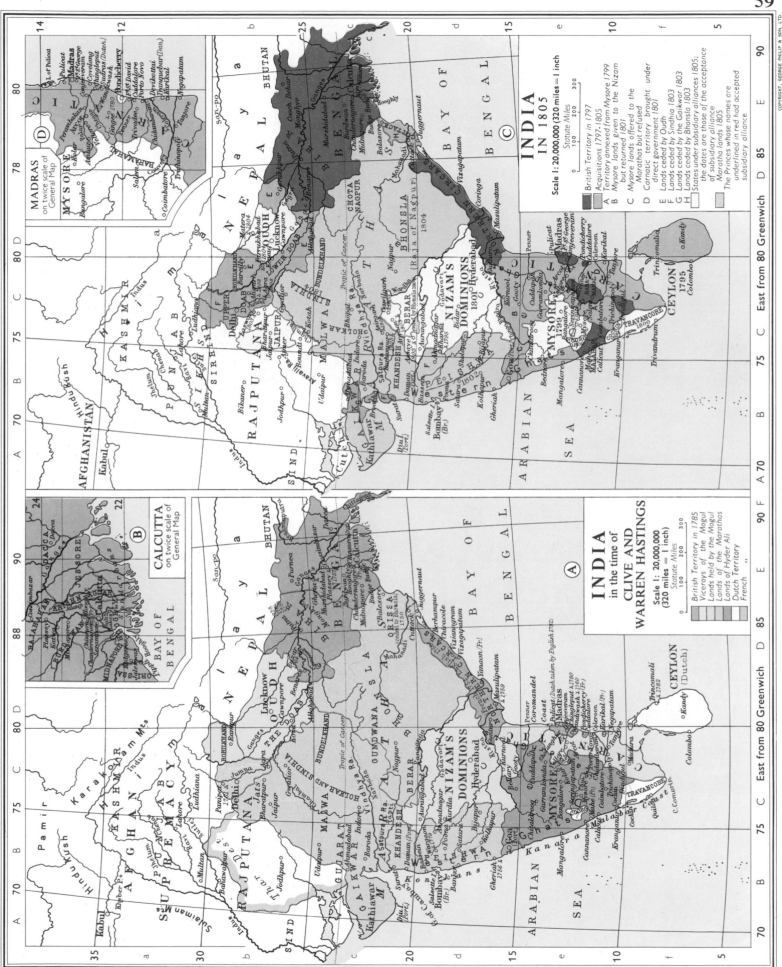

INDIA
IN 1805

Scale 1: 20,000,000 (320 miles = 1 inch)

Statute Miles
0   100   200   300

British Territory in 1797
A Acquisitions 1797-1805
B Territory annexed from Mysore 1799
   Mysore lands given to the Nizam
C Mysore lands offered to the
   Marathas but refused
   but returned 1801
D Carnatic territory brought under
   direct government 1801
E Lands ceded by Oudh
F Lands ceded by Sindhia 1803
G Lands ceded by the Gaikwar 1803
H Lands ceded by Bhonsla 1803
   States under subsidiary alliances 1805:
   the dates are those of the acceptance
   of subsidiary alliance
   Maratha lands 1805
   The Princes whose names are
   underlined in red had accepted
   subsidiary alliance

MADRAS
on twice scale of General Map

MYSORE

CALCUTTA
on twice scale of General Map

INDIA
in the time of
CLIVE AND
WARREN HASTINGS

Scale 1: 20,000,000
(320 miles = 1 inch)

Statute Miles
0   100   200   300

British Territory in 1785
Viceroys of the Mogul
Lands held by the Mogul
Lands of the Marathas
Lands of Hyder Ali
Dutch Territory
French "

East from 80 Greenwich

COPYRIGHT, GEORGE PHILIP & SON, LTD.

Map A

THE GROWTH OF BRANDENBURG-PRUSSIA

Scale 1:6,000,000 (96 miles = 1 inch)

Statute Miles
0   25   50   75   100

- Brandenburg at death of Frederick I. 1440
- Acquisitions 1440-1608
- Acquisitions 1608-1624
- Acquisitions under the Great Elector, 1640-1688
- Acquisitions under Frederick III, (I. of Prussia) 1689-1713 & Frederick William I., 1713-1740
- Acquisitions under Frederick the Great 1740-1786
- Acquisitions under Frederick William II., 1786-1797
- Second Partition of Poland
- Third Partition of Poland
- Acquisitions under Frederick William III., 1797-1807

Map labels (A): NORTH SEA · Heligoland (Dan.1714-1807, Br.1807-90) · SCHLESWIG · HOLSTEIN · BALTIC SEA · Memel · Tauroggen 1691,1793 · Tilsit · Niemen · Königsberg · Pregel · Gt. Jägersdorf · Pillau · EAST PRUSSIA · Eylau · Friedland · Serrey 1691-1793, 1795 · Heilsberg · ERMLAND 1618 · Grodno · Marienwerder · Elbing · Danzig · Oliva 1793 · Lauenburg 1657 · NEW EAST PRUSSIA 1795 (Third Partition) · Tannenberg · WEST PRUSSIA 1772 (First Partition) · Marienburg · Kolberg · KAMMIN 1648 1657 · Stralsund 1657 · Rostock · Stettin · Draheim 1657 · Thorn · Netze · Bromberg · Vistula · Plock · Bug · Hamburg · Stade · Kloster Zeven · Lüneburg · MECKLENBURG · W. POMERANIA 1720 · EASTERN POMERANIA · Bahn 1679 · UKERMARK 1472 · Bremen · Verden · Elbe · Celle · PRIEGNITZ · Ruppin 1524 · NEUMARK 1455 · Küstrin · Gnesen · SOUTH PRUSSIA · Posen · Warsaw · EAST FRIESLAND Emden 1744 · Tingen 1702 · B'PRIC OF MINDEN 1648 · Hanover · Brunswick · ALTMARK Stendal · Havelberg · MITTELMARK · Brandenburg 1537 · Berlin · Spandau · Küstrin · Kunersdorf 1680 · Zorndorf · Meseritz · Warthe 1793 · Tecklenburg 1707 · Osnabrück · Minden 1648 · Hildesheim 1803 · RAVENSBERG 1614 · Bielefeld · HALBERSTADT 1648 · Magdeburg 1680 · Potsdam · Zossen 1490 · Storkow 1571 · Frankfurt 1686-95,1742 · Zullichau · Warthe · Ravenstein · CLEVES 1614 · Wesel 1609 · Hamm · MARK 1614 · Paderborn 1803 · Warburg · Wernigerode · HARZ · HOHENSTEIN 1680 · MANSFELD 1780 · Halle 1680 · Wittenberg · Luckenwalde · Barwalde 1462 · KOTTBUS 1462 · LOWER LAUSITZ · GUELDERS 1715-1801 · Crefeld · BERG · Essen 1803 · Verden 1803 · Corbach · EICHSFELD 1803 · Lutterburg · Merseburg 1680 · Rossbach · Torgau · Hubertusburg · UPPER LAUSITZ · Glogau · LOWER SILESIA · Wohlau · Liegnitz · Breslau · Jülich · Gimborn · Cassel · Fulda · Weimar 1803 · Erfurt 1803 · Gotha · Leipzig · Chemnitz · SAXONY · Kesselsdorf · Görlitz · Hennersdorf · Leuthen · Aix-la-Chapelle · Cologne · Rhine · Marburg · THURINGIAN FOREST · Freiberg · Dresden · Pillnitz · Bautzen · Hochkirch · Hirschberg · Landeshut · Hohenfriedberg · Schweidnitz · UPPER SILESIA · Mollwitz 1740 · Brieg · Coblenz · Frankfurt · Hanau · Dettingen · Ore Mts. · Maxen · Pirna · Lobositz · Soor · Glatz 1742 · Neisse 1741 · Neisse · Kosel · Beuthen 1603-7,1750 · Klein Schnellendorf · NEW SILESIA 1795 · Mainz · Worms · Würzburg · Fulda · BAYREUTH 1426 40,1470-86, Bayreuth 1791 · Bamberg · Eger · Bohemian Forest · Prague · Königgrätz · Kolin · Czaslau · Chotusitz · Troppau · Jägerndorf 1603,7,21 · AUSTRIAN SILESIA · Teschen · Ansbach 1415 40,1470-86 · Nuremberg · ANSBACH · BOHEMIA · LIMPURG 1713-42 1791 · BAVARIA · Pilsen · Tisek · Olmütz · Brünn · Neuchâtel 1707 (Fr.)

Map B

THE GROWTH OF PRUSSIA

Scale 1:6,000,000 (96 miles = 1 inch)

Statute Miles
0   25   50   75   100

- Prussia at the Treaty of Tilsit 1807
- Territory regained by the Treaty of Vienna 1815
- New territory acquired by the Treaty of Vienna, 1815
- Acquisitions 1815-1866
- *Bonn* University Towns

Map labels (B): NORTH SEA · Heligoland (Ger. 1890, Pruss. 1891) · DENMARK · Malmö · SCHLESWIG · Alsen · Düppel · HOLSTEIN · Kiel 1866 · Fehmarn · BALTIC SEA · Rügen I. · Stralsund · Greifswald · POMERANIA · Kolberg · Rep. of Danzig · Königsberg · Tilsit · Niemen · Eylau · EAST PRUSSIA · Bartenstein · Marienburg · Marienwerder · United 1824-78 · WEST PRUSSIA · Kulm · Thorn · Ostrolenka · Eider · Cuxhaven · Lübeck · Wismar · SCHWERIN · MECKLENBURG · STRELITZ · Lauenburg 1865 · Stettin · BRANDENBURG · POSEN 1815 · Warthe · Vistula · Bug · Pultusk · Warsaw · NETHERLANDS · Emden · Bremerhaven · Bremen · PR. OF OLDENBURG 1854 · HANOVER · Celle · Lüneburg · Elbe · ALTMARK · Schönhausen · Potsdam · Berlin · Spree · Küstrin · Frankfurt · Grossbeeren · Oder · POSEN · RUSSIA · Osnabrück · Minden · Hanover · Detmold · Brunswick · Brandenburg · Magdeburg · Dennewitz · ANHALT · Wittenberg · LOWER LAUSITZ 1815 · Glogau · Kalisz · Pilica · Cleves · Münster · WESTPHALIA 1815 · Halberstadt · HARZ · Göttingen · Halle · Torgau · UPPER LAUSITZ · Hainau · Bautzen · Glogau · SILESIA · Breslau · Crefeld · Düsseldorf · RHINE PROVINCE 1815 · Aix · Cologne · Bonn · HESSEN · Cassel · Jerra · Langensalza · Weimar · Erfurt · Gotha · Jena · Leipzig · Lützen · Chemnitz · SAXONY · Dresden · Kulm 1815 · Teplitz · Giant Mts. · Wahlstatt · Schweidnitz · Brieg · Reichenbach · Sudetes · Trautenau · Moshle · Coblenz · NASSAU · Marburg · Giessen · HESSE DARMSTADT · Weilzar · Ems · Frankfurt · Ore Mts. · Münchengrätz · Gotschin · Sadowa · Königgrätz · Oder · Troppau · Treves · Meisenheim (to Oldenburg) · Wiesbaden · Mainz · Würzburg · BOHEMIA · Prague · Teplitz · HOHENZOLLERN 1849 SIGMARINGEN · Hechingen · Neuchâtel 1815-52 (Pr.) · Doubs · Danube

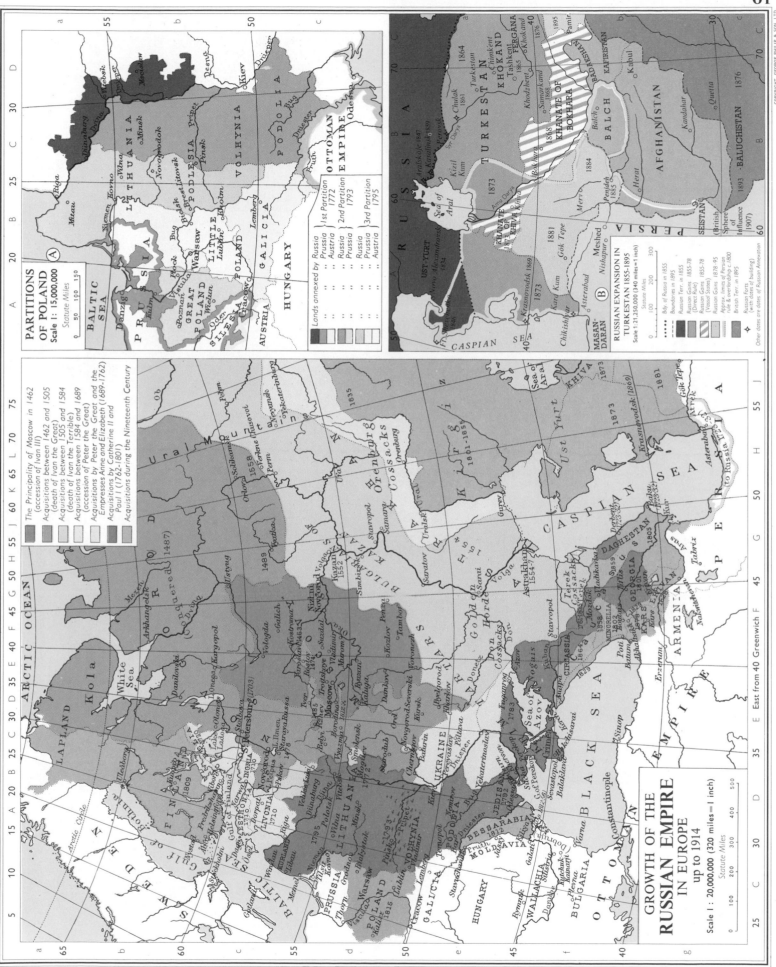

PARTITIONS OF POLAND
Scale 1: 15,000,000

Statute Miles
0   50   100   150

Lands annexed by Russia
Prussia
Austria } 1st Partition 1772

Russia
Prussia
Austria } 2nd Partition 1793

Russia
Prussia
Austria } 3rd Partition 1795

Ⓐ

BALTIC SEA

Mitau Riga
Niemen Kovno Vilna Minsk
LITHUANIA

Danzig Kulm
Bielsk Brest-Litovsk Pinsk Pripet PODLESIA
Novogrodok PODOLIA
Bug Dnieper

PRUSSIA
Odzno Plock
Poznan GREAT POLAND Warsaw LITTLE Lublin Kholm VOLHYNIA
Oder Wielun POLAND
SILESIA Cracow GALICIA Lemberg
AUSTRIA HUNGARY

Drebesk Smolensk
Moscow
Desna
Kiev Dnieper
OTTOMAN EMPIRE Odessa

RUSSIAN EXPANSION IN TURKESTAN 1855-1895
Scale 1:21,250,000 (340 miles=1 inch)

Ⓑ

Bdy. of Russia in 1855
Boundaries in 1895
Russian Terr. in 1855
Russian Gains 1855-78 (Direct Rule)
Russian Gains 1855-78 (Vassal States)
Russian Gains 1878-95
Approx. limits of Persian rule & overlordship c.1800
British Terr. in 1895
Russian Forts (with dates of building)

Statute Miles
0 100 200 300

Other dates are dates of Russian Annexation

R U S S I A
UST-YURT
Hulakoje 1859 Turkistan 1864
Kizil Kum
Sea of Aral
Novo Alexandrovsk 1834
Irgadii 1847 Kasalinsk 1859
Perovsk
Syr Darya
TURKESTAN Chimkent 1864 Tashkent 1865
Khodzhent 1866
Samarkand 1868
Bokhara KHANATE OF BOKHARA 1868
FERGANA Khokand Khokand 1876
Margelan 1875
Pamir 1895
BADAKHSHAN

KHANATE OF KHIVA Khiva 1873
1873 Amu Darya
1873

Krasnovodsk 1869
Gok Tepe 1881
Kizil Kum
Kand Kum
Merv 1884
Penjdeh 1885
Askabad

BALCH Balch
Kabul KAFIRISTAN
AFGHANISTAN Kandahar Quetta 1876
Herat
BALUCHISTAN 1876
1893 SEISTAN
British Sphere of Influence (1907)
Meshed Nishapur
Asterabad PERSIA
MASAN-DARAN
Chikishlyar
CASPIAN SEA

GROWTH OF THE RUSSIAN EMPIRE
IN EUROPE up to 1914

Scale 1 : 20,000,000 (320 miles=1 inch)

Statute Miles
0 100 200 300 400 500

The Principality of Moscow in 1462 (accession of Ivan III)
Acquisitions between 1462 and 1505 (death of Ivan the Great)
Acquisitions between 1505 and 1584 (death of Ivan the Terrible)
Acquisitions between 1584 and 1689 (accession of Peter the Great)
Acquisitions by Peter the Great and the Empresses Anne and Elizabeth (1689-1762)
Acquisitions by Catherine II and Paul I (1762-1801)
Acquisitions during the Nineteenth Century

ARCTIC OCEAN
Arctic Circle
Kola
LAPLAND White Sea
SWEDEN Lapland
Gulf of Bothnia FINLAND
Mezen
Arkhangel
Onega
Kargopol
Ural Mountains
Ob
Tobolsk
Ekaterinburg 1835
Perm 1558
Cherdyn
Vyatka
Vologda
Galich 1463
Conquered 1487
Ustyug
Dvina

NORWAY SWEDEN
Abo Helsingfors Petersburg (1703)
ESTHONIA 1710
Dorpat 1710
LIVONIA 1710 Pskov
Novgorod 1478
Tver 1485
Moscow 1300
Kaluga
Vladimir
Nizhni Novgorod
Kazan 1552
Simbirsk
Samara
Saratov
Ufa
Orenburg
Orenburg Cossacks
1489

KURLAND Riga Dvinsk
LITHUANIA Vilna Vitebsk
Polotsk Smolensk 1772
Minsk 1793
POLAND Warsaw 1815
PRUSSIA Thorn Grodno Kalisz
GALICIA Cracow Lemberg
VOLHYNIA 1795
PODOLIA
AUSTRIA HUNGARY

Kiev 1667
UKRAINE
Dnieper
Ekaterinoslav
Kharkov Belgorod-Seversk Kursk
Voronezh Tambov Penza
BULGARS
KAZAN
Simbirsk
K I R G I Z
1801-1855
Ust Yurt
KHIVA 1873 1873
1881

Don Cossacks Don
Tsaritsyn Volga Astrakhan 1554-7
GOLDEN HORDE
Sarai

Sea of Azov 1783
BLACK SEA
Crimea Sevastopol Perekop
BESSARABIA 1812
MOLDAVIA
WALLACHIA BULGARIA
Bucharest Danube Pruth Dniester
OTTOMAN EMPIRE
Constantinople Sinop

CAUCASUS
Kuban Nogais CIRCASSIA 1829
Terek Cossacks DAGHESTAN
Kutais GEORGIA Tiflis 1801 1859
MINGRELIA Batum 1878 Kars 1878
Poti ARMENIA Erzeram
Erivan Kars Alexandropol Nakhichevan Tabriz

CASPIAN SEA
Baku 1806 Derbent
Krasnovodsk (1869) 1873
Asterabad
Gok Tepe 1881 Atrek
(to Russia 1731)
PERSIA

East from 40 Greenwich

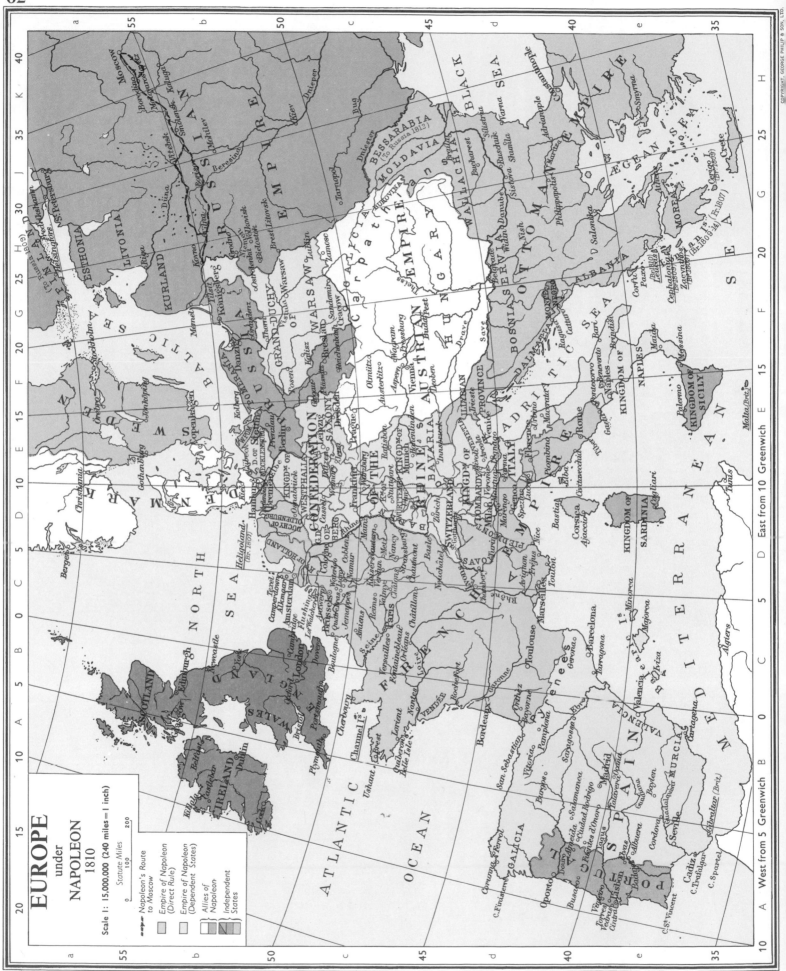

EUROPE
under
NAPOLEON
1810

Scale 1: 15,000,000 (240 miles = 1 inch)

Statute Miles
100   200

Napoleon's Route to Moscow
Empire of Napoleon (Direct Rule)
Empire of Napoleon (Dependent States)
Allies of Napoleon
Independent States

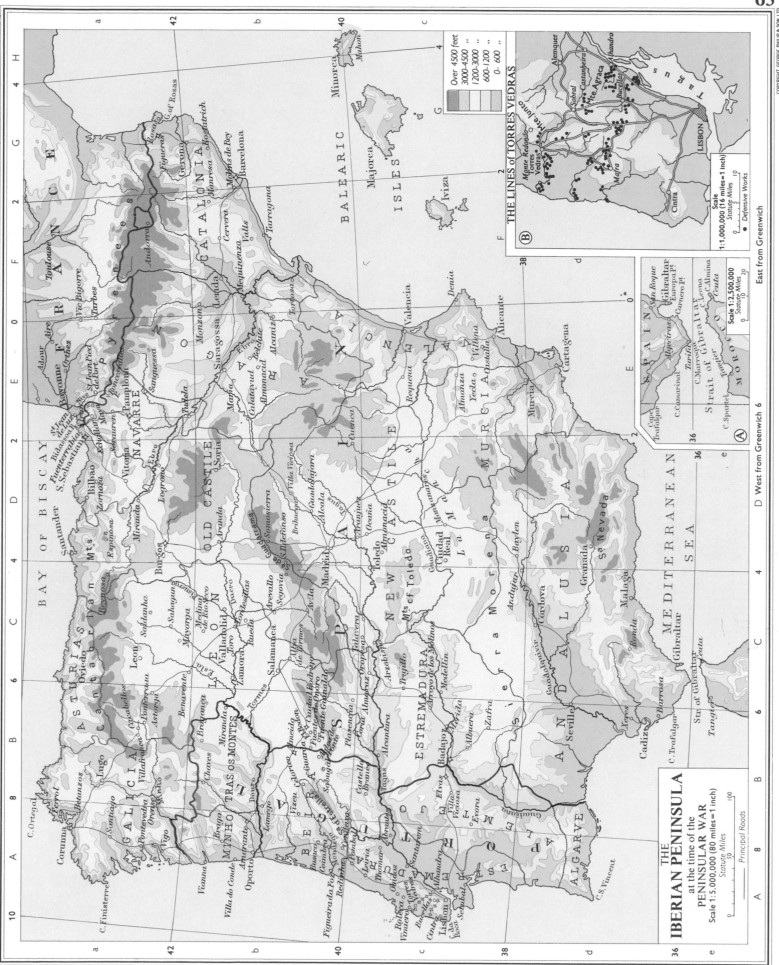

THE
IBERIAN PENINSULA
at the time of the
PENINSULAR WAR
Scale 1:5,000,000 (80 miles=1 inch)

Statute Miles
Principal Roads

THE LINES OF TORRES VEDRAS

Scale
1:1,000,000 (16 miles=1 inch)
Statute Miles
● Defensive Works

Over 4500 feet
3000-4500
1200-3000
600-1200
0- 600

Scale 1:2,500,000
Statute Miles

West from Greenwich   East from Greenwich

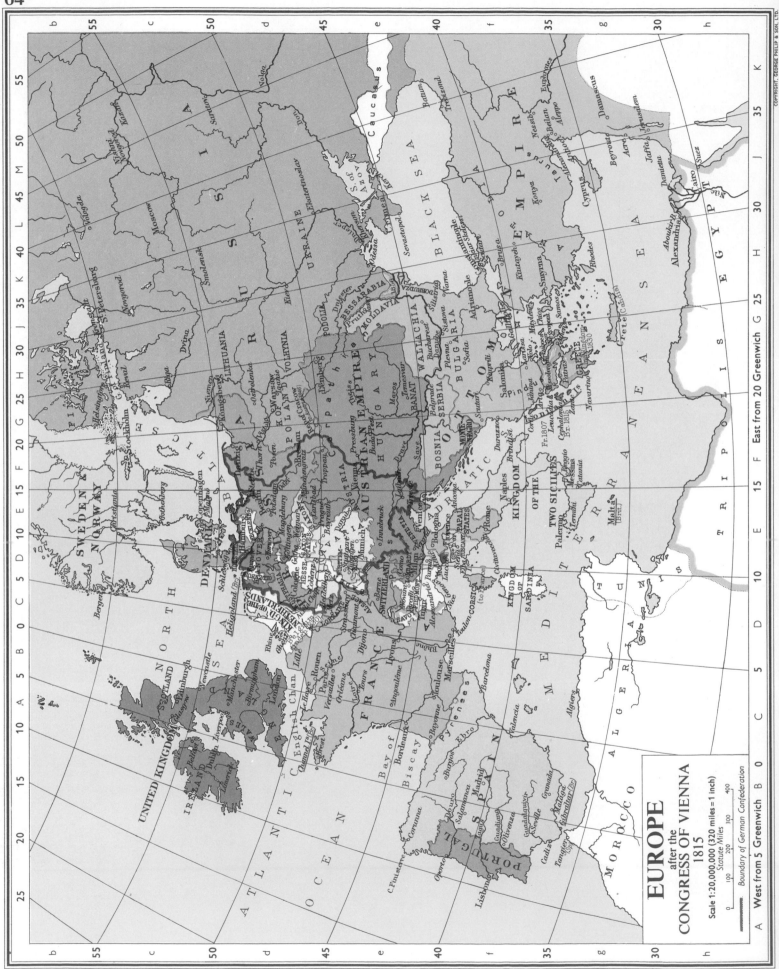

EUROPE
after the
CONGRESS OF VIENNA
1815

Scale 1:20,000,000 (320 miles = 1 inch)

Statute Miles
0   100   200   300   400

▬▬▬▬ Boundary of German Confederation

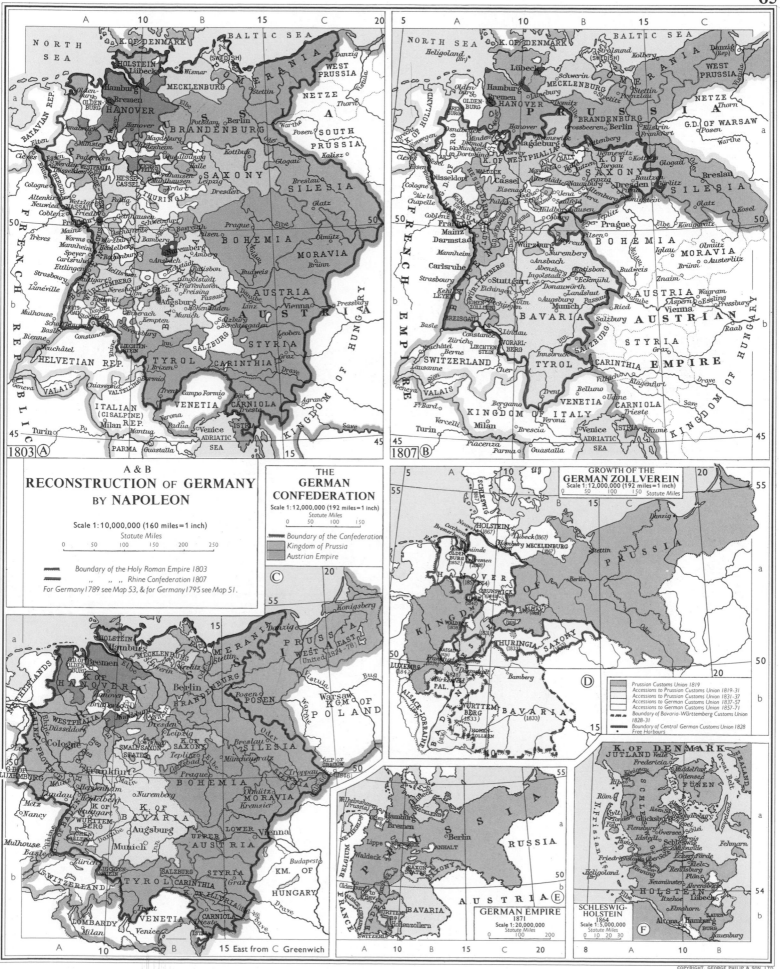

1803 Ⓐ

1807 Ⓑ

A & B
RECONSTRUCTION of GERMANY BY NAPOLEON

Scale 1:10,000,000 (160 miles = 1 inch)

Statute Miles

0   50   100   150   200   250

〰〰〰 Boundary of the Holy Roman Empire 1803
═══   „   „   „   Rhine Confederation 1807
For Germany 1789 see Map 53, & for Germany 1795 see Map 51.

THE GERMAN CONFEDERATION
Scale 1:12,000,000 (192 miles = 1 inch)

Statute Miles
0   50   100   150

〰〰 *Boundary of the Confederation*
Kingdom of Prussia
Austrian Empire

Ⓒ

GROWTH OF THE GERMAN ZOLLVEREIN
Scale 1:12,000,000 (192 miles = 1 inch)
0   50   100   150
Statute Miles

Ⓓ

Prussian Customs Union 1819
Accessions to Prussian Customs Union 1819-31
Accessions to Prussian Customs Union 1831-37
Accessions to Prussian Customs Union 1837-57
Accessions to German Customs Union 1857-71
Boundary of Bavaria-Württemberg Customs Union 1828-31
Boundary of Central German Customs Union 1828
Free Harbours

Ⓔ

GERMAN EMPIRE 1871
Scale 1:20,000,000
0   100   200
Statute Miles

Ⓕ

SCHLESWIG-HOLSTEIN 1864
Scale 1:5,000,000
0 10 20 30
Statute Miles

15 East from Greenwich

COPYRIGHT, GEORGE PHILIP & SON, LTD.

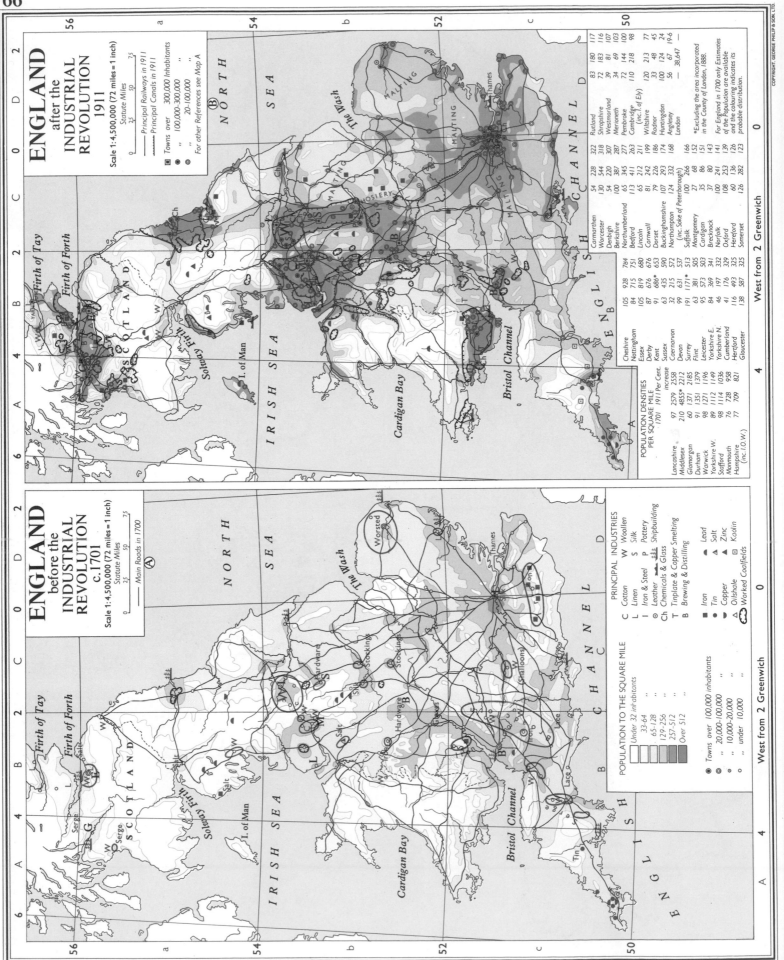

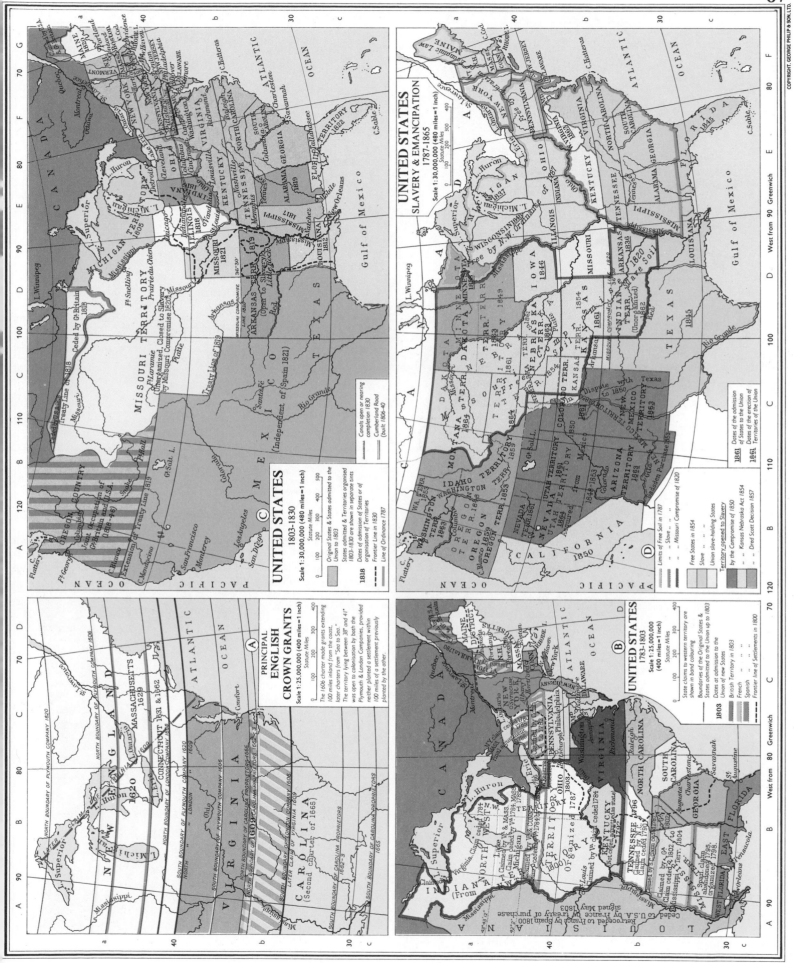

SOUTH AMERICA
in the
XIX & XX CENTURIES
Scale 1:30,000,000 (480 miles=1 inch)
Statute Miles

0   200   400   600

- Approximate Boundaries of States in 1830
- Boundaries subsequently & finally adjusted
- Boundary of Greater Colombia, 1819-30
- Boundary of Federation of Bolivia & Peru 1835-39

West from 50 Greenwich

GUYANA
BOUNDARY
Scale 1:24,000,000 (384 miles=1 inch)
Statute Miles

0   100   200   300

- Present Bdy. of Guyana
- Br. Guiana. Bdy. settlement 1899
- Original Schomburgk Line
- Extension of Schomburgk Line
- Extreme Venezuelan Claim
- Extreme British Claim

NORTH WEST
SOUTH AMERICA
Conflicting Territorial Claims
Scale 1:40,000,000 (640 miles=1 inch)
Statute Miles

0   200   400   600

Boundaries fixed by Treaty

The conflicting claims of the various states are shown by narrow bands of their respective colours.

COPYRIGHT. GEORGE PHILIP & SON, LTD.

THE WORLD
IN 1830
(A)

On Mollweide's Equivalent Projection
Scale 1:165,000,000

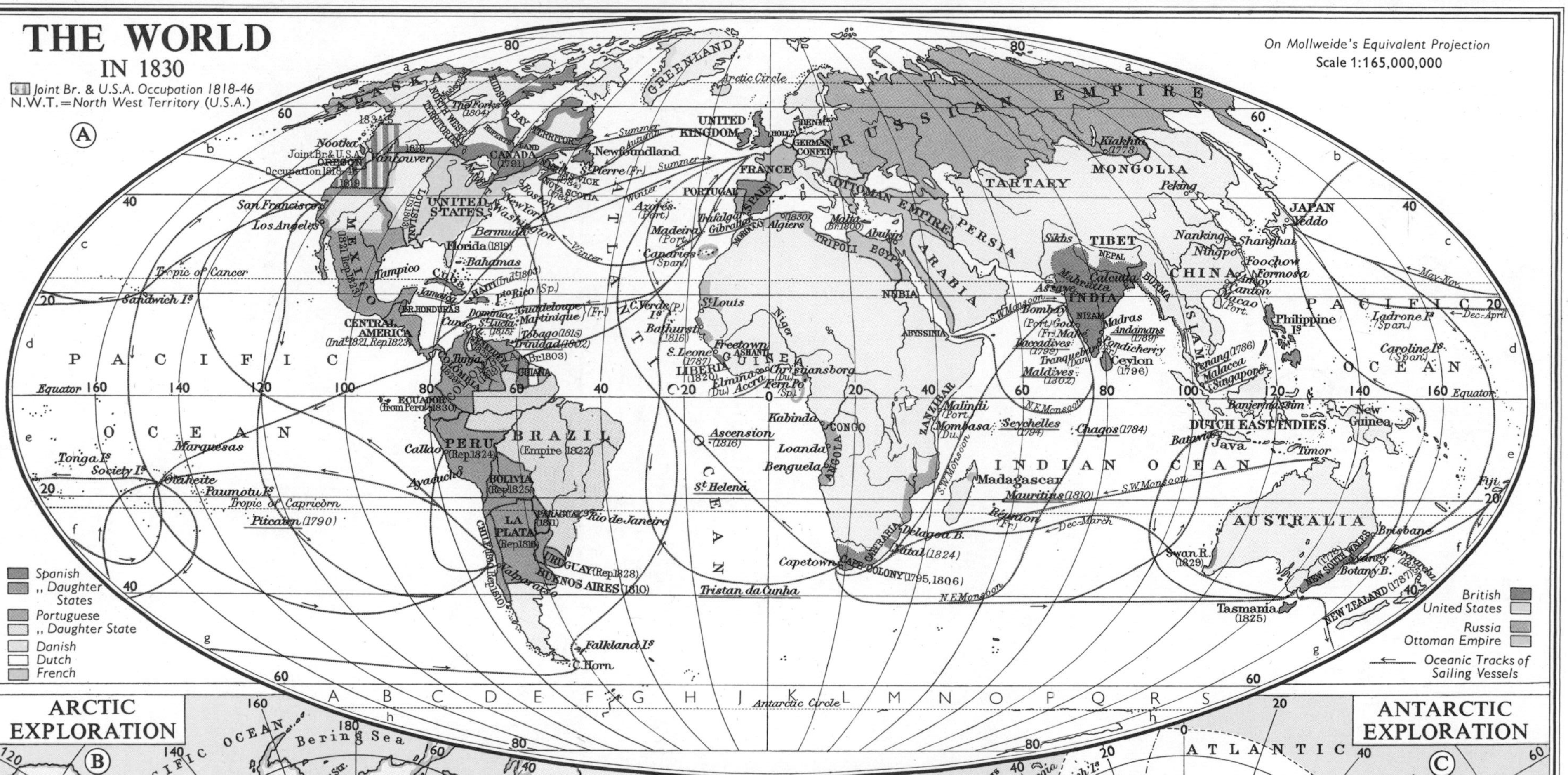

Joint Br. & U.S.A. Occupation 1818-46
N.W.T. = North West Territory (U.S.A.)

Spanish | Daughter States
Portuguese " Daughter State
Danish
Dutch
French

British
United States
Russia
Ottoman Empire
Oceanic Tracks of Sailing Vessels

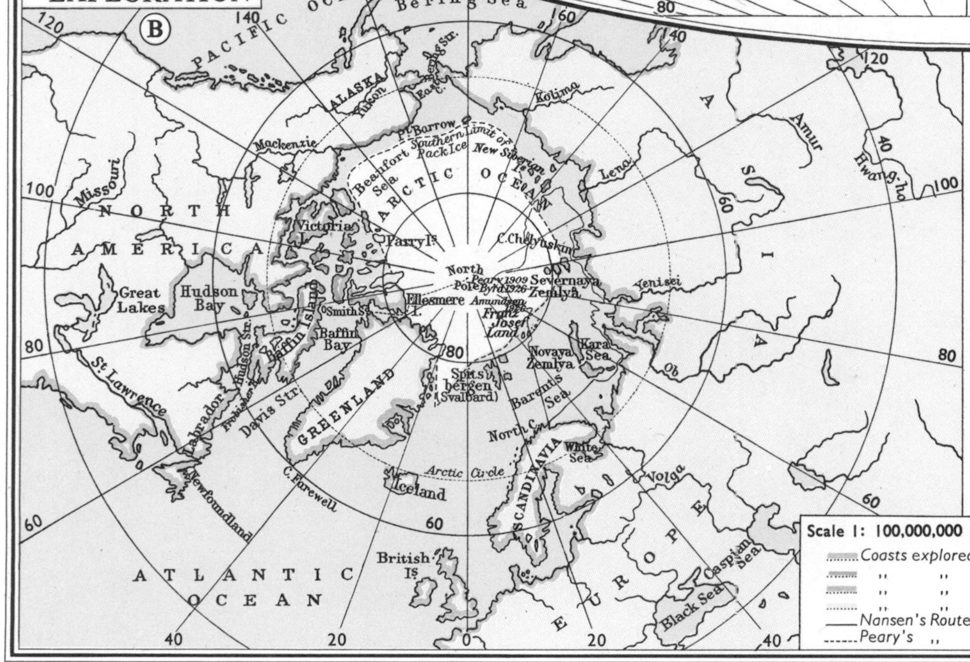

ANTARCTIC EXPLORATION
(C)

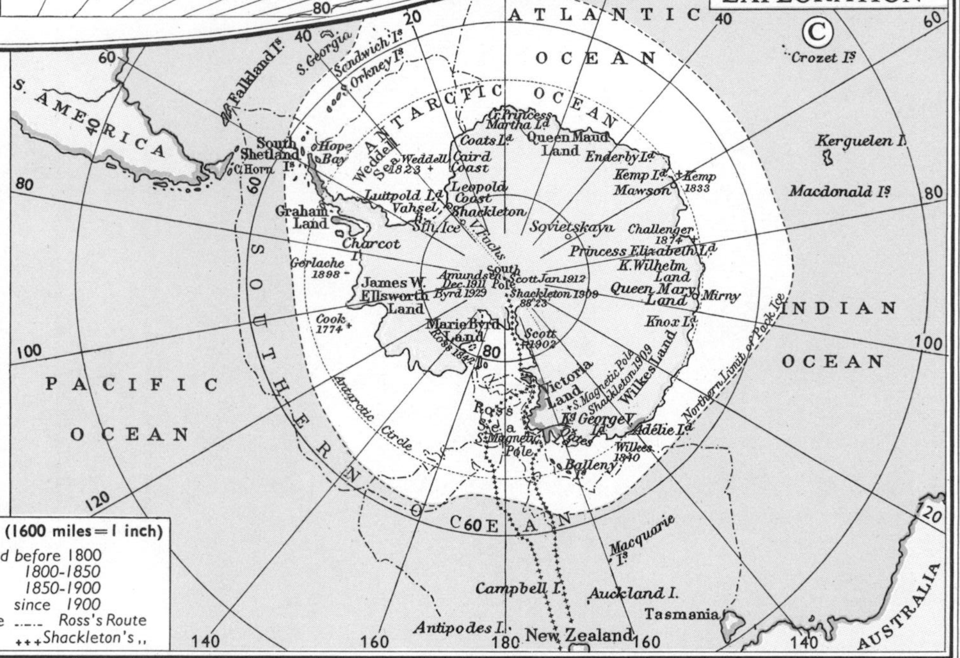

Scale 1: 100,000,000 (1600 miles = 1 inch)

Coasts explored before 1800
" " 1800-1850
" " 1850-1900
" " since 1900
Nansen's Route
Peary's "
Ross's Route
Shackleton's "

ARCTIC EXPLORATION
(B)

ALASKA 140 A 130 B 120 C 110 D 100 E 90 F 80 G 70 H

British North America

The Colonies in 1841
The Provinces of the Dominion
The Territories of the Dominion
Former boundaries of territories

Dates shown thus **1784** *are those of the organisation of the various colonies, and thus* **1867** *of the admission of the various provinces to the Dominion.*

Principal Trails & Mail Routes

═OT═ Oregon Trail
═SFT═ Santa Fé Trail
═ST═ Spanish Trail
═PE═ Pony Express
═BOM═ Butterfield Overland Mail

Principal Railroads

In operation up to 1848
" " 1848 to 1869
" " 1869 to 1890

C 110 D 100 West from E Greenwich 90 F 80

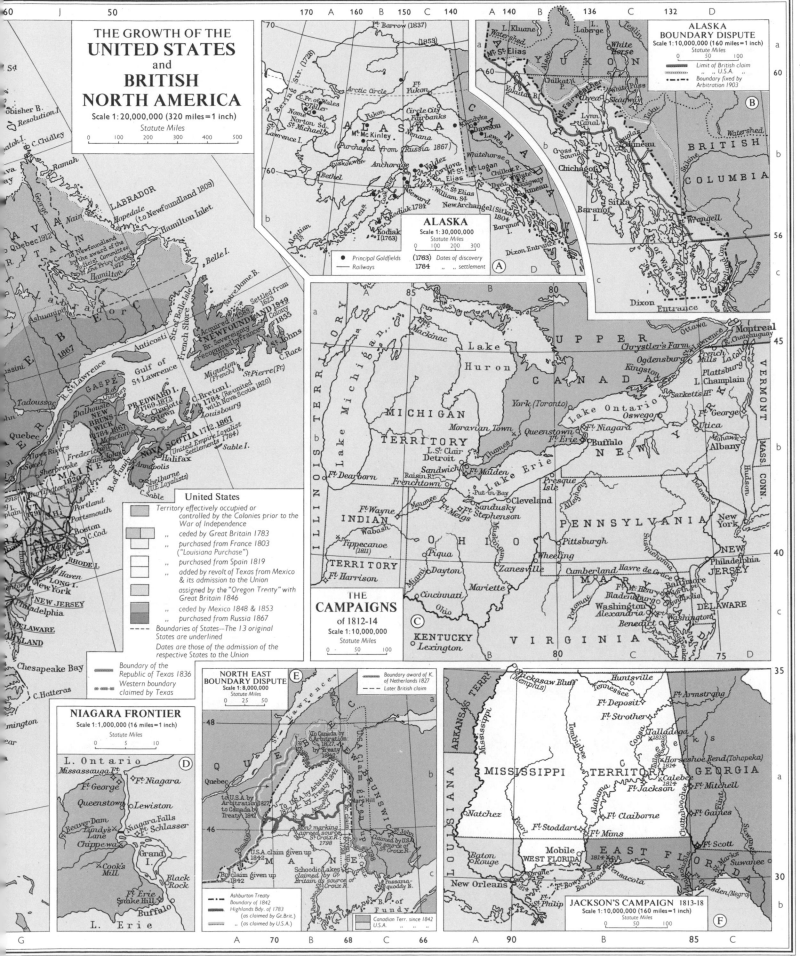

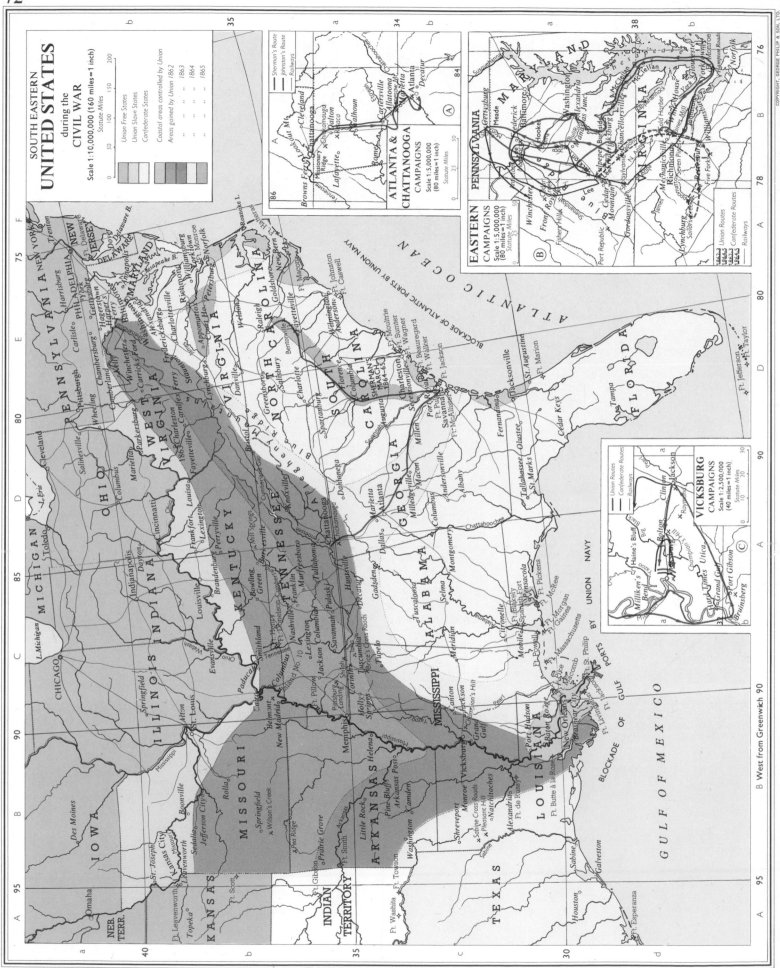

72

SOUTH EASTERN
UNITED STATES
during the
CIVIL WAR
Scale 1:10,000,000 (160 miles=1 inch)
Statute Miles

Union Free States
Union Slave States
Confederate States
Coastal areas controlled by Union 1862
Areas gained by Union 1862
" " " " 1863
" " " " 1864
" " " " 1865

ATLANTA &
CHATTANOOGA
CAMPAIGNS
Scale 1:5,000,000
(80 miles=1 inch)
Statute Miles

— Sherman's Route
— Johnston's Route
Railways

A

EASTERN
CAMPAIGNS
Scale 1:5,000,000
(80 miles=1 inch)
Statute Miles

Union Routes
Confederate Routes
Railways

B

VICKSBURG
CAMPAIGNS
Scale 1:2,500,000
(40 miles=1 inch)
Statute Miles

— Union Routes
— Confederate Routes
Railways

C

ATLANTIC OCEAN

BLOCKADE OF ATLANTIC PORTS BY UNION NAVY

GULF OF MEXICO

BLOCKADE OF GULF PORTS BY UNION NAVY

COPYRIGHT. GEORGE PHILIP & SON, LTD.

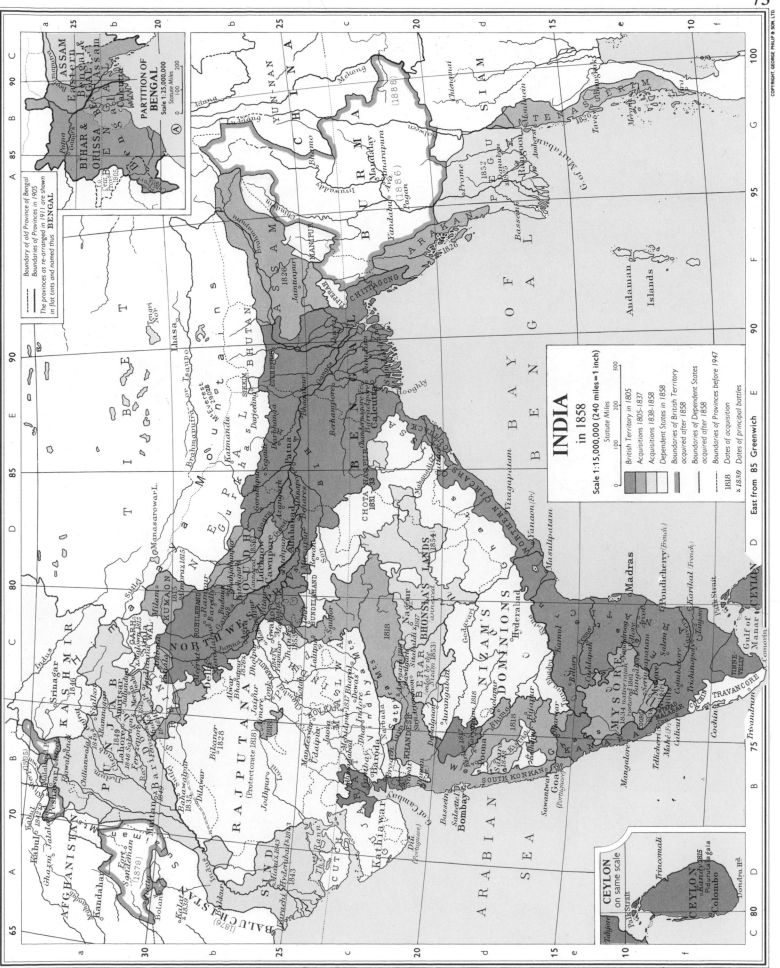

PARTITION OF BENGAL

Scale 1:25,000,000

Boundary of old Province of Bengal
Boundaries of Provinces in 1905
The provinces as re-arranged in 1911 are shown in flat tints and named thus BENGAL

ASSAM
Eastern Bengal
BIHAR & ORISSA
BENGAL

INDIA in 1858

Scale 1:15,000,000 (240 miles = 1 inch)
Statute Miles

British Territory in 1805
Acquisitions 1805–1837
Acquisitions 1838–1858
Dependent States in 1858
Boundaries of British Territory acquired after 1858
Boundaries of Dependent States acquired after 1858
Boundaries of Provinces before 1947
1818 Dates of acquisition
✕1839 Dates of principal battles

East from 85 Greenwich

CEYLON on same scale

COPYRIGHT. GEORGE PHILIP & SON, LTD.

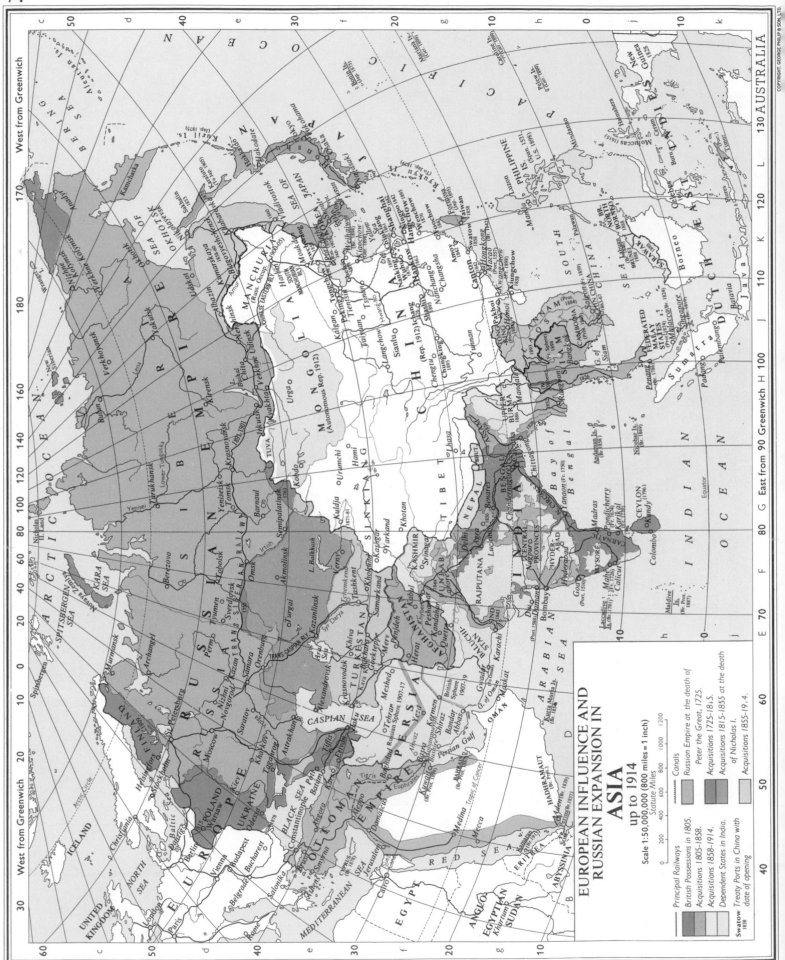

EUROPEAN INFLUENCE AND
RUSSIAN EXPANSION IN
ASIA
up to 1914

Scale 1:50,000,000 (800 miles = 1 inch)

Statute Miles

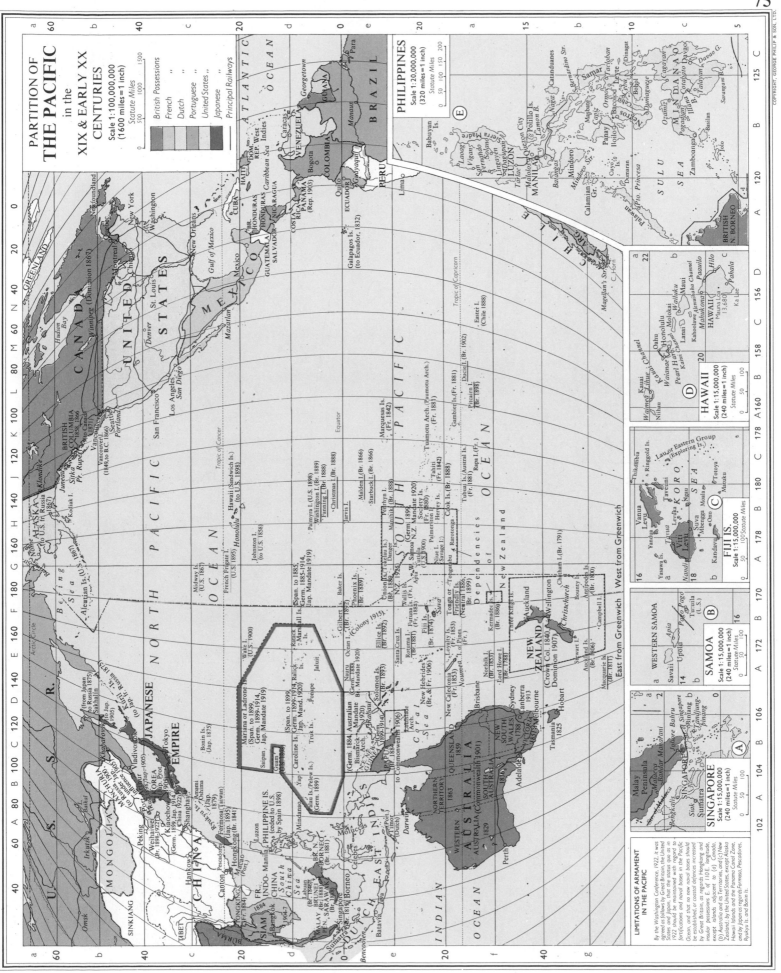

PARTITION OF
THE PACIFIC
in the
XIX & EARLY XX
CENTURIES

Scale 1:100,000,000
(1600 miles = 1 inch)

Statute Miles

British Possessions
French   "
Dutch   "
Portuguese "
United States, "
Japanese   "
Principal Railways

PHILIPPINES
Scale 1:20,000,000
(320 miles=1 inch)
Statute Miles

HAWAII
Scale 1:15,000,000
(240 miles=1 inch)
Statute Miles

FIJI IS.
Scale 1:15,000,000
Statute Miles

WESTERN SAMOA

SAMOA
Scale 1:15,000,000
(240 miles=1 inch)
Statute Miles

SINGAPORE
Scale 1:15,000,000
(240 miles=1 inch)
Statute Miles

LIMITATIONS OF ARMAMENT
IN THE PACIFIC

By the Washington Conference, 1922, it was
agreed as follows:- by Great Britain, the United
States and Japan, that the status quo as in
1922 should be maintained with regard to
fortifications and naval bases in the Pacific
Ocean, and that no new naval bases should
be established, or coastal defences increased
by Great Britain, as regards Hong Kong and
insular possessions E. of 110 E. longitude,
except islands adjacent to (a) Canada,
(b) Australia and its Territories, and (c) New
Zealand; by the United States, except Alaska,
Hawaii Islands and the Panama Canal Zone,
and by Japan as regards Formosa, Pescadores,
Ryukyu Is. and Bonin Is.

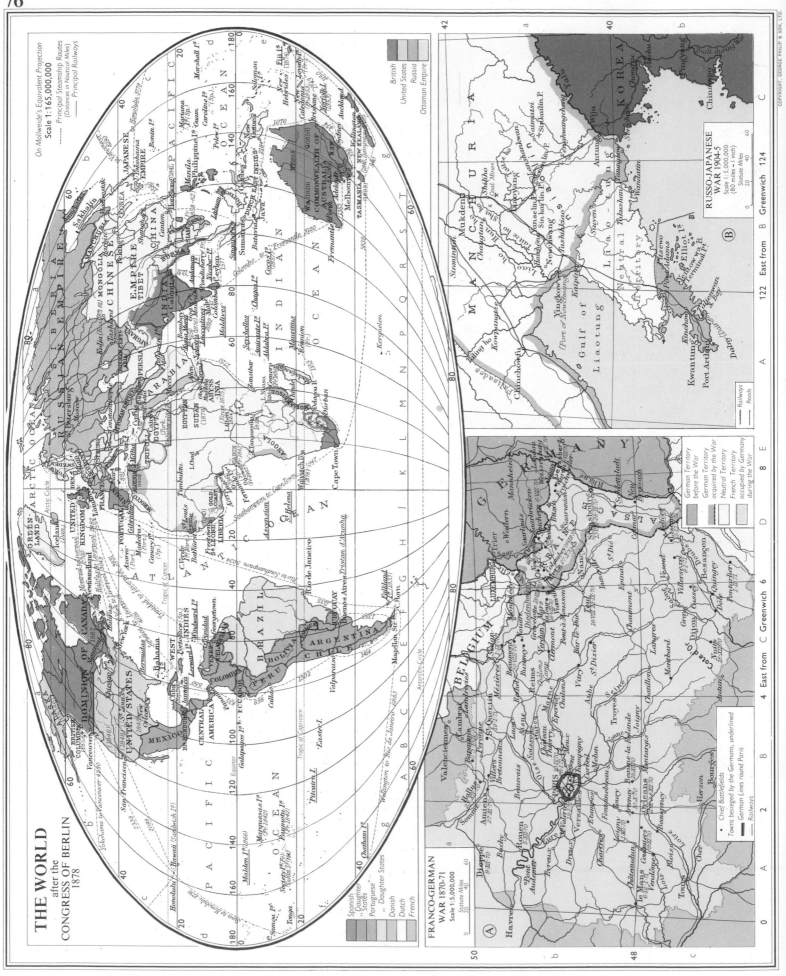

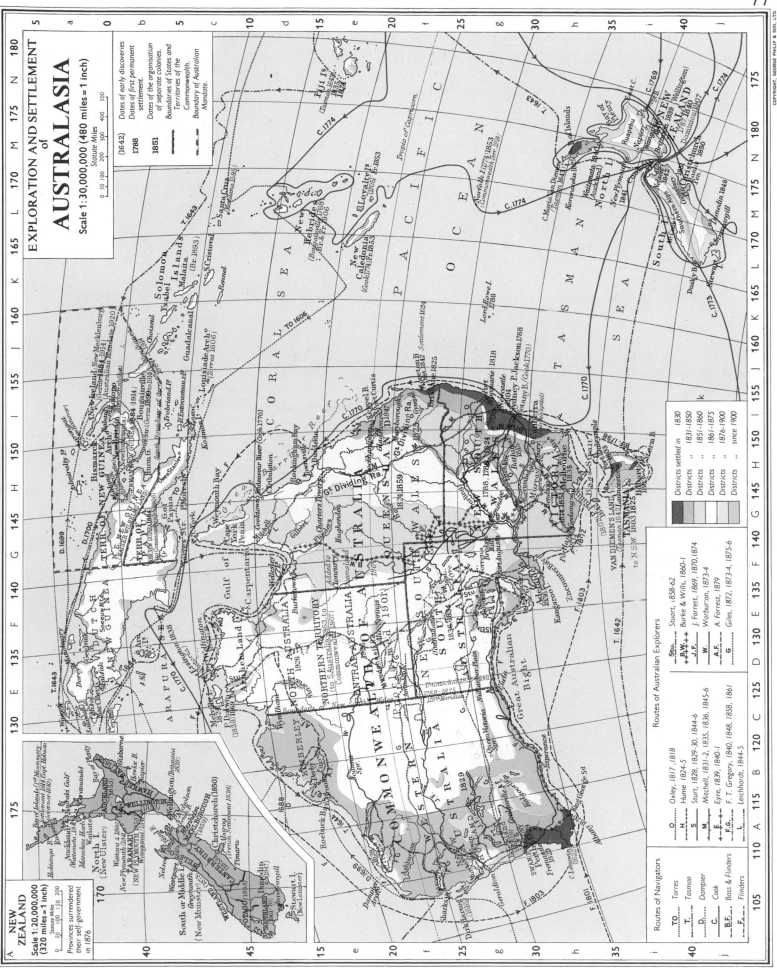

EXPLORATION AND SETTLEMENT
of
AUSTRALASIA

Scale 1:30,000,000 (480 miles = 1 inch)

Statute Miles

(1642) Dates of early discoveries
1788 Dates of first permanent settlement.
1851 Dates of the organisation of separate colonies.
Boundaries of States and Territories of the Commonwealth.
Boundary of Australian Mandate.

NEW ZEALAND
Scale 1:20,000,000
(320 miles = 1 inch)

Statute Miles
0 50 100 150 200

Provinces surrendered their self-government in 1876

Districts settled in 1830
Districts " 1831-1850
Districts " 1851-1860
Districts " 1861-1875
Districts " 1876-1900
Districts " since 1900

Routes of Navigators
T.O. — Torres
T. — Tasman
D. — Dampier
C. — Cook
B.F. — Bass & Flinders
F. — Flinders

Routes of Australian Explorers
O — Oxley, 1817, 1818
H — Hume 1824-5
S — Sturt, 1828, 1829-30, 1844-6
M — Mitchell, 1831-2, 1835, 1836, 1845-6
E — Eyre, 1839, 1840-1
F.G. — F. T. Gregory, 1840, 1848, 1858, 1861
L — Leichhardt, 1844-5
Stu. — Stuart, 1858-62
B.W. — Burke & Wills, 1860-1
J.F. — J. Forrest, 1869, 1870, 1874
W. — Warburton, 1873-4
A.F. — A. Forrest, 1879
G — Giles, 1872, 1873-4, 1875-6

COPYRIGHT, GEORGE PHILIP & SON, LTD.

78

THE DECLINE OF THE
OTTOMAN EMPIRE
1683-1924

Scale 1:15,000,000 (240 miles=1 inch)

Statute Miles

Losses

| 1683-99 (T. of Carlowitz) |
| 1700-18 (T. of Passarowitz) |
| 1719-74 (T. of Kutchuk-Kainarji) |
| 1775-1812 (T. of Bucharest) |
| 1813-29 (T. of Adrianople) |

| 1830-78 (T. of Berlin) |
| 1879-1915 (Ts. of London & Bucharest) |
| 1916-23 (T. of Lausanne) |
| Turkey in 1923 |
| Boundary after Treaty of Sèvres 1920 |
| Boundary after Treaty of Lausanne 1923 |
| Boundary after Hatay, to Turkey 1939 |

Boundaries of Spheres of Influence in Anatolia after the 1914-18 War.

Dates of Russian acquisitions in W. Caucasus thus:—1829

LIST OF ABBREVIATIONS
ABK.	ABKHAZIA	IM.	IMERETIA
ACH.	ACHALZICH	MIN.	MINGRELIA
B.	BATUM	MONT.	MONTENEGRO
C.	CATTARO	N.	NOVIBAZAR
G.	GURIA	P.	POTI
HA.	HATAY	V.	VONITSA
HER.	HERZEGOVINA		

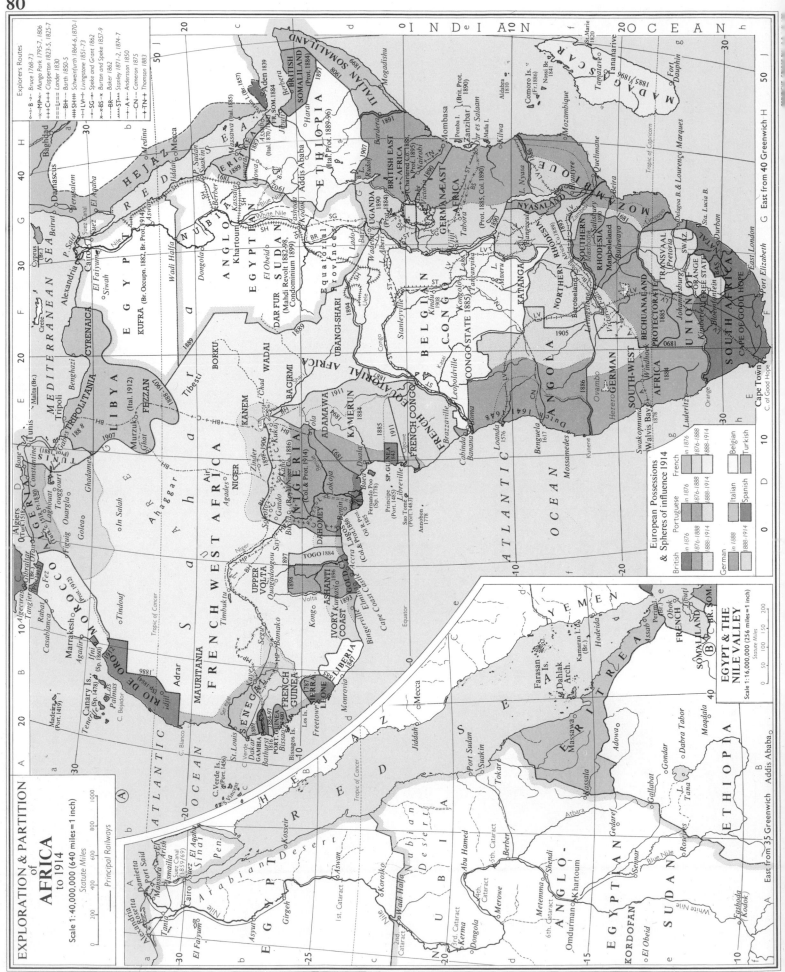

EXPLORATION & PARTITION of AFRICA to 1914

Scale 1: 40,000,000 (640 miles = 1 inch)

Statute Miles

——— Principal Railways

Ⓐ

Explorers Routes

B ○○ Bruce 1768-73
MP○ Mungo Park 1795-7, 1806
C++ Clapperton 1823-5, 1825-7
L═══ Lander 1830
BH━━ Barth 1850-5
SH╋╋╋ Schweinfurth 1864-6, 1870-1
LW━━ Livingstone 1851-73
SG×× Speke and Grant 1862
BS×× Burton and Speke 1857-9
BR━━ Baker 1862
A▲▲ Anderson 1850
CN━━ Cameron 1875
TN╋╋ Thomson 1883

European Possessions & Spheres of influence 1914

British
In 1876 | 1876–1888 | 1888–1914

French
In 1876 | 1876–1888 | 1888–1914

Portuguese
In 1876 | 1876–1888 | 1888–1914

German
In 1888 | 1888–1914

Belgian | Turkish

Italian | Spanish

B EGYPT & THE NILE VALLEY

Scale 1:16,000,000 (256 miles=1 inch)

Statute Miles
0   50   100 150 200

East from 35 Greenwich B East from 40 Greenwich

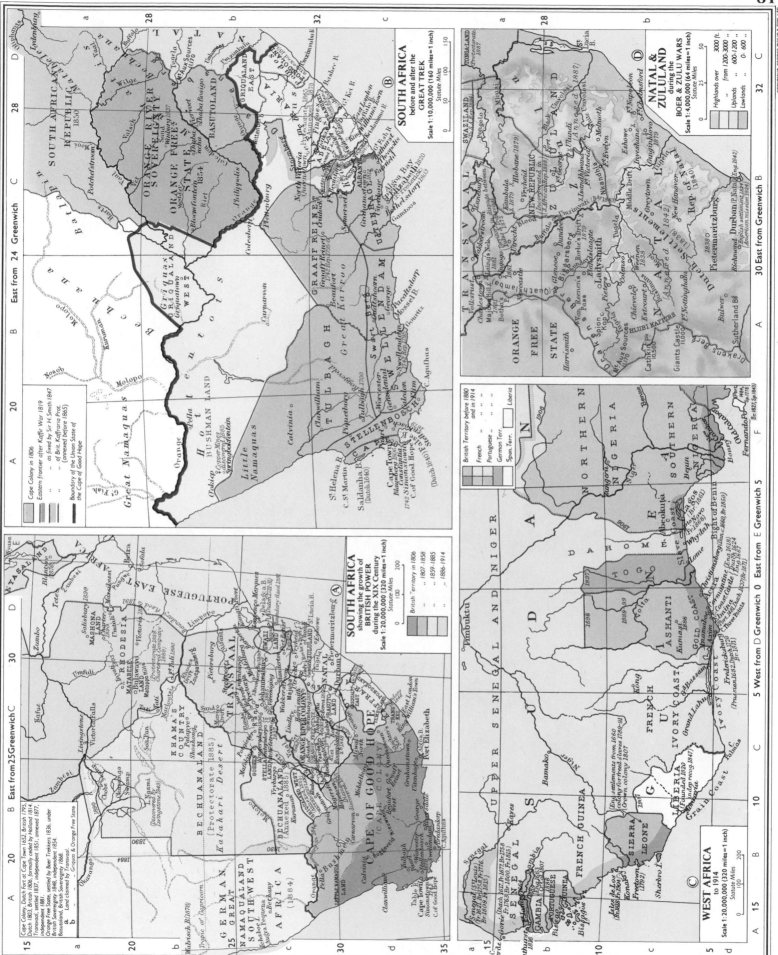

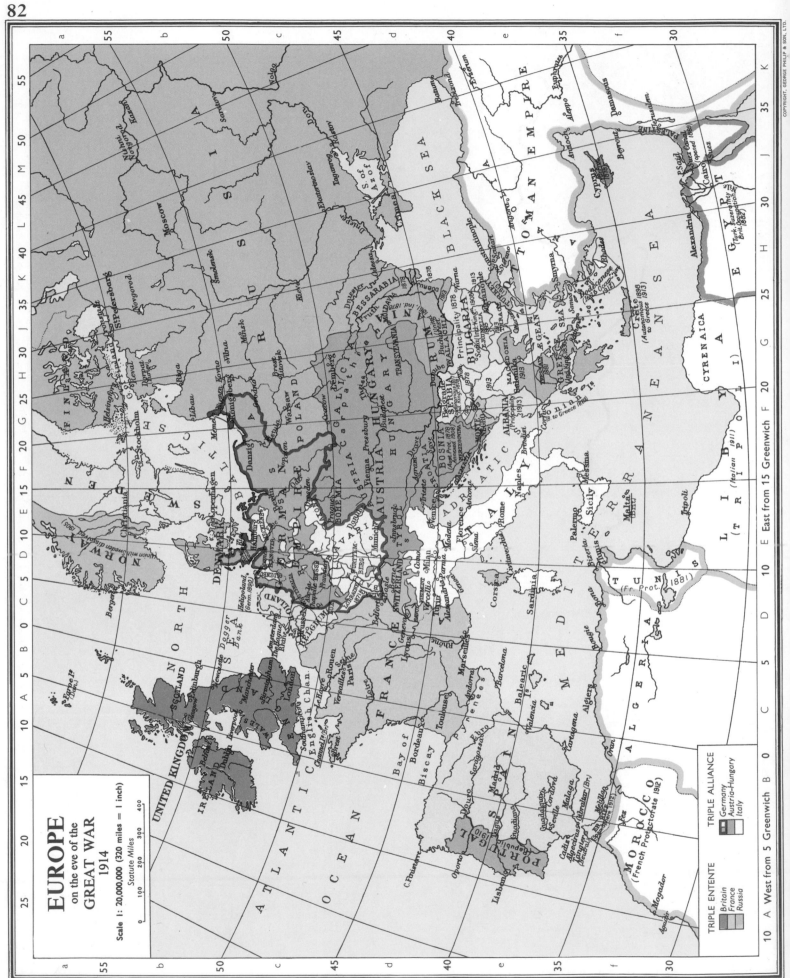

EUROPE
on the eve of the
GREAT WAR
1914

Scale 1 : 20,000,000 (320 miles = 1 inch)

Statute Miles

0   100   200   300   400

TRIPLE ENTENTE
Britain
France
Russia

TRIPLE ALLIANCE
Germany
Austria-Hungary
Italy

THE WORLD
at the Outbreak of the GREAT WAR 1914

On Mollweide's Equivalent Projection
Scale 1:165,000,000

- - - - Principal Steamship Routes
(Distances in Nautical Miles)
———— Principal Railways

Triple Alliance
Germany
Austria Hungary
Italy

Triple Entente
Britain
France
Russia
Japan (in Alliance with Britain)

Spain " & Daughter States
" " " & Daughter States
Portugal " & Daughter States

United States
Dutch
Belgian
Ottoman Empire

Belligerent States with dates of declaration of War

Allied Powers
British Empire 4-VIII-14
Russia 1-VIII-14
Belgium 2-VIII-14
France 3-VIII-14
Montenegro 28-VII-14, Rumano 27-VIII-16
Albania 1-16, Greece VI-17

Italy 23-V-15
Portugal 9-III-16
Japan 23-VIII-14
China 14-VIII-17
Siam VII-17, Liberia 17
United States 6-IV-17
Brazil X-17, Guatemala IV-18,
Nicaragua V-18, Costa Rica V-18,
Honduras VII-18
Cuba IV-17, Panama IV-17

Central Powers
Germany I-VIII-14
Austria-Hungary 28-VII-14
Turkey 4-XI-14 Bulgaria 5-X-15

THE WESTERN FRONT

B Scale 1:3,000,000 (48 miles = 1 inch)

Statute Miles

- - - Chief Battlefields and Sieges
Limit of German advance 1914
Allied Gains
Line of prolonged Trench Warfare
Enemy Gains
German Retreat, March 1917
Hindenburg Line
Limit of German advance 1918
Armistice Line, 11 Nov. 1918
French Acquisitions by the Treaty of Versailles
Belgian Saar Basin, mines assigned to France, under Control of League of Nations 1919-1934
Area in Occupation of the Allies (1918-1920)
Railways

COPYRIGHT, GEORGE PHILIP & SON, LTD.

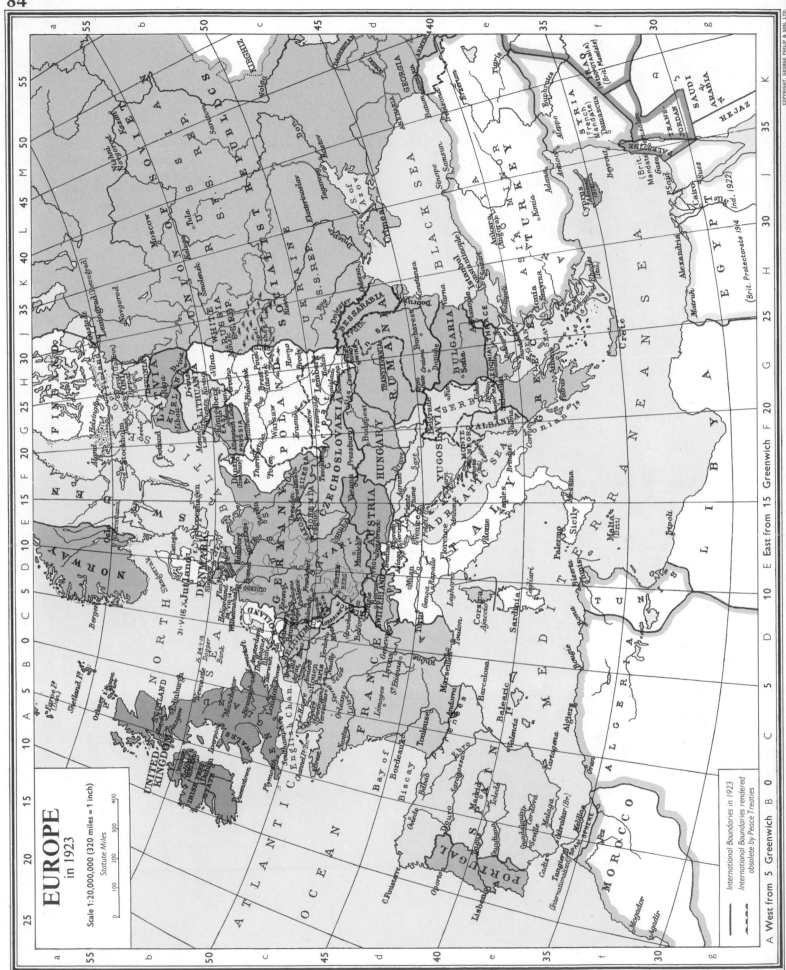

84

EUROPE
in 1923

Scale 1:20,000,000 (320 miles = 1 inch)

Statute Miles

International Boundaries in 1923
International Boundaries rendered
obsolete by Peace Treaties

A West from 5 Greenwich B 0 C East from 15 Greenwich F 20 E

COPYRIGHT, GEORGE PHILIP & SON, LTD.

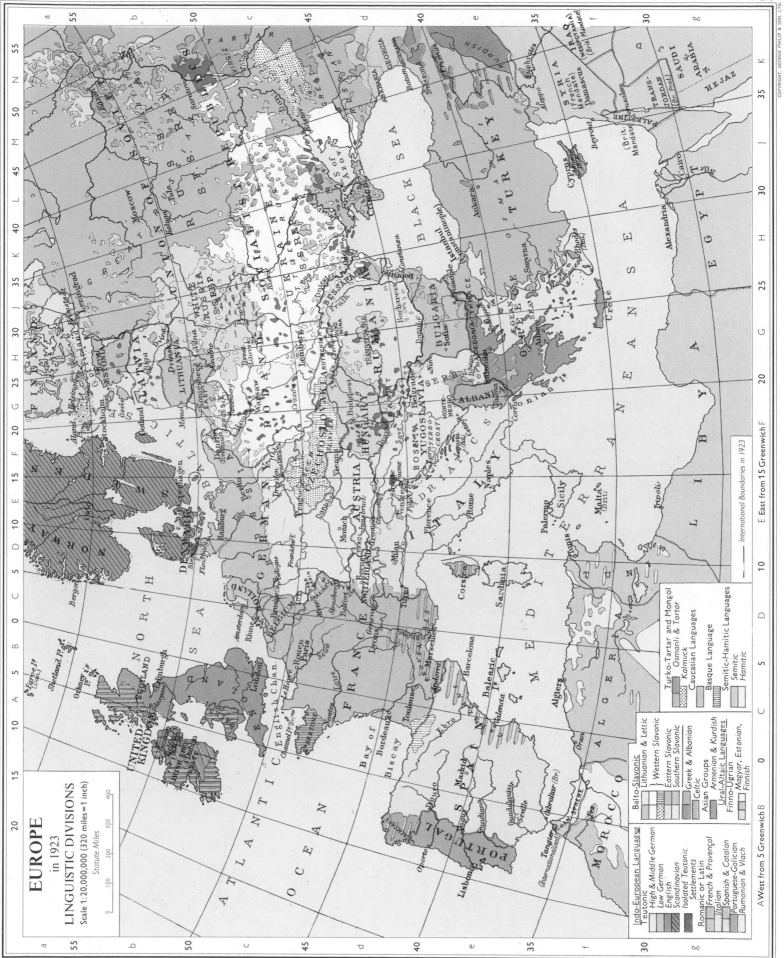

EUROPE
in 1923
LINGUISTIC DIVISIONS

Scale 1:20,000,000 (320 miles=1 inch)

Statute Miles

Indo-European Languages

Teutonic
High & Middle German
Low German
English
Scandinavian
Isolated Teutonic
  Settlements

Romanic or Latin
French & Provençal
Italian
Spanish & Catalan
Portuguese-Galician
Rumanian & Vlach

Balto-Slavonic
Lithuanian & Lettic
Western Slavonic
Eastern Slavonic
Southern Slavonic

Greek & Albanian
Celtic

Asian Groups
Armenian & Kurdish

Ural-Altaic Languages
Finno-Ugrian
Magyar, Estonian,
  Finnish

Turko-Tartar and Mongol
Osmanli & Tartar
Kalmuck

Caucasian Languages

Basque Language

Semitic-Hamitic Languages
Semitic
Hamitic

International Boundaries in 1923

A West from 5 Greenwich B   E East from 15 Greenwich F

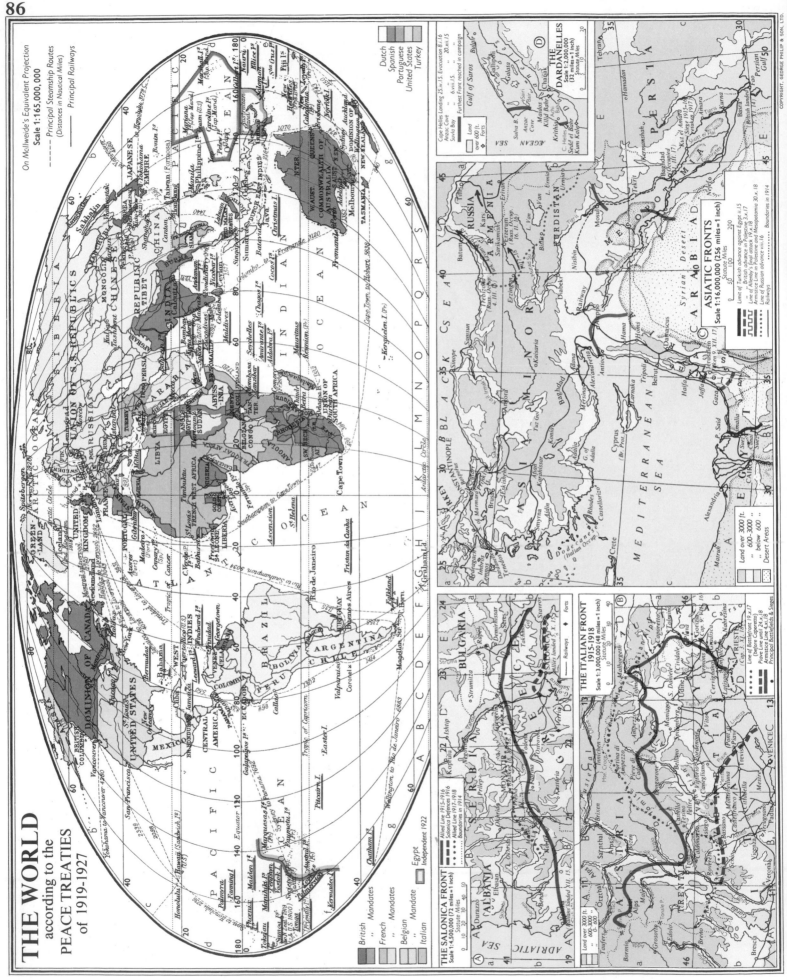

THE WORLD
according to the
PEACE TREATIES
of 1919-1927

On Mollweide's Equivalent Projection
Scale 1:165,000,000

------ Principal Steamship Routes
(Distances in Nautical Miles)
—— Principal Railways

British   Mandates
"   Mandates
French   Mandates
Belgian   Mandate
Italian

Dutch
Spanish
Portuguese
United States
Turkey

Egypt
Independent 1922

THE DARDANELLES
Scale 1:2,000,000
(32 miles = 1 inch)

Cape Helles Landing 25.iv.15. Evacuation 8.i.16
Anzac Cove   20.xii.15.
Suvla Bay   6.viii.15.
Furthest Front reached in campaign
Land over 600 ft.   Forts

ASIATIC FRONTS
Scale 1:16,000,000 (256 miles = 1 inch)

Limit of Turkish advance against Egypt ii.15
British advance in Palestine 3.xi.17
Last of Allies' advance 30.x.18
Armistice Line in Palestine and Mesopotamia 30.x.18
Line of Russian advance viii.16
Boundaries in 1914
Railways

Land over 3000 ft.
" 600-3000 "
" below 600 "
Desert Areas

THE ITALIAN FRONT
1915-1918
Scale 1:3,000,000 (48 miles = 1 inch)

Line of Battlefront 9.xi.17
Piave Line until 24.x.18
Armistice Line 4.xi.18
Principal Battlefields & Sieges

THE SALONICA FRONT
Scale 1:4,500,000 (72 miles = 1 inch)

Allied Line 1915-1916
Salonica Defences 1916
Allied Line 1917-1918
Boundaries in 1914
Land over 3000 ft.
600-3000
below 600
Railways   Forts

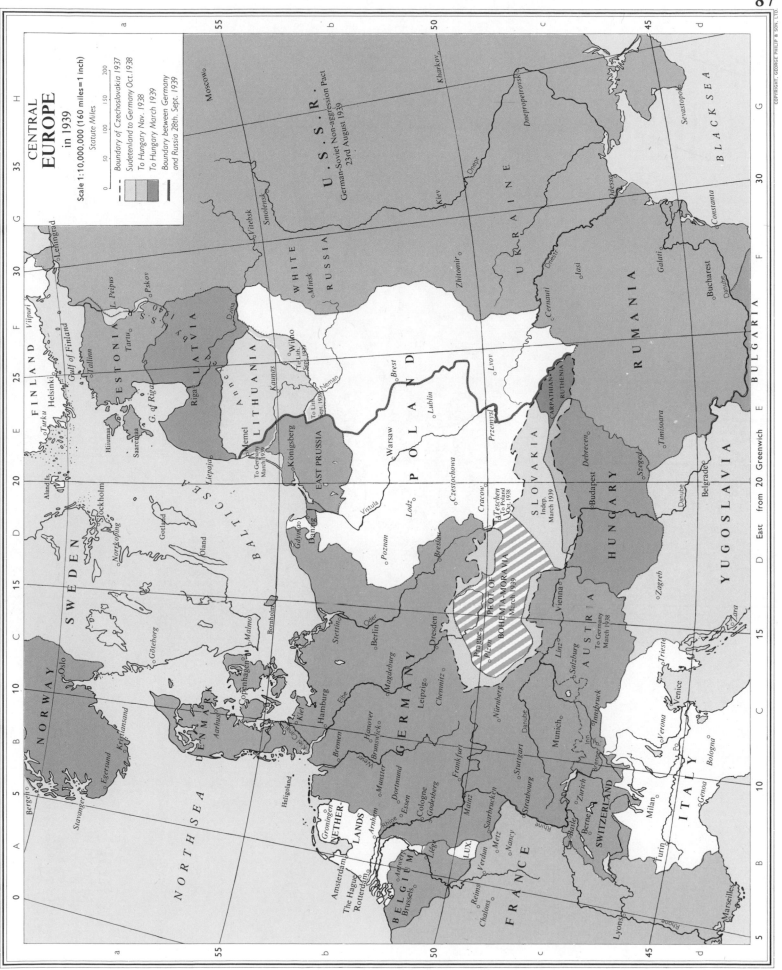

CENTRAL
EUROPE
in 1939

Scale 1:10,000,000 (160 miles = 1 inch)
Statute Miles

Boundary of Czechoslovakia 1937
Sudetenland to Germany Oct. 1938
To Hungary Nov. 1938
To Hungary March 1939
Boundary between Germany
and Russia 28th. Sept. 1939

German-Soviet Non-aggression Pact
23rd August 1939

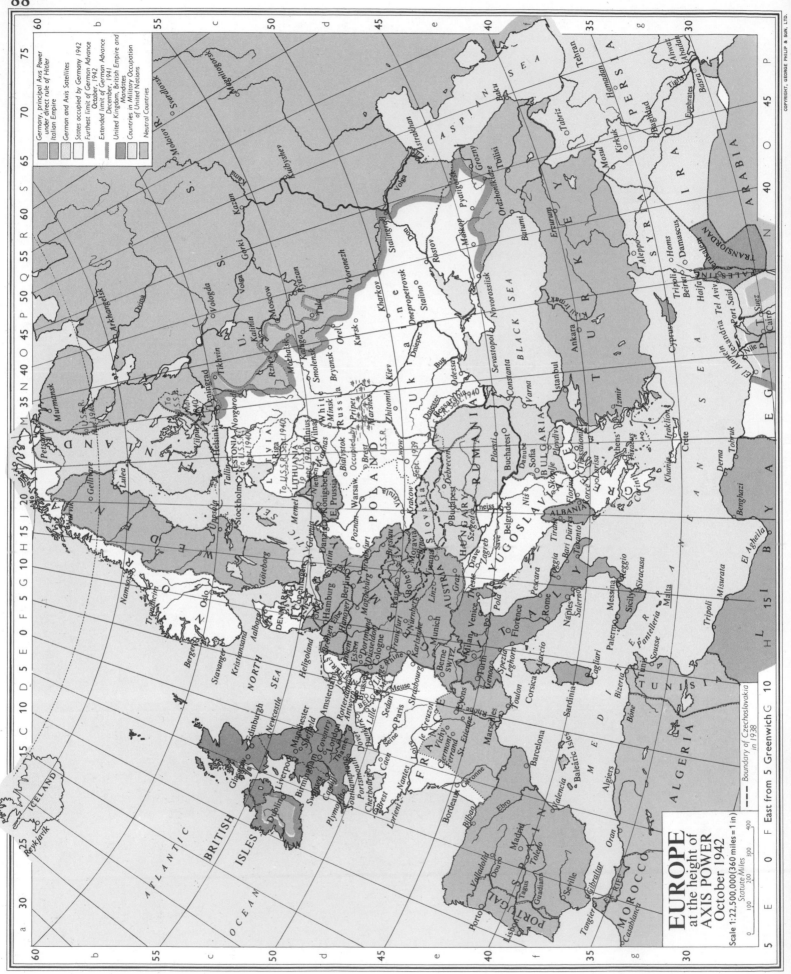

EUROPE
at the height of
AXIS POWER
October 1942

Scale 1:22,500,000(360 miles = 1 in)

Statute Miles
0   100   200   300   400

Germany, principal Axis Power
under direct rule of Hitler
Italian Empire

German and Axis Satellites

States occupied by Germany 1942

Furthest limit of German Advance
October, 1942

Extended limit of German Advance
December, 1941

United Kingdom, British Empire and
Mandates

Countries in Military Occupation
of United Nations

Neutral Countries

Boundary of Czechoslovakia
in 1938

East from 5 Greenwich 10

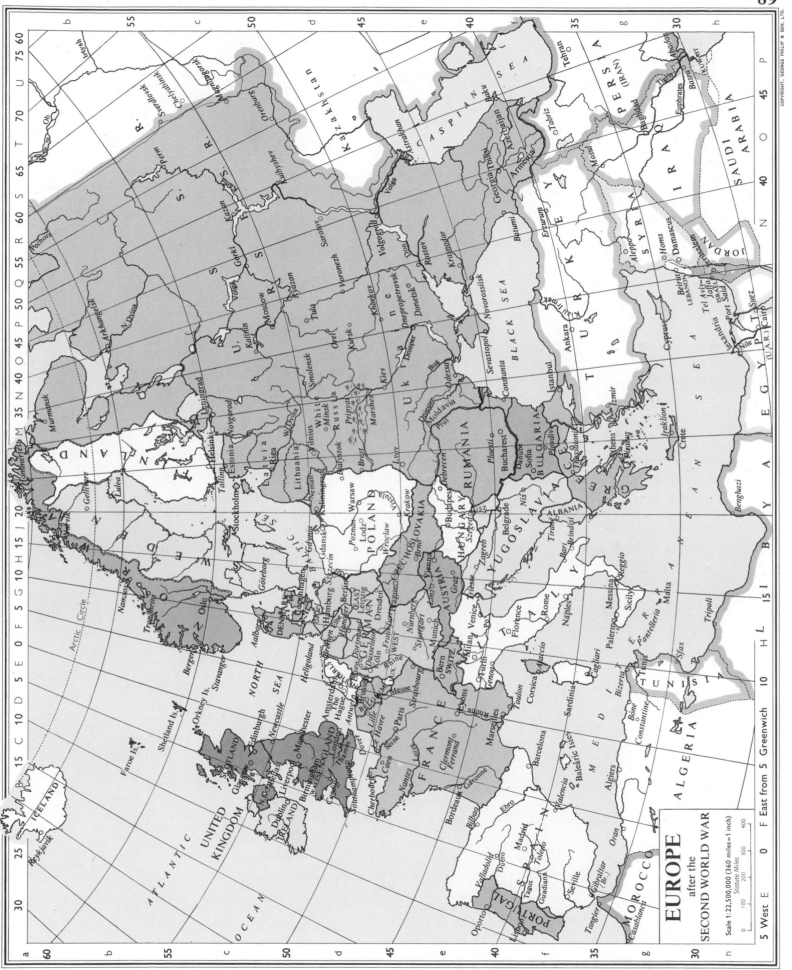

EUROPE
after the
SECOND WORLD WAR

Scale 1:22,500,000 (360 miles=1 inch)

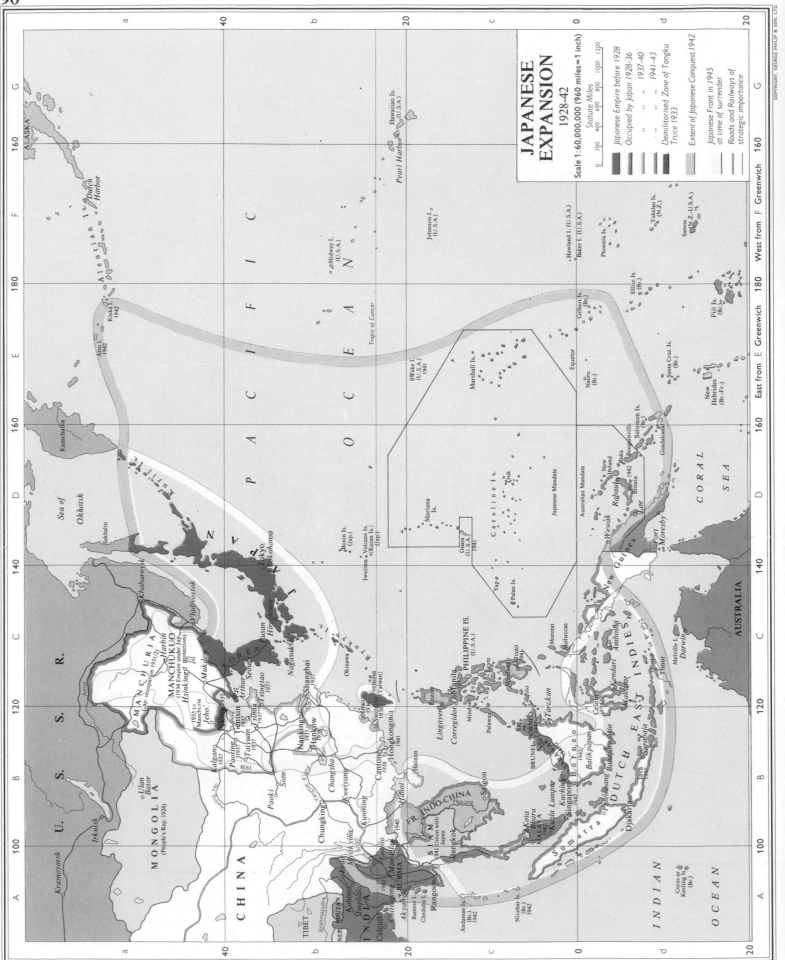

JAPANESE
EXPANSION
1928-42

Scale 1:60,000,000 (960 miles = 1 inch)

Statute Miles

Japanese Empire before 1928
Occupied by Japan 1928-36
"   "   "   1937-40
"   "   "   1941-43
Demilitarised Zone of Tangku
Truce 1933
Extent of Japanese Conquest 1942

Japanese Front in 1945
at time of surrender
Roads and Railways of
strategic importance

EASTERN
ASIA
1945-1969

Scale 1:30,000,000 (480 miles = 1 inch)

Statute Miles

0   100   200   300   400   500

—— *Principal Railways*

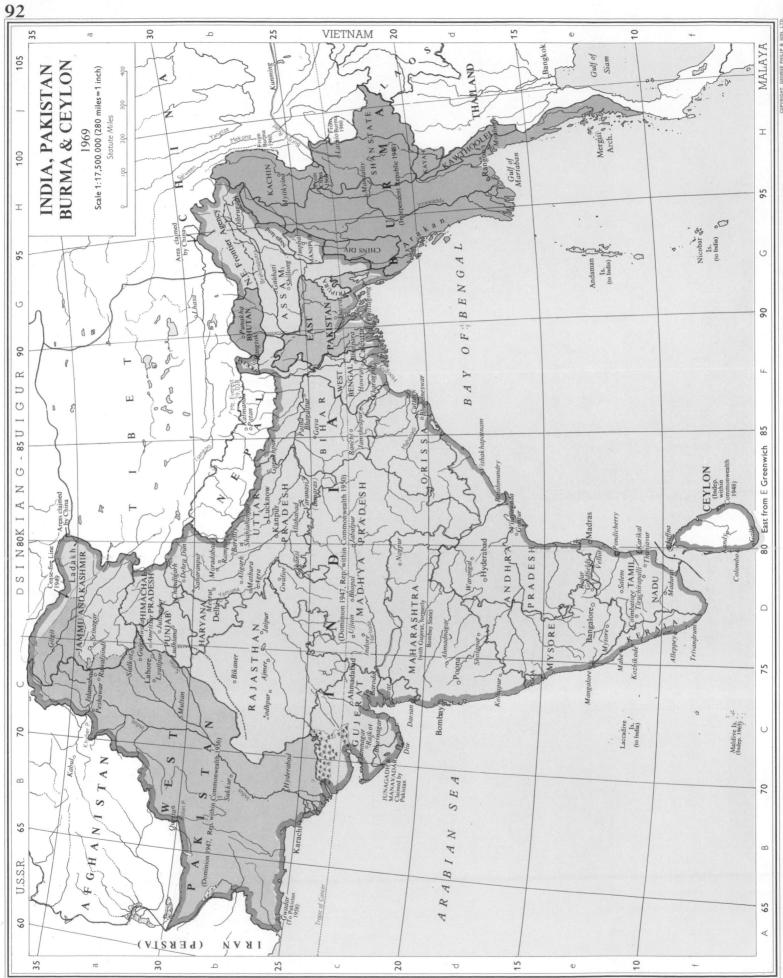

INDIA, PAKISTAN BURMA & CEYLON
1969
Scale 1:17,500,000 (280 miles=1 inch)
Statute Miles

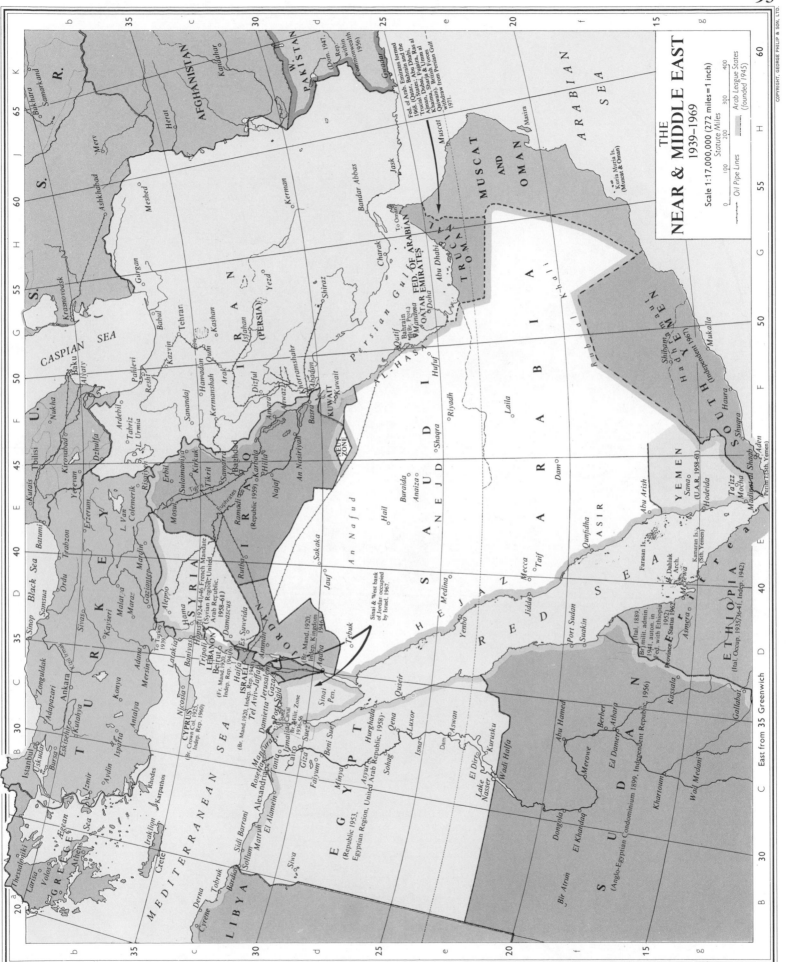

THE
NEAR & MIDDLE EAST
1939-1969

Scale 1:17,000,000 (272 miles=1 inch)
Statute Miles

Oil Pipe Lines

Arab League States
(founded 1945)

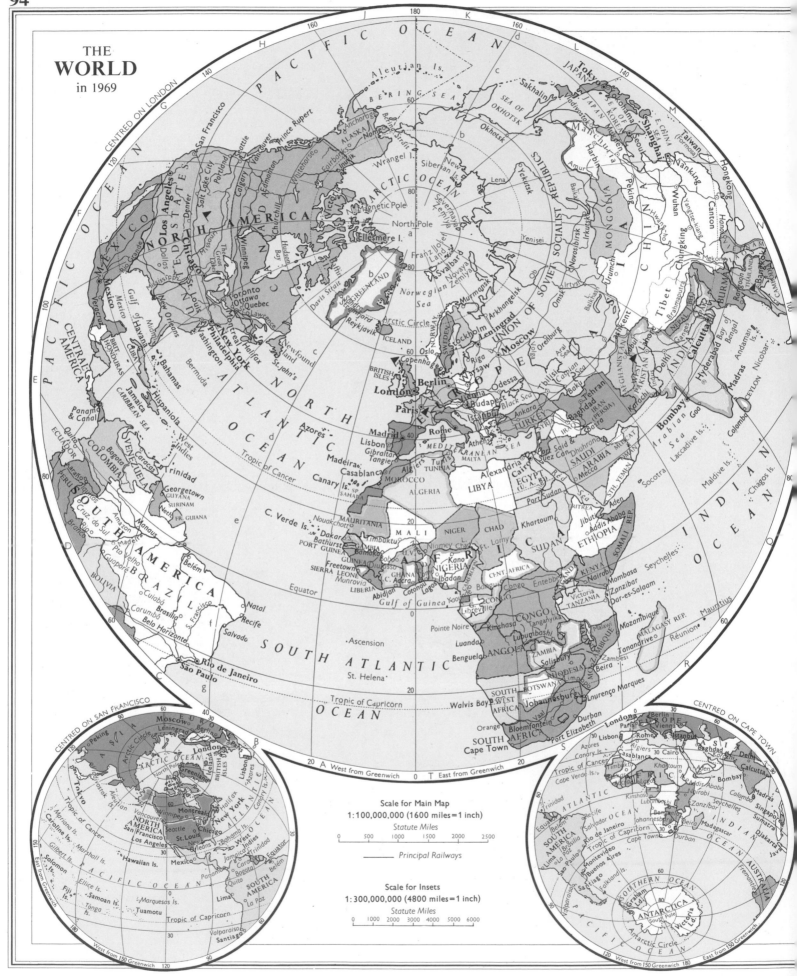

THE
WORLD
in 1969

Scale for Main Map
1:100,000,000 (1600 miles=1 inch)

Statute Miles

0   500   1000   1500   2000   2500

—— Principal Railways

Scale for Insets
1:300,000,000 (4800 miles=1 inch)

Statute Miles

0   1000   2000   3000   4000   5000   6000

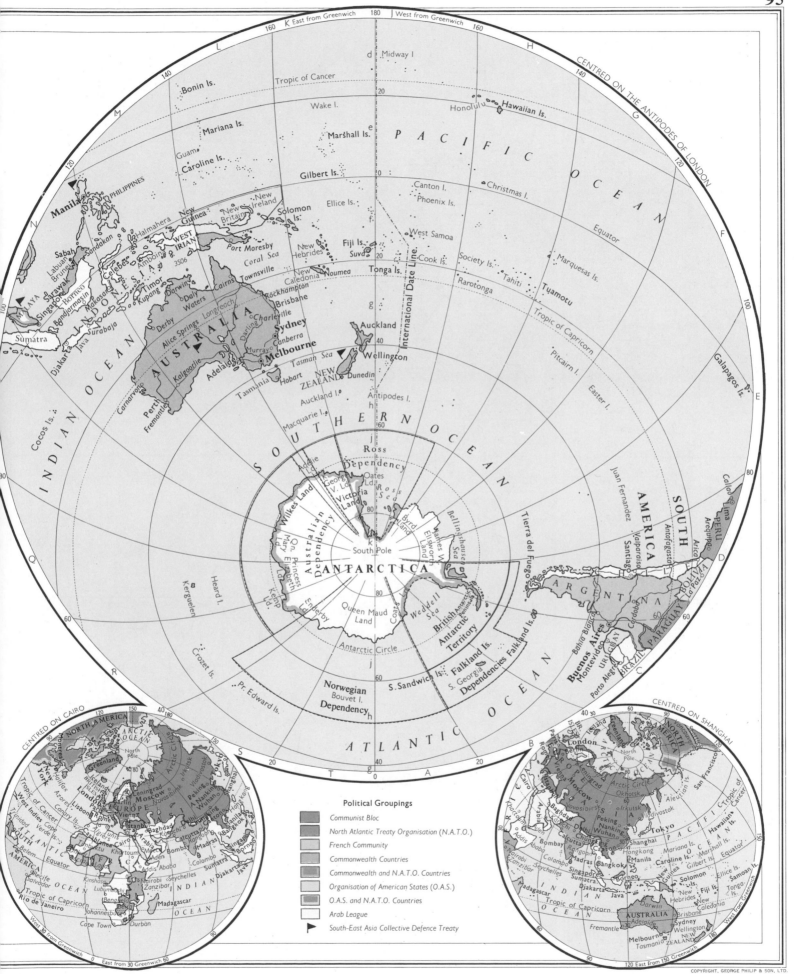

95

CENTRED ON THE ANTIPODES OF LONDON

d Midway I.

Tropic of Cancer

Bonin Is.

Wake I.

Honolulu Hawaiian Is.

20

Mariana Is.

e

Guam

Caroline Is.

Marshall Is.

Gilbert Is.

PACIFIC OCEAN

Manila

PHILIPPINES

Canton I.

Christmas I.

Phoenix Is.

Equator

New Ireland

Ellice Is.

f

Halmahera

New Britain

Solomon Is.

New Guinea

WEST IRIAN

Port Moresby

New Hebrides

Fiji Is.

Suva

West Samoa

20

Cook Is.

Society Is.

Marquesas Is.

Sabah

Sandakan

Labuan

Brunei

Celebes

Amboina

Timor

Coral Sea

New Caledonia

Noumea

Tonga Is.

Tahiti

Tuamotu

Rarotonga

Tropic of Capricorn

Townsville

INDONESIA

3506

Cairns

Rockhampton

Pitcairn I.

Easter I.

Sumatra

Djakarta

Java

Surabaja

Makasar

Kupang

Darwin

Daly Waters

Derby

Alice Springs

Longreach

Charleville

Brisbane

AUSTRALIA

Darling

Sydney

Canberra

Auckland

Galapagos Is.

E

INDIAN OCEAN

Carnarvon

Kalgoorlie

Adelaide

Melbourne

Murray

Tasman Sea

Wellington

Cocos Is.

Perth

Fremantle

Hobart

NEW ZEALAND

Dunedin

Tasmania

Auckland Is.

Antipodes I.

h

Macquarie I.

60

SOUTHERN OCEAN

Juan Fernandez

Valparaiso

Santiago

SOUTH AMERICA

80

Kerguelen

Ross Dependency

Adelie Ld.

George V. Ld.

Oates Ld.

Ross Sea

Byrd Land

Bellingshausen Sea

Tierra del Fuego

Callao Lima PERU

Arequipa

D

Heard I.

Wilkes Land

Victoria Land

80

James W. Ellsworth Land

Antofagasta

BOLIVIA La Paz

Australian Dependency

South Pole

k

ANTARCTICA

ARGENTINA

PARAGUAY

BRAZIL

60

Crozet Is.

On. Princess Mary Elizabeth Ld.

Kemp Ld.

Enderby Ld.

80

Queen Maud Land

Coats Ld.

Weddell Sea

British Antarctic Territory

Antarctic Peninsula

Bahia Blanca

Cordoba

Buenos Aires

Montevideo

URUGUAY

Porto Alegre

C

Pr. Edward Is.

Antarctic Circle

Falkland Is.

Falkland Is. Dependencies

j

Norwegian Bouvet I. Dependency

S. Sandwich Is.

S. Georgia

h

ATLANTIC OCEAN

Political Groupings

Communist Bloc

North Atlantic Treaty Organisation (N.A.T.O.)

French Community

Commonwealth Countries

Commonwealth and N.A.T.O. Countries

Organisation of American States (O.A.S.)

O.A.S. and N.A.T.O. Countries

Arab League

South-East Asia Collective Defence Treaty

CENTRED ON CAIRO

CENTRED ON SHANGHAI

COPYRIGHT, GEORGE PHILIP & SON, LTD.

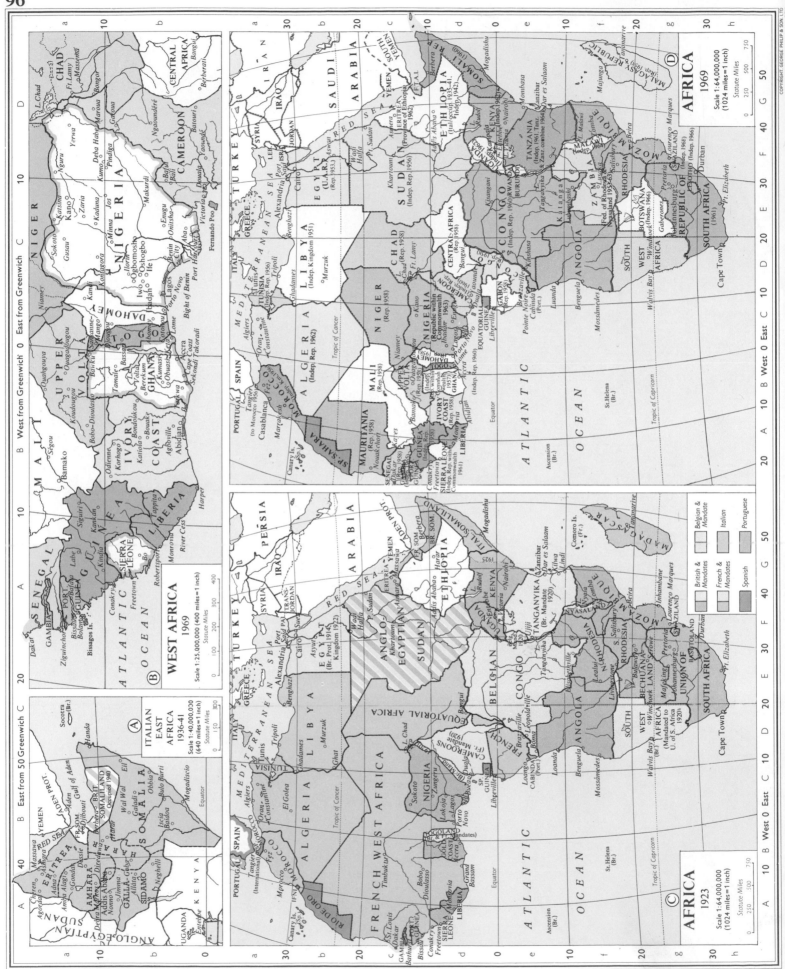

WEST AFRICA
1969
Scale 1:25,000,000 (400 miles=1 inch)
Statute Miles
0 100 200 300 400

ITALIAN EAST AFRICA
1936-41
Scale 1:40,000,030 (640 miles=1 inch)
Statute Miles
0 150 300

AFRICA
1969
Scale 1:64,000,000 (1024 miles=1 inch)
Statute Miles
0 250 500 750

AFRICA
1923
Scale 1:64,000,000 (1024 miles=1 inch)
Statute Miles
0 250 500 750

British & Mandates
French & Mandates
Spanish
Belgian & Mandate
Italian
Portuguese

INDEX

ABBREVIATIONS

AACHEN, 8, Da; 12, Fd; 38, Gc
Aalborg, 26, Db; 88, Gb
Aalen, 30, Hd; 53, Hc
Aar, R., 29B, Ba
Aarau, 29B, Ca
Aargau, canton, 29B, Ca
Aargau, reg., 10, Ce
Aarhus, 26, Db
Aba, 96B, Cb
Abadan, 93, Fc
Abancay, 68, Bd
Abbasid Caliphate, 8, He
Abbendone (Abingdon), 13, Ee
Abbéville, 38, Dc; 83A, Aa
Abbotsbury, 36, Dg
Abedesberie (Abbotsbury), 13, Df
Abenaki, 56, Fa
Abensberg, 29A, Da
Abeokuta, 81C, Ec
Aberdeen, 14, Fb; 37A, Cb
Aberdeen, co., 37A, Cb
Aberdour, 14, Eb
Aberfeldy, 37A, Cb; 49A, Cb
Aberfoyle, 37A, Bb; 48B, Aa
Abergavenny, 27, Ce
Abergwili, 27, Be; 28A, Bc
Aberlleiniog, 13, Ba
Abernethy, 14, Ec
Abidjan, 96B, Bb
Abingdon, 27, Ee
Abitibi, L., 45A, Ba
Abkhazia, 79, Hb
Åbo, 26 Fa
Abomey, 96B, Cb
Abone (Sea Mills), 3A, De
Abotrites, 8, Ea
Aboukir B., 64, Jf
Abraham, Heights of, 56A
Abrantes, 63, Ac
Abruzzi, reg., 32A, Ec
Abruzzo, 22, Ec
Abu Arish, 93, Ef
Abu Dhabi, 93, Ge
Abu Hamed, 80B, Ad
Abus Fl. (The Humber), 3A, Gc
Abydos, 19, Dd
Abydus, 4B, Hc
Abyssinia (Ethiopia), 6, Ed
Acadia, 45A, Ea; 55B, Db
Acajutla, 55B, Be
Acapulco, 43A, Cc
Accia, 22, Dc
Accompong, 43A, Ec
Accra, 81C, Dc
Acerenza, 22, Fc
Acerenza, eccl. prov., 22, Fc
Achaia, 1, Ed
Achaia, Pr. of, 19, Ce
Achalzich, 79, Hb
Achi Baba, 86D
Achill I., 15, Ac
Achonry, 15, Cb
Achusi (Pensacola), 43A, Da
Acklin I., 43A, Eb
Acqui, 20, Hf; 23B, Bb
Acra (Acre), 13, Gd
Acre, 16, Kf
Acre, terr., 68, Bc
Acre (Akko), 18C, Cf
Acton Burnell, 27, Dd
Actune (Acton), 13, De
Adalia, 6, Eb; 86C, Bb
Adalia, G. of, 86C, Bb
Adamawa, 80A, Ed
Adana (Aden), 1, Gf
Adana, Turkey, 18C, Ca
Adapazari, 93, Ca
Adda, R., 5, Bb
Addis Ababa, 96A, Ab
Adelaide, Australia, 77, Fl
Adelaide, S. Africa, 81B, C
Adélie Land, 69C
Adelingle (Atheiney), 13, De
Adelsberg, 39, Lf
Aden, 80A, Hc; 93, Fg
Aden, G. of, 96A, Ba
Adige, R., 5, Cb; 86B, Bd
Adirondack Mts., 57, Ea
Admiralty Is., 77, Hb

Adna, 96A, Aa
Adour, R., 11, Ce; 63, Ea
Adowa, 80B, Be
Adramyttium, 19, De
Adrar, 80A, Bb
Adrian, 70, Fc
Adrianople, 78, Fe
Adriatic Sea, 5, Ec
Adwalton Moor, 48A, Cc
Adzharia, 84, Ld
Ægean Sea, 78, Ef
Ægina, 78, Dg
Ægyptus, 2, Jg
Aegidius & Syagrius, King. of, 8, Bb
Aerschot, 83A, Ca
Aesica (Great Chesters), 3C
Aesium, 5B, Bb
Afghan Supremacy, 59A, Ba
Afghanistan, 61B, Bb; 92, Aa
Afiun Karahissar, 86C, Bb
Africa, 2, Eg; 4A, Dd
Africa, Exarchate of, 4B, Cd
Afyon, 79, Fc
Agades, 80A, Dc
Agadir, 80A, Ba; 82, Af
Agali, 22, Bc
Agamenticus (York), 45B, Db
Agawam (Ipswich), 45B, Db
Agboville, 96B, Bb
Agde, 11, Ee
Agder, 12, Fb
Agemundrenesse (Amunderness), 18, Dc
Agen, 11, Dd; 17A, Cd
Agenais, 17, Ff
Aggersborg, 12, Gb
Aggershuus (Christiania), 34, Ea
Aghadoe, 15, Bd
Aghlabids, 8, Dd
Aghlabids, King. of, 6B, Ca
Agincourt, 28D, Da
Agnadello, 32A, Cb
Agordat, 96A, Ae
Agra, 73, Cb
Agraca, Mte., 63B
Agram, 21, Mf; 39, Lf
Agrigentum (Girgenti), 5, Df
Aguilar, 23D, Ca
Agulhas, C., 81B, Bc
Ahaggar, 80A, Db
Ahausen, 29A, Da
Ahmadabad, 73, Bc; 92, Cc
Ahmadnagar, 59A, Bd; 92, Cd
Ahrensböck, 65F, Ba
Ahwaz, 6A, Db; 93, Fc
Aidin, 78, Fg; 86C, Ab
Aigle, 29B, Ab
Aiguesmortes, 20, Fg
Aiguillon, 53, De
Aila, 6A, Bc; 18C, Cj
Ailech, 7A, Ca
Ailsa Craig, 49A, Bc
Aimargues, 38, Fg
Ain, R., 29A, Ab
Aintab, 18C, Ea
Air, 80A, Dc
Airds Moss, 49A, Bc
Aire, Flanders, 17, Gc
Aire, Gascony, 22, Bc
Aire, R., 7C, Cb
Airgialla, 7A, Ba
Aisne, R., 17, Hd; 83A, Bb
Aix, 11, Fe
Aix la Chapelle, 10, Bc
Ajaccio, 30, Hg; 84, Dd
Ajmere, 73, Bb
Ajnadain, 6A, Ab
Akaroa, 77A
Akeman Street, 3A, Ee
Akerman, 51, Gd; 78, Hb
Akhaltsikh, 61, Ff
Akhlat, 19, Ge
Akko (Acre), 18C, Cf
Akmolinsk, 74, Fc
Akpatok I., 71, Ha
Akyab, 90, Ac
al Anbar, 6A, cb
al Dahna, 6, Fc

Al-Hasa, 79, Je
al Jawf, 6, Ec
al Kufah, 6A, Cb
al Nufud, 6, Fc
al Raqqah, 6A, Ba
al Ruha, 6A, Ba
Alabama, R., 56, Bd; 57A, Bc
Alabama, st., 72, Cc
Alagoas, 68, Fc
Alais, 30, Ff
Åland Is., 26, Ea
Alamanni, 7A, Fb
Alani, 2, Ld
Alans, 6, Fa; 19, Gd
Alarcos, 23C, Cc
Alasehir, 79, Ec
Alaska, 69B; 71A, Ba
Alaska Pen., 71A, Bb
Alatri, 22A
Alauna (Maryport), 3A, Ba
Alava, 23C, Da
Alba, 5, Ab
Alba de Tormes, 63, Cb
Alban, 7C, Aa; 14, Db
Albania, 78, Be
Albanian Pr., 24, Fe
Albanians, 18B, Cb
Albano, 22A
Albany, Georgia, 72, Dc
Albany, New York, 57, Eb
Albany, W. Australia, 77, Bl
Albany, reg., 81B, Cc
Albany, R., 70, Fb
Albara, 18C, Dc
Albaracin, 22, Bc; 23C, Eb
Albazin, 74, Lc
Albemarle, 45B, Ae
Albemarle Sd., 57, Ce
Albert, 83A, Ba
Albert, L., 80A, Fd
Alberta, 70, Cb
Albi, 11, Ee; 22, Dc
Albiac, 38, Df
Albis, R., 2, Fc
Albistan, 19, Fe
Albon, 30, Ff
Albret, 17, Ef
Albret, S. of, 30, Cf
Albuera, 23D, Bc; 63, Bc
Albury, 77, Hl
Alcacer do Sal, 23C, Ac
Alcala, 22, Bc; 63, Db
Alcala de Henares, 23C, Db
Alcaniz, 63, Eb
Alcantara, Brazil, 68, Ec
Alcantara, Spain, 23C, Bc; 63, Bc
Alcazar, 34, Be
Alchester, 3A, Ee
Alcira, 23C, Ec
Alclyde, 7B, Aa
Alclyde (Dumbarton), 14, Dd
Alcoboça, 22, Ad
Aldabra, 80A, He
Aldbury, 36, Ff
Alderney, 17, Dd
Aleksandrovsk, 91, Ha
Alemquer, 63B
Alemtejo, 23C, Ac; 63, Bc
Alençon, 11, Db
Alençon, D. of, 30, Dd
Alenuihaha Chan., 75D, Cb
Aleppo (Haleb), 18C, Eb
Aleria, 5, Bc; 53, Bf
Alessandria, 32A, Cb
Aleutian Is., 71A, Ab
Alexandretta, 18C, Ea
Alexandria, Egypt, 80B, Aa
Alexandria, Louisiana, 72, Bc
Alexandria, Virginia, 57, Cd
Alexandrovsk, 74, Dd
Alford, 37A, Cb
Algarve, 23C, Ad; 63, Ad
Algarve de Alem Mar, 47, Ae
Algeciras, 23C, Cd; 63A
Algeria, 24, Cf; 80A, Da
Algeria, Pashalik of, 47, Ce
Algiers, 34, Ce; 80A, Da

Algiers, Sultanate of, 34, De
Algoa B., 81B, Cc
Algonkins, 45A, Ca
Alhandra, 63B
Alhama, 52C, Cb; 90, Cd
Alicante, 23C, Ec; 63, Ec
Alice Springs, 77, Ef
Alids, King. of, 6B, Ga
Aligarh, 59C, Cb; 92, Db
Aliwal, 73, Ca
Aliwal North, 81A, Cd
Aljubarrota, 23D, Ac
Aljustro, 23C, Ad
Alkmaar, 46A, Db
Allahabad, 73, Db
Allata, 96A, Ab
Allatoona, 72A, Aa
Allegheny Mts., 57, Bd
Allegheny, R., 45A, Bb
Allemanni, 2, Ed; 4A, Db
Allen, Bog of, 15, Ec
Allen, L., 15, Cb
Allenstein, 84, Gb
Alleppey, 92, Df
Aller, R., 10, Cb; 55A, Hb
Allerdale, 28B, Bc
Allier, R., 11, Ed
Allstedt, 39C, Bb
Allumette Is., 45A, Ba
Alma Ata, 91, Ab
Almada, 23D, Ac
Almalik, 25, Hb
Almanza, 47, Be; 63, Ec
Almaraz, 63, Cc
Almeida, 23C, Bb; 63, Bb
Almeria, 23C, Db; 23C, Dd
Almina, C., 63A
Almissa, 22, Fc
Almohad Empire, 18A, Ac
Almonacid, Aragon, 63, Eb
Almonacid, New Castile, 63, Dc
Almora, 73, Cb
Almoravids, 16, Be
Aln, R., 28B, Db
Alnwick, 13, Ea
Alost, 46A, Cd
Alpes, 1, Cc; 2, Fd
Alps, The, 5, Ca; 10, De
Alpuente, 23C, Ec
Alresford, 27, Ee
Alsace, 10, Bd; 39B, Db
Alsace-Lorraine, 65D, Ab
Alsebruge (Axbridge), 13, De
Alsek, R., 71B, Ba
Alsen, 60B, Ba; 65F, Aa
Alsen Sd., 65F, Aa
Alsh, L., 49A, Bb
Alston, 13, Db
Alt, R., 78, Ec
Alt Breisach, 39B, Db
Altenburg, 10, Fd; 21, Kc
Altenkirchen, 53, Gb
Altkirch, 39B, Dc; 83B, Bb
Altmark, 30, Jb; 60A, Cb
Altomünster, 22, Eb
Alton, England, 27, Fe
Alton, Illinois, 72, Cb
Altona, 51, Bc; 65F, Ab
Altorf, 29B, Cb
Altranstadt, 50,
Aluta, R., 19, Cd; 78, Ec
Alvarado, 43A, Cc
Alvertune (Allerton, Northallerton), 13, Eb
Alwar, 73, Cb
Alwinestune (Carisbrooke), 13, Ef
Alyaty, 93, Fb
Alyth, 37A, Cb

Amadeus, L., 77, Ef
Amalfi, 5, Ed
Amami-Oshima, 75, Dc
Amapa, 68, Db
Amara, 86C, Ec; 93, Fc
Amarante, 63, Ab
Amarapura, 73, Gc
Amasia, 9, Kd
Amasra, 24, Je
Amastris, 19, Ed
Amatola Mts., 81B, Cc

Amazon, R., 68, Dc
Amazonas, 68, Cc
Amba Alagi, 96A, Aa
Ambala, 73, Ca
Amberg, 29A, Da
Amboina, 52C, Cb; 90, Cd
Amboise, 11, Dc
Ambra, 32E, Bb
Ambresberie (Amesbury), 13, Ee
Ambur, 59D
Ameland, 46A, Ea
Amelia, 57, Ce
Ameria, 5B, Bb
Amersfoort, 46A, Eb
Amersham, 27, Fe
Amhara, 96A, Aa
Amherst, 73, Gd
Amichel, 43A, Cb
Amida, 2, Mf; 6A, Ca
Amida (Diarbekr), 33A, Fc
Amiens, 11, Eb; 83A, Bb
Amirante Is., 83, Me
Amisus, 18B, Fb; 24, Ke
Amiterno, 21A, Ba
Amman, 79, Gd
Amorgos, 78, Fg
Amorium, 9, Je
Amoy, 91, Ed
Ampezzo, 86B, Ca
Ampurias, 23C, Ga
Amritsar, 73, Ba
Amsterdam, 31A, Ca; 46A, Db
Amsterdam, I., 42B
Amu Darya, R., 61B, Ba
Amur, R., 25, Ma; 91, Fa
An Nafud, 93, Ed
An Nasiriyah, 93, Fc
Anadirsk, 42, Aa
Anadyr, 74, Qb
Anagni, 22A; 32A, Ed
Anahuac, 43A, Cc
Anaiza, 93, Ed
Anamaboe, 81C, Dc
Anapa, 61, Ef
Anas, R., 2, Bf
Anatolia, 33A, Dc; 64, Jf
Anatolic Theme, 9, Je
Ancénis, 20, Ce
Anchialus, 8, Hc
Anchorage, 71A, Ca
Anchu, 76B, Cb
Ancona, 5, Ec
Ancona, M. of, 21, Kg
Ancud, 68, Bf
Ancyra, 2, Ke; 8, Jd
Andalusia, 23C, Cd; 63, Cd
Andaman Is., 73, Fe
Andastes, 45B, Bc
Andechs, 20, Je
Anderida (Pevensey), 3A, Gf
Anderida Silva, 3A, Ff
Andernach, 10, Bc
Anderson, 72, Ec
Andersonville, 72, Dc
Andes, 68, Bc
Andhra, 1, Kf
Andhra Pradesh, 92, Dd
Andorra, 30, Dg; 63, Fa
Andover, 27, Ee
Andredsweald (The Weald), 13, Ge
Andria, 21A, Db
Andros, I., 78, Eg
Andros Is., 43A, Eb
Androscoggin, R., 45B, Da
Andrusov, 50, Gc; 54, Jb
Andujar, 23C, Cc; 63, Cc
Angara, R., 91, Da
Angermanland, 26, Ea
Angers, 11, Cc; 17, Ee
Anghaile, 37B, Dc
Angles, 2A, Ba; 4A, Ba
Anglesey, 27, Bc
Angli, 2, Ec
Anglo-Egyptian Sudan, 80A, Fc
Angol, 68, Bf
Angola, 80A, Ef
Angora, 19, Ee; 86C, Bb

1

Angostura (Ciudad Bolivar), 68, Cb
Angoulême, 11, Dd; 17A, Cd
Angoulême, Co. of, 11, Dd
Angoumois, 17, Ef; 38, Df
Angra Pequena, 81A, Ac
Anguilla, 43A, Fc
Angus, 14, Fc
Anhalt, 20, Jc; 30, Jc
Ani, 9, Ld
Anjala, 51, Fa
Anjou, 28C, Bc; 38, Ce
Anjou, Co. of, 11, Dc; 17, Ee
Ankara, 79, Fb
Anklam, 26, Dc
Ann, 45B, Ad
Annale, R., 49B, Db
Annaly, 15, Dc
Annam, 25, Kd; 74, Jg
Annan, 49A, Cc
Annandale, 14, Ed; 28B, Bb
Annapolis (Port Royal), 45A, Db; 71, Hc
Annecy, 30, Gf
Annobon, 80A, De
Annonay, 30, Ff
Annone, 23B, Bb
Ansbach, 38, Jd
Ansbach, Pr., 53, Jc
Anstruther, 49A, Cb
Antalya, 79, Fc
Antarctic Ocean, 69 C
Antarctica, 95, Ak
Antequera, 23D, Cd
Antibes, 38, Gg
Anticosti, 45A, Ea
Antietam, 72B, Ba
Antigua, 43A, Fc
Antioch, 6A, Ba; 18C, Db
Antioch, Pr. of, 18C, Dc
Antiochia, 16, He
Antipodes I., 69C, 75, Fg
Antivari, 22, Fc; 78, Bd
Antofagasta, 68, Be
Antofagasta, st., 68 ,Ce
Antoing, 46A, Cd
Antrim, co., 37C; 49B, Eb
Antrim, Mts. of, 15, Eb
Antung, 76B, Ca
Antwerp, 17A, Ea; 46A, Dc
Anzac Cove, 86D
Aosta, 5, Ab
Apalachee, 56 ,Cd
Apalachicola, R., 71F, Ba
Apamea (Famia), 18C, Dc
Apcher, 30, Ef
Apennines, 5, Dc
Apia, 75B, Ba
Appalache, 43A, Da
Appalache Bay, 43A, Db
Appalachian Mts., 70, Fd
Appenzell, 29B, Da
Appenzell, canton, 29B, Da
Appin, 49A, Bb
Appleby, 13, Db; 27, Db
Appledore, 7C, Dc
Appomattox Court House, 72, Eb
Appomattox, R., 72B, A6
Apt, 22, Dc; 30, Fg
Apulia, 4B, Fc; 5, Ed
Apulia, D. of, 16, Fd
Apure, R., 43A, Ed
Apurímac, R., 41B, Be
Aqaba, 93, Dd
Aquae (Buxton), 3A, Ec
Aquae Sulis (Bath), 3A, De
Aquidatan, 68, De
Aquila, 23B, Dc; 39, Kg
Aqui'eia, 5, Db
Aquileia, eccl. prov., 22, Eb
Aquino, 21A, Bb; 22, Ec
Aquitaine, 4A, Cc
Aquitaine, D. of. 17, Fe
Aquitania, 2, Dd;
Ar, 65B, Aa
Arabia, 1, Ge; 6, Fc
Arabia Deserta, 1, Ge
Arabia Felix, 1, Fe
Arabian Desert, 80B, Ab
Arabian Sea, 25, Fe
Aracaju, 68, Fd
Aracena, 23D, Bd
Arachosia, 1, Jd
Arad, 33C, Eb
Arafura Sea, 77, Ec; 91, Fg
Aragon, 23C, Cc; 63, Eb
Aragon, King. of, 23C, Eb
Araguaia, R., 68, Dd
Arak, 93, Fc
Arakan, 73, Fc; 92, Gd
Aral, L., 6, Ga; 25, Eb
Aralskoje, 61B, Ba
Aran I., 15, Ca
Aran Is., 15, Bc
Aranda, 63, Db
Aranjuez, 54, Be
Ararguez, 54, Be
Aras, R., 19, He
Aravalli Ra., 59C, Bb
Arbe, 22, Ec

Arbo, 23B, Eb
Arboga, 26, Eb
Arborea, 23B, Bd
Arbre Croche, 56, Ca
Arbroath, 37A, Cb
Arc, 28D, Ec
Arcenefeld (Archenfield), 13, De
Arces, 5B, Bc
Archa, 18C, Dd
Arcole. 29A, Dc
Arcos, 23C, Bb
Arcot, 59D; 73, Ce
Arctic Ocean, 69B
Arcugnano, 86B, Bb
Ardagh, 15, Dc
Ardagh, bp., 15A, Bb
Ardebil, 19, He; 93, Fb
Arden, 7B, Cc
Arden, Forest of, 3A, Ed
Ardennes, 11, Fb; 83A, Ca
Ardfert, 15, Bd
Ardfinnan, 15, Dd
Ardgour, 14, Cc
Ardnamurchan Pt., 49A, Ab
Ardoch, 49A, Cb
Ardstraw, bp., 15A, Ba
Arelate (Upper King. of Burgundy), 10, Bf
Aremberg, 53, Gb
Aremburg, 65B, Aa
Arequipa, 68, Bd
Arevallo, 63, Cb
Arezzo, 21, Jg; 32E, Bb
Argaon, 59C, Cc
Argentan, 17, Fd
Argentina, 68, Ce; 83, Ff
Argentine Confederation, 68, Cf
Argentine Rep., 68, Cf
Argenton, 38, De
Arghandab, R., 73, Aa
Argonne, 83A, Cb
Argos, 78, Dg
Argostolion, 78, Cf
Arguin, 35, Hc; 52, Jc
Argyll, 14, Cc
Argyll, bp., 14A, Bb
Argyll, co., 49A, Bb
Argyll and Tarbert, co., 37A, Fb
Aria, 1, Jd
Ariano, 21A, Cb
Arica, 68, Bd
Ariminum (Rimini), 5, Db
Arinos, R., 68, Dd
Arinsol, 23C, Cd
Arisaig, 49A, Bb
Arizona, 70, Cd
Arizona Terr., 67D, Bb
Arkansas, 72, Bc
Arkansas Post, 72, Bc
Arkansas, R., 70, Dd
Arkansas Terr., 67C, Db
Arkhangelsk, 61, Fb; 88, Oa
Arklow, 15, Ed
Arlberg Pass, 29A, Dc
Arles, 11, Fe; 17A, Ee
Arles, King. of, 20, Ff
Armagh, 15, Eb
Armagh, co., 37C; 49B, Eb
Armagnac, Co. of, 11, Ce
Armenia, 19, Ge; 79, Hc
Armenia, King. of, 19, Ee
Armeniac Theme, 9, Kd
Armenians, 18C, Ca
Armentieres, 46A, Bd
Armorica, 2, Cd; 4A, Bb
Armstrong, 28B, Bb
Arnhem, 46A, Eb
Arnhem Land, 77, Ed
Arnis, 65F, Aa
Arno, R., 5. Cc; 21B, Db
Arnsberg, 20, Hc; 38, Hc
Arnstadt, 38, Jc
Arnswalde, 21, Lb
Aroche, 23D, Bd
Aroostook, R., 71E, Bb
Arpinum, 5B, Bc
Arques, 20, Ab
Arran, 14, Cd
Arras, 17, Gc; 46A, Bd
Arroyo de los Molinos, 63, Bc
Arsamosata, 9, Ke
Arsuf, 18C, Bf
Arta, 64, Gf; 78, Cf
Artaxata, 1, Gc
Artenay, 76A, Ab
Artois, 17, Gc; 83A, Ba
Aru Is., 77, Ec
Aruba, 41B, Cb
Arundel, England, 27, Ff
Arundel, Maryland, 45B, Ad
Arve, R., 29B, Ab
Arwystli, 13, Cd
Arzobispo, 63, Cc
Ascalon, 6A, Ab; 18C, Bg
Ascension, 40, Je; 96C, Ae
Aschaffenburg, 29A, Ca
Ascoli, 5, Dc
Ashanti, 81C, Dc
Ashburton, 27, Cf

Ashburton, R., 77, Bf
Ashby-de-la-Zouch, 48A, Cc
Ashdown, 7B, Cc
Ashkhabad, 93, Hb
Ashridge, 36, Ff
Ashuanipi, L., 71, Hb
Asia, cont., 94, Pc
Asia, diocese, 2, Kf
Asia, reg., 1, Ed
Asia Minor, 86C, Bb
Asir, 93, Ef
Asirgarh, 73, Cc
Askeaton, 37B, Cd; 49B, Cd
Asmara, 80A, Gc
Asmera, 93, Df
Asoka Empire, 1, Ke
Aspadana, 1, Hd
Aspern, 29A, Ga
Aspinwall, 43D, Ed; 68, Bb
Aspromonte, 32C, Ee
Aspropotamos, R., 78, Cf
Assab, 80B, Ce
Assam, 25, Jd; 73, Fb
Assandun, 12, Ed
Assassins, 18C, Dc
Assaye, 59C, Cc; 69A, Nc
Assiette, Col d', 29A, Bc
Assiniboia, 70, Db
Assisi, 5, Dc
Assuan, 6, Ec
Assynt, 14, Ca
Astarac, Co. of, 11, De
Asterabad, 61, Hd
Astico, R., 86B, Bb
Astorga, 23C, Ba; 63, Ba
Astrakhan, 19, Hc
Astrakhan, reg., 61, Hd
Asturias, 23C, Ca; 63, Ba
Asuncion, 68, De
Aswan, 80B, Ac; 96D, Fb
Aswan Dam, 93, Ce
Asyut, 80B, Ab
Atacama Desert, 68, Be
Atapuerca, 23C, Da
Athara, 93, Cf
Athara, R., 80B, Bd
Atelkuza, 9, Hc
Atella, 32A, Bc
Ath, 46A, Cd; 53, Eb
Athabaska, 70, Cb
Athabaska L., 70, Db
Athabaska, R., 70, Cb
Athboy, 49B, Ec
Athelney, 7C, Bc; 36, Df
Athenae, 2, Hf
Athenry, 37B, Cc; 49B, Cc
Athens, 78, Df
Athens, D. of, 19, Ce
Athlone, 15, Dc
Atholl, 14, Dc
Athos, Mt., 9, Gd; 18B, Cb
Athy, 15, Ed
Atlanta, 72A, Ab
Atlantic Ocean, 35, Hd
Atrato, R., 43A, Ed
Atrebates, 3A, Ec
Atrek, R., 61, Jg
Atri, 21, Kg
Atropatene, 2, Nf
Attalia, 19, Ee
Attock, 73, Ba
Attu, L., 90, Ea
Aube, R., 76A, Cb
Auberoche, 28C, Cd
Aubigny, 53, Ed
Auch, 11, De
Auch, eccl. prov., 22, Bc
Auchterarder, 49A, Cb
Auckland, 75, Ff; 77A
Auckland, prov., 77A
Auckland (Waitemata), 77, Ml
Auerstädt, 65B, Ba
Aughrim, 49B, Cc
Augsburg, 10, Dd
Augusta (Fort Cornwallis), 57D, Ab
Augusta, Georgia, 72, Dc
Augusta, Maine, 67B, Ca
Augusta Taurinorum (Turin), 5, Ab
Auldearn, 37A, Cb
Aumale, 17, Fd
Aunis, 30, Ce
Aurangabad, 73, Cd
Auray, 28C, Ac; 55A, Be
Aureliani, 2, Dd
Aurillac, 17, Gf; 30, Ef
Aussig, 31, Lc
Austerfield, 7B, Cb
Austerlitz, 29A, Ga
Austin, 70, Ed
Austral (Tubuai) Is., 75, Hf; 83, Bf
Australia, 69A, Qf
Australia, Commonwealth of, 77, Ef
Australian Alps, 77, Hl

Australian Dependency, 95, PJ
Australasia, 7A, Eb; 8, Da
Austria, 50, Dd; 65A, Cb
Austria, reg., Italy, 5, Cb
Austria, March of, 10, Fd
Austria-Hungary, 82, Fc
Austrian Empire, 62, Fc; 65B, Cb
Austrian Netherlands, 54, Db
Austrian Silesia, 60A, Fc
Autun, 8B, Bb; 11, Fc
Auvergne, 11, Ed; 20, Ef
Auvergne, Co. of, 11, Ed
Auxerre, 11, Ec
Auximum, 5B, Bb
Auximum (Osimo), 5, Dc
Auxonne, 30, Fe
Ava, 41A, Gb; 73, Gc
Avalon, 45A, Ga
Avars, 8, Gb; 9, Fc
Aveiro, 22, Ac
Aventine, 5A
Aversa, 32A, Fd
Avesnes, 46A, Cd
Avignon, 11, Fe; 17, Hf
Avila, 22, Bc; 63, Cb
Avisio, R., 86B, Ba
Avlona, 18A, Ba
Avoca, R., 15, Ed
Avon, R., Bristol, 27, De
Avon, R., Hants., 27, Ef
Avon, R., Warwick, 27, Ed
Avondale, 28B, Ab
Avranches, 11, Dc
Awe, L., 14, Ce
Avretone (Overton, Richard's Castle), 13, Dd
Ax, 11, Ce
Axtridge, 27, De
Axim, 40, Jd; 81C, Dc
Ayacucho, 68, Bd; 69A, Fe
Ayas, 19, De; 93, Bb
Aydin, 19, De; 79, Fc
Aylesbury, 7A, Cb; 48A, Cd
Aylesford, 7B, Dc
Ayr, co., 37A, Bc; 49A, Bc
Ayr, R., 14, Dd
Ayton, 37A, Cc
Ayubale, 56, Cd
Ayubites, Empire of the, 18B, Ed
Azangarh, 73, Db
Azerbaijan, 79, Jc; 89, Pe
Azores, 55B, Hc
Azov, 24, Kd; 79, Ga
Azov, Sea of, 19, Fc
Aztec Kingdom, 35, Dc
Aztecs, 43A, Bb

BAALBEK, 6A, Bb
Baalbek (Heliopolis), 18C, De
Babul, 93, Gb
Babuyan Is., 75E, Ba
Babylon, 2, Mg
Bacalhaos, 35, Hd
Bacan, 52C, Cb
Bacharach, 29A, Ba
Bacolod, 75E, Bb
Bactria, I, Jd
Badajoz, 22, Ad; 63, Bc
Badakshan, 61B, Cb
Bade (Bath), 13, De
Baden, 20, Hd; 29B, Ca
Baden, Marg. of, 30, Hd
Baden Baden, 29A, Ca
Badenoch, 14, Eb; 37A, Bb
Badissin, 31, Lc
Baentone (Bampton), 13, Cf
Baeza, 23C, Dd
Bafata, 96B, Aa
Baffin Bay, 44, Ha; 69B
Baffin L., 44, Ga
Bafut, 96B, Db
Bagdad, 6A, Cb; 9, Lf
Baghdad, Caliphate of, 18A, Gc
Baghdad Railway, 86C, Bb
Bagirmi, 80A, Ec
Bagnolo, 32D, Bb
Bahama Is., 43A, Eb
Bahawalpur, 73, Bb
Bahia (Salvador), 68, Fd
Bahia, st., 68, Ed
Bahia Blanca, 68, Cf
Bahn, 60A, Eb
Bahrein, 6, Gc; 79, Ke
Baikal, L., 25, Ka; 91, Da
Baker, I, 90, Fd
Bakewell, 7C, Cb
Bakhchisarai, 51, Ge
Baku, 19, Hd; 79, Jb
Balaguer, 23C, Fb
Balakhava, 61, Df
Balasore, 59A, Ec
Balassaghun, 25, Gb
Balaton, L., 31, Me; 33c, Db
Balch, 61B, Bb
Balchik, 78, Gd
Baleares Insulae, 2, Df
Balearic Is., 23C, Gc; 63, Gc

Bali, 96B, Db
Balidon Hill, 28B, Cb
Balikpapan, 90, Bd
Balkans, 78, Ed
Balkh, 6, Hb; 25, Fc
Balkhash, L., 25, Gb; 91, Ab
Ballachulish, 49A, Bb
Ballater, 49A, Cb
Balleny Is., 69C
Ballinamuck, 49B, Dc
Bai.iol. 28B, Db
Ballycastle, 49B, Ea
Ballymena, 49B, Eb
Ballymore, 49B, Dc
Balneum Regis, 5B, Bb
Balta, 51, Fd; 78, Gb
Baltic Sea, 22, Ea; 26, Eb
Baltimore, Maryland, 57, Cd; 72 B, Ba
Baluchistan, 61B, Bc; 74 Ef
Bamako, 80A, Cc; 81C, Cb
Bamberg, 10, Dd
Bamforough, 27, Ea
Banana, 80A, Ee
Banaras (Varanasi), 92, Eb
Banat of Craiova, 33C, Ec
Banat of Temesvar, 33C, Eb
Banbury, 27, Ed
Banda Is, 52 C, Cb
Banda Oriental, 68, Df
Bandar Abtas, 93, Hd
Bandar Maharani, 75A, Aa
Bandjarmasin, 91, Eg
Bandon, 49B, Ce
Bandon, R., 15, Ce
Banff, co., 37A, Cb; 49A, Cb
Bangalore, 73, Ce
Bangaya Is., 52C, Bb
Bangkok, 73, Ge; 92, Je
Bangor, Caernarvon, 13, Bc; 36, Bd
Bangor, Flint, 7A, Ca; 13, Dc
Bangor, Ireland, 37B, Fb
Bangor, Maine, 71, Hc
Bangor, bp, 36, Be
Bangtok, 92, Fb
Bangui, 96D, Dd
Bangweulu, L., 80A, Gf
Baniyas, 93, Db
Banjermasin, 69A, Pe
Bankot, 59A, Bd
Banks I., 44, Ba
Banks Pen., 77, Mj
Bann, R., 15, Eb; 37C
Bannaventa (Whilton Lodge) 3A, Ed
Bannockburn, 28B, Aa
Bannow, B., 15, Ed
Bantam, 41A, He
Bantry, 49B, Be
Bantry B., 15, Be
Banwelle (Banwell), 13, De
Banyaluka, 39, Mf; 78, Ac
Bapaume, 30, Ec; 83A, Ba
Bar, 17A, Eb; 39B, Bb
Bar, D. of, 30, Fd; 39B, Ba
Bar-le-Duc, 17, Hd; 29A, Aa
Bar-sur-Aube, 11, Fb
Bar-sur-Seine, 11, Fb
Bar Hill, 3A, Ba
Bararmahal, 59C, Ce
Baranof I., 71B, Db
Baranow, 26, Fc
Barataria Bay, 43A, Db
Barawa, 40, Md; 41A, Bd
Barbados, 43A, Gc
Bartarike, I, Je
Barbary, 40, Kc
Barbastre, 22, Cc
Barberton, 81A, Dc
Bartuda, 43A, Fc
Barcastro, 23C, Fa
Barcelona, Spain, 23C, Gb; 63, Gb
Barcelona, Venezuela, 68, Ca
Barcelona, Co. of, 23C, Ga
Barcelona, Co. of (Spanish March), 11, De
Barcelonnette, 38, Gf
Barcelos, 23C, Cc
Barcoo, R., 77 Gg
Bardera, 80A, Hd
Bardia, 93, Ac
Bardney, 36, Fd
Bardsey, I., 7C, Ab
Fareilly, 73, Cb
Barents Sea, 69B
Barfleur, 28C, Bb; 55A, Cd
Bari, Africa, 80A, Gd
Bari, Italy, 5, Fd; 32A, Gd
Bari Doab, 73, Ba
Barka, 6, Db; 9, Gf
Barking, 13, Ge; 36, Gf
Barletta, 32A, Gd
Barlings, 36, Fd
Barmen, 83A, Da
Barnard Castle, 27, Eb
Barnaul, 91, Ba
Barnestable (Barnstaple), 13, Be

Barnet, 27, Fe
Barnstaple, England, 27, Ce
Barnstable, Massachusetts, 45B, Dc
Baroda, 73, Bc
Barotseland, 80A, Ff
Barra, 43A, Ec
Barra, I., 14, Ac
Barrackpore, 73, Ec
Barranquilla, 68, Ba
Barrois Mouvant, 39B, Bb
Barrosa, 63, Bd
Barrow, Ft., 71A, Ba
Barrow, R., 15, Ed; 37B, Ed
Bartenstein, 60B, Ha
Barth, 31, Ea
Barton-on-Humber, 27, Fc
Bartzo, 23B, Fc
Baruth, 39C, Da
Bärwalde, 39, Lb; 60A, Dc
Basel (Basle), 29B, Ba
Bashee B., 81B, Dc
Basilan, 75E, Bc
Basilicata, 5, Fd
Basing, 7C, Cc; 48A, Cd
Basinges (Basingstoke), 13, Ee
Basingstoke, 27, Ee
Basle (Basel), 29B, Ba
Basle, canton, 29B, Ba
Basle, Bp. of, 29B, Ba
Basques, 8C, Bb
Basra, 6A, Dc
Basra (Bassorah), 41A, Ba
Bass Rock, 28B, Ca
Bass Str., 77, Hi
Bassano, 32D, Bb; 86B, Bb
Bassari, 96B, Cb
Basse, Fontaine, 22, Cb
Bassein, Burma, 73, Fd
Bassein, India, 73, Bd
Bassignano, 32B, Bb; 51, Bd
Bassigny, 39B, Bb
Bassorah, 33A, Gd
Bassorah (Basra), 41A, Ba
Bastarnae, 2, Jc
Bastia, 20, Hg
Bastogne, 83A, Ca
Basutoland, 81B, Db
Batak, 78, Ee
Batangas, 75E, Bb
Batanta, 52C, Db
Batavia, 74, Jj
Batavian Rep., 51, Bc
Bath, England, 27, De
Bath, N. Carolina, 56, Dc
Bath and Wells, bp., 36, Cf
Bathurst, C. Prov., 81B, Cc
Bathurst, Gambia, 81C, Ab
Bathurst, New South Wales, 77, Hh
Bathurst Inlet, 70, Da
Batlapin, 81B, Bc
Batoche, 70, Db
Baton Rouge, 56, Ad
Batouri, 96B, Db
Battle, 12, Ed; 36, Gg
Battleford, 70, Db
Batuchina, 52B, Aa
Batum, 33A, Fb; 79, Hb
Batum, reg., 79, Hb
Batumi, 88, Oe
Baturin, 50, Gc
Baugé, 28D, Bc
Baugy, 38, Ee
Bautzen, 10, Fc; 53, Lb
Bavaria, 10, Ed; 21, Ke
Bavaria, D. of, 30, Jd
Bavaria-Landshut, D. of, 31, Kd
Bavaria-Munich, D. of, 30, Jd
Bavarians, 4A, Eb; 8B, Db
Bawku, 96B, Ba
Bay Is., 43B, Bc
Bayeux, 11, Cb
Baylen, 62, Be; 63, Dc
Bayonne, 11, Ce; 63, Ea
Bayreuth, 20, Jd; 53, Jc
Bayreuth, pr., 38, Jc
Baza, 23C, Dd
Bazarchik, 78, Fd
Bazas, 11, Cd
Beachy Hd., 55A, Dc
Beacon Hill, 56B
Beacons, 27, Ce
Béarn, V. of, 11, Ce
Beaucaire, 17, Hg
Beaufort, France, 38, Ce
Beaufort, Georgia, 57D, Ab
Beaufort, S. Africa, 81B, Bc
Beaufort, Syria, 18C, Ce
Beaufort Bay, 44, Aa
Beaufort Sea, 69B
Beaufort West, 81A, Bd
Beaugency, 20, De; 76A, Ac
Beaujeu, 11, Fc
Beaujeu, S. of, 20, Fe
Beaulieu, England, 36, Eg
Beaulieu, France, 22, Cb
Beauly, 49A, Bb
Beaumaris, 27, Bc
Beaumont, 30, Ed; 76A, Cb
Beaune, 30, Fe

Beaune-la-Rolande, 76A, Bb
Beaupréau, 53, Cd
Beauséjour, 45A, Ea
Beauvais, 11, Eb; 83A, Bb
Beauvais, Co. of, 11, Eb
Beauvale, 36, Ed
Beauvoir, 38, Be
Beaver Dam, 71D
Bebbanburh (Banburgh), 13, Ea
Bec, 17, Fd; 22, Cb
Beccles, 13, Hd
Bechuana, 81B, Ba
Bechuanaland, 81A, Bb; 96C, Eg
Bechuanaland Prot., 80A, Fg; 81A, Bc
Bedale, 27, Eb
Bedeforde (Bedford), 13, Fd
Bedefordscire (Bedfordshire), 13, Fd
Bedford, England, 27, Fd
Bedford, Virginia, 57, Be
Bedford, co., 27, Fd
Bedlington, 27, Ea
Bednore, 59C, Ce
Bedr, 6, Ec
Bedvinde (Great Bedwyn), 13, Ee
Bedwin, 27, Ee
Beeston Castle, 48A, Bc
Bega, 6, Ec
Beilan, 64, Kf
Beira, 81A, Da
Beira, prov., 63, Ab
Beirut, 79, Gd; 80A, Ga
Beisan, 18C, Cf
Beja, 23C, Bc
Belata, 23C, Ac
Belbuck, 22, Fa
Belcher Is., 70, Fb
Belchite, 63, Eb
Belem, 22, Ad
Belem (Para), 41B, Ed; 68, Ec
Belerium Prom., 3A, Af
Belfast, 37B, Fb; 49B, Fb
Belfort, 29A, Bb; 39B, Cc
Belgae, 3A, De
Belgard, 21, Mb
Belgian Congo, 80A, Fe
Belgium, 83A, Ca; 87, Ab
Belgrade, 78, Cc
Belin, 38, Cf
Belinas (Paneas), 18C, Ce
Belize, 43A, Dc
Bellary, 73, Cd
Belle I., Canada, 71, Jb
Belle I., France, 11, Bc
Belle Isle, Str. of, 71, Jb
Belleek, 49B, Cb
Bellegarde, 53, Ef
Bellême, 11, Db; 17, Fd
Belley, 11, Fd; 22, Db
Bellingshausen Sea, 95, Ej
Bellingtun (Bedlington), 13, Ea
Bellinzona, 5, Ba; 29B, Db
Belluno, 5, Da; 86B, Ca
Belmont, U.S.A., 72, Cb
Belo Horizonte, 68, Ee
Belturbet, 49B, Db
Belvedoir (Belvoir), 13, Fd
Belvoir, England, 36, Fe
Belvoir, Syria, 18C, Cf
Belyi, 61, Dc
Bemis Heights, 57, Eb
Benares, 25, Hd; 73, Db
Benauges, 11, Cd
Benavente, 63, Ca
Benbecula, 14, Ab
Benburb, 49B, Eb
Bencoolen, 52, Qe; 75, Ce
Bender, 50, Fd; 78, Gb
Bendigo, 77, Gi
Benedict, 71C, Cc
Benevento (Beneventum), 5, Ed
Benevento, D. of, 23A, Ec
Beneventum (Benevento), 5, Ed
Beneventum, D. of, 4B, Fc
Benfleet, 7C, Dc
Bengal, 25, Hd; 73, Ec
Bengal, Bay of, 25, He
Benghazi, 80A, Ea
Bengkalis, 75A, Ab
Benguela, 80A, Ef
Beni Suef, 93, Cd
Benin, 81C, Fc
Benin City, 96B, Cb
Benin, Bight of, 81C, Ed
Bennington, 57, Eb
Benon, 30, Ce
Bensington, 7B, Cc
Bent's Fort, 70, Dd
Bentheim, 20, Hd
Bentheim, Co. of, 46C, C
Bentonville, 72, Eb
Benue, R., 81C, Fc
Beorn, 12, Dc
Berar, 73, Cc
Berat, 86A, Ab

Berber, 80B, Ad
Berbera, 96A, Ba
Berberati, 96B, Db
Berbers, 6, Bc
Berbice, reg., 41B, Dc
Berbice, R., 68B, Ea
Berchamstede (Berkhamsted), 13, Fe
Berchelai (Berkeley), 13, De
Berchtesgaden, 21, Ke
Bere, 28A, Cb
Bere I., 15, Be
Berea, 81A, Cc
Berekum, 96B, Bb
Beresina, R., 50, Fc
Berewic (Berwick), 13, Da
Berezovo, 74, Eb
Berg, Co. of, 20, Gc
Berg, D. of, 38, Gc; 46C, Cb
Bergamo (Bergamum), 5, Bb
Bergen, Nassau, 29A, Ca
Bergen, Netherlands, 46A, Db
Bergen, Norway, 26, Ca
Bergen, Rügen, 22, Ea
Bergen op Zoom, 46A, Dc
Bergerac, 20, Df; 28C, Cd
Bergues, 53, Eb
Berhampore, 73, Ec
Berhampur, 59A, Dd
Beri (Berry Pomeroy), 13, Cf
Bering Sea, 74, Qc
Bering Str., 69B
Berkeley, England, 27, De
Berkeley, Maryland, 45B, Ae
Berkeley, reg., 45A, Bd
Berkhamsted, 27, Fe
Berkshire, 27, Ee
Berkshire Hills, 57, Eb
Berlad, 33A, Ca
Berlin, 21, Kb
Bermejo, R., 68, Cc
Bermuda Hundred, 45B, Ae
Bermuda I., 55B, Dc
Bermudas (Somers Is.), 43A, Fa
Bernardino Pass, 5, Ba
Bernburg, 53, Jb
Berne, 10, Be; 29B, Bb
Berne, canton, 29B, Bb
Bernicia, 7B, Ca; 12, Dc
Bernina, 29A, Db
Berrochescire (Berkshire), 13, Ee
Berry, 17A, Cc
Berry, D. of, 30, Ee
Berthier, 56, Ea
Bervie, 49A, Cb
Berwick, 14, Fd
Berwick, co., 37A, Cc
Berwick upon Tweed, 28B, Cb
Besalú, 22, Cc
Besançon, 11, Gc; 29A, Bb
Besançon, eccl. prov., 22, Db
Beshbalik, 25, Jb
Bessarabia, 50, Fd; 78, Gb
Bessin, 8, Bb
Bessingen, 20, Hd
Betanzos, 63, Aa
Bethany, 81A, Ac
Bethel, 71A, Aa
Bethelsdorp, 81B, Cc
Bethesda, Pool of, 18D
Bethlehem, 18C, Cg
Béthune, 28B, Ba; 46A, Bd
Betwa, R., 52A, Bb
Beuthen, 21, Nc
Beverley, 27, Fc
Beverley Manor, 56, Dc
Beverlie (Beverley), 13, Fc
Bewcastle, 7B, Ba; 13, Da
Beyrout, 6A, Bb; 18C, Ce
Béziers, 11, Ee; 17A, De
Bhagalpur, 73, Eb
Bhamo, 73, Gc
Bharatpur, 73, Cb
Bhatpara, 92, Fc
Bhavnagar, 92, Cc
Bhima, R., 73, Cd
Bhonsla's Lands, 73, Cc
Bhopal, 59C, Cc; 73, Cc
Bhubaneswar, 92, Fc
Bhutan, 73, Fb
Bialystok, 51, Ec
Biar, 23C, Ec
Biberach, 20, Hd
Bicocca, 32A, Cb
Bidar, 59C, Cd
Bidassoa, R., 63, Ea
Biddeford, 57, Fb
Bideford, 48A, Ad
Biel (Bienne), 29B, Ba
Biel, L., 29B, Ba
Bielefeld, 30, Hb; 53, Ha
Bielgorod, 19, Fb
Biella, 32A, Cb
Bielostok, 26, Fc; 84, Gb
Bielsk, 61A, Bb
Bienne, 65A, Ab
Bienne (Biel), 29B, Ba
Big, R., 70, Gb
Big Black, R., 72C, Aa
Biggarsberg, 81D, Bb

Bigorre, 17, Fg
Bigorre, Co. of, 11, De
Bihacs, 31, Lf; 39, Lf
Bihar, 73, Eb
Bihar and Orissa, 73A, Bb
Bijapur, 52A, Bc; 73, Cd
Bijayah, 6, Bb
Bikaner, 73, Bb
Bilbao, 23D, Da; 63, Dd
Billings, Lds. of the, 10, Db
Billungs, M. of the, 10, Ea
Biloxi, 56, Ad
Binche, 46A, Dd
Bingerville, 80A, Cd
Binkath, 6, Ha
Bintang, 75A, Bb
Bir Atrun, 93, Bf
Birkenfeld, 39B, Da; 65D, Ab
Birmingham, 64, Bc
Birr, 15, Dc
Birthen, 10, Bc
Biscay, B. of, 11, Bd
Bischofsheim, 20, Jc
Bishop's Stortford, 27, Ge
Bisignano, 21A, Dc
Bismarck (Fort Mandant), 70, Dc
Bismarck Arch., 77, Hb
Bissagos Is., 81C, Ab; 96B, Aa
Bissao, 81C, Ab
Bissau, 96B, Aa
Bistritz, 24, Gd
Bithur, 73, Db
Bithynia, 2, Ke; 16, Jd
Bitlis, 9, Le; 86C, Db
Bitolia (Monastir), 78, Ce
Bitonto, 32B, Fd; 54, Fd
Bitsch, 76A, Db
Bizerta, 34, De
Black Castle, 15, Ed
Black Elster, R., 39C, Db
Black Forest, 10, Cd; 29A, Bb
Black Mts., 27, Ce
Black, R., 57, Db
Black River, 43A, Dc
Black Rock, 71D
Black Russia, 50, Ec
Black Sea, 4A, Jc; 19, Ed
Black Umvolosi, R., 81D, Bb
Blacksod B., 49B, Ab
Blackstocks, 57D, Aa
Blackwater, R., Meath. 49B, Ec
Blackwater, R., Munster, 15, Cd
Blackwater, R., Ulster, 15, Db
Bladensburg, 71C, Cc
Blagovyeshchensk, 74, Lc
Blair Atholl, 37A, Cb; 49A, Cb
Blairgowrie, 37A, Cb
Blakeney, 27, Gd
Blamont, 30, Gd; 39B, Cb
Blanc, Mt., 29A, Bc
Blanchegarde, 18C, Bg
Blanco, C., Africa, 80A, Bb
Blanco, C., Oregon, 67C, Aa
Blanco (North), C., 55B, Kc
Blandford, 27, Df
Blankenberghe, 46A, Cc
Blantyre, 80A, Gf; 81A, Ea
Blatno, 9, Fc
Blatobulgium, (Birrens), 3A, Ca
Blauwberg, 81B, Ac
Blaye, 17, Ef
Bleichfeld, 10, Dd
Blekinge 26, Eb
Bléneau, 53 Ed
Blenheim, Germany, 29A, Da
Blenheim, New Zealand, 77A
Bletchingley, 27, Fe
Blewfields, 43B, Bc
Blida (Blyth), 13, Ec
Blind B., 77A
Bloemfontein, 81B, Cb
Blois, 11, Dc
Blois, Co. of, 11, Dc
Blood, R., 81D, Ba
Bloody Foreland, 49B, Ca
Blore Heath, 27, Dd
Blue Mts., 77, Ih
Blue Nile, R., 80B, Ae
Blue Ridge Mts., 57, Be
Bluestack, 15, Cb
Blumenau, 68, Ee
Blunkenburg, 30, Jc
Bo, 96B, Ab
Bobbio, 22, Dc
Bobo-Dioulasso, 96B, Ba
Boca de Navios, 43A, Gd
Boca del Toro, 43A, Dd
Bochingeham (Buckingham), 13, Fe
Bochingehamscire (Buckinghamshire), 13, Fe
Böckelheim, 10, Bd
Bodele (Bootle), 13, Cb
Bodmin, 27, Bf
Bodotria Aest. (Firth of Forth), 3A, Da

Bogesund, 26, Db
Boggerah Mts., 15, Bd
Bogota, 68, Bb
Bohemia, King. of, 21, Ld
Bohemia-Moravia, Prot. of, 87, Dc
Bohemian Forest, 60A, Dd
Bohemond, 16, Fd
Bohemond, Castle of, 18E
Bohol, 75E, Bc
Bohun, 28A, Cc
Bohns, 26, Db
Behuslan, 50, Cb
Bois le Duc, 46A, Ec
Boisdale L., 49A, Ab
Boise, 70, Cc
Bojador, C., 55B, Jd
Bokhara, I, Jd; 6, Hb
Bokhara, Khanate of, 61B, B5
Bolama, 96B, Aa
Bolan Pass, 73, Ab; 92, Bb
Bolchen, 39B, Ca
Bolinbroc (Bolingbroke), 13, Gc
Bolingbroke, 27, Fc
Bolivar, 68, Cf
Bolivia, 68, Cd
Bologna (Bononia), 5, Cb
Bolsena, L., 32A, Dc
Bolsover, 13, Ec
Bolton, England, 48A, Bc
Bolton, Massachusetts, 72C, Aa
Bolton Abbey, 36, Ed
Bolton Castle, 48A, Cb
Bolzen, 5, Ca
Boma, 80A, Ee
Bombay, 73, Bd
Bona, 16, De; 47, De
Bonacca, 43A, Dc
Bonar Bridge, 49A, Bb
Bonaventure, 45A, Ea
Bonavista, B., 45A, Ga
Bonavista, C., 45A, Ga
Bondoukou, 96B, Bb
Bone, 80A, Da
Bongor, 96B, Da
Boni, 52C, Bb
Bonifacio, 23A, Dc; 53, Bf
Bonin Is., 74, Nf; 90, Db
Bonn, 10, Bc; 83A, Da
Bonny, 81C, Fd
Bononia, 5B, Aa
Booma Pass, 81B, Cc
Boomplaats, 81A, Cc
Boonesboro, 57A, Cb
Boonesborough, 56, Cc
Boonville, 72, Bb
Boothia Pen., 44, Ea
Bopüngen, 20, Jd
Boppard, 20, Gc
Bordeaux, 11, Cd
Bordeaux, eccl. prov., 22, Bb
Bordesley, 36, Ee
Börglum, 26, Cb
Borgne, L., 71F, Ba
Borisov, 62, Hb
Borku, 80A, Ec
Bormio, 29B, Eb; 32A, Ba
Borne (Eastbourne), 13, Gf
Borneo, 40, Pd; 91, Ef
Borneo (Java Major), 35, Pd
Bornholm, 26, Eb
Bornhöved, 20, Ja
Borodino, 62, Ka
Boroughbridge, 27, Eb
Borthwick, 37A, Cc
Boshof, 81A, Cc
Bosna, R., 78, Bc
Bosnia, 21, Mf; 78, Ac
Bosporus, 78, Ge; 86C, Aa
Bosra, 6A, Bb
Boston, England, 27, Fd
Boston, Massachusetts, 45B, Db; 56B
Boston Neck, 56B
Bostra, 18C, Df
Bosworth, 27, Ed
Botany B., 77, Ih
Botha's Pass, 81D, Aa
Bothnia, G. of, 26, Fa
Bothwell, 28B, Ab
Bothwell Bridge, 49A, Bc
Boswana, 96D, Eg
Botzen, 10, De
Bouake, 96B, Bb
Boudonitza, 19, Ce
Bougainville, 77, Ic; 90, Db
Bouillon, 46A, Ee; 53, Fc
Boulogne, 11, Da
Boulonnais, 53, Db
Boundi, 59C, Cb
Bounty I., 75, Fg
Bourbon, 17, Ge; 42, Mf
Bourbon, S. of, 20, Ee
Bourbon l'Ancy, 30, Ee
Bourbon l'Archambault, 53, Ed
Bourbonnais, 17, Ee
Bourg, Guyenne, 20, Cf
Bourg, Savoy, 30, Fe
Bourganeuf, 30, Df
Bourges, 11, Ec
Bourges, eccl. prov., 22, Cb

Bourges, V. of, 11, Ec
Bourgneuf Bay, 28C, Ac
Bourne, 36, Fe
Boutières, 38, Ff
Bouvet I., 95, Th
Bouvines, 17, Gc; 46A, Cd
Bovino, 22, Fc
Bowes, 13, Db
Bowling Green, Virginia, 57, Cd
Bowness, 3C
Boxley, 36, Gf
Boxtel, 46A, Ec
Boyata, 68, Bb
Boyne, R., 15, Ec; 37B, Ec
Brabant, 46A, Dd
Brabant, D. of, 17, Hc; 46, Bb
Bracciano, 39, Kg
Brackley, 27, Ed
Bradeford (Bradford-on-Avon), 13, De
Bradenstock, 36, Ef
Bradford, Wilts., 27, De
Bradford, Yorks., 48A, Cc
Bradninch, 27, Cf
Bradock Down, 48A, Ad
Braemar, 37A, Cb; 49A, Cb
Braga, 22, Ac; 63, Ab
Braga, eccl. prov., 22, Ac
Braganca, Brazil, 68, Dd
Bragança, Portugal, 63, Bb
Brahmanabad, 6, Hd
Brahmaputra (Tsanpo), R., 73, Eb
Braila, 51, Fd; 78, Fc
Bramber and Steyning, 27, Ff
Brampton, 49A, Cc
Branco, R., 68, Cc
Brancepeth, 27, Eb
Brandenburg, Germany, 10, Eb
Brandenburg, Kentucky, 72, Cb
Brandenburg, M. of, 21, Kb
Brandon, 45B, Ae
Brandon B., 49B, Ad
Brandon Hill, 15, Ad
Brandywine, R., 57. Dd
Branford, 45B, Cc
Brännkyrka, 26, Eb
Branodunum (Brancaster), 3A, Gd
Bras d'Or. L., 45A, Ea
Brashear City, 72, Bd
Brasilia, 68, Ed
Braunau, 21, Kd; 29A, Ea
Braunsberg, 26, Ec; 39, Na
Bravo del Norte (Rio Grande), R., 43A, Bb
Bravoniacum (Kirkby Thore), 3A, Db
Bravonium (Leintwardine), 3A, Dd
Brazil, 41B, Ee; 68, Dd
Brazos, R., 70, Ed
Brazos Santiago, 70, Ee
Brazzaville, 80A, Ee
Brechin, 14, Fc
Brecon, 27, Ce
Breda, 46A, Dc
Breda, Barony of, 46C, Bb
Brederode, 46, Ec
Breedevoort, 46A, Fc
Breedon, 7B, Cb
Breeds Hill, 56B
Breffny, 15, Db
Breisach, 29A, Ba; 38, Gd
Breisgau, 30, Ge; 38, Ge
Breitenfeld, 39, Kc
Breitenwang, 20, Je
Brembre (Bramber), 13, Ff
Bremen, 10, Cb
Bremen, eccl. prov., 22, Da
Bremen, Abp. of, 30, Hb
Bremenium (High Rochester), 3A, Da
Bremerhaven, 55A, Hb; 65D, Aa
Bremetennacum (Ribchester), 3A, Dc
Brenner Pass, 5, Ca; 10, De
Breno, 86B, Ab
Brenta, R., 5, Cb; 86B, B b
Brentford, 48A, Cd
Brescello, 32D, Bb
Brescia, 5, Cb; 29A, Dc
Breslau, 21, Mc
Bresse, 17A, Ec; 38, Fe
Bressuire, 20, Ce
Brest, 30, Ad
Brest Litovsk, 26, Fc
Breteuil, 11, Eb; 30, Dd
Bretigny, 24, Cd; 28C, Cb
Bretlinton (Bridlington), 13, Fb
Breton C., 45A, Fa
Bretons, 8B, Ab; 85, Bc
Breuckelen, 45B, Cc
Briancon, 20, Gf
Briansk, 26, Hc

Briar Creek, 57D, Ab
Brice's Cross Roads, 72, Cc
Brideport (Bridport), 13, Df
Bridgetown, 43A, Gc
Bridgnorth, 27, Dd
Bridgwater, 27, De
Bridiers, 20, De
Bridlington, 36, Fc
Bridport, 27, Df
Brieg, 31, Mc; 39, Mc
Brienne, 11, Fb
Brienz, 29B, Bb
Brienz, L., 29B, Bb
Driey, 20, Fd; 39B, Ba
Brig, 29B, Bb
Brigantes, 3A, Db
Brighton, 48B, Cd
Brignoles, 20, Gg
Brihuega, 63, Db
Brill, 46A, Dc
Brindisi (Brindisium), 5, Fd
Brioude, 11, Ed
Brisbane, 77, Ig
Brissac, 53, Cd
Bristol, England, 27, De
Bristol, Rhode I., 57, Fe
Bristol, Tennessee, 72, Db
Bristol, bp., 36, Df
Bristol Channel, 27, Ce
Bristou (Bristol), 13, De
Britain, 2A, Aa
Britannia, 2, Cc
British Columbia, 70, Bb
British East Africa, 80A, Gd
British Guiana, 43D, Gd; 68B, Bb
British Honduras, 55B, Ae
British Isles, 69B
British Kaffraria, 81B, Db
British New Guinea (Terr. of Papua), 77, Gc
British North Borneo, 74, Kh; 90, Bc
British Somaliland, 96A, Bb
British South Africa Company, 80A, Ff
Brittania (Wellington), 77, Nj
Brittany, 7A, Cb
Brittany, D. of, 30, Bd
Brive, 20, Df
Briwetone (Bruton), 13, De
Brixen, 10, De; 20, Je
Brixworth, 7B, Cb
Broach, 73, Bc
Broad, R., 57D, Aa
Brocavum (Brougham), 3A, Db
Brocolitia (Carrowburgh), 3c
Brod, 78, Ac
Brodick, 37A, Bc
Brody, 50, Fc; 84, Hb
Broken Hill, 77, Gh
Bromberg, 54, Fb; 60A, Fb
Brömsebro, 47, Fa; 50, Db
Bromsgrove, 27, Dd
Bromyard, 27, Dd
Brondolo, 32D, Cb
Bronker's Spruit, 81A, Cc
Brookline, 56B
Brooklyn, 57B
Broom, L., 14, Cb
Broome, 77, Ce
Brosna, R., 15, Dc
Brouage, 53, Ce
Brough, 13, Db; 23B, Cc
Brougham, 28B, Cc
Browns Ferry, 72A, Aa
Bruchhausen, 20, Hb
Bruck, 21, Le
Bruffe, 49B, Cd
Bruges, 17, Gc; 46A, Cc
Bruinsberg, 72C, Ab
Brunanburh, 7C, Ba
Brundisium, 2, Ge
Brunei, 91, Ff
Brunig Pass, 29B, Cb
Brunkeberg, 26, Eb
Brünn, 21, Md; 29A, Ga
Brunnen, 29B, Cb
Brunswick, Georgia, 56, Cd
Brunswick, Germany, 10, Db; 38, Hb
Brunswick, Maine, 57, Gb
Brunswick-Lüneburg, D. of, 20, Jb
Brunswick-Wolfenbüttel, D. of, 30, Hb
Brusa, 19, Dd; 86c, Aa
Brussa, 6, Da
Brussels, 28D, Ea; 46A, Dd
Bruttium, 4B, Fd; 5, Fe
Bryansk, 88, Mc
Brycheiniog, 7B, Bc; 13, Ce
Byron, I., 45A, Ea
Bucaramanga, 68, Bb
Bucellas, 63B
Bucfestre (Buckfastleigh), 13, Cf
Buch, 17, Ef
Buchan, 14, Fb
Buchanan, 48B, Aa

Bucharest, 78, Fc
Buchau, 20, Hd
Buchhorn, 20, He; 53, Hd
Buchy, 76A, Ab
Buckingham, 27, Fe
Buckland (Cornwall), 36, Bg
Buckland (Somerset), 36, Cf
Buczacz, 50, Fd
Buda, 39, Ne
Budapest, 33C, Db; 87, Dc
Budaun, 73, Cb
Budge Budge, 59A, Ec
Budua, 22, Fc
Budweis, 21, Ld; 29A, Fa
Buea, 80A, Dd
Buellt, 7B, Bb; 13, Cd
Buen Ayre, 43A, Fc
Buenaventura, 41B, Bc
Buenos Aires, 68, Df
Buffalo, 71C, Cb
Buffalo, R., C. Prov., 81B, Bc
Buffalo (Umzimyati), R., 81D, Bb
Bug, R., Poland, 26, Fc; 39, Qb
Bug, R., Ukraine, 9, Jc; 50, Gd
Bugey, 38, Fe
Bugia, 34, De
Builth, 27, Cd
Bujids, King. of, 6B, Gb
Buka, 90, Dd
Bukeilarian, Theme, 9, Jd
Bukhara, 93, Jb
Bukkur, 73, Ab
Bukovina, 33C, Fb
Bulair, 78, Fe; 86D
Bulawayo, 81A, Cb
Bulgar, 9, Mb; 19, Ha
Bulgaria, 78, Ed
Bulgaria, King. of, 19, Cd
Bulgarians, 8, Jb
Bulgarians of Kazan, 61, Gd
Bulgars, 8C, Db; 25, Da
Bull Run, 72B, Ba
Bulo Burti, 96A, Bb
Bulun, 74, La
Bulwer, 81D, Ab
Bundelkhand, 73, Cc
Bundoran, 49B, Cb
Bungay, 27, Hd
Bunker Hill, 56B
Bunzlau, 21, Lc
Buraburg, 8A, Ca
Buraida, 93, Ed
Burdas, 9, Mb
Burdekin, R., 77, He
Burdigala, 2, Ce
Burdwan, 59A, Ec; 59B
Burford, 7B, Cc; 27, Ee
Burg, 39, Kb
Burg (Peterborough), 13, Fd
Burgas, 78, Fc
Burgau, 20, Jd
Burgdorf, 29B, Ba
Burgh by Sands, 3C
Burgh on Sands, 28B, Bc
Burgos, 22, Bc; 63, Da
Burgos, eccl. prov., 22, Bc
Burgundian Kingdom, 4A, Db
Burgundians, 2A, Bb; 8C, Bb
Burgundiones, 2, Fd
Burgundy, Co. of, 10, Be; 11, Fc
Burgundy, D. of, 11, Fc
Burgundy, King. of (Arelate), 11, Fd
Burhampur, 59C, Cc
Burke (De Burgh), 37B, Cc
Burkesville, 72, Cb
Burketown, 77, Fe
Burlington, New Jersey, 45B, Bc
Burlington, Vermont, 57, Ea
Burma, 73, Gc
Burma (Mien), 25, Jd
Burma Road, 91, Cd
Burpham, 7C, Cc
Burrium (Usk), 3A, De
Burton upon Trent, 36, Ee
Burtone (Burton), 13, Ed
Buru, 52C, Db; 91, Fg
Burundi, 96, Ee
Bury St. Edmunds, 27, Gd
Busaco, 63, Ab
Bushman Land, 81B, Ab
Bushmans, R., 81D, Ab
Bushmen, 81A, Ac
Bushy Run, 57, Bc
Bussa, 80A, Dc
Bute, 14, Cd
Bute, co., 37A, Bc
Butera, 21A, Cd
Butler, 37B, Dd
Butley, 36, He
Buton, 52C, Bb
Bütow, 31, Ma
Butte des Mortes, 56, Bb
Butterworth, 48B, Cc
Buttington, 7C, Bb
Buxar, 59A, Db

Buxtehude, 26, Cc
Buzakha, 6, Fc
Buzancy, 76A, Cb
Buzzard B., 45B, Dc
Byblos (Gibelet), 18C, Cd
Bydgoszcz, 31, Nb
Byelgorod, 61, Gd
Byland, 36, Ec
Byrd Land, 95, Gj
Byzantine Empire. 9, Ge
Byzantium, 1, Ec

CABELLUM, 5B, Aa
Cabinda, 80A, Ee
Cabinda, col., 96C, De
Cabot Str., 45A, Fa
Cacabellos, 63, Ba
Caceres, 23C, Bc
Cachoeira, 68, Fd
Caconda, 52, Ke
Cadore, 32A, Ea
Cadiz, 23C, Bd; 63, Bd
Cadodachos, 43A, Ca
Cadzand, 46A, Cc
Caen, 11, Cb
Caer Gai, 3A, Cd
Caer Segeini, 7B, Ab
Caer Segont, 13, Bc
Caer Sws, 3A, Cd
Caerdydd (Cardiff), 13, Ce
Caerlaverock, 28B, Bb
Caerleon, 13, De; 28A, Dc
Caerphilly, 27, Ce; 28A, Cc
Caesar Augusta, 2, Cc
Caesarea, Africa, 2, Df; 4A, Cd
Caesarea, Km. of Jerusalem, 18C, Cc
Caesarea, Syria, 18C, Dc
Caesarea, Turkey, 6, Eb; 19, Fe
Caffraria, 69A, Lf
Cagayan, 75E, Bc
Cagliari, 23A, Bd; 32B, Be
Cagliari, eccl. prov., 22, Dd; 23A, Bd
Cahokia, 56, Ac
Cahors, 11, Dd ;17A, Cd
Caicos, 43A, Eb
Caird Coast, 69C
Cairns, 95, Lf
Cairo (Fustat), 6A, Ab
Cairo, Egypt, 80B, Ab
Cairo, Illinois, 72, Cb
Caistor, Lincs., 3A, Fc
Caistor, Norfolk, 7B, Db
Caithness, 14, Da
Cajamarca, 41B ,Bd
Calabria, 5, Fd; 21A, Dc
Calabria Theme, 9, Fe
Calahorra, 22, Bc; 23C, Da
Calais, 17A, Ca; 30, Dc
Calamian Group, 75E, Ab
Calatafimi, 32C, De
Calatayud, 23C. Db; 63, Eb
Calatrava, 22, Bd; 23C, Dc
Calcaria (Tadcaster), 3A, Ec
Calcutta, 59B
Caldera, 68, Be
Caldiero, 29A, Dc
Caledon, 81B, Ac
Caledon, R., 81B, Cb
Caledonia, 2, Bb; 14, Eb
Calgary, 70, Cb
Calhoun, 72A, Aa
Cali, 68, Bb
Calicut, 73, Ce
California, 43A, Ab; 70, Cd
California, G. of, 43A, Ab
Callander, 49A, Bb
Callao, 68, Bd
Calleva Atrebatum (Silchester), 3A, Ee
Callinicum, 2, Lf; 4B. Kd
Calmar, 26, Eb
Calmar, Union of, 35, Ka
Calne, 27, De
Caltabellotta, 21A, Bd
Caltanisetta, 21A, Cd
Calvi, 53, Bf
Calvinet, 38, Ef
Calvinia, 81B, Ab
Camaldoli, 21, Ec; 23A, Cb
Camarinal, C., 63A
Cambay, 35, Nc; 73, Bc
Cambay, G. of, 73, Bc
Cambodia, 91, De
Camboglanna (Birdoswald), 3C
Cambolu, 35, Pb
Cambrai, 46A, Cd
Cambrai, Bp of, 46C, Ab
Cambrésis, 46A, Cd
Cambridge, England, 27, Gd
Cambridge, Massachusetts, 45B, Db, 56B
Cambridge, co., 27, Gd
Cambridge (Charles), R., 56B
Cambuskenneth, 14, Ec
Camden, Arkansas, 72, Bc
Camden, S. Carolina, 57D, Ab
Camelon, 3A, Ca
Camerino, 5, Dc

Cameron, 37A, Bb
Cameroon, 96D, Dd
Cameroons, 96C, Dd
Cameta, 68, Ec
Camisards, 54, Cd
Campagna, 32A, Ed
Campaldino, 32E, Bb
Campania, 5, Dd
Campbell, 28B, Aa; 37A, Bb
Campbell I., 69C; 75, Fg
Campbelltown, 49A, Bc
Campeche, 43A, Cc
Campeche, st., 43A, Cc
Campeche. G. of, 43A, Cb
Camperdown, 55A, Fb
Campinas, 68, Ee
Campo Formio, 65A, Bb
Campobasso, 32A, Fd
Campos, 68, Ee
Camulodunum (Colchester), 3A, Ge
Canada, 45A, Ba; 69A, Fb
Canadian, R., 70, Dd
Canal Zone, 68, Ab
Canary Is., 80A, Bb
Canaveral, C., 70, Fe
Canberra, 77, Hi
Cancelleria, 5A
Candia, 19, De; 78, Eh
Canea, 78, Dh
Canigou, 22, Cc
Canna, 15, Bb
Cannae, 21A, Db
Cannanore, 59A, Ce
Cannes, 30, Gg
Canossa, 23B, Cb
Canovium (Caerhun), 3A, Cc
Canso, C., 45A, Ea
Cantabria, 4A ,Bc; 8, Bc
Cantabrian Mts., 63, Ca
Canterbury, England, 27, He
Canterbury, N.Z., 77A
Canterbury, bp., 36, Gf
Canterbury, eccl. prov., 22, Ba
Canterbury Plain, 77, Mj
Cantii, 3A, Ge
Canton, China, 25, Ld; 91, Ed
Canton, Mississippi, 72, Bc
Cantuaria (Canterbury), 13, He
Cantware, 7A, Db
Canusium, 5, Fd
Cão, 35, Kf
Cap Francois, 43A, Ec
Capdenac, 38, Ef
Cape, 81B, Ac
Cape Ann (Gloucester), 45B, Db
Cape Breton I., 71, Hc
Cape Breton I. (Ile Royale), 45A, Ea
Cape Coast, 96B, Bb
Cape Coast Castle, 81C, Dc
Cape Cod B., 45B, Dc
Cape Colony, 69A, Lf
Cape Colony (Cape of Good Hope), 81A, Bd
Cape Fear, R., 57, Bf; 57D, Ba
Cape Fear (Charles), R., 45A, Bc
Cape of Good Hope (Cape Colony, 81A), Bd
Cape Porpoise, 45B, Db
Cape Town, 81B, Ac
Caper Verde Is., 80A, Ac
Cape York Pen., 77, Gd
Capetown, 52, Kf
Capitanata, 32A, Fd
Capitol, 5A
Capiz, 75E, Bb
Capo d'Istria, 22, Eb; 32D, Cb
Cappadocia, 2, Lf
Cappadocia Theme, 9, Je
Caporetto. 84, Ec; 86B, Da
Caprera I., 32C, Bd
Capri, 5, Ed
Capsa, 6, Bb
Capua, 5, Ed; 32A, Fd
Capua, D. of, 23A, Ec
Capua, Pr. of, 21A, Cb
Caqueta, R., 68, Bc
Carabobo, 68, Cb
Caracas, 41B, Cc; 68, Cb
Caradeña, 22, Bc
Caralis, 2, Ef
Caramania, 33A, Dc
Caravaggio, 32D, Ab
Carberry House, 37A, Cc
Carbisdale, 37A, Bb
Carcassonne, 11, Ee
Cardaillac, 38, Df
Cardiff, 3A, Ce; 27, Ce
Cardigan, 13, Db; 28A, Bb
Cardigan, co., 27, Bd
Cardigan B., 27, Bd
Carelia, 26, Ha; 47, Ja
Carentan, 38, Cd
Carhaix, 11, Bb
Carham, 14, Fa
Caribbean Sea, 43A, Ec
Caribs, 43A, Fd
Carignano, 29A, Bc; 30, Gf

Carinthia, D. of, 10, Fe; 21, Ke
Carisbrooke Castle, 48B, Cd
Carlat, 17, Gf; 30, Ef
Carleol (Carlisle), 13, Db
Carlisle, England, 27, Db
Carlisle, N. America, 57, Cc
Carlisle, bp., 36, Gc
Carlow, 15, Ed
Carlow, co., 37C; 49B, Ed
Carlowitz, 33C, Db; 79, Ca
Carlsbad, 64, Ec; 65C, Ba
Carlsruhe, 65A, Ab
Carmanaia, 1, He
Carmarthen, 27, Be; 36, Bf
Carmarthen, co., 27, Be; 28A, Bc
Carmel, Mt., 18C, Cf
Carmona, 23C, Cd
Carnarvon, Australia, 95, Ng
Carnarvon, S. Africa, 81B, Bb
Carnarvon, Wales, 27, Bc
Carnarvon, co., 27, Bd
Carnatic, 73, Ce
Carnero Pt., 63A
Carnic Alps, 29A, Eb; 86B ,Ca
Carnifex Ferry, 72, Db
Carniola, 10, Ff
Carniola, D. of, 21, Lf
Carnsore Pt., 15, Ed
Carolina, 45A, Ad
Caroline Is., 74, Mg; 90, Dc
Carolines, 40, Rd
Carpathian Mts., 8, Gb; 50, Ed
Carpathian Ruthenia, 87, Ec
Carpatus Mons, 2, Hd
Carpentaria, G. of, 77, Fd
Carpentras, 22, Dc
Carpi, 32A, Db
Carrantuohill, 15, Be
Carrara, 22B, Cb
Carrick, Galloway, 14, Dd
Carrick, Leitrim, 49B, Cc
Carrick, Tipperary, 49B, Dd
Carrickfergus, 37B, Fb; 49B, Fb
Carricks Ford, 72, Eb
Carriden, 3A, Ca
Carse of Gowrie, 28B, Da
Carso, 86B, Db
Cartagena, Columbia, 43A, Ec
Cartagena, Spain, 4A, Bd; 23C, Ed; 63, Ed
Cartago, 41B, Bc
Cartersville, 72A, Aa
Carthage, 4A, Ed; 9, Ee
Carthage, U.S.A., 70, Ed
Carthago, 2, Ff
Carthago Nova, 2, Cf
Cartmel, 28B, Cc; 36, Dc
Carumnassa, R., 59A, Db
Casablanca, 80A, Ca; 96D, Ba
Casale, 32A, Db
Casalmaggiore, 32D, Bb
Casco B., 57, Fb
Casco (Fort Loyal) (Falmouth), 45B, Db
Caseros, 68, Df
Cashel, 15, Dd
Caspe, 23C, Eb; 23D, Eb
Caspian Sea, 19, Hd; 25, Eb
Cassanitae, 1, Ge
Cassano, Calabria, 22, Fd
Cassano, Lombardy, 29A, Cc
Cassel, Flanders, 20, Fc
Cassel, Thuringia, 20, Hc
Cassett, 30, Ee
Castalla, 63, Ec
Castamon, 18A, Ea
Castanheira, 63B
Castel Branco, 22, Ad
Castel Jaloux, 38, Df
Castel Sardo, 23B, Bd
Castelbaldo, 32D, Bb
Castelfranco, 86B, Bb
Castell Collen, 3A, Cd
Castellamare, 32C, Ed
Castello, 22A
Castello Branco, 63, Bc
Castello Tesino, 86B, Ba
Castellon Alani (Richmond), 13 Eb
Castellon Harundel (Arundel), 13, Ff
Castellon Warham (Corfe Castle), 13 Df
Castelnau, 20, Dg
Castelnaudary, 30, Dg
Castelnuovo, 78, Bd
Castelorizo, 86C, Ab
Castelsagrat, 38, Df
Castets, 38, Cf
Castiglione, Lombardy, 29A, Dc
Castiglione, Tuscany, 20, Jg
Castile, King. of, 23C, Cb
Castilia do Oro, 43A, Dd
Castillon, 11, Cd
Castle I., 56B
Castle Dermot, 49B, Ed

Castle Douglas, 49A, Cc
Castle Flemish, 3A, Be
Castle of St. Angelo, 5A
Castle Rising, 48A, Dc
Castlebar, 49B, Bc
Castlecary, 3A, Ca
Castledykes, 3A, Ca
Castlefinn, 49B, Db
Castlehill, 3A, Ba
Castlejordan, 15, Dc
Castlekevin, 37B, Ec
Castlereagh, 49B, Cc
Castleroe, 37B, Ea
Castles, B. of the, 55B, Ea
Castlesteads, 3C
Castleton, 57, Bb
Castletown, 48A, Ab
Castra Exploratum (Netherby), 3A, Ca
Castres, 20, Eg; 22, Cc
Castro, 22, Ec; 32B, Cc
Castro Giovanni, 23A, Ef
Castrum Felicitatis, 5B, Bb
Cat I., 43A, Eb
Catalans, 85, Cd
Catalonia, 23C, Fb; 63, Fb
Catalonia, Pr. of, 16, Cd
Catamarca, 68, Ce
Catanduanes, 75E, Bb
Catania, 21A, Cd; 22, Fd
Catanzaro, 22, Fd
Cataractonium (Catterick Bridge), 3A, Eb
Cateau Cambrésis, 34, Cb
Cathay, 25, Kc
Cathkin Peak, 81D, Ab
Catóche, C., 43A, Db
Catric (Catterick), 13, Eb
Catrone, 22, Fd
Catskill Mts., 57, Db
Cattaro, 22, Fc; 78, Bd
Cattegat, 84, Ea
Catterick, 7A, Ca
Catuvellauni, 3A, Fe
Cauca, R., 68, Bb
Caucasus, 19, Gd; 33A, Fb
Caucasus Mons, 2, Me
Caudebec, 20, Dd
Cauna (Calne), 13, De
Causennae (Ancaster), 3A, Fd
Caus, 13, Dd; 28A, Db
Causse, 38, Eg
Cauvery, R., 73, Ce
Cavan, 49B, Dc
Cavan, co., 37C; 49B, Dc
Cavour, 32C, Ab
Cawnpore, 73, Db
Cawood Castle, 48A, Cc
Cayenne, 43B, Ed; 68, Db
Cayman Is., 43A, Dc
Cayo Romano, 43A, Eb
Cayoan, 52B, Aa
Cayugas, 45A, Bb
Ceara, 41B, Fd
Ceara (Fortaleza), 68, Fc
Ceara, st., 68, Fc
Cebu, 75E, Bb
Cebu, I., 75E, Bb
Ceccanum, 5B, Bc
Cedar Creek, 72B, Aa
Cedar Keys, 72, Dd
Cedar Mountain, 72B, Aa
Cedar Rapids, 57, Ea
Cefalu, 21A, Cc; 22, Ed
Celebes, 52C, Bb; 74, Lj
Celebes (Sulawesi), 91, Eg
Celebes Sea, 91, Ff
Celle, 30, Jb
Celorico, 63, Bb
Celtic Lands, 4A, Aa
Celts, 8C, Aa
Cembala, 19, Ed
Ceneda, 22, Bb
Central Africa, rep., 96D, Dd
Central America, rep., 69A, Ed
Central Australia, 77, Ef
Central Provinces, India, 74, Ff
Cephallenia Theme, 9, Ge
Cephalonia, 78, Cf
Cephalonia, Co. of, 24, Gf
Ceprano, 23B, Dd
Ceram, 52C, Cb; 77, Db; 91, Fg
Cerami, 23A, Ef
Ceramix, 21A, Cd
Cerdagne, 30, Dg
Cerdana, 23C, Ga
Ceredigion (Cardigan), 7B, Ab; 13, Bd
Ceri, 13, Cd
Cerignola, 32A, Fd
Cerigo, 18B, Cc; 78, Dg
Cerisolo, 29A, Bc
Cernauti, 87, Fc
Cerne, 36, Dg
Cerneli (Cerne Abbas), 13, Df
Cerralvo, 43A, Cb
Cerro de Pasco, 68, Bd
Certesyg (Chertsey), 13, Fe
Cervera, 63, Fb
Cervignano, 86B, Db
Cesena, 32A, Eb

Cesenae, 5B, Ba
Cesme, 51, Ff
Cestre (Chester), 13, Dc
Cestrescire (Cheshire), 13, Dc
Cetinje, 78, Bd
Cette, 30, Eg
Ceuta, 23C, Ce; 34, Ac; 63A
Cevennes, 11, Ed
Ceylon, 73, Df
Ceylon (Seilan), 25, Hf
Chabats, 78, Bc
Chablais, 29B, Ab
Chacabuco, 68, Bf
Chaco, 68, Ce
Chad, L., 96B, Da
Chad, rep., 96D, Dc
Chads Ford, 57, Dd
Chagos Is., 69A, Ne; 94, Qf
Chagres, 43A, Ed
Chalcedon, 2, Je; 8, Hc
Chalchuites, 43A, Bb
Chalcis, 4B, Kd
Chaldea Theme, 9, Kd
Chaldiran, 33A, Fb
Chaleur B., 45A, Ea
Chalgrove Field, 48A, Cd
Challon, 29B, Ab
Chalon, 11, Fc
Chalôns, 11, Fb; 83A, Cb
Châlons Camp, 76A, Cb
Chaluz, 17, Ff
Cham, 21, Kd
Chambal, R., 73, Cb
Chambersburg, 72, Eb
Chambéry, 20, Ff; 30, Ff
Chambly, 56, Ea
Champa, 25, Ke
Champagne, 11, Eb; 83A, Cb
Champagne, Co. of, 20, Fb
Champigny, 76A, Bb
Champion's Hill, 72C, Aa
Champlain L., 57, Ea
Chanak, 86D
Chancellorsville, 72B, Ba
Chandax, 9, He
Chandernagore, 59B
Chandière, R., 71E, Ac
Chang-an, 1, Nd
Changchow, 41A, Jb
Changchun, 91, Fb
Changsha, 91, Ed
Changtan, 76B, Ba
Channel Is., 11, Bb
Chantoceaux, 20, Ce
Chapelle St. Lambert, 46B
Charak, 93, Gd
Charcot I., 69C
Chard, 27, Df; 48A, Bd
Charente, R., 17, Ef
Charing Cross, 27A
Charleroi, 46A, Dd
Charles, C., 45B, Be
Charles, King. of, 8A, Bc
Charles (Cambridge), R., 56B
Charles (Cape Fear), R., 45A, Bc
Charles City, 45B, Ae
Charles Fort, 45A, Ad
Charles Town, 45A, Ad
Charleston, Massachusetts, 45B, Db
Charleston, S. Carolina, 57D, Bb
Charleston, W. Virginia, 72, Db
Charleston (Stephen's Fort), 57, Eb
Charlestown, Massachusetts, 56B
Charlestown, Natal, 81D, Aa
Charleville, Australia, 95, Lg
Charleville, France, 53, Cb
Charlotte, 57, Af
Charlottesville, 57, Be
Charlottetown, 71, Hc
Charolais, 30, Fe; 38, Fe
Charolles, 17, He
Charolles, Co., 31A, Gd
Charost, 53, Ed
Charroux, 22, Cb
Charsianon Theme, 9, Je
Charter, 81A, Da
Charters Towers, 77 Hf
Chartres, 11, Db; 17A, Cb
Chartreux, 11, Fa
Chatalja, 78, Ge
Château Chinon, 30, Ee
Château Dauphin, 53, Ge
Château d'If, 38, Fg
Château des Dames, 83A, Bb
Château Gaillard, 20, Dd
Château Neuf, 20, Ee
Château Thierry, 17, Gd
Châteaubriant, 38, Ce
Châteaudun, 11, Db
Châteauguay, R., 71C, Da
Châteauroux, 17, Fe
Châteauroux, S. of, 20, De
Châtellerault, 11, Dc
Chatham, 55A, Dc
Chatham I., 75, Gg
Châtillon, 38, Cd; 76A, Cc

Chattahoochee, R., 72, Cc
Chattanooga, 72A, Aa
Chaudière, R., 56, Ea
Chaumont, 20, Fd; 76A, Cb
Chaves, 23C, Bb; 63, Bb
Cheat, R., 57, Bd
Cheduba I., 90, Ac
Chefoo, 74, Le
Chegar, R., 59D
Chelm, 26, Fc; 33C, Ea
Chelmsford, 27, Ge
Chelsea, 56B
Chelyabinsk, 89, Sb
Chelyuskin, C., 69B
Chemnitz, 31, Kc; 53, Kb
Chenab, R., 73, Ba
Chenaresburg (Knaresborough), 13, Eb
Chengtu, 25, Kc; 91, Dc
Chenth (Kent), 13, Ge
Chepstow, 27, De
Cher, R., 11, Dc; 17, Ge
Chera, 1, Kf
Cherasco, 32B, Ab; 47, Dd
Cheraw, 57D, Ba
Cherbourg, 28D, Bb; 30, Cd
Cherchebi (Kirkby Lonsdale), 13, Db
Cheren, 96A, Aa
Cheriton, 48A, Cd
Cherkassy, 79, Fa
Cherkess, 45A, Ac
Cherna, R., 86A, Ca
Chernigov, 19, Eb; 26, Hc
Cherry Valley, 57, Db
Cherso, 23B, Eb
Cherson, 2A, Eb; 19, Ed
Cherson Theme, 9, Jd
Chertsey, 36, Ff
Chesapeake B., 57, Cd
Chester, England, 27, Dc
Chester, Illinois, 70, Fd
Chester, Pennsylvania, 57, Dd
Chester (Fort New Korsholm), 45B, Bd
Chester, bp., 36, Gd
Chester, Co. Palatine of, 27, Dc
Chesterfield Inlet, 70, Ea
Chesterford, 3A, Fd
Chester-le-Street, 3A, Eb; 7C, Ca
Chetsteven (Kesteven), 13, Fd
Cheviot Hills, 27, Da; 28B, Cb
Cheyenne, 70, Dc
Chiangmai, 91, Ce
Chiao Chow, 1, Oe
Chiapas, 43A, Cc
Chiavenna, 5, Ba; 23B, Bd
Chiavenna, Co. of, 29B, Db
Chicacole, 59A, Dd
Chicago, 56, Bb
Chichagof I., 71B, Db
Chichester, 27, Ff
Chichester, bp., 36, Fg
Chickamauga, 72A, Aa
Chickasaw Bluff (Memphis), 71F, Aa
Chickasaws, Alabama, 43A,Da, Ac
Chickasaws, W. Virginia, 45A, Ac
Chiclayo, 68, Bc
Chicora, 43A, Da
Chidambaram, 59D
Chidley, C., 71, Ha
Chiem L., 29A, Eb
Chiemsee, 22, Ef
Chiengmai, 73, Gd
Chiese, R., 5, Cb; 86B, Ab
Chieti, 5, Ec
Chieveley, 81D, Ab
Chigirin, 50, Gd
Chignecto, C., 45A, Ea
Chihuahua, 43A, Bb
Chikishlyar, 61B, Ab
Chikt B., 71B, Bb
Chilanwala, 73, Ba
Chile, 42, Ff; 68, Be
Chilian, 68, Bf
Chillicothe, 56, Cc
Chiloe I., 68, Bg
Chiltern Hills, 27, Fe
Chilternsaetan, 7B, Cc
Chimay, 30, Fc; 46A, Dd
Chimkent, 61B, Ba
China, 41A, Ja; 74, Je
China Sea, 25, Le
Chinampo, 76B, Db
Chincha Is., 68, Bd
Chinchowfu, 76B, Aa
Chinde, 83, Le
Chindwin, R., 73, Gb
Chinese Eastern Railway, 74, Ld
Chinese Empire, 83, Oc
Chinese Rep., 91, Dc
Ching Chow, 1, Oe
Chingleput, 59D
Chingkiang, 25, Lc; 74, Le
Chinon, 17, Fe; 28C, Cc
Chins Division, 92, Gc
Chinsura, 59B
Chiny, 20, Fd

Chioggia, 32D, Cb
Chios, 24, Hf; 78, Ef
Chippenham, 7C, Bc; 27, De
Chippewa, 71D
Chipping Norton, 27, Ee
Chirbury, 13, Cd
Chirk, 27, Cd
Chisholm, 37A, Bb
Chita, 91, Ea
Chitaldroog, 59A, Ce
Chitor, 25, Gd; 52A, Bb
Chittagong, 92, Gc
Chittagong, st., 73, Fc
Chiusi, 5, Cc
Chobe Swamp, 81A, Ba
Choctaws, 56, Bd
Choczim, 50, Fd; 54, Hc
Choiseul, E. Indies, 77, Jc
Choiseul, France, 53, Cb
Chola, 1, Kf
Cholas, 25, Ge
Cholula, 43A, Cc
Chongju, 76B, Cb
Chonos Arch., 68, Bg
Chorasmia, 1, Jc
Chorlu (Tzurulum), 19, Dd
Chota Nagpur, 73, Dc
Chotusitz, 29A, Fa
Chowan, R., 45B, Ae
Christchurch, England, 27, Ef
Christchurch, N.Z., 77A
Christiania, 50, Cb; 54, Ea
Christiansand, 26, Cb
Christiansborg, 69A, Kd; 81C, Dc
Christianstad, 51, Cb
Christmas I., Indian Ocean, 83, Pe
Christmas I., Pacific Ocean, 75, Hd
Christopolis, 19, Cd
Chrysler's Farm, 71C, Ca
Chu, R., 91, Ab
Chubut (Rawson), 68, Cg
Chubut, R., 68, Cg
Chudes, 9, Ha
Chulak, 61B, Ba
Chungking, 91, Dd
Chur, 5, Ba; 29B, Db
Church, States of the, 32A, Ec
Church of the Holy Sepulchre, 18D
Churchill, 70, Eb
Churchill, R., 70, Db
Cibalae, 2, Gd
Cibyrrhaeot Theme, 9, Je
Cicestre (Chichester), 13, Ff
Cilgerran, 28A, Bb
Cilicia, 2A, Ec; 18C, Cb
Cilicia Theme, 2, Kf
Cilli, 21, Le
Cilurnum (Chesters), 3C
Cimarron, R., 70, Ed
Cin, Sea of, 25, Md
Cinbretune (Kinderton), 13,Dc
Cincinnati, 57A, Cb; 71C, Bc
Cintra, 23C, Ac; 63B
Circassia, 61
Circesium, 2, Mg; 4A, Ld
Circle City, 71A, Ca
Cirencester, 27, Se
Cirencestre (Cirencester), 13, Ee
Cirey, 83B, Ba
Cirta, 2, Ef
Cisalpine (Italian) Rep., 65A, Ab
Citatea, 78, Dc
Citeaux, 11, Fc
Citra, 32A, Fd
Citronelle, 72, Cc
Citta di Castello, 32A, Ec
Cittadella, 86B, Bb
Cittavecchia, 22, Fc
City Pt., 57, Ce
Ciudad Bolivar (Angostura), 68, Cb
Ciudad Real, 23C, Ce; 63, Dc
Ciudad Rodrigo, 23C, Bb; 63, Bb
Ciudad Victoria, 43A, Cb
Ciudadela, 22, Cc
Cividale, 21, Ke; 86B, Da
Civita, 23B, Bd
Civita Vecchia, 5, Cc
Civitate, 21A, Cb
Civitella, 32A, Ec
Clackmannan, co., 37A, Cb; 49A, Cb
Cladyford, 49B, Db
Clair-sur-Epte, 11, Db
Clairac, 22, Cc; 38, Df
Clairvaux, 11, Fb
Clanwilliam, 81B, Ac
Clara (Clare), 13, Cd
Clare, England, 27, Gd
Clare, Ireland, 37B, Cd
Clare, Wales, 28A, Cc
Clare, co., Ireland, 37C; 49B, Cd
Clare, R., 15, Cc

Clarendon, England, 17, Ec
Clarendon, N. Carolina, 45A, Bd
Classis, 23A, Da
Clausentum (Bitterne), 3A, Ef
Clear, C., 15, Be
Cleeve, 36, Cf
Clermont, Auvergne, 8B, Bb; 11, Ed
Clermont, Champagne, 39B, Ba; 76A, Cb
Clermont, Co. of, 20, Ed; 39B, Ba
Clermont Ferrand, 53, Ee
Cleve, Netherlands, 46A, Fc
Cleve, Co. of, Netherlands, 46A, Fc
Cleveland, Ohio, 71C, Bb
Cleveland, Tennessee, 72A, Aa
Cleves, 53, Db
Clew B., 15, Bc; 49B, Bc
Clifford, Scotland, 28B, Cc
Clifford, Wales, 13, Cd
Clifford, Co. of., Wales, 28A, Cb
Clifton, 49A, Cb
Clinton, 72C, Aa
Clisson, 28C, Bc
Clissow, 50, Ec
Clogher, 15, Db
Clonard, 15, Dc
Cloncurry, 77, Gf
Clones, 37B, Db; 49B, Db
Clonfert, 15, Cc; 49B, Cc
Clonlish, 49B, Bd
Clonmacnoise, 15, Dc
Clonmel, 37B, Db; 49B, Dd
Clontarf, 12, Cc; 49B, Ec
Cloudy B., 77A
Cloyne, 15, Ce
Clun, 27, Cd; 28A, Cb
Cluny, 11, Fc
Clydesdale, 14, Ed; 28B, Bb
Clyde, R., 14, Ed; 28B, Ab
Clyde, Firth of, 14, Dd
Clyveland (Cleveland), 13, Eb
Coahuila, 70, Dd
Coats I., 70, Fa
Coats Land, 69C
Cobh (Queenstown), 49B, Ce
Cobija, Bolivia, 68, Cd
Cobija, Chile, 68, Be
Coblenz, 10, Bc; 38, Gc
Coburg, 30, Jc
Cochem, 20, Gc
Cochin, 59A, Ce; 73, Cf
Cochin, st., 59C, Ce; 73, Ce
Cochin China, 74, Jg
Cockburn Chan., 68, Bh
Cockermouth, 27, Cb
Cocos (Keeling) Is., 83, Oe; 90, Ad
Cod, C., 45B, Db
Coevorden, 46A, Fb
Coggeshall, 36, Gf
Cognac, 38, Df
Cohoes, 57, Eb
Coiba I., 43A, Dd
Coigny, 53, Cc
Coimbatore, 73, Ce
Coimbra, 22, Ac; 63, Ab
Colchester, 27, Ge
Cold Harbor, 72B, Bb
Coldstream, 36, Db; 37A, Cc
Colecestra (Colchester), 13, Ge
Colemerik, 93, Eb
Colenso, 81D, Ab
Coleraine, 49B, Ea
Coleroon, R., 52A, Cc; 59D
Colesberg, 81B, Cb
Coligny, 20, Fe
Colima, 43A, Bc
Coll, 14, Bc
Colle, 32E, Bh
Colleton, 45A, Ad
Collioure, 23D, Ga; 53, Ef
Colmar, 8A, Cb; 10, Bd
Colmars, 53, Ge
Cologne, 10, Bc; 83A, Da
Cologne, Abp. of, 46C, Cb
Cologne, eccl. prov., 22, Da
Colombey, 76A, Db
Colombia, 68, Bb
Colombia, Confederation of, 43D, Fd
Colombia, Rep. of, 68, Bb
Colombia, U.S. of, 68, Bb
Colombo, 73, Cf
Colon (Aspinwall), 43D, Ed
Colonea Theme, 9, Kd
Colonia, 68, Df
Colonia Agrippina, 2, Ec
Colonia del Sacramento, 41B, Dg
Colonna, C., 23A, Fd
Colonsay, 14, Bc
Colooney, 49B, Cb
Colorado, R., Argentina, 68, Cf
Colorado, R., U.S.A., 44, Ee
Colorado, st., 70, Dd
Colorado Terr., 67D, Cb

Colosseum, 5A
Columbia, S. Carolina, 57D, Aa
Columbia, Tennessee, 72, Cb
Columbia, Virginia, 56, Dc
Columbia, R., 70, Cb
Columbus, Kentucky, 72, Cb
Columbus, Ohio, 72, Db
Colwyn, 28A, Cb
Comacchio, 5, Db
Combermere, 36, De
Comeragh Mts., 15, Dd
Comfort Pt., 67A, Cb
Comiaclum, 5B, Ba
Cominges, 17, Fg; 20, Dg
Cominges, Co. of, 11, De
Commercy, 39B, Bb
Comminges, 22, Cc
Como, 5, Bb; 29A, Cc
Como, L., 5, Ba
Comorin, C., 73, Cf
Comoro Is., 80A, Hf
Compiègne, 17, Gd; 31A, B
Compludo, 22, Ac
Compoalla, 43A, Cc
Compostela, 43A, Bb
Compostella, 16, Ad
Conakry, 96B, Ab
Concepcion, Chile, 68, Bf
Concepcion, Paraguay, 68, De
Concepcion, Uruguay, 68, Df
Concord, 45B, Db
Concordia, 68, Df
Conde, 46A, Cd
Condeixa, 63, Ab
Condercum (Benwell), 3C
Condom, 53, Df
Conegliano, 86B, Da
Conflans, 30, Ed; 83A, Cb
Congaree, R., 57D, Ad
Congo, rep., (formerly Belgian) 96D, Ee
Congo, rep. (formerly French) 96D, De
Congo, R., 80A, Fd
Congo State, 80A, Fe
Coni, 20, Gf
Coningesburg (Conisborough), 13, Ec
Conisborough, 27, Ec
Conjeeveram, 59D
Connacht, 15, Cc
Connaught, 37B, Cc; 49C
Connecticut, 45B, Cc
Connecticut, R., 45A, Cb
Conn, L., 15, Bb; 37B, Bc
Connor, 15, Eb; 49B, Eb
Consentia (Cosenza), 5, Fe
Constance, 10, Ce; 29B, Da
Constance, L. of, 29B, Da
Constanta, 78, Gc
Constantia, 81B, Ac
Constantine, 80A, Da
Constantinople, 18E; 78, Ge
Constantinopolis (Byzantium), 2, Je
Constantsa, 24, He
Constitucion, 68, Bf
Conti, 53, Ec
Convent Garden, 27A
Conversano, 21A, Db
Conza, 21, Fc
Cooch Behar, 59C, Eb
Cook Inlet, 71A, Bb
Cook Is., 75, Hf
Cook, Mt., 77, Lj
Cook Str., 77, Mj
Cook's Mill, 71D
Cooktown, 77, Ge
Coolgardie, 77, Ch
Coombe, 36, Ee
Cooper's Creek, 77, Gg
Coorg, 73, Ce
Coosa, R., 56, Bd
Copenhagen, 26, Db
Copiapo, 41B, Bf; 68, Be
Coppermine, R., 70, Ca
Coquet, R., 28B, Db; 48A, Bb
Coquimbo, 68, Bf
Coral Sea, 77, Je; 90, Dd
Corato, 21A, Db
Corbach, 60A, Bc
Corbeil, 11, Eb
Corbet, 28A, Db
Corbie, 11, Eb; 22, Ca
Corbridge, 27, Ea
Cordoba, 68, Cf
Cordova, Alaska, 71A, Ca
Cordova, Spain, 22, Bd; 63, Cd
Cordova, Emirate of, 8, Bd
Crieff, 49A, Cb
Corduba, 2, Cf
Corfe Castle, 27, Df
Corfu, 78, Bf
Coria, 22, Ac; 63, Bc
Coringa, 59C, Dd
Corinium (Cirencester), 3A, Ee
Corinth, Greece, 2, Hf
Corinth, U.S.A., 72, Cc
Corinth, G. of, 78, Df
Coritani, 3A, Fc
Cork, 15, Ce
Cork, co., 37C; 49B, Ce

Cork Harbour, 37B, Ce
Cormantine, 81C, Dc
Cormons, 86B, Da
Cornbie (Carn Brea), 13, Af
Corneto, 22A; 23B, Cc
Cornouaille, Co. of, 11, Bb
Cornovii, 3A, Dd
Cornvalge (Cornwall), 13, Bf
Cornwall, Canada, 57, Da
Cornwall, co., 27, Bf
Coro, 43A, Fc
Coromandel, 77A
Coromandel Coast, 59A, De
Coron, 19, Ce
Coronel, 86, Ff
Corpus Christi, 70, Ee
Correggio, 32A, Db
Corregidor, 90, Cc
Corrib, L., 15, Bc; 37B, Bc
Corrientes, 68, De
Corrientes, C., Cuba, 43A, Db
Corrientes, C., Mexico, 43A, Bb
Corrieyairack Pass, 49A, Bb
Corsewall Pt., 49A, Bc
Corsica, 5, Bc
Corstopitum (Corbridge), 3C
Cortenuova, 20, Hf
Cortina di Ampezzo, 86B, Ca
Cortona, Bruttium, 5, Fe
Cortona, Florence, 21, Kg
Corumba, 68, Dd; 94, Cf
Corunna, 23D, Aa; 63, Aa
Corvey, 22, Da; 65B, Aa
Cos, 78, Fg
Cosenza, 23A, Fd
Cosenza (Consentia), 5, Fe
Cossacks, 50, Gd
Cossimbazar, 59B
Costa Rica, 43D, Dc
Cotabato, 75E, Cc
Côte d'Or, 76A, Cc
Coteau du Lac, 57, Da
Cotentin, 8, Bb; 17, Ed
Cotonou, 94, Te; 96B, Cb
Cotrone, 23A, Fd
Cotswold Hills, 27, De
Cottian Alps, 29A, Bc
Couci, 11, Eb
Couci, S. of, 20, Ed
Coudres, I. aux, 45A, Ca
Coulmiers, 76A, Ac
Countisbury, 7C, Cb
Coupland, 28B, Bc
Courantyne, 68, Db
Courtrai, 28C, Da; 46A, Cd
Coutances, 11, Cb
Coutras, 38, Cf
Covadonga, 22, Bc
Covelong, 59D
Coventreu (Coventry), 13, Ed
Coventry, 27, Ed
Cowal, 14, Cd
Cowans Ford, 57, Af
Cowens, 56, Cc; 57D, Aa
Cowpens, 56, Cc; 57D, Aa
Cozumel, 43A, Db
Crac de la Pierre (Krak), 18C, Cg
Cracow, 21, Nc
Cracow, Rep. of, 64, Gc
Cradock, 81B, Cc
Craigmillar, 37A, Cc
Crail, 49A, Cb
Craiova, 54, Gd; 78, Ec
Cramond, 3A, Ca
Craon, 20, Ce
Craonne, 83A, Bb
Crati, R., 21A, Dc
Crave (Craven), 13, Db
Craven, 45A, Bd
Crawford, 37A, Cc
Crecy, 28C, Ca
Crediton, 27, Cf; 36, Cg
Creeks, 56, Bd; 71F, Hb
Crefeld, 46A, Fc
Creil, 83A, Bb
Crema, 32D, Ab
Cremona, 5, Cb
Creneburne (Cranborne) 13, Ef
Crépy, 53, Ec
Crespy, 38, Ed
Creta, 2, Jf
Crete, 19, Ce; 78, Eh
Crevant, 28D, Dc
Crewkerne, 48B, Ec
Criccieth, 28A, Bb
Crichelade (Cricklade), 13, Ee
Crickhowell, 28A, Cc
Cricklade, 27, Ee
Crim, Khanate of, 79, Ga
Crim Tartary, 33A, Ea
Crimea, 50, Gd
Croagh Patrick, 15, Bc
Croatan L., 45A, Bc
Croatia, 21, Lf
Croats, 9, Fc
Croce, Mte., 86B, Ca
Croceraguel, 36, Bb
Crococalana (Brough), 3A, Fc
Croisic, 55A, Be
Cromarty, 37A, Bb; 49A, Bb

Cromarty, co., 37A, Bb
Cromarty Firth, 14, Db
Cropredy Bridge, 48A, Cc
Cross Sd., 71B, Bb
Crossen, 31, Lb
Croton, 57, Ec
Crowland, 7B, Cb; 7C, Cb; 36, Fe
Crown Point, 57, Eb
Crown Princess Martha Land, 69C
Crows Nest Pass, 44, Cd
Croxton, 36, Fe
Crozet Is., 69C
Cruces (Venta Cruz), 43A, Ed
Cruilande (Crowland), 13, Fd
Crussol, 20, Ff
Cruz, C. de, 43A, Ec
Cruzeiro do Sul, 94, Df
Csanad, 19, Cc
Ctesiphon, 1, Gd; 6A, Db
Cuba, 43A, Db
Cuch Behar, 73, Eb
Cucui, 68, Cb
Cucuta, 68, Bb
Cuddalore, 59D
Cuddapah, 73, Ce
Cuenca, Ecuador, 68, Bc
Cuenca, Spain, 22, Bc
Cuiaba, 68, Dd
Cuillins, 14, Bb
Culebra B., 43A, Dc
Culiacan, 43A, Bb
Cullen, 49A, Cb
Culloden, 49A, Bb
Culpeper, 72B, Ba
Cumana, 43A, Fc
Cumans, 19, Dc
Cumberland, 71C, Cc
Cumberland, co., 27, Cb
Cumberland Gap, 72, Db
Cumberland House, 44, Dc
Cumberland Mts., 56, Cc
Cumberland, R., 56, Bc
Cumberland Sd., 70, Ha
Cumbria, 7B, Ba; 13, Db
Cumbrian Hills, 27, Cb
Cumnock, 37A, Bc; 49A, Bc
Cuncacestre (Chester-le-Street), 13, Eb
Cuneo, 32A, Bb
Cunningham, 14, Dd
Cupar, 37A, Cb
Curacura, 23B, Fc
Curico, 68, Bf
Curitiba, 68 Ee
Curzola, 22, Fc
Cushendun, 49B, Ea
Cussey, 76A, Cc
Custozza, 32C, Cb
Cutch, 73, Ac
Cuttack, 73, Ec
Cuttack, st., 73, Ec
Cuxhaven, 55A, Hb; 60B, Bb
Cuyo Is., 75E, Bb
Cuyuni, R., 68B, Ba
Cuzco, 68, Bd
Cyclades, 78, Eg
Cydewain, 13, Cd
Cydnus, R., 18C, Ba
Cynllaith, 13, Cd
Cyprus, 2, Kg; 4A, Je; 6A, Ab
Cyprus, King. of, 18A, Eb
Cyprus Theme, 9, Je
Cyrenaica, 1, Ed; 80A, Fa
Cyrene, 2, Hg; 4A, Ge; 93, Ac
Cythnos, 78, Eg
Cyzicus, 8, Hc
Czarnikow, 31, Mb
Czartorysk, 51, Fc
Czaslau, 60A, Ed
Czech, 8C, Cb; 85, Fc
Czechoslovakia, 84, Fc
Czechs, 8, Fb
Czernowitz, 33C, Fb; 78, Ea
Czerwinsk, 26, Fc
Czestochowa, 21, Nc; 87, Db

Dabra Tabor, 80B, Be
Dacca, 59B; 73, Fc
Dachstein, 29A, Eb
Dacia, 2, He
Dacre, 7C, Ba
Dadislela (Tickhill), 13, Ec
Daghestan, 79, Jb; 84, Md
Dagö, 26, Fb
Dagsburg, 39B, Db
Dagsestune, 14, Ea
Dagupan, 75E, Ba
Dahlak Arch., 80B, Cd
Dahlonega, 72, Dc
Dahomé, 81C, Ec
Dahomey, 96B, Cb
Daibul, 6, Hc
Dairen, 91, Fd
Dairen (Dalny), 76B, Ab
Daix, R., 1, Hb
Dakar, 80A, Bc; 96B, Aa
Dakota Terr., 67D, Ca
Dal, 26, Db

Dal Arridhe, 15, Eb
Dalecarlia, 26, Da
Dalhousie, 71, Hc
Dalkeith, 37A, Cc; 48A, Bb
Dalkey, 37B, Ec
Dallas, Georgia, 72, Dc
Dallas, Texas, 94, Ed
Dalmally, 49A, Bb
Dalmatia, 32A, Gc; 78, Ad
Dalnaspidal, 49A, Bb
Dalny (Dairen), 76b, Ab
Dalriada, 14, Cc; 15, Ea
Dalriada Scots, 7B, Aa
Dalriada Ulaid, 7A, Ba
Dalry, Ayrshire, 37A, Bc
Dalry, Kirkcudbright, 49A, Bc
Dalton, 72A, Aa
Daltune (Dalton), 13, Cb
Dalwhinnie, 49A, Bb
Daly Waters, 95, Mf
Dam, 93, Ee
Daman, 73, Bc
Damariscotta, 45B, Ea
Damascus, 2, Lg; 18C, De
Damascus, Emirs of, 18C, De
Damietta, 6A, Ab; 9, Jf
Damm, 50, Cc
Dammartin, 20, Ed
Damme, 17, Gc, 55, Ec
Damnonii, 3A, Ba
Dampier Arch., 77, Bf
Dampier Str., 77, Hc
Dampierre, 20, Fd
Damvillers, 39B, Ba; 53, Fc
Dan, R., 57, Be
Danes, 2A, Ca; 7A, Fa; 8, E
Danewerk, 65F, Aa
Danilovski, 61, Eb
Danish Mercia, 7C, Cb
Dankov, 61, Ed
Danube, R., 21, Me; 33C, Ec
Danubius, R., 1, Ec; 2, He
Danubyu, 73, Gd
Danum, (Doncaster), 3A, Ec
Danville, 57, Be
Danzig, 21, Na
Danzig, Rep. of, 60B, Ga
Dar es Salaam, 80A, Ge
Dar Fur, 80A, Fc
Darabjird, 6, Gc
Daras, 4B, Ld
Darbhanga, 73, Eb
Dardanelles, 78, Fe; 86D
Dargun, 22, Ea
Darien, Central America, 43A, Ed
Darien, Georgia, 56, Cd
Darien, G. of, 43A, Ed
Darjeeling, 73, Eb
Darley, 36, Ee
Darling, R., 77, Gh
Darmstadt, 29A, Ca
Daroca, 23C, Eb
Dartford, 36, Gf
Dartmoor, 27, Cf
Dartmouth, England, 27, Cf
Dartmouth, Nova Scotia, 45A, Eb
Dartmouth College, 57, Eb
Darum, 18C, Bg
Darwin, 90, Cd
Dassel, 20, Hc
Dauphiné, 20, Ff; 30, Ff
Davao, 75E, Cc
Davao G., 75E, Cc
Davenport, 72, Bb
David Comnenus, 18B, Eb
David Street, 18D
David's Gate, 18D
David's Tower, 18D
Davis Str., 44, Jb,; 69B
Davos, 29B, Db
Dawson, 71A, Da
Dax, 22, Bc; 28C, Be; 30, Cg
Dayton, 71C, Bc; 72, Db
De Aveiro, 36, Kd
De Burgh (Burke), 37B, Cc
De Courcy, 17, Ba
De Leuwin, 42B
De Witts Land, 42, Qe
Deabolis, 18A, Ca
Dead Sea, 18C, Cg
Deal, 27, He
Dean, Forest of, 3A, De
Deba Habe, 96B, Da
Debra Markos, 96A, Aa
Debrecen, 87, Ec
Debreczin, 33C, Eb
Decatur, Alabama, 72, Cc
Decatur, Georgia, 72A, Ab
Deccan, 41A, Ec; 73, Cd
Deceangli, 3A, Cc
Decies, 15, Dd
Deddington, 27, Ed
Dedeagach, 78, Ee; 86C, Aa
Dee, R., Aberdeenshire, 14, Fb
Dee, R., Galloway, 36, Bb
Dee, R., Wales, 27, Dc
Deer, 14, Eb
Deer I., 56B
Deerfield, 45B, Cb

Deganwy, 13, Cc; 28A, Ca
Deheubarth, 13, Be; 17, Cc
Dehra Dun, 92, Da
Deira, 7B, Ca
Delagoa B., 81A, Dc
Delaware B., 45B, Bd; 57, Dd
Delaware, R., 45B, Bc; 57, Dc
Delft, 30, Fb; 46A, Db
Delgado, C., 58, Me
Delhi, 25, Gd; 73, Cb
Delhi, Sultanate of, 25, Gd
Demerara (Georgetown), 43D, Gd
Demerara, R., 68B, Ba
Demetae, 3A, Bd
Demirhissar, 86A, Ea
Demmin, 21, Kb; 39, Kb
Demotika, 9, Hd
Denain, 54, Cb
Denbigh, 27, Cc
Dendermonde, 46A, Dc
Dene (Dean), 13, De
Denia, 23C, Fc; 63, Fc
Denmark, 12, Gc
Denmark, King. of, 26, Db
Denmark and Norway, 54, Da
Dennewitz, 60B, Dc
D'Entrecasteaux Is., 77, Ic
Denver, 70, Dd
Deogir, 25, Gd
Deols, 11, Dc
Depenbeck, 13, Dc
Deptford, 13, Ge
Derbent, 6, Fa; 19, Hd
Derby, Connecticut, 45B, Cc
Derby, England, 13, Ed
Derby, W. Australia, 77, Ce
Derby, co., 27, Ec
Derbyscire (Derbyshire), 13, Ec
Derevlyans, 9, Hb
Derg, L., 15, Cc
Derg, R., 15, Db
Derlington (Darlington), 13, Eb
Derna, 79, Dd
Derry, 15, Db
Derwent, R., 27, Ec; 48A, Cc
Des Moines, 70, Ec
Deshima, 52, Rc
Desmond, 15, Be
Desna, R., 9, Jb; 61A, Db
Dessie, 96A, Aa
Dessau, 31, Kc; 39, Kc
Desterro (Florianopolis), 68, Ee
Detmold, 10, Cc; 60B, Bc
Detroit, 45A, Db
Dettingen, 54, Dc; 60A, Bc
Deutsch Brod, 31, Ld
Deva (Chester), 3A, Dc
Devenescire (Devon), 13, Cf
Deventer, 22, Da; 46A, Fb
Devernaki Pass, 78, Dg
Deveron, R., 14, Eb
Devikottai, 59D
Devizes, 27, De
Devol, R., 86A, Bb
Devon, 27, Cf
Devonport, 55A, Ac
Dewalgaon, 73, Cc
Dewas, 73, Cc
Dewsland, 27, Ae
Dhahran, 94, Rd
Dhar, 73, Cc
Dharwar, 73, Cd
Dholpur, 73, Cb
Diakova, 78, Cd
Diamantina, 68, Ed
Diarbekr, 19, Fe
Diarbekr (Amida), 33A, Fc
Dibrugarh, 92, Hb
Die, 11, Fd; 22, Dc; 38, Ff
Diedenhofen (Thionville), 10, Bd; 76A, Cb
Diepholz, 30, Hb
Dieppe, 30, Dd; 83A, Ab
Dieren, 46A, Fb
Dieulacres, 36, Dd
Digne, 22, Dc; 38, Gf
Dijon, 11, Fc
Dilawar, 73, Bb
Dimotika, 78, Fe
Dinagat, 75E, Cb
Dinan, 11, Bb
Dinant, 46A, Dd
Dinapore, 73, Db
Dinaric Alps, 78, Ac
Dinas, 28A, Cb
Dinas Bran, 28A, Cb
Dindigul, 59A, Ce
Dinevor, 13, Be
Dingle, 49B, Ad
Dingle B., 15, Ad
Dingwall, 14, Db
Dinkelsbühl, 53, Jc
Dioclea, 9, Fd
Diocletian, Baths of, 5A
Dioscoridis I., 1, Hf
Diredawa, 96A, Bb
Direlton, 28B, Ca
Dirk Hartog I., 77, Ag

Disentis, 20, He; 29B, Cb
Ditmarsh, 26, Cc
Diu, 73, Bc
Dixmude, 46A, Bc
Dixon Entrance, 71B, Cc
Dizful, 93, Fc
Djagatai Empire, 25, Hb
Djakarta, 91, Dg
Djerba, 16, Ef
Djibouti, 96A, Ba
Djokjakarta, 91, Eg
Djougou, 96B, Cb
Dnieper, R., 50, Gc; 87, Gc
Dniester, R., 8, Hb; 87, Fc
Doab, The, 59A, Db
Dobb's Ferry, 57, Ec
Doberan, 22, Ea
Dobruja, 78, Gc
Dobrzyn, 21, Nb
Dobunni, 3A, Bf
Doce Leguas, Cays de, 43A, Eb
Dodecanese, 79, Ec
Dodinga, 52B, Aa
Dogger Bank, 82, Cb
Doha, 93, Gd
Doiran, 78, De
Dol, 11, Cb; 30, Cd
Dôle, 20, Fe; 38, Fe
Dolforwyn, 28A, Cb
Dolomites, 86B, Ba
Dolores, 43C, Ab
Dolwyddelan, 28A, Ca
Dombes, 53, Fd
Domfront, 17, Ed
Dominica, 43A, Fc
Dömitz, 38, Jb
Domrémy, 28D, Eb
Don, R., Russia, 16, Lc; 19, Fb
Don, R., Scotland, 14, Fb
Don Cossacks, 61, Fe
Donauwörth, 29A, Da
Doncaster, 27, Ec
Dondra Hd., 73, Df
Donegal, co., 37C; 49B, Cb
Donegal Abbey, 37B, Cb
Doneham (Dunham Massey), 13, Dc
Donets, R., 19, Fc; 61, Ee
Donetsk, 89, Nd
Dongola, 80B, Ad
Donnington Castle, 48B, Cd
Donzy, 17, Ge; 31A, Bd
Dora Baltea, R., 5, Ab
Dorat, 53, Dd
Dorcestre (Dorchester), 13, Df
Dorchester, Dorset, 27, Df
Dorchester, Massachusetts, 45B, Db; 56B
Dorchester, New Jersey, 45B, Bd
Dorchester, Oxon., 3A, Ee; 7B, Cc
Dorchester Heights, 56B
Dorchester Neck, 56B
Dorchester Pt., 56B
Dordogne, R., 11, Dd
Dore, 7B, Dc
Dorey, 77, Eb
Dordrecht, 26, Bc; 53, Fb
Dornach, 29B, Ba
Dornoch, 37A, Bb; 49A, Cb
Dornoch, bp., of, 14A, Bf
Dornoch Firth, 14, Eb
Dorostol, 9, Hd
Dorpat, 26, Gb
Dorset, 27, Df
Dorsete (Dorset), 13, Df
Dort, 46A, Dc
Dortmund, 10, Bc
Dorylaeum, 9, Je
Douai, 30, Ec; 46A, Cd
Doubs, R., 11, Fc; 29A, Bb
Douglas, Alaska, 71B, Cb
Douglas, Scotland, 37A, Cc
Douglas, clan, 28B, Ab
Douglas Castle, 28B, Bb
Dourdan, 38, Ed
Douro, R., 22, Ac; 63, Bb
Dover, Delaware, 57, Dd
Dover, England, 27, He
Dover, New England, 45B, Db
Dover, Str. of., 11, Da
Dovere (Dover), 13, He
Down, 15, Fb
Down, co., 37C; 49B, Eb
Downham Market, 48B, Dc
Downpatrick, 37B, Fb; 49B, Fb
Downpatrick, bp., 15A, Ca
Downs, The, 55A, Dc
Downton, 27, Ee
Dragasani, 78, Ec
Dragashan, 78, Ec
Draguignan, 20, Gg; 30, Gg
Draheim, 60A, Fb
Drakens Berg (Quathlamba), 81D, Ab
Drakensberg, 81B, Db
Drangiana, 1, Jd
Draper's Meadow, 56, Cc
Drave, R., 8, Fb; 21, Le
Dregoviches, 9, Gb

Drenthe, 46A, Fb
Dresden, 21, Kc; 31, Kc
Dreux 11, Db; 76A, Ab
Dreznik, 33C, Dc
Drina, R., 78, Bc
Drogheda, 37B, Ec; 49B, Ec
Droitwich, 27, Dd
Dromore, 49B, Eb
Dromore, bp., 15A, Ba
Drumburgh, 3C
Drumclog, 49A, Bc
Drumlog, 49A, Bc
Dryslwyn, 28A, Bc
Duala, 80A, Dd; 96B, Db
Dubawnt L., 44, Db
Dubienka, 51, Ec
Dublin, 15, Ec
Dublin, abp., 15A, Bb
Dublin, co., 37C; 49B, Ec
Dübnik, 78, Ed
Dubris (Dover), 3A, He
Ducatus Venetianus, 23B, Db
Ducie I., 75, Jf
Dudelei (Dudley), 13, Dd
Dudley, 27, Dd
Duero, R., 22, Bc; 63, Cb
Duich, L., 49A, Bb
Duisburg, 20, Gc; 46A, Fc
Duiveland, 46A, Cc
Dulce, R., 41B, Cf
Dulcigno, 22, Fc; 78, Be
Duleek, 15, Ec
Dull, 14, Ec
Duluth, 70, Ec
Dumaguete, 75E, Bc
Dumaran, 75E, Ab
Dumbarton, 37A, Bc; 48A, Ab
Dumbarton, co., 37A, Bb; 49A, Bc
Dumdum, 73, Bc
Dumfries, 28B, Bb; 36, Cb
Dumfries, co., 37A, Cc; 49A, Cc
Dumio, 22, Ac
Dumnonii, 3A, Bf
Dun, 20, Ee
Dun Laoghaire (Kingstown), 49B, Ec
Düna, 26, Gb
Dünaburg, 26, Gb
Dunbar, 14, Fc
Dunblane, 14, Ec; 49A, Cb
Duncannon, 49B, Ed
Duncansby Hd., 14, Ea; 49A, Ca
Dundalk, 37B, Ec; 49B, Ec
Dundee, Natal, 81D, Bb
Dundee, Scotland, 28B, Ca; 48A, Ba
Dundonald Castle, 28B, Ab
Dundrennan, 14, Ee
Dundrum, 37B, Fb
Dunewic (Dunwich), 13, Hd
Dunfermline, 14, Ec
Dungannon, 49B, Eb
Dungarvan, 37B, Dd; 49B, Dd
Dungeness, 55A, Dc
Dungiven, 49B, Eb
Dunhevet (Dunheved, Launceston), 13, Bf
Dunholm (Durham), 13, Eb
Dunkeld, 14, Ec
Dunkeswell, 36, Cg
Dunkirk, 46A, Bc
Dunlavin, 49B, Ec
Dunmore Hd., 15, Ad
Dunnet Hd., 14, Ea
Dunnottar, 37A, Cb
Dunois, 30, Dd
Dunrobin, 37A, Cb
Dunrobin Castle, 49A, Cb
Duns, 37A, Cc; 48A, Bb
Dunstable, 27, Fe
Dunstaffnage, 49A, Ab
Dunstanburgh, 27, Ea
Dunster, 27, Ce; 48A, Bd
Dunvegan, 49A, Ab
Dunwich, 27, Hd; 36A
Duppel, 65F, Aa
Dupplin Moor, 28B, Ba
Durance, R., 11, Fe; 29A, Ad
Durango, 43A, Bb
Duras, 53, De
Durazzo, 78, Be
Durban (Port Natal), 81D, Bb
Düren, 20, Gc
Durham, England, 27, Eb
Durham, New Hampshire, 57, Fb
Durham, Bb. of, 28B, Dc; 36, Db
Durham, Palatinate of, 27, Eb
Durinish, 14, Bb
Durlach, 38, Gd
Durnkrüt, 19, Kc
Durness, 14, Da
Durnovaria (Dorchester), 3A, Df
Durobrivae (Rochester), 3A, Ge

Durobrivae (Water Newton), 3A, Fd
Durocobrivae (Dunstable), 3A, Fe
Durolipons (Cambridge), 3A, Gd
Durotriges, 3A, Df
Durovernum (Canterbury), 3A, He
Durovigatum (Godmanchester), 3A, Fd
Dürrenstein, 29A, Fa
Dürres, 88, Je
Durstede, 12, Fc
Dusky B., 77, Lk
Düsseldorf, 38, Gc; 83A, Da
Dutch Brazil, 41B, Ed; 42, He
Dutch East Indies, 74, Kj; 90, Bd
Dutch Harbor, 90, Fa
Dutch New Guinea, 77, Fb
Duxbury, 45B, Db; 57, Fb
Dvina, R., (N.), 61, Fb; 88, Oa
Dvina, R., (W.), 50, Fb; 64, Hb
Dvinsk, 84, Ha
Dyea, 71B, Cb
Dyfed, 7B, Ac; 13, Be
Dyle, R., 46B; 83A, Ca
Dynefwr, 28A, Bc
Dyrrhachium, 2, Ge; 4A, Fc
Dzhulfa, 93, Fb

EALONDSCIRE, (ISLANDSHIRE), 13, Ea
Eamont, 7C, Ba
Earn, L., 14, Dc
Easby, 7B, Ca
East C., Asia, 69B
East C., New Zealand, 77, Ni
East, Pref. of the., 2, Kf
East Angles, 7A, Da
East Anglia, 7B, Db; 12, Ec
East China Sea, 91 Fd
East Florida, 71F, Ba
East Franconia, 10, Dd
East Friesland, Co. of, 30, Gb
East Germany, 89, Hc
East London, 81B, Cc
East Main, R., 70, Gb
East March, 28B, Cb
East Mark, 8A, Db
East of March, 27, Cd
East Pakistan, 92, Gc
East Prussia, 39, Pb
East Roman Empire, 2, Kf
East Saxons, 7A, Db
Easter I., 75, Kf
Eastern Association, 48A, Cc
Eastern Bengal and Assam, 73A, Cb
Eastern Ghats, 73, Dd
Eastern Roman Empire, 8, Gd
Eastern Rumelia, 78, Ed
Eastham, 45B, Dc
Easthampton, 45B, Cc
Easton, 57, Dc
Eastphalia, 10, Db
Ebbsfleet, 36, Hf
Ebenezer, 57D, Ab
Eboracum (Evrvic) (York), 13, Eb
Eburacum (York), 3A, Ec
Ecbatana, 1, Gd; 6, Fb
Ecclefechan, 49A, Cc
Ecclesia de Labatailge (Battle), 13, Gf
Echallar, 63, Da
Echallens, 29B, Ab
Eckernförde, 65F, Aa
Eckmühl, 65B, Bb
Ecuador, 68, Bc
Edam 46A, Eb
Eddisbury, 7C, Bb
Edelsland, 42B; 77, Bh
Eden, R., 7C, Ba; 27, Db
Edenton, 57, Ce
Edessa, 2, Lf; 6, Eb; 19, Fe
Edessa, Co. of, 16, Ke
Edeyrnion, 13, Cd
Edge Hill, 48A, Cc
Edgecot, 27, Ed
Edinburgh (Dunedin), 14, Ed
Edinburgh, co., 49A, Cc
Edington, 36, Df
Edisto, R., 57D, Ab
Edmonton, 70, Cb
Edolo, 86B, Aa
Eger, Bohemia, 21, Kc
Eger, Hungary, 33C, Eb
Eger, R., 21, Kc
Egersund, 87, Ba
Eggmühl, 29A, Ea
Egisheim, 39B, Db
Egitama, 22, Ad
Eglesham (Eynsham), 13, Ee
Egmont, 22, Ca; 46A, Db

Egremont, 27, Cb
Egri Palanka, 78, Dd
Egripo, 78, Df
Egypt, 80A, Fb; 93, Bd
Egypt (Misr), 6, Dc
Egyptian Sudan, 83, Ld
Ehrenbreitstein, 51, Bc
Eia (Eye), 13, Gd
Eichsfeld, 20, Hc
Eichstadt, 10, Dd
Eider, R., 60B, Ba; 65F, Aa
Eifel, 83A, Da
Eigg, 14, Bc
Eight Emirates, 24, Jf
Eil, 95A, Bb
Eilean Donan, 49A, Bb
Einsiedeln, 22, Db; 29B, Ca
Eire, 49B, Dc
Eisenach, 20, Jc; 39C, Ac
Eisenburg, 39C, Bc
Eisenburg (Vasvar), 29A, Gb
Ekaterinoslav, 64, Kd
El Agheila, 88, Jg
El Alamein, 93, Bc
El Aqaba, 80B, Ab
El Arish, 80B, Aa
El Bodon, 63, Bb
El Damer, 93, Cf
El Dirr, 93, Ce
El Dorado, 43A, Fd
El Faiyum, 80B, Ab
El Golea, 96C, Ca
El Khandaq, 93, Cf
El Morro, 43A, Db
El Obeid, 80A, Fc
El Paso, 70, Dd
Elands, R., 81A, Cc
Elandslaagte, 81D, Ab
Elassona, 78, Df
Elba, 5, Cc
Elbasan, 86A, Ba
Elbe, R., 10, Cb; 60A, Ec
Elberfeld, 53, Gb; 60B, Ac
Elbeuf, 23C, Cb; 38, Dd
Elbing, 21, Na; 39, Na
Elburz, 19, Je
Elche, 23C, Ec
Elchingen, 22, Eb; 29A, Da
Elderslie, 28B, Ab
Electoral Palatinate, 30, Hd
Eleuthera I., 43A, Eb
Elfael, 13, Cd
Elfsborg, 5J, Cb
Elgin, 37A, Cb
Elgin, bp., 14A, Cb
Elgin, co., 49A, Cb
Elgin and Forres. co., 37A, Cb
Elim, 81B, Ac
Elisabethville, 96C, Ef
Elizabeth, New Jersey, 45B, Bc
Elizabeth, Virginia, 45B, Ae
Elizabeth, C., 45B, Db
Elizabethtown, 57B
Elk Hill, 57, Be
Elkton, 57, Dd
Ellandun, 7B, Cc
Ellesmere, 28A, Db
Ellesmere I., 44, Ga
Ellice Is., 90, Ed
Ellichpur, 52A, Bh
Elliot, 28B, Cb
Elliot Is., 76B, Bb
Ellwangen, 22, Eb
Elmeslae (Helmsley), 13, Eb
Elmet, 7A, Ca
Elmham, 7B, Db; 36A
Elmham, bp., 36A
Elmina, 35, Jd; 81C, Dc
Elmshorn, 65F, Ab
Elne, 11, Ee
Elnestow (Elstow), 13, Fd
Elphin, 15, Cc
Elster, R., 10, Ec
Elstow, 36, Fe
Elten, 65A, Aa
Elvas, 23C, Bc; 63, Bc
Ely, 27, Gd
Ely, bp., 36, Ge
Ely, I. of, 27, Gd
Elyg (Ely), 13, Gd
Embrun, 11, Gd
Emden, 38, Gb; 65D, Aa
Emesa, 9, Ke
Emilia, 32A, Db
Emirs of Damascus, 18C, De
Emly, 15, Cd
Empingham (Losecoat Field), 27, Fd
Empire, The, 16, Dc; 54, Eb
Ems, 60B, Ac
Ems, R., 10, Bb; 38, Gb
Enaghdun, 15, Cc
Encounter B., 77, Fl
Endeavour R., 77, He
Enderby Land, 69C
Engadi, 18C, Cg
Engadin, 29B, Eb
Engelberg, 10, Cc
Engelberg, Abbey of, 29B, Cb
Engern, 10, Cb
Enghien, 46A, Dd

England, 34, Bb; 55A, Cb
England, King. of, 20, Cc
English, R., 70, Eb
English Channel, 7B, Cc
English Mercia, 7C, Bb
Enkhuizen, 46A, Eb
Enköping, 26, Eb
Ennis, 49B, Cd
Enniscorthy, 15, Ed
Enniskillen, 49B, Db
Enns, R., 29A, Fb
Enos, 78, Fe
Entebbe, 96C, Fd
Enugu, 96B, Db
Eperjes, 33C, Eb
Épernay, 83A, Bb
Ephesus, 8, Hd
Epidaurus, 79, Dc
Epidium Prom., 3A, Aa
Epila, 23D, Eb
Épinal, 20, Gd; 83B, Ba
Epirus, 1, Ed; 79, Dc
Epirus, Despotate of, 19, Ce
Eppenstein, 10, Fe
Epworth, 3A, Fd
Equatorial Guinea, 96D, Cd
Equatorial Provs., 80A, Fd
Erbach, 38, Hd
Erbil, 93, Eb
Ericht, L., 49A Bb
Erfurt, 10, Ec; 39C, Bc
Eriboll, 49A, Ba
Ericht, L., 49A Bb
Erie, 70, Fc
Erie, L., 45A, Ab
Eries, 45A, Ab
Eriska, 49A, Ab
Eritrea, 80B, Ce; 96A, Aa
Erivan, 61, Ff; 79, Hb
Erlau, 31, Pe; 33A, Ba
Ermeland, 39, Pb
Ermine Street, 3A, Fd
Erne, L., 15, Db
Erne, Upper L., 49B, Db
Errigal, 15, Ca
Erz Gebirge, 10, Ec
Erzerum, 6, Fb; 79, Hc
Erzingan, 86C, Cb
Es Suweida, 93, Dc
Escewelle (Ashwell), 13, Gd
Escomb, 7B, Ca
Eshowe, 81D, Db
Eskdale, 14, Ed
Eskisehir, 79, Fc
Eskishehr, 86C, Bb
Esla, R., 63, Cb
Esmeraldas, 68, Bb
Esopus, 45B, Cc
Española(Hispaniola),43A,Ec
Esperance, 77, Ch
Esperance, C.d', 45A, Ea
Espinosa, 63, Da
Espirito Santo, 68, Ed
Essek, 33C, Db
Essen, 53, Gb; 87, Bb
Essequibo, 41B, Db
Essequibo, R., 68, Db
Essex, 27, Ge
Essling, 29A, Ga
Esslingen, 30, Hd
Essonnes, 38, Ed
Est-Treding (East Riding), 13, Fc
Estavayer, 29B, Ab
Estcourt, 81D, Ab
Este, 23B, Cb; 32D, Bb
Este (D. of Ferrara), 32A, Db
Este (D. of Modena), 32A, Db
Esthonia, 26, Gb
Esthonians, 9, Ha
Estonia, 87, Fa
Estrella, Sierra d', 63, Bb
Estremadura, Portugal, 63, Ac
Estremadura, Spain, 63, Bc
Étampes, 11, Eb; 17, Gd
Étaples, 30 Dc
Ethandun, 7C, Bc
Ethiopia, 6, Ed; 80A, Gd
Etna, Mt., 5 Ef
Etowah, R., 72A, Aa
Ettlingen, 65A, Ab
Ettrick, R., 14, Ed
Ettrick Forest, 28B, Bb
Eu, 11, Db; 17, Fd; 30, Dc
Eucla, 77, Dh
Eugubium, 5B, Bb
Eupàtoria (Kozlov), 50, Gd
Eupen, 83A, Da
Euphrates, R., 2, Mg; 6A, Cb
Eure, R., 76A, Ab
Europa Pt., 63A
Eustria, 8, Cb
Eutaw Springs, 57D, Ab
Evansville, 72, Cc
Evaux, 30, Ee
Everest, Mt., 73, Eb; 92, Fb
Everglades, 43A, Db
Evesham, 13, Ed; 27, Ed
Evora, 22, Ad; 63, Bc
Evora, eccl. prov., 22, Ad
Evreux, 11, Db; 17, Fd

Evrvicscire (Yorkshire), 13, Eb
Ewias, 13, De
Ewisdale, 28B, Bb
Ewyas, 7C, Bc
Ewyas Lacy, 32A, Dc
Exarchate, 5, Cb
Exe, R., 27, Cf; 48B, Bd
Exeter, England, 27, Cf
Exeter, New Hampshire, 45B, Db
Exeter, bp., 36, Bg
Exilles, 38, Gf
Exmoor, 27, Ce
Exonia (Exeter), 13, Cf
Exploring Is. (Lau Group), 75C, Ca
Exsessa (Essex), 13, Ge
Eye, 27, Hd
Eylau, 60A, Ha; 60B, Ha
Eyre, L., 77, Fg

FAENZA, 5, Cb
Faesulae, 5, Cc
Fair Hd., 49B, Ea
Fairbanks, 71A, Ca
Fairfield, Connecticut, 45B, Cc
Fairfield, S. Africa, 81B, Cc
Faiyum, 93, Cd
Fakfak, 77, Eb
Falaise, 11, Cb
Falkenburg, 39B, Ca
Falkenstein, Austria, 33C, Cb
Falkenstein, Swabia, 10, Cd
Falkirk, 28B, Bb; 49A, Cc
Falkland Is., 68, Dh
Falkland Is. Dependencies, 95, Cj
Falköping, 26, Db
Falmouth, England, 55A, Ac
Falmouth, Maine, 57, Fb
Falmouth (Casco) (For Loyal), 45B, Db
False B., 81B, Ac
Falsterbo, 26, Db
Falun, 26, Ea
Famagusta, 16, Je
Famia (Apamea), 18C, Dc
Fanning I., 75, Hd
Fano, 32A, Ec
Fanum, 5B, Bb
Fao, 86C, Ec
Farasan Is., 80B, Cd
Farenam, 27, Ef
Farewell, C., 69B
Farmingham, 45B, Cc
Farnea, Is. (Farne Is.), 13, Ea
Farnham, 27, Fe
Faro, 22, Ad
Faroe Is., 12, Ca; 82, Ja
Farquharson, 37A, Cb
Farrukhabad, 59C, Cb
Fars, 6, Gb
Fashoda (Kodak), 80B, Ae
Fast Castle, 28B, Cb
Fatehgarh, 73, Cb
Fatehpur, 73, Bb
Fatimite anti-Caliphate, 6B, Ba
Fatimite Caliphs, 16, Jg
Faucigny, 30, Ge
Faventia, 5B, Aa
Faversham, 27, Ge
Fayetteville, N. Carolina, 57, Bf; W. Virginia, 72, Db
Fayum, 6A, Ac
Fear, C., 57F, Aa
Fécamp, 11, Db
Federal District, Brazil, 68, Bd
Federated Malay States, 74, Jh
Fed. of Arabian Emirates, 93, Gd
Fehmarn, 60B, Ca; 65F, Ba
Fehrbellin, 60A, Db
Felipinas, Islas (Philippine Is.), 41A, Kc
Feltre, 5, Ca; 86B, Ba
Fenestrelles, 53, Ge
Fenghwangcheng, 76B, Ca
Fentsch, 39B, Ba
Fer, Pointe au, 57, Ea
Ferette, 31A, Dd
Fergana, 61B, Ca
Ferghana, 6, Ja
Fergus, R., 15, Cd
Ferle (Firle), 13, Gf
Fermanagh, 49B, Db
Fermanagh, co., 37C
Fermo (Firmum), 5, Dc
Fermoy, 49B, Cd
Fernandina, 72, Dc
Fernando Poo, 80A, Dd
Ferns, 15, Ed
Ferrara, 5, Cb; 29A, Dc
Ferrara, D. of (Este), 32A, Db
Formentera, 23C, Fc
Ferreus (Orontes), R., 18C, Dc
Ferrol, 55B, Kb; 63, Aa
Ferry Land, 45A, Ga
Ferrybridge, 27, Ec
Feurs, 11, Fd

Fez, 9. Bf; 40, Jc; 80A, Ca
Fez, Sultanate of (Watasios), 34, Be
Fezensac, Co. of, 11, De
Fezzan, 6, Cc; 80A, Eb
Fiesole, 32A, Dc
Fife, 14, Ec
Fife, co., 37A, Cb; 49A, Cb
Fifth Cataract, 80B, Ad
Figeac, 17, Gf
Figueira da Foz, 63, Ab
Figueras, 63, Ga
Figuig, 80A, Ca
Fiji Is., 75C; 77, Ne
Filey, 3A, Fb
Finale, 54, Dd
Findhord, 49A, Cb
Findhorn, R., 37A, Cb
Findon, 49A, Cb
Fingoes, 81B, Dc
Finisterre, C., 63, Aa
Finland, 26, Ga; 88, La
Finland, G. of, 26, Gb
Finnish Peoples, 19, Ca
Finsiaolin, 76B, Ba
Finsteraarhorn, 29B, Cb
Finstingen, 39B, Bb
Firmana, 23A, Db
Firmum (Fermo), 5, Dc
First Cataract, 80B, Ac
Fischhausen, 26, Ec
Fishers Hill, 72B, Aa
Fishguard, 55A, Ac
Fishkill, 57, Ec
Fitero, 22, Bc
Fitzalan, 28A, Db; 28B, Dc
Fitzgerald, 37B, Ec
Fitzgibbon, 37B, Cd
Fitzmaurice, 37B, Bd
Fitzroy, R., 77, Ce
Fiume, 39, Lf
Five Forks, 72B, Bb
Fivizzano, 32A, Db
Flanders, 46A, Bd
Flarchheim, 10, Dc
Flatbush, 57B
Flattery, C., 67C, Aa
Flavigny, 22, Cb
Fleet, R., 27A
Flensburg, 26, Cc; 60B, Ba
Fleurus, 38, Fc; 46B
Fleury, Languedoc, 53, Ef
Fleury, Sens, 22, Cb
Flinders, R., 77, Gf
Flint, 28A, Ca
Flint, co., 28A, Ca
Flint, R., 71F, Ca
Flodden, 28B, Cb
Flodden Field, 37A, Cc
Florchingen, 39B, Ca
Florence, Italy, 32E, Bb
Florence, U.S.A., 72, Ec
Florence, Rep. of, 32A, Dc
Flores, Azores, 55B, Hc
Flores, E. Indies, 52C, Ec
Florianopolis (Desterro), 68, Ee
Florida, 56, Bd; 72, Dd
Florida, C., 55B, Md
Florida Terr., 67C, Ec
Florina, 86A, Cb; 88, Ke
Fluelen, 29B, Cb
Flushing, 46A, Cc
Fochabers, 37A, Cb
Focsani, 51, Fd; 78, Fc
Foggia, 23B, Ed; 32A, Fd
Föhr, 65F, Aa
Foix, 11, De; 17, Fg
Folchingeham (Folkingeham), 13, Fd
Folkstone, 13, He; 27, He
Fondi, 21A, Bb; 22, Ec
Fonseca, G. of, 43A, Dc
Fontaine, 46B
Fontainebleau, 47, Cc
Fontanet, 8A, Bb
Fontenay, 30, Ce
Fontenoy, 46A, Cd; 54, Cb
Fontevrault, 17, Ee
Font-Marigny, 22, Cb
Foochow, 25, Ld; 91, Ed
Forbach, 39B, Ca
Forbes, 37A, Cb
Forcalquier, 20, Fg; 30, Fg
Forchheim, 8, Eb, 22, Eb
Ford, 36, Cg
Forden, 3A, Cd
Foresta, 13, De
Forewic (Fordwich), 13, He
Forez, Co. of, 11, Ed
Forfar, 49A, Cb
Forfar, co., 37A, Cb
Forglen, 14, Ed
Forks, The, 69A, Da
Forli, 32A, Eb
Forlimpopoli, 21, Kf
Formentera, 23C, Fc
Formigny, 28D, Bb
Formosa (Taiwan), 91, Fd
Fornbi (Formby) 13, Cc
Fornovo, 32A, Db
Forres, 37A, Cb

Fort, 81D, Bb
Fort Albany, 70, Fb
Fort Alexander, 70, Eb
Fort Amsterdam, 45B, Bc
Fort Ann, 57, Eb
Fort Argyll, 56, Cd
Fort Armstrong, Mississippi Terr., 71F, Ba
FortArmstrong, Pennsylvania, 57, Bc
Fort Assomption, 57C, Ab
Fort Assumption (Memphis), 56, Bc
Fort Augusta, Georgia, 56, Cd
Fort Augusta, Pennsylvania, 56, Db
Fort Augustus, 37A, Bb
Fort Bard, 65B, Ab
Fort Bariancas, 71F, Ba
Fort Barraux, 38, Ff
Fort Beafort, 81B, Cc
Fort Beauharnais, 56, Ab
Fort Beauregard, 72, Dc
Fort Bedford, 57, Bd
Fort Benton, 70, Cc
Fort Bird, 56, Db
Fort Blakely, 72, Cc
Fort Boise, 44, Cd
Fort Bowyer, 71F, Ba
Fort Brewerton, 57, Cb
Fort Bridger, 70, Cc
Fort Bull, 57, Db
Fort Bute (Manchac), 56, Ad
Fort Butte à la Rose, 72, Bc
Fort Caroline, 43A, Da
Fort Caswell, 72, Ec
Fort Chambly, 57, Ea
Fort Charlotte, 56, Bd
Fort Chartres, 56, Ac
Fort Chelmsford, 81D, Bb
Fort Chequemagon, 56, Ba
Fort Chipewyan, 70, Cb
Fort Chiswell, 57, Ae
Fort Christina (Newcastle), 45B, Bd
Fort Claiborne, 71F, Ba
Fort Clinton, New York, 57, Dc
Fort Clinton, Vermont, 57. Eb
Fort Cornwallis (Augusta), 57D, Ab
Fort Crèvecœur, 56, Ab
Fort Crown Point, 56, Eb
Fort Cumberland, 57, Bd
Fort Dauphin, Canada, 44, Ec
Fort Dauphin, Madagascar, 80A, Hg
Fort de la Presentation, 56, Db
57, Da
Fort de Russy, 72, Bc
Fort Dearborn, 71C, Ab
Fort Delaware, 72, Eb
Fort Deposit, 71F, Ba
Fort des Abitibis, 45A, Ba
Fort Detroit, 56, Cb
Fort Dobbs, 56, Cc
Fort Donelson, 72, Cb
Fort Dummer (Hinsdale), 57, Eb
Fort Duquesne (Fort Pitt), 57, Bc
Fort Edward, 57, Eb
Fort Erie, 71C, Cb; 71D
Fort Esperanza, 72, Ad
Fort Evelyn, 81D, Bb
Fort Frédéric, 56, Eb
Fort Frederica, 56, Cd
Fort Frederick (Port Eliza-beth), 81B, Cc
Fort Frontenac, 57, Ca
Fort Gadsden (Negro), 71F, Ba
Fort Gaines, Alabama, 72, Cc
Fort Gaines, Georgia, 71F, Ca
Fort George, British Columbia, 44, Bc
Fort George, Natal, 81D, Bb
Fort George, New York, 57, Eb
Fort George, Ontario, 71D
Fort George, Oregon, 67C, Aa
Fort George, Scotland, 49A, Bb
Fort Gibson, 72, Ab
Fort Granby, 57D, Ab
Fort Halifax, 56, Fb
Fort Hall, 70, Cc
Fort Harris, 57, Cc
Fort Harrison, 71C, Ac
Fort Hatteras, 72, Eb
Fort Henry, Ohio, 56, Cc
Fort Henry, Tennessee, 72, Cb
Fort Herkimer, 57, Db
Fort Hunter, 56 Eb
Fort Independence, 57, Eb
Fort Jackson, Georgia, 72, Dc
Fort Jackson, Louisiana, 72, Cd
Fort Jackson, Mississippi Terr., 71F, Ba
Fort James, 81C, Ab
Fort Jefferson, 72, De

Fort Johnston, 72, Ec
Fort King George, 56, Cd
Fort la Baye, 56, Bb
Fort la Galette, 56, Db
Fort La Reine, 44, Ed
Fort Lamotte, 45A, Cb
Fort Lamy, 96B, Db
Fort Laramie, 67C, Ca
Fort Lawrence, 45A, Ea
Forte le Boeuf, 57, Bc
Fort Leavenworth, 72, Bb
Fort Lee, 57B
Fort Lifou, 52C, Dc
Fort Ligonier, 57, Bc
Fort Livingston, 72, Cd
Fort Loudoun, 56, Cd
Fort Louis, 56, Bd
Fort Loyal(Casco)(Falmouth), 45B, Db
Fort McAllister, 72, Dc
Fort McHenry, 71C, Cc
Fort Mackinac, 56, Ca
Fort McMurray, 70, Cb
Fort Macomb, 72, Cc
Fort Macon, 72, Ec
Fort McRee, 72, Cc
Fort Malden, 71C, Bb
Fort Mandant (Bismarck), 70, Dc
Fort Marion, 72, Dd
Fort Massac, 56, Bc
Fort Massachusetts, 72, Cc
Fort Maurepas, 44, Ec
Fort Meigs, 71C, Bb
Fort Miami, 56, Cb
Fort Mims, 71F, Ba
Fort Mitchell, 71F, Ca
Fort Monroe, 72, Eb
Fort Montgomery, 57, Dc
Fort Moore, 56, Cd
Fort Morgan, 72, Cc
Fort Motte, 57D, Ab
Fort Moultrie, 57D, Bb
Fort Mufflin, 57, Dd
Fort Napoleon, 81D, Bb
Fort Nassau, Moluccas, 52B, Aa
Fort Nassau, New Jersey, 45B, Bd
Fort Nassau (Fort Orange), 45B, Cb
Fort Necessity, 57, Bd
Fort New Elfsborg, 45B, Bd
Fort New Gothenburg, 45B, Bd
Fort New Korsholm (Chester), 45B, Bd
Fort Niagara, 57, Bb
Fort Norman, 70, Ba
Fort Nottingham, 81D, Ab
Fort Ontario, 57, Cb
Fort Orange (Fort Nassau), 45B, Cb
Fort Orleans, 56, Ac
Fort Oswego, 57, Cb
Fort Pentagöet (Penobscot), 45B, Ea
Fort Pickens, 72, Cc
Fort Pike, 72, Cc
Fort Pillow, 72, Cb
Fort Pitt (Fort Duquesne), 57, Bc
Fort Pitt (Pittsburgh), 57A, Ca
Fort Powell, 72, Cc
Fort Presqu'ile, 57, Ab
Fort Prince George (Savan-nah), 56, Cd
Fort Providence, 70, Ca
Fort Prudhomme, 56, Bc
Fort Pulaski, 72, Dc
Fort Quiatanon, 57A, Ba
Fort Rae, 70, Ca
Fort Resolution, 70, Ca
Fort Richelieu, 45A, Ca
Fort Rouille (Fort Toronto), 56, Db
Fort Royal, 43A, Fc
Fort St. David, 59D
Fort St. Esprit (La Pointe), 56, Aa
Fort St. George, 59D
Fort St. Jean, 57, Ea
Fort St. John, 70, Bb
Fort St. Joseph, L. Huron, 45A, Ab
Fort St. Joseph, L. Michigan, 56, Bb
Fort St. Louis, Illinois, 56, Bb
Fort St. Louis, Nova Scotia, 45A, Db
Fort St. Louis, Texas, 43A, Cb
Fort St. Philip, 72, Cd
Fort St. Philippe, 57A, Bd
Fort St. Therese, 45A, Ca
Fort Sandeman, 73, Aa
Fort Sandusky, 56, Cb
Fort Schlosser, 57, Bb
Fort Schuyler, 57, Db
Fort Scott, Georgia, 71F, Ca
Fort Scott, Kansas, 72, Bb
Fort Severn, 70, Fb
Fort Shevchenko, 61B, Aa

Fort Simpson, 70, Ba
Fort Smith, 72, Bb
Fort Snelling, 67C, Da
Fort Stanwix, 57, Db
Fort Stephenson, 71C, Bb
Fort Stoddard, 71F, Ba
Fort Strother, 71F, Ba
Fort Sumter, 72, Ec
Fort Taylor, 72, De
Fort Ticonderoga, 56, Eb
Fort Tombécbé (Fort York), 56, Bd
Fort Toronto (Fort Rouille), 56, Db
Fort Toulouse, 56, Bd
Fort Towson, 72, Ac
Fort Tuli, 81A, Cb
Fort Union, 70, Dc
Fort Vancouver, 44, Bd
Fort Venango, 57, Bc
Fort Victoria, Canada, 44, Bd
Fort Victoria, Natal, 81D, Bb
Fort Wagner, 72, Dc
Fort Walker, 72, Dc
Fort Washington, Maryland, 71C, Cc
Fort Washington, New Jersey, 57B
Fort Washita, 72, Ac
Fort Watson, 57D, Ab
Fort Wayne, 71C, Ab
Fort Wellington, 57, Ed
Fort Western, 56, Fb
Fort William, Bengal, 59C, Ec
Fort William, Canada, 70, Fc
Fort William, Scotland, 37A, Bb
Fort William Henry, 57, Eb
Fort Wiltshire, 81B, Cc
Fort Wrangell, 71B, Cb
Fort York (Fort Tombécbé), 56, Bd
Fort Yukon, 71A, Ca
Fortaleza (Ceara), 68, Fc
Forteviot, 49A, Cb
Forth, R., 28B, Aa
Forth, Firth of, 14, Fc
Fortore, R., 21A, Cb
Fossalta, 20, Jf
Fosse Way, 3A, Ed
Fotheringhay, 27, Fd
Fougères, 20, Cd; 28D, Bb
Fountains, 36, Cc
Four Cantons, L. of the, 29B, Cb
Fourth Cataract, 80B, Ad
Fowey, 48B, Ad
Foyle, L., 15, Da
Foyle, R., 37B, Db
Framlingham, 27, Hd
France, I. de, Indian Ocean, 58, Me
France, King of, 20, De
France Antarctique, 41B, Ef
Franche Comté, 30, Fe
Franci, 2, Ec
Francia, 11, Eb
Franconia, 10, Cc
Frankenthal, 38, Hd
Frankfort, U.S.A., 72, Db
Frankfurt, R. Main, 10, Cc
Frankfurt, R. Oder, 21, Lb
Frankfurt, G.D. of, 65B, Aa
Frankish Empire, 8, Cb
Frankish Kingdom, 4A, Cb
Franklin, 72, Cb
Franklin, terr., 70, Ga
Franks, 2A, Ba; 8C, Ba
Franz Josef Land, 69B
Frascati (Tusculum), 22A
Fraser, R., 70, Bb
Fraserburgh, 49A, Cb
Fraustadt, 31, Mc
Fraxinet, 11, Ge
Fraxinetum, 23A, Ab
Fray Bentos, 68, Df
Frazer, 37A, Bb
Fredericia, 65F, Aa
Frederick, 72B, Ba
Fredericksburg, Virginia, 72B, Ba
Fredericksburg, W. Africa, 81C, Dd
Frederickstown, 57, Cd
Fredericton, 56, Fa; 71, Hc
Frederikssten, 50, Cb
Fredrikshald, 51, Cb
Fredrikshamn, 62, Ha
Freeman's Farm, 57, Eb
Freeport, 70, Fc
Freetown, 81C, Bc
Freiberg, 53, Kb
Freiburg, Germany, 31, Kc
Freiburg, Switzerland, 10, Be; 29A, Ba
Freising, 10, Dd; 31B, Cb
Fréjus, 22, Dc; 38, Gg
Fremantle, 77, Bh
Fremington, 27, Be
French, R., 45A, Aa
French Congo, 80A, Ee
French Empire, 62, Cc

French Equatorial Africa, 80A, Ed
French Frigate I., 75, Gc
French Guiana, 68, Db
French Guinea, 81C, Bb
French Indo-China, 90, Bc
French Ivory Coast, 81C, Cc
French Mills, 57, Da
French Post, 57A, Bc
French Rep., 51, Bd
French Somaliland, 80B, Ce
F. Terr. of Afars and Issas, 96D, Gc
French West Africa, 80A, Cc
Frenchtown, 71C, Bb
Fresnillo, 43A, Bb
Frew, Ford of, 49A, Bb
Fribourg (Freiburg), 29B, Bb
Fribourg, canton, 29B, Bb
Friedberg, Austria, 31, Me
Friedberg, Germany, 53, Hb
Friedland, Bohemia, 47, Fb; East Prussia, 60A, Ha
Friedrich Wilhelmshafen (Madang), 77, Hc
Friedrichstadt, 65F, Aa
Friendly (Tonga) Is., 75, Gf
Friesach, 21, Le
Friesland, 46A, Ea
Frio, C., 68, Ee
Frisia, 20, Gb
Frisian Is., 55A, Fb
Frisians, 2A, Ba; 7A, Ea
Frisii, 2, Ec
Fritzlar, 8, Da; 10, Cc
Friuli, 5, Da
Friuli, M. of, 23B, Da
Frobisher, B., 71, Ha
Frome, 7B, Bc
Fronsac, 11, Cd; 20, Cf
Front Royal, 72B, Aa
Frontenai, 20, Ce
Froschweiler, 76A, Db
Frosham (Frodsham), 13, Dc
Frutigen, 29B, Bb
Fuego, vol., 43A, Cc
Fuente Guinaldo, 63, Bb
Fuenterrabia, 23C, Ea; 63, Ea
Fuentes, de Onoro, 63, Bb
Fulda, 10, Cc
Fulda, R., 10, Cc; 20, Hc
Fulford, 13, Ec
Fulham, 7C, Cc
Funchal, 55B, Jc
Fundy, B. of, 45A, Da
Fünen, 51, Cb; 65F, Ba
Fünfkirchen, 22, Fb; 39, Ne
Furka Pass, 29B, Cb
Furnes, 46A, Bc
Furness, 36, Cc
Fürstenberg, 30, He
Fürstenwalde, 22, Ea
Fürth, Bavaria, 38, Jd
Fürth, Bohemia, 29A, Ea
Fusan, 74, Le
Fushun, 91, Fb
Füssen, 29A, Db
Futhernesse (Furness), 13, Cb
Futuna Is., 75, Fe
Fyne, L., 14, Cc
Fyvie, 37A, Cb

GABARAS B., 45A, Fa
Gabarret, 20, Dg
Gabbards, 55A, Dc
Gaberones, 96D, Eg
Gabes, 6, Cb; 80A, Da
Gabon, 96D, De
Gabrova, 78, Ed
Gabun, 76, Kd
Gadara, 18C, Cf
Gades, 2, Bf
Gadsden, 72, Cc
Gaeta, 5, Dd
Gaikas, 81B, Cc
Gaikwar, 59A, Bc
Gaines Mill, 72B, Bb
Gainesburg (Gainsborough), 13, Fc
Gainesville, 72B, Ba
Gainsborough, 48A, Cc
Gairloch, 49A, Bb
Galadi, 96A, Bb
Galapagos Is., 75, Le
Galata, 86D
Galati, 61, Be
Galatia, 2, Kf
Galatz, 51, Fd; 78, Fc
Galekas, 81B, Dc
Galford, 7B, Ac
Galich, 19, Cc
Galicia, Poland, 33C, Eb
Galicia, Spain, 63, Ba
Galicians, 85, Ad
Galilee, Sea of, 18C, Cf
Galitch, 19, Ga
Galla, 80A, Gd
Gallabat, 80B, Be
Galla-Sidamo, 96A, Ab
Galle, 92, Ef
Gallegos, 68, Ch
Gallia, 2, Dd

Gallinas, C., 43A, Ec
Gallipoli, Italy, 21A, Eb
Gallipoli, Turkey, 78, Fe
Galloway, 14, De
Gallura, 23B, Bd
Galtellia, 23B, Bd
Galty Mts., 15, Cd
Galveston, 72, Bd
Galway, 37B, Bc; 49B, Bc
Galway, co., 37C; 49B, Bc
Galway B., 37B, Bc
Gamalama, 52B, Aa
Gambia, 81C, Ab; 96B, Aa
Gambia, R., 81C, Bb
Gambier Is., 75, Jf
Gandersheim, 22, Da
Gandhara, 1, Kd
Gandia, 23D, Ec
Gando, 80A, Dc
Ganga, R., 91, Bd
Ganganorum Prom., 3A, Bd
Ganges, R., 25, Hd; 73, Ec
Gangra, 16, Jd
Gap, 22, Dc; 30, Gf; 38, Gf
Garamantes, 6, Cc
Garda, L., 5, Cb
Gardelegen, 20, Jb
Gardner, L., 77, Fh
Garfagna, 32E, Ba
Gargano, Mte., 5, Fd
Garhwal, 73, Ca
Garlannonum (Burgh Castle), 3A, Hd
Garigliano, R., 5, Dd
Garonne, R., 11, Dd
Garoua, 96B, Db
Gartagnana, 23B, Cb
Gartz, 31, Lb; 39, Lb
Gascony, D. of, 11, Ce
Gascoyne, R., 77, Af
Gaspé, 45A, Da
Gaspé, C., 45A, Ea
Gaspereau, 45A, Ea
Gassentino, 32E, Bb
Gastein, 21, Ke
Gateshead (Gateshead), 13, Eb
Gatinais, 17, Gd
Gatinais, Co. of, 11, Eb
Gatton, 27, Fe
Gauhati, 92, db
Gaul, Pref. of, 2, Dd
Gaur, 52A, Cb
Gava, 92, Fc
Gavle, 50, Da
Gavre, 46A, Cd
Gawilgarh, 73, Cc
Gaza, 9, Jf; 18C, Bg; 79, Hj
Gaziantep, 79, Gc
Gdansk, 89, Jc
Gdow, 33C, Eb
Gdynia, 87, Db
Gedaref, 80B, Be
Gedrosia, 1, Je
Geelong, 77, Gi
Geelvink, B., 77, Fb
Geestemünde, 65D, Aa
Gefle, 26, Ea
Geissberg, 76A, Eb
Gelderland, 46A, Eb
Geldern, 20, Gc
Gelligaer, 3A, Ce
Gellivare, 88, Ka
Gelnhausen, 20, Hc; 65A, Aa
Gemar, 39B, Db
Gembloux, 46B
Gemlik, 78, Ge
Gemmi Pass, 29B, Bb
Genadental, 81B, Ac
Genappe, 46B
Generality, Lands of the, 46A, Dc
Geneva, 11, Gc; 29B, Ab
Geneva, L. of, 29B, Ab
Gengenbach, 53, Hc
Genoa (Genova), 5, Bb
Genoa, eccl. prov., 22, Dc
Genoa, G. of, 5, Bb
Genoa, Rep. of, 32A, Cb
Genova (Genoa), 5, Bb
George, 81B, Bc
George, L., 45A, Cb; 57, Eb
George, R., 71, Hb
Georgetown (Demerara), 43D, Gd; 68B, Ba
Georgetown, Delaware, 57, Dd
Georgetown, S. Carolina, 57D, Bb
Georgia, U.S.A., 43C, Ca; 56, Cd
Georgia, U.S.S.R., 19, Gd; 25, Db; 79, Hb
Georgian B., 45A, Aa
Gepidae, 2, Hd; 4A, Gb
Gera, 21, Kc; 65B, Ba
Gerace, 22, Fd
Geraldton, 77, Ag
Gerba, 6, Cb
Geringswalde, 22, Ea
German Confederation, 69A, Kb
German East Africa, 80A, Ge

German Flats, 57, Db
German New Guinea, 77, Hc
German South-West Africa, 81A, Ac
Germani, 1, Db
Germanna, 56, Dc
Germantown, 57, Dc
Germany, 87, Cb
Germany, King. of, 16, Db; 20, Jc
Germiyan, 19, Ee
Gernemutha (Yarmouth), 13, Hd
Gerolstein, 53, Gb
Gerona, 11, Ef; 63, Gb
Gerresheim, 22, Da
Gerrha, 1, He
Gerrhaei, 1, Ge
Gersau, 29B, Ca
Gerstungen, 10, Cc
Gertruidenberg, 46A, Dc
Gesoriacum (Boulogne), 3A, Hf
Gettysburg, 72B, Ba
Gévaudan, Co. of, 11, Ed
Gèvres, 53, Dc
Gex, 38, Fe
Ghadames, 80A, Da; 96C, Cb
Ghana, 96B, Bb
Ghassanids, 6A, Bb
Ghat, 80A, Db
Ghaznah, 6, Hb
Ghazni, 25, Fc; 73, Aa
Ghent, 17, Gc; 46A, Cc
Gheria, 59A, Ec
Gheriah, 59A, Bd
Ghillinges (Gilling), 13, Eb
Ghomera, 6, Ab
Giants Castle, 81D, Ab
Gibelet (Byblos), 18C, Cd
Gibelin, 18C, Bg
Gibraltar, Europe, 23D, Cd; 63A
Gibraltar, S. America, 43A, Ed
Gibraltar, Str. of, 63A
Gien, 17, Ge; 30, Fd
Giengen, 20, Jd; 38, Jd
Giessen, 60B, Ba
Gifford, 28A, Bc
Gijon, 23D, Ca
Gila, R., 67D, Bb; 70, Cd
Gilbert Is., 90, Ed
Gilbert, R., 77, Ge
Gildeford (Guildford), 13, Fe
Gilgit, 92, Ca
Gilolo, 52C, Ca
Gimborn, 60A, Ac
Gingee, 59D
Ginginhlovo, 81D, Bb
Giornico, 29B, Cb
Giovenazzo, 21A, Db
Gipewiz (Ipswich), 13, Hd
Girgeh, 80B, Ab
Girgenti (Agrigentum), 5, Df
Gironde, R., 17, Ef; 28C, Bd
Girvan, 49A, Bc
Gisborne, 77A
Gisors, 20, Dd; 83A, Ab
Gitschin, 39, Lc
Giurgevo, 78, Ed
Givelcestre (Ilchester), 13, Df
Givet, 53, Fb; 83A, Ca
Giza, 93, Cd
Gjevgelu, 86A, Da
Gladbach, 83A, Da
Gladstone, 77, If
Glama, R., 12, Ga
Glamorgan, Lordship of, 27, Ce
Glandève, 20, Gg; 22, Dc
Glannaventa (Ravenglass), 3A, Cb
Glarus, 29B, Da
Glarus, canton, 29B, Db
Glasgow, 14, Dd
Glasgow, bp., 14A, Bc
Glastingeberie (Glastonbury), 13, De
Glastonbury, 27, De
Glatz, 21, Mc; 39, Mc
Glatz. co., 39, Mc
Glauchau, 39C, Cc; 53, Kb
Gleichen 39C, Ac
Glen Affric, 14, Db
Glen Coe, 49A, Bb
Glen Elchaig, 49A, Bb
Glen Finnan, 49A, Bb
Glen Garry, 14, Dc
Glen Lyon, 49A, Bb
Glen Moriston, 14, Db
Glen Orchy, 49A, Bb
Glen Shiel, 49A, Bb
Glen Spean, 14, Dc
Glencoe, Natal, 81D, Bb
Glendalough, 15, Ec
Glenlochar, 3A, Bb
Glenluce, 36, Bc; 49A, Bc
Glenmore, 14, Db
Glevum (Gloucester), 3A, De
Gloucester, England, 27, De
Gloucester, Virginia, 45B, Ae

Gloucester (Cape Ann), 45B, Db; 57, Fb
Gloucester, bp., 36, Df
Gloucester, co., 27, De
Glowecestre (Gloucester), 13, De
Glowecestrescire (Gloucester shire), 13, De
Glücksburg, 65F, Aa
Glückstadt, 38, Hb
Glywising, 7B, Bc
Gmünd, 20, Hd; 38, Hd
Gmunden, 39, Ke
Gnesen, 21, Mb
Gnesen, eccl. prov., 22, Fa
Goa, 73, Bd
Goba, 96A, Ab
Gobbio, 23B, Dc
Godavari, R., 25, He; 73, Cd
Godesberg, 87, Bb
Godfrey of Bouillon, 16, Gd
Gödöllö, 33C, Db
Godwin, 12, Dd
Goes, 46A, Cc
Gogra, R., 73, Db
Goias, 68, Dd
Goias, st., 68, Ed
Gok Tepe, 61, Jg
Gokcha, L., 19, Hd
Golconda, 52A, Bc
Golconda Coast, 81C, Dc
Gold Coast, 81C, Dc
Goldeminge, (Godalming), 13, Fe
Golden Gate, Constantinople, 18E
Golden Gate, Jerusalem, 18D
Golden Horde, 25, Da; 61, Fe
Golden Horde, Khanate of the, 19, Gb
Golden Horn, 18E
Golden Vale, 15, Cd
Goldenkron, 22, Eb
Goldsboro, 72, Eb
Goldsborough, 3A, Fb
Golea, 80A, Da
Göllersdorf, 39, Md
Gollnow, 26, Ec
Golspie, 49A, Bb
Gommern, 39C, Ba
Gonave, 43A, Ec
Gondar, 80B, Be; 96A, Aa
Gondrecourt, 39B, Bb
Gondwana, 52A, Cb
Gonzaga, 20, Jf
Gonzaga (Marq. of Mantua), 32A, Db
Good Hope, C. of (Tormentoso), 35, Kf; 81B, Ac
Gooshland, 57, Cd
Gooty, 59A, Cd
Gorakhpur, 73, Db
Gordon, 37A, Bc; 37A, Cb
Gordon Castle, 37A, Cb
Gordonsville, 57, Bd; 72B, Aa
Gorée, 81C, Ab
Gorinchem, 46A, Dc
Gorizia, 23B, Db; 84, Ec
Görlitz, 21, Lc
Gorski, 84, Ld
Görz, 21, Kf; 39, Ke
Görz, Co. of, 39, Ke
Gorze, 39B, Ba
Goshen, 81A, Bc
Goslar, 10, Dc
Gosselies, 46B
Göteborg, 87, Cb
Gotha, 30, Jc; 54, Eb
Gothenburg, 47, Ea; 50, Cb
Gothia, Marq. of, 11, Ee
Gotland, 26, Eb; 34, Ea
Gottesgab, 39C, Cc
Göttingen, 26, Dc; 38, Hc
Gottorp, 51, Bc
Gourdon, 17, Ff
Gouritz, R., 81B, Bc
Governors I., 56B
Gower, 27, Ce
Gowna, L., 15, Dc
Goya, 68, De
Graaff Reinet, 81B, Cc
Graaff Reinet, dist., 81B, Cc
Gracias á Dios, 43A, Dc
Gradisca, 32A, Eb; 86B, Db
Grado, 32D, Cb
Grafenau, 31, Kd
Graham, 37A, Bb
Graham Land, 69C
Grahamstown, 81B, Cc
Graian Alps, 29A, Bc
Grain Coast, 81C, Bc
Grammont, 22, Ca; 46A, Cd
Grampians, 14, Dc
Gran, 22, Fb; 39, Ne
Gran, R., 31, Nd
Gran Chaco, 68, Ce
Granada, Nicaragua, 43A, Dc
Granada, Spain, 23C, Dd; 63, Dd
Granada, eccl. prov., 22, Bd

Granada, King, of, 23C, Dd
Granadine Confederation, 68, Bb
Granard, 15, Dc
Grand Canal, 25, Lc
Grand Canyon, 70, Cd
Grand Gulf, 72C, Aa
Grand I., New York, 71D
Grand I., Vermont, 57, Ea
Grand Lahu, 81C, Dc
Grand Portage, 44, Ed
Grand Pré, 45A, Ea
Grand, R., 70, Dd
Grand Tartary, 42, Ob
Grande Chartreuse, 22, Db
Grande Gette, R., 46B
Grandpré, 30, Fd
Grandson, 29B, Ab
Granson, 30, Ge
Grant, 37A, Bb
Grantham, 13, Fd
Grantown, 49A, Cb
Granville, 55A, Cd
Grappa, Mt., 86B, Bb
Grasse, 22, Dc
Graudenz, 62, Fb
Grauer Bund, 29B, Db
Graus, 23C, Fa
Grave, 46A, Ec
Gravelines, 46A, Bc
Gravelotte, 76A, Cb
Gravesend, 45B, Cc; 57B
Gravina, 21A, Db
Gravosa, 39, Ng
Gray, 38, Fe; 76A, Cc
Grays Inn, 27A
Graz, 21, Le; 29A, Fb
Great Abaco I., 43A, Eb
Great Australian Bight, 77, Dh
Great Bahama I., 43A, Eb
Great Bear L., 70, Ca
Great Belt, 65F, Ba
Great Bridge, 57, Ce
Great Bulgaria, 19, Jb
Great Cayman, 43A, Dc
Great Dividing Ra., 77, Hf
Great Exuma, 43A, Eb
Great Fish, R., Cape Prov., 81B, Cc
Great Fish, R., S.W. Africa, 81B, Aa
Great Inagua, 43A, Eb
Great Kel, R., 81B, Dc
Great Lakes, 69B
Great Manitoulin I., 45A, Aa
Great Marlow, 48A, Cd
Great Namaqualand, 81A, Ac
Great Namaquas, 81B, Aa
Great Ouse, R., 27, Gd
Great Pedee, R., 45A, Ed
Great Poland, 39, Mb
Great Russian, 85, Gb
Great St. Bernard Pass, 29A, Bc
Great Salt L., 70, Cc
Great Slave L., 70, Ca
Great Slave, R., 70, Ca
Great Whale, R., 70, Gb
Great Zab, R., 6A, Ca
Greater Antilles, 43A, Ec
Greece, 78, Dg
Green B., 56, Ba
Green Mts., 45A, Cb
Green, R., 70, Cd
Green Bay, 70, Fc
Greenbrier, R., 57, Ad
Greencastle, 37B, Eb
Greenland, 69B
Greenlaw, 48A, Bb
Greenock, 49A, Bc
Greensboro, 72, Eb
Greenwich, 45B, Cc
Greifswald, 22, Ea; 39, Ka
Greiz, 39C, Cc; 53, Kb
Grenada, 43A, Fc
Grenadines, 43A, Fc
Grenoble, 11, Fd
Grentebrige (Cambridge), 13, Gd
Grentebrigescire (Cambridge-shire), 13, Gd
Gretna, 28B, Bb; 49A, Cc
Greymouth, 77A
Greytown, 81D, Bb
Grèzes, 17A, Dd
Griffen, 39, Le
Griffin's Wharfe, 56B
Grimesbi (Grimsby), 13, Fc
Grimsby, 27, Fc
Grimsel Pass, 29B, Cb
Grinstead, 27, Fe
Griqualand East, 81B, Db
Griqualand West, 81B, Bb
Griquas, 81B, Bb
Griquatown, 81B, Bb
Gris Nez, C., 55A, Dc
Grislingen, 30, Hd
Grisons (Rhaetian Leagues), 29B, Db
Grobe, 22, Ea
Gröbming, 31, Ke; 39, Ke

Grodno, 26, Fc; 60A, Jb
Groll, 46A, Fb
Groningen, 46A, Fa
Groningen, prov., 46A, Fa
Grosmont, 28A, Dc
Grosotto, 86B, Aa
Gross Jägersdorf, 51, Ec
Gross Mariazell, 22, Fb
Grossbeeren, 60B, Db
Grosseto, 20, Jg; 22, Ec
Grosswardein, 33C, Cb
Grotska, 33C, Ec; 51, Ee
Grozny, 88, Pe
Gruffyd ap Llywelyn, Pr. of, 12, Dc
Gruyères, 29B, Ab
Guadalajara, Mexico, 43A, Bb
Guadalajara, Spain, 63, Db
Guadalcanal, 77, Jc; 90, Dd
Guadalquivir, R., 63, Cd
Guadalupe, 22, Ad
Guadarrama, Sierra de, 63, Db
Guadeloupe, 43A, Fc
Guadenhutten, 56, Cb
Guadiana, R., 63, Bd
Guadix, 22, Bd; 23C, Db
Guam, 40, Qd; 90, Dc
Guanahani, 40, Fc
Guanajuato, 43A, Bb
Guapora, R., 68, Cd
Guaporé, 94, Df
Guarda, 22, Ac; 63, Bb
Guastalla, 32A, Db
Guatemala, 43A, Cc
Guatulco, 42, Ed
Guaviare, R., 68, Cb
Guayaquil, 68, Ac
Guben, 31, Lc
Guelders, 60A, Ac
Guelders, Co. of, 46C, Ba
Guelders, D. of, 31A, Cb
Gueldres, 46A, Fc
Guérande, 30, Be
Gueret, 30, De
Guermistr (Warminster),13, Ee
Guernsey, 17, Dd
Guiana, 68, Db
Guienne, D. of (Aquitaine), 11, Dd
Guildford, 27, Fe
Guilford, 45B, Cc
Guilford Court House, 57, Be
Guillon, 28C, Ec
Guimaraes, 23D, Ab
Guinea, 81C, Dc; 96B, Ab
Guinea, G. of, 94, Te
Guinegate, 30, Ec
Guines, 11, Da; 17, Fc
Guingamp, 22, Bb; 38, Bd
Guipuzcoa, 23C, Da
Guise, 17, Gd; 30, Ed; 53, Ec
Gultres, 22, Bb
Gujarat, 25, Gd; 73, Bc
Gujranwala, 92, Ca
Gujrat, 73, Ba
Gumti, R., 73, Db
Gundwana, 59A, Cc
Güns, 39, Me
Guntur, 59A, Cd; 92, Ed
Gurev, 61, Ma
Gurganj, 6, Ga
Gurgan, 93, Gb
Guria, 79, Hb
Gurk, 22, Ea
Gurkhas, 73, Db
Gurramkonda, 59A, Ce
Gurupa, 41B, Dd
Gusau, 96B, Ca
Güstrow, 39, Kb
Guthrum's King., 7C, Db
Guyana, 68. Db
Guyenne, 20, Df; 28C, Cd
Gwadar, 92, Ab
Gwalior, 25, Gd; 73, Cb
Gwent, 28A, Dc
Gwynedd, 13, Bc; 28A, Dc
Gympie, 77, Ig
Gyrwe (Jarrow), 13, Eb

HAARLEM, 46A, Db
Habitancum (Risingham), 3A, Da
Habsburg, 11, Gc; 29B, Ca
Hackensack, 57B
Haddeby, 12, Gc
Hadby-Schleswig, 12, Gc
Haddington, 49A, Cc
Haddington, co., 49A, Cc
Hadhramaut, 93, Ff
Hadjach, 50, Gc
Hadrianopolis, 2, Je
Hadrian's Wall, 3C
Hafir, 6, Fc
Hafrsfjord, 12, Fb
Hafsids, 24, Eg
Hafsids (Sultanate of Tunis), 34, De
Hagenau, 20, Gd; 29A, Ba
Hagerstown, 72, Eb
Hague, C. de la, 55A, Cd
Hague, The, 46A, Db

Hagustalham (Hexsham) (Hexham), 13, Db
Haifa, 18C, Cf; 93, Cc
Hail, 93, Ed
Hailes, 36, Ef
Hainan, 25, Ke; 91, De
Hainau, 60B, Dc
Hainaut, 10, Ac; 46A, Cd
Haine, R., 46B
Haine's Bluff, 72C, Aa
Haingeham (Hedingham), 13, Gd
Haiti, 43A, Ec
Hakodate, 91, Hb
Halberstadt, 10, Dc
Haleb (Aleppo), 18C, Eb
Halesowen, 36, De
Halifax, England, 48A, Cc
Halifax, N. Carolina, 57, Ce
Halifax, Nova Scotia, 45A, Eb
Hall, 20, Hd; 53, Hc
Halland, 26, Db; 47, Ea
Halle, 10, Ec; 31B, Dc
Hallue, 76A, Bb
Halmahera, 91, Ff
Halmstad, 26, Db
Halton, 27, Dc
Halys, R., 18A, Ea; 24, Jf
Ham, 30, Ed
Hama, 18C, Dc; 93, Db
Hamadan, 6A, Db; 93, Fc
Hamar, 26, Da
Hamburg, 10, Cb
Hamdan, 6, Fd
Hamdanids, King of, 6B, Fa
Hami, 74, Hd
Hamid, 19, Ee
Hamilton, Canada, 70, Fc
Hamilton, Scotland, 37A, Bc
Hamilton Inlet, 71, Jb
Hamilton, R., 71, Hb
Hamm, 60A, Ac
Hammadids, 16, Ce
Hampshire, 27, Ec
Hampton, New Hampshire, 45B, Db
Hampton, Virginia, 45B, Ae
Hampton Roads, 72B, Bb
Hamton, 7B, Ac
Han Dominions, 1, Od
Hanau, 29A, Ca; 30. Hc
Hanchong, 76B, Ba
Han-chung, 1, Nd
Handa, 96A, Ca
Hangchow, 74, Lf; 91, Ec
Hangchow (Quinsay) (Lin-gan), 25, Mc
Hanging Rock, 57D, Aa
Hankow, 74, Ke; 90, Dd
Hanoi, 25, Kd; 91, Dd
Hanover, Germany, 26, Cc
Hanover, Virginia, 57, Ce
Hanover, El., 53, Ha
Hantescire (Hampshire), 13, Ee
Hantune (Southampton), 13, Ef
Harar, 96A, Bb
Harar, prov., 96A, Bb
Harbin (Pinkiang), 90, Ca; 91, Fb
Harcourt, 17, Fd; 53, Cc
Hard Times, 72C, Aa
Hardangerfjord, 12, Fb
Hardknot, 3A, Cb
Harenc, 18C, Db
Harfleur, 30, Dd; 53, Dc
Harlech, 27, Bd
Harmazia, 1, He
Harold, 12, Dd
Harper, 96B, Bb
Harper's Ferry, 56, Dc
Harran, 6A, Ba
Harris, 14, Db; 37A, Ab
Harrisburg, 72, Ea
Harrismith ,81A, Cc; 81D, Ab
Harrodsburg, 56, Cc
Hartford, 45B, Cc
Hartland, 36 Bg
Hartmannswillerkopf,83B,Bb
Harts, R., 81A, Cc
Harwich, 27, He
Haryana, 92, Db
Harz, 60A, Dc
Harz, mts., 10, Dc
Harzburg, 10, Dc
Hasselt, 26, Cc; 83A, Ca
Hastenbeck, 60A, Bb
Hastings, 27, He
Hastinges (Hastings), 13, Gf
Hatay, 79, Gc
Hatfield, 7B, Cc
Hatteras, C., 45A, Bf; 57, Df
Hattin, 18C, Cf
Haughmond, 36, De
Haura, 93, Fg
Hauraki, G., 77A
Hauterive, 22, Db
Havana, 43A, Db
Havelberg, 10, Eb; 30, Kb
Haverfordwest, 27, Ae

Haverhill, 45B, Db
Havre, 76A, Ab
Havre de Grâce (Le Havre), 38, Dd
Havre de Grace, Maryland, 71C, Cc
Haw, R., 57, Be
Hawaii, 75D, Cc
Hawaiian Is., 90, Gb
Hawarden, 13, Cc; 27, Cc
Hawke B., 77A
Hawkes Bay, 77A
Hawick, 28B, Cb
Hay, 28A, Cb
Hayingen, 30, Hd
Haymarket, 27A
Heard L., 95, Qh
Heathfield, 7A, Ca
Hebrides, 37A, Ab; 49A, Ab
Hebron, Palestine, 18C, Cg
Hebron, Transvaal, 81A, Cc
Hechingen, 60B, Cc; 65B, Ab
Heda (Hythe), 13, He
Hedgley Moor, 27, Da
Hedmark, 12, Ga
Hedon, 27, Fc
Heidelburg, 29A, Ca
Heilbronn, 29A, Ca
Heiligenkreuz, 22, Fb
Heiligerlee, 46A, Fa
Heilsberg, 26, Fc; 60A, Ha
Heinsberg, 46C, Cb
Hejaz, 6, Fc; 80B, Bc
Hejer, 6, Fc
Helder, 46A, Db
Heldernesse (Holderness), 13, Fc
Helena, Arkansas, 72, Bc
Helena, Montana, 70, Cc
Heletune (Halton), 13, Dc
Heligoland, 55A, Ga; 60A, Aa
Heligoland Bight, 55A, Ga
Heliopolis (Baalbek), 18C, De
Hellas, 9, Ge
Helles, C., 86D
Hellespont, 34, He
Hellespontus, 2, Jf
Helluland, 35, Gb
Helmsdale, 49A, Ca
Helsingborg, 26, Db
Helsingfors, 26, Fa
Helsingland, 26, Ea
Helsingor, 26, Lb
Helsinki, 87, Ea
Helston, 27, Af
Helvetian Rep., 65A, Ab
Hemmingstedt, 26, Cc; 30, Ha
Hempstead, 45B, Cc
Hendaye, 53, Cf
Hengistdun, 7B, Ac
Hennebont, 28C, Ac; 55A, Be
Hennersdorf, 60A, Ec
Henrico, 45B, Ae
Henry, C., 45B, Be
Heppenheim, 65C, Ab
Heraclea, Iconium, 16, Je
Heraclea, Nicaea, 19, Ed
Herakleia, 18C, Ba
Herat, 25, Fc; 61B, Bb
Herbertshöhe (Kokopo), 77, Ib
Herculis Prom., 3A, Be
Herdeslege, (Eardisley), 13, Dd
Hereford, 13, Dd
Hereford, bp., 36, De
Hereford, co., 27, Dd
Herefordscire (Hereford-shire), 13, Dd
Hereke, 33A, Cb
Herero, 80A, Ef
Héricourt, 31A, Dd
Héristal, 7A, Eb; 8, Da
Heijdalen, 26, Da
Hermannstadt (Sibin), 19, Cc
Hermannstadt, Hungary, 24 Gd; 78, Ec
Hermitage, 28B, Cb
Hermon, Mt., 18C, De
Hernösand, 26, Ea
Hersfeld, 10, Cc; 30, Hc
Herteforde (Hertford), 13, Fe
Hertefordscire (Hertford-shire), 13, Fe
Hertford, 27, Fe
Hertford, co., 27, Fe
Heruli, 2, Kd
Hervey Is., 75, He
Herzegovina, 39, Mg; 78, Ad
Hesdin, 53, Eb
Hesse, 10, Cc
Hesse, G. D. of, 65C, Aa
Hesse, Land. of, 30, Hc
Hesse-Cassel, Land., 38, Hc
Hesse-Darmstadt, Land., 38, Hc
Hessen, 60B, Bc
Hevellians, 10, Eb
Heversham, 7B, Ba
Hexham, 27, Db; 36A
Heytesbury, 27, De
Hibernia, 2, Bc

Hierapolis, 2, Lf; 4B, Kd
Hierosolyma, 1, Fd
High Bridge, 49A, Bb
High Street, 3A, Db
Hiiumaa, 87, Ea
Hildburghausen, 39C, Ac
Hildesheim, 10, Cb
Hilla, 93, Ec
Hillsborough, 57, Be
Hilo, 75D, Cc
Himachal Pradesh, 92, Da
Himalaya Mts., 73, Ca
Hims, 6A, Bb
Hindon, 27, De
Hindu Kush, 59A, Ba
Hindu States, 25, Ge
Hindustan, 40, Nc
Hingham, 45B, Db
Hinsdale (Fort Dummer), 57, Eb
Hippo, 4A, Dd; 8, Dd
Hippo Regius, 2, Ef
Hira, 6A, Cb
Hiroshima, 91, Gc
Hirschau, 22 Db
Hirschberg, 39, Lc; 60A, Ec
Hirson, 83A, Cb
Hirsova, 78, Fc
Hispania, 2, Be
Hispaniola (Española), 43A, Ec
Hit, 6A, Cb
Hitchin, 36, Ff
Hlobane, 81D, Ba
Hlubi Kaffirs, 81D, Ab
Hobart, 77, Hj
Hobkirk's Hill, 57D, Aa
Hoboken, 45B, Cc
Hochkirch, 60A, Ec
Hochschwab, 29A, Fb
Höchst, 38, Hc
Höchstadt, 29A, Da
Hodeida, 80B, Ce; 93, Eg
Hofburg, 20, Gd
Hog I., 56B
Hohe Tauern, 29A, Eb
Höhen, 10, Ec
Hohenburg, Bavaria, 20, Jd
Hohenburg, Swabia, 20, Hd
Hohenfriedeberg, 60A, Fc
Hohenlinden, 29A, Da
Hohenlohe, 20, Jd
Hohenstein, 60A, Dc
Hohenzollern, 38, Hd
Hohnstein, 60A, Ec
Hokianga B., 77A
Hokkaido, 91, Hb
Holborn, 27A
Holkar, 73, Cc
Holkar and Sindhia, 59A, Cc
Hollabrünn, 29A, Ga
Holland, Co. of, 17, Hb; 46A, Db
Holland, dist., England, 13 Gd
Holland, King. of, 65F, Aa
Holly Springs, 72, Cc
Holme Cultram, 36, Cc
Holme St. Benet, 36, He
Holstein, 10, Cb
Holt, 28A, Da; 48B, Bc
Holy I., 12, Dc; 36, Eb
Holyhead, 3A, Bc
Holy Roman Empire, 20, Jd
Holy Sepulchre, Church of the, 18D
Holyhead, 3A, Bc
Holyrood, 14, Ed
Homburg, 30, Gc; 39B, Ca
Home, 28B, Cb
Homildon Hill, 27, Da
Homs, 18C, Dd; 79, Gd; 93, Dc
Honduras, 43D, Dc
Honduras, I., 43B, Bc
Honduras, G. of, 43A, Dc
Honfleur, 28D, Db; 55A, Dd
Hongkong, 91, Ed
Honiton, 27, Cf
Honolulu, 75, Hc; 75D, Cb
Honshu, 91, Gc
Hooghly, 59B
Hooghly, R., 59B; 92, Fc
Hoogstracten, 46A, Dc
Hoorn, 30, Fc; 46A, Eb
Hope, 28A, Ca
Hope Bay, 69C
Hopedale, 71, Hb
Hopetown, 81A, Bc
Hopton Heath, 48A, Bc
Horburg, 39B, Db
Horgen, 29B, Ca
Horn, 46C, Bb
Horn, C., 68, Ch
Horncastle, 3A, Fc
Horseshoe Bend (Tohopeka), 71F, Ba
Horsham, 27, Fe
Horta, 3, Gb
Hostatrich 63, Gb
Hottentots, 81B, Bb
Houdan, 38, Dd
Housatonic, R., 45B, Cc
Houston, 72, Ad

Hovedene (Howden), 13, Fc
Howland I., 90, Fc
Howrah, 92, Fc
Howth, 49B, Ec
Howth Hd., 15, Ec
Hoy, 49A, Ca
Hoya, 20, Hb
Hoysalas, 25, Ge
Hradisch, 22, Fb
Hsi-Liao, R., 91, Fb
Hsinking, 90, Ca
Hsu Chow, 1, Od
Huanuco, 68, Bc
Huaras, 68, Bc
Hubbardton, 57, Eb
Hubertusbrug, 60A, Dc
Hudson B., 70, Fb
Hudson, R., 57, Dc
Hudson (North), R., 45B, Bc
Hudson Str., 70, Ga
Hudson Bay Company Terr., 44, Eb
Hué, 91, De
Huelgas, 22, Bc
Huelva, 23C, Bd
Huesca, Granada, 23D, Dd
Huesca, Saragossa, 23C, Ea
Hufuf, 93, Fd
Hughenden, 77, Gf
Huilier, Fort d', 56, Ab
Hull, 27, Fc
Hulme, 48B, Bc
Hulst, 46A, Dc
Humana, 5B, Bb
Humanita, 68, De
Humber, 27, Gc
Humboldt, R., 70, Cc
Hume Castle, 28B, Bd
Hungarian Ore Mts., 50, Dd
Hungary, 33C, Db; 87, Dc
Hungary, King. of, 16, Fc
Hungshui-Ho, R., 91, Dd
Hun-ho, R., 76B, Ba
Hüningen, 53, Gd
Hunni, 2, Ld
Huns, 2A, Fb
Hunsrück, 83A, Db
Huntcliff, 3A, Fc
Huntedun (Huntingdon), 13, Fd
Huntedunscire (Huntingdon-shire), 13, Fd
Hunter, R., 77, Ih
Huntingdon, 27, Fd
Huntingdon, co., 27, Fd
Huntly, 37A, Cb; 49A, Cb
Huntsville, 72, Cc; 71F, Ba
Huon G., 77, Hc
Hurghada, 93, Cd
Huron, L., 45A, Ab
Huron Mission, 45A, Ab
Hurons, 45A, Ab
Hush, 54, Hc
Hussinetz, 31, Ld
Husum, 65F, Aa
Huy, 53, Fb
Hvitramannaland, 35, Fc
Hwang-ho, R., 25, Lc
Hwicce, 7B, Bc
Hy (Iona), 14, Bc
Hyderabad, Nizam's Domini-ons, 73, Cd
Hyderabad, Sind, 73, Ab
Hydra, 78, Dg
Hyères, 30, Gg
Hyères, Is. d', 53, Gf
Hyrcania, I, Hd
Hythe, 27, He

IAL, 13, Cc
Iambia, 1, Fe
Iarum (Yarm), 13, Eb
Iasi, 87, Fc
Iazyges, 1, Ec
Ibadan, 96B, Cb
Ibelim, 18C, Bg
Iberia, 19, Gd
Iberus, R., 2, Ce
Ica, 68, Bd
Icaria, 19, De
Iceland, 88, Ba
Iceni, 3A, Gd
Ichaboe I., 81A, Ac
Ichang, 74, Ke
Icknield Way, 3A, Fe
Iconium (Konieh), 18A, Eb; 19, Ee
Iconium (Seljuk Sultanate of Rum), 16, Je
Ida, Mt., 78, Eh
Idaho, 70, Cc
Idaho Terr., 67D, Ba
Idjil, 80A, Bb
Idrisids, 8, Ae
Idrisids, King. of, 6B, Aa
Idstedt, 65F, Aa
Ife, 96B, Cb
Ifni, 80A, Bb
Ifni, col., 96C, Ab
Iganie, 64, Gc
Iglau, 31, Ld; 39, Ld
Ikhshids, King. of, 6B, Eb

Ilchester, 27, De
Ile Bouchard, 38, De
Ilfracombe, 48B, Ad
Ilha, 41B, Ee
Ilheus, 68, Fd
Ili, R., 91, Ab
Ilkhan Empire, 25, Ec
Ilkley, 7B, Cb
Ill, R., 39B, Db
Ilana B., 75E, Bc
Ilapel, 68, Bf
Iler, R., 10, Dd; 29A, Db
Illinois, 56, Bc; 72, Cb
Illinois, R., 56, Bb
Illinois Terr., 71C, Ab
Illyria, King. of, 65C, Bb
Illyria, Pref. of, 2, Hf
Illyrian Prov., 62, Ec
Illyricum, 4A, Gc
Illyricum, Diocese, 2, Gd
Ilmen, L., 26, Hb
Iloilo, 75E, Bb
Ilorin, 96B, Cb
Imbros, 78, Ee
Imeretia, 79, Hb
Imperial Hungary, 39, Me
Imphal, 92, Gc
In Salah, 80A, Db
Inca King., 35, Fe
Inchcolm, 14, Ec
Inchtuthill, 14, Ec
Inde, 43A, Bb
Independence, 70, Ed
India, 92, Dc
Indian Ocean, 35, Ne
Indian Terr., 67D, Db
Indiana, 72, Cb
Indiana Terr., 67B, Aa
Indianapolis, 72, Cb
Indies, 42, Oc
Indonesia, 91, Eg
Indore, 73, Cc
Indraprastha, 1, Ke
Indus, R., 1, Kd; 73, Ab
Ingelheim, 10, Cd
Ingogo, 81D, Aa
Ingolstadt, 22, Eb; 29A, Da
Innichen, 86B, Ca
Inner Mongolia, 91, Eb
Innsbruck, 29A, Db
Inny, R., 15, Dc
Inter Ripam et Mersham, 13, Dc
Interlaken, 29B, Bb
Inuvik, 94, Gb
Inveraray, 37A, Bb; 49A, Bb
Inveravon, 3A, Ca
Invercargill, 77A
Inveresk, 3A, Ca
Inverey, 49A, Cb
Invergarry, 49A, Bb
Invergordon, 49A, Bb
Invergowrie, 14, Ec
Inverkeithing, 37A, Cb; 48B, Ba
Inverlochy, 49A, Bb
Inverness, 14, Db
Inverness, co., 37A, Bb; 49A, Bb
Inverurie, 49A, Cb
Invola, 32A, Db
Inyati, 81A, Ca
Inyeshane, 81D, Bb
Iona (Hy), 14, Bc; 49A, Ab
Ionia, 84, He
Ionian Is., 62, Ge; 78, Cf
Ionian Sea, 78, Bf
Iowa, 70, Ec
Iowas, 56, Bb
Ipswich (Agawam), 45B, Db; 57, Fb
Ipswich, England, 27, Hd
Iquique, 68, Be
Iquitos, 68, Bc
Iran (Persia), 89, Pg; 93, Gc
Iraq, 6A, Db; 79, Hd
Irchester, 3A, Fd
Ireland, 15; 49A
Irish Free State, 84, Ab
Irish Sea, 15, Fc; 28B, Ac
Irkutsk, 91, Da
Iron Gate, 78, Dc
Iroquois, 45A, Bb
Irrawaddy, R., 73, Gc; 92, Hd
Iroslavl, 19, Fa
Irthing, R., 28B, Cc
Irtysh, R., 25, Ga; 91, Aa
Irun, 63, Ea
Irvine, 49A, Bc
Isabella, 43A, Ec
Isandhlwana, 81D, Bb
Isar, R., 10, Ed
Isauria, 2, Kf
Isca (Caerleon), 3A, De

Isca Dumnoniorum (Exeter), 3A, Cf
Ischia, 32B, Dd
Iscia Baidoa, 96A, Bb
Isère, R., 11, Fd; 32A, Bb
Isernia, 22, Ec
Isfahan, 25, Ec; 93, Gc
Ishtip, 86A, Da
Isker, R., 78, Dd
Islamabad, 92, Ca
Island Number Ten, 72, Cb
Islands, B. of, 77A
Isle of France, 38, Ed
Isles, King. of the, 14, Bb
Isles, The, bp., 14A, Ab
Ismail, 51, Fd; 78, Gc
Ismailia, 80B, Aa; 86C, Bc
Isna, 93, Cd
Isny, 30, Je
Isola, 32D, Bb
Isonzo, 2A, Cb
Isonzo, R., 5, Db; 86B, Da
Ispahan, 6, Gb
Isparta, 93, Cc
Israel, 89, Mg; 93, Cc
Issoire, 30, Ef
Issoudun, 11, Dc
Istanbul, 93, Ba
Istria, 5, Db; 10, Ef
Isurium (Aldborough), 3A, Eb
Italia, 2, Fe
Italian (Cisalpine) Rep., 65A, Ab
Italian Somaliland, 80A, Hd
Italy, 88, He
Italy, Exarchate of, 4B, Ec
Italy, King. of, 20, Jf
Italy, Pref. of, 2, Fe
Itil, 9, Mc
Ituna Aest. (Solway Firth), 3A, Cb
Itzehoe, 65F, Ab
Iuka, 72, Cc
Iviza, 23C, Fc; 63, Fc
Ivory Coast, 81C, Cd
Ivrea, 5, Ab
Ivry, 38, Dd
Iwo, 96B, Cb
Iwojima, 90, Db
Izborsk, 9, Ha
Izmir, 93, Bb

JABALPUR, 92, Ec
Jabia, 6A, Bb
Jablunkau, 39, Nd
Jaca 22, Bc; 23C, Ea
Jackson, Mississippi, 72C, Aa
Jackson, Tennessee, 72, Cb
Jacksonville, 72, Dc
Jaen, 22, Bd; 23C, Dd
Jaffa, 86C, Bc
Jaffa (Joppa), 18C, Bf
Jaffna, 92, Ef
Jagellons, Lands of the, 31, Md
Jagerndorf, 31, Mc; 33C, Da
Jaintiapur, 73, Fb
Jaipur, 73, Cb
Jaipur, st., 59C, Cb
Jajce, 39, Mf
Jalalabad, 73, Ba
Jalangi, R., 59B
Jalayas, Dominions of the, 24, Mf
Jaleswar, 59B
Jaluit, 75, Fd
Jamaica, 45B, Cc
Jamaica, I., 43A, Ec
Jamaica B., 57B
James B., 70, Fb
James, R., 57, Ce; 72B, Ab
James City, 45B, Ae
James W. Ellsworth Land, 69C
Jamestown, 45B, Ae
Jammu and Kashmir, 92, Da
Jamnagar, 92, Cc
Jamshedpur, 92, Fc
Jamtland, 12, Ha
Janer, 31, Mc
Janina, 78, Cf
Jankau, 38, Ld
Jaora, 73, Cc
Japan, 91, Gc
Japan (Zipangu), 25, Nc
Japan, Sea of, 91, Gc
Japanese Empire, 75, Ec
Japura, R., 68, Cc
Jargeau, 28D, Dc
Jarnac, 38, Cf
Jaroslau, 26, Fc
Jaroslavl, 19, Fa
Jarrow, 36, Ec
Jarvis I., 75, He
Jask, 93, Hd
Jassy, 50, Fd; 78, Fb
Jativa, 23C, Ec
Jats, 59A, Cb
Jauf, 93, Dd
Java, 42B; 91, Dg
Java Major (Borneo), 35, Pd
Java Minor (Sumatra), 35, Oe

Java Sea, 91, Eg
Jaxartes, R., 1, Jc
Jebel Hamrin, 19, Ge
Jebel Tarik, 9, Ae
Jedburgh, 14, Fd
Jeddah, 6, Ec
Jedisan, 50, Gd; 78. Gb
Jefferson City, 72, Bb
Jehol, 90, Ba
Jehoshophat's Gate, 18D
Jelling, 12, Gc
Jemappes, 46A, Cd; 62, Cb
Jemmingen, 46A, Ga
Jemtland, 26, Da
Jena, 30, Jc; 38, Jc; 62, Eb
Jericho, 18C, Cg
Jersey, 17, Dd
Jerusalem, 18A, Bb; 18C, Cg
Jerusalem, Kingdom of, 18C, Cf
Jervaulx, 36, Ee
Jessore, 59B
Jever, 30, Gb; 38, Gb
Jhansi, 73, Cb
Jhelum, R., 73, Ba
Jibuti, 80B, Ce; 94, Re
Jiddah, 80B, Bc
Jimma, 96A, Ab
Jitomir, 50, Fc
Joanna Spring, 77, Cf
Jodhpur, 73, Bb
Johannesburg, 81A, Cc
Johore, 58, Pd
Johore Bahru, 75A, Bb
Johnston, 28B, Bb
Johnston I., 90, Fc
Johnstone, 28B, Bb
Joigny, 11, Ec
Jolo, 75E, Bc
Jönköping, 26, Db
Joppa, 18A, Ec
Joppa (Jaffa), 18C, Bf
Jordan, 89, Ng; 93, Dc
Jordan, R., 18C, Cf
Jos, 96B, Cb
Joscelin, Lordship of, 18C, Eb
Josselin, 30, Be
Joux, 53, Gd
Juan de Fuca Str., 70, Bc
Juan Fernandez Is., 68, Bf
Jucar, R., 23C, Ec
Juggernaut, 59A, Ed
Jujuy, 41B, Cf
Julian Alps, 86B, Da
Jülich, 20, Gc; 46A, Fd
Jülich, D. of, 46A, Fd
Juliers, Co. of, 46C, Cb
Jullundur, 73, Ca
Jumièges, 22, Dc
Jumna, R., 73, Cb
Junagadh and Manavadar, 92, Cc
Juneau, 71B, Cb
Junin, Argentina, 68, Cf
Junin, Peru, 68, Bd
Junto, Mte., 63B
Jura, I., 14, Cc
Jura, mts., 11, Gc
Jura, Sd. of, 14, Cd
Jurjan, 6, Gb
Jurua, R., 68, Cc
Jussy, 29B, Ab
Justingen, 30, Hd
Jüterbog, 53, Kb
Jutes, 4A, Ba; 7A, Fa
Juti, 2, Eb
Jutland, 55B, La; 84, Da
Juzajan, 6, Hb

KA LAE, pt., 75D, Dc
Kaanbaligh (Peking), 25, Lc
Kabul, 6, Hb; 25, Fc; 73, Aa
Kabul, R., 73, Aa
Kabusi, R., 81B, Cc
Kachin, 92, Hb
Kadisiya, 6A, Cb
Kaduna, 96B, Ca
Kaffa, 19, Fd; 25, Cb
Kaffraria, 81A, Cd
Kafiristan, 61B, Cb
Kagoshima, 91, Gc
Kahoolawe, 75D, Cb
Kaifeng, 25, Lc
Kaiping, 76B, Ba
Kairwan, 8, Ed
Kaisaria, 33A, Ec; 86C, Cb
Kaiser Wilhelm Land, Antarctica, 69C
Kaiser Wilhelms Land (North-East New Guinea), 77, Gc
Kaiserslautern, 29A, Ba
Kaiserswerth, 10, Bc
Kaiwi Chan., 75D, Cb
Kalahari Desert, 81A, Bb
Kalamata, 78, Dg
Kalat, 73, Ab
Kalau, 39C, Db
Kalavryta, 78, Df
Kalgan, 74, Kd; 90, Ba
Kalgoorlie, 77, Ch
Kalimantan, 91, Eg

Kalinga, 1, Lf
Kaliningrad, 89, Kc
Kalinjar, 52A, Cb
Kalisz, 21, Nc; 31, Nc
Kalka, 19, Fc
Kalmuck, 85, Lc
Kalocsa, 22, Fb; 24, Fd
Kalocsa, eccl. prov., 22, Fc
Kalpi, 73, Cb
Kaluga, 24, Kc; 50, Hc
Kama, R., 19, Ja; 88, Qb
Kamakura, 25, Nc
Kamaran, 40, Md
Kamaran I., 80B, Cd; 93, Ef
Kambula, 81D, Ba
Kamchatka, 74, Oc; 90, Da
Kamchik, R., 78, Fd
Kamenets Podolski, 79, Ea
Kamerun, 80A, Ed
Kaminiec, 50, Fd
Kamioops, 70, Eb
Kammin, 21, Lb
Kammin, Bp. of, 31, Ma
Kamp, 22, Da
Kampala, 96D, Fd
Kanara, 59A, Be; 73, Be
Kanauj, 25, Hd
Kanawha, R., 57, Ad
Kanazawa, 91, Gc
Kandahar, 61B, Bb; 73, Aa
Kandavu, 75C, Bb
Kandi, 96B, Ca
Kandy, 73, Df
Kanem, 80A, Ec
Kangaroo I., 77, Fi
Kanizsa, 39, Me
Kankan, 96B, Ba
Kano, 96B, Ca
Kanpur, 92, Eb
Kansas, 70, Ed
Kansas, R., 44, Ee
Kansas City, 72, Bb
Kansas Terr., 67D, Cb
Kapolna, 33C, Eb
Kappel, 29B, Ca
Kaprivshtitza, 78, Ed
Kara Kum, 61B, Ab
Kara Kuyunli, 24, Lf
Kara Sea, 74, Ea
Karabagh, 79, Jc
Karachi, 73, Ab
Karaganda, 91, Ab
Karakakua B., 58, Bd
Karakoram Mts., 59A, Ca
Karaman, Amirate of, 19, Ee
Karansebes, 33C, Eb
Kara-shahr, 1, Lc
Karassi, 33A, Cc
Karauli, 73, Cb
Karawanken, 29A, Fb
Karbala, 79, Hd
Kardis, 50, Fb; 54, Ha
Kargopol, 61, Eb
Karikal, 59D
Karlovo, 78, Ed
Karlsbad, 31B, Ca
Karlskrona, 51, Db; 54, Fa
Karlsruhe, 83A, Eb
Karmati, King. of, 6B, Fb
Karnul, 73, Cd
Karpathos, 93, Bb
Kars, 19, Gd; 61, Ff; 79, Hb
Karystos, 78, Ef
Karytaena, 78, Df
Kasai, R., 80A, Ee
Kasalinsk, 61B, Ba
Kaschau, 31, Pd; 50, Ed
Kashan, 93, Gc
Kashgar, 1, Kd
Kashmir, 1, Kd; 73, Ca
Kaskaskia, 56, Bc
Käsmark, 21, Pd
Kasogs (Cherkes es), 9, Lc
Kassa, 33C, Eb
Kassala, 80B, Bd
Kastamuni, 33A, Do
Kastoria, 86A, Cb
Kasvin, 19, He
Kat, R., 81B, Cc
Katanga, 80A, Ff; 96D, Ee
Kath, 6, Ha
Kathiawar, 73, Bc
Katiola, 96B, Bb
Katmandu, 73, Eb
Katrine, L., 14, Dc
Katsina, 96B, Ca
Kattegat, 12, Gb
Katwa, 59B
Kauai, 75D, Ba
Kauai Chan., 75D, Bb
Kaufbeuren, 20, Je
Kaunas, 87, Eb
Kavalla, 78, Ee; 84, Gd
Kawita, 56, Cd
Kawthoolei, 92, Hd
Kayah, 92, Hd
Kayes, 81C, Bb
Kayseri, 79, Gc
Kaysersburg, 39B, Db
Kazam, 19, Ha

Kazan Is., 90, Db
Kazanlik, 78, Ed
Kazanlinsk, 74, Ed
Kazvin, 93, Gb
Ke Chow, 1, Od
Kearney, 70, Ec
Kecskemet, 33C, Db
Kedgeree, 59B
Keeling (Cocos) Is., 90, Ad
Keewatin, 70, Ea
Kehl, 39B, Db; 65B, Ab
Kei Is., 52C, Dc
Keiskamma, R., 81B, Cc
Keith, 37A, Cb
Kells, 15, Ec; 49B, Ec
Kelly, 72, Eb
Kelso, 14, Fd; 37A, Cc
Kemi, 26, Fa
Kemp Land, 69C
Kempten, 20, Je
Kenauj, 59C, Cb
Kendal, 27, Db
Kendari, 90, Cd
Kenesaw Mt., 72A, Aa
Kenilworth, 27, Ed
Kenmare, R., 15, Be
Kennebec, R., 45A, Da
Kennedy, 28B, Ab
Kent, co., 27, Ge
Kent I., 45B, Ad
Kentucky, 72, Cb
Kenya, 96C, Fd
Keppel B., 77, If
Kerala, 92, De
Kerbela, 6A, Cb
Kerch, 9, Kc; 79, Ga
Kerguelen I., 69C, 76, Ng
Kerma, 80B, Ad
Kermadec Is., 75, Gf
Kerman, 25, Ed; 93, Hc
Kermanshah, 79, Jd
Kermian, 33A, Cc
Kerrera I., 14, Cc
Kerry, co., 37C; 49B, Bd
Kerulen, R., 91, Eb
Kesselsdorf, 60A, Dc
Keta, 96B, Cb
Kexholm, 50, Ga
Key West, 43A, Db
Keynsham, 36, Df
Khabarovsk, 91, Cb
Khama, 88, Kf
Khama's Country, 81A, Cb
Khanate, 50, Gd
Khandesh, 73, Bc
Kharagpur, 92, Fc
Kharda, 59C, Cd
Kharkov, 9, Kc
Khartoum, 80B, Ad; 96D, Fc
Khazar Empire, 9, Lc
Khazars, 9, Lc
Kherson 8, Jc; 50, Gd
Khiva, 6, Ga; 61B, Ba
Khiva, Khanate of, 61B, Aa
Khmer Empire, 25, Ke
Khmyelnik, 19, Cb
Khodzhent, 61B, Ba
Khojand, 6, Ja
Khokand, 25, Gb; 61B, Ca
Kholm, 61A, Bb
Khorasan, 6, Gb; 25, Ec
Khorramshahr, 93, Fc
Khotan, 1, Ld
Khuzistan, 6, Gb
Khwarizm, 6, Ha; 25, Eb
Khyber Pass, 73, Ba; 74, Fe
Kiakhta, 69A, Pb
Kiaochow, 74, Le
Kichinef, 51, Fd
Kicking Horse Pass, 70, Cb
Kidderminster, 27, Dd
Kidwelly, 27, Be; 28A, Bc
Kiel, 26, Dc; 51, Bc; 60B, Ca
Kiel Canal, 87, Bb
Kielce, 21, Pc
Kiev, 19, Eb; 50, Gc; 82, Jb
Kilcullen, 37B, Ec
Kildare, 15, Ec; 49B, Ec
Kildare, co., 37C; 49B, Ec
Kildrummy, 49A, Cb
Kilfenora, 15, Bd; 49B, Bd
Kilia, 51, Fd; 78, Gc
Kilia Mouth, 78, Gc
Kilid Bahr, 86D
Kilimane, 40, Le
Kilkenny, 15, Dd
Kilkenny, co., 37C
Killala, 15, Bb
Killaloe, 15, Cd
Killarney, 49B, Bd
Killarney, Lakes of, 15, Bd
Killiecrankie Pass, 14, Ec
Killybegs, 49B, Cb
Kilmacduagh, 15, Cc
Kilmacrenan, 49B, Da
Kilmallock, 37B, Cd
Kilrush, 49B, Bd
Kilsyth, 37A, Bc; 48B, Ab
Kilwa, 80A, Ge; 96C, Fe
Kimberley, S. Africa, 81A, Bc
Kimberley, W. Australia, 77, De
Kinburn, 51, Gd; 61, De

Kincardine, co., 37A, Cb
Kinchow, 76B, Ab
Kindah, 6, Fc
Kindia, 96B, Aa
Kindu, 80A, Fe
King George Sd., 77, Bi
King George V. Land, 69C,
King William's Town, 81B,Cc
King's Co., 37C; 49B, Dc
Kings Lynn, 24, Cc; 48A, Dc
Kings Mountain, 56, Cc
Kingston, Canada, 71C, Cb
Kingston, England, 27, Fe
Kingston, Georgia, 56, Cd
Kingston, Jamaica, 43A, Ec
Kingston, New York, 57, Cc
Kingston upon Hull, 36, Fd
Kingstown (Dun Laoghaire),
    49B, Ec
Kingswood, 36, Df
Kington, 27, Cd
Kinloss, 14, Eb
Kinross, 37A, Cb
Kinross, co., 49A, Cb
Kinsale, 37B, Ce; 49B, Ce
Kinshasa, 96D, De
Kintore, 37A, Cb
Kintyre, 14, Cd
Kintyre, Mull of, 49A, Bc
Kipchaks (Polovtsi), 19, Gc
Kippure, 15, Ec
Kirchhayn, 30, Hc
Kirensk, 74, Jc
Kirgiz, 25, Ja; 61, Je
Kirin, 91, Fb
Kirk Kilisse, 78, Fe
Kirkcaldy, 49A, Cb
Kirkcudbright, 28B, Bc
Kirkcudbright, co., 37A, Bc
Kirkee, 73, Bd
Kirkham, 36, Fc
Kirkpatrick, 28B, Bb
Kirkstall, 36, Ed
Kirkstead, 36, Fd
Kirkuk, 79, Hc
Kirkwall, 37A, Ca
Kirman, 6, Gc
Kirmisin, 6A, Db
Kirovabad, 93, Fa
Kirriemuir, 37A, Cb
Kisangani, 96D, Ed
Kiska I., 90, Ea
Kistna, R., 1, Kf; 73, Cd
Kitakyushu, 91, Gc
Kittery, 45B, Db
Kiungchow, 74, Kg
Kiutayeh, 64, Jf
Kizil Ahmadli, Amirate of,
    19, Ed
Kizil Irmak, R., 19, Ed
Kizil Kum, 61B, Ba
Kladrau, 21, Kd
Klagenfurt, 29A, Fb
Klattau, 21, Kd; 53, Kc
Klausenburg (Kolosvar), 33C,
    Eb
Klein Schnellendorf, 60A, Fc
Klip, R., 81A, Cc
Klondyke, 71A, Da
Kloster Zeven, 60A, Bb
Klostergrab, 39, Kc
Klosterneuburg, 22, Fb
Kluane, L., 71B, Ba
Knapdale, 14, Cd; 37A, Bc
Knäred, 50, Cb
Knaresborough, 27, Eb
Knights of the Sword, 34, Ga
Knights Templar, Hospital of
    the, 18D
Knin, 22, Fc
Knocke, 46A, Bd
Knockin, 28A, Db
Knockmealdown Mts., 15, Cd
Knocktopher, 49B, Dd
Knoidart, 14, Cb
Knox Land, 69C
Knoxville, 72, Db
Kobdo, 74, Hd
Kobe, 91, Gc
Koblenz, 83A, Da
Kodiak, 71A, Bb
Kodiak I., 71A, Bb
Kodok (Fashoda), 80B, Ae
Kohima, 90, Ab
Kokenhusen, 26, Gb
Kokopo (Herbertshöhe), 77, Ib
Kola, 42, La; 61, Ea
Kolar, 59A, Ce; 59D
Kolar Goldfields, 92, De
Kolberg, 21, La
Kolhapur, 73, Bd
Kolima, R., 69B
Kolin, 29A, Fa; 31, Lc
Kölln, 26, Dc
Köln, 89, Gc
Kolomea, 84, Gc
Kolomna, 19, Fa
Kolozsvar (Klausenburg),
    33C, Eb; 34, Gc
Komati Poort, 81A, Dc
Kommotau, 21, Kc

Komorn, 39, Ne
Konakry, 81C, Bc
Kong, 80A, Cd; 81C, Dc
Kongolo, 80A, Fe
Konia, 24, Jf
Konieh (Iconium), 18A, Eb
Königgratz, 21, Lc; 60A, Ec
Königsau, R., 65F, Aa
Königsberg, Bavaria, 39C, Ac
Konigsberg, E. Prussia, 21, Pa
Königstein, 65B, Ba
Konitz, 21, Mb
Konkan, 1, Kf
Konkans, 59A, Bd
Konya, 19, Fc
Koonap, R., 81B, Cc
Koporje, 26, Gb
Köprülü, 86A, Ca
Kora, 59A, Db
Korçë, 88, Ke
Kordofan, 80B, Ae
Korea, 91, Fc
Korhogo, 96B, Bb
Koritza, 86A, Bb
Koro Sea, 75C, Ba
Koroni, 78, Cg
Kororareka, 77, Mi
Korosko, 80B, Ac
Korygaum, 73, Bd
Kosas, 81B, Cc
Kosel, 60A, Gc; 65B, Ca
Koselsk, 19, Fb
Koslin, 31, Ma; 54, Fb
Kosman, I., 77, Id
Kosseir, 80B, Ab
Kossovo, 24, Ge; 78, Cd
Kossovopolye, 50, Ee
Kostroma, 24, Lb; 61, Fc
Kota Bharu, 90, Bc
Kota Kinabalu, 91, Ef
Kotah, 59C, Cb; 73, Cb
Kotchana, 78, De
Köthen, 39C, Bb
Kottbus, 21, Lc; 31, Lc
Koudougou, 96B, Ba
Kovno, 26, Fb
Kowpangtze, 76B, Ba
Kozhikode, 92, De
Kozlov, 61, Fd
Kozlov (Eupatoria), 50, Gd
Kra, 73, Ge
Kraguyevats, 78, Cc
Krak, 18C, Dd; (Crac de la
    Pierre), 18C, Dc
Krakow, 88, Kd
Kranganur, 59A, Ce
Krasnik, 26, Fc; 84, Gb
Krasnodar, 89, Nd
Krasnovodsk, 61, Hf; 93, Ga
Krasnoyarsk, 74, Hc; 90, Aa
Krefeld, 83A, Da
Kremnitz, 21, Nd
Krems, 10, Fd
Kremsier, 31, Md; 65C, Cb
Kremsmünster, 22, Eb
Kressenbrunn, 21, Md
Kreuznach, 29A, Ba
Kreuzschanze, 46A, Dc
Kriechingen, 39B, Ca
Krim Tartars, 61, Ee
Krishnagar, 59B
Kristiansand, 87, Ba
Krithia, 86D
Kriviches, 9, Ha
Krcja, 19, Bd
Kronstadt, Hungary, 34, Hc
Kronstadt, Russia, 51, Ga
Krossen, 21, Lb
Krumau, 39, Ld
Krushevatz, 78, Cd
Kuala Lumpur, 91, Df
Kuban, R., 19, Fc
Kubans, 16, Lc
Kublai Khan, Empire of, 25,
    Kc
Kucha, 1, Lc
Kuching, 91, Ef
Kufra, 80A, Fb
Kufstein, 39, Ke
Kuibyshev, 88, Qc
Kuka, 80A, Ec
Kuldja, 74, Gd
Kulikovo, 19, Fb
Kulm, Poland, 21, Nb
Kulm, Saxony, 60B, Dc
Kumaon, 73, Ca
Kumarskaya, 74, Lc
Kumasi, 81C, Dc; 96B, Bb
Kumo, 96B, Da
Kuma, R., 33A, Gb
Kumamoto, 91, Gc
Kumanovo, 78, Cd
Kunene, R., 80A, Df
Kunersdorf, 54, Eb; 60A, Eb
Kunming, 91, Dd
Kuopio, 61, Gb
Kupang, 95, Mf
Kur, R., 33A, Gb
Kura, R., 19, Hd

Kurdish, 85, Le
Kurdistan, 79, Hc
Kurdla, 59A, Cd
Kuria Muria Is., 93, Hf
Kuril Is., 74, Od; 90, Da
Kurland, 26, Fb
Kurna, 86C, Ec
Kursk, 19, Fb; 88, Nc
Kuruman, 81A, Bc
Kuruman, R., 81B, Ba
Kuruska, 93, Ce
Kushan Dominions, 1, Jd
Kuskokwim, R., 71A, Ba
Kuskuskie, 57, Cc
Kustendil, 78, Dd
Küstrin, 31, Lb
Kut-el-Amara, 79, Jd
Kutahya, 33A, Cc; 93, Cb
Kutais, 33A, Fb; 93, Ea
Kutchuk Kainarji, 78, Fd
Kuttenberg, 31, Ld
Kuwait, 79, Je; 93, Fd
Kwangchow, 74, Kf
Kwangtung, 76B, Ab
Kweiyang, 91, Dd
Kyakhta, 74, Jc
Kyle, 14, Dd
Kyoto, 25, Nc; 91, Gc
Kyritz, 26, Dc

La Bahia, 43C, Bb
La Balize, 56, Be
La Bassee, 83A, Ba
La Belle Alliance, 46B
La Charité, 28D, Dc; 38, Ee
La Colle, 71C, Db
La Colombe, 22, Cb
la Conception, 45A, Ab
La Fère, 28D, Db; 83A, Bb
La Ferté, 22, Db
La Ferté Vidame, 38, Dd
La Garnache, 38, Ce
La Guaira, 68, Df
La Haye Sainte, 46B
La Higuera, 23D, Dd
La Hougue, 55A, Cd
La Mancha, 23D, Dc; 63, Dc
La Manche (English Channel),
    55A, Dc
La Marche, 39B, Bb
La Marche, Co. of, 11, Dc
La Motte, I., 57, Ea
La Paz, 68, Cd
La Plata, Argentina, 68, Df
La Plata, Bolivia, 41B, Ce
La Plata, dist., 41B, Cf; 42, Ff
La Plata, rep., 69A, Ff
La Plata, Rio de, 68, Df
La Plata, United Provs. of, 68,
    Cf
La Pointe (Fort St. Esprit),
    56, Aa
La Réole, 17, Ff
La Roche, 53, Cd
La Roche Bernard, 38, Be
La Roche Derien, 28C, Ab
La Rochelle, 11, Cc; 53, Cd
La Serena, 68, Bf
La Teste de Buch, 28C, Bd
La Tour, 30, Ef
La Trappe, 22, Cb
La Tremouille, 30, De
Labe, 96B, Aa
Laberge, L., 71B, Ca
Labiau, 39, Pa; 50, Ec
Labrador, 71, Hb
Labrador, Pen. of, 71, Hb
Labuan, 91, Ef
Lachine, 57, Ea
Lachlan, R., 77, Hh
Lactodorum (Towcester), 3A,
    Fd
Lacy, 17, Bb
Ladakh, 92, Da
Lade, 12, Ga
Lado, 80A, Ad
Ladoga, 19, Ea
Ladoga, L., 26, Ha
Ladrones, 40, Rd
Ladysmith, 81D, Ab
Lae, 90, Dd
Lafayette, 72A, Aa
Lafayetteville, 56, Dc
Lagan, R., 15, Fb
Lagen, R., 12, Ga
Lagentium (Castleford), 3A, Ec
Laghouat, 80A, Da
Lagos, Nigeria, 80, Dc; 81C, Ec
Lagos, Portugal, 4B, Ad; 23C,
    Ad
Lagosta, 84, Fd
Laguna, 68, Ee
Lahave, 45A, Eb
Lahn, R., 10, Cc; 83A, Ea
Lahore, 25, Gc; 73, Ba
Lahr, 30, Gd
Laibach, 10, Fe
Laighin (Leinster), 15, Ed
Laila, 93, Fe
Laing's Nek, 81D, Aa

Lakhmids, 6A, Cb
Lalitpur, 73, Cc
Lamballe, 17, Dd; 20, Bd
Lambertville, 57, Dc
Lambeth, 27A
Lamego, 22, Ac; 23C, Bb
Lammermuir Hill, 14, Fd
Lamon B., 75E, Bb
Lampadar, 27, Bd
Lampsacus, 78, Fe
Lamu, 40, Me
Lanai, 75D, Cb
Lanark, 28B, Db
Lanark, co., 37A, Cc; 49A, Cc
Lancaster, England, 3A, Db;
    27, Db
Lancaster, Pennsylvania, 57, Cc
Lancaster, clan, 28B, Db
Lancaster, lordship, 28A, Bc
Lancaster, Co. Palatine of, 27,
    Dc
Lancaster Sd., 44, Ga
Lanchow, 91, Dc
Landau, 29A, Ca; 76A, Eb
Landeck, 20, Je
Landeshut, 60A, Ec
Landrecies, 46A, Cd
Landriano, 32A, Cb
Land's End, 55A, Ac
Landsberg, Brandenburg, 21,
    Lb
Landsberg, Osterland, 21, Kc
Landsberg, Styria, 31, Le
Landshut, 21, Kd
Landstuhl, 39B, Da
Lanercost, 36, Dc
Langarone, 86B, Ca
Langeac, 20, Ef
Langeland, 65F, Ba
Langensalza, 39C, Ab; 60B, Cc
Langford House, 48B, Cd
Langholm, 28B, Bb
Langobardi, 2, Fc
Langport, 27, De
Langres, 11, Fc
Langside, 37A, Bc
Languedoc, 17A, De; 20, Eg
Lanporth (Langport), 13, De
Lansdown, 48A, Bd
Lanshankwan, 76B, Ba
Lanstavetone (Launceston),
    13, Bf
Lanthony, 36, Cd
Laoag, 75E, Ba
Laodicea, 2, Lf; 18, Cc
Laon, 11, Eb; 83A, Bb
Laos, 91, De
Lapland, 61, Ca
Laprairie, 56, Ea
Laramie, 70, Dc
Larantuka, 52C, Bc
Larche, Col de, 29A, Dc
Laredo, 43A, Cb
Largs, 14, Dd; 37A, Bc
Larissa, 19, Ce; 78, Df
Larnaka, 86C, Ec
Laron, 20, Df
Las Navas de Tolosa, 23C, Dc
Las Palmas, 80A, Bb
Las Vegas, 44, Ce; 70, Dd
Lasalle, 70, Fc
Lashio, 92, Hc
Lastingham, 7B, Ca
Laswari, 59C, Cb
Latakia, 79, Gc
Lateran, 5A
Lathom, 48A, Bc
Latin States, 24, Gf
Latins, 8C, Bb
Latisana, 86B, Db
Latvia, 87, Fa
Lau (Eastern) Group, 75C, Ca
Lau Group (Exploring Is.),
    75C, Ca
Lauder, 49A, Cc
Lauderdale, 28B, Cb
Laudenburg, Holstein, 20, Jb;
    65F, Bb
Lauenburg, Pomerania, 21, Ma
Lauenburg, D., 65F, Bb
Lauenstein, 39C, Dc
Laufen, 29B, Ba
Laun, 39, Kc
Launceston, England, 27, Bf
Launceston, Tasmania, 77, HJ
Laund, 36, Fe
Laupen, 29B, Bb
Laurencekirk, 49A, Cb
Lausanne, 11, Gc; 29B, Ab
Lausitz, 10, Ec
Lausitz, M. of, 21, Lc
Lauter, R., 76A, Eb
Lautrec, 20, Eg
Lavagna, 20, Hf
Laval, 20, Cd
Lavant, 22, Eb
Lavatrae (Bowes), 3A, Eb
Lavaur, 20, Dg
Lavongai(NewHanover), 77. Ib
Lavoro, Terra de, 32A, FJ
Lawes (Lewes), 13, Ff

Lawless, 37B, Bb
Lazica, 19, Gd
Le Cateau, 83A, Ba
Le Creuzot, 88, Fd
Le Havre (Havre de Grace), 38, Dd; 89, Fd
Le Mans, 11, Dc
Le Puiset, 17, Fd
Le Puy, 11, Ed
Lea, R., 7C, Cc
Leaf, R., 70, Gb
League of God's House, 29B, Db
League of Ten Jurisdictions, 29B, Db
Lealui, 96C, Ef
Leavenworth, 70, Ed; 72, Bb
Lebanon, 18C, Ce; 79, Gd
Lebu, 68, Bf
Lebus, 21, Lb; 60A, Eb
Lecce, 5, Gd
Lech, R., 10, De; 30, Jd
Leck, R., 46A, Dc
Lectoure, 11, De
Ledbury, 27, Dd
Ledecestre (Leicester), 13, Ed
Ledecestrescire (Leicestershire), 13, Ed
Ledo, 90, Ab
Lee, R., 15, Ce
Leeds, Kent, 27, Ge; 36, Gf
Leeds, Yorks, 48A, Cc
Leer 30, Gb
Leesburg, 57, Cd
Leeuwarden, 46A, Ea
Leeuwin, C., 77, Bh
Leghorn, 23B, Cc; 32E, Bb
Legnago, 29A, Dc; 62, Ec
Legnano, 20, Hf
Leicester, 27, Ed
Leicester, co., 27, Ed
Leicester, diocese, 36A
Leighlin, 15, Ed
Leinster, 37B, Dd; 49C
Leinster (Laighin), 15, Ed
Leinster Irish, 49C
Leipzig, 10, Ec
Leire, 12, Gc
Leiria, 23C, Ac; 63, Ac
Leith, 37A, Cc; 48A, Bb
Leitmeritz, 21, Lc
Leitrim, 17, Ba; 49B, Cc
Leitrim, co., 37C; 49B, Cb
Leix 37B, Dd
Lemberg, 26, Fd; 33C, Eb
Lemnos, 19, De; 78, Ef
Lena, R., 25, Ma; 91, Da
Leningrad, 87, Ga
Lenne, R., 83A, Da
Lennox, 14, Dd
Lens, 17, Gc; 83A, Ba
Lenteurde (Leintwardine), 13, Dd
Lenton, 36, Ee
Leoben, 29A, Fb; 65A, Cb
Leofminstre (Leominster), 13, Dd
Leofric, 12, Dc
Leominster, 27, Dd; 48B, Bc
Léon, France, 11, Ab
Leon, Nicaragua, 43A, Dc
Leon, Spain, 63, Ca
Leon, King. of, 23C, Ba
Leon, prov., 63, Cb
Leon and Castile, King. of, 23C, Cb
Leona, C., 63A
Leonine City, 5A
Leontini, 5, Ef
Leopold Coast, 69C
Leopoldville, 80A, Ee
Lepanto, 18B, Cc; 78, Cf
Lepontine Alps, 29A, Cb
Leptis, 6, Cb
Lerida, 23D, Fb; 63, Fb
Les Clairets, 22, Cb
Lesbos, 19, De
Lescar, 11, Ce
Lesgians, 19, Hd
Lesina, 22, Fc
Lesina, I., 23B, Fc
Lesna, 54, Jb
Lesotho, 96D, Eg
Lesser Antilles, 43A, Ec
Lesser Armenia, 25, Cc
Lessines, 46A, Cd
Lethbridge, 70, Cc
Lethington, 37A, Cc
Letocetum (Wall), 3A, Ed
Letterkenny, 49B, Db
Leucadia, 64, Gf
Leucas, 62, Ge; 78, Cf
Leuchtenburg, 21, Kd
Leuk, 29B, Bb
Leuthen, 54, Fb; 60A, Fc
Leutkirch, 53, Fd
Leutschau, 19, Cc; 31, Pd
Leven, L., Inverness, 14, Cc
Leven, L., Kinross, 14, Ec
Levis, 57C, Ba
Levis, Pt., 56A
Levuka, 75C, Ba

Lewes, 27, Gf
Lewes, R., 71A, Da
Lewis, 14, Ba
Lewiston, 71D
Lexington, Kentucky, 56, Cc
Lexington, Mass., 57, Fb
Lexington, Tennessee, 72, Cb
Leyden, 46A, Db
Leyen, 65B, Ab
Leyre, 22, Bc
Leyte, 75E, Bb
Lhasa, 25, Jd; 73, Fb
Liang Chow, 1, Nd
Liao-ho, R., 76B, Ba
Liao-tung, 76B, Ba
Liaotung, G. of, 76B, Aa
Liaoyang, 76B, Ba
Liard, 70, Ba
Liard, R., 70, Ba
Libau, 26, Fb
Libava, 51, Eb
Liberia, 81C, Cc
Libreville, 80A, Dd
Libya, 80A, Eb; 93, Ac
Licata, 21A, Bd
Licefelle (Lichfield), 13, Ed
Lichfensteig, 29B, Da
Lichfield, 27, Ed
Lichfield, bp., 36, De
Lichsfeld, bp., 30, Jc
Lichtenberg, 39B, Db
Lida, 26, Gc
Liddisdale, 14, Fd; 28B, Cb
Lideforde (Lidford), 13, Bf
Liechtenstein, 65A, Ab
Liège, 46A, Ed
Liège, Bp. of, 46A, Ed
Liegnitz, 19, Bb; 21, Mc
Lienz, 31, Ke
Liepaja, 87, Ea
Lier, 46A, Dc
Lierkenshoek, 46A, Dc
Liffey, R., 15, Ec
Lifford, 37B, Db
Liger, R., 2, Dd
Ligny, Belgium, 46B
Ligny, France, 39B, Bb
Liguria, 5, Bb; 32C, Bb
Lihue, 75D, Bb
Lille, 28D, Da; 46A, Cd
Lillebonne, 17, Fd
Lillo, 46A, Dc
Lilybaeum, 5, Df
Lima, 68, Bd
Limasol, 18A, Ec
Limburg, Germany, 60A, Bd
Limburg, Netherlands, 46A, Ed
Limburg, Co. of, 46C, Bb
Limerick, 15, Cd
Limerick, co., 37C; 49B, Cd
Limia, 23C, Ab
Limoges, 11, Dd; 84, Cc
Limousin, V. of, 11, Dd
Limoux, 20, Eg
Limpopo, R., 81A, Db
Lincluden, 36, Cb
Lincolescire (Lincolnshire), 13, Fc
Lincolia (Lincoln), 13, Fc
Lincoln, 7B, Ch; 27, Fc
Lincoln, bp., 36, Fe
Lincoln, co., 27, Fc
Lincoln, lordship, 28A, Ca
Lincoln Wolds, 27, Fc
Lincolns Inn, 27A
Lindau, 30, He
Lindi, 96C, Fe
Lindinis (Ilchester), 3A, De
Lindisfarna (Lindisfarne), 13, Ea
Lindisfarne, 36, Eb; 36A
Lindley, 81A, Cc
Lindsay, 28B, Ca; 37A, Cb
Lindsey, 7B, Cb
Lindum (Lincoln), 3A, Fc
Lingan (Quinsay) (Hangchow), 25, Mc
Lingayen, 75E, Ba
Lingen, 60A, Ab
Lingen, co., 38, Gb
Linköping, 26, Eb
Linlithgow, 28B, Bb
Linlithgow, co., 37A, Cc
Linnhe, L., 14, Cc
Linz, 10, Fd; 33C, Cb
Lion, G. of the, 17, Gg
Lipari Is., 5, Ee
Lippa, 33C, Eb
Lippe, 65D, Aa
Lippe, Co., 30, Hc
Lippe, R., 20, Gc
Lisaine, 76A, Dc
Lisbon, Ireland, 15, Ed
Lisbon, eccl. prov., 22, Ad
Lisburn, 49B, Eb
Lisieux, 11, Db
Liskeard, 27, Bf
L'Isle Jourdain, 30, Dg
Lismore, Ireland, 15, Dd
Lismore, Scotland, 14, Cc
Lismore, bp., 14A, Bb

Lissa, 32C, Fc; 87, Ea
Lithuania, 50, Fc; 87, Ea
Lithuania, G.D. of, 26, Gc
Lithuanians, 9, Ga
Little Belt, 65F, Aa
Little Harbour (Rye), 45B, Db
Little Minch, 14, Bb
Little Namaqua Land, 81A, Ac
Little Namaquas, 81B, Ab
Little Poland, 39, Pc
Little Rock, 72, Bc
Little Russia, 51, Gc
Little Russian, 85, Jc
Little St. Bernard Pass, 5, Ab
Littlechester, 3A, Ed
Litus Saxonicum, 3A, Hd
Livadia, 78, Df
Livenza, R., 86B, Cb
Liverpool, 27, Dc
Livingstone, 81A, Ca
Livno, 38, Ff
Livonia, 26, Gb
Livonians, 9, Ga
Livorno, 32A, Dc
Livron, 38, Ff
Lixheim, 29A, Ba; 39B, Db
Lizard, 55A, Ac
Llanbadarn, 28A, Bb
Llanbadarn Fawr, 13, Bd
Llandaf (Llandaff), 13, Ce
Llandaff, 27, Ce
Llandaff, bp., 36, Cf
Llandovery, 3A, Cd; 27, Cc
Llanelwy, 13, Cc
Llanfaes, 7B, Ab
Llangollen, 48B, Bc
Llanio, 3A, Bd
Llanthony, 36, Cf
Llantwit, 28A, Cc
Loanda, 80A, Ee
Loango, 80A, Dc
Loano, 29A, Cc; 38, Hf
Lobenstein, 39C, Bc
Lobositz, 54, Eb; 60A, Ec
Locarno, 29B, Cb
Loches, 11, Dc; 17, Fe
Lochaber, 14, Dc
Lochmaben, 28B, Bb
Lochnannagh, 49A, Bb
Lockerbie, 49A, Cc
Locri, 5, Fe
Löcse, 39, Pd
Lodève, 11, Ee
Lodi, 32A, Cc
Lodz, 87, Db; 89, Jc
Logan, Mt., 70, Aa
Logans, 56, Cc
Logia Sinus, 3A, Ab
Logno, 23D, Da; 63, Da
Logstown, 57, Ac
Logudoro, 23B, Bd
Loigny, 76A, Ab
Loir, R., 11, Dc
Loire, R., 11, Cc; 22, Cb
Loitz, 31, Ka
Loja, 68, Bc
Lokoja, 80A, Dd; 96C, Cd
Lombard Alps, 29A, Dc
Lombard King., 5, Bb
Lombards, 4A, Fb
Lombardy, 20, Hf; 32C, Bb
Lombardy, King. of, 23A, Ba
Lombartzyde, 46A, Bc
Lombers, 20, Eg
Lome, 81C, Ec; 94, Te
Lomond, L., 14, Dc
Lonato, 32D, Bb
Loncastre (Lancaster), 13, Db
Londinium (London), 3A, Fe
London, Canada, 70, Gc
London, England, 27, Fe
London, bp., 36, Gf
London Bridge, 27A
Londonderry, co., 37C; 49B, Eb
Long B., 57D, Bb
Long I., Bahamas, 43A, Eb
Long I., Massachusetts, 56B
Long I., New York, 45B, Cc; 56, Eb
Long Island Sound, 57, Ec
Long, L., 14, Dc
Longford, co., 37C; 49B, Dc
Longibardia, 9, Fd
Longjumeau, 38, Ed
Longone, 32B, Cc
Longreach, 95, Lg
Longtown, 49A, Cc
Longueuil, 57, Ea
Longueville, 20, Dd
Longwy, 39B, Ba; 83A, Cb
Lookout Mt., 72A, Aa
Loop Hd., 15, Bd
Lopadium, 19, Dd
Lorch, 8, Hd
Lörchingen, 39B, Db
Loreto, 21, Kg
Lorient, 53, Bd; 55A, Be
Loritello, 21A, Cb
Lorne, 14, Cc

Lorne, Firth of, 14, Cc
Lorraine, 83B, Ba
Lorraine, C. de, 45A, Ea
Lorraine, D. of, 20,Gd; 39B,Cb
Lorris, 20, Ee
Lorsch, 8, Dd
Los, Is. de, 81C, Bc
Los Adaes, 43A, Ca
Los Angeles, 70, Cd
Los Diabolos, 40, Fc
Los Tiburones, I. de, 40, Be
Losecoat Field (Empingham), 27, Fd
Lostwithiel, 27, Bf
Lot, R., 11, Dd; 22, Cc
Lothar, King. of, 8A, Dc
Lotharingia, 8A, Ca
Lotharingia, D., 10, Ac
Lothian, 14, Ed
Lothian, co., 37A, Cc
Loudoun Hill, 3A, Ba
Loudun, 20, De
Loughbrickland, 49B, Eb
Loughrea, 37B, Cc; 49B, Cc
Louis, King. of, 8A, Db
Louisa, 72, Db
Louisburg, 45A, Fa
Louise, 57, Cd
Louisiade Arch., 77, Id
Louisiana, 56, Bd
Louisiana, st., 72, Bc
Louisville, 72, Cb
Lourenço Marques, 81A, Dc
Lourmarin, 38, Fg
Louth, England, 27, Fc
Louth, Ireland, 37B, Ec
Louth, co., 37C; 49B, Ec
Louvain, 46A, Dd
Lovat, R., 19, Ea
Lovcha, 78, Ed
Lowell, 45B, Db
Lower Alsace, Land. of, 20, Gd
Lower Austria, 65C, Cb
Lower Burgundy (Regnum Provinciae), 11, Ec
Lower California, 42, Dc; 43D Ab
Lower Canada, 71, Gc
Lower Doab, 59C, Db
Lower Lausitz, Marg. of, 31, Lc
Lower Lorraine, 20, Fc
Lower Lotharingia, 10, Ac
Lower Palatinate, 34, Dc; 38, Hd
Lower Peru, 41B, Be
Lower Silesia, 60A, Fc
Lower Tunguska, R., 74, Hb
Lowestoft, 54, Cb; 55A, Db
Loyalty Is., 77, Lf
Loyang, 1, Od
Luang Prabang, 91, Dd
Lübben, 39C, Db
Lubeck, 10, Db
Lublin, 26, Fc
Lucca, 5, Cc
Lucca, Rep. of, 32A, Dc
Luce, B., 14, De
Lucena, 23D, Cd
Lucera, 5, Ed
Lucerne, 10, Ce; 29B, Ca
Lucerne, canton, 29B, Ca
Luckenwalde, 60A, Db
Lucknow, 73, Db
Luçon, 20, Ce; 47, Bc
Lucy, 28B, Bc
Luderitz, 80A, Eg
Ludes (Louth), 13, Fc
Ludgershall, 27, Ee
Ludhiana, 73, Ca
Ludlow, 13, Dd; 27, Dd
Lug, R., 28A, Db
Lugano, 29B, Cb
Lugdunum, 2, Dd
Lugnaquillia, 15, Ed
Lugo, 23C, Ba; 63, Ba
Luguvalium (Carlisle), 3C
Lujan, 68, Cf
Lu-kiang, R., 73, Gb
Lule Burgas, 78, Fe
Lulea, 88, Ka
Luna, 20, Jf
Lund, 16, Ea; 26, Db
Lund, eccl. prov., 22, Ea
Lundonia (London), 13, Ge
Lundy's Lane, 71D
Lune, R., 48B, Bb
Lüneburg, Germany, 10, Db
Luneburg, Transvaal, 81D, Ba
Lunel, 38, Fg
Lunenburg, 45A, Eb
Lunéville, 10, Bd; 39B, Cb
Lung-Hsi, 1, Nd
Luni, R., 73, Bb
Lunigiana, 32E, Ba
Luray, 72B, Aa
Luristan, 79, Jd
Lusatia (Lausitz), 10, Fc
Lusatia, M. of, 16, Eb
Lusatians, 10, Eb

Lusignan, 11, Dc
Lussac, 28C, Cc
Lussina, 23B, Eb
Lutetia, 2, Dd
Lutsk, 19, Db
Lutter, 38, Jc
Lutterberg, 60A, Bc
Lutterworth, 27, Ed
Lützelburg, 39B, Db
Lützelburg (Luxemburg), Co of, 20, Fd
Lützen, 38, Jc; 60B, Dc
Luvre (Oswestry), 13, Cd
Luxembourg, 31A, Dc; 46A, Fe
Luxemburg (Lützelburg), Co. of, 20, Fd
Luxemburg, D., 46A, Ee
Luxeuil, 10, Be; 39B, Cc
Luxor, 93, Cd
Luynes, 53, Dd
Luzon, 75E, Ba
Lvov, 87, Ec
Lyallpur, 92, Ca
Lycia, 1, Fd
Lydda (St. George), 18C, Dg
Lydenburg, 81B, Da
Lydford, 7C, Ac; 27, Bf
Lydia, 2, Jf
Lykandos, 9, Ke
Lym (Lyme Regis), 13, Df
Lyme Regis, 27, Df
Lynchburg, 57, Be; 72B, Ab
Lynn, 17, Fb; 27, Gd
Lynn Canal, 71B, Cb
Lyonnais, 17, Hf; 38, Ef
Lyons, 11, Fd
Lyons, eccl. prov., 22, Cb
Lyons, Co. of, 11, Fd
Lys, R., 46A, Cd
Lyubech, 9, Jb

MAABAR, 35, Nd
Maas, R., 20, Fc; 30, Fc
Maastricht, 83A, Ca
Macae, 1, Me
MacAllister, 37A, Bc
Macao, 91, Ed
Macapa, 68, Db
Macaria, 22, Fc
Macassar, 52C, A
McCarthy, 15, Cd
MacCluer G., 77, Eb
MacDonald, 37A, Ab
Macdonald Is., 69C
MacDonald of Clanranald, 37A, Bb
MacDonald of Glencoe, 37A, Bb
MacDonald of Glengarry, 37A, Bb
MacDonald of Inverlochy, 37A, Bb
MacDonald of Keppoch, 37A, Bb
McDonnell, 37B, Ea
Macdonnell Ra., 77, Ef
McDouall, 28B, Ac
Macedonia, 2, Hf; 78, De
Maceio, 68, Fc
Macerata, 22, Ec
Macfie, 37A, Ab
Macgillicuddys Reeks, 15, Bd
McGillipatrick, 15, Dd
Macgregor, 28B, Aa
McGuire, 37B, Db
Machecoul, 30, Ce
Macintosh, 37A, Bb
Mackay, 37A, Ba
Mackenzie, clan, 37A, Bb
Mackenzie, district, 70, Ca
Mackenzie, R., 44, Bb
McKinley, Mt., 71A, Ba
Maclachlan, 37A, Bb
Maclean, 37A, Bb
MacLeod, 37A, Aa
Macloutsie, R., 81A, Cb
MacMahon, 37B, Bd
McMahon, 37B, Eb
MacMurrough, 15, Ed
McMurrough, 37B, Ed
Macnab, 28B, Aa
Mâcon, France, 11, Fc
Macon, U.S.A., 72, Dc
Macpherson, 37A, Bb
Macquarie Is., 69C; 75, Eg
Macroom, 49B, Cc
Mactan, 40, Qd
Macziewice, 51, Ec
Madagascar, 80A, Hf
Madang (Friedrich Wilhelmshafen), 77, Hc
Maddy, L., 49A, Ab
Madeira, 80A, Ba
Madeira, R., 41B, Ce; 68, Cc
Madhya Pradesh, 92, Dc
Madinat al Shaab, 93, Eg
Madras, 59D; 92, Ee
Madre de Dios L., 68, Bh
Madrid, 23C, Db; 63, Db
Madura, 25, Gf; 59A, Cf
Madurai, 92, Df

Maelienydd, 13, Cd
Maelor, 13, Dc
Maeotis Palus, 2, Ld
Maestricht, 46A, Ed
Mafeking, 81A, Cc; 96C, Eg
Mafia I., 80A, Ge
Mafra, 63B
Magadha, I., Le
Magdala, 83, Ld
Magdalen Is., 45A, Ea
Magdalena, R., 68, Bb
Magdalena (Rio Grande), R. 43A, Ed
Magdeburg, 10, Db; 21, Jb
Magdeburg, eccl. prov., 22, Ea
Magdeburg, Abp. of, 30, Jb
Magellan's Str., 68, Bh
Magennis, 37B, Eb
Magenta, 29A; Cc; 32C, Bb
Magersfontein, 81A, Bc
Maggiore, L., 5, Bb
Maghreb, 9, Bf
Maghreb-al-Aqsa, 6, Ab
Maghreb-al-Awsat, 6, Bb
Magnano, 29A, Bc
Magnis (Carvoran), 3C
Magnis (Kenchester), 3A, Dd
Magnitogorsk, 88, Rc
Magnus Portus (Portsmouth Harb.), 3A, Ef
Magog, 57C, Ab
Maguelonne, 11, Ee
Magus Muir, 37A, Cb
Magyar, 85, Fc
Magyars, 8, Hb; 9, Hc
Mahanadi, R., 73, Dc
Maharajpur, 73, Cb
Maharashtra, 92, Dc
Mahé, 73, Ce
Mahon, 63, Hc
Mahra, 6, Gd
Mahratta, 69A, Nc
Mahukona, 75D, Cb
Maida, 62, Fe
Maidenhead, 48B, Cd
Maidos, 86D
Maidstone, 48A, Dd
Maikop, 88, Oe
Maillezais, 22, Bb; 38, Ce
Main, R., Germany, 10, Cd
Main, R., Ireland, 15, Eb
Maine, prov., France, 38, Dd
Maine, st., U.S.A., 71E, Kc
Maine, terr., N.Amer., 45A, Cb
Maine, Co. of., 11, Cb
Mainland, 49A, Ca
Mainz, 10, Cd; 83A, Eb
Mainz, abp., 30, Hc
Mainz, eccl. prov., 22, Ea
Maipu, 68, Bf
Majapahit, 40, Pe
Majorca, 23C, Gc; 63, Gc
Majorca, King. of, 23D, Gc
Majuba Hill, 81D, Aa
Majunga, 96D, Gf
Makasar, 90, Cd
Makran, 6, Hc
Makurdi, 96B, Cb
Makyan, 52B, Aa
Malabar Coast, 59A, Ce
Malacca, 75A, Aa; 91, Df
Malacca, Str. of, 75A, Aa
Malaga, 23C, Cd; 63, Cd
Malagasy Rep., 96D, Gg
Malaita, 77, Kc
Malakand Pass, 73, Ba
Malamocco, 32D, Cb
Malatya, 79, Gc
Malawi, 96D, Ff
Malawi L., 96D, Ff
Malay Pen., 75, Cd
Malaya, 91, Df
Malborgeth, 86B, Da
Malchin, 31, Kb
Malden I., 75, He
Malden, R., 56B
Maldive Is., 92, Cf
Maldon, 27, Ge; 48A, Dd
Maldonado, 68, Df
Malduna (Maldon), 13, Ge
Male, 86B, Aa
Mali, 96D, Bc
Malia, C., 78, Dg
Malik L., 86A, Bb
Malin Hd., 15, Da
Malindi, 69A, Me
Malines, 51, Ac; 83A, Ca
Malling, 36, Gf
Mallow, 49B, Cd
Malmédy, 46A, Kd; 83A, Da
Malmesberie (Malmesbury), 13, De
Malmesbury, 27, De; 48A, Bd
Malmö, 26, Db; 60B, Da
Maloja Pass, 29B, Db
Malolos, 75E, Bb
Malown, 73, Ca
Malpas, 27, Dc
Malplaquet, 46A, Cd; 54, Cb
Malta, 8, Ed; 34, Ee
Malton, 27, Fb
Malvasia, 18B, Cc; 78, Dg

Malvern, England, 36, De
Malvern, Virginia, 57, Ce
Malwa, 1, Ke; 73, Cc
Mamecastre (Manchester), 18, Dc
Mameln, 38, Hb
Mameluke Sultans, 24, Hg
Mamistra, 18C, Ca
Mamore, R., 68, Cd
Mamucium (Manchester), 3A, Dc
Man, I. of, 7B, Aa; 34, Bb
Managua, 43D, Dc
Manama, 93, Gd
Manassas Junction, 72B, Ba
Manau, 14, Dc
Manaus, 68, Dc
Manbedj, 18C, Eb
Manchac (Fort Bute), 56, Ad
Manchester, England, 7C, Bb
Manchester, New York, 57, Eb
Manchu, 42, Qb
Manchukuo, 90, Ca
Manchuria, 74, Ld; 90, Ca
Mandalay, 73, Gc
Mandan Village, 44, Dd
Mandeswar, 73, Cc
Manfredonia, 32A, Fd
Mangalore, 73, Be
Mangi, 35, Pc
Mangi (Song Empire), 25, Kd
Manhattan I., 45B, Cc; 57B
Maniago, 86B, Ca
Manihiki, 75, He
Manila, 75E, Bb
Manipur, 73, Fc
Manissa, 78, Ff
Manitoba, 70, Eb
Mannheim, 29A, Ca; 83A, Eb
Manokvary, 77, Eb
Manresa, 23C, Fb; 63, Fb
Mansel, I., 70, Fa
Mansfeld, 20, Jc; 60A, Cc
Mansura, Egypt, 80B, Aa
Mansura, India, 6, Hc
Mansurabad, 6, Db
Mansurah, 18A, Ec
Mantatis, 81B, Da
Mantes, 17, Fd
Mantua, 5, Cb; 22, Eb
Mantua, Marq. of (Gonzaga), 32A, Db
Manukau Harbour, 77A
Manzanares, 63, Dc
Manzanillo, 43D, Bc
Manzikert, 16, Le
Maputa, R., 81A, Dc
Maqdala, 80B, Be
Mar, 14, Fb
Mar del Plata, 68, Df
Maracaibo, 43A, Ec
Maracaibo, L., 43A, Ed
Marajo I., 68, Ec
Maranhão, 41B, Ed
Maranhao (Sao Luis), 68, Ec
Maranhao, st., 68, Ec
Marañon, R., 68, Bc
Marans, 38, Ce
Marar, G. of, 73, Cf
Maras, 93, Db
Marash, 18C, Da
Maratha, 59A, Cc
Marbella, 23D, Cd
Marble Head, 57, Fb
Marburg, 20, Hc
March, R., 21, Md
Marches, The, 32A, Ec
Marchfield, 21, Md
Marcianopolis, 4A, Hc
Marcomanni, 2, Gd
Mardin, 18A, Gb; 93, Eb
Mare Adriaticum, 2, Ge
Mare Ægæum, 2, Jf
Mare Cantabricum, 1, Bc
Mare Caspium, 1, Gc
Mare Internum, 1, Cd
Mare Ionium, 2, Gf
Mare Suevicum, 2, Gb
Mare Tyrrhenum, 2, Ff
Maree, L., 14, Cb
Marengo, 29A, Cc; 62, Dd
Margam, 7B, Bc
Margarita, 43A, Fc
Margiana, 1, Jd
Margidunum(Castle H.),3A,Fd
Maria, 63, Eb
Maria Van Diemen, C., 77, Mh
Mariana Is., 74, Ng; 90, Dc
Marib, 6, Fd
Marico Drift, 81A, Cb
Marie Byrd Land, 69C
Marie Galante, 43A, Fc
Marienbourg, 46A, Dd
Marienburg, 21, Na
Marienthal, 22, Ea
Marienwalde, 22, Fa
Marienwerder, 21, Nb
Marietta, Georgia, 72A, Ab
Marietta, Ohio, 56, Cc
Mariette, 71C, Bc
Marignano, 29, Cc; 32A, Cb

Marinids, 24, Ag
Maritime Alps, 29A, Db
Maritza, 78, Ed
Maritza, R., 78, Fe
Mark, 12, Ga
Mark, Co. of, 20, Gc; 46C, Cb
Market Drayton, 48B, Bc
Markirch, 39B, Db
Markland, 35, Fb
Marlborough, England, 27, Ee
Marlborough, N.Z., 77A
Marle, 11, Eb
Marlow, 27, Fe
Marmande, 30, Df
Marmara, Sea of, 78, Ge
Marmolada, 29A, Eb
Marmoutier, 22, Cb
Marne, R., 11, Eb
Maros, R., 33C, Eb; 78, Dc
Maroua, 96B, Da
Marquesas Is., 75, Je
Marra, 18C, Dc
Marrakesh, 80A, Ca; 96D, Ba
Marrana, 23B, Cc
Marroqui, C., 63A, Cc
Mars Hill, 71E, Cb
Mars la Tour, 76A, Cc
Marsaglia, 29A, Cc
Marsal, 39B, Cc
Marsala, 32C, De
Marsalquivir, 34, Be
Marseilles, 11, Fe; 29A, Ad
Marshall Is., 90, Ec
Marshfield, 45B, Db
Marsi, 21A, Bb
Marsia, 23A, Dc
Marsico, 21A, Cb; 22, Fc
Marston Moor, 48A, Cc
Martaban, G. of, 73, Gd
Martello, The, 86B, Cb
Martha's Vineyard, 45B, Dc
Martigny, 29B, Bb
Martinique, 43A, Fc
Martirano, 21A, Dc
Martyropolis, 4B, Ld
Marvejols, 38, Ef
Maryborough, Australia, 77, Ig
Maryborough, Ireland, 49B, Dc
Maryland, 57, Cd; 72B, Ba
Masan-daran, 61B, Ab
Masbate, 75E, Bb
Mascarenhas, 40, Mf
Mashona, 80A, Gf
Mashona Land, 81A, Da
Masira, 93, He
Mask, L., 15, Bc
Maskat, 41A, Cb; 74, Df
Masmünster, 39B, Dc
Mason and Dixon's Line, 56, Dc
Masovia, 26, Fc
Masper, 45B, Cc
Massa, 22, Ec; 32A, Db
Massachusetts, 45B, Db
Massagetae, 1, Hc
Massawa, 80B, Bd
Massema, 96B, Da
Massikessi, 81A, Da
Massilia, 2, Ee
Masulipatam, 73, Dd
Masurian Lakes, 84, Gb
Matabele, 81B, Da
Matabeleland, 81A, Ca
Matagorda Bay, 43A, Cb
Matamoros, 43A, Cb
Matanzas, 43A, Db
Matapan, C., 78, Dg
Matatana, 40, Mf
Matera, India, 59C, Db
Matera, Italy, 21A, Db
Mathura, 73, Cc
Mato Grosso (V. Bella), 68, Cd
Mato Grosso, prov., 68, Dd
Matoppo Hills, 27, De
Matruh, 84, Hf; 93, Bc
Mattapony, R., 72B, Ba
Matuku, 75C, Bb
Maturin, 68, Cf
Maubeuge, 46A. Cd
Maui, 75D, Cb
Mauléon, 20, Cg
Maumee, R., 57A, Ca; 71C, Bb
Mauna Loa, 75D, Dc
Mauretania, 2, Df
Mauriac, 20, Ef
Mauritania, 80A, Bc
Mauritania, rep., 96D, Ac
Mauritia (Pernambuco), 42, He
Mauritius, 42, Mf; 69A, Ne
Mauvezin, 38, Dg
Mawddach, R., Bb
Mawson, 69C
Maxen, 60A, Dc
Maxwell, 28B, Bb; 37A, Cc
May, C., 45B, Bd
May, I. of, 28B, Ca
Maya, 63, Ea
Mayas, 43A, Cc
Maybole, 28B, Ab
Mayence, 33C, Bb
Mayenne, 17, Ed
Mayenne, R., 53, Cc

Maynooth, 49B, Ec
Mayo, 15, Bc
Mayo, co., 37C; 49B, Bc
Mayorga, 63, Ca
Mazagan, 42, Jc
Mazapil, 43A, Bb
Mazaltan, 43A, Bb
Mazovia, 39, Pb
Mazzara, 21A, Bd; 22, Ed
Mbengga, 75C, Bb
Meander, R., 19, De
Mearns, 14, Fc
Meath, 17, Bb; 37B, Dc
Meath (Midhe), 15, Dc
Meath, co., 49B, Ec
Meaux, England, 36, Fd
Meaux, France, 11, Eb
Mecca, 6, Fc; 25, Dd; 80B, Bc
Mechanicsville, 72B, Bb
Mechlin, 46A, Dc
Mecklenburg, 10, Db
Mecklenburg, D. of, 10, Db
Medan, 91, Cf
Medellin, Colombia, 68, Bb
Medellin, Spain, 63, Cc
Medelpad, 26, Ea
Medeltune (Melton Mowbray), 13, Fd
Media, I., Gd
Medicine Hat, 70, Cb
Medina, 25, Dd; 93, De
Medina (Yathreb), 6, Fc
Medina de Rio Seco, 63, Cc
Medina Sidonia, 23C, Cd
Mediolanum (Milan), 5, Bb
Mediterranean Sea, 8, Fd
Meean Doab, 73, Ca
Meerut, 73, Cb
Mehadia, 78, Dc
Mehdiya, 9, Ee
Mehidpur, 73, Cc
Meiningen, 20, Jc; 30, Jc
Meirionydd (Merioneth), 13, Db
Meisenheim, 60B, Ad
Meissen, 10, Ec
Meissen, March of, 10, Fc
Mejillones, 68, Be
Mekong, R., 25, Ke; 91, De
Melandra Castle, 3A, Ec
Melbourne, 77, Hi
Melcombe Regis, 27, Df
Meldorf, 20, Ha
Melfi, 21A, Cb; 22, Fc
Melilla, 34, Be; 40, Jc
Melinde, 41A, Be
Melite I., 2, Ff
Melitene, 6A, Ba
Melk, 21, Ld
Mellrichstadt, 10, Dc
Melnik, 19, Cd
Meloria I., 24, De
Melrose, 14, Fd; 28B, Bb
Melton Mowbray, 27, Fd
Melun, 11, Eb; 17, Gd
Melville I., Australia, 77, Ed
Melville I., Canada, 44, Ca
Melville Pen., 44, Fb
Memel, 26, Fb; 60A, Ha
Memel, R., 26, Fb
Memleben, 10, Dc
Memmingen, 20, Jd; 29A, Da
Memphis, Egypt, 2, Kh
Memphis, U.S.A., 72, Bb
Memphis (Chickasaw Bluff), 71F, Aa
Memphis (Fort Assumption), 56, Bc
Menado, 52C, Ba
Mende, 11, Ed; 17, Gf
Menderes, R., 24, Hf
Mendip Hills, 27, De
Mendocino, C., 70, Bc
Mendoza, 68, Cf
Mendrisio, 29B, Cc
Menin, 46A, Cd; 53, Eb
Menindee, 77, Gh
Mentana, 32C, Dc
Menteith, 14, Dc
Menteshe, 19, De
Menzies, 37A, Bb
Meonware, 7A, Cb
Meppen, 20, Gb
Mequinenza, 23C, Fb; 63, Fb
Meran, 10, De; 86B, Ba
Mercia, 7B, Cb; 12, Dc
Mercians, 7A, Ca
Mere, 27, De
Meresberie (Maesbury), 13, Cd
Merevale, 36, Ee
Mergui, 73, Ge
Mergui Arch., 92, He
Merida, Spain, 63, Bc
Merida, Venezuela, 43A, Ed
Meridian, 72, Cc
Merioneth, co., 27, Cd
Merleberge (Marlborough), 13, Ee
Meroe, 35, Ld
Merowe, 80B, Ad
Merrimac, R., 45B, Db

Merry Mount (Quincey), 45B, Db
Merse (Mersea I.), 13, Ge
Merse, The, 14, Fd
Mersea, 7C, Dc
Merseburg, 10, Dc; 39C, Bb
Merseburg, M. of, 10, Ec
Mersen, 8A, Ca; 9, Db
Mersey, R., 27, Dc
Mersha, R. (Mersey), 13, Cc
Mersin, 93, Cb
Mersina, 86C, Bb
Mertola, 23C, Bd
Merton, 36, Ff
Merv, 6, Hb; 25, Fc; 61B, Bb
Mesembria, 8, Hc
Meseritz, 22, Fa; 31, Lb
Mesewa, 80, Bd
Meshed, 61B, Ab; 93, Hb
Mesopotamia, 1, Gd; 6A, Ca
Messana, 2, Gf
Messina, 5, Ee
Messina, eccl. prov., 22, Ed
Messines, 83A, Ba
Mesta, R., 78, Ee
Mestre, 86B, Cb
Meta, R., 43A, Ed; 68, Cb
Metaris Aest. (The Wash), 3A, Gc
Metemma, 80B, Ad
Methone, 9, Ge
Methven, 28B, Ba
Metis, R., 71E, Ba
Metsovo, 78, Cf
Metz, 10, Bd; 83A, Db
Metz, Bp. of, 30, Gd; 39B, Ca
Meuse, R., 10, Ac; 17, Hc
Meuse, Mouth of, the, 46A, Cc
Mexico, city, 43A, Cc
Mexico, st., 43A, Bb
Mexico, G. of, 43A, Cb
Mezen, R., 61, Ga
Mézières, 46A, De, 53, Fc
Miami, 94, Ed
Miami, R., 71C, Bc
Miamis, 45A, Ab; 56, Bb
Miani, 73, Ab
Michigan, 70, Fc
Michigan, L., 56, Bb
Michigan Terr., 67C, Da
Michillimackinac I., 45A, Aa
Michoacan, 43A, Bc
Micmacs, 45A, Da
Mics, 31, Kd
Middelburg, C. of Good Hope, 81A, Bd
Middelburg, Netherlands, 46A, Cc
Middelburg, Tr'vaal, 81A, Cc
Middelfart, 65F, Aa
Middle I. (South I., N.Z.), 77A
Middle Angles, 7A, Ca
Middle Drift, 81D, Bb
Middle March, 28B, Bb
Middle Saxons, 7A, Cb
Middleham, 27, Eb
Middlesex, 27, Fe
Middleton, 37A, Cb
Middletown, Connecticut, 45B, Cc
Middletown, New Jersey, 45B, Bc
Midelsexe (Middlesex), 13, Fe
Midhe (Meath), 15, Dc
Midhurst, 27, Fe
Midia, 78, Ge
Midnapore, 59A, Ec; 59B
Midway I., 90, Fb
Miedniki, 26, Fb
Mien (Burma), 25, Jd
Mierdyk, 46A, Dc
Milam, 73, Da
Milan (Mediolanum), 5, Bb
Milan, eccl. prov., 22, Db
Milan, D. of, 32A, Cb
Milazzo, 21A, Cc; 32C, Ee
Milborne Port, 27, Df
Mileburne (Milborne Port), 13, Df
Miletus, 19, De
Milford, Connecticut, 45B, Cc
Milford, Wales, 27, Ae
Milford Haven, 55A, Ac
Milhau, 11, Ed
Mill Springs, 72, Bb
Milledgeville, 72, Dc
Millen, 72, Dc
Millikens Bend, 72C, Aa
Milos, 78, Ee
Milton, 7C, Dc
Milwaukee, 70, Fc
Milzienians, 10, Fc
Min Yueh, 1, Oe
Minaei, 1, Gf
Minas Gerais, 68, Ed
Minch, The, 14, Bb
Mincio, R., 5, Cb
Mindanao, 75E, Bc
Mindelheim, 53, Jc
Minden, 10, Cb
Minden, Bp. of, 60A, Cb
Mindoro, 75E, Bb

Mindoro Str., 75E, Bb
Mingrelia, 61, Ff; 79, Hb
Minho, 63, Ab
Minho, R., 63, Ba
Minna, 96B, Cb
Minneapolis, 70, Ec
Minnesota, 70, Ec
Minnesota Terr., 67D, Da
Minorca, 23C, Gb; 63, Gb
Minsk, 26, Gc; 87, Fb
Minster, 7B, Dc
Minto, L., 70, Gb
Minya, 93, Cd
Miquelon, 45A, Fa
Mirabeau, 17, Fe
Mirabel, 18C, Cf
Mirambeau, 20, Cf
Miramichi B., 45A, Ea
Miranda, Brazil, 68, De
Miranda, Portugal, 22, Ac; 63, Bb
Miranda, Spain, 63, Da
Mirande, 53, Df
Mirandola, 32A, Db
Mirepoix, 22, Cc; 38, Dg
Mirny, 69C
Mirzapur, 59B; 73, Db
Misilmeri, 21A, Bd
Miskolcz, 31, Pd
Misol, 52C, Cb; 77, Eb
Misr (Egypt), 6, Dc
Missassauga Fort, 71D
Missenden, 36, Ff
Missionary Ridge, 72A, Aa
Mississippi, R., 56, Ab; 70, Ec
Mississippi, st., 70, Fd
Mississippi, Delta of the, 43A, Db
Mississippi Terr., 67B, Bb; 71F, Ba
Missolonghi, 78, Cf
Missouri, R., 70, Ec; 72, Bb
Missouri, st., 72, Bb
Missouri Terr., 67C, Ca
Missunde, 65F, Aa
Mistassini, L., 70, Gb
Mistra, 19, Ce
Misurata, 88, Jg
Mitau, 50, Eb; 61A, Ba
Mitchell, R., 77, Ge
Mitchelstown, 49B, Cd
Mittelmark, 31, Kb; 60A, Db
Mitylene, 78, Ef
Mizen Hd., 15, Be
Mkusi, R., 81D, Ba
Mlava, 21, Pb
Moala, 75C, Bb
Mobile, 56, Bd; 67C, Eb
Mocha, 93, Eg
Modbury, 27, Cf
Modder, R., 81B, Cb
Modena, 8A, Dc
Modena (Mutina), 5, Cb
Modena, D. of (Este), 32A, Db
Modon, 78, Cg
Modrusch, 2, Fb
Moesia, 1, Ec; 4A, Gc
Moffat, 37A, Cc
Mogador, 82, Af
Mogadiscio (Mogadishu), 96A, Bb
Mogadishu, 80A, Hd; 96C, Gd
Mogul Empire, 52A, Bb
Moguntiacum, 2, Ec
Mohacs, 33C, Db; 39, Ne
Mohammed Abtin, Dominions of, 24, Kf
Mohawk, R., 57, Db
Mohawks, 45A, Cb; 57, Db
Mohi, 19, Cc
Mohilev, 26, Hc; 50, Gc
Moidart, 14, Cc; 49A, Bb
Mojaisk, 19, Fa
Mold, 27, Cc
Moldau, R., 21, Ld
Moldavia, 50, Fd; 78, Fb
Molème 22, Cb
Molfetta, 23B, Fd
Molina, 23D, Eb
Mo.i is de Rey, 63, Gb
Molise, 23B, Ed; 32A, Fd
Mollendo, 68, Bd
Molloy, 37B, Dc
Mollwitz, 60A, Fc
Molokai, 75D, Cb
Molopo, R., 81B, Ba
Molotov, 88, Rb
Moloyaroslavetz, 62, Ka
Molucca Passage, 52C, Ca
Moluccas, 52C, Cb; 91, Ff
Mölzen, 10, Ec
Mombasa, 80A, Ge; 96D, Fe
Momonia (Mumha) (Munster), 15, Cd
Mömpelgard, 39B, Cc
Mon, I. (Anglesey), 7B, Ab; 13, Bc
Mona (Angelsey), 3A, Bc
Mona Passage, 43A, Fc
Monaco, 32A, Bc
Monaghan, 49B, Eb
Monaghan, co., 37C; 49B, Eb

Monastir (Bitolia), 78, Ce
Monavia (I. of Man), 3A, Bb
Monclova, 43A, Bb
Moncton, 71, Hc
Mondego, R., 63, Ab
Mondoñedo, 22, Ac
Mondovi, 29A, Cc
Mondovia, 32A, Bb
Monemude (Monmouth), 13, De
Monemvasia, 19, Ce
Monfalcone, 86B, Db
Monflanquin, 38, Df
Monforte, 22, Ac
Monghyr, 59A, Eb
Mongol Il-Khans, Empire of the, 19, He
Mongolia, rep., 91, Db
Monks Bretton, 36, Ed
Monks Corner, 57D, Ab
Monmouth, 27, De
Monmouth Court House, 56, Eb; 57, Dc
Monnow, R., 28A, Dc
Monocacy, 72B, Ba
Monocacy, R., 72B, Ba
Monomotapa, 52, Lf
Monongahela, R., 45A, Bb
Monopoli, 32A, Gd
Monreal (Mons Regalis), 18C, Ch
Monreale, 21A, Bc; 22, Ed
Monreale, eccl. prov., 22, Ed
Monroe, 72, Bc
Monrovia, 81C, Bc
Mons, 46A, Cd
Mons Regalis (Monreal), 18C, Ch
Mont Cenis Pass, 5, Ab
Mont de Marsan, 38, Cg
Mont Genèvre Pass, 32A, Bb
Mont Louis, 53, Ef
Mont St. Jean, 46B
Mont St. Michel, 17, Ed
Mont Valerien, 76A, Ab
Montacute, 27, Df
Montagnais, 45A, Ca
Montagud (Montacute), 13, Df
Montaigu, 20, Hd
Montalto, 39, Kg
Montana, 70, Dc
Montana Terr., 67D, Ba
Montaperto, 23B, Cc
Montargis, 17, Gd; 38, Ed
Montauban, Provence, 20, Ff
Montauban, Toulouse, 11, Dd
Montaut, 38, Dg
Montbard, 76A, Cc
Montbazon, 53, Dd
Montbéliard, 20, Ge
Montbrison, 30, Ef
Montcenis, 38, Fe
Montdidier, 31A, Bc; 83A, Bb
Monte Cassino, 5, Dd
Monte Peloso, 21A, Db
Monte Redondo, 63B
Monte San Angelo, 21A, Db
Montebello, Milan, 29A, Cc
Montebello, Pavia, 29A, Cc
Montecatini, 32E, Bb
Montefeltro, 32A, Ec
Montelcone, 21A, Dc
Montélimar, 30, Ef
Montendre, 38, Cf
Montenegro, 39, Ng; 78, Bd
Montenotte, 29A, Cc
Montepulciano, 32E, Bb
Montereau, 28D, Db; 31A, Bc
Monterey, California, 70, Bd
Monterey, Mexico, 43A, Bb
Montescaglioso, 21A, Db
Montevideo, 68, Df
Montfaucon, 22, Db
Montferrat, Marq. of, 32A, Cb
Montfort, 11, Db; 30, Dd
Montgomery, Alabama, 72, Cc
Montgomery, Wales, 27, Cd
Montgomery, family, 28B, Ab
Montiel, 23D, Dc
Montlaur, 30, Ef
Montlhéry, 30, Ed; 31A, Bc
Montluçon, 53, Ed
Montmédy, 29A, Aa; 83A, Cb
Montmorency, 53, Ec
Montpellier, 11, Ee
Montpensier, 30, Ee
Montreal, 45A, Ca; 57, Ea
Montreuil, 11, Da; 83A, Aa
Montrose, 49A, Cb
Montserrat, 22, Cc
Montserrat, I., 43A, Fc
Monza, 4B, Eb; 5, Bb
Monzon, 63, Fb
Mooi, R., 81A, Cc
Mook, 46A, Ec
Moore's Creek, R., 57Γ, Ba
Moorfields, 27A
Moorfoot Hills, 28B, Bb
Moors, 2A, Ac
Moose, R., 70, Fb
Moose Factory, 70, Fb
Moquegua, 68, Bd
Mora, 26, Da

Moradabad, 73, Cb
Morant, 43A, Ec
Morar, 73, Cb
Morar, L., 14, Cc
Morat, 29B, Bb; 31A, Dd
Morava, R., 78, Cc
Moravia, 8A, Eb; 33C, Db
Moravia, M. of, 21, Md
Moravian Empire, 9, Fc
Moravian Town, 71C, Bb
Moravians, 8, Fb
Moray, 14, Db; 37A, Bb
Moray Firth, 14, Eb
Morea, 78, Dg
Morecambe B., 27, Cc
Morella, 23C, Eb
Morena, Sierra, 63, Cc
Moresnet, 83A, Da
Moret, 20, Ed
Moreton B., 77, Ig
Morgannwg, 7C, Bc; 12, Dd
Morgannwg (Glamorgan), 13, Ce
Morgarten, 29B, Ca
Morhange, 83B, Ba
Moriah, 18D
Moridunum (Carmarthen), 3A, Be
Morimont, 22, Db
Morlaix, 28C, Ab; 38, Bd
Moro, 52B, Aa
Morocco, 96C, Ba
Morocco, King., 80A, Ca
Morotai, 90, Cc
Morpeth, 13, Ea
Morrisburg, 57, Da
Morristown, 57, Dc
Mors, 60A, Ac
Mortagne, 11, Db; 30, Dd
Mortain, 11, Cb
Mortara, 32C, Bb
Mortemart, 53, Dd
Mortie, 52C, Ca
Mortimer, Ireland, 37B, Dd
Mortimer, Wales, 28A, Bc
Mortimers Cross, 27, Dd
Morven, 14, Cc
Mosbach, 20, Hd
Moscow, 19, Fa
Moscow, Pr. of, 24, Kb
Moselle, R., 10, Bd; 39B, Cb
Mosquito Coast, 43A, Dc
Mossamedes, 80A, Ef
Mossel B., 81B, Bc
Mostar, 39, Mg; 78, Ad
Mosul, 6A, Ca; 25, Dc
Motien lin Pass, 76B, Ba
Motir, 52B, Aa
Motrone, 32E, Bb
Moulins, 30, Ee
Moulmein, 73, Gd; 92, Hd
Mount Desert I., 45B, Ea
Mount Grace, 36, Ec
Mount Vernon, 57, Cd
Mountmellick, 49B, Dc
Moura, 23C, Bc
Mourne Mts., 15, Eb
Mourne, R., 15, Db
Moutiers, 11, Gd
Mouzon, 22, Db
Moy, 49A, Bb
Moyenvic, 39B, Cb
Mozambique, 80A, Hf
Mozambique, col., 80A, Gf
Mozdok, 61, Ff
Mozhaisk, 88, Nb
Mscislaw, 51, Gc; 61A, Db
Mstof, 26, Ec
Muck, 14, Bc
Mudania, 79, Eb
Mudki, 73, Ba
Mugello, 32E, Bb
Mügeln, 39C, Db
Mühlberg, 34, Eb; 39C, Db
Mühldorf, 10, Ed
Mühlhausen, 20, Jc
Muiden, 46A, Eb
Muilrea, 15, Bc
Mukalla, 93, Fg
Mukden, 76B, Ba
Mukden (Shenyang), 91, Fb
Mukha, 6, Fd
Mulde, R., 39C, Cb
Mulgrave, 27, Fb
Mulhausen, 30, Ge
Mulhouse, 29A, Bb; 83B, Bb
Mulkaid, 52A, Bc
Mull, 14, Cc
Mullingar, 49B, Dc
Multan, 25, Gc; 73, Ba
Multun, 6, Jb
Mumha (Momonia, Munster), 15, Cd
Muncaster, 13, Cb
Münchengrätz, 60B, Ec
Münden, 53, Hb
Mundelsheim, 29A, Ca
Munich, 29A, Da
Munkacz, 50, Ed; 54, Gc
Münster, Germany, 10, Bc
Munster, Ireland, 37B, Cd

Munster (Mumha, Momonia), 15, Ca
Münster, Bp. of, 30, Gb
Munster Irish, 49C
Munster Thal, 29B, Eb
Münsterberg, 31, Mc
Mur, R., 21, Le
Murad Su, R., 19, Ge
Murat, 30, Ef
Murbach, 20, Ge; 39B, Dc
Murchison, R., 77, Eg
Murcia, 22, Bd; 63, Ed
Murcia, prov., 63, Ec
Muret, 11, De; 22, Ed
Murfreesboro, 72, Cb
Muri, 29B, Ca
Murmansk, 74, Bb; 88, Ma
Murom, 19, Ga
Murom-Riazan, 19, Fb
Murray, 28B, Ba; 37A, Ba
Murray, R., 77, Hi
Murrumbidgee, R., 77, Hh
Mursa, 2, Gd
Murshidabad, 59A, Ec
Murten, 30, Ge
Murviedro, 23C, Ec
Murzuk, 80A, Eb; 96C, Db
Muscat, 40, Mc; 93, He
Muscovy, 35, Mb; 61, Fc
Muskingum, R., 71C, Bb
Musselburgh, 49A, Cc
Mustapha Pasha, 78, Fe
Muta, 6A, Bb
Mutina (Modena), 5, Cb
Mweru, L., 80A, Fe
Myitkyina, 92, Hb
Mynyw (St. David's), 13, Ae
Myriocephalon, 18A, Eb
Mysore, 59A, Ce; 73, Ce
Mysore, st., 59D; 73, Ce
Mystic, R., 56B
Myton, 28B, Dc

NAARDEN, 46A, Eb
Naas, 49B, Ec
Nablus, 18C, Cf
Nabresina, 86B, Db
Nachod, 33C, Da
Nafels, 29B, Da
Naga, 75E, Bb
Nagaland, 92, Gb
Nagasaki, 91, Fc
Nagoya, 91, Gc
Nagpur, 73, Cc
Nagy Sarlo, 33C, Db
Nahuas, 43A, Bc
Naiman, 25, Hb
Nain, 71, Hb
Nairn, 37A, Cb
Nairn, co., 37A, Cb; 49A, Cb
Nairn, R., 37A, Cb
Nairobi, 80A, Ge
Naissus, 2, He; 4A, Gc
Najaf, 93, Ec
Najera, 23D, Da; 28C, Ae
Nakhijevan, 9, Me
Namos, 88, Ha
Namur, 28D, Ea; 46A, Dd
Namur, Co. of, 46C, Bb
Nanaimo, 70, Bc
Nanchang, 91, Ed
Nancy, 10, Bd; 39B, Cb
Nandi, 75C, Aa
Nandidroog, 73, Cc
Nanking, 91, Ec
Nanning, 91, Dd
Nantasket, 45B, Db
Nantes, 11, Cc; 17, Ee
Nantes, Co. of, 11, Cc
Nantucket, 45B, Ec
Nantwich, 48A, Bc
Napier, 77A
Naples (Neapolis), 5, Ed
Naples, King. of, 32A, Fd
Napo, R., 68, Bc
Narbada, R., 25, Gd; 73, Cc
Narberth, 28A, Bc
Narbo, 2, De
Narbonne, 11, Ee
Narbonne, eccl. prov., 22, Cc
Narenta, R., 78, Ad
Narew, R., 31, Pb; 39, Qb
Narke, 50, Db
Narnia, 5B, Bb
Naro, 21A, Bd
Narragansett B., 45B, Db
Narragh, 15, Ec
Narva, 26, Gb; 54, Ha
Narvik, 88, Ja
Naseby 48B, Cc
Nashborough, 56, Bc
Nashville (Nashborough), 56, Bc
Nass, R., 71B, Dc
Nassau, 43A, Eb
Nassau, Co. of, 20, Hc
Nasser, L., 93, Ce
Natal, Brazil, 68, Fc
Natal, Rep. of, 81D, Bb
Natchez, 56, Ad
Natchitoches, 70, Ed

Nauders, 29A, Db
Naugard, 31, Lb
Naumburg, 21, Jc; 38, Jc
Naumkeag (Salem), 45B, Db
Naupactus, 19, Ce
Nauplia, 78, Dg
Nauplia, 18A, Cb
Nauru, 90, Ed
Nauta, 68, Bc
Navan, 49B, Ec
Navarino, 78, Cg
Navarre, 63, Ea
Navarreins, 38, Cg
Navio (Brough), 3A, Ec
Naworth, 27, Db
Naxos, 78, Eg
Naxos, D. of, 24, Hf; 34, Ge
Naxcuat, 56, Fa
Nay, 38, Cg
Nazareth, Italy, 22, Fc
Nazareth, Palestine, 18C, Cf
Naze, The, 55A, Dc
Neagh, L., 15, Eb
Neapolis, 2, Fe
Neapolis (Naples), 5, Ed
Neath, 28A, Bc
Neath, R., 28A, Bc
Nebbio, 22, Ac
Nebraska, 70, Dc
Nebraska Terr., 67D, Ca
Nechtansmere, 14, Ec
Neckar, R., 10, Cd
Neerwinden, 53, Fb
Negapatam, 59D
Neghelli, 96A, Ab
Negotin, 86A, Da
Negrepelisse, 38, Df
Negro (Fort Gadsden), 71F, Ba
Negro, R., Argentina, 68, Cf
Negro, R., Brazil, 68, Ca
Negroponte, 78, Ef
Negros, 75E, Bb
Nehavend, 6A, Db
Neisse, 21, Mc
Neisse, R., 10, Fc; 60A, Ec
Neiva, 41B, Bc
Nejd, 6, Fc; 84, Kg; 93, Ed
Nejef, 86C, Dc
Nejran, 6, Fd
Nellore, 52A, Cc
Nelson, 77A
Nelson, prov., 77A
Nelson, R., 70, Eb
Neman, R., 87, Eb
Nemirov, 51, Fd
Nemours, 30, Ed
Nemours, D. of, 30, Ed
Nen, R., 27, Gd; 36, Ge
Nenagh, 37B, Cd; 49B, Cd
Nenana, 71A, Ca
Neocaesarea, 18A, Fa
Nepal, 73, Db
Nephin, 15, Bb
Nepi, 22A
Nepomuk, 22, Eb
Nérac, 38, Df
Nerchinsk, 52, Qb; 74, Kc
Nereisheim, 65A, Bb
Nesjar, 12, Gb
Nesle, 20, Ed
Ness, L., 14, Db
Nesse, 13, De
Nessib, 64, Kf
Netherby, 28B, Bb
Netherlands, 46A; 53, Fb
Netherlands, King. of the, 64, Dc
Netherlands Guiana, 68, Db
Netley, 36, Eg
Netz, 65A, Ca
Netze R., 31, Me; 39, Mb
Neu Breisach, 76A, Db
Neu-Sandec, 39, Pd
Neuburg, 38, Jd; 47, Ec
Neuchâtel, 10, Be; 29B, Aa
Neuchâtel, canton, 29B, Aa
Neuchâtel, L. of, 29B, Ab
Neuenburg, 20, Ge
Neuf Brisach, 83B, Ba
Neufchâteau, 29A, Aa
Neufchâtel, 53, Ec
Neuhäusel, 33C, Db
Neuilly, 84, Cc
Neumark, 31, Lb
Neumarkt, 29A, Db
Neumünster, 65F, Aa
Neuse, R., 57, Cf
Neuss, 46A, Cc
Neustadt, Austria, 21, Me
Neustadt, Hungary, 33C, Db
Neustadt, Moravia, 51, Dd
Neustadt, Palatinate, 39B, Ea
Neustadt, Saxony, 38, Jc
Neustria, France, 4A, Bb
Neustria, Italy, 5, Bb
Neutra, 21, Nd
Neuwerk, 65D, Aa
Neuwied, 53, Gb
Neva, R., 19, Ea
Nevada, 70, Cd
Nevada, Sierra, Spain, 63, Dd
Nevada, Sierra, U.S.A., 70, Bd

Nevada Terr., 67D, Ba
Nevers, 11, Ec
Nevers, Co. of, 11, Ec
Neville, 28B, Cc
Neville's Cross, 27, Eb
Nevis, 43A, Fc
Nevis, L., 49A, Bb
Nevyansk, 61, Kc
New Albion, 42, Dc
New Amsterdam, Guiana, 68B, Ba
New Amsterdam, N. America, 42, Fb
New Archangel (Sitka), 71A, Db
New Biscay, 43A, Bb
New Britain, Canada, 71, Hb
New Britain, I., 90, Dd
New Britain (New Pomerania), I., 77, Ib
New Brunswick, Canada, 71, Hc
New Brunswick, New Jersey, 57, Dc
New Calabar, 81C, Fd
New Caledonia, 70, Bb
New Caledonia, I., 77, Lf
New Castile, 63, Dc
New Dorp, 45B, Bc
New East Prussia, 60A, Hb
New England, 45B, Db
New France, 52, Fb
New Galicia, 43A, Bb
New Granada, Captain-Generalship of, 41B, Bc
New Granada, Rep., 68, Bb
New Granada, U.S. of, 68, Bb
New Guinea, 90, Dd
New Guinea, Terr. of, 77, Hb
New Hampshire, 45B, Db
New Hanover, 81D, Bb
New Hanover (Lavongai), 77, Ib
New Haven, 45B, Cc
New Hebrides, 77, Le
New Holland, 42B; 77, Bg
New Ireland, 90, Dd
New Ireland (New Mecklenburg), 77, Ib
New Jersey, 45A, Cc; 57, Dc
New Leinster (Stewart I.), 77A
New Leon, 43A, Cb
New London, 45B, Cc
New Madrid, 72, Cb
New Mecklenburg (New Ireland), 77, Ib
New Mexico, 70, Dd
New Mexico Terr., 67D, Cb
New Munster (South I., N.Z.), 77A
New Navarre, 43A, Aa
New Netherland, 45B, Bc
New Orleans, 56, Ae
New Plymouth, 77A
New Point Comfort, 45B, Ae
New Pomerania, 60B, Da
New Pomerania (New Britain), 77, Ib
New Providence, 43A, Eb
New Republic, 81D, Ba
New Ross, 49B, Ed
New Santander, 43C, Bb
New Siberian Is., 74, Na
New Silesia, 60A, Gc
New South Wales, Australia, 77, Hh
New South Wales, Canada, 70, Eb
New Sweden, 45B, Bd
New Toledo, 41B, Ce
New Ulster (North I., N.Z.), 77A
New York, 57B
New York, st., 57, Db
New Zealand, 77, NJ
Newark, England, 27, Fc
Newark, New York, 57B
Newbattle, 14, Ed
Newbern, 56, Dc
Newburn, 48A, Cb
Newbury, England, 27, Ee
Newbury, Massachusetts, 45B Db
Newburyport, 56, Eb
Newcastle, Delaware, 57, Dd
Newcastle, England, 27, Eb
Newcastle, Leinster, 37B, Ec
Newcastle, Limerick, 49B, Bd
Newcastle, Natal, 81D, Aa
Newcastle, New South Wales, 77, Ih
Newcastle, Ulster, 37B, Ea
Newcastle, Wales, 28A, Cb
Newcastle (Fort Christina), 45B, Bd
Newcastle-under-Lyme, 27, Dc
Newchwang, 74, Ld; 76B, Ba
Newerche (Newark), 13, Fc
Newfoundland, 45A, Fa
Newmarket, 48B, Dc
Newport, I. of W., 27, Ef
Newport, Monmouth, 28A, Cc

Newport, Rhode I., 45B, Dc
Newport, Wales, 28A, Bb
Newport News, 45B, Ae
Newport Pagnell, 48A, Cc
Newry, 49B, Eb
Newstead, 36, Ed
Newtown, 48B, Bc
Newtown Butler, 49B, Dt
Newtownards, 49B, Fb
Ngami, L., 81A, Bb
Ngaoundéré, 96B, Db
Ngau, 75C, Ba
Nguru, 96B, Da
Niagara, 70, Gc
Niagara Falls, 57, Bb; 71D
Niamey, 96B, Ca
Nias, 91, Cf
Nicaea, 2, Je; 19, Dd; 79, Eb
Nicaea, Empire of, 19, De
Nicaragua, 43D, Dc
Nicaragua, L., 43D, Dc
Nicastro, 21A, Dc
Nice, 5, Ac; 11, Ge
Nice, Co. of, 38, Gg
Nicholas II Land, 74, Ga
Nickerie, 68B, Ba
Nicobar Is., 92, Gf
Nicomedia, 2, Ke; 19, Ed
Nicopolis, Bulgaria, 78, Ed
Nicopolis, Turkey, 19, Ed
Nicopolis Theme, 9, Ge
Nicosia, 18A, Ec
Nicoya, G. of, 43A, Dd
Nidaros (Trondheim), 26, Da
Nidda, 20, Hc
Nidum (Neath), 3A, Ce
Niebla, 23C, Bd
Niemen, R., 19, Ca; 50, Fc
Nieuport, 46A, Bc
Nieuwveld, 81A, Bd
Niger, rep., 96D, Cc
Niger, R., 81C, Fc
Niger, terr., 80A, Dc
Nigeria, 80A, Dc; 96B, Db
Nigeria, Federation of, 96D, Cd
Nigritia, 52, Kd
Niigata, 91, Gc
Nijni Kamchatsk, 52, Sb
Nikolayevsk, 74, Nc
Nikolsburg, 33C, Db; 39, Md
Nile, R., 25, Cd; 80B, Ab
Nilgiri Hills, 73, Ce
Nîmes, 11, Fe
Nimwegen, 20, Fc; 46A, Ec
Ninety Six, 57D, Aa
Ningpo, 41A, Kb; 74, Lf
Ninus, 2, Mf; 4A, Ld
Niort, 30, Ce
Nipigon, L., 70, Fb
Nipissing, L., 45A, Ba
Niš, 88, Ke
Nish (Nissa), 78, Cd
Nishapur, 25, Ec; 61B, Ab
Nishni Novgorod, 19, Ga
Nisibis, 2, Mf; 6A, Ca
Nissa, 8, Gc
Nissa (Nish), 78, Cd
Nith, R., 36, Cb
Nithsdale, 14, Ed; 28B, Bb
Niue (Savage) I., 75, Ge
Nive, R., 63, Ea
Nivelles, 46B
Nivernais, 17, Ge
Nizam's Dominions, 73, Cd
Nizhne Kolymsk, 74, Pb
Nkandhla, mts., 81D, Bb
Noce, R., 86B, Aa
Nocera, 22, Ec
Noddles I., 56B
Nogais, 61, Ee
Nogent le Roi, 30, Dd
Nogent-le-Rotrou, 38, Dd
Nogent-sur-Marne, 76A, Bb
Nogent-sur-Seine, 30, Ed
Noirmoutier, 9, Bc; 53, Bd
Noisseville, 76A, Db
Noix, I. aux, 57, Ea
Nola, 22, Ec
Noli, 23B, Ba
Nomadic Arab Tribes, 16, Fg
Nombre de Dios, Mexico, 43A, Bb
Nombre de Dios, Panama, 43A, Ed
Nome, 71A, Aa
Nomeny, 39B, Cb
Nona, 22, Fc
Nonette, 20, Ef
Nonno, 96A, Ab
Nootka, 69A, Cb
Norden, 10 Bb
Nordfulc (Norfolk), 13, Gd
Nordgau, Marg. of, 10, Dd
Nordhausen, 10, Dc
Nordheim, 10, Cc
Nördlingen, 29A, Da
Nordmark, 10, Eb
Nordreys, 12, Cb; 14, Bb
Nore, 55A, Dc
Nore, R., 15, Dd
Norfolk, 45B, Ae; 72B, Bb

Norfolk, co., 27, Hd
Norfolk I., 77, Lg
Norham, 27, Da; 28B, Cb
Norhamscire (Norhamshire), 13, Da
Noric Alps, 29A, Fb
Noricum, 2, Fd; 2A, Cb
Norman King., 18A, Bb
Normands, Iles, 17, Dd
Normandy, D. of, 11, Cb
Norrköping, 51, Db; 54, Fa
North C., 69B
North Chan., 14, Cd; 37A, Bc
North I. (New Ulster), 77A
North Pt., 71C, Cc
North (Hudson), R., 45B, Bc
North (Hudson) 1, Cd; 4B, Dd
North Sea, 12, Eb; 55A, Eb
North Anna, R., 72B, Bb
North Atlantic Ocean, 94, Cc
North Australia, 77, Ee
North Berwick, 49A, Cb
North Dakota, 70, Dc
North Downs, 27, Ge
North Dvina, R., 89, Oa
North-East Frontier Agency, 91, Cd
North-East New Guinea (Kaiser Wilhelms Land), 77, Gc
North Esk, R., 14, Fc
North Foreland, 55A, Dc
North Frisian Is., 65F, Aa
North Kanara, 52A, Bc
North Konkan, 52A, Bc
North Korea, 91, Fb
North Pacific Ocean, 75, Gc
North Platte, R., 70, Dc
North Pole, 69B
North Potomac, R., 57, Bd
North Saskatchewan, R., 70, Cb
North Somerset I., 44, Ea
North Uist, 14, Ab
North Victoria (Queenstown), 81B, Cb
North Vietnam, 91, Dd
North Wales, 36A
North West Provs., 73, Cb
North West Terr., 67B, Ba
North-West Terrs., 70, Ea
Northallerton, 27, Eb
Northampton, England, 27, Fd
Northampton, Massachusetts, 45B, Cb
Northampton, co., 27, Fd
Northantone (Northampton), 13, Fd
Northantonescire (Northamptonshire), 13, Fd
Northern Circars, 73, Dd
Northern Hiung-nu, 1, Kb
Northern Ireland, 49B, Eb
Northern Nigeria, 81C, Fc
Northern Rhodesia, 80A, Ff
Northern Slav Peoples, 8C, Ca
Northern Terr., Australia, 77, Ee
Northfield, 57, Eb
Northumbria, 7B, Ba
Northymbraland (Northumberland), 13, Da
Norton Sd., 71A, Aa
Nor-Treding (North Riding, Lincolnshire), 13, Fc
Nor-Treding (North Riding, Yorkshire), 13, Eb
Norway, 12, Ga; 82, Aa
Norway, King. of, 26, Da
Norwegian Sea, 94, Tb
Norwic (Norwich), 13, Hd
Norwich, 27, Hd
Norwich, bp., 36, He
Nosob, R., 81B, Ba
Nossi Be, 80A, Hf
Notley, 36, Ff
Noto, 21A, Cd
Notre Dame B., 71, Jc
Notre Dame de la Grasse, 22, Cc
Nottingham, 7C, Cb; 27, Ed
Nottingham, co., 27, Ec
Nouakchott, 96D, Ac
Nouart, 76A, Cb
Noumea, 75, Ff
Nova Coimbra, 41B, De
Nova Foresta (New Forest), 13, Ef
Nova Scotia, 45A, Eb
Novae, 2, Je; 4A, Hc
Novantae, 3A, Bb
Novara, 5, Bb
Novaya Zemlya, 74, Da
Novgorod, Poland, 47, Hb
Novgorod, Russia, 26, Hb
Novgorod, Pr., 61, Eb
Novgorod, Rep. of, 19, Ga
Novgorod Severski, 50, Gc
Novi, 29A, Cc
Novibazar, 78, Cd

Noviomagus (Chichester), 3A, Ff
Novo Alexandrovsk, 61B, Aa
Novogrodek, 26, Gc
Novokuznetsk, 91, Ba
Novorossiisk, 88, Ne
Novosibirsk, 91, Ba; 94, Pc
Noyon, 11, Eb; 83A, Bb
Nubia, 80B, Ac
Nubian Desert, 80B, Ac
Nubians, 6, Ec
Nugent, 37B, Dc
Nuits, 76A, Cc
Nukha, 93, Fa
Nullarbor Plain, 77, Dh
Numidia, 1, Cd; 4B, Dd
Nuneaton, 36, Ee
Nuremberg, 10, Dd
Nuremburg, Bur. of, 30, Jd
Nürnberg, 87, Cc
Nursia, 5, Dc; 23B, Dc
Nyasa, L., 80A, Gf
Nyasaland, 80A, Gf
Nyköping, 26, Eb
Nymphaeum, 19, De
Nymphenburg, 53, Jc
Nyons, 38, Ff
Nystad, 51, Ea; 61, Bb

Oahu, 75D, Cb
Oakham, 27, Fd
Oates Land, 95, Kj
Oaxaca, 43A, Cc
Ob, R., 25, Fa; 61, Lb; 91, Ba
Obbia, 96A, Bb
Ober Selk, 65F, Aa
Oberehnheim, 39B, Db
Oberland, 29B, Bb
Obi, 52C, Cb
Obidos, Brazil, 68, Dc
Obidos, Portugal, 63, Ac
Obok, 80B, Ce; 83, Ld
Ototrites, 10, Db
O'Brien, 15, Cd; 37B, Bd
Obuasi, 96B, Bb
O'Byrne, 37B, Ec
Ocaña, Colombia, 68, Bb
Ocaña, Spain, 62, Be; 63, Dc
O'Carroll, 15, Db
Ocean I., 75, Fe
Oceanus Atlanticus, 2, Ad
Oceanus Germanicus, 2, Dc
Oceanus Hibernicus (Irish Sea), 3A, Bc
Ochakov, 51, Gd
Ochementone (Okehampton) 13, Bf
Ochil Hills, 23B, Ba
O'Connor, 15, Cc; 37B, Cc
Ocrinum Prom., 3A, Af
Octapitarum Pr., 3A, Ae
Odenburg, 16, Fc
Oder, R., 21, Lb; 31, Lb
Oderberg, 39, Nd
Odessa, 50, Gd; 51, Gd
Odessus, 4B, Gc
Odham, 27, Fe
Odoacer, King. of, 2A, Cb
Odienne, 96B, Bb
Odorber, 32B, Cc; 38, Jg
Orchies, 46A, Cd
Ordovices, 3A, Cd
Ordu, 93, Dd
Ordzhonikidze, 88, Oe
Ore Mts., 60A, Dc
Örebro, 26, Eb
Oregon, 70, Bc
Oregon City, 70, Bc
Oregon Country, 70, Cc
Oregon Terr., 67D, Aa
O'Reilly, 15, Dc
Orel, 61, Ed; 88, Nc
Orenburg, 61, Jd; 89, Rc
Orenburg Cossacks, 61, Jd
Orense, 23C, Ba; 63, Ba
Orewyn Bridge, 27, Cd
Orford, 13, Hd, 27, Hd
Oria, 21A, Db
Orientis, 2, Lg
Orinoco, Delta of the, 43A, Fd
Orinoco, R., 68, Cb
Oriskany, 57, Db
Orissa, 25, Hd; 73, Ec
Oristano, 22, Dd
Oristano, eccl. prov., 22, Dd
Orizaba, 43A, Cc
Orkney, co., 37A, Ca
Orkney Is., 14, Fa
Orléanais, 38, Dc
Orléans, 11, Dc; 28C, Dc
Orléans, D. of, 30, Ee
Orléans, I. d', 57C, Ba
Orlov, 61, Jc
Ormoc, 75E, Bb
Ormond, 15, Cd
Ormskirk, 48A, Bc
Ormuz, 25, Ed
Orneau, R., 46B
Orontes, R., 6A, Ba; 18A, Fc
Orontes (Ferreus), R., 18C, Dc
Oropesa, 63, Cc

Öland, 26, Eb
Olavarria, 68, Cf
Old Bridge, 49B, Ec
Old Calabar, 81C, Fd
Old Castle, 63, Db
Old Castle, 37B, Db
Old Charles Town, 45A, Bd
Old Fort Franklin, 70, Ba
Old Head of Kinsale, 15, Ce
Old Kilpatrick, 3A, Ba
Old Orsova, 33C, Cc
Old Point Comfort, 45B, Ae
Old Providence I., 43A, Dc
Old Sarai, 25, Db
Old Sarum 27 ,Ee
Oldenburg, 20, Hb; 30, Hb
Oldenburg, Co. of, 38, Hb
Oldenzaal, 46A, Fb
Oléron, 11, Cd
Olicana (Ilkley), 3A, Ec
Olifants, R., 81A, Db
Oliva, 21, Na
Olivenza, 64, Af
Olmütz, 21, Md; 33C, Db
Olonets, 26, Ha
Oloron, 11, Ce; 38, Cg
Öls, 39, Mc
Oltenitza, 78, Fc
Olustee, 72, Bc
Omagh, 37B, Db; 49B, Db
Omaha, 70, Ec
O'Malley, 37B, Bc
Oman, 6, Gc; 25, Ed; 93, He
Oman, G. of, 74, Df
Ombai, 52C, Bc
Omdurman, 80B, Ad
Ominitae, 1, Hf
Ommeyad Emirate, 6B, Aa
Omont, Co. of, 11, Fb
O'More, 37B, Dc
Omsk, 91, Aa
Oneida, L., 57, Cb
Oneidas, 45A, Bb
Onega, L., 26, Ja
Oneglia, 38, Hg
O'Neill, 15, Db
Onitsha, 96B, Cb
Onnum (Halton), 3C
Ono, 75C, Ba
Onondagas, 45A, Bb
Ontario, 70, Fc
Ontario, L., 57, Cb
Oodnadatta, 77, Fg
O'okiep, 81B, Ab
Opland, 12, Ga
Opsikion, 9, Hd
Optimaton, 9, Jd
Oran, 16, Be; 33B, Aa; 80, Ca
Orange, France, 11, Fd
Orange, R., 81B, Cb
Orange Free State, 81B, Cb
Orange River Colony, 81A, Cc
Orange River Sovereignty 81B, Cb
Orangeburg, 57D, Ab
Oranmore, 49B, Cc
Orbe, 9, Dc; 29B, Ab
Oklahoma, 70, Ed
Oklahoma Indian Territory 70, Ed

O'Rourke, 15, Cb
Oroya, 68, Bd
Orsova, 78, Dc
Orsoy, 53, Gb
Orta, 23B, Bb
Ortegal, C., 63, Aa
Ortenau, 33C, Bb
Orthez, 30, Cg; 63, Ea
Ortles, 29A, Db
Ortona, 21, Lg
Oruba, 43A, Fc
Oruro, 68, Cd
Orvieto, 5, Dc
Osaka, 91, Gc
Ösel, 26, Fb
Osero, 22, Ec
O'Shaughnessy, 15, Cc
Oshogbo, 96B, Cb
Osiek, 26, Fc
Osimo, 21, Kg
Osimo (Auximum), 5, Dc
Oslo, 26, Db; 84, Ea
Osma, 22, Bc
Osmanli, 85, Je
Osnabrück, 10, Cb
Ossory, 15, Dd
Ostend, 46A, Bc; 47, Cb
Öster-Götland, 26, Eb
Ostheim, 39C, Ac
Ostia, 5, Dd; 22A
Ostmark, 10, Ec
Ostrach, 29A, Cb
Ostrogothi, 2, Jd
Ostrogothic Kingdom, 4A, Eb
Ostrogoths, 2A, Db
Ostrolenka, 60B, Hb; 64, Gc
Ostrovo L., 86A, Cb
Oswego, 70, Gc; 71C, Cb
Oswestry, 13, Cd; 27, Cd
Otadini, 3A, Da
Otago, 77A
Otaheite, 69A, Be
Otchakov, 54, Jc
Otford, 7B, Dc
Othona (Bradwell), 3A, Ge
O'Toole, 15, Ed; 37B, Bc
Otranto, 5, Gd; 32A, Gd
Otrar, 25, Fb
Ottawa, 70, Gc
Ottawa, R., 45A, Ba; 71C, Ca
Ottawas, 45A, Aa
Otterburn, 27, Da
Ottery St. Mary, 36, Cg
Ottoman Empire, 50, Ee
Ottoman Turks, 24, Hf
Ouagadougou, 96B, Ba
Ouahgouya, 96B, Ba
Ouargla, 80A, Da
Oudenarde, 46A, Cd; 54, Cb
Oudh, 73, Db
Oudon, 20, Ce
Oudtshoorn, 81B, Bc
Oulatanon, 56, Bb
Oujitsa, 78, Bd
Ourcq, R., 76A, Bb
Ourique, 23C, Ad
Ourthe, R., 83A, Ca
Ouse, R., 27, Ec; 36, Fd
Ovambo, 80A, Ef
Översee, 65F, Aa
Overton, 27, Ee
Overyssel, 46A, Fb
Oviedo, 23C, Ca; 63, Bb
Owen Stanley Ra., 77, Hc
Ox Mts., 15, Cb
Oxeneford (Oxford), 13, Ee
Oxenefordscire (Oxfordshire),
13, Ee
Oxford, England, 27, Ee
Oxford, Maryland, 45B, Ad
Oxford, bp., 36, Ef
Oxford, co., 27, Ee
Oxus, R., 1, Jd; 6, Hb; 25, Fc
Oyster Bay, 45B, Dc
Ozamiz, 75E, Bc

PAARDE BERG, 81A, Cc
Paarl, 81B, Ac
Paauilo, 75D, Db
Pacaltsdorp, 81B, Bc
Pachacamac, 41B, Be
Pacific Ocean, 40, Cd; 75
Padang, 91, Dg
Paderborn, 10, Cc
Padua (Patavium), 5, Cb;
86B, Bb
Paducah, 72, Db
Paestum, 5, Ed
Pagadian, 75E, Bc
Pagan, 25, Jd; 73, Gc
Pago Pago, 75B, Bb
Pahala, 75D, Dc
Pahang, 41A, Hd
Pahlevi, 93, Fb
Paithan, 1, Kf
Pakhoi, 73, Jf
Palace, Constantinople, 18E
Palapye, 81A, Cb
Palar, R., 59D
Palatine, 5A
Palato, eccl. prov., 22, Fc
Palau Is., 90, Cc

Palawan, 75E, Ac; 90, Bc
Palazzo di Venezia, 5A
Palembang, 91, Dg
Palencia, 22, Bc
Palenque, 43A, Cc
Palermo, eccl. prov., 22, Ed
Palermo (Panormus), 5, De
Palestine, 6A, Ab; 79, Gd
Palestrina, 22A
Palma, 22, Cd; 23C, Gc
Palmas, C., 81C, Cd
Palmella, 23C, Ac
Palmerston I., 75, He
Palmyra, 2, Lg; 4A, Ke
Palmyra I., 75, Hd
Palos, 23D, Bd
Pamiers, 17, Fg; 22, Cc
Pamir, 59A, Ba; 61B, Cb
Pamlico, R., 57, Cf
Pamlico Sound, 45B, Af
Pamphylia, 2, Jf
Pamplona, 22, Bc; 23C, Ea
Panama, 43A, Ed; 68, Bb
Panay, 75E, Bb
Pandhya, 1, Kf
Pandyas, 25, Ge
Paneas (Belinas), 18C, Ce
Panganga, R., 59A, Cd
Panipat, 59A, Cb
Panniar, 73, Cb
Pannonia, 2, Gd; 9, Fc
Panormus (Palermo), 5, De
Panton, 57, Ea
Pantelleria, 88, Hf
Pantheon, 5A
Panuco, 43A, Cb
Panuco, R., 43A, Cb
Paoki, 90, Bb
Paoting, 90, Bb
Paotow, 91, Eb
Papal States, 32B, Dc; 34, Ed
Papua, G. of, 77, Gc
Papua, Terr. of (British New
Guinea), 77, Gc
Para (Belem), 41B, Ed; 68, Ec
Para, st., 68, Dc
Paradies, 22, Fa
Paraguay, 68, De
Paraguay, Jesuit Mission
State of, 41B, Df
Paraguay R., 41B, De
Paraiba, 68, Fc
Paraiba, st., 68, Fc
Paramaribo, 68, Db
Parana, 68, Cf
Parana, R., 41B, Df; 68, De
Parana, st., 68, De
Paranagua, 68, Ef
Parchim, 21, Jb
Parenzo, 22, Eb; 23B, Db
Parga, 54, Ge; 78, Cf
Parintins, 68, Dc
Paris, 11, Eb; 17, Gd
Parisii, 3A, Fc
Parkersburg, 72, Db
Parma, 5, Cb; 38, Jf
Parma, D. of, 38, Jf; 54, Dd
Parnaiba, 68, Ec
Parnaiba, R., 68, Ec
Paros, 78, Eg
Parret, R., 7B, Bc
Parry Is., 69B
Parthenay, 11, Cc
Parthia, 1, Hd
Parthian Empire, 1, Hd
Partenkirchen, 22, Eb
Passamaquoddy B., 45A, Da;
71E, Cc
Passaro, C., 32B, Ee
Passarowitz, 33C, Ec; 78, Cc
Passau, 10, Ed
Passchendaele, 83A, Ba
Passo Fundo, 68, De
Pasto, 68, Bb
Patagonia, 68, Cg
Pataliputra, 1, Le
Patan, 92, Fb
Patavium (Padua), 5, Cb
Patay, 28D, Cb
Patchefstroom, 81A, Cc
Patiala, 73, Ca
Patillos, 68, Bc
Patna, 73, Eb
Patras, 78, Cf
Patriarch's Pond, 18D
Patrimonium, 23B, Dd
Patrimony of St. Peter, 16,
Ed; 32A, Ed
Patti, 22, Fd
Patzinaks (Pechenegs), 9, Jc
Pau, 30, Cg
Paumotu Arch. (Tuamotu
Arch.), 69A, Ce; 75, He
Pavia, 6, Ba
Pavia (Picinum), 5, Bb
Pawtucket, 45B, Dc
Paxo, 62, Ge
Paxton, 57, Cc
Paysandu, 68, Df

Pea Ridge, 72, Bb
Peace, R., 44, Cc; 70, Cb
Peak, The, 27, Ec
Pearl, R., 71F, Ba; 72C, Aa
Pearl Coast, 43A, Fc
Pearl Harbor, 75D, Bb; 90, Gb
Pearl Is., 43A, Ed
Pecfers (Peak), 13, Ec
Pecos, R., 44, De
Pecs, 19, Bc; 33C, Db
Pedee, R., 57D, Ba
Pedir, 40, Od
Peebles, 49A, Cc
Peebles, co., 37A, Cc; 49A, Cc
Peekskill, 57, Ec
Pegu, 25, Je; 73, Gd
Peipus, L., 26, Gb
Peishwa, 59A, Bd
Peking, 91, Ec
Peking (Kaanbaligh), 25, Lc
Pelagonia, 19, Cd
Pelew Is., 74, Mh
Pella, 81B, Ab
Pelly, R., 70, Aa
Pelotas, 68, Df
Pelplin, 22, Fa
Pelusium, 18A, Ec
Pelvoux, Mt., 29A, Bc
Pemaquid, 45A, Db; 45B, Eb
Pemba I., 80A, Ge
Pembroke, 27, Be
Pembroke, Co. Palatine of, 27,
Be
Pelim, 61, Kc
Penafiel, 23D, Cb
Peñan de Alger, 34, Ce
Penang, 91, Df
Penbroc (Pembroke), 13, Be
Pendennis, 48A, Ad
Penedo, 68, Fd
Peneverdant (Penwortham),
13, Dc
Penicola, 23D, Fb
Peniscola, 23D, Fb
Penjdeh, 61B, Bb; 74, Ee
Penkridge 13, Dd
Pennal, 3A, Cd
Penner, R., 59D; 73, Ce
Pennine Alps, 29A, Bb
Pennine Chain, 27, Db; 28B,
Cc
Pennsylvania, 57, Cc; 72B, Ba
Penobscot (Fort Pentagöet),
45B, Ea
Penobscot B., 45B Ea
Penobscot, R., 45A, Da; 71E,
Bc
Penrith, 27, Db
Penryn, 48A, Ad
Penrhyn I., 75, He
Pensacola, 56, Bd; 67B, Bb
Pensacola (Achusi), 43A, Da
Penselwood, 7B Bc
Pentapolis, Africa, 2, Hg; 4B,
Ge
Pentapolis, Italy, 5, Dc
Pentegoet, 56, Fb
Penthièvre, 17, Dd
Pentland Firth, 14, Ea
Pentland Hills, 14, Ed
Penukonda, 52A, Bc
Penza, 61, Fd
Peoria, 56, Bb
Pera, 18E; 19, Dd
Perambakan, 59D
Perche, 17, Fd; 30, Dd
Perekop, 51, Gd; 61, Db
Perekop, G. of, 61, De
Pereyaslav, 19, Eb
Pergamum, 9, He; 18A, Db
Perigord, Co. of, 11, Dd
Perigueux, 11, Dd
Perim I., 80B, Ce
Perm, 61, Jc; 89, Rb
Pernambuco (Mauritia), 42, He
Pernambuco (Recife), 68, Fc
Pernambuco, st., 68, Fc
Pernau, 26, Fb
Péronne, 11, Eb; 83A, Bb
Perovsk, 61B, Ba
Perpignan, 11, Ee
Perryville, 72, Db
Persarum Regnum, 2, Og
Persepolis, 1, Hd
Pershore, 27, Dd
Persia, 6, Gb; 33A, Hd; 74, De
Persia (Iran), 89, Pg; 93, Gc
Persian Empire, 2A, Fc
Persian Gulf, 6, Gc; 93, Gd
Persis, 1, Hd
Persore (Pershore), 13, Dd
Perth, Scotland, 14, Ec
Perth, W. Australia, 77, Bh
Perth, co., 37A, Cb; 49A, Cb
Peru, 68, Bd
Peru, Viceroyalty of, 41B, Be;
42, Ee
Perugia, 5, Dc; 21, Kg
Perusia, 5B, Bb
Pesaro, 8A, Dc; 21, Kg
Pesaro (Pisaurum), 5, Dc
Pisco, 68, Bd
Pisek, 21, Ld; 60A, Ed

Pescadores, 75, Cc
Pescara, 32A, Fc
Peschiera, 29A, Dc; 32D, Bb
Peshawar, 25, Gc; 73, Ba
Pessinus, 2, Kf
Pest, 39, Ne
Peterborough, 36, Fe
Peterborough, bp., 36, Fe
Peterhead, 37A, Db
Petersburg, 57, Ce; 72B, Bb
Petersfield, 27, Ef; 48A, Cd
Peterwardein, 50, Dd
Petra, 6A, Bb
Petrianae, 3A, Cb
Petropavlovsk, 58, Rb
Petropolis, 68, Ee
Petsamo, 88, Ma
Pettau, 9, Fc
Petuaria (Brough), 3A, Fc
Pevenesel (Pevensey), 13, Gf
Pevensey, 27, Gf
Pfaffenhofen, 65A, Bb
Pfalzburg, 39B, Ac
Pfävers, 29B, Db
Pfirt, 39B, Dc
Pfullendorf, 53, Hd
Pharsalus, 9, Ge
Philadelphia, Nicaea, 19, De
Philadelphia, Pennsylvania,
57, Dd
Philiphaugh, 37A, Cc; 48B, Bb
Philippeville, 46A, Dd
Philippine Is., 74, Lg
Philippine Is. (Felipinas,
Islas), 41A, Kc
Philippines (St. Lazaro Arch.),
40, Qd
Philippolis, 81B, Cb
Philippopolis, 2, Je; 78, Ed
Philippsburg, 29A, Ca
Philipstown, 49B, Dc
Philomelion, 18A, Eb
Fhnom, Fenh, 91, De
Phoenicia, 1, Fd
Phoenix Is., 90, Fd
Phrygia, 2, Jf
Piacenza (Placentia), 5, Bb
Piaui, 68, Ec
Piave, R., 5, Db; 86B, Cb
Picardy, 28D, Db; 83A, Bb
Pichincha, 68, Bc
Picinum (Pavia), 5, Bb
Pickawillany, 56, Cb
Pickering, 27, Fb
Pickeringham (Pickering), 13,
Fb
Picquigny, 30, Ed
Picti, 2, Cb
Picts, 7B, Ba
Pidurutalagala, 73, Df
Piedmont, 32A, Bb
Piedmont, Pr. of, 38, Gf
Piedra, 22, Bc
Piet Retief, 81A, Dc
Pietermaritzburg, 81D, Bb
Pieters, 81D, Ab
Pietersburg, 81A, Cb
Pietra Santa, 38, Jg
Pieve di Cadore, 86B, Ca
Pike's Peak, 70, Dd
Pilar, 68, De
Pilcomayo, R., 68, Ce
Pilica, 60A, Hc
Pilica, R., 31, Pc; 33C, Ea
Pillau, 39, Na
Pilinitz, 60A, Dc
Pilsen, 10, Ed; 39, Kd
Pilten, 26, Fb
Pilton, 7C, Ac
Piltune (Pilton), 13, Be
Pinar del Rio, 43A, Db
Pindari, 73, Cb
Pindiga, 96B, Db
Pindus, 50, Ee
Pine Bluff, 72, Bc
Pinerolo, 32A, Bb
Pines, I. of, 75, Ff
Pines, I. de Cuba, 43A, Db
Pinos, I. de, Panama, 43A, Ed
Pinsk, 34, Hb; 50, Fc; 84, Hb
Piombino, 5, Cc
Pippli, 59B
Piqua, 71C, Bb
Piquetberg, 81B, Ac
Piraeus, 78, Dg; 88, Kf
Pirapora, 68, Ed
Pirmasens, 83A, Db
Pirna, 31, Kc; 39C, Dc
Pirot, 78, Dc
Pisa, 5, Cc; 8A, Dc
Pisaurum (Pesaro), 5, Dc
Piscataqua B. (Portsmouth),
45B, Db

Pisidia, 2, Kf
Pisino, 22, Eb
Pistoia, 32E, Ba
Pisuerga, R., 63, Ca
Pitcairn I., 75, Jf
Pitiqui, 43C, Ab
Pitsewo, 76B, Bb
Pittsburg Landing, 72, Cb
Pittsburgh, 71C, Cb
Pittsburgh (Fort Pitt), 57A, Ca
Pityus, 2, Me
Piura, 68, Ac
Placentia, 45A, Ga; 52, Gb
Placentia (Piacenza), 5, Bb
Plaine Selve, 22, Bb
Plancenoit, 46B
Plasencia, 22, Ac; 63, Bb
Plassey, 59A, Ec
Pläswitz, 62, Fb
Platte, R., 70, Dc
Plattsburg, 57, Ea
Plauen, 21, Kc
Plava, 86B, Da
Pleasant Hill, 72, Bc
Plenty, B. of, 77A
Pleshey, 27, Fe
Pless, 31, Nd; 39, Nd
Plessis-les-Tours, 30, Dd
Plettenburg, 81B, Cb
Pleven, 79, Dd
Plevna, 78, Ed
Plintone (Plympton), 13, Br
Plock, 21, Nb
Ploërmel, 20, Be
Ploesti, 88, Ld
Ploughed Hill, 56B
Plovdiv, 79, Db
Plunket, 37B, Ec
Plymouth, England, 27, Bf
Plymouth, Massachusetts,
45B, Dc
Plympton, 27, Bf; 36, Bg
Plzen, 87, Cc
Po, R., 5, Cb; 21B, Bc; 38, Gf
Poblet, 22, Cc
Poclinton (Pocklington), 13, Fc
Podiebrad, 31, Lc
Podlesia, 50, Fd
Podolia, 50, Fd
Poetovia, 2, Gd
Poggibonsi, 32E, Bb
Pohlde, 10, De
Pointe Noire, 96D, De
Poissy, 11, Db; 38, Ed
Poitiers, 11, Cc
Poitou, 30, De
Poitou, Co. of, 11, Cc
Pola, 5, Db
Poland, 50, Ec; 87, Eb
Poland, King. of, 21, Nc
Poles, 8, Hb; 9, Fb
Polesina, 32D, Db
Policastro, 32A, Fd
Poligny, 30, Fe
Polillo Is., 75E, Bb
Polling, 10, De
Polotsk, 26, Gb
Polotsk, Pr. of, 19, Db
Polovtsi (Kipchaks), 19, Gc
Poltava, 50, Gd
Polygars, 52A, Bc
Pombal, 63, Ac
Pomerania, D. of, 21, Mb
Pomeranian, 8, Fa
Pomerelia, 19, Bb; 31, Na
Pompadour, 53, De
Ponape, 75, Ed
Pondicherry, 59D
Pondoland, 81B, Db
Pondos, 81B, Db
Ponferrada, 63, Ba
Pongolo, R., 81D, Ba
Poniec, 50, Cf
Pons, 20, Cf
Pons Aelius (Newcastle), 3C
Pont à Mousson, 39B, Cb
Pont Audemer, 20, Dd
Pont di Piave, 86B, Cb
Pontarlier, 30, Ge; 76A, Dc
Pontecorvo 32A, Ed
Pontefract, 27, Ec; 48A, Cc
Pontes (Staines), 3A, Fe
Ponthieu, Co. of, 11, Da
Pontiac, 71C, Bb
Pontigny, 22, Cb; 28C, Cb
Pontivy, 38, Bd
Pontoise, 20, Dd
Pontremoli, 32A, Cb
Pontus, 2, Kf
Pontus Euxinus, 2, Ke
Pontvallain, 28C, Cc
Ponza, 32A, Ed
Pool, 28A, Cb
Poole, 27, Df
Poole, family, 28A, Cb
Poona, 73, Bd
Popayan, 68, Bb
Popocatopetl, 43A, Cc
Poprad, 31, Pd
Populonium, 5B, Ab

Porcestre (Porchester), 13, Ef
Porcien, Co. of, 11, Fb
Pordenone, 32D, Cb; 86B, Cb
Port Adams, 76B, Bb
Port Antonio, 43A, Ec
Port Arthur, Canada, 70, Fc
Port Arthur, China, 91, Fc
Port au Port, 45A, Fa
Port au Prince, 43C, Dc
Port Augusta, 77, Fh
Port aux Basques, 45A, Fa
Port Bonnel, 18C, Cb
Port Curtis, 77, If
Port Dalrymple, 77, HJ
Port Darwin, 77, Ed
Port Dieu, 29B, Bb
Port Elizabeth (Fort Frederick), 81B, Cc
Port Essington (Port Victoria), 77, Ed
Port Gibson, 72C, Ab
Port Harcourt, 96B, Cb
Port Hudson, 72, Bc
Port Jackson (Sydney), 77, Ih
Port Macquarie, 77, Ih
Port Mahon, 54, Ce
Port Moresby, 77, Hc
Port Mouton, 45A, Eb
Port Natal (Durban), 81D, Bb
Port Nelson, 70, Eb
Port Nicholson, 77A
Port of Spain, 43A, Fc
Port Phillip, 77, Gi
Port Pleasant, 57A, Cb
Port Republic, 72B, Aa
Port Royal (Annapolis), 45A, Db
Port Royal (Stuart Town), 45A, Ad
Port Royal, Jamaica, 43A, Ec
Port Said, 80B, Aa
Port St. Julian, 41B, Ch
Port Simpson, 70, Ab
Port Sudan, 80B, Bd; 96D, Fc
Port Victoria (Port Essington), 77, Ed
Portadown, 49B, Eb
Portage la Prairie, 70, Eb
Portalegre, 22, Ad
Portarlington, 49B, Dc
Portland, England, 7C, Bc
Portland, Maine, 56, Eb
Portland, Oregon, 70, Bc
Portland, Victoria, 77, Gi
Portland Canal, 71B, Dc
Portloc (Porlock), 13, Ce
Porto, 22A
Porto Alegre, 68, Df
Porto Novo, India, 59D
Porto Novo, Dahomé, 81C, Ec
Porto Praya, 55B, He
Porto Rico, 43A, Fc
Porto Seguro, 68, Fd
Porto Seguro, prov., 41B, Ee
Porto Velho, 94, Df
Porto Viejo, 68, Ac
Portree, 49A, Ab
Portsmouth (Piscataqua B.), 45B, Db
Portsmouth, England, 27, Ef
Portsmouth, New Hampshire, 45B, Db
Portsmouth, Ohio, 70, Fd
Portsmouth, Rhode I., 45B, Dc
Portsmouth, Virginia, 57, Ce
Portsoy, 49A, Cb
Portugal, 63, Ac
Portugal, Co. of, 23C, Bb
Portugal, King. of, 23D, Bb
Portuguese East Africa, 81A, Db
Portuguese Guinea, 81C, Ab; 96B, Aa
Portus Adurni (Porchester), 3A, Ef
Portus Lemanis (Lympne), 3A, He
Posadas, 68, De
Poschiavo, 29B, Eb
Posen, 21, Mb
Posen, reg., 60B, Fb
Potawatomis, 45A, Ab
Potchefstroom, 81B, Ca
Potgieter, 81A, Cc
Poti, 61, Ff; 79, Hb
Potomac, R., 57, Cd; 72B, Ba
Potosi, 68, Cd
Potsdam, 54, Eb; 60A, Db
Poughkeepsie, 57, Ec
Pounanen, 19, De
Poverty B., 77, Ni
Powder, R., 70, Dc
Powderham, 13, Cf
Powhatans, 45A, Bc
Powick Bridge, 48A, Bc
Powys, 7C, Bb; 13, Cd; 27, Cd
Pozières, 83A, Ba
Poznań, 61A, Ab; 87, Db
Praga, 51, Ec
Prague, 21, Lc
Prague, eccl. prov., 22, Fb

Prairie du Chien, 67C, Da
Prairie Grove, 72, Bb
Praslin, 53, Fc
Prato, 20, Jg; 32E, Bb
Prättigau, 29B, Db
Pravadi, 78, Fd
Prayaga, 52A, Cb
Pregel, R., 60A, Ha
Prèmontrè, 22, Cb
Prenzlau, 21, Kb; 65B, Ba
Presba L., 86A, Cb
Presidios, 32B, Cc; 38, Jg
Preslav, 9, Hd
Presque Isle, 71C, Bb
Presqu'île, 56, Cb
Pressburg, 10, Gd
Preston, 27, Dc
Prestonpans, 49A, Cc
Prestune (Preston), 18, Dc
Pretoria, 80A, Fg; 81A, Cc
Prettin, 39C, Cb
Preveza, 78, Cf
Priegnitz, 31B, Ca; 60A, Cb
Prilep, 19, Cd; 86A, Ca
Prince Albert, 70, Ab
Prince Edward I., 71, Hc
Prince Edward I. (Ile de St. Jean), 45A, Ea
Prince Edward Is., 95, Sh
Prince of Wales, C., 71A, Aa
Prince of Wales I., Alaska, 71B, Cc
Prince of Wales I., Canada, 44, Ea
Prince Rupert, 70, Bb
Prince Willem's Is., 42B
Prince William Sd., 71A, Ca
Princess Elizabeth Land, 69C
Princeton, 57, Dc
Principato, 32A, Fd
Principato Salerno, 21A, Cb
Principe, 80A, Dd
Prinkipo Is., 86C, Aa
Pripet, R., 50, Fc
Pripet Marshes, 84, Hb
Pristhina, 78, Cd
Pritzwalk, 21, Kb
Prizren, 19, Cd
Prome, 25, Je; 73, Gd
Prospect Hill, 56B
Prosperous, 49B, Ec
Provencals, 85, Cd
Provence, 8A, Cc; 9, Dd
Provence, Co. of, 11, Gd
Provence, Marq. of, 20, Ff
Providence, Maryland, 45B, Ad
Providence, Rhode I., 45B, Dc
Provincia, 2A, Bb
Provins, 17, Gd
Prüm, 20, Gc
Prussia, 51, Dc; 65A, Ba
Prussians, 8, Ga
Pruth, R., 50, Fd; 78, Fb
Przemysl, 26, Fd; 87, Ec
Psara, 78, Ef
Pskov, 26, Gb
Pueblo, 70, Dd
Puerto Bello, 43A, Ed
Puerto Cabello, 68, Ca
Puerto de Caballos, 43A, Dc
Puerto Deseado, 68, Cg
Puerto Madryn, 68, Cg
Puerto Montt, 68, Bg
Puerto Princesa, 75E, Ac
Puerto Principe, 43A, Eb
Pularoon, 52C, Cb
Pulaski, 72, Cb
Pulaway, 52C, Cb
Pulicat, 59D
Pulicat, L. of, 59D
Pultusk, 31, Pb; 54, Gb
Punakha, 92, Gb
Pungwe, R., 81A, Da
Punjab, 73, Ba; 74, Fe
Puno, 68, Bd
Punta Arenas, 68, Bh
Purdysburg, 57D, Ab
Purnea, 59A, Eb
Purus, R., 68, Cc
Pusan, 91, Fc
Pustat (Cairo), 6A, Ab
Pustertal, 29A, Db; 86B, Ca
Put-in-Bay, 71C, Bb
Putivl, 19, Eb
Puttlingen, 20, Gd; 39B, Da
Putumayo, R., 68, Bc
Puylaurens, 38, Eg
Pwllheli, 28A, Bb
Pyatigorsk, 88, Oe
Pyrenæ Montes, 2, De
Pyrenees, 11, De; 63, Fa
Pyritz, 10, Fb

Qayin, 6, Gb
Qatar, 93, Gd
Qatif, 93, Gd
Qena, 93, Cd
Qivira, 44, Ee
Quadi, 2, Gd
Quatford, 13, Dd

Quathlamba (Drakens Berg), 81D, Ab
Quatre Bras, 46B; 62, Cb
Quebec, 45A, Ca; 56A; 57C, Ba
Quebec, prov., 56, Da
Quedlinburg, 10, Dc; 65A, Ba
Queen Charlotte Is., 70, Ab
Queen Charlotte Sd., 70, Bb
Queen Mary Land, 69C
Queen Maud Land, 69C
Queen Victoria Spring, 77, Ch
Queen's Co., 37C; 49B, Dd
Queensferry, 49A, Cc
Queensland, 77, Gf
Queenstown (Cobh), 49B, Ce
Queenstown (North Victoria), 81B, Cb
Queenstown, Canada, 71C, Cb
Queenstown, Cape Colony, 81A, Cd
Quelimane, 80A, Gf
Quemoy, 91, Ed
Quensanfu, 25, Kc
Quentovic, 12, Ed
Quercy, 17, Ff; 28C, Cd
Quetta, 61B, Bb; 73, Aa
Quezon City, 75E, Ac
Quiberon, 53, Bd; 55A, Be
Quilon, 59A, Cf
Quimper, 11, Ab
Quimperlé, 22, Bb; 28D, Ac
Quincey (Merry Mount), 45B, Db
Quincy, 70, Ed
Quingey, 76A, Cc
Quinsay (Lingan, Hangchow), 25, Mc
Quito, 68, Bc
Qum, 93, Gc
Qunfidha, 93, Ef
Quseir, 93, Cd

Raab, 21, Me
Raab, R., 31, Me; 39, Me
Raasay, 49A, Ab
Rabast, C. de, 45A, Ea
Rabat, 80A, Ca
Rabaul, 77, Ib; 90, Dd
Raby, 27, Eb
Raccoon Ford, 57, Cd
Race, C., 45A, Ga
Radcot Bridge, 27, Ee
Raddenore (Radnor), 13, Cd
Radicofani, 23B, Cc
Radimiches, 9, Jb
Radnor, 27, Cd
Radom, 31, Pc; 39, Pc
Radstadt, 21, Ke
Radzyn, 51, Ec
Raeburnfoot, 3A, Ca
Rageneia (Rayleigh), 13, Ge
Raglan, 48A, Bd
Ragnit, 26, Fb
Ragusa, 39, Ng; 78, Bd
Ragusa, eccl. prov., 22, Fc
Ragusa, Rep. of, 54, Fd
Rain, 29A, Da
Rainy, R., 70, Ec
Rais, 17, Ee; 30, Ce
Raisin, R., 71C, Bb
Rajahahan, 59B
Rajahmundry, 92, Ed
Rajasthan, 92, Cb
Rajkot, 92, Cc
Rajputana, 73, Bb
Rakka, 18A, Fb
Rakonitz, 39, Kc
Raleigh, 57, Bf
Raleigh's Virginia Colony, 45A, Bc
Ralick Is., 75, Fd
Ralph, 12, Dc
Ramadi, 93, Ec
Ramah, 71, Hb
Ramesyg (Ramsey), 13, Fd
Ramillies, 46A, Dd
Ramle, 18C, Bg
Ramleh, 46A, Ab
Rammekens, 46A, Cc
Ramnagar, 73, Ba
Rampur, 73, Cb
Ramree I., 90, Ac
Ramsay's Mills, 57, Bf
Ramsbury, 36A
Ramsey, 36, Fe
Ranchi, 92, Fc
Rand, 81A, Cc
Rangoon, 73, Gd; 92, Hd
Rann, The, 73, Bc
Rannoch, L., 49A, Bb
Rannoch Moor, 49A, Bb
Rapa I., 75, Hf
Rapallo, 32A, Cb
Raphoe, 15, Db
Rappahannock, R., 57, Cd
Rapperswyl, 29B, Ca
Rappoltstein, 39B, Db
Raquette, R., 57, Cd
Raraton ga, 75, Gf
Ras el Ain, 6A, Ca
Rasgrad, 78, Fd
Raslawice, 51, Ec

Rastatt, 29A, Ca
Rat Portage, 70, Ec
Ratack Is., 75, Fd
Ratae (Leicester), 3A, Ed
Rathfarnham, 49B, Ec
Rathlin I., 15, Ea
Rathmines, 49B, Ec
Rathmore, 37B, Ec
Rathmullan, 49B, Da
Ratibor, 21, Nc
Ratisbon, 8A, Db
Ratisbon (Regensburg), 10, Ed
Ratzeburg, 22, Ea; 30, Jb
Ravenglass, 48B, Bb
Ravenna, 5, Db; 23B, Cb
Ravenna, eccl. prov., 22, Ec
Ravensberg, Co. of, 30, Hb
Ravensburg, 20, He; 30, He
Ravenscar, 3A, Fb
Ravenspur, 27, Gc
Ravenstein, 46A, Ec
Ravi, R., 73, Ba
Rawa, 21, Pc
Rawalpindi, 73, Ba
Rawson (Chubut), 68, Cg
Raymond, 72C, Aa
Raymond of Toulouse, 16, Fd
Ré, I. de, 17, Ee
Reading, England, 27, Fe
Reading, Massachusetts, 57, Cc
Reate, 5, Dc
Recife (Pernambuco), 68, Fc
Recklinghausen, 20, Gc
Reculver, 7B, Dc
Red, R., Canada, 70, Ec
Red, R., U.S.A., 70, Ed
Red River Colony, 70, Ec
Red Russia, 50, Ed
Red Sea, 6, Ec; 25, Cd
Redarians, 10, Eb
Redesdale, 13, Da; 28B, Cb
Redinges (Reading), 13, Ee
Redinha, 63, Ab
Redstone (Fort Burd), 57, Bc
Ree, L., 15, Dc
Regensburg, 8, Eb; 31B, Cb
Reggio (Rhegium), Bruttium, 5, Ee
Reggio (Rhegium), Lombardy, 5, Cb
Reggio, eccl. prov., 22, Fd
Regina, 70, Db
Regni, 3A, Ff
Regulbium (Reculver), 3A, He
Rehdaniya, 33A, Dd
Rei, 19, Je
Reichenau, 22, Db
Reichenbach, 33C, Ca
Reigate, 27, Fe
Reims, 11, Ff; 83A, Cb
Reims, eccl. prov., 22, Cb
Remagen, 20, Gc
Remington, 57, Cd
Remiremont, 39B, Cb
Rendsburg, 38, Ha; 65F, Aa
Renfrew, 14, Dd
Renfrew, co., 37A, Bc
Rennel, 77, Kd
Rennes, 11, Cb
Reno, R., 5, Cb; 29A, Dc
Rense, 30, Gc
Rensselaerwyk, 45B, Cb
Requena, 63, Ec
Rerigonius Sinus, 3A, Ba
Resaca, 72A, Aa
Resht, 93, Fb
Resino, 22, Ec
Resolution I., 71, Ha
Rethel, 20, Fd; 31A, Cc
Retford, 27, Fc; 48A, Cc
Réunion, 69A, Mf
Reuss, 39C, Cc
Reuss, Co. of, 30, Kc; 38, Jc
Reuss, R., 29D, Ca
Reutlingen, 20, Hd
Reval, 26, Gb; 54, Ga
Revesby, 36, Fd
Rewah, 73, Dc
Reykjavik, 88, Aa
Reynosa, 63, Ca
Rha, R., 1, Gc
Rhaetia, 2, Fd; 8, Db
Rhætian Alps, 29A, Cb
Rhætian Leagues (Grisons), 29B, Db
Rhagae, 1, Hd
Rhayader, 28A, Cb
Rhegium (Reggio), Bruttium, 5, Ee
Rhegium (Reggio), Lombardy, 5, Cb
Rheinau, 29B, Ca
Rheinberg, 46A, Fc
Rheinfelden, 29A, Bb
Rhenus, R., 2, Ed
Rhine, R., 10, Bc; 46A, Db
Rhine, Confederation of the, 62, Ec
Rhine Prov., 60B, Ac
Rhineland, 83A, Da
Rhodanus, R., 2, De
Rhode Island, 45B, Dc

Rhodes, 78, Gg
Rhodes Drift, 81A, Cb
Rhodesia, 81A, Da; 96D, Ef
Rhodesia and Nyasaland, Federation of, 96D, Ef
Rhodope, 9, Gd; 50, Ee
Rhodri Mawr, Pr. of, 7C, Bb
Rhodus, 2, Jf
Rhône, R., 11, Fd; 30, Ff
Rhos, 13, Cc
Rhuddlan, 27, Cc
Rhufoniog, 13, Cc
Riade, 10, Ec
Ribacoa, 23D, Bb
Ribagorza, 23C, Fa
Ribble, R., 27, Ec
Ribe, 12, Gc; 65F, Aa
Riccall, 12, Dc
Richard's Castle, 28A, Db
Richelieu, 47, Cc; 53, Dd
Richelieu, R., 45A, Ca
Richmond, Canada, 57, Ea
Richmond, Natal, 81D, Bb
Richmond, Surrey, 48B, Cd
Richmond, Virginia, 57, Ce
Richmond, Yorkshire, 27, Eb
Ried, 65B, Bb
Rieneck, 53, Hb
Rienzi, House of, 5A
Rier, R., 81B, Cb
Rieti, 32C, Dc
Rieux, 22, Dc
Riez, 22, Dc
Riga, 26, Fb
Riga, eccl. prov., 22, Ga
Riga, G. of, 26, Fb
Rimini (Ariminum), 5, Db
Rincoede (Ringwood), 13, Ef
Ringgold Is., 75C, Ca
Rio Branco, 94, Df
Rio Branco, prov., 68, Cb
Rio de Janeiro, 68, Ee
Rio de la Hacha, 43A, Ec
Rio de Oro, 80A, Bb
Rio Grande, 68, Df
Rio Grande (Bravo del Norte), R., 43A, Bb
Rio Grande (Magdalena), R., 43A, Ed
Rio Grande, R., Central America, 43A, Dc
Rio Grande do Norte, prov., 68, Fc
Rio Grande do Sul (San Pedro do Rio Grande), 41B, Dg
Rio Grande do Sul, prov., 68, De
Rio Pardo, 68, De
Rio Pecos, R., 70, Dd
Rio Salado, 23D, Bd
Rioja, 23C. Da
Riom, 17, Gf; 20, Ef
Ripa, R. (Ribble), 18, Dc
Ripoli, 22, Cc
Ripon. 27, Eb
Ripuarians, 8b, Ca
Ripuarii, 2, Ec
Ripun (Ripon), 13, Eb
Risaiyeh, 93, Eb
Risti, 22, Ec
Ristovatz, 78, Cd
Ritzebüttel, 30, Hb; 38, Hb
Riva, 20, Jf; 32D, Bb
Rivaulx, 36, Ec
River Cess, 96B, Bb
Riversdale, 81A, Bd
Riviera, 29A, Cc
Rivière du Loup, 45A, Da
Rivoli, Piedmont, 29A, Bc
Rivoli, Veneto, 29A, Dc
Riyadh, 93, Fe
Björneborg, 26, Fa
Roanne, 38, Fe
Roanoke, 70, Gd
Roanoke I., 45B, Bf
Roanoke, R., 45A, Bc
Roanoke Sd., 55B, Cc
Robe, R., 15, Bc
Robert of Flanders, 16, Ed
Robertsbridge, 36, Gg
Robertson, 37A, Bb
Robertsport, 96B, Ab
Robogdium Prom., 3A, Aa
Roca, C. da, 63, Ac
Rocca San Casiano, 32E, Ba
Roccasecca, 32A, Ed
Roche, 36, Ed
Rochefort, 30, Cf; 53, Ce
Rochester, 27, Ge
Rochester, bp., 36, Gf
Rochingeham (Rockingham), 13, Fd
Rochlitz, 39, Kc; 39C, Cb
Rockhampton, 77, If
Rockhill, 57, Af
Rockingham, 27, Fd
Rockingham B., 77, He
Rockingham Forest, 3A, Fd
Rocky Mount, 57D, Aa
Rocky Mts., 70, Bb
Rocourt, 46A, Ed

Rocroy, 38, Fd
Rodemackern, 39B, Ca
Rodez, 11, Ed
Rodney and de Grasse, 55B, De
Rodosto, 8, Hc; 78, Fe
Roebuck B., 77, Ce
Roelant (Rhuddlan), 13, Cc
Roer, R., 83A, Da
Roeskilde, 26, Db
Rogaland, 12, Fb
Roger's Rock, 57, Eb
Roggeveld, 81B, Bc
Rohan, 17, Dd
Rohilkhand, 73, Cb
Roleca, 63, Ac
Röm, 65F, Aa
Roma (Rome), 2, Fe; 5, Dd
Romagna, 20, Jf; 32A, Dc
Roman Empire, 1, Dc; 4A, Jd
Roman Empire (under Syagrius), 2A, Bb
Romaniola, 23B, Cb
Rome (Roma), 5, Dd
Rome, U.S.A., 72A, Aa
Rome, eccl. prov., 22, Ec
Romenel (Romney), 13, Gf
Romesey (Romsey), 13, Ef
Romney, 27, Gf
Romsey, 36, Eg
Roncaglia, 10, Cf; 20, Hf
Roncesvalles, 8, Bc; 22, Bc
Roncesvalles Pass, 63, Ea
Ronciglione, 39, Kg
Ronda, 23C, Cd; 63, Cd
Rondonia, 68, Cd
Roraima, 68, Cd
Rorke's Drift, 81A, Dc; 81D, Bb
Rosa, Mte., 29A, Bc; 29B, Bc
Rosario, 68, Cf
Rosas, 63, Ga
Roscommon, 15, Cc
Roscommon, co., 37C; 49B, Cc
Roscrea, 37B, Dd; 49B, Dd
Rose Castle, 28B, Bc
Roseires, 80B, Ae
Roseljae, 5B, Ab
Rosemarkie, bp., 14A, Bb
Rosenheim, 53, Kd
Rosetta, 6A, Ab; 80B, Aa
Roskilde, 12, Hc
Rosheim, 39B, Db
Rosnay, 11, Fb
Rosoy, 38, Ed
Ross, England, 27, De
Ross, Ireland, 15, Be
Ross, co., 37A, Bb
Ross, dist., 14, Db
Ross Dependency, 95, Kj
Ross Sea, 69C
Rossano, 22, Fd
Rossbach, 60A, Cc
Rosslyn, 36, Cb
Rostock, 21, Ka; 22, Ea
Rostov (-on-Don), 19, Fc; 79, Ga
Rostov, Suzdal, 19, Fa
Rosyth, 84, Ba
Roteland (Rutland), 13, Fd
Rothbury, 28B, Db
Rothenburg, 20, Jd; 60A, Eb
Rothesay, 37A, Bc
Rotterdam, 46A, Dc
Rotterdam, I., 42B
Rottweil, 20, Hd; 30, Hd
Rotuma I., 75, Fe
Roubaix, 83A, Ba
Roucy, 20, Ed; 30, Ed
Rouecestre (Rochester), 13, Ge
Rouen, 11, Db; 83A, Ab
Rouen, eccl. prov., 22, Cb
Rouergue, Co. of, 11, Ed; 28C, De
Rough Castle, 3A, Ca
Roundway Down, 48A, Cd
Rouses Pt., 57, Ea
Roussillon, Co. of, 11, Ee
Rouvray, 28D, Cb
Roveredo, 32D, Bb
Rovereto, 38, Jf; 86B, Bb
Rovigo, 32D, Bb
Rovno, 84, Hb
Rowley, 45B, Db
Rowton, 48B, Bc
Roxburgh, 14, Fd
Roxburgh, co., 37A, Cc; 49A, Cc
Roxbury, 56B
Roxolani, 1, Fc
Royal Niger Company, 80A, Dc
Royal Palace, Jerusalem, 18D
Royale, I. (Cape Breton I.), 45A, Ea
Royan, 38, Cf
Roye, 20, Ed; 81A, Bb
Ruapehu, 77, Ni
Rub al Khali, 93, Gf

Rueda, 63, Cb
Rufford, 36, Ed
Rudolf, L., 80A, Gd
Rudolstadt, 30, Jc; 39C, Bc
Rügen I., 10, Ea
Rügenwalde, 31, Ma
Rugii, 2, Fc; 2, Hd
Ruhr, R., 10, Bc
Rullion Green, 49A, Cc
Rum, I., 14. Bc
Rum, Seljuk Sultanate of (Iconium), 16, Je
Rum or Iconium, King. of, 18A, Fb
Rumania, 78, Ec
Rumelia, 50, Ee
Runcorn, 7C, Bb
Runnymede, 27, Fe
Rupel, 86A, Ea
Rupel Pass, 19, Cd
Rupert, R., 70, Gb
Rupert's Land, 45A, Ba; 70, Fb
Ruphia, R., 78, Cg
Ruppin, 21, Kb
Ruremonde, 46A, Ec
Rus, King. of, 16, Jb
Ruschuk, 78, Ed
Russell, 77A
Russia, 26, Hb; 34, Ja
Russia, Prs. of, 19, Ga
Russian Central Asia, 83, Mc
Russian Empire, 62, Hb; 74, Gc
Russian Soviet Federal Socialist Rep., 84, Lb
Russian States, 24, Kb
Rustenburg, 81A, Cc
Rutba, 93, Ec
Ruthenian, 85, Gc
Rutherglen, 49A, Bc
Ruthin, 27, Ae
Ruthven, 37A, Cb
Ruthwell, 7B, Ba
Rutland, 27, Fd
Rutli, 29B, Cb
Rüttgen, 39B, Ca
Rutupiae (Richborough), 3A, He
Rwanda, 96D, Ee
Ryazan, 19, Fb; 88, Nc
Rye, 13, Gf; 27, Gf
Rye (Little Harbour), 45B, Db
Ryknield Way, 3A, Ed
Rymnik, 61, Ae
Ryswyk, 46A, Db
Ryukyu Is., 91, Fd
Rzeszow, 26, Fc
Rzhev, 61, Dc; 88, Mb

SAALE, R., 10, Dc; 39C, Bb
Saalfeld, 20, Jc; 39C, Bc
Saanen, 29B, Bb
Saar, R., 39B, Ca; 83A, Db
Saar Basin, 83A, Db
Saarbrücken, 10, Bd; 83A, Db
Saareguemines, 83A, Db
Saaremaa, 87, Ea
Saarlonis, 53, Gc; 76A, Db
Saarumon, 76A, Db
Saarwerden, 39B, Db
Saaz, 21, Kc
Saba. 43A, Fc
Sabah, 91, Ef
Sabancuy, 43A, Cc
Sabina, 32A, Ec
Sabina, bp., 22A
Sabine, 72, Bd
Sabine, R., 72, Bc
Sabine Cross Roads, 72, Bc
Sabinensis, 5B, Bb
Sabino, 45B, Eb
Sable, C., Florida, 70, Fe
Sable, C., Nova Scotia, 45A, Db
Sable L., 71, Jc
Sabrina Aest. (Severn), 3A, Ce
Sabugal, 63, Bb
Sachsenburg, 53, Kd
Sacile, 29A, Ec
Säckingen, 22, Db; 29B, Ba
Saco, 45B, Db
Saco, R., 45B, Db
Sacramento, California, 70, Bd
Sacramento, Uruguay, 42, Gf
Sacramento, R., 70, Bd
Sada, 6, Fd
Sadowa, 60B, Ec
Saffarids, King. of, 6B, Hb
Sagan, 31, Lc; 39, Lc
Saginaw B., 45A, Ab
Sagitta (Sidon), 18C, Ce
Sagona, 20, Hg
Sagres, 35, Jc
Saguenay, R., 45A, Ca
Sahagun, 22, Ac; 63, Ca
Sahara, 80A, Db
Saharanpur, 92, Db
Saigon, 90, Bc
Saigon-Cholon, 91, De
Sailors Creek, 72B, Ab
Saimatsi, 76B, Ca

St. Achebrannus, 13, Af
St. Aignan, 53, Dd
St. Albans, 27, Fe
St. Amand, 46A, Cd; 46B
St. Amand-Montrond, 38, Ee
St. Andrew I., 43A, Dc
St. Andrews, 14, Fc; 37, Cb
St. Andrews, bp., 14A, Cb; 36, Db
St. Angelo, Castle of, 5A
St. Anne, Church of, 18D
St. Anns, 43A, Ec
St. Antonin, 38, Df
St. Asaph, 27, Cc
St. Asaph, bp., 36, Ce
St. Augustine, 72, Dd
St. Austell, 48B, Ad
St. Avold, 76A, Db
St. Bartholomew, 43A, Fc
St. Bees, 36, Cc
St. Benedictus de Holme (St. Benedict's Abbey), 13, Hd
St. Bernard, Hospice of, 22, Db
St. Berrione (St. Buryan), 13, Af
St. Bertrand, 38, Dg
St. Blazey, 48B, Ad
St. Brieuc, 11, Bb
St. Carentochus (Crantock), 13, Af
St. Cast, 55A, Bd
St. Charles, 56, Ac
St. Charles, R., 56A
St. Christopher, 43B, Dc; 55B, De
St. Clair, 45A, Ab
St. Clair, L., 45A, Ab
St. Claude, 20, Fe
St. Croix, R., 45A, Da; 56, Fa
St. Cuthbertes-Lond, 13, Eb
St. David's, 27, Ae
St. David's, bp., 36, Ce
St. Denis, France, 22, Cb
St. Denis, Louisiana, 56, Bc
St. Dié, 22, Db; 83B, Ba
St. Dizier, 76A, Cb
St. Edmundi (Bury St. Edmunds), 13, Gd
St. Elias, C., 71A, Ca
St. Elias, Mt., 71B, Aa
St. Eustatius, 43A, Fc
St. Fargeau, 20, Ee
St. Flour, 20, Ef; 22, Cc
St. Francis, L., Quebec, 57C, Bb
St. Francis, L., St. Lawrence R., 57, Da
St. Francis, R., 71E, Bb
St. Francis de Sales Mission, 45A, Ca
St. Gall, 10, Ce; 29B, Da
St. Gallen, 29B, Da
St. Geneviève, 56, Ac
St. George (Lydda), 18C, Bg
St. George, Str. of, 18E
St. George's, 45A, Bd
St. Germain, 53, Dc; 84, Cc
St. Germain, C., 45A, Fa
St. Germans, 36, Bg
St. Germanus, 13, Bf
St. Giles, 27A
St. Gilles, Languedoc, 20, Fg
St. Gilles, Poitou, 53, Cd
St. Goar, 22, Da
St. Gotthard, 29A, Gb; 33C, Db
St. Gotthard Pass, 29B, Cb
St. Helena, 40, Je; 96C, Bf
St. Helena B., 81B, Ac
St. Helens, 55A, Cc
St. Hyacinthe, 57, Ea
St. Ignace Mission, 45A, Aa
St. Ives, Cornwall, 55A, Ac
St. Ives, Hunts, 13, Fd; 48A, Cc
St. Jacob, 30, Ge
St. James Church, Jerusalem, 18D
St. Jean, I. de, (Prince Edward I.), 45A, Ea
St. Jean d'Angely, 20, Cf
St. Jean de Luz, 63, Ea
St. Jean de Maurienne, 11, Gd
St. Jean Pied de Port, 30, Cg; 63, Ea
St. Jehan, I., 45A, Da
St. John, 45A, Da
St. John, Hospital of, 18D
St. John, I., 43A, Fc
St. John, L., 71, Gc
St. John, R., 45A, Da; 71E, Cc
St. John the Baptist, Church of, 18D
St. John's (San Juan), 56, Cd
St. John's, Newfoundland, 45A, Ga
St. Johns, Quebec, 56, Ea
St. John's R., 43A, Da
St. Joseph, 72, Bb
St. Jullian, B. de, 45A, Fa

St. Kitts, 43A, Fc
St. Lawrence, G. of, 45A, Ea
St. Lawrence I., 71A, Aa
St. Lawrence, R., 45A, Da; 57, Da
St. Lazaro Arch. (Philippines), 40, Qd
St. Lizier, 11, De
St. Lo, 22, Bb; 28C, Bb
St. Louis (Senegal), 81C, Aa
St. Louis, Missouri, 56, Ac; 57A, Ab
St. Louis, W. Africa, 80A, Bc; 96C, Ac
St. Loys, C., 45A, Ea
St. Lucia, 43A, Db
St. Lucia B., 81D, Bb
St. Lucia, I., 43A, Fc; 43C, Ec
St. Maixent, 22, Bd; 38, Ce
St. Malo, 20, Cd; 28C, Ab
St. Maria in Mt. Zion, 18D
St. Marie, 80A, Hf
St. Marks, 71F, Ca; 72, Dc
St. Martin, 43A, Fc
St. Martin, C., 81B, Ac
St. Martin, Church of, 18D
St. Mary Magdalen, Church of, 18D
St. Mary's (Santa Maria), 56, Cd
St. Mary's, Canada, 45A, Ba; 56, Db
St. Mary's, Maryland, 45B, Ad
St. Mary's Hospital, 18D
St. Maur, 30, Ed
St. Maurice, R., 57C, Aa
St. Michael (St. Michael's Mount), 13, Af
St. Michael, Alaska, 71A, Aa
St. Mihiel, 83A, Cb
St. Moritz, 29B, Db
St. Neots, 36, Fe
St. Neotus, 13, Bf
St. Omer, 22, Ca; 46A, Bd
St. Osyth, 36, Hf
St. Paul, France, 22, Cc; 53, Fe
St. Paul, Minnesota, 70, Ec
St. Pauls, 27A
St. Peter, Church of, Jerusalem, 18D
St. Peter's, Rome, 5A
St. Petersburg, 51, Gb; 61, Dc
St. Philippe, 56, Be
St. Pieranus (St. Piran), 13, Af
St. Pierre, 45A, Fa
St. Pierre, L., 57C, Aa
St. Pol, 46A, Bd
St. Pol, prov., 46A, Bd
St. Pol de Leon, 17, Cd
St. Pölten, 21, Ld
St. Probus (Probus), 13, Bf
St. Quentin, 11, Eb; 83A, Bb
St. Regis, 57, Da
St. Riquier, 17, Cd
St. Sauveur, 45A, Db
St. Seurin, 22, Bc
St. Sever, 22, Cc
St. Simon's I., 56, Cd
St. Sophia, 18E
St. Stephen's Gate, 18D
St. Symeon (Seleucia), 18C, Cb
St. Thomas, 43A, Fc
St. Thomas' Tomb, 35, Od
St. Trond, 22, Da; 46A, Ed
St. Urban, 29B, Ba
St. Vaast, 22, Ca; 28C, Bb
St. Valery en Caux, 55A, Bd
St. Valery sur Somme, 28C, Ca
St. Veit, 21, Le
St. Vincent, 80A, Ac
St. Vincent, C., 63, Ad
St. Vincent, I., 43A, Fc
Ste. Foy, 38, Df
Ste. Katherine, 45A, Ga
Saintes, 11, Cd; 30, Cf
Saintonge, 38, Cf
Saintonge, Co. of, 11, Cd
Saipan, 75, Ed
Sajits, King. of, 6B, Fa
Sakaka, 93, Ec
Sakaria, R., 86C, Ba
Sakas, 1, Ke
Sakhalin, 91, Ha
Saladin and the Ayubites, Empire of, 18A, Ee
Salado, R., N. Argentina, 68, Ce
Salado, R., S. Argentina, 68, Cf
Salamanca, 23C, Cb; 63, Cb
Salamis, 9, Je
Salawati, 52C, Db; 77, Eb
Salces, 23D, Ga; 53, Ef
Saldanha, 63, Ca
Saldanha B., 81B, Ac
Salem (Naumkeag), 45B, Db
Salem (Varkinskii), 45B, Bd
Salem, India, 59C, Ce
Salem, Massachusetts, 57, Fb
Salem, Oregon, 70, Bc

Salemi, 32C, De
Salerno (Salernum), 5, Ed
Salerno, D. of, 23A, Ec
Salerno, Pr. of, 21A, Cb
Salernum (Salerno), 5, Ed
Sallans, 8B, Ba
Salii, 2, Ce
Salinae (Droitwich), 3A, Dd
Salinesville, 72, Da
Salins, 20, Fe; 31A, Cd
Salisbury, England, 27, Ee
Salisbury, New Hampshire, 45B, Db
Salisbury, North Carolina, 57, Af
Salisbury, Rhodesia, 81A, Da
Salisbury, bp., 36, Ef
Salm, Alsace, 20, Gd
Salm, Luxemburg, 20, Fc
Salm, king., 65B, Aa
Salmon Falls, 45B, Db
Salo, 29A, Dc
Salobrena, 23C, Dd
Salom, 2A, Cb
Salona, Dalmatia, 23B, Fc
Salona, Greece, 19, Ce
Salonae, 2, Ge
Salonica, 78, De
Salonica, G. of, 86A, Db
Salonica, King. of, 19, Cd
Salsette I., 73, Bd
Salt Lake City, 70, Cc
Salt Lakes, 59B
Salta, 68, Ce
Saltillo, 43A, Bb
Salto, 68, Df
Saluda, R., 57D, Aa
Saluzzo, 32A, Bb
Saluzzo, Marq. of, 32A, Bb
Salvador, 43D, Dc
Salvador (Bahia), 68, Fd
Salvatierra, 28C, Ae
Salween, R., 25, Jd; 73, Gc
Salza, 20, Jc
Salzach, R., 29A, Eb
Salzburg, 10, Ee
Salzburg, eccl. prov., 22, Eb
Salzburg, Abp. of, 31, Ke
Salzwedel, 10, Db; 26, Dc
Samana, C., 43A, Fc
Samandar, 9, Md
Samanids, King. of, 6B, Ha
Samar, 75E, Cb
Samara, 61, Hd
Samarkand, 6, Hb; 25, Fc
Samarra, 6A, Cb; 9, Ld
Sambre, R., 46A, Cc
Samoa, 90, Fd
Samoa Is., 83, Ae
Samogitia, 26, Fb
Samos, I., 78, Ee
Samos, theme, 9, He
Samosata, 8, Kd
Samothrace, 78, Ee
Samsun, 19, Fd; 93, Da
San, R., 19, Cb
San Agostino, 5A
San Ambrosio, 68, Be
San Antonio, 70, Ee
San Antonio Bay, 44, Ef
San Antonio, C., 43A, Db
San Bernardino Str., 75E, Bb
San Blas, G. of, 43A, Ed
San Cesareo, 5A
San Christobal, 43A, Cc
San Clemente, 5A
San Cosmo y Damiano, 22, Ac
San Cristoval, 77, Kd
San Daniele, 32D, Ca
San Diego, 70, Cd
San Domingo, 43A, Fc
San Domingo, st., 43A, Ec
San Felipe, Chile, 68, Bf
San Felipe, Venezuela, 43A, Fc
San Felix, 68, Ae
San Fernando, Philippines, 75E, Ba
San Fernando, Venezuela, 68, Cb
San Francisco, 70, Bd
San Germano, 23B, Dd
San Geronimo, 43A, Ba
San Geronimo de Yuste, 22, Ac
San Gimignano, 32E, Db
San Giovanni, 29A, Cc
San Grisogono, 5A
San Ildefonso, 63, Db
San Jorge, G. de, 68, Cg
San José, 43A, Bd
San Juan (St. John's), 56, Cd
San Juan, Argentina, 68, Cf
San Juan, Mexico, 43A, Bb
San Juan, Porto Rico, 43A, Fc
San Juan de la Peña, 22, Bc
San Juan de los Remedios, 43A, Eb
San Juan de Nicaragua, 43A, Dc
San Juan de Ulloa, 43A, Cc
San Leopoldo, 68, De

San Lorenzo del Escorial, 22, Bc
San Lorenzo Fuori le Mura, 5A
San Lorenzo in Damaso, 5A
San Lorenzo in Lucina, 5A
San Lucas, Mexico, 43A, Bb
San Lucas, Spain, 23C, Bd
San Lucas, C., 43A, Ab
San Luis, Argentina, 42, Ge
San Luis, Brazil, 68, Cf
San Luis, Texas, 43A, Ca
San Luis de Caceres, 68, Dd
San Luis Potosi, 43A, Bb
San Marco, 21A, Dc; 22, Fd
San Marino, 32A, Ec
San Martin, Mexico, 43A, Bb
San Martin, Spain, 22, Cd
San Miguel de Piura, 41B, Bd
San Miniato, 32E, Bb
San Nicolas, 68, Cf
San Pablo, L., 40, Ce
San Pedro do Rio Grande (Rio Grande do Sul), 41B, Dg
San Pietro, 5A
San Prassede, 5A
San Quattro Coronati, 5A
San Rafael, 68, Cf
San Roque, 63A
San Salvador, 43C, Dc
San Salvador, I., 43A, Eb
San Salvador de Bahia, 41B, Fe
San Sebastian, Colombia, 43A, Ed
San Sebastian, Spain, 63, Ea
San Sepolcro, 32E, Cb
San Severina, 22, Fd
San Silvestro, 5A
San Sisto, 5A
San Stefano, Rome, 5A
San Stefano, Turkey, 78, Ge
San Susanna, 5A
San Thomé, 43B, Dd
San Vito, 32D, Cb; 86B, Cb
San Xavier, 43A, Ca
San Zoilo, 22, Bc
Sana, 6, Fd; 93, Ef
Sanandaj, 93, Fb
Sancerre, 17, Ge
Sand, R., 81A, Cb
Sandakan, 95, Ne
Sandal, 27, Ec
Sandalwood I. (Sumba), 52C, Bc
Sanday, 49A, Ca
Sandec, 31, Pd
Sandomir, 31, Pc
Sandusky, 71C, Bb
Sandwic (Sandwich), 13, He
Sandwich, England, 7B, Dc
Sandwich, Massachusetts, 45B, Dc
Sandwich, Michigan Terr., 71C, Bb
Sandwich Is., Antarctic Ocean, 69C
Sandwich Is., Pacific Ocean, 42, Bc
Sandy Hook, 57B
Sangarius, R., 19, Ed
Sangir Is., 52C, Ca
Sanguessa, 63, Ea
Sanquhar, 49A, Cc
Sansanne-Mango, 96B, Ca
Santa Agata, 5A
Santa Balbina, 5A
Santa Barbara, 43A, Bb
Santa Barbara Is., 42, Cc
Santa Catalina, 56, Cd
Santa Catarina, 68, Ee
Santa Catarina, st., 68, De
Santa Cecilia, 5A
Santa Croce, 5A
Santa Cruz, Argentina, 68, Ch
Santa Cruz, Bolivia, 68, Cd
Santa Cruz, Brazil, 41B, Fe
Santa Cruz, Canary Is., 55B, Jd
Santa Cruz, I., Pacific Ocean, 77, Ld
Santa Cruz, I., West Indies, 43A, Fc
Santa Elena B., 43D, Dc
Santa Fé, Argentina, 68, Cf
Santa Fé, Florida, 56, Cd
Santa Fé, New Mexico, 70, Dd
Santa Fé, Spain, 22, Bd
Santa Fé de Bogota, 41B, Bc
Santa Isabel, 68, Cc
Santa Lucia B., 80A, Gg
Santa Maria, 68, De
Santa Maria (St. Mary's), 56, Cd
Santa Maria in Trastevere, 5A
Santa Maria Maggiore, 5A
Santa Marta, 43A, Cc
Santa Maura, 50, Ef
Santa Prisca, 5A
Santa Rosa, 43A, Bb
Santa Sabina, 5A
Santander, 23C, Da; 63, Da

Santarem, Brazil, 68, Dc
Santarem, Portugal, 63, Ac
Santarem, W. Africa, 35, Kd
Santas Creus, 22, Cc
Santee, R., 45A, Bd; 57D, Bb
Santiago, Chile, 68, Bf
Santiago, San Domingo, 43A, Ec
Santiago, Spain, 63, Aa
Santiago, ecci prov., 22, Ac
Santiago de Compostella, 8, Ac; 22, Ac; 23D, Aa
Santiago de Cuba, 43A, Ec
Santorin, 78, Eg
Santos, 68, Ee
Sao Borja, 68, De
Sao Francisco, 68, Ee
Sao Francisco, R., 68, Ec
Sao José de Rio Negro, 41B, Dd
Sao Luis (Maranhao), 68, Ec
Sao Manuel, 68, Dc
Sao Paulo, 68, Ee
Sao Paulo, st., 68, Ee
Sao Tomé, 80A, Dd
São Vicente, Brazil, 41B, Ef
São Vicente, Portugal, 22, Ad
Saône, R., 11, Fc; 20, Fe
Sapporo, 91, Hb
Saragossa, 23C, Eb; 63, Eb
Saragossa, eccl. prov., 22, Cc
Sarai, 19, Hc; 25, Db; 61, Ge
Sarajevo, 39, Ng; 78, Bb
Saranac, R., 57, Da
Sarandi, 68, Df
Sarangani B., 75E, Cc
Saratoga, 57, Eb
Saratov, 61, Gd
Sarawak, 91, Ef
Sardes, 9, He
Sardica, 4B, Hc; 8, Gc
Sardinia, 5, Bd
Sardinia, King. of, 32B, Ad
Sardis, 18A, Dd
Sarepta, 18C, Ce
Sargans, 29B, Da
Sargans, canton, 29B, Db
Sari Bair, 86D
Sarikamish, 86C, Da
Sarisberie (Salisbury), 13, Ee
Sark, 17, Dd
Sarkel, 9, Kc
Sarlat, 20, Df
Sarmatia, 1, Fb
Sarnem, 29B, Cb
Sarnthal Alps, 86B, Ba
Saros, G. of, 86D
Saros-Patak, 33C, Cb
Sarrebourg, 83B, Ba
Sarthe, R., 11, Cc
Sarukham, 33A, Cc
Sarum, 7A, Cb
Sarzana, 22, Dc; 32E, Aa
Saskatchewan, 70, Db
Sassbach, 29A, Ca
Satara, 73, Bd
Satpura Mts., 73, Cc
Saucourt, 9, Cb
Saudi Arabia, 93, Ed; 96D, Gb
Sauer, R., 83A, Cb
Saugerties, 56, Eb
Saugor, 73, Cc
Sault Ste. Marie, 45A, Aa
Saumur, 11, Cc
Saumurois, 53, Cd
Saurashtra, I, Ke
Sauveterre, 38, Cg
Savage (Niue) I., 75, Ge
Savaii, 75B, Aa
Savana, 22, Ec
Savannah (Fort Prince George), 56, Cd
Savannah, Georgia, 56, Cd; 72, Dc
Savannah, Tenn., 72, Cb
Savannah, R., 56, Cd; 72, Dc
Save, R., 22, Fb; 78, Bc
Savona, 5, Bb
Savoy, 28C, Ed; 32A, Ab
Savoy, Co. of, 11, Fd; 20, Ff
Savoy, D. of, 32A, Bb
Sawantwari, 73, Bd
Sawley, 36, Dd
Saxe-Weimar, 51, Cc
Saxon States, 47, Eb
Saxones, 2, Ec
Saxonia, 12, Gc
Saxons, 4A, Ba; 7A, Fa
Saxony, Duchies of, 53, Jb
Saxony, Elec. of, 31, Kc
Say, 80A, Dc
Saybrook, 45B, Cc
Sayda, 39C, Dc
Sayn, 20, Gc
Sayn, Co. of, 30, Gc
Scalea, 21A, Cc
Scandalion, 18C, Ce
Scandia, 2, Fa
Scandinavia, 69B
Scania, 26, Db; 47, Ea
Scapa Flow, 55B, Ka; 84, Ba

Scarboro, 57, Fb
Scarborough, 3A, Fb; 27, Fb
Scardonia, 22, Fc
Scarpanto, 18B, Dc
Sceptesberie (Shaftsbury), 13, De
Schaffhausen, 29B, Ca; 65A, Ab
Schaffhausen, canton, 29B, Ca
Schärding, 21, Kd
Schässburg, 19, Dd
Schauenburg, 20, Hb
Schaumberg, 21, Kd
Scheidungen, 8B, Da
Schelde, R., 46A, Cd
Schemnitz, 31, Nd
Schenectady, 57, Eb
Schenk, 38, Gc
Schesel, 8, Ea
Schio, 86B, Bb
Schirmeck, 39B, Db
Schlei, R., 65F, Ba
Schleiz, 39C, Bc
Schleswig, 26, Cc; 65F, Aa
Schleswig, D., 30, Ha; 65F, Aa
Schleswig, M. of, 10, Ca
Schlettstadt, 20, Gd; 76A, Db
Schleusingen, 39C, Ac
Schmalkalden, 34, Eb
Schmölln, 39C, Cc
Schober Pass, 29A, Fb
Schönhausen, 60B, Cb
Schoodic Lakes, 71E, Bc
Schoonhoven, 46A, Dc
Schouwen, 46A, Cc
Schuylkill, R., 45B, Bc; 57, Dc
Schwarzburg, 39C, Ab
Schwarzburg, Pr., 38, Jc, 39C, Bc
Schwarzenberg, 39C, Cc
Schwarzenburg, 29B, Bb
Schwechat, 33C, Db
Schwedt, 39, Lb
Schweidnitz, 31, Mc; 39, Mc
Schweinfurt, 30, Jc; 38, Jc
Schwerin, 10, Db; 20, Jb
Schwerin, D., 38, Jb
Schwiebus, 39, Lb
Schwyz, 29B, Ca
Schwyz, canton, 29B, Ca
Scilly Is., 55B, Kb
Sciptone (Skipton), 18, Dc
Scireburne (Sherborne), 13, Df
Scireburne (Sherburn), 13, Ec
Sciropesberie (Shrewsbury), 13, Dd
Sciropescire (Shropshire), 13, Dd
Scituate, 45B, Db
Scone, 14, Ec
Scopia, 16, Gd
Scotl, 2, Bc
Scotland, 12, Cb; 34, Ba
Scots, 15, Bb
Scott, 28B, Cb
Scutari, 78, Ge; 86C, Aa
Scutari (Skodra), 78, Bd
Scyros, 78, Ef
Scythia, 1, Kb
Seaford, 27, Gf
Seattle, 70, Bc
Sebago L., 45B, Db
Sebaste, 18C, Cf
Sebastea, 8, Kd; 9, Ke
Sebenico, 31, Lg; 32A, Fc
Secessionville, 72, Dc
Seckau, 22, Eb
Second Cataract, 80B, Ac
Sedalia, 72, Bb
Sedan, 29A, Aa; 88, Fd
Sedberuie (Sadbe ge), 13, Eb
Sedd el Bahr, 86D
Sedgemoor, 48B, Bd
Sées, 22, Cb
Segauli, 73, Eb
Segeberg, 22, Ea; 38, Jb
Segedunum (Wallsend), 3C
Segelocum (Littleborough), 3A, Fc
Segni, 22A
Segontium (Caernarvon), 3A, Bc
Segorbe, 22, Bd
Ségou, 96B, Ba
Segovia, 23D, Cb; 63, Cb
Segre, R., 20, Dd
Segu, 80A, Cc
Seilan (Ceylon), 25, Hf
Seine, R., 11, Db, 76A, Cb
Seistan (Sijistan), 6, Hb; 61B, Bb
Seisyllwg, 7C, Ab
Sekondi Takoradi, 96B, Bb
Selby, 36, Ed; 48A, Cc
Selenga, R., 91, Db
Seleucia, 8, Jd; 9, Ke
Seleucia (St. Symeon), 18C, Cb
Selgovae, 3A, Ca
Seljuk Empire, 16, Le
Seljuk Empire of Rum or Iconium, 18B, Ec

Seljuk Kingdom of Rum or Iconium, 19, Fe
Seljuk Turks, 24, Jf
Selkirk, Canada, 70, Eb
Selkirk, Scotland, 14, Fd
Selkirk, co., 37A, Cc
Selma, 72, Cc
Selsey, 7A, Cb; 36A
Selsey, diocese, 36A
Selwood, 7B, Bc
Selymbria, 19, Dd
Selz, 39B, Eb
Semarang, 91, Eg
Semendria, 78, Cc
Semeni, R., 86A, Ab
Semipalatinsk, 91, Ba
Semlin, 78, Cc
Semmering Pass, 29A, Fb
Semoy, R., 46A, Ee
Sempach, 29B, Ca
Sempringham, 36, Fe
Semur, 11, Fc; 30, Fe
Sendai, 91, Hc
Senecas, 45A, Bb
Seneffe, 46A, Dd
Senegal (St. Louis), 81C, Aa
Senegal, rep., 96, Ac
Senegal, terr., 81C, Bb
Senegal, R., 81C, Ba
Senez, 22, Ec
Senigallia, 39, Kg
Senlis, 11, Eb; 83A, Bb
Sennar, 80B, Ae
Senne, R., 46B
Senogalliae, 5B, Bb
Sens, 11, Eb; 17, Gd
Sens, eccl. prov., 22, Cb
Seoul, 91, Fc
Sept Iles, 45A, Da
Septimania, 4A, Cc; 8, Cc
Sequana, R., 2, Dd
Serai, 24, Md
Serampore, 59B
Serbia, 78, Cd
Serbia, King. of, 18B, Bb
Serbs, 9, Fd
Serdica, 2, He; 78A
Seres, 78, De; 86A, Ea
Sereth, R., 50, Fd; 78, Fb
Sergipe, 68, Fd
Seringapatam, 73, Ce
Seriphos, 78, Eg
Serowe, 96C, Eg
Serpa, 23D, Bd
Serpent's Mouth, 43B, Dc
Serres, 38, Ff
Serrey, 60A, Ja
Servia, 9, Fd; 78, De
Servian Princes, 24, Ge
Sesia, R., 29A, Cc
Sessa, 22, Ec
Seteia Aest., 3A., Cc
Setif, 8, Dd
Seton, clan, 28B, Ba; 37A, Cb
Setubal, 63, Ac
Sevastopol, 51, Ge
Seven Pines, 72B, Bb
Severn, R., Britain, 36, De
Severn, R., Canada, 70, Eb
Severnaya Zemlya, 69B
Severski, 19, Eb
Severyans, 9, Jb
Seville, 23C, Cd; 63, Bd
Seville, eccl. prov., 22, Ad
Sèvres, 84, Cc
Seward, 71A, Cb
Seychelles, 69A, Me; 94, Rf
Sfax, 89, Hg
Shackleton, 69C
Shaftesbury, 27, Df
Shahjahanpur, 73, Db
Sha-ho, R., 76B, Ba
Shan State, 92, Hc
Shanghai, 91, Fc
Shantgu, 25, Lb
Shannon, R., 15, Cc; 37B, Cc
Shap, 36, Dc; 49A, Cc
Shaqra, 93, Fd
Shari, R., 80A, Ed
Sharks B., 77, Af
Shashi, 74, Ke
Shatt el Hai, R., 86C, Dc
Shawnees, 45B, Cd; 56, Bc
Sheelin, L., 15, Dc
Sheen, 36, Ff
Sheerness, 54, Cb
Sheffield, 27, Ec; 48A, Cc
Shelburne, 71, Hc
Shenandoah, R., 57, Bd; 72B, Aa
Shendi, 80B, Ad
Shenyang (Mukden), 91, Fb
Sheppey, 7C, Dc
Sherborne, 27, Df; 36, Df
Sherborne, diocese, 36A
Sherbro I., 81C, Bc
Sherbrook, 57C, Bb
Sherbrooke, 71, Gc
Sherburn, 48B, Cc
Sheriffmuir, 37A, Cb
Sherman's March, 72, Dc

Sherwood, 7B, Cb
Sherwood Forest, 3A, Ec
Shetland Is., 12, Da; 34, Ba
Shibam, 93, Ff
Shiel, L., 49A, Bb
Shiliho, 76B, Ba
Shillong, 92, Gb
Shiloh, 72, Cb
Shipka Pass, 78, Ed
Shiraz, 6, Gc; 93, Gd
Shirley, 45B, Ae
Shiz, 6A, Da
Shoeburyness, 7C, Dc
Sholanghur, 59A, Ce
Sholapur, 73, Cd
Shoreditch, 27A
Shoreham, England, 27, Ff
Shoreham, Vermont, 57, Eb
Shoshong, 81A, Cb
Shreveport, 70, Ed; 72, Bc
Shrewsbury, England, 27, Dd
Shrewsbury, New Jersey, 45B, Bc
Shropshire, 27, Dd; 28A, Db
Shumla, 62, Hd; 78, Fd
Shuqra, 93, Fg
Shushan (Susa), 6A, Db
Siak, 75A, Ad
Sialkot, 73, Ba
Siam (Thailand), 74, Jg; 90, Bc
Siam, G. of, 91, De
Sian, 91, Dc
Sianfu, 74, Je
Siberia, 74, Jb; 83, Pa
Siberut, 91, Cg
Sibin (Hermannstadt), 19, Cc
Sibir, 25, Fa; 40, Na
Sibir, Khanate of, 25, Ga
Sibton, 36, He
Sicilia, 2, Ff
Sicily, 5, Df
Sicily, Co. of, 16, Ee
Sicily, King. of, 23B, Ed
Side, 19, Ee
Sidi Barrani, 93, Bc
Sidlaw Hills, 14, Ec
Sidnacester, 36A
Sidnacester, diocese, 36A
Sidon (Sagitta), 18C, Ce
Siegburg, 20, Gc
Siegen, 53, Hb; 83A, Ea
Siena, 5, Cc
Siena, Rep. of, 32A, Dc
Sieradz, 31, Nc
Sierra Leone, 81C, Bc
Sierra Madre, 43A, Bb
Siffin, 6A, Cc
Sigmaringen, 10, Cd; 60B, Cd
Sigüenza, 22, Cc
Siguiri, 96B, Ba
Sijistan (Seistan), 6, Hb
Sikhs, 59C, Ba
Si-Kiang, R., 91, Ed
Sikkim, 73, Eb; 92, Fb
Sikri, 52A, Bb
Silesia, 33C, Db
Silesia, D. of, 21, Mc
Silistra, 78, Fc
Silistria, 19, Dd
Sillery, 45A, Ca
Silos, 22, Cc
Silures, 3A, Ce
Silves, 22, Ad
Simancas, 23C, Cb
Simbach, 29A, Ea
Simbirsk, 61, Gd
Simcoe, L., 45A, Bb
Simeulve, 91, Cf
Simla, 73, Ca
Simnitza, 78, Ed
Simonstown, 81B, Ac
Simplon Pass, 29B, Cb
Sinai, 6A, Ac
Sinai Peninsula, 18A, Ed; 80B, Ab
Sinaloa, 43A, Bb
Sinclair, 37A, Ca
Sind, 1, Je; 73, Ab
Sindhia, 73, Cc
Singapore, 75A, Bb; 91, Df
Singapore, Str. of, 75A, Bb
Singara, 2, Mf
Singidunum, 4A, Gc
Siniglaglia, 8A, Dc; 32A, Eb
Sinkailin Pass, 76B, Ba
Sinkailin Pass, 76B, Ca
Sinkiang-Uigur, 91, Bc
Sinmintun, 76B, Ba
Sinope, 19, Fd; 79, Gb
Sinsheim, 29A, Ca
Sinus Arabicus, 1, Fe
Sinus Aualites, 1, Gf
Sinus Oxianus, 1, Hc
Sinus Persicus, 1, He
Sion, 11, Gc
Sion (Sitten), 29B, Bb
Siponto, 23B, Ed
Sirhind, 52A, Ba; 73, Ca
Sirji Arjengaon, 73, Cc
Sirmium, 2, Ge; 4A, Fc
Sis, 18C, Ca; 19, Fe
Siscia, 2, Gd

Sissek, 31, Mf; 33A, Aa
Sissonne, 83A, Bb
Sisteron, 22, Dc; 30, Ff
Sistova, 78, Ed
Sita, 19, Fa
Sitabaldi, 73, Cc
Sitcha, 61, De
Sitka, 71B, Cb
Sitka (New Archangel), 71A, Db
Sitten (Sion), 29B, Bb
Sitvatorok, 33C, Db
Siuyen, 76B, Ba
Sivas, 79, Gc
Siwah, 80A, Fb; 93, Bd
Siward, 12, Dc
Siwas, 16, Ke; 18A, Fb
Six Nations, 57, Cb
Sixth Cataract, 80B, Ad
Skagerrak, 12, Gb; 84, Da
Skagway, 71B, Cb
Skara, 26, Db
Skaw, The, 12, Gb
Skeena, R., 70, Bb
Skelleftea, 26, Fa
Skelton, 27, Fb
Skenesboro, 57, Eb
Skenfrith, 28A, Dc
Skeninge, 26, Db
Skhumbi, R., 78, Be
Skibbereen, 49B, Be
Skipsea, 13, Fc
Skipton, 27, Dc
Skiringssal, 12, Gb
Skodra (Scutari), 78, Bd
Skog, 50, Da
Skopje (Uskub), 78, Cd
Skreen, 15, Ec
Skumbi, R., 86A, Aa
Skye, 14, Bb
Slachter's Nek, 81A, Cd
Slane, 49B, Ec
Slaney, R., 15, Ed; 37B, Ed
Slave Coast, 81C, Ec
Slavinia, 21B, Cb
Slavinia, D. of, 21, Lb
Slavonia, 39, Mf
Slavonic Peoples, 8A, Da
Slavs, 4A, Hb; 8, Ha
Sleat, 14, Cb
Sleat, Sd. of, 14, Cb
Slieve Bloom, 15, Dc
Slieve League, 15, Cb
Sligo, 37B, Cb; 49B, Cb
Sligo, co., 37C; 49B, Cb
Slivnitza, 78, Dd
Slovak, 85, Fc
Slovakia, 87, Ec
Slovenes, 9, Fc
Sluys, 28C, Da; 46A, Cc
Slyne Hd., 49B, Ac
Smaland, 26, Db
Small Saxon States, 65C, Ba
Smerwick, 49B, Ad
Smith Sd., 42, Ga; 69B
Smithfield, 57, Ce
Smithland, 72, Cb
Smolensk, 19, Eb; 26, Hc
Smolensk, Pr., 19, Ea
Smyrna, 78, Ff
Snake, R., 44, Cd; 70, Cc
Snake Hill, 71D
Sneeuw Mts., 77, Fb
Snotingeham (Nottingham), 13, Ed
Snotinghamscire (Notting-hamshire), 13, Fc
Snowdon, 27, Cc
Soa Pan, 81A, Cb
Soana, 23B, Cc
Sobral, 63B
Sobraon, 73, Ba
Sobrarbe, 23C, Ea
Society Is., 75, He
Socorro, 70, Dd
Socotra, 94, Re; 96A, Ca
Söderhamn, 26, Ea
Söderköping, 34, Fa; 50, Db
Södermanland, 26, Eb
Sodor and Man, bp., 36, Bc
Soest, 20, Hc
Sofala, 40, Le; 81A, Db
Sofia, 78, Dd
Sogdiana, 1, Jc; 6, Ha
Sognefjord, 12, Fa
Sohag, 93, Cd
Soignes, Forest of, 46B
Soignies, 46B
Soissons, 11, Eb; 83A, Eb
Sokol, 78, Bc
Sokoto, 96B, Cb
Sokotra, 41A, Cc; 83, Md
Solano, 75E, Ba
Soldaia, 19, Ed
Soldin, 21, Lb
Sole Bay, 55A, Db
Soleure (Solothurn), 29B, Ba
Solferino, 29A, Dc; 32C, Cb
Solikamsk, 61, Jc
Solms, 30, Hc
Solomon Is., 77, Kc; 90, Dd

Solothurn (Soleure), 29B, Ba
Solothurn, canton, 29B, Ba
Solsona, 22, Cc
Solway Firth, 14, Ee
Solway Moss, 37A, Cc
Somali Rep., 96D, Gd
Somalia, 96A, Bb
Somberete, 43A, Bb
Somers Is. (Bermudas), 43A, Fa
Somerset, 27, De
Somerset East, 81B, Cc
Somerton, 7B, Bc
Somme, R., 11, Eb; 83A, Bb
Somnath, 52A, Ab; 25, Gd
Somosierra, 63, Db
Son, R., 73, Dc
Sonchön, 76B, Db
Soncino, 32D, Ab
Sonderburg, 65F, Aa
Sondershausen, 39C, Ab
Sondre Stromfjord, 94, Cb
Sondrio, 29B, Bb
Song Empire (Mangi), 25, Kd
Sonora, 43A, Ab
Sonora, R., 43A, Ab
Soor, 60A, Ec
Sora, 5B, Bc
Sorauren, 63, Ea
Sorbs, 8, Ea
Sorel, 57C, Aa
Soria, 23C, Db; 63, Db
Sorrento, 5, Ed
Squillace, 5, Fe
Sorviodunum (Salisbury), 3A, Ee
Soule. 17, Eg; 30, Cg
Sources, Mont Aux, 81D, Ab
South (Middle) I. (New Munster), 77A
South Africa, Rep. of, 96D, Eh
South Africa, Union of, 80A Fg
South African Republic, 81B, Ca
South Anna, R., 72B, Bb
South Atlantic Ocean, 94, Af
South Australia, 77, Eg
South Beveland, 46A, Cc
South Carolina, 57D, Ab
South China Sea, 91, Ef
South Dakota, 70, Dc
South Downs, 27, Ff
South Esk, R., 14, Fc
South Georgia, 69C
South Ice, 69C
South Kanara, 52A, Bc
South Konkan, 73, Bd
South Korea, 91, Fc
South Manchurian Railway, 74, Ld
South Molton, 27, Cf
South Orkney Is., 69C
South Pacific Ocean, 75, He
South Pass, 44, Dd
South Pole, 69C
South Potomac, R., 57, Bd
South Prussia, 60A, Fb
South Ronaldsay, 49A, Ca
South Saskatchewan, R., 70, Db
South Saxons, 7A, Cb
South Sea, 40, Cd
South Shetland Is., 69C
South Shields, 3C
South Uist, 14, Ab
South Vietnam, 91, De
South West Africa, 96C, Dg
South Yemen, 93, Ff
Southampton, England, 27, Ef
Southampton, Long I., 45B, Cc
Southampton I., 70, Fa
Southern Alps, N.Z., 77, Mj
Southern Hiung-nu, 1, Nc
Southern Nigeria, 81C, Cc
Southern Ocean, 69C
Southern Rhodesia, 80A, Ff
Southern Slavs, 8C, Cb
Southland, 77A
Southold, 45B, Cc
Southwark, 27, Fe; 27A
Southwell, 36, Fd; 48B, Cc
Southwold, 55A, Db
Souvigny, 22, Jb
Sovietskaya, 69C
Sozopolis, 18A, Eb
Sozusa, 4B, Ge
Spa, 46A, Ed
Spain, 34, Bd; 63, Db
Spalato, 5, Fc; 78, Ad
Spalding, 27, Fd
Spallinge (Spalding), 13, Fd
Spandau, 60A, Db
Spanish Fort, 72, Cc
Spanish Guinea, 80A, Dd
Spanish Main, 43A, Ec
Spanish March, 8, Cc
Spanish Morocco, 96C, Ca
Spanish Netherlands, 38, Fc
Spanish Sahara, 96D, Ab
Spanish Town, 43A, Ec
Sparta, 78, Dg
Spartanburg, 72, Dc

Spartel, C., 62, Ae; 63A
Spectacle I., 56B
Spencer G., 77, Fh
Sperrin Mts., 15, Db
Spey, R., 14, Eb
Speyer, 29A, Ca; 83A, Eb
Speyer (Spires), 20, Hd
Spezia, 32A, Cb
Spezzia, 78, Dg
Spichern, 76A, Db
Spilimberg, 86B, Ca
Spinalonga, 79, Ec
Spinis (Speen), 3A, Ee
Spion Kop, 81D, Ab
Spires (Speyer), 20, Hd
Spithead, 55A, Cc
Spitzbergen, 42, Ka; 74, Aa
Spitzbergen Sea, 74, Ba
Splügen Pass, 29B, Db
Spoleto (Spoletium), 5, Dc
Spoleto, D. of, 5, Dc; 21, Kg
Sponheim, 20, Gd
Sporades, 78, Df
Spotsylvania, 72B, Ba
Spree, R., 10, Eb
Springbokfontein, 81B, Ab
Springfield, Illinois, 72, Cb
Springfield, Massachusetts, 45B, Cb
Springfield, Missouri, 72, Bb
Spurn Hd., 55A, Db
Srinagar, 25, Gc; 73, Ca
Srivijaya, 25, Jf
Staaten Land, 42, Sf
Stade, 20, Hb
Stadford (Stafford), 13, Dd
Stadfordscire (Staffordshire), 13, Dd
Stadtlohn, 38, Gb
Staete Land, 42B
Staffarda, 29A, Bc; 50, Be
Stafford, 27, Dd
Stafford, co., 27, Dd
Stagno, 22, Fc
Stalingrad, 88, Od
Stalino, 88, Nd
Stamford, Connecticut, 45B, Cc
Stamford, England, 27, Fd
Stamford Bridge, 12, Dc
Standerton, 81A, Cc
Stanes (Staines), 13, Fe
Stanford (Stamford), 13, Fd
Stanfordbrycge (Stamford Bridge), 13, Fb
Stångebro, 26, Eb
Stanislau, 84, Gc
Stanleyville, 80A, Fd
Stantune (Long Stanton), 13, Dd
Stanwix, 3C
Stanz, 29B, Cb
Stara Zagora, 78, Ed
Staraya Russa, 61, Dc
Starbuck I., 75, He
Stargard, 21, Lb; 31, Kb
Starodub, 19, Ga; 61, Dd
Staten I., 45B, Bc; 57B
Stau (Stow), 13, Fc
Staufen, 10, Cd
Staunton, 56, Dc
Staunton, R., 57, Be
Stavanger, 12, Fb; 47, Da
Stavelot, 22, Da; 46A, Ed
Staveren, 26, Cc
Stavropol, Astrakhan, 61, Fe
Stavropol, Kazan, 61, Gd
Stavros, 86A, Eb
Stavuchanak, 61, Ce
Stayninges (Steyning), 13, Ff
Steelpoort, 81A, Db
Steenkerque, 46A, Dd
Steenwyk, 46A, Fb
Steier, 21, Ld
Steinamanger, 21, Me
Steinau, 39, Mc
Stella Land, 81A, Bc
Stellenbosch, 81B, Ac
Stellenbosch, dist., 81B, Ac
Stelvio Pass, 29B, Eb
Stenay, 38, Fd
Stendal, 20, Jb
Stephen Dushan, Emp. of, 24, Ge
Stephen's Fort (Charleston), 57, Eb
Sternberg, 21, Lb
Stettin, 31, Lb; 39, Cb
Stewart, 28B, Ab; 37A, Bb
Stewart I. (New Leinster), 77A
Stikine, R., 71B, Db
Stiklestad, 12, Ga
Stillwater, 57, Eb
Stirling, 14, Ec; 37A, Cb
Stirling, co., 37A, Bb; 49A, Bb
Stockach, 29A, Cb
Stockholm, 26, Eb
Stoke Courcy, 27, Ce
Stolbova, 47, Ja; 50, Gb
Stollhofen, 29A, Ba
Stolp, 21, La

Stolpen, 39C, Eb
Stonehaven, 49A, Cb
Stonington, 45B, Dc
Stony Pt., 57, Dc
Storkow, 31, Kb
Storkyro, 50, Ea
Storm B., 77, Hj
Stormberg, 81B, Cb
Stornoway, 49A, Aa
Stoss Pass, 29B, Da
Stour, R., 27, Ge
Strabane, 49B, Db
Stradella, 29A, Cc
Stralsund, 26, Dc; 31B, Ca
Strand, 27A
Strängnäs, 26, Eb
Stranraer, 49A, Bc
Strasbourg, 7A, Eb; 83B, Ba
Strassburg, 10, Cd
Strata Florida, 36, Ce
Strata Marcella, 36, Ce
Stratford, 45B, Cc
Strath Earn, 14, Ec
Strath Spey, 14, Eb
Strathaven, 28B, Ab
Strathclyde, 14, Ed; 36A
Strathfillan, 49A, Bb
Strathmore, 14, Ec
Strathnaver, 14, Da
Stratton, 48A, Ad
Straubing, 39, Kd
Strelitz, 60B, Db; 65B, Ba
Striguil, 13, De; 28A, Dc
Stromness, 49A, Ca
Stronsay, 49A, Ca
Strumna, R., 78, De; 86A, Ea
Strumnitza, 78, De
Strymon, 9, Gd
Stuart Town (Port Royal), 45A, Ad
Stuhlweissenburg, 33C, Db
Stuhm, 39, Nb
Stuhmsdorf, 50, Dc
Stumitza, 86A, Da
Sturgeon L., 45A, Bb
Stuttgart, 29A, Ca
Styria, 10, Fe
Styria, D. of, 21, Le
Styrian Alps, 29A, Fb
Suakin, 80B, Bd
Suana, 5B, Ab
Suck, R., 15, Cc
Sucre, 68, Cd
Suda Bay, 79, Dc
Sudan, reg., 81C, Db
Sudan, rep., 96D, Ec
Sudberie (Sudbury), 13, Gd
Sudbury, Canada, 70, Fc
Sudetes, 60A, Fc
Sudfulc (Suffolk), 13, Hd
Sudras, 59D
Sudreys, 12, Cb; 14, Bc
Sudrie (Surrey), 13, Fe
Sudsexe (Sussex), 13, Ff
Sud-Treding (South Riding), 13, Gc
Sudwelle (Southwell), 13, Ec
Sudwerca (Southwark), 13, Fe
Suevi, 2, Ed; 4A, Ac
Suez, 80B, Ah
Suez Canal, 80B, Aa
Suffolk, Virginia, 57, Ce
Suffolk, co., 27, Hd
Sugar Hill, 57, Eb
Suir, R., 15, Dd; 37B, Dd
Sukhumi, 79, Hb
Sukkur, 92, Bb
Sula Is., 52C, Bb
Sula Sea, 75E, Bc
Sulaiman Mts., 73, Aa
Sulaimaniya, 93, Fb
Sulawesi (Celebes), 91, Eg
Sulina, 78, Gc
Sullana, 68, Ac
Sullivan, 15, Be
Sully, 38, Ee
Sulzbach, 21, Jd
Sumatra (Java Minor), 35, Oe
Sumatra, 35, Od
Sumatra, I., 91, Dg
Sumba, 91, Fg
Sumba (Sandelwood I.), 52C, Bc
Sumbawa, 91, Eg
Sumorsete (Somerset), 13, Ce
Sunart, 14, Cc
Sunbury, 56, Cd
Sunda Sea, 91, Fg
Sundarbans, 59B, 73, Ec
Sunday, R., 81D, Bb
Sundgau, 30, Ge; 39B, Dc
Superior, L., 56, Ba; 70, Fc
Supplingenburg, 20, Jb
Sur (Tyre), 18C, Cc
Surabaja, 91, Eg
Surat, 73, Bc
Surinam, 41B, Dc; 42, Gd; 94, Cc
Surrey, 7A, Cb; 27, Fe
Susa, Italy, 5, Ab
Susa, N. Africa, 6, Cb; 24, Ef

Susa (Shushan), 1, Gd; 6A, Db
Susquehanna, R., 45A, Bb; 57, Db
Sussex, 27, Ff
Sutherland, 14, Da
Sutherland Berg, 81D, Ab
Sutlej, R., 73, Da
Sutri, 21, Kg; 23B, Dc
Sutrium, 5, Dc
Suva, 75, Fe; 75C, Bb
Suvla B., 86D
Suwanee, 71F, Ca
Suwanee, R., 71F, Ca
Suzdal, 19, Ga
Suzdal, dist., 19, Ga
Suzzara, 29A, Dc
Svalbard, 94, Rb
Sveaborg, 51, Fa
Svendborg, 26, Db
Sverdlovsk, 74, Ec; 88, Sb
Sverdrup Is., 44, Da
Swaanendael, 45B, Bd
Swabia, 10, Ce; 20, He
Swabian Jura, 10, Cd
Swakopmund, 80A, Eg
Swale, R., 12, Dc
Swan River Colony, 77, Bh
Swanage, 7C, Cc
Swansea, Rhode I., 45B, Dc
Swansea, Wales, 27, Ce; 28A, Bc
Swart Berg, 81B, Bc
Swat, R., 73, Ba
Swatow, 74, Kf; 90, Bb
Swaziland, 80A, Gg; 81A, Dc
Sweden, 26, Ea; 47, Fa; 82, Ea
Sweden and Norway, 64, Ea
Swedish Pomerania, 51, Cc
Sweetheart Abbey, 36, Cc
Swellendam, 81B, Bc
Swellendam, dist., 81B, Bc
Sweyn, 12, Bd
Swilly L., 15, Da
Swiss Confederation, The, 29B; 30, He
Switzerland, 47, Dc; 54, Db
Sycamore Shoals, 57A, Cb
Sydney (Port Jackson), 77, Ih
Sylt, 65F, Aa
Syr Darya, R., 25, Fb; 61B, Ba
Syracusae, 2, Gf
Syracuse (Syracusa), 5, Ef
Syracuse, New York, 57, Cb; 67B, Ca
Syria, 1, Fd; 6A, Bb; 79, Gc
Syriam, 40, Cl
Syrian Desert, 86C, Cc
Syrtis Major, 2, Fg
Syrtis Minor, 2, Gg
Szabacs, 33C, Dc
Szathmar, 33C, Eb
Szczelankemen, 33C, Eb
Szczebrzeszyn, 26, Fc
Szczekociny, 51, Ec
Szczecin, 89, Hc
Sze Chow, 1, Od
Szeged, 87, Ec
Szegedin, 33C, Eb; 39, Pe
Sziget, 33C, Db

TABARISTAN, 6, Gb
Tabasco, 43A, Cc
Tabatinga, 68, Cc
Table B., 81A, Ad
Taboga I., 43A, Ed
Tabor, 31, Ld; 33C, Cb
Tabora, 80A, Ge
Tabriz, 6, Fb; 19, He; 79, Jc
Tacloban, 75E, Bb
Tacna, Chile, 68, Bd
Tacna, Peru, 68, Cd
Tacuba, 43A, Cc
Tacutu, R., 68B, Bb
Tadcaster, 48A, Cc
Tadkin, R., 57, Ae
Tadmor, 6A, Bb; 9, Kf
Tadoussac, 45A, Da; 71, Hc
Tafosoho, 81A, Db
Taganrog, 61, Ee
Taginae, 5, Dc
Tagliacozzo, 21, Kg
Tagliamento, R., 29A, Ec
Tagus, R., 23C, Cc; 63, Bc
Tahirids, King. of, 6B, Ga
Tahiti, 75, He
Tai Yuan, 1, Od
Taif, 6, Fc; 93, Be
Taillebourg, 17, Ef
Tain, 37A, Bb; 49A, Bb
Tainan, 91, Fd
Tainan, 91, Fd
Taipei, 91, Fd
Taitze-ho, R., 76B, Ba
Taiwan, 74, Lf
Taiwan (Formosa), 91, Fd
Taiyuan, 91, Ec
Ta'iz, 93, Ef
Takhires Gol, L., 86A, Eb
Takrit, 6, Fb
Taku, R., 71B, Cb
Takushan, 76B, Bb
Talangama, 52B, Aa
Talavera, 62, Be; 63, Cc

Talayan, 75E, Bc
Talca, 68, Bf
Talcaguano, 68, Bf
Tali, 25, Kd
Talienwan, 76B, Ab
Talienwan B., 76B, Ab
Talikot, 52A, Bc
Taling Ho, R., 76B, Aa
Talladega, 71F, Ba
Tallahassee, 72, Dc
Tallapoosa, R., 71F, Ba
Tallard, 38, Gf
Tallinn, 87, Fa
Talmont, 20, Ce
Tamale, 96B, Bb
Tamar, R., 27, Bf
Tamatave, 80A, Hf
Tambof, 61, Fd
Tamesis (R. Thames), 3A, Ge
Tamil Nadu, 92, De
Tampa, 72, Dd
Tampa B., 44, Ff; 70, Fe
Tampico, 43A, Cb
Tamrush, 78, Ee
Tamworde (Tamworth), 13, Ed
Tamworth, 7B, Cb; 48A, Cc
Tana, India, 35, Nd
Tana, Russia, 19, Fc
Tana, L., 80B, Be
Tananarive, 80A, Hf
Tanaro, R., 29A, Bc
Tancrids Tower, 18D
Tandil, 68, Df
Tandjungpinang, 75A, Bb
Tanega Shima, 41A, La
Tanganyika, 96C, Fe
Tanganyika, L., 80A, Fe
Tangermünde, 30, Kb
Tangier, 23D, Ce; 63A
Tanjore, 59D
Tann, 29A, Ea
Tannenberg, 31, Pb; 84, Gb
Tanner's Gate, 18D
Tanta, 80B, Aa
Tantallon Castle, 28B, Ca
Tantone (Taunton), 13, Ce
Tanzania, 96D, Fe
Taormina, 21A, Cd
Taormina (Tauromenium), 5,
    Ef
Tapajos, 68, Dc
Tappita, 96B, Bb
Tapti, R., 73, Bc
Tara, 15, Ec
Tarakan, 90, Bc
Taranaki, 77A
Taranto, 32A, Gd
Taranto, G. of, 32B, Fd
Tarapaca, Chile, 68, Cd
Tarapaca, Colombia, 68, Cc
Tarascon, 38, Dg
Tarasp, 29B, Eb
Tarazona, 22, Bc; 23C, Eb
Tarbes, 11, Ce; 63, Fa
Tarentaise, 22, Db
Tarentaise, eccl. prov., 22, Db
Targowica, 51, Gd
Tarifa, 23D, Cd; 63A
Tarija, 68, Ce
Tarim, R., 25, Hb; 91, Bb
Tarki, 19, Hd
Tarkwa, 96B, Bb
Tarlac, 75E, Ba
Tarn, R., 11, Ed
Tarnof, 26, Fc
Tarnopol, 33C, Fb; 62, Hc
Tarnow, 33C, Ea
Taron, 18C, Ce
Tarraco, 2, Je
Tarragona, 23C, Fb; 63, Fb
Tarragona, eccl. prov., 22, Cc
Tarsus, 6A, Ba; 18C, Bb
Tartar, 85, Mb
Tartary, 35, Nb; 69A, Nb
Tartas, 30, Cg
Tartu, 87, Fa
Tashihkiao, 76B, Ba
Tashkent, 25, Fb; 61B, Ba
Tasman Sea, 77, Ki
Tasmania, 77, Gj
Tateshale (Tanshelf), 13, Ec
Tati, 81A, Cb
Tati, R., 81A, Cb
Tattershall, 27, Fc
Tatungkow, 76B, Cb
Taufers, 86B, Aa
Taunton, England, 27, Ce
Taunton, Rhode I., 45B, Dc
Taunus, 83A, Ea
Taurica, 2, Kd
Tauroggen, 60A, Ja
Tauromenium (Taormina), 5,
    Ef
Taurus, 2, Kf; 19, Ee
Taus, 31, Kd
Tavastehus, 26, Fa
Tavestoche (Tavistock), 13, Bf
Taveuni, 75C, Ba
Tavira, 23C, Bd
Tavistock, 27, Bf
Tavoy, 73, Ge
Tavua, 75C, Aa

Tawarik, 6, Bc
Taxila, 1, Kd
Tay, Firth of, 14, Fc
Tay, L., 14, Dc
Tay, R., 14, Ec
Tbilisi, 93, Ea
Tchirman, 33A, Cb
Tebuk, 93, Dd
Tecklenburg, 20, Gb
Tecklenburg, co., 46C, Ca
Tees, R., 27, Eb
Teesdale, 28B, Cc
Tefe, 68, Cc
Tegeingl, 13, Ce
Tegesta, 43A, Db
Tehama, 6, Fd
Tehran, 93, Gb
Tehri, 73, Dc
Tehuantepec, 43A, Cc
Tehuantepec, Isthmus of, 43A,
    Cc
Teifi, R., 27, Bd
Teith, R., 14, Dc
Tekke, Amirate of, 19, Ee
Tekrit, 86C, Dc
Tel Aviv-Jaffa, 79, Fd
Tell-basher (Turbessel), 18C,
    Eb
Teller, 71A, Aa
Tellicherri, 73, Ce
Tembuland, 81A, Cd
Tembus, 81B, Cb
Teme, R., 28A, Cb
Temesvar, 33C, Eb
Temple, Jerusalem, 18D
Temple, London, 27A
Temple Bar, 27A
Templeborough, 3A, Ec
Templin, 31, Kb
Temuco, 68, Bf
Tenasserim, 73, Ge
Tenby, 27, Be
Tenda, 32A, Bb
Tenda, Coc di, 29A, Bc
Tenedos, 78, Ef; 86C, Ab
Tenerife, 80A, Bb
Tenes, 16, Ce
Tengri Nor, L., 73, Fa
Tennessee, R., 56, Bd
Tennessee, st., 72, Cb
Tenterden, 27, Ge
Teodekesberie (Tewkesbury),
    13, De
Teofilo-Otoni, 68, Ed
Tephrik, 16, Ke
Tepl, 22, Eb
Teplitz, 33C, Ca; 60B, Dc
Terek, R., 19, Hd; 61, Ff
Terek Cossacks, 61, Gf
Teresina, 68, Ec
Tergovist, 24, Hd
Terminal Pt., 76B, Bb
Termoli, 32A, Fc
Ternate, 52B, Aa
Terni, 22, Ec; 39, Kg
Terracina, 5, Dd; 22A
Terschelling, 46A, Ea
Tertry, 7A, Db; 8B, Bb
Teruel, 22, Bc; 23C, Eb
Teschen, 21, Nd; 87, Dc
Teslin, L., 70, Aa
Teslin, R., 71B, Ca
Tete, 42, Le; 81A, Da
Tetford (Thetford), 13, Gd
Tettenhall, 7C, Bb; 13, Dd
Tetuan, 16, Ae
Teupitz, 60A, Db
Teutonic Knights, 21B, Db;
    26, Gb
Teviot, R., 48A, Bb
Teviotdale, 28B, Cb
Tewkesbury, 27, De; 36, Df
Texas, 70, Ed
Texel, 46A, Da
Tezcuco, 43A, Cc
Thaba Bosigo, 81B, Cb
Thabanchu, 81B, Cb
Thailand, 91, De
Thame, 36, Ff
Thames, R., Canada, 45A, Ab
Thames, R., Connecticut, 45B,
    Cc
Thames, R., England, 27, Ee
Thanet, 7B, Dc
Thanjavur, 92, De
Thann, 39B, Dc
Thapsus, 2, Ff
Thar Desert, 59A, Bb
Tharandt, 39C, Dc
Thasos, 78, Ee
The Forks, 69A, Da
The Hague, 46A, Db
Theanum, 5B, Bc
Thebes, 19, Ce
Theiss, R., 22, Gb; 33C, Eb
Thelwall, 7C, Bb
Theodosiopolis (Erzerum), 4A,
    Ld
Theopolis, 81B, Cc
Thérouanne, 22, Ca; 46A, Bd
Thessalonica, 8, Gc; 9, Gd
Thessalonica Theme, 9, Gd

Thessaly, 78, Df
Thetford, 7C, Db; 36, Ge
Thiers, 30, Ef
Thikombia, 75C, Ca
Thimer, 11, Db
Thionville, 29A, Ba; 83A, Db
Third Cataract, 80B, Ad
Thirsk, 27, Eb
Tholen, 46A, Dc
Tnoley, 39B, Da
Thomar, 23C, Ac; 63, Ac
Thomastown, 49B, Cd
Thomond, 15, Cd
Thompsons I., 56B
Thorn, 21, Nb
Thorney, 36, Fe
Thouars, 11, Cc
Thousand Is., L. of, 57, Ca
Thrace, 8, Hc; 78, Fe
Thrace Theme, 9, Hd
Thracesian Theme, 9, He
Thracia, 2, Je
Threave, 14, Ee
Threave Castle, 28B, Ac
Three Kings I., 75, Ff
Three Points, C., 81C, Dd
Three Rivers, 57C, Aa
Thun, 29B, Bb
Thun, L., 29B, Bb
Thur, R., 29B, Ca
Thurgau, 10, Ce; 29B, Da
Thuringia, 10, Dc; 39C, Ac
Thuringia, Land. of, 21B, Cb
Thuringia, March of, 10, Fc
Thuringian Forest, 10, Dc
Thuringians, 4A, Ea; 7A, Fb
Thurles, 49B, Dd
Thurso, 37A, Ca
Tibbu, 6, Cc
Tiber, R., 5, Dc; 32A, Ec
Tiberias, 18C, Cf
Tibesti, 80A, Eb
Tibet, 25, Hc; 92, Fa
Tiburon, C., 43A, Ec
Ticino, canton, 29B, Cb
Ticino, R., 5, Bb
Tickhill, 27, Ec
Ticonderoga, 57, Eb
Tidor, 52B, Aa
Tientsin, 74, Ke; 91, Ec
Tierra del Fuego, 68, Ch
Tierra Firme, 43A, Fd
Tiflis, 19, Gd; 79, Hb
Tigris, R., 2, Mg; 6A, Ca
Tikhvin, 88, Mb
Tikrit, 93, Ec
Till, R., 28B, Cb; 48A, Cb
Tilsit, 60A, Ha; 61, Bc
Timaru, 77A
Timbuktu, 81C, Da
Timbuktu (Tombuto), 35, Jd
Timisoara, 87, Ec
Timor, 52C, Cc; 91, Fg
Timor Laut, 52C, Dc
Tinchebrai, 17, Ed
Tindouf, 80A, Cb
Tinemuthe (Tynem'th), 13, Ea
Tingitana, 2, Cg
Tinnevelly, 73, Cf
Tinos, 78, Eg
Tioga, 56, Db
Tippecanoe, 71C, Ab
Tipperah, 73, Fc
Tipperary, 37B, Cd
Tipperary, co., 49B, Dd
Tippermuir, 37A, Cb
Tiranë, 88, Je
Tiree, 14, Bc
Tirlemont, 46A, Dd
Tirnova, 78, Dc
Tiruchirapalli, 92, De
Tisz, R., 89, Kd
Titicaca, L., 68, Cd
Titus, Baths of, 5A
Tiverton, 27, Cf
Tivoli, 22A; 32A, Ed
Tlaxcala, 43A, Cc
Tlemsen, 6, Ab; 9, Bf
Tmatarakhan, 9, Kc
Tobago, 43A, Fc
Tobermory, 49A, Ab
Tobolsk, 74, Ec
Tobruk, 93, Ac
Tocantins, R., 68, Ec
Toce, R., 29B, Cb
Togean Is., 52C, Bb
Toggenburg, 29B, Ca; 30, He
Toggenburg, canton, 29B, Da
Togo, 81C, Ec; 96B, Cb
Togoland, 96C, Cd
Tohopeka (Horseshoe Bend),
    71F, Ba
Tokar, 80B, Bd
Tokat, 33A, Kd
Tokay, 33C, Eb
Tokelau Is., 83, Ae; 90, Fd
Tokelau (Union) Is., 75, Ge
Tokyo, 91, Gc
Toledo, Ohio, 70, Fc

Toledo, Spain, 23C, Cc; 63, Cc
Toledo, eccl. prov., 22, Bc
Toledo, Mts. of, 63, Cc
Toliman, 52B, Ab
To.lhuys, 53, Gb
Tolmezzo, 86B, Da
Tolmino, 86B, Da
Tolosa, 2, De
Tols, 53, Jd
Tolu, 43A, Ed
Tombigbee, R., 43A, Da
Tombuto (Timbuktu), 35, Jd
Tomen-y-mur, 3A, Cd
Tomini, Gulf of, 52C, Bb
Tomsk, 42, Ob; 74, Gc
Tonale Pass, 29A, Db
Tonbridge, 27, Ge
Tondern, 65F, Aa
Tonebridge (Tonbridge), 13,
    Ge
Tonga (Friendly) Is., 75, Gf
Tonga Land, 81D, Ca
Tongatabu, 75, Gf
Tongking, 74, Jf
Tongue, Kyle of, 49A, Ba
Tongueland, 36, Bc
Tonk, 73, Cb
Tonnai, 20, Cf
Tonnerre, 11, Fc; 17A, Dc
Tönning, 65F, Aa
Tonsberg, 26, Db
Toome, 37B, Bb
Topeka, 10, Ed
Tor B., 55A, Dc
Tormentoso, C. (C. of Good
    Hope), 35, Kf
Tormes, R., 63, Bb
Torni (Thorney), 13, Fd
Toro, 23C, Cb; 63, Cb
Toronto, 70, Gc
Toronto (York), 71C, Cb
Toropets, 19, Ea
Torre, Devon, 36, Cg
Torre, Somerset, 13, Ce
Torrens, L., 77, Fh
Torres, 23B, Bd
Torres, eccl. prov., 22, Dc
Torres Str., 77, Gc
Torres Vedras, 63B
Torridon, L., 14, Cb
Tortola, 43A, Fc
Tortona, 5, Bb
Tortosa, 23C, Fb; 63, Fb
Tortue (Tortuga), 43D, Eb
Tortuga, I., Haiti, 43A, Eb
Tortuga, I., Venezuela, 43A,
    Fc
Tory I., 15, Ca
Tostar, 6A, Db
Toteberie (Tutbury), 13, Ed
Totenais (Totnes), 13, Cf
Totnes, 27, Cf
Totoya, 75C, Cb
Touggourt, 80A, Da
Toul, 10, Ad; 39B, Bb
Toulon, 11, Fe; 29A, Ad
Toulouse, 11, De
Toulouse, Co. of, 11, De
Touraine, 11, Dc
Tourcoing, 46A, Cd
Tournai, 46A, Cd
Tournon, 17, Hf; 38, Df
Tours, 11, Dc
Tours, eccl. prov., 22, Bb
Toury, 76A, Ab
Towcester, 7C, Cb; 48B, Cc
Tower, 27A
Townsville, 77, He
Towton, 27, Ec
Towy, R., 28A, Cb
Toxandria, 8b, Ba
Trabzon, 93, Ea
Trafalgar, 55B, Kc; 69A, Jc
Trafalgar, C., 63A
Tralee, 37B, Bd; 49B, Bd
Trani, 32A, Gd
Tranquebar, 42, Od; 59D
Trans Tiberis, 5A
Trans-Caspian Rail'y, 74, Dd
Trans-Jordan, 79, Gd
Transkei, 81B, Dc
Transmarine Algarve, 35, Jc
Trans-Siberian Railway, 74,
    Ec
Transvaal, 81A, Cb
Transylvania, Europe, 33C, Eb
Transylvania, N. America,
    57A, Bb
Transylvanian Alps, 50, Ed
Trapani, 5, De
Trapezus, 2, Le; 4A, Kc
Traquair, 28B, Bb
Tras os Montes, 63, Bb
Trasimene, L., 5, Dc
Trastamara, 23D, Aa

Trau, 22, Fc
Traungau, 10, Fd
Traunstein, 53, Kd
Trautenau, 60B, Ec
Travancore, 73, Cf
Travnik, 78, Ac
Trebbio, R., 5, Bb
Trebizond, 19, Fd; 79, Gb
Trebizond, Empircof, 19, Fd
Trebnitz, 22, Fa
Tregony, 27, Bf
Tréguier, 11, Bb
Trelleborg, 12, Gc
Tremetone (Trematon), 13, Bf
Trencsen, 21, Nd
Trent, 5, Da
Trent, Bp. of, 30, Je; 33C, Cb
Trent, R., 27, Fc
Trentino, 84, Ec; 86B, Aa
Trenton, 45A, Cb; 57, Dc
Tresch (Thirsk), 13, Eb
Trèves, 10, Bd; 83A, Db
Trèves, Abp. of, 22, Db; 46C,
    Cb
Treviglio, 32A, Cb
Treviso, 5, Db; 86B, Cb
Treviso, M. of, 23B, Cb
Trévoux, 53, Ee
Tribulation, C., 77, He
Tribur, 10, Cd
Trichinopoly, 59D
Triebl, 39, Kd
Trier, 31A, Dc; 76A, Db
Trieste, 5, Db
Triglav, 29A, Fb
Trim, 15, Ec; 49B, Ec
Trim, bp., 15A, Bb
Trimontium (Newstead), 3A,
    Da
Trincomali, 73, Df
Trinidad, Bolivia, 68, Cd
Trinidad, Cuba, 43A, Eb
Trinidad, I., 43A, Fc
Trinity B., 45A, Ga
Trinovantes, 3A, Ge
Tripoli, Libya, 6, Cb; 80A, Ea
Tripoli, Syria, 6A, Bb; 18C, Cd
Tripoli, Volhynia, 19, Dc
Tripoli, Co. of, 18C, Dd
Tripolis, 2, Fg
Tripolitana, 4B, Ee
Tripolitania, 80A, Ea
Tripolitza, 78, Dg
Tripura, 92, Gc
Trisameron, 4B, Dd
Trisanna, R., 29B, Ea
Tristan da Cunha, 69A, Jf
Trivadee, 59D
Trivandrum, 73, Cf
Trivento, 22, Ec
Trobriand Is., 77, Ic
Trocala, 5, Df
Troia, 21A, Cb
Troina, 21A, Cd
Troitskoye, 61, Ec
Trondelag, 12, Ga
Trondheim (Nidaros), 26, Da;
    88, Ha
Trondhjem, 50, Ca
Trondhjem, prov., 50, Ca
Tronto, R., 21A, Ba
Troppau, 31, Md; 39, Md
Tropea, 22, Fd
Trostan, 15, Ea
Trotternish, 14, Bb
Troy, 57, Eb
Troyes, 2, Dd; 28D, Db
Troyes, Co. of, 11, Eb
Trucial Oman, 93, Ge
Trujillo, Peru, 68, Bc
Trujillo, Spain, 23C, Cc; 63,
    Cc
Trujillo, Venezuela, 68, Bb
Truk, 90, Dc
Truro, 27, Af
Truxillo, 43A, Dc
Tsang-Wu, 1, Oe
Tsanpo (Brahmaputra), R.,
    73, Eb
Tsaribrod, 78, Dd
Tschaslau, 31, Ld
Tsinan, 91, Ec
Tsingtao, 91, Fc
Tsympe, 33A, Cb
Tuam, 15, Cc
Tuamotu Arch. (Paumotu
    Arch.), 75, He
Tuareg, 80A, Db
Tübingen, 10, Cd; 64, Dd
Tubuai (Austral) Is., 75, Hf
Tucson, 70, Cd
Tucuman, 41B, Cf; 68, Ce
Tudela, 23C, Ea; 63, Ea
Tuder. 5, Dc
Tugela, R., 81D, Bb
Tukharistan, 6, Jb
Tula, 84, Kb; 88, Nc
Tulbagh, 81B, Ae
Tulbagh, dist., 81B, Bc
Tulcea, 78, Gc
Tullagh, 37B, Ec

Tullahoma, 72, Cb
Tullamore, 49B, Dc
Tulle, 22, Cb; 30, Df
Tulunid Dominions, 9, Hf
Tulunids, King. of, 6B, Db
Tumbez, 68, Ac
Tummel, R., 49A, Bb
Tun, 6, Gb
Tunga Bhadra, R., 73, Cd
Tungchow, 74, Kd
Tunis, 24, Df; 80A, Da
Tunis, prot., 80A, Da
Tunis, Pashalik of, 47, De
Tunis, Sultanate of (Hafsids) 34, De
Tunisia, 96C, Ca; 96D, Ca
Tunja, 68, Bb
Tunja, R., 78, Fd
Tupelo, 72, Cc
Turbessel (Tell-basher), 18C, Eb
Turenne, 11, Dd
Turenne, V. of, 11, Dd
Turgai, 74, Ed
Turkestan, 61B, Ba
Turkestan, reg., 61B, Ba
Turkey, 93, Db
Turkheim, 29A, Ba; 39B, Db
Turkish Hungary, 39, Ne
Turkomans, 24, Lf
Turks Is., 43A, Eb
Turku, 87, Ea
Turin, 20, Gf; 32C, Ab
Turin (Augusta Taurinorum), 5, Ab
Turmid, 6, Hb
Turnberry, 14, Dd
Turneffe, 43A, Dc
Turnham Green, 48A, Cd
Turnhout, 46A, Dc
Turov, 26, Gc
Turriff, 37A, Cb
Turukhansk, 74, Gb
Tus, 6, Gb
Tuscaloosa, 72, Cc
Tuscan Presidios, 47, Ed
Tuscany, 5, Ce
Tuscana, 5B, Ab
Tuscany, D. of, 23A, Cb
Tuscany, G. D. of, 32B, Cc; 38, Jg
Tuscaroras, 45A, Bc
Tusculum (Frascati), 22A
Tuscumbia, 72, Cc
Tutbury, 27, Ed
Tutuila, 75, Ge; 75B, Bb
Tuva, 74, Hc
Tuy, 22, Ac; 23C, Aa
Tuz Gol, L., 86C, Bb
Tuzi, 78, Bd
Tver, 19, Fa
Tvinam (Twineham, Christ-church), 13, Ef
Tweed, R., 14, Ed; 28B, Bb
Twelve Pins, 15, Bc
Two Sicilies, King. of, 18B, Bc; 21, Kg; 32B, Ed
Tyburn, 27A
Tyne, R., 27, Eb; 28B, Dc
Tynedale, 13, Db
Tynedale, Franchise of, 28D, Cb
Tynemouth, 27, Ea
Tyr Connell, 15, Cb
Tyr Owen, 15, Db
Tyras, R., 2, Jd
Tyre, 2, Lg; 16, Kf
Tyre (Sur), 18C, Ce
Tyrnau, 39, Md
Tyrol, 20, Je
Tyrol, Co. of, 20, Je
Tyrone, 37B, Db
Tyrone, co., 49B, Db
Tyrrell, 37B, Dc
Tyrrhenian Sea, 5, Dd
Tyumen, 74, Ec
Tzurulum (Chorlu), 19, Dd

UBANGI-SHARI, 80A, Fd
Ubeda, 23C, Dc
Uberaba, 68, Ed
Uberlingen, 20, He
Ucayali, R., 68, Bc
Uch, 25, Gd
Uckermark, 31B, Ca
Ucles, 23C, Dc
Udaipur, 73, Bc
Udine, 22, Eb; 29A, Eb
Udskot, 74, Mc
Uele, R., 80A, Fd
Uexküll, 26, Fb
Ufa, 61, Jd
Ufa, R., 19, Ka
Uganda, 80A, Gd
Uighur, 25, Hb
Uitenhage, 81A, Cd
Uitenhage, dist., 81B, Cc
Ujiji, 80A, Fe
Ujjain, 1, Ke; 92, Dc
Ukermark, 60A, Db
Ukraine, 19, Eb; 50, Gd

Ukraine Soviet Socialist Rep., 84, Jc
Ukrians, 10, Eb
Uladh (Ultonia, Ulster), 15, Db
Ulan Bator, 91, Db
Ulan Ude, 91, Da
Uleåborg, 61, Cb
Ullapool, 49A, Bb
Ulm, 10, Cd; 29A, Ca
Ulster, 37B, Db; 49C
Ulster (Uladh, Ultonia), 15, Db
Ulster Irish, 49C
Ultonia (Uladh, Ulster), 15, Db
Ulundi, 81D, Bb
Ülzen, 26, Dc
Umarkot, 52A, Ab
Umbria, 5, Dc; 32A, Ec
Umeå, 26, Fa
Umfraville, 28B, Cb
Unfuli, R., 81A, Ca
Umkomaas, R., 81B, Db
Umtali, 81A, Da
Umzimkulu, R., 81B, Db
Umzimvubu, R., 81B, Db
Umzimyati (Buffalo), R., 81D, Bb
Una, R., 33C, Dc
Ungava, 70, Gb
Ungava B., 44, Hc; 71, Hb
Union (Tokelau) Is., 75, Ge
Union of Soviet Socialist Republics, 94, Qc
United Arab Republic, 96D, Fb
United Kingdom, 64, Ab
United Provinces, Rep. of, 38, Fb
United St. of America, 70-71
United States of Brazil, 68, Dd
Unklar Skelessi, 79, Eb
Unterwalden, 29B, Cb
Upland, New Sweden, 45B, Bd
Upland, Sweden, 26, Ea
Upolu, 75B, Ba
Upper Alsace, 31A, Dd
Upper Alsace, Land. of, 20, Ge
Upper Austria, 65C, Bb
Upper Burgundy (Regnum Jurense), 11, Gc
Upper Burma, 74, Hf
Upper Canada, 71C, Ca
Upper Doab, 59C, Cb
Upper Lausitz, Marg. of, 31, Lc
Upper Lorraine, 20, Gd
Upper Lotharingia, 10, Bd
Upper Lotharingia, 10, Ad
Upper Palatinate, 30, Jd
Upper Peru, 41B, Ce
Upper Senegal and Niger, 81C, Da
Upper Silesia, 60A, Fc
Upper Volta, 80A, Cc
Upper Volta, St., 96B, Bc
Upsala, 26, Eb
Uraba, G. of, 43A, Ed
Ural Mts., 19, Ka
Ural, R., 19, Kb; 61, Hd
Uralsk, 61, Hd
Urbino, 5, Dc; 8A, Dc
Urbinum, 5B, Bb
Urfa, 79, Gc
Urga, 74, Jd
Urgel, 11, De; 23C, Fa
Urgenj, 25, Eb
Uri, 29B, Cb
Uriel, 37B, Eb
Uriel (Oirghealla), 15, Db
Urmia, 86C, Db
Urmia, L., 6A, Da
Urseren, 29B, Cb
Uruaiana, 68, De
Uruguay, 68, Df
Uruguay, R., 68, De
Urumchi, 91, Bb
Usak, 79, Ec
Usedom, 10, Eb; 31, Kb
Ushant, 11, Ab
Usingen, 65B, Aa
Usk, 28A, Dc
Usk, R., 27, De; 28, Cb
Uskub (Skoplje), 78, Cd
Uskudar, 93, Ba
Ust Yurt, 61, Jf
Ustyug, 61, Gb
Utah, 70, Cd
Utah L., 44, Cd
Utah Terr., 67D, Bb
Utica, Mississippi, 72C, Aa
Utica, New York, 57, Db
Utrecht, Natal, 81D, Ba
Utrecht, Netherlands, 46A, Eb
Utrecht, prov., 46A, Eb
Utrecht, Bp. of, 46C, Ca
Uttar Pradesh, 92, Eb
Uttoxeter, 48B, Cc
Uxbridge, 48B, Cd
Uyuni, 68, Ce
Uzés, 11, Fe
Uzes (Cumans), 9, Mc
Uznach, 29B, Da

VAAL, R., 81A, Cc

Vabres, 22, Cc
Vadstena, 26, Db
Vaduz, 38, He
Vahsel B., 69C
Vaigeu, 52C, Db
Vaison, 22, Dc
Val d'Aran, 23D, Fa
Val Leventina, 29B, Cb
Val Maggia, 29B, Cb
Valais, 29B, Bb
Valais, Co. of, 11, Gc
Valcour I., 57, Ea
Valdemoni, 21A, Cc
Valdez, 71A, Ca
Valdivia, 68, Bg
Vale Royal, 36, Dd
Valence, 11, Fd
Valence, family, 37B, Ed
Valencia, Spain, 63, Ec
Valencia, Venezuela, 68, Cb
Valencia, eccl. prov., 22, Bd
Valencia, prov., 63, Ec
Valenciennes, 46A, Cd
Valentia I., 49B, Ae
Valladolid, 23C, Cb; 63, Cb
Valle Crucis, 36, Ce
Valley Forge, 57, Dc
Vallombrosa, 32A, Dc
Valls, 63, Fb
Vallum Antonini, 3A, Ba
Valmy, 62, Cc
Valognes, 11, Cb
Valois, 17, Gd
Valois, Co. of, 11, Eb
Valona, 16, Fd; 78, Be
Valparaiso, 68, Bf
Valromey, 53, Fe
Valsainte, 29B, Bb
Valsch, R., 81B, Ca
Valteline, 29B, Db
Valverde, 23D, Bc
Van, 19, Ge; 86C, Db
Van, L., 6A, Ca
Van Diemen's Land, 77, Gj
Van Reenen's Pass, 81D, Ab
Vancouver, Canada, 70, Bc
Vancouver, U.S.A., 70, Bc
Vancouver I., 70, Bc
Vandal Kingdom, 4A, Dd
Vandali, 2, Gc
Vandalia, 67C, Eb
Vandals, 2A, Ac
Vannes, 11, Bc
Vanua Levu, 75C, Ba
Var, R., 29A, Bd
Värälä, 51, Fa
Varanasi (Banaras), 92, Eb
Varazdin, 21, Me
Vardar, R., 78, De; 86A, Da
Varennes, 29A, Aa; 31A, Cc
Varey, 20, Ff
Varilhes, 53, Dg
Varkinskil (Salem), 45B, Bd
Varna, 78, Fd
Vasa, 26, Fa
Vasconia, 4A, Bc
Vassy, 38, Fd
Vasvar, 33C, Db
Vasvar (Eisenburg), 29A, Gb
Vaternish, 14, Bb
Vatersay, 49A, Ab
Vatican, 5A
Vatter, L., 26, Db
Vauclair, 22, Cb
Vaucouleurs, 28D, Eb
Vaud, 29B, Ab
Vaud, Co. of, 11, Gc
Vaudemont, 20, Fd; 39B, Cb
Vaudreuil, 57, Da
Vechte, R., 46A, Gb
Vectis (I. of Wight), 3A, Ef
Veglia, 22, Eb
Veile, 65F, Aa
Velay, Co. of, 11, Fd
Velikie Luki, 61, Dc
Velletri, 32B, Dd
Vellinghausen, 60A, Ac
Vellore, 59D
Venaissin, 30, Ff
Vendée, 53, Cd; 62, Bc
Venden, 26, Gb
Vendôme, 11, Dc
Venedae, 1, Fb
Vener, L., 26, Db
Venetia, 5, Db; 32C, Db
Venetian Alps, 29A, Dc
Venezuela, 43C, Ed; 68, Cb
Venezuela, G. of, 43A, Ec
Venice, 32D, Cb
Venice, D. of, 10, Ef
Venice, G. of, 29A, Ec
Venlo, 46A, Fc
Venonae (High Cross), 3A, Ed
Venta Belgarum (Winchester), 3A, Ee
Venta Cruz (Cruces), 43A, Ed
Venta Icenorum (Caister), 3A, Hd
Venta Silurum (Caerwent), 3A, De
Ventadour, 17, Gf; 53, Ee
Ventersdorp, 81A, Cc

Ventimiglia, 5, Ac; 20, Gg
Vera Cruz, 43A, Cc
Vera Cruz, Terra da, 40, He
Veragua, 43A, Dd
Veragua, prov., 43A, Dd
Vercelli, 5, Bb; 29A, Cc
Verchères, 57, Ea
Vercovicium (Housesteads), 3C
Verde, C., 80A, Bc; 81C, Ab
Verden, 10, Cb; 60A, Ac
Verden, Bp. of, 38, Hb
Verdon, R., 29A, Bd
Verdun, Gascony, 38, Dg
Verdun, Lotharingia, 10, Ad
Verdun, Bp. of, 39B, Ba
Vereeniging, 81A, Cc
Veria, 78, De
Verkhne Kolymsk, 74, Ob
Verkhne Udinsk, 74, Jc
Verkhoyansk, 74, Mb
Verkne Chusovoi, 61, Jc
Verlucio (Sandy Lane), 3A, De
Vermandois, Co. of, 11, Eb
Vermland, 26, Db
Vermont, 67C, Fa; 71, Gc
Vernemetum (Willoughby), 3A, Fe
Verneuil, 17, Fd
Verny, 74, Fd
Verona, 5, Cb; 32D, Bb
Verona, M. of, 10, Ef; 20, Jf
Verria, 86A, Db
Versailles, 53, Ec; 76A, Bb
Verterae (Brough), 3A, Db
Vertus, 38, Fd
Veruela, 22, Bc
Verviers, 46A, Ed
Vervins, 38, Ed
Vesle, R., 83A, Bb
Vesoul, 20, Ge; 83B, Bb
Vester-Götland, 26, Db
Vesterås, 26, Eb
Vesterbotten, 26, Fa
Vestmanland, 26, Eb
Veszprem, 21, Me
Vet (Sand), R., 81A, Cc
Vevey, 29B, Ab
Vexin, Co. of, 11, Db
Vexins, 38, Ce
Vézelay, 20, Ee; 31A, Bd
Via Dolorosa, 18D
Viadua, R., 2, Gc
Vianen, 46A, Ec
Vianna, 23D, Ab; 63, Ab
Viatka, 19, Ha
Viborg, Denmark, 26, Cb
Viborg, Finland, 26, Ga
Vic, 39B, Cb
Vic Bigorre, 63, Fa
Vicenza, 5, Cb; 38, Jf
Vich, 11, Ef
Vichy, 88, Fd
Vicksburg, 72C, Aa
Victoria, British Columbia, 70, Bc
Victoria, Cameroon, 96B, Cb
Victoria, Rhodesia, 81A, Db
Victoria, dist., S. Africa, 81B, Cc
Victoria Falls, 81A, Ca
Victoria I., Canada, 44, Ca
Victoria, I., Moluccas, 52C, Cb
Victoria, L., 80A, Ge
Victoria Land, 69C
Victoria, R., 77, Ee
Victoria, st., 77, Gi
Vidin, 33A, Bb
Viedma, 68, Cg
Vienna, Austria, 10, Gd
Vienna, Gaul, 2, Dd
Vienne, 11, Fd; 17A, Ed
Vienne, eccl. prov., 22, Db
Vienne, R., 11, Dc; 30, De
Vientiane, 91, De
Vietnam, 91, De
Vigan, 75E, Ba
Vigo, 63, Aa
Viipuri, 87, Fa
Vijayanagar, 52A, Ab
Vijayanagar, king., 41A, Ec
Vijayawada, 92, Ed
Viken, 12, Gb
Vilagos, 33C, Eb
Vilaine, R., 30, Be
Vilkomir, 26, Fb
Villa Bella (Mato Grosso), 68, Cd
Villa do Conde, 63, Ab
Villa Dolores, 68, Cf
Villa St. Albani (St. Albans), 13, Fe
Villa Viciosa, Portugal, 63, Bc
Villa Viciosa, Spain, 63, Db
Villach, 10, Ee; 29A, Eb
Villafranca, Italy, 32C, Cb
Villafranca, Spain, 63, Ba
Villarrica, 68, De

Villefranche, Guyenne, 53, Ee
Villefranche, Lyonnais, 53, Fe
Villemaur, 31A, Bc
Villena, 23C, Ec; 63, Ec
Villeneuve, 20, Df
Villers Bretonneux, 76A, Bb
Villers Cotterets, 83A, Bb
Villersexel, 76A, Dc
Vilna, 26, Gc
Vimiero, 63, Ac
Viminacium, 2, He
Vimy, 83A, Ba
Vincennes, 56, Bc
Vindhya Mts., 73, Cc
Vindocladia (Badbury), 3A, Df
Vindolanda (Chesterholm), 3C
Vindomora (Ebchester), 3C
Vindovala (Rudchester), 3C
Vinegar Hill, 49B, Ed
Vinland, 35, Fb
Vinnitsa, 79, Ea
Vinovia (Binchester), 3A, Eb
Vionville, 76A, Cb
Vire, 53, Cc
Virgin Is., 43A, Fc
Virginia, 57, Ce; 72B, Bb
Virginia Colony, Raleigh's, 45A, Bc
Viroconium (Wroxeter), 3A, Dd
Visconti, Lands of, 24, Dd
Visé, 83A, Ca
Viseu, 23C, Ab
Vishakhapatnam, 92, Ed
Vishegorod, 19, Da
Visigothi, 2, Hd
Visigothic Kingdom, 4A, Bc
Viso, Mte., 29A, Bc
Visp, 29B, Bb
Vistula, R., 31, Pc; 33C, Ea
Vitebsk, 26, Gb
Viterbo, 5, Dc
Viti Levu, 75C, Aa
Vitichev, 9, Jb
Vitoria, Brazil, 68, Ee
Vitoria, Spain, 63, Da
Vitoria la Conquista, 68, Ed
Vitré, 20, Cd
Vitry, 11, Fb
Vitry, Co. of, 11, Fb
Vittoria, 4B, Cb
Vittorio, 86B, Cb
Viviers, 11, Fd; 17, Hf
Vizagapatam, 73, Dd
Vizcaya, 23C, Da
Vizeu, 22, Ac; 63, Bb
Vizianagram, 59A, Dc
Vizye, 19, Dd
Vlach, 8C, Db
Vlachs, 19, Dc
Vladikavkaz, 61, Ff
Vladimir, Poland, 26, Fc
Vladimir, Russia, 19, Ga
Vladimir Volinski, 19, Cb
Vladivostok, 91, Gb
Vlieland, 46A, Da
Vodena, 86A, Db
Vogtland, 21, Kc
Volcano Is., 90, Db
Volga, R., 19, Hc; 24, Md
Volgograd, 89, Qd
Volhynia, 50, Fc
Volkovisk, 62, Gb
Volksrust, 81D, Aa
Volmeringen, 39B, Ca
Vologda, 19, Fa
Volos, 78, Df
Volta, L., 96B, Bb
Volta, R., 81C, Dc
Volterra, 32E, Bb
Voltri, R., 32C, Dd
Voltutara, 22, Fc
Vorarlberg, 33C, Cb
Voronezh, 61, Ed; 88, Nc
Vosges, 10, Bd; 83B, Ba
Vostok I., 83, Be
Votyaks, 19, Ja
Vouillé, 4A, Bb; 8B, Ab
Vrania, 78, Cd
Vryburg, 81A, Bc
Vryheid, 81A, Dc; 81D, Ba
Vyatiches, 9, Ka
Vyazma, 19, Ea

WAAG, R., 21, Nd
Waal, R., 46A, Ec
Wabash, R., 56, Bc; 57A, Bb
Wachefeld (Wakefield), 13, Ec
Wad Medani, 93, Cg
Wadai, 80A, Ec
Wadelai, 80A, Gd
Wadern, 76A, Db
Wadi Halfa, 80B, Ac
Wagram, 29A, Ga
Wagrians, 10, Da
Wahlstatt, 60B, Fc
Waianae, 75D, Bb
Waiblingen, 10, Cd
Waidhaus, 39, Kd
Waidhofen, 21, Le
Waigen, 77, Eb

Waikato, R., 77A
Wailuku, 75D, Cb
Waimea, 75D, Bb
Waitara, 77A
Waitemata (Auckland), 77, Mi
Waitzen, 22, Fb
Wake I., 90, Ec
Wakkerstroom, 81D, Ba
Wal Wal, 96A, Bb
Walachia, 78, Ec
Walcheren, 46A, Cc
Waldeck, 30, Hc
Waldeck, co., 38, Hc
Walden, 36, Ge
Waldsassen, 22, Eb
Waledana (Saffron Walden), 13, Gd
Walenstadt, 29B, Da
Wales, 28A; 34, Bb; 55A, Bb
Wales, Pr. of, 27, Cd
Wales, The March of, 17, Dc
Walila, 6, Ab
Walingeford (Wallingford), 13, Ee
Walla Walla, 70, Cc
Wallhof, 50, Eb
Wallingford, 27, Ee
Wallis Is., 75, Ge
Walpole, 57, Eb
Walsingham, 36, Ge
Walsleben, 10, Db
Waltham, 13, Ge; 36, Gf
Walton Castle, 3A, He
Walvis Bay, 80A, Eg
Walvisch B., 81A, Ab
Wandatin, 76B, Bb
Wandiwash, 59D
Wangama, 77A
Wanganui, 77, Nj
Wangen, 30, He
Wantage, 7C, Cc; 48B, Cd
Warberg, 26, Db
Wardha, R., 59C, Cc
Wardour Castle, 48A, Bd
Wareham, 27, Df
Wargaon, 59A, Bd
Warham (Wareham), 13, Df
Wark, 27, Da; 28B, Cb
Warkworth, 27, Ea
Warnabians, 10, Eb
Warneton, 46A, Bd
Warnstedt, 10, Dc
Warren, 28A, Ca
Warrington, 3A, Dc; 48A, Bc
Warsaw, 21, Pb
Warsaw, G. D. of, 62, Gb
Warta, R., 21B, Db; 31, Db
Wartburg, 20, Jc; 39C, Ac
Warthe, R., 21, Lb; 22, Fa
Warwic (Warwick), 13, Ed
Warwick, England, 27, Ed
Warwick, Rhode I., 45B, Dc
Warwick, co., 27, Ed
Warwicscire (Warwickshire), 13, Ed
Wash, The, 27, Gd; 36, Ge
Washington, Arkansas, 72, Bc
Washington, Dist. of Columbia, 71C, Cc; 72B, Ba
Washington, st., 70, Bc
Washington I., 75, Hd
Washington Terr., 67D, Aa
Wasit, 6A, Db
Watasios (Sultanate of Fez), 34, Be
Watauga Association, 57A, Cb
Watchet, 27, Ce
Waterboer's Land, 81A, Bc
Wateree, R., 57D, Aa
Waterford, 15, Dd
Waterford, co., 49B, Dd
Waterloo, 46B
Watford, 48B, Cd
Watkins Pt., 45B, Be
Watling Street, 3A, Ed
Wattignies, 46A, Dd
Watton, 36, Fd
Waverley, 36, Ff
Wavre, 46A, Dd; 46B
Waxhaw Creek, 57, Af
Weardale, 28B, Cc
Weare, 27, De
Wearmouth, 36, Ec
Weddell Sea, 69C
Wedmore, 7C, Bc
Wedone (Weedon), 13, Ed
Weenen, 81D, Bb
Wehlau, 39, Pa; 50, Ec
Weiden, 38, Jd
Weihaiwei, 74, Le
Weil, 30, Hd; 38, Hd
Weilerthal, 39B, Db
Weimar, 10, Dc
Weinsberg, 10, Cd
Weissenburg, Alsace, 39B, Da
Weissenburg, Germany, 20, Jd; 29A, Da
Weissenfels, 39C, Bb
Weitburg, 65B, Aa

Welbeck, 36, Ed
Weldon, 72, Eb
Welfesholz, 10, Dc
Wella (Wells), 13, Gd
Welland, R., 27, Fd
Welle (Wells), 13, De
Wellesley, 37B, Ec
Wellesley Is., 77, Fe
Wellington, 75, Fg
Wellington (Brittania), 77, Nj
Wellington, prov., 77A
Wells, 27, De
Welshpool, 27, Cd
Wenchow, 74, Lf
Wendover, 27, Fe
Wener, L., 12, Hb
Wenloch (Wenlock), 13, Dd
Wenlock, 27, Dd
Weobley, 27, Dd; 23, Db
Werben, 10, Db; 38, Jb
Werc (Wark), 13, Da
Werdenfels, 53, Jd
Weremuthe (Wearmouth), 13, Eb
Werle, 21, Kb
Wernigerode, 60A, Cc
Werra, R., 10, Dc; 20, Hc
Wertheim, 53, Hc
Wes-Treding (West Riding, Lincolnshire), 13, Fc
Wes-Treding (West Riding, Yorkshire), 13, Ec
Wesel, 20, Gc; 60A, Ac
Wesel (Oberwesel), 20, Gc
Weser, R., 10, Cb; 30, Hb
Wessaugusset (Weymouth), 45B, Db
Wessex, 7B, Bc; 12, Dd
West Bengal, 92, Fc
West Dvina, R., 89, Lb
West Florida, 56, Bd
West Franconia, 10, Cd
West Germany, 89, Gd
West Indies, 55B, Dd
West Irian, 91, Gg
West Looe, 27, Bf
West March, 28B, Bb
West Meath, co., 49B, Dc
West New Jersey, 45A, Cc
West Pakistan, 92, Bb
West Point, 57, Dc
West Prussia, 31, Nb
West Roman Empire, 2, Fe
West Saxons, 7A, Cb
West Schelde, R., 54, Cb
West Virginia, 72, Db
West Wales, 7B, Ac; 36A
Westderbei (West Derby), 18, Dc
Wester Wald, 10, Cc
Western Australia, 77, Cg
Western Ghats, 73, Bd
Western Pomerania, 39, Kb
Western Samoa, 75, Ge; 75B
Westerwald, 83A, Da
Westland, 77A
Westmeath, co., 37C
Westminster, 27A; 36, Ff
Westminster, Palace of, 27A
Westminster Abbey, 27A
Westmonasterium (Westminster), 13, Fe
Westmorland, 27, Db
Westover, 45B, Ae; 57, Ce
Westphalia, 10, Bb; 20, Hc
Westport, Missouri, 70, Ed
Westport, New Zealand, 77A
Westray, 49A, Ca
Wetherby, 48B, Cc
Wethersfield, 45B, Cc
Wetter, I., 52C, Cc
Wettin, 10, Dc; 39C, Bb
Wettingen, 29B, Ca
Wetzlar, 10, Cc
Wewak, 90, Dd
Wexford, 15, Ed
Wexford, co., 37C; 49B, Ed
Wexio, 26, Db
Weymouth, 27, Df; 55A, Bc
Weymouth (Wessaugusset), 45B, Db
Weymouth B., 77, Gd
Whalley, 36, Dd
Wheeling, 57, Ac
Wherwell, 36, Ef
Whitby, 27, Fb
Whitchurch, 48B, Cd
White Castle, 28A, Dc
White Croats, 9, Gb
White Horse, 71B, Ca
White House, 72B, Bb
White Huns, 6, Ha
White Marsh, 57, Dc
White Mts., 45A, Cb
White Nile, R., 80B, Ae
White Pass, 71B, Cb
White Plains, 57, Ec
White Russia, 51, Gc
White Sea, 61, Ea
White Umvolosi, R., 81D, Bb

Whitehall, 27A
Whitern, 7B, Aa
Whithorn, 14, De
Whitland, 36, Bf
Whitsand B., 55A, Ac
Whydah 81C, Ec
Wiceford (Witchford), 13, Gd
Wich (Nantwich), 13, Dc
Wiche (Droitwich), 13, Dd
Wick, 49A, Ca
Wicklow, 15, Ed
Wicklow, co., 37C; 49B, Ed
Wicklow Hd., 15, Ed
Wicklow Mts., 15, Ed
Wicumbe (High Wycombe), 13, Fe
Widin, 19, Cd; 78, Dc
Wied, 20, Gc
Wielun, 61A, Ab
Wiesbaden, 60B, Bc; 83A, Ea
Wiesloch, 38, Hd
Wigan, 3A, Dc; 27, Dc
Wigemor (Wigmore), 13, Cd
Wight, I. of, 27, Ef
Wigmore, 28A, Db
Wigtown, 14, De
Wigtown, co., 37A, Bc
Wigtown B., 28B, Ac
Wiht, Is. de (I. of Wight), 13, Ef
Wiju, 76B, Ca
Wildhaus, 29B, Da
Wildspitze, 29A, Db
Wilge, R., 81B, Da
Wilhelmshaven, 55A, Hb
Wilkes Land, 69C
Wilkesbarre, 56, Db
Willebroek, 46A, Dc
Willemstadt, 52B, Aa
Williamsburg, 57, Ce
Williamsport, 70, Gc
Willis Creek, 56B
Willmanstrand, 51, Fa
Willsboro, 57, Ea
Wilmington, Delaware, 57, Dd
Wilmington, North Carolina, 57D, Ba
Wilno, 87, Fb
Wilson's Creek, 72, Bb
Wiltberg, 20, Jc
Wilten, 10, De
Wiltescire (Wiltshire), 13, Ee
Wilton, 27, Ee
Wiltshire, 27, Ee
Wiltunie (Wilton), 13, Ee
Wiltzes, 8, Ea; 10, Eb
Wimborne, 7C, Cc
Wimpfen, 10, Cd
Winburg, 81A, Cc
Winburne (Wimborne Minster), 13, Ef
Winceby, 48A, Cc
Wincelcumbe (Winchcomb), 13, Ee
Winchelsea, 17, Fc; 27, Gf
Winchester, England, 27, Ee
Winchester, Virginia, 57, Bd
Winchester, bp., 36, Ef
Windau, 26, Fb
Windesores (Windsor), 13, Fe
Windhoek, 80A, Eg
Windsheim, 22, Eb; 30, Jd
Windsor, Connecticut, 45B, Cc
Windsor, England, 27, Fe
Windward Passage, 43A, Ec
Winnebago, L., 56, Bb
Winnepesaukee, L., 45B, Db
Winnipeg, 70, Ec
Winnipeg, L., 70, Eb
Winnipegosis, L., 70, Eb
Winnisimet, 56B
Winnsboro, 57D, Aa
Winter Hill, 56B
Winterberg Mts., 81B, Cc
Winterthur, 29B, Ca
Wintonia (Winchester), 13, Ee
Wirecestre (Worcester), 13, Dd
Wirecestrescire (Worcestershire), 13, Dd
Wisbeche (Wisbech), 13, Gd
Wisby, 26, Eb
Wischerhrad, 31, Lc
Wisconsin, 70, Ec
Wisconsin, R., 56, Bb
Wislica, 31, Pc
Wismar, 26, Dc; 31B, Ca
Wissembourg, 29A, Ba
Witebl (Whitby), 13, Fb
Witham, Essex, 7C, Dc
Witham, Wiltshire, 36, Df
Witham, R., 27, Fc
Witney, 27, Ee
Witteland, 42B
Witteland West, 77, Bf
Wittelsbach, 20, Jd
Wittenberg, 21, Kc; 31B, Ca
Wittenberg, mts., 81B, Cb
Wittgenstein, 30, Hc
Wittstock, 21, Kb
Wloclawek, 22, Fa

Woburn, 36, Ff
Woerden, 46A, Db
Woëvre, The, 83A, Cb
Wohlau, 39, Mc
Wolfenbüttel, 20, Jb
Wolgast, 21, Ka
Wollin (Jomsburg), 10, Fb
Wolmar, 50, Fb
Wölpe, 20, Hb
Woods, L. of the, 70, Ec
Woodstock, England, 27, Ee
Wooler, 49A, Cc
Worcester, England, 27, Ed
Worcester, Massachusetts, 57, Fb
Worcester, S. Africa, 81B, Ac
Worcester, bp., 36, De
Worcester, co., 27, Dd
Wordingborg, 26, Db
Worksop, 36, Ed
Worms, 10, Cd; 83A, Eb
Wörth, 39B, Ea; 76A, Db
Wurzburg, G. D. of, 65B, Ba
Wragby, 36, Ed
Wrangel I., 74, Qa; 94, Jb
Wrath, C., 14, Ca
Wrexham, 48B, Bc
Wroclaw, 89, Jc
Wuhan, 91, Ec
Wuhu, 74, Ke
Württemberg, 10, Cd; 20, Hd
Würzburg, 10, Cd; 29A, Da
Wurzen, 39C, Cb
Wychwood, 7B, Cc
Wycombe, 27, Fe
Wye, R., 27, De; 36, De
Wymondham, 36, He
Wynaad Malabar, 73, Ce
Wyndham, 77, De
Wynendael, 46A, Bc
Wyoming, 57, Cc
Wyoming, st., 70, Dc

Xanten, 46A, Fc
Xeres, 23C, Bd; 63, Bd
Xingu, R., 68, Dc

Y Gaer, 3A, Cd
Yadavas, 25, Gd
Yakutat B., 71B, Bb
Yakutsk, 74, Lb
Yalu, R., 76B, Ca
Yamasees, 45A, Bc
Yamuna, R., 92, Db
Yanaon, 73, Dd
Yanbu, 6, Ec
Yandabu, 73, Gc
Yandua, 75C, Ba
Yang Chow, 1, Oe
Yangtze-Kiang, R., 91, Dc
Yanselin Pass, 76B, Ba
Yantra, R., 78, Ed
Yaoundé, 96B, Db
Yap, 90, Cc
Yaqui, Pico de, 43D, Ec
Yarkand, 1, Kd; 74, Fe
Yarm, 27, Eb
Yarmak, 6A, Bb
Yarmouth, I. of W., 27, Ef
Yarmouth, Maine, 57, Fb
Yarmouth, Massachusetts, 45B, Dc
Yarmouth, Norfolk, 27, Hd
Yarmouth, Nova Scotia, 56, Fb
Yasawa Is., 75C, Aa
Yathreb (Medina), 6, Fc
Yavanas, 1, Je
Yazoo, R., 56, Ad; 72C, Aa
Yecla, 63, Ec
Yeddo, 69A, Qc
Yekaterinburg, 61, Kc
Yekaterinoslav, 51, Gd
Yellow Ford, 49B, Eb
Yellow Sea, 91, Fc
Yellowhead Pass, 44, Cc
Yellowstone, R., 70, Dc
Yellowstone National Park, 70, Dc
Yemen, 6, Fd; 25, De; 93, Ef
Yenbo, 93, De
Yenisei, R., 25, Ha
Yeniseisk, 74, Ke
Yentowwa B., 76B, Bb
Yerevan, 93, Ea
Yerwa, 96B, Da
Yeu, 53, Bd
Yewin, 77, Bg
Yezd, 6, Gb; 93, Gc
Yih Chow, 1, Nd
Yingkow, 76B, Ba
Ynys Enlli, 7B, Ab
Yokohama, 91, Gc
Yola, 80A, Ed
Yonne, R., 11, Ec
York (Agamenticus), 45B, Db
York, England, 27, Ec; 36A
York, Maine, 57, Fb
York, Pennsylvania, 57, Cd
York (Toronto), 71C, Cb
York, abp., 36, Ed

York, C., 77, Gd
York, eccl. prov., 22, Ba
York, Norse King. of, 7C, Ca
York, R., 72B, Bb
York Factory, 70, Eb
York Moors, 27, Fb
York Wolds, 27, Fb
Yorkshire, 27, Eb
Yorktown, 57, Ce; 72B, Bb
Youghal, 37B, De; 49B, De
Ypres, 17, Gc; 46A, Bd
Ysabel, 77, Jc
Ystrad Towy, 7B, Ac
Ythancester, 7B, Dc
Yu Chow, 1, Od
Yucatan, 43A, Db
Yu-chang, 1, Oe
Yugoslavia, 84, Fd
Yukon, 71B, Ba
Yukon, R., 71A, Ba
Yunnan, 74, Jf
Yun-nan, prov., 73, Gb
Yverdon, 29B, Ab
Yxninga (Exning), 13, Gd

Zabern, 38, Gd
Zablat, 39, Ld
Zabid, 6, Fd
Zacatecas, 43A, Bb
Zacatula, 43A, Bc
Zacynthos (Zante) I., 78, Cg
Zafra, 63, Bc
Zagreb, 16, Fc
Zahringen, 10, Bd; 20, Gd
Zaitun, 25, Ld; 35, Pc
Zallaca, 23C, Bc
Zambesi, R., 81A, Da
Zambia, 96D, Ef
Zamboanga, 75E, Bc
Zamora, 23C, Cb; 63, Cb
Zamosc, 50, Ec; 62, Gb
Zanesville, 71C, Bc
Zanj, 6, Fd
Zante, 78, Cg
Zante (Zacynthos) I., 78, Cg
Zanzibar, 80A, Ge
Zapetra, 8, Kd
Zara, 5, Eb; 32A, Fb
Zara, eccl. prov., 22, Ec
Zaranj, 6, Hb
Zaria, 96B, Ca
Zator, 31, Nd
Zduny, 26, Ec
Zealand, 65F, Ba
Zeebrugge, 83A, Ba
Zeeland, Denmark, 51, Cb
Zeeland, Netherlands, 46A, Cc
Zehdenick, 22, Ea
Zeila, 40, Md
Zeitz, 21, Kc; 39C, Cb
Zeitz, March of, 10, Ec
Zell, 53, Hc
Zengg, 21, Lf
Zenta, 33C, Eb
Zerbst, 21, Kc
Zettin, 33C, Db
Zevenbergen, 46A, Dc
Zhitomir, 87, Fb
Zidon, 18A, Fc
Ziegenhain, 20, Hc
Zierikzee, 46A, Cc
Ziguinchor, 96B, Aa
Zinder, 80A, Dc
Zion Gate, 18D
Zipangu (Japan), 25, Nc
Zips, 24, Gd; 33C, Eb; 50, Ed
Zirids, 16, Df
Zittau, 21, Lc
Ziyanids, 24, Cg
Znaim, 21, Md; 31B, Db
Zobor, 9, Ec
Zollern, 10, Cd; 30, Hd
Zomba, 96C, Ff
Zonguldak, 79, Fb
Zorndorf, 54, Eb; 60A, Eb
Zornoza, 63, Da
Zossen, 60A, Db
Zoutpansberg, 81A, Cb
Zug, 29B, Ca
Zug, canton, 29B, Ca
Zug, L., 29B, Ca
Zuider Zee, 46A, Eb
Zulpich, 4B, Da
Zulu, 81D, Bb
Zululand, 81D, Bb
Zumbo, 81A, Da
Zungeru, 81C, Fc; 96C, Cd
Zurawno, 50, Ed
Zürich, 10, Ce; 29B, Ca
Zürich, canton, 29B, Ca
Zürich, L. of, 29B, Ca
Zutphen, 46A, Fb
Zutphen, prov., 46A, Fb
Zvenigorod, 19, Dc
Zweibrücken, 29A, Ba
Zweibrücken, Pr. of, 53, Gc
Zwettl, 39, Ld
Zwickau, 21, Kc; 39C, Cc
Zwolle, 46A, Fb

PRINTED IN GREAT BRITAIN BY GEORGE PHILIP PRINTERS, LIMITED, LONDON